Starting his career as a fire-cadet at sixteen the author rose to senior
rank, always in an operational role. A steady 'plodder' more than a
high flier he learnt his trade craft serving, and commanding, the
Capital's busiest and most challenging fire station, Brixton. Awarded
the Queen's Commendation for Brave Conduct he also rowed himself
into the Guinness Book of Records whilst raising many thousands of
pounds for charity. A talented organiser he was involved in delivering
some of the London Fire Brigade's most high-profile public events
during the 1990s including royal visits and the unveiling of the
national Blitz memorial by St Paul's Cathedral. A fireman first and
foremost he provides a valuable human story into the life and history
of the London Fire Brigade from 1965 to the late 1990s.

BEYOND THE FLAMES

Nominated for the People's Book Prize 2014 and finalist in the UK's
Non-fiction Category.

Dedicated to the ultimate supreme sacrifice of firefighters everywhere and to my daughter Abby – taken too soon.

David C. Pike

BEYOND THE FLAMES

AUSTIN MACAULEY
PUBLISHERS LTD.

A CIP catalogue record for this title is available from the British Library.

ISBN 978 184963 396 3

www.austinmacauley.com

First Published (2013)
Austin Macauley Publishers Ltd.
25 Canada Square
Canary Wharf
London
E14 5LB

Printed and bound in Great Britain

Acknowledgements

London Fire Brigade.

Roger Stuart Vaughan – a guiding light.

Brian 'Bill' Butler MBE OStJ. QFSM – a guiding hand.

Christopher J. Thompson – friend and mentor.

Mary Evans – a picture library.

Robin Griffiths – an ace with apostrophes.

Contents

Introduction

This is a personal memoir. It offers glimpses and snapshots that gave definition to a fire service career that spanned the last four decades of the twentieth century. Whilst the tales cover the people and events that shaped and influenced my working life, it also offers a special reminiscence of the life and times in the long history of the London Fire Brigade, highlighting personalities, acts of courage, and the ultimate sacrifice that any firefighter can make, to give their life in the performance of their duty. All of which made this so much more than just a job. This story is dedicated to them, the fallen.

Riding the engine...

"One of my early childhood memories was that of running to the front window of our home to watch the fire engines when I heard their clanging bells as they drove up Waller Road, a steep thoroughfare in South London. My parents occupied the top floor flat of my grandmother's three-storey Victorian house. I had a grandstand view of the big red fire engines, with their wooden ladders, as they seemed to fill the tree-lined road, which in the early fifties was bereft of any parked cars. New Cross fire station was located at the bottom of the hill and Waller Road was a frequent transit route for these engines responding to some urgent call. The sight of these magnificent engines with the firemen getting dressed into their fire tunics and black helmets always filled my childhood mind with excitement and the hope of one day being able to join in their adventure."

Chapter 1

Every Cloud

Selection

I left secondary school in 1965. I left it much as I joined it, hopefully a bit wiser but without a worthwhile academic qualification to my name. The school, Samuel Pepys, was a South London secondary modern. Comprehensives were not that common then and this school was the destination for many boys in the local area who had not or could not pass their 11 plus exam. I did eventually get a school certificate when I left at sixteen. This meant that I attended school more than I missed it and managed to get to most classes on time. At school *"spilling and grimmer"* were never my best subjects, probably on a par with my maths. I found French and algebra totally bewildering and algebra still is! I was not much of a sportsman either. I played rugby and hockey because I had to and not because I was any good at them. My only saving grace was that I could swim, and very well. I represented both my school and the local borough of Deptford. This gave me some "street cred" at school with both my peers and some of the teaching staff. It was largely thanks to an extremely enthusiastic physical education teacher that I was introduced into Sub Aqua swimming. I took to it like the proverbial duck to water, soon passing all the snorkelling tests, which qualified me to use the compressed air tanks at the nearby swimming pool where the weekly training took place. The pool was located on the top floor of a three-storey health centre in New Cross. Originally built in the early fifties, it was then state of the art but now looked tired, neglected and in need of considerable renovation. The pool training, however, was great and having twelve feet deep-end helped develop my snorkelling skills. The open water training was even better and was undertaken at various lakes in Kent and Essex and harbours along the south coast. I was soon able to qualify as a diver, third class.

In the fifth form, my last school year, the form master was a Mr Mills. He was a quietly spoken Welshman in his mid-fifties. He had a halo of white wispy hair surrounding his shiny bald head. As a teacher he was okay but thirty years of teaching teenage boys, overloaded with the trials and tribulations of puberty and high on increasing levels of testosterone, had taken its toll on his enthusiasm for teaching. When teaching his own subject, maths, the bright and talented boys were clearly targeted whilst those, like me, were left to our own devices, working from a teach-yourself maths textbook. Mr Mills also doubled up as the school's career master, a task that he probably performed to increase his weekly pay packet rather than for any altruistic reason. He had a simple career philosophy for those boys, who like me, had no natural academic flair; it was simple, "Go to MOLINS boy." He called every pupil "boy." Molins was a large local engineering firm, located in the depths of Deptford near the River Thames. We were convinced that Mr Mills actually worked for Molins as their recruitment officer rather than a teacher, especially given the large number of boys who ended up there as apprentices as soon as they left school.

I had other ideas. It was no engineering factory for me, nor working in the newspaper industry as my father did. I wanted something different, something exciting and something that did not require at least ten GCEs to get it. The Metropolitan Police Cadet scheme caught my eye, which all too soon proved to be ironic! I sent off my application and much to my surprise I got an interview date at the Police Selection Centre in Borough Road, near London Bridge. On the appointed day I went proudly wearing my school uniform, which consisted of a rather worn school blazer, my faded and discoloured school badge, a prefect's badge and my school swimming colours. I was out to impress but it was all, sadly, very short lived.

First came the police medical examination. This included stripping naked, then standing on a pair of white footprints painted on the floor and having to face the wall! We had certain teachers who may have liked to get us into that position at school but surely not here? Anyway, whatever was inspected appeared satisfactory and was followed by the eyesight and hearing tests. The medical examination was immediately followed by the written tests. Directed into a large room with individual desks thirty or so of us hopeful boys each found a desk, sat and waited. We were briefed by a uniformed police sergeant on what was to happen next and were provided with the question papers. I was ready for this test and was even feeling reasonably confident. No sooner I had put my name on the answer sheet than I was told to leave the examination room. Another uniformed police sergeant told me I had failed my eyesight test. Giving me my train fare home he unceremoniously sent me on my way.

I was disappointed, shocked and upset. I did not wear glasses and thought that I could see perfectly well. Then the mind games started. Maybe what they said at school about playing with yourself was true after all? Did it really send you blind? Thinking my dad would surely put two and two together and come up with the obvious cause for my early failing eyesight my mind was working overtime. Many of my uncles wore glasses so maybe the problem ran in the family? Confused and worried just what to tell my parents I choose to delay the inevitable and walked for a while. In truth I could not actually find my way back to London Bridge railway station! Whilst trying to think of possible excuses to offer for my failure, I came upon a large semi-derelict Victorian frontage next to Southwark Fire Station in Southwark Bridge Road. It turned out to be the defunct exterior of the London Fire Brigade's training school and recruitment centre. On its wall was a weathered notice board containing an advert for their

Junior Fireman scheme. I thought I would give that a try and apply to join the Fire Brigade as a cadet. Looking at the state of the building I thought their standards could not be as high as those of the Police. I went in and found the Training School office and asked for an application form. On the way home I promised not to play with myself ever again or, at least, until after the eyesight test!

I was nearly sixteen and old enough to apply to become a Junior Fireman in the London Fire Brigade. It was late 1964 and the London County Council (LCC) was preparing to become the newly created Greater London Council (GLC). Among its many responsibilities the GLC would be the Fire Authority for the Greater London area and the London Fire Brigade would become one of the largest Fire Brigades in the world. The GLC would absorb parts of Kent, Surrey, the whole of Middlesex, Croydon Borough and other county areas and Boroughs such as East Ham and West Ham that surrounded the old LCC boundary.

There was, thankfully, no family inquest into my failure at the Police medical and no boxing gloves left for me on my bed. I thought my parents were very supportive of me joining the Fire Brigade as a cadet but it could have been they were just pleased I was looking for work, any work! My application form duly completed it was posted back to the Fire Brigade Headquarters. Now the wait for a reply. What my application clearly lacked in any national exam results and academic prowess was made up for by selling my Sub Aqua skills for all it was worth. Whether this actually made any difference I never discovered. But just after my sixteenth birthday, in January 1965, I was invited to attend the Cadets' next selection tests at Southwark. I was to attend pure in mind, body and spirit. I also, as a precaution, had my eyesight tested at the local opticians to ensure I would not fall at that particular hurdle again.

The London Fire Brigade's training school had previously been the Headquarters of the Metropolitan Fire Brigade and the home of its most famous Chief Fire Officer, Sir Eyre Massey Shaw. Sadly the site showed none of its former glory and was now hidden behind its semi-derelict four storey frontage facing on Southwark Bridge Road. Behind this frontage was a random collection of unprepossessing Victorian brick buildings and fire brigade training facilities. The recruitment hut, for that is all it was, a wooden hut, was located at the far northern side of the training school at the end of a long narrow cobbled yard. The civilian staff welcomed us and checked our names off the list of that day's candidates, a collection of hopeful, but nervous, adolescent lads. We were in stark contrast to the other fire-fighter recruits at the training school who all looked at least ten years older, much stronger, and far more self-assured.

There were about twenty of us expectant cadets in that day's selection intake. We were all required to take an educational test; undertake physical exercises; and undergo a through medical examination at County Hall. Finally, and if we got that far, attend an interview at Brigade Headquarters, located at Lambeth. Shown into a classroom in the hut we each sat at single desks. An unsmiling and aged looking man took us through the English, maths and dictation examinations. It was fortunate that they used the same tests more than once because written on my wooden desk, and on the issued ruler, were answers to the sums and some of the more difficult spellings. With the aid of the desk and ruler I thought the tests were manageable, or was it we just had to prove we could actually read and write? Maybe fate would be kinder to me this time?

Next came the two strength tests. These were done outside in the cobbled courtyard and taken by someone wearing a fire brigade uniform. He introduced himself as, "Sub Officer Billingham." Squat in stature he looked extremely powerful. In a surly voice he explained what was expected of us whilst trying, at the same time, to put us at our ease, despite our nervousness about what we had to do. We had to pass these two separate strength tests to go on to the next stage of the selection process.

Divided into pairs, each pair being approximately the same height and weight, we were required to perform a fireman's lift and carry our partner one hundred yards in less than one minute. By way of a demonstration, and without a pause for breath, the Sub Officer hoisted the largest of our group onto his shoulder and briskly walked down the drill yard and about turned at the drill tower, fifty yards away. He effortlessly paced his way back to the starting point without the faintest hint of tiring and walking as though he was not even carrying anyone. Now it was our turn. The first ten to carry moved towards and faced their partners. Three of those being lifted either fell off completely or slid down the backs of those doing the lifting. One poor unfortunate soul was lifted with such gusto that he was thrown completely over the shoulder of this Hercules, landing in an undignified heap on the ground. Sub Officer Billingham's sudden outburst would have done credit to a Smithfield or Covent Garden porter as his colourful language turned the air blue and its tone made us all quake in our boots. He told the power lifter, in no uncertain terms, that he was meant to hold onto his partner and he was not trying to "toss an effing caber!" Meanwhile the poor lad, lying prostrate on the ground, was feeling the lump on his forehead grow ever larger. He got little sympathy from the still berating Billingham, who seemed unimpressed by the antics of his juvenile charges.

Whilst encouraging us to get our act together he dispatched the first pairs off down the yard, some clearly staggering under the weight on their backs. All made it, except for one. I was in this first group and one rather tubby chap was clearly having trouble. As we were coming back up the yard he was still going down, huffing and puffing and struggling with his charge. The Sub Officer was not as hard-hearted as he made out. He let the sweating, and heavily breathing potential firefighter, catch his breath and try again. Sadly he fared no better the second time and was sent back to the hut. We did not see him again.

Our number depleted by one, we moved onto the second test. It involved winding the handle on the side of a metal A-frame that was firmly secured to the ground. There was a wire running from a central drum, over a pulley and connected to a large weight that stood on the ground. The weight had to be lifted up by turning the handle. This was geared to make the lift the equivalent of winding up a fifty-foot wheeled escape ladder, which we had seen the recruits using in the main drill yard. Sub Officer Billingham again demonstrated what was expected of us by turning the winding handle. He did it with ease and we watched the weight rise smoothly and rapidly to the top of the frame. "That's it my lovelies, just do that in one minute." He had done it in well under the time allowed. Hercules, the guy who had thrown his partner over his shoulder, elected to go first and we looked on in horror as he struggled to raise the weight in the time. Red faced, he was obviously relieved that he made it. Sadly, another of our number, even after a second attempt, failed and he was on his way home too. The rest of us managed it but not without a struggle.

Before lunch those remaining were given the results of the educational tests, fire brigade fashion that is. Two names were called out and told to go to the wooden hut. We did not see them again either. The rest of us were sent off to lunch in the training school canteen. It was here we got our first glimpse of real junior firemen, who seemed rather puny against the other adult recruits. Our small group of potential future cadets felt very conspicuous in our civilian clothes when everyone else was wearing various types of firemen's uniform and kit. We huddled together at a large corner table at the back of the canteen, kept our heads down, ate our lunch and said very little.

Following lunch we were driven to County Hall, on the South Bank, for the medical examinations. County Hall was the headquarters of the then LCC and would become the new home of the enlarged GLC. Conversation was nervous and consisted mainly of where we each lived, school and football. I was never a football fan so probably made a complete ass of myself trying to talk about something I knew nothing of. Driven in a green box van that had no side windows, we sat on the two rows of hard wooden bench seats located down each side. The driver, a grey haired, middle-aged stout fireman was wearing worn blue overalls. His weathered overall trousers were held up by a wide black leather belt, as it tried in vain to contain his enormous beer gut. He seemed to enjoy the short journey from Southwark, deriving great pleasure by throwing us out of our seats as he turned the corners too fast or braking hard when he had to stop, which seemed all too frequently. We arrived somewhat shaken and dishevelled at the steps of County Hall, a large white stone-faced office complex.

We were directed by our grinning driver to its main entrance and told to ask at reception for the medical department. The complex was large, very large, and much bigger than most of us had experienced before. It was certainly more complicated than finding your way around school. Eventually, after various people pointed us in the right direction, we found the medical department on one of the upper floors. We were immediately greeted by a nurse who handed out strange flute shaped glass containers that we were told to pee in. This was like the police medical but for one of our number it was a totally new and embarrassing experience as his flushed face clearly demonstrated. Tentatively he walked into the small cubical, only to return to the nurse saying that he could not pee. Obviously used to such problems, the nurse made him drink what seemed like a gallon of water and told him to come back later. The rest of us supplied the requisite sample without too much difficulty.

The medical continued; poking around in our ears; sticking wooden sticks in our mouths; reading from eyesight charts and having our hearing checked. The examinations were performed by a doctor, at least he said he was? He looked incredibly old. He had pale wrinkly skin, sunken eyes and a narrow unsmiling mouth, he was small and seemingly very frail, his white medical coat came down almost to his shoes. Whilst he listened to our own breathing he wheezed noisily, his nicotine stained fingers giving a clue as to the cause, before he took our blood pressure. It was here the medical took a very different direction from our normal school medicals and I felt distinctly uncomfortable. Told to drop my trousers and remove my underpants I had to expose my private parts so they could undergo his professional scrutiny. I was instructed to cough whilst his shaky hand cupped my testicles. I prayed his hand would stop shaking long enough whilst holding them so as not to cause unwanted stirrings. Fortunately "Percy" remained flaccid and pointing downward, no doubt in shock. Much relieved, I quickly pulled my trousers back up and the medical was over.

The height requirement, then, for a man joining the London Fire Brigade was five feet eight inches. If you joined the Junior Firemen scheme you had to be at least five feet six inches and reach five feet eight inches by your eighteenth birthday. How was this growth potential determined? Well it was all in your ball size apparently. Some clever individual came up with the incredible theory that the size of your balls at sixteen could determine your height by eighteen. It was this medical "fact" that indicated which of those under five feet eight inches had the potential to grow taller. I was already over five feet eight inches so it was not a problem for me. This was just a well as I was already one ball short due to a childhood accident. This anomaly seemed to bemuse the doctor during the cradling of my manhood, as he spent some time searching for the missing one. At least, that is what I hoped he was doing. Sadly for some height-impaired cadets it was discovered that this very dubious measuring system was not infallible. By the time they reached their eighteenth birthday some balls clearly had earlier had delusions of grandeur and their size proved to be no indication of their owner's ability to reach the required height. The old adage that you shouldn't judge a book by its cover seemed apt. Only in this case, just don't judge a cadet's potential height by the contents of his scrotum!

The last round of the day were the selection interviews. They were conducted at the Brigade's Headquarters at Lambeth, located on the Albert Embankment. We were again transported in the box-van and escorted to the second floor on our arrival. Told to wait in an office we were called one by one for interview. Our numbers dwindled as individual candidates were called for and then made their way home without returning to the office. Eventually my turn came and I was shown into an imposing office overlooking the River Thames. Two uniformed senior officers were seated behind a wide wooden desk. Whilst one of the officers introduced themselves the other picked up a file and asked me to confirm if the details he read out were accurate? Clear recall of the interview has now faded but the officers appeared more interested in my swimming and sub aqua achievements rather than anything else. Having rehearsed some really impressive reasons for wanting to join the Fire Brigade I was never asked why I actually wanted to join, something I always found strange. They did mention my failure at the previous eyesight test with the police and pointed out that this is something they would have to look into with the Medical Officer. They said they would be in touch and let me know if I had been accepted or not. The "or not" sounded rather ominous. Their decision would be notified by letter, and it was.

The letter duly arrived at my parent's home in Chelsfield, Kent. I had been accepted and I was delighted, not least because I could tell Mr Mills that I would not end up having to go to Molins! My starting date with the Brigade was the 1st April 1965, the day the Greater London Council was to be officially created. It was also another special day; one famous for its practical jokes. Was I the recipient of some cruel practical joke? Dad rang the telephone number given on the letter and confirmed that it was genuine. My last day at school was only a few weeks away, or so I thought. The school, however, had other plans and wanted my start date delayed so I could sit my GCEs, which I subsequently failed with a capital F. So it was not until the 13th September 1965 that I excitedly set off by train to London Bridge and then made the short walk to Southwark Training School. My first day of training in the London Fire Brigade.

Chapter 2

F Squad

Basic Training

I was no stranger to commuting, my parents having moved from South London to Chelsfield a year earlier. This meant I travelled back and forth to school each day by train, getting off at New Cross and walking the couple of miles to school in Brockley. Today, however, I stayed on the train to London Bridge and then walked to the training school. I was filled with a mixture of nervousness and excited anticipation as I began my first day of real paid work. I was to be paid the princely sum of £5.10s.0d per week, which was considerably more than the apprentice rates at Molins.

Walking through the arched entrance of the training school I passed unnoticed as I joined the adult recruits, their training instructors and firemen from Southwark fire station either reporting for duty or that day's training. My letter had instructed me to report to the Training School office and to report to Station Officer Charlie Swanton. He was not at all what I had expected to find, but we were to discover that Charlie Swanton had been a long-time serving fire officer with a reputation as an excellent "governor" and an experienced "smoke eater." Sadly, he was now crippled with disfigured hands and joints because of his severe arthritis. He had not wanted to leave the Brigade and had been transferred into this post, which meant that he was no longer an operational officer. He and his wife lived in Brigade accommodation above Southwark fire station and, conveniently, next door to the adjoining Goldsmiths Arms public house, his favourite haunt. Despite his considerable pain, he possessed a wonderful sense of humour and it was impossible to faze him no matter what problems he was presented with. This included, among many other things, dealing with the Council's auditors, who on finding the petty cash short challenged Charlie, prompted no doubt by an IOU he had placed in the office safe in lieu of the money he had borrowed and naturally intended to, and would, replace!

Together with the other first day cadets we were redirected to the same hut where we had undertaken our initial selection tests. It was here we re-assembled to meet our training instructors. Our names ticked off, we were divided into two separate groups, each group told to sit and wait in one of the two classrooms in the hut. There were ten of us now sitting down together and making uneasy small talk when the door opened and in walked a powerfully built uniformed officer in his mid-thirties. He had a round stern face, with no hint of a smile, no neck, and a head that sat directly on top of his shoulders. He instructed us to stand in a clear authoritative voice, which stopped all conversation dead. He strutted to a lectern at the front of the class and eyed the now apprehensive and attentive gathering. "Good morning gentlemen my name is Station Officer Knight and until you complete you training, or fail it, I am your instructor. Sit down." It was probably the one time he ever called us gentlemen. He was, however, very inventive with his other choice phrases used to describe our collective or individual efforts during our basic training.

Removing his cap he revealed a US marine style crew cut, which did little to improve the looks of his lived-in face. The toecaps of his black service shoes shone like mirrors. He called the roll and we each had to stand up in turn to introduce ourselves when our name was read out aloud. As we each stood, he gave us all a cursory inspection and said, "Hair cut by tomorrow." With roll call completed his face softened into a smile and he even managed to look friendly. "Welcome lads; you are now officially F Squad, my Squad. My name is Len but you will call me Sir." We did not know it then but it was his first day too, having been selected to join the Training School as one of an enlarged team of Junior Firemen cadet instructors.

The first day was a mixture of introductions to the site; allocation of lockers and getting haircuts (then some getting it cut again!). By the afternoon we were travelling to the GLC stores depot in South West London to be issued with our uniform and personal kit. It was a drawn-out affair. We were first measured then issued with uniform that did not always fit anyway. We were given three styles of uniform; fire kit consisting of rubber fireboots, (only recruits were issued with the heavy leather fireboots), rubberised black leggings; black thick woollen fire tunic with two lines of chrome buttons down the front, a wide webbing belt and the fireman's axe plus, of course, the large black cork fire helmet. Second was our walking-out uniform including the cap with the red band that indicated that we were junior firemen. This was something that in the months ahead adult recruits would constantly remind us of. We were issued with blue shirts that had detachable collars, but no collar studs! (Both my grandfathers had died before I was born but I had seen pictures of them with their stiff starched collars and collar studs.) I had never used collar studs, and when I did, the bloody things would bore their way into your Adam's apple within seconds of putting them on. For some strange reason, known only to the Fire Brigade, the black naval style double-breasted jacket and trousers was called an **undress** uniform. It was only worn on smart occasions or if you were in trouble and were to get a bollocking by a senior officer. Finally the work overalls comprising separate blue dungaree trousers and jacket. The issued shoes did not have the highly polished toecaps that our instructor shoes had. That was to come and we would soon learn the meaning and art of "spit and polish."

We were getting to learn each other's names and recognise faces. We would grow much closer during the months ahead; some friendships and associations would last throughout our careers. For now "F" Squad was no more than a bunch of youngsters all with the common aim of wanting to become firemen. The squad was made up of Reg Banks, Mike Brown, Peter Cox, Kit Carson, David Melbourne, John Norris, Keith Popple, Dennis Stevens, Bill Wise and me. It was far too early to determine individual personalities or abilities that would come later.

Basic training in the first few weeks was aptly named. It would be weeks before we even got near a fire engine. Those early days consisted of learning to march; keeping in step; running out heavy canvas hose, joining hoses together and connecting a nozzle (which firemen call a branch); putting a standpipe on a water hydrant; turning the water on, then trying to control the hose against the pressure of water coming out the nozzle. We learnt about ropes (called lines), practised tying different knots used in the Brigade, plus we did lots and lots of cleaning. We cleaned everything; the drill yard, the toilets, our locker room and classrooms. We could certainly handle a mop and bucket by the end of the first couple of weeks even if we could not do much else. As for our progress with the training, but especially the marching, it was not long before Len Knight demonstrated his particular oratory skills and his sense of the dramatic. His frustration at our pitiful efforts at trying to do things the way he had just told us to do them resulted in him pulling off his cap, throwing it to the ground and telling us in no uncertain terms what he thought of us. Our initial attempts at marching as a squad were pitiful. Some would be turning right when they should be turning left or kept on going forward when they should be about-turning. We could also manage to fall over the hose when rolling it along the ground, or worse still, try to join identical hose couplings together, which is something that is impossible to do, although we tried!

Each lad was issued with a personal set of the Brigade's *Standard Technical Notes.* These notes, and instructions would make up the major theoretical part of our training course. It was the accepted teaching practice then (and would be for many years to come) to place a lot of emphasis on facts and figures concerning weight, size, diameters, construction, and what things were made from and why. Many of the notes had remained unchanged for years and contained information that would only have been useful in a firemen's trivia quiz. Some of the information was far more important however and gave valuable details and instruction on building construction; hydraulics; pumps and pumping water, and elements in the art of practical firemanship. This information, useful or otherwise, had to be committed to memory over the coming months but used rarely in practice after that. Some information, however, was important straight away. This included how equipment was tested, how to make certain it was safe to use and when to test it. These *Standard Notes*, as they were called, were the same as issued to all recruits, but the adult recruits had to absorb the contents within their twelve to fourteen weeks of basic training before their final examinations and passing out as firemen.

Junior Firemen also attended the City of London day college, located near the Barbican. This was to provide additional educational training as well as technical studies including chemistry and physics. A highlight was the hydraulics and building study sessions but only because the unassuming tutor was a sixth Dan Karate expert. If the session got a bit heavy, he could often be talked into breaking a brick or two! Our sister squad, G squad, combined with us for these twice weekly afternoon college sessions and we regularly joined forces to annoy our teenage college rivals, trainees from the Post Office, also on day release.

In those early days of intense training the historical background of the Brigade's training school made little or no real impression on us. Our world consisted of the locker room, classrooms, drill yards and towers; the canteens and, of course, the loos which we seemed to be forever cleaning. Yet the site, which now formed the training school, had a long and colourful history long before the Fire Brigade got its hands on it in 1878, nearly ninety years earlier. Once a burial site for the Great Plague victims in the mid-1600s, it later became a pleasure ground in the eighteenth century before a three-storey hat factory was finally erected together with the owner's twenty-room home called Winchester House. The Victorian factory remained, as did Winchester House, which still retains the name today. The original hat factory buildings formed a major part of the current training school site.

London's fire brigade, then called the London Fire Engine Establishment, originally had its Headquarters located in the City of London but had outgrown the site. The site at Southwark was purchased and impressive new buildings and facilities were added to the existing hat factory. It became the new Headquarters of the renamed Metropolitan Fire Brigade under the command of its first Chief Officer, Captain Eyre Massey Shaw. He was to live in the twenty-room house and became quite a celebrity on London's privileged social scene and enjoyed in his circle of acquaintances the then Prince of Wales. His home, in later years, would become an important listed building and heritage site and the home to the Brigade's unique "niche" museum.

But in 1965 the site had lacked funds for maintenance and had done so for some time. With the transfer of the Brigade's Headquarters in 1937 to a new location in Lambeth much of the Victorian frontage facing Southwark Bridge Road, built of red brick with magnificent white carved stonework and ornate features, lay unused. Time, and the lack of maintenance, had taken its toll. The building looked forlorn and tired with much of it being left semi-derelict. When first built this impressive frontage, some two hundred and fifty feet in length and five storeys high, sent out a clear message about the standing and pride of the Metropolitan Fire Brigade. An imposing arched entrance was incorporated in this new frontage that gave access to the private courtyard in front of Winchester House, the Chief Officer's private residence. On either side of this arch were large hand carved reliefs, sculpted in Portland stone, depicting heroic scenes of the Fire Brigade's derring-do and showing firemen and their engines in action. Above the arch, and again in hand carved stonework, was the new crest of the Metropolitan Fire Brigade. Built on the roof was a tall latticed signalling tower, used to semaphore messages to other local fire stations, which looked much like a church steeple with two arms located at its tip. At the southern end of the building, on the ground floor, was the Headquarters' fire station. Its three fire appliance bays housed the hose-carts and horse drawn manual fire engines. Later it would hold the latest in innovative fire engine design, steam fire engines drawn by teams of horses. The Metropolitan firemen manning those engines were on call twenty-four hours a day. They lived with their families at the station in accommodation above the engine room. The unmarried firemen shared barracks also located in the Headquarters site.

Now this dilapidated and sad looking frontage of the former Headquarters building was unoccupied except, that is, for the hundreds of pigeons who called it home and probably a large rat or two. It did have some human occupants however; Junior Firemen. We had been allocated a ground floor area that was called the "B" Locker room. This locker room was meant to keep us safe and sound and distant from possible interference from the grown-up recruits in the main locker room on the far side of the training school. Even bunking with the grown-ups would have been preferable to the constant smell of rotting bird shit that we had to endure. The remainder of the training school site consisted of former stores; stables and the old Brigade's workshop building. All had been adapted and converted over the years to provide the range of training facilities that the fire brigade needed to meet the requirements of the day. Its drill yards were nearly all laid to cobblestones and it was once reputed to be the largest enclosed cobbled area in London. There had been some recent improvements to the site, which included modernisation of some classrooms in the old hat factory and a new eight storey concrete drill tower that was meant to be dedicated to the Junior Fireman scheme. However, demand for scarce training resources caused occasional clashes. It was not unknown for recruit and junior firemen instructors to come eyeball-to-eyeball, haggling over who was to get priority on the tower or a drill yard.

Weeks quickly turned into months and we were getting our act together. I was now capable of performing hose drills; carrying and pitching a ladder into a drill tower and even made my first exploratory ascent on a hook ladder. The hook ladder was a test of nerve and climbing ability. This ladder was climbed on the outside of the drill tower, suspended from a steel hook that was secured over the windowsill. To start, the ladder would be lifted and placed up against the tower with the extended steel hook secured over the first-floor sill. You would climb using the right hand and foot together, then the left hand and foot, so as to maintain a natural balance on the ladder. On reaching the head of the hook ladder you would grip the top, whilst swinging one leg into the tower and, with your bum on the sill, the other leg would be taken off the ladder and your foot would now point down the outside of the tower. Lifting the hook ladder out of the drill tower, with the hook pointing away from you, and grasping the ladder on either side you pushed it up, hand over hand to the next windowsill and then swing the hook back in again securing the hook on the sill above you. Climbing back on to the hook ladder and by repeating the process at each floor you could eventually reach the required height. But that was still some way down the line. For us, just lifting the ladder off the ground demonstrated one of the reasons why the strength tests were necessary in the selection process. By the end of our course, and in order to pass out as a fireman, I would have to climb the hook ladder to the fifth floor, firstly on my own and then in a two-man crew (with lowering lines carried on our backs) to the same level. Oh joy!

Outward Bound

Just before Christmas 1965 we were allocated our Outward Bound Course schools which are located in various places around Great Britain. This course formed an integral part of the syllabus for all Junior Firemen. Although the four Junior Firemen squads were at various stages of their training it was decided that we should all attend at the same time. We thought the Brigade probably got a cheaper rate sending us in the middle of winter, when no one else in their right mind would want to go, which actually proved not to be the case. The individual squads were split up and cadets divided equally between the three different locations. The schools were in Wales, Yorkshire and Devon. I was allocated to Ashburton near Newton Abbot in South Devon.

On the 3rd January 1966 and still recovering from an over-indulgence of cider after the New Year celebrations, I found myself bound for Newton Abbot by train. Upon arrival I was collected, with a gang of other lads armed with either suitcases or backpacks, and put on a coach and driven off into the night. It was incredibly dark! Living in London I had not realised just how dark the night sky could be without light filtering from streetlamps, factories and people's homes. We eventually arrived at an isolated country house, its lights illuminating the tall, uncovered windows. Ushered inside by the staff we were greeted by the Director of the Outward Bound School and joined other lads, already waiting, in a grand room for the Director's introduction to the course. He quickly outlined the four-week programme and set out the house rules. No smoking. No drinking and definitely no sex! As none of us had seen any sign of a female the last rule did not seem too hard to manage. Just good old-fashioned fun and hard work. We were then sorted into prearranged mixed groups. I joined twelve other lads, all under eighteen, that formed our team.

A tall, lean, bespectacled man in his late twenties joined us and introduced himself as Michael Vinney-Wilson. He was our team instructor and told us he was a former RAF pilot (Flight Lieutenant). He showed us around the school which contained several communal dormitories, a canteen, the sick-bay, which seemed ominous, and the staff quarters. They were strictly off limits to us lads. Then it was into supper and off to bed. Vinney-Wilson said he would see us again in the morning, early.

What with the general chitchat, chatter, and introductions it was not until the early hours of the morning before anyone got to off to sleep. We were rudely woken at 5.30 am by Vinney-Wilson turning all the lights on and standing there in his running kit for the first of our daily 6 o'clock morning runs. There was no trainers or running shoes for the Junior Firemen just fire brigade issue black rubber and canvas, very cheap, plimsolls. They were crap and horrible to run in. Led by Vinney-Wilson we joined all the other teams and their instructors and started running, almost blindly, in the still near total darkness. Following the dimly lit path we stumbled around the four-mile route until we got back to the school with our chests heaving and lungs burning. None of us were prepared for what that followed next, a very cold shower! However, some lads quickly got to grips with this early morning treat by blocking up the centre holes of the shower heads with soap and standing in a water free cone. The course was clearly already working and developing our personal initiative and survival skills.

We were a mixed bag, coming from a variety of organisations that sent its under-eighteens on the course. Some were cadets from Police or other fire brigade cadet schemes. Others came from larger companies that ran apprentice training. The London junior firemen, however, made up the largest single grouping. To counter this, we were evenly divided amongst the other teams. I joined eleven others that included two older London junior firemen, Ray Ford and Mike French. Mike was the size of a *giant,* well over 6ft tall and built like the proverbial "brick shithouse." Over the next four weeks the course's aim was to develop and stretch us both mentally and physically. It would help build our physical strength and, hopefully, increase personal confidence besides showing us the benefits of working as a team. However, some lads were already showing signs of being confident, to the point of arrogance.

Most of the instructional staff, like Vinney-Wilson, had a military background. They were ex-army, marines or the RAF. They all seemed in their late twenties to early thirties, were extremely fit and highly motivated. Whilst they could, and did, push us hard at times, they were not out to undermine our confidence or prove that they were better or stronger than us, which of course they were. They all possessed an excellent attitude towards their role and their teenage charges. If we played up at times, and we did, they knew exactly how to handle us in a firm but friendly manner leaving us in no doubt as to who was in charge. This is more than can be said of our own people skills. For when tensions or conflict arose, between individuals or groups, it occasionally resulted in fists being used to settle the argument. Thankfully, I managed to avoid those situations but by some strange coincidence it always seemed to involve the police cadets and it was not always entirely their own fault.

The course was out of this world. I had not experienced anything like it before. It was both testing and varied. We had adventures climbing the tors of Dartmoor; abseiling into deep quarries; caving on Exmoor; canoeing down the River Dart and performing cliff rescues on near sheer cliff faces at Berry Head (well they seemed sheer at the time!) The exercises had been developed to make us work and think together as a team and to bring out individual leadership skills. Such tasks involved, for example, getting large heavy objects from one side of an area to the other, but without them touching the ground. We had to utilise the equipment given to us, to improvise and we were given no direction as how to achieve the task. Mostly we managed it, after a fashion, but sometimes we got our knickers in a real twist and it all went horribly wrong. The debrief afterwards let us know how to arrive at a possible solution and how we might have worked better as a team. There were also various hikes and extended forced walks. These started with easy half-day excursions that built up to the twenty-four-hour solo hike on Dartmoor and a three-day endurance hike from North Devon back to Ashburton.

My own twenty-four-hour solo hike tested my fear of the dark and my overactive imagination. One very cold morning we were taken to separate locations on Dartmoor. Each lad was given his map bearings and told to make his way back to the school by breakfast the following day. Issued with only a small tent, primus, billy-can and food for twenty-four hours we each set off from our individual starting points in the direction of Ashburton. Some dry clothing was packed in our backpacks but mainly what you wore was it. Thankfully, despite the cold, it was a bright, clear winter's day with thick frost covering the ground. I enjoyed the walking and even read the map correctly managing not to take compass bearings on moving sheep! This was something I had achieved in my compass practice much to my embarrassment and to the amusement of the others on the training session out on the moor.

I found the required landmarks for the route I had planned without too much difficulty. With all ten of us on the moor, although taking different individual routes, it still felt strange not to see anyone else not even the instructional staff that were meant to be keeping a watchful, if distant, eye on us, in case we got lost or injured. Their only contact came in the early evening when a staff member checked up on each lad to make sure things were alright and we had set up camp properly for the night.

To say I was enthusiastic about camping out on Dartmoor, on my own, and in the dark, would be a gross overstatement. I was shitting myself. I made my hot drink and cooked and ate my ration pack, which tasted utterly disgusting. Tented down I climbed fully clothed, less boots, into my sleeping bag and drifted off into a fretful sleep. The evening mist that came down when I set up camp had cleared and now a bright shining full moon was illuminating the star filled night sky when I awoke in the very early hours of the following day. In fact it was so bright you could walk around without a torch lighting your way. I thought it was a good move to make tracks, regardless of the time, and head off back to the school. After a quick hot drink and breaking camp I set off across the moor looking forward to my cooked breakfast back upon my return. It was about 3 am and my early start would put me ahead of schedule. I could get back in time to see the others having to endure that bloody early morning run.

Although the moor was lit by moonlight, I still had to navigate by compass as it was difficult, if not impossible, to make out distant landmarks clearly. I kept to my bearings and knew that I had to locate a stone slab bridge that crossed a stream, if I was to follow my chosen route. I could see moonlight reflected in the stream and looking ahead I could see the glistening slabs of a granite bridge crossing the stream in the distance. I was really pleased with myself; maybe being on your own at night was not so bad after all. I have always had a fear of the dark but this was not dark was it? But here on my own, on Dartmoor, I still had my imagination to contend with.

Moving purposefully towards the bridge I suddenly froze. I felt cold and clammy as the blood drained from my face and I could feel my heart pounding violently in my chest. In the distance, sitting or crouching just by the side of the bridge, was somebody or was it something? My recollection is as clear today as it was then. This something, that my rational brain told me was only a boulder or jagged rock, had the distinct outline of an old hag or witch sitting there, waiting. For what; me? My imagination overruled my rational thoughts and there was no effing way I was going anywhere near that bridge. So leaving whoever or whatever it was behind me I turned and walked quickly in the opposite direction out onto the open moor. Within a short time I had got myself totally lost. Not quite sure where I was, I saw a light in the far distance and made for it, falling waist deep into a bog in the process. Now wet, cold, and getting colder by the minute I made my way towards the light. It came from a barn next to an isolated moorland farmhouse. Exhausted I lay down on some straw and fell into a deep sleep only to be woken by the farmer inspecting this strange new addition to his livestock. A kind and friendly man, he quickly guessed I was yet another lost outward-bounder. After giving me a cup of hot tea he pointed me in the right direction and sent me on my way. I left the farm at about 6 am and even made it back to the school for breakfast. As I grew nearer my goal, the hike almost over, I met up with other equally weary hikers heading back to Ashburton. None of us, it seemed, had an *easy* night on the moor?

During the course it was strongly rumoured by us, not so worldly wise, lads that our drinks were laced with bromide so as to keep our sexual arousal and activity in check. This was probably untrue but, even so, the early morning cross-country running, cold showers and long active days did not leave much energy for playing with oneself or anyone else for that matter (male or female). Nevertheless, the subject was a popular topic of conversation at lights out. The lure of the attractive matron's underwear, left hanging in the laundry, became a magnet to those needing an antidote to the alleged effects of the bromide. Ray was determined to publicly disprove the bromide theory. One night in our dormitory and in the privacy of his own bed, thankfully, Ray gave a narrated "wank." It turned into a highly amusing, one-handed, affair with a string of Ray's sexual exploits thrown in to set the mood. His climax was greeted with loud cheers and a round of applause. Although from the look of some of the faces around the room they had already disproved the bromide theory for themselves.

With most of the course completed, only the final three-day hike was left. This was a strenuous hike against the clock that would test both our resolve and team spirit. Split into groups of sixes or sevens and provided with maps, camping equipment and food we were dropped off seventy miles from the school on the northern side of Dartmoor and told to get on with it. We had to phone the school on the first and second evenings to report progress and were expected to arrive back on the third day. Each group had to select its own leader and much to my surprise, especially as Mike the gentle giant was in our group, I was elected. It was to be Mike that stood out as the champion of our small band of hikers, however, and showed what determination under adversity was all about.

All those attending the school had been issued with hiking boots from their parent organisation or had bought their own. The fire brigade had issued walking boots to the Junior Firemen. (Army surplus, what else, although I am not sure from which war!) Whilst we had to wear these "army" boots, Mike had feet to match his height, size fourteen! Apparently, nothing was available in that size from the army surplus stock. The GLC Supplies Dept had had to find Mike suitable sized boots, which they eventually did. His only problem was that they were mountaineering boots and not walking boots. These boots had rigid soles and were not meant for normal hiking. Short hikes for Mike had been uncomfortable, but he had coped. Now he had to cover over seventy miles in three days. Without the three-day expedition under your belt you could not complete the course, which was something none of us wanted to happen but especially Mike.

For late January the weather was exceptionally kind. We had experienced some flurries of snow high on the moor; the occasional passing sleet shower, but in the main it was dry, bright and cold. We camped at night with two sharing a tent and managed not to fall out over the allocation of chores. Day one had taken its toll on Mike's feet. We had covered nearly thirty miles that first day, but Mike had walked more slowly in the last hour and we decided to let him set the pace, prior to camping for the night. When he eventually took off his boots, he had painful raw blisters on each foot but there was not much we could do about them.

Day two started at about 6 am. At least there was no cross-country run and cold shower out here. After porridge, we packed our gear and set off again. Mike had decided to burst his blisters and had put plasters on them during the night. He was quiet during the morning's hike, clearly in some discomfort, but never asked us to stop or for others to help with his backpack. We had agreed, prior to starting the three-day event, that we would try to be the first group back to Ashburton but we recognised we had lost time on our self-imposed schedule. Our designated route combined moorland, across open country and road walking. The roads seemed worst of all for Mike and his feet were obviously hurting yet he never once complained except, that is, of what he thought about the bloody boots he had to wear. On the second night I had reported in, from a telephone call box, and told the instructor that Mike was suffering badly from sore feet but that he wanted to continue the walk tomorrow, our final day. When Mike removed his boots that evening, we looked on in horror as we saw his socks soaked in blood. The boots had rubbed his feet raw or, at least, it looked like they had. After washing his feet they did not look quite so bad but the blistered areas had grown in size and looked painfully sore which, Mike assured us, they were. Refusing any special treatment, he undertook his share of the tasks as we set up camp for the night.

The weather on day three matched our mood; grey and overcast. We knew we would never be first back now. We agreed this was not a problem; now it was just a matter of getting back together as a team. Even putting his boots back on hurt Mike but his determination to complete the hike was obvious. Despite his protests we divided his backpack contents between us so that he only had to walk; although limp would be a more apt description. We had to stop more frequently so Mike could rest his feet but only once was it at his request. Mike was probably the biggest and strongest of all those attending the winter school yet never pushed his weight about. His strength was always focussed on getting the job done and not wanting to let others down. By the afternoon he was walking with his boots undone, the laces removed to ease the pressure on his feet. We were now ambling along rather than walking and Mike's only concern was he was letting us all down. We said, with a few extra choice expletives thrown in, that the stupid bastard who issued the boots should be walking in them.

Late afternoon and with the last few miles to go it was clear, no matter how hard he wanted to finish, Mike's feet were not going to let him. The instructional staff were now watching the routes around the school and they transported Mike the last couple of miles to the school and into the sick bay for treatment. It was a privilege to have shared the company of Mike over those three days and understand what determination and commitment to a team can mean. Thankfully Mike's feet, no longer encased in those boots, made a rapid recovery. We never saw Mike in those bloody boots again and they were last seen floating down the River Dart towards the sea. Because of his resolve Mike was deemed to have completed the hike.

It had been a great fun filled four weeks and most of us seemed sad that it was now all over. We had learnt things about ourselves and each other. We had faced up to some of our fears and tried to overcome them. Not always successfully; I remain fearful of the dark but can now hide it better. On the final morning, after the Course Director addressed us all, we returned to say farewell to individual team instructors. Vinney-Wilson had been an excellent tutor, a great guy, funny and intelligent. We had all gained from what he taught us, most of all about ourselves. We had clubbed together to get him a couple of bottles of whisky, which seemed to genuinely surprise him and he was moved to receive them. It was not the only surprise of the morning. In each group the instructor awarded a special Outward Bound tie to the individual who had made a noteworthy or outstanding contribution to the team over the four weeks. I naturally thought of Mike or even Ray's wank as news of his disproving the bromide myth had travelled far and wide! When my name was called and Vinney-Wilson presented me with the tie I was speechless. (I still have the tie as a memento of a wonderful time and a unique experience.) After a group photo it was off to the railway station, home for the weekend and back to training at Southwark on the Monday morning. But not for long because we cadets were being moved to a new dedicated college. We were off to Swanley in Kent.

Junior fireman learning hose drill and how to control a jet at Southwark Training School. 1964.

Copyright. *London Fire Brigade/Mary Evans Picture Library.*

Junior firemen combining hose and ladder work at Southwark training school. 1965.

Copyright. *London Fire Brigade/Mary Evans Picture Library.*

The London Fire Brigade opens its new Junior Firemen College in 1966.

Copyright. *London Fire Brigade/Mary Evans Picture Library.*

Junior firemen learn the science of firemanship whilst visiting the scene of a major riverside warehouse fire. 1965.

Copyright. *London Fire Brigade/Mary Evans Picture Library.*

F Squad-the one and only squad picture. Early days at Swanley with Sub Officer John Berry. 1966.

The former, defunct, MFB and LFB headquarters main entrance and accommodation block prior to its demolition by the GLC in 1969. Located in Southwark Bridge Road, SE1, the junior fireman's locker room was to the left of the arch on the ground floor.

Copyright. *London Fire Brigade/Mary Evans Picture Library.*

Chapter 3

Swanley

New Start

Returning to Southwark Training School in late January 1966 heralded a new direction in our regime. Cadets' training was to become residential. A former care institution, standing in its own extensive wooded grounds on the Kent and London border had been purchased by the GLC. It was located on the outskirts of Swanley, a sprawling village near Sidcup. The building had once been, a Victorian isolation hospital, later a residential care facility and, most recently, a care home for children with behavioural problems run by Kent County Council. We should fit in there just fine.

The move to Swanley was to take place in late March, or early April. Our training would continue at Southwark until then, but with the addition of excursions to the new site transporting equipment and with us acting as removal men, cleaners and odd job crews. The two senior Junior Firemen squads were to remain at Southwark as they had nearly completed their training and would have been hampered by the distraction and interruptions caused by the move. The remaining five squads, E: F: G: H and J (the new boys) were to be the first boarders at what was to become known as the Junior Firemen's Training College. The work routines there were as uncertain as the training facilities. The building was neither designed nor intended for training firemen, junior or otherwise. Someone obviously had had a vision of the site's potential, but when our instructors returned from increasingly frequent planning meetings about the future of the college, they were largely unimpressed. Len Knight confided to us, "There's no effing drill tower, no pressure in the hydrants, a fire engine that no one wants and facilities that only exist on paper." Poor Len's cap took another battering as he threw it to the ground in frustration and despair. But he had taught us, at an early stage in our training, that to be a successful fireman you have to be extremely adaptable, and that is what Len said we would be. We would make it work and be the best squad at the college. He was proved to be right.

The college, as it was now called, looked like somewhere David Copperfield or Tom Brown might have attended as a boarder in the nineteenth century. This red-brick building had a long wide frontage and was three storeys high. It had two higher domed square towers at either side of the main entrance that were separated by a central ornate pointed turret which made the whole building look much taller. Tiny round windows near the top of the towers added an air of mystery and intrigue. The combination of towers and turrets with numerous tall brick chimneystacks gave it the appearance of having once been a posh Victorian school for the sons of the wealthy, but its remoteness and isolation meant it was more likely to have been a hospital for contagious diseases or perhaps a lunatic asylum. The main building had an imposing front entrance with striking solid wooden double doors. On either side, and along the front of the building, were arched walkways that extended outwards providing balconies on the first floor. A long tree lined driveway led uphill from the main entrance gate and its adjacent lodge house, which was half a mile from the main college building. In addition to the main college building there were a range of other single and two-storey buildings that included an expansive chapel, two semi-detached houses, extensive garages and storerooms, a boiler house and a mixture of various out-houses.

Work was still very much in progress, getting ready for our imminent arrival. Piles of old iron hospital beds and mattresses filled the courtyard near the chapel. It was clear that the last owners had not much cared for garden maintenance as the once laid out shrubbery and flowerbeds had been left unattended for some considerable time. Large rhododendron bushes filled the undergrowth along the driveway, whilst extensive woodland made up the college's enclosed grounds and which were interlaced with pathways and vehicle tracks. The college was adjacent to what would eventually become junction three of the M25, but for now it was surrounded by unspoilt Kentish countryside.

During my cadet training, both at Southwark and now at Swanley, I had managed to maintain my regular weekly commitment to my Sub Aqua club and had progressed to become a third-class diver. On Saturday 12th February, a national Sub Aqua Championship was held at the Crystal Palace National Recreation Centre. I was to represent my diving club and had also entered in the individual competition. This involved a series of pool tests and activities to demonstrate diving and snorkelling skills, combined with swimming endurance. All the events were to be completed against the clock. Competing in the under eighteen category I had never once finished first, always coming second or third. Teams and individuals from diving clubs came from all over the UK to compete in these demanding and wide-ranging tests of skills. At the conclusion of these tests aggregated scores were totalled and to my delight I was named the individual overall winner, thus becoming the Under Eighteen Indoor Sub Aqua Champion of Great Britain. Quite a day, much helped by my training at Southwark that had increased my body strength and stamina dramatically.

The week before our move we were at Swanley each day; normal training having been abandoned. We were cleaning, sorting out gear and shifting equipment. The ground floor of the college was given over to senior officer offices, instructional rooms, canteen, kitchen, staffroom and our recreation rooms. The dormitories were situated on the first floor. They were a mix of smaller rooms that four cadets shared, or larger dormitories that would accommodate a whole squad, as ours did. The instructors also had their accommodation on this floor. They were required to sleep at the college on a rota basis to baby-sit us each night and over the weekends. The second floor was converted into residential family accommodation for the two senior officers who were responsible for the Junior Fireman training college. They were to move in and live permanently at the college with their wives and children.

Our training had been progressing well according to our instructor. We had a long way to go but could *"mount and dismount"* a fire engine without falling over each other. We were able to *"slip and pitch"* a wheeled fifty-foot escape and a thirty-foot extension ladder. This meant getting the ladder off the fire engine, wheeling or carrying it into position, then winding or pulling it up to the required height on the drill tower. Hose drills had progressed to incorporate pump drills and we could connect hose to a fire engine and work and control the pressure of the water coming out the end of the nozzle. We could now even climb hook ladders to the third floor in solo drills and we were learning two-man drills. All things considered our knowledge and skills were developing and we enjoyed every day at Southwark. So when the time came to leave it was a feeling of uncertainty rather than sadness that we shared with each other. Naturally we all mixed with other squad members and had got to know each other but now we were off to live together, day and night. Some cadets had never been away from home before, going home each night since childhood. Our parents had been informed about the forthcoming changes but they received no invitation to see the embryonic college. That was not the Fire Brigade's way of doing things.

On moving day we were to be transported from Southwark by coach to the new College. We had already taken our kit bags and fire kit earlier in the week. On this day we wore our undress uniforms and looked remarkably smart. Our shoes were highly polished and our red-banded caps proudly pointed out that we were Junior Firemen. The five squads were paraded in the main drill yard for the last time and we were inspected by the Commandant of the Training School, (a title that *political correctness* would ensure was changed in later years.) Our collection of big and small suitcases, containing civvies and personal belongings were loaded on the coaches, as we wondered how different things would be tomorrow.

Settling in at the College took remarkably little time. We were allocated dormitories and dumped our suitcases on the beds. A great deal of work had been done in the days before our arrival and the main building had an almost overpowering smell of new paint, polish and bleach. The dormitory was clean, new beds had been provided and an individual personal locker placed by each one. Army style blankets, sheets and a pillow were made up in a tight bedroll at the head of each bed. A task we had to repeat every morning, only being let off this particular chore at the weekend if you stayed at the college. The ground floor had been transformed by the contractors and builders. Lecture rooms were now fitted out with desks and chairs, blackboards and other visual aid materials.

The dining room, which doubled as the assembly hall, had an enormous picture portrait of the Queen at one end. The place had the distinct feel of a school about it. Some of those, who had previously been sent to boarding school, commented that they had joined the cadets to get away from all that and now they were going back again.

In the afternoon we were all to be addressed by the new uniformed Head of the College, Assistant Divisional Officer Ferdy Hurcombe. We gathered in the dining room and waited. We knew of him from Southwark but had had little actual contact with him before today. He was a squat powerful looking man who always managed to maintain an uncompromising look on his rounded face. Given a beadle's hat and coat he could have easily have passed for Mr Bumble from Dickens's *Oliver Twist*. He stood on the raised dais, hands on his hips, looking very self-important. He could have been addressing troops prior to going into battle rather than just sixty junior firemen and their instructors, his captive audience. He told us we had to get used to new daily routines; earlier starts each day with room inspections; varied timetables that catered for the different intakes of new squads; increased weekly sport; swimming and daily fitness training.

The college was in Kent County Council's area and the nearest Kent fire station did not have either a full-time crew or a respectable drill tower. With none of the previous fire brigade training facilities available that we had enjoyed at Southwark we had to travel to the nearest London fire stations, Orpington and Sidcup, to get access to a drill tower. The academic part of the course was now to be provided at Dartford College. Our daily free time would start at 6.30 pm Mondays to Thursdays. "Lights out" was at 11 pm but this was a rule that some "duty" instructors found harder to enforce than others. We were allowed home every weekend with an added concession that we could leave College at 4 pm on Fridays. This meant that those with long distances to travel could make the bus and train connections at mainline stations. Some cadets, however, lived in far-flung parts of the country and this meant they stayed at the college most weekends but occasionally went home with other cadets for a weekend leave. For those found guilty of misdemeanours, or other punishable offences, there was no weekend leave, and you would be confined to barracks. Actually it was not that bad as I was, all too soon, to find out. Everyone had to return to the College by 10pm on Sunday evenings.

It was inevitable, with over sixty physically fit and active adolescent boys in College wanting to let off steam, that fun and high spirits would sometimes get out of hand. More serious disagreements between individual cadets were settled in the gym in the boxing ring under the supervision of an instructor. This was, however, an infrequent occurrence.

John "Noddy" Norris was a fellow F Squad member who came from Bury St Edmonds in Suffolk. He had a broad East Anglian accent and was considered, light-heartedly, to be a country bumpkin by his London squad members. It was customary to take the mickey out of one another, each giving as good as he got.

I was mimicking John's yokel country accent, and generally taking the piss, when John grabbed one of his fireboots and hurled it across the dormitory in retaliation. It missed me completely. This just added fuel to the fire as a chorus of "oo ah" went up and the others in the squad lampooned his poor throwing ability and abysmal aim. Incensed, he gave chase, armed with his other fireboot, determined not to miss a second time. I legged it out of the dorm and into the corridor at the end of which was a tall closed window. He ran after me into the corridor and the second fireboot came flying through the air, missing me entirely but not the wide windowpane! An enormous crash and the tinkling of broken glass followed as the boot sailed clear out into the night air. We had hurriedly disappeared back to our dorm, put the lights out, and were tucked up in our beds before the duty Instructor threw open the door and said, "Norris, clear up the bloody mess and report to ADO Hurcombe immediately after breakfast." John and I cleaned up the broken glass and we were the topic of considerable conversation about what would happen the following morning. The general consensus of opinion was that it would be better to be hung, drawn and quartered than be expelled from College.

I joined John the following morning as we stood to attention outside the ADO's office door. We were both dressed in our best undress uniform that had creases down the trousers you could have cut your finger on and shoes you could see your face in. We waited pensively for ADO Hurcombe to arrive. His stern face seemed to spell bad news as he walked gruffly into his office, ordering us to follow him. He sat down and we stood to attention looking at him across his enormous desk with a solitary fireboot standing on it. "What are you doing here Pike?" he demanded. "It was my fault sir, I ducked." This unexpected confession seemed to take the wind out of his sails or maybe he was human after all? "You two will lose your next two weekend passes." John could not give a hoot about this, as he had to stay weekends anyway. But we had to pay for the replacement windowpane and that hurt, at least in our pockets. It amounted to almost two weeks' pay and our meagre £6.0s.0d a week did not get us very far as it was. He ordered us out of his office telling John to take the evidence with him, a fireboot with his name; **J.E.P. Norris**, clearly written inside it.

A great deal of activity occurred over the next few weeks and considerable changes occurred at the College. The Brigade had recruited a Principal to run the College, an ex-Major from the army. He was a grey suited and a grey-haired individual who looked better placed to running a prep school rather than a Fire Service college. In fact he had had a distinguished army career and had been awarded medals for gallantry, but still he looked and acted like a headmaster. The fact that he was still involved with a uniformed service seemed to us the only thread of commonality between his own background and the Fire Brigade's ways. It may seem arrogant but we were not meant to be boy soldiers, or officer cadets, or whatever he thought we should be. It was clear that his view of what was needed came into conflict with the college's senior fire officers and uniformed instructional staff. Whatever his priorities were, they did not seem to match those of our instructors, who would look increasingly frustrated at the change of management style and worse having to report to a civvy! Sadly ADO Hurcombe could not take to this new regime and chose to return to operational duties, although it was strongly rumoured that he was pushed out; by guess who? So ADO Hurcombe had to uproot and relocate his family yet again. It was widely considered by cadets and staff that it was one to the ex-Major and nil to the Brigade. On his last day at the college it was an emotional ADO that said goodbye to all the squads in turn and it is to his great credit that he encouraged us all to make a go of the College and to ensure our endeavours helped make it a success. ADO Hurcombe, plus family in tow, went back to the A Division, which covered London's West End and the districts of Mayfair and Paddington. He would be later be commended for his bravery in the rescue of a woman threatening to jump off a building and later rose to become the Divisional Commander.

Motor driving course

Sub Officer John Berry was a tall, lean, almost skinny, man. In his mid-forties, with a long face and a beaky nose, he was one of the Brigade's full-time driving instructors. Like everyone else in the Brigade, he had started his career as an operational fireman, serving at South London fire stations before transferring to day duties as a driving instructor. Now he worked at the College and taught junior firemen how to drive. Shortly after their seventeenth birthdays junior firemen had to be able to drive as part of their course. Three of us, now aged seventeen, had been put on a driving course. Ray Smith from E squad, Mick Brown and I were put in the care of John Berry. It would be nice to say that I was a natural driver, but I was not. We did not learn to drive in a car either; it was a diesel Commer twelve-seater personnel carrier. We started, like all novice drivers, learning the basics, driving around the quiet back streets of Sidcup and then some manoeuvring on the wide-open spaces of Dartford Common. My driving ability, or rather lack of it, tested the patience of John Berry who did not normally swear. But it was not long, once I was behind the wheel, before his first then his second expletive led into a full flow of sexually descriptive phrases that sounded physically impossible but which John Berry clearly thought my driving capable of. Whilst Mike and Ray were getting the hang of this driving lark and managing three-point turns and reversing I was still checking my rear-view mirrors and changing from first to second gear. The weekend could not come soon enough. I spent a fretful Saturday and Sunday at home knowing that Monday was rapidly approaching and it was back behind that damned wheel again.

With a new week came a new driver. Not necessarily a better driver but more confident at least, which was just as well because the honeymoon was over. We were driving in London's traffic, initially around Southwark and Clapham then moving north of the river, somewhere! After a better day, with less crunching of the gears and even less swearing from John Berry, it fell to me to get us home via the Elephant and Castle. It was by now rush hour and it was there and then that it all fell apart! Other than those immediately behind me very few of the hundreds of delayed motorists would ever know that the cause of their painfully slow journey home was a learner driver, me; stalling his way down the New and Old Kent Roads. I was in a cold sweat by the time I got to Lewisham and John Berry was in danger of severe apoplexy. I was in such a sorry state by the time we finally returned to college that I just took to my bed. The new dawn saw no improvement in the situation and I took myself off to the sick bay complaining of chronic stomach ache, but I knew it was just the fear of another day's driving. I think that John Berry knew what the real problem was too. Wednesday seemed to go better and by Thursday I actually got the hang of this driving malarkey and was not sworn at once, much to everyone's amazement, especially mine.

Our driving test was scheduled for early the following week. I was not confident of a pass. The examiner, a Station Officer, seemed devoid of all human emotion and spoke in monosyllabic tones. "Turn right: Take the next left Do a three-point turn here." Needless to say I failed. Which was not exactly true as I was not allowed to fail but had to retake the test the following day. Mike and Ray passed with flying colours so I had the benefit of intensive revision all the way back to College and also on the return to the testing centre at Southwark the next day. John Berry was both encouraging and positive about my second attempt, which in part, helped with my nervousness. Again the same examiner gave the instructions and I followed them to the letter. Either my driving was actually better or John Berry had pleaded with the examiner not to make him teach me anymore. I passed, much to my surprise and John Berry's delight. If this was because he did not have to put up with me anymore; well he did not admit to it.

Making the best of it

After that unforgettable episode it was back to squad training at the College. Whilst it was easier to carry out our technical and academic studies at Swanley, the practical side remained more difficult due to the lack of equipment and on-site training facilities. The College grounds did not have an adequate hydrant system and the pressure was described professionally by the instructors as "piss poor." To overcome this problem we were given training that wartime firemen, during London's Blitz, would have found familiar. Erected in the grounds were a series of "emergency" dams, each containing about five thousand gallons of water. Our fire engine was a Government surplus "green" one-ton trailer pump that was probably last used in the war. It had to be hand cranked to start the damn thing and was pulled or pushed manually into position, and with its suction hose connected, we would lift water from the dams. Jets of water that we got to work were directed back into the dams to conserve the limited water supply. I unsurprisingly cannot remember seeing the firemen from Southwark Fire Station pulling these heavy trailer pumps out of the fire station when they got a call. However I am sure it was not what we were expected to be doing in 1966.

We did have a fire engine or two but they were far too heavy to drive around the grounds of the College that were more cart tracks than roads. The fire engines were used for off-site training or static drills at the College. We took the ladders off the engines then pitched them against the only available college structure, a tall metal fire escape at one end of the main building. Our other ladder drills took on a completely new meaning, and were certainly not in the Fire Service Drill Book, our "Bible." The inventive instructional staff had constructed an obstacle course using a combination of various fire service ladders. These ladders gave us access to the treetops which were linked by rope bridges, some thirty to fifty feet off the ground. If nothing else, by the end of our training, we would excel at rescuing cats from trees. The instructors also constructed a ten-foot high climbing wall out of thick timber boards that required both excellent team effort and co-ordination to climb over as a squad; this would have challenged the SAS to get over the damn thing.

Climbing trees with ladders attached, pulling trailer pumps, scaling climbing walls, plus lots of sport, swimming and physical training was turning us into very fit young men. So much so, that squads would race each other around the grounds pulling the one-ton trailer pump with its hose and equipment then getting the pump to work at each of the three emergency dams, over the distance of about a mile. We were timed to see who had completed the course the quickest. E squad had a built-in advantage in the form of Nobby Clark and Graham Holloway. Nobby was short and squat whilst Graham was tall and wide, both were built like brick shithouses and could have picked up and ran with the bloody trailer pump all on their own. We always came a close second and only moved into first place when E squad returned to Southwark to complete the final phase of their training. As this was probably the Brigade's only trailer pump if the Soviet Union did *nuke* the West, as was widely feared in the late 1960s, it would be Junior Firemen who would come to the rescue! The only ones trained in the lost art of pulling and working ancient trailer pumps.

The cadets' high level of physical strength did have some unforeseen advantages, especially when it came to dealing with problems that we encountered with the local lads living around Swanley. We were more than capable of looking after ourselves. Having sixty teenage boys descend on Swanley had upset the natural order that previously existed between the local population of teenage boys and the available and willing, snoggable girls. We were all under the legal age for drinking alcohol but local landlords did not mind turning a blind eye and taking our money, particularly in pubs off the beaten track. But in Swanley village the Kent Constabulary were a lot hotter and some of us got a clip around the ear for trying our luck by drinking in the town. It was not as if we could blend in easily either; firstly we were not local, and our short haircuts made us stand out like a sore thumb. The local lads had the latest in fashionable hair styles or just plain long hair, and did not look at all like the "Fire College boys." If a fracas developed, and they did from time to time, we were more than capable of taking care of ourselves, and each other.

With cadet numbers un-depleted by local lynch mobs looking to string up randy junior firemen, for deflowering the young maidens of Swanley, we were preparing to welcome the then Home Secretary, the Rt Hon Roy Jenkins MP, in the late spring of 1966. He was to formally open the College and unveil a commemorative plaque. The Brigade's top brass turned out in force together with, as if by some miracle, red fire engines (that actually worked!) with which cadets could show off their talents to Mr Jenkins. Unfortunately he looked as though he wanted to be somewhere else. It was a carefully choreographed tour of inspection. We were paraded as a welcoming guard of honour, along the drive leading to the main entrance to await his arrival. Greeted by the Principal, he inspected us and I was even spoken to by the great man himself, while standing on parade. He had a strange lispy voice and a soft gentle handshake. As he disappeared in the front door of the College, we were all hastily ushered via the back entrance into the main hall to listen to his speech. He spoke about things we did not really understand and seemed to have very little to do with us or our training. It must have been important though because everyone on the dais was nodding wisely in agreement. We clapped loudly, on cue, just as we had been instructed during the rehearsal for the speech. Whilst all the bigwigs had their tea and biscuits, or whatever they devoured, we were ushered outside again and regrouped into our squads. Some changed into fire kit, others into undress uniform or gym strip ready to demonstrate the various activities that encompassed College training. I was in my fire kit and the Home Secretary could hardly contain his excitement as he watched us run-out and then roll up hose along the drive. We were not allowed water in case we got him wet! The activities actually looked quite impressive as we cadets showed off our ability at drill; fitness training; dragging the dreaded trailer pump around the grounds; pumping water; plus pitching ladders. Cadets in the classroom portrayed the technical side of the college's curriculum, whilst a couple more demonstrated three-point turns and their learner driver training. A task I was not asked to demonstrate.

Whilst my fire brigade training had been on going at Swanley I still managed to keep up my Sub Aqua course at New Cross, on Friday nights. I even fitted in the occasional weekend open water training sessions at lakes and on the south coast. It was helping me achieve my second-Class Diver's certificate and become a Dive Leader; that was, of course, when I was not restricted to barracks for some misdemeanour or other. I was already taking other novices through their basic snorkel training and theory tests. Although none of my own squad fancied taking the plunge, a number of other cadets did and it was not long before we had one of the Instructors, a Station Officer, joining in too. That particular Station Officer was a former soldier in the Guards Regiment and had "doctored" his cap peak to prove it, cut so that it lay flat on his forehead. He marched around with a guardsman's swagger and we hated it when he took us for marching drill, which he did frequently. It was like trooping the colour with him barking out his drill orders, well not quite, but you get my meaning. He was also a very heavy smoker and training was interspersed with smoke breaks so he could scrounge a fag off anyone that was silly enough to give him one. Sadly the smoking would be the death of him a few years later when he returned to a fire station. Whilst there he later developed lung cancer and died.

All this swimming activity plus my UK championship success, and role as a 'lay' Sub Aqua teacher, got to the ears of the College Principal. The Major was seeking ways to up the College's profile within the local community and get the College some good press coverage into the bargain. My Instructor, Len Knight, and I were summoned to see the Major one afternoon. We looked equally bemused as to what it was all about. It transpired that a group of special needs children, who went swimming each Friday morning at a local pool in Hextable (a village near Swanley) required some assistance in helping them with their swimming sessions. It demanded a high ratio of helpers to children to cater for the children's enthusiasm in the pool. I was requested to "volunteer" and to find some other cadets willing to assist in the task. This was subject to Len agreeing to release me from training for a couple of hours each Friday morning. He agreed and a small group of us attended the pool the next Friday to meet the carers and the children for the first time.

The special needs children numbered about fifteen boys and girls aged between nine and fourteen years old. There were to be four carers and now five additional "volunteer" cadets, including myself. The majority of the children had Down's syndrome whilst others had severe learning difficulties. They all had one thing in common however, they loved the water. Whilst some were able to swim, a couple thought they could but could not as they sank every time their feet left the bottom of the pool. The look of joy on all their faces was incredibly moving seeing them splash around and play carefree, and safe, in the water with their minders. In no time we made friends with the children, some of who were young teenagers themselves. It was not a structured swimming lesson, although some seemed eager to learn and we obliged them. As there were more children than helpers, we had at times two or more hanging from around our necks or pulling at our arms. The children were incredibly caring and affectionate. They were also extremely strong for their age; some were almost as big as us. With a couple of children holding on to you it took a lot of effort to keep your balance and head above water. At the end of the 90-minute session we were knackered but it did not matter, seeing the enjoyment this activity brought to them. We promised to return the following week and the relationship between the school and the College grew and lasted until the Junior Fireman scheme and the College was closed on financial grounds in 1970. The local paper picked up on the story probably prompted by the College Principal. We became famous for a day or two. Far more important was the privilege of meeting and helping such wonderful young people whose thanks, each week, we saw in their joyful welcome and smiles at the poolside.

Spring turned to summer. England famously won the World Cup beating Germany 4-2. We celebrated by throwing everyone who had stayed over the weekend to watch the match into the dams, including the instructors. Our fitness levels continued to grow, as did our knowledge and skills in what the College had to offer. This remained targeted more on the technical side than practical thanks to the influence of the Principal. It was believed by many in the wider Brigade that the College was training the Brigade's future senior and principal officers. A Fire Brigade Sandhurst or West Point! They had only to look at some of our school records to shoot that particular theory down in flames, although time would prove that very many of those passing through the Junior Fireman scheme would actually progress to senior rank, some even higher. If this ratio was greater than a similar number passing through recruit training, nobody ever took the trouble to analyse the statistics. So who knows?

Many of the College's instructional staff were characters in their own right, each with their own particular and individual methods of training. Station Officer Peter Carnell was a fitness fanatic, an excellent cross-country runner and sportsman. A Brigade champion runner, he would effortlessly trot off into the distance as we tried to keep up, whether in the college grounds or out in the surrounding Kentish countryside. He could be heard shouting his personal catch phrase, "Come on my side," as he rapidly disappeared over some hill or other. He was also a talented rugby player and coach. We were convinced his incentive to become an instructor at the College was to use it as a private fitness club. I believe he achieved his goal.

Norman Everard was another of the college instructors. A Station Officer in his early thirties he also was an excellent athlete and talented cross-country runner. He was lean, fit and had a distinctive jutting jaw. He sounded just like the famous 1960's television personality Derek Nimmo. Norman called everyone, "Cock. Alright cock?" would be his educated and softly spoken greeting heard about the College corridors as he spoke to the cadets. Seemingly unflappable, his party piece however was defying the laws of gravity. When taking hook ladder drills, he would stand in front of the tower with his feet slightly apart. He would watch cadets ascend the tower and occasionally call, "Come on cock, punch that bloody ladder up faster," whilst some poor sod struggled to push the twenty-eight pound ladder to the next level; this whilst balancing with one foot on the ladder they had just climbed and secured to the ladder by only the hook belt. Other instructors would tilt their head backwards as the trainees climbed higher, sill to sill. Not Norman. His whole body, hinged from his ankles, leant backwards eventually to an angle of nearly forty-five degrees! His body appeared to be firmly glued to the ground by only his feet supporting this strange stance angle. It was a sight you had to see to believe, that anyone could actually stand like that.

The autumn of 1966 saw us say goodbye to the college and return to Southwark Training School, still together but no longer F Squad. Our instructor, Len Knight, had a new intake, a new F squad. We now had a recruit instructor, Station Officer Dave Rees, who was to take us through our conversion course.

Chapter 4

Conversion

No more Mr Nice guy

The conversion course was just under five weeks' duration. Its aim was to bring us up to recruit standard so we could pass-out as firemen. Station Officer Rees, at our very first meeting, left none of us in any doubt that we were in for some very hard work. Whilst we could sail through the technical exams, the practical side was a completely different story. The poor training facilities and lack of fire engines at the college had meant we had not even touched some of the drills we were required to cover and to be able to demonstrate them proficiently. We had the basics but had not combined the drills in a way that was required of our pass-out drills nor, more importantly, to use at real fires. In the main we had used one fire engine with some of its equipment and now we had to use two engines and most of the equipment they carried in a safe and competent manner. Plus there were the live rescue drills. Until our conversion course we had been prevented from undertaking this type of training as it was considered too risky by the powers that be. Now we would be carrying each other down a fifty-foot wheeled escape ladder and lowering each other from the drill tower using a lowering line. All of a sudden, those five weeks did not seem very much time.

Station Officer Dave Rees, who was to become a close colleague in later years, can best be described as firm but fair. No longer at Swanley I now went home at the end of each day, exhausted. In the first few days we clearly demonstrated the practical failings of the College's drill regime, at least to the standards expected of our new instructor. We undertook a very intense refresher of the basic elements before starting to combine them. Working with three other cadets with just one ladder was different to ten of us working at the same time using multiple ladders, hose lines, hydrants, and pumping water. Regardless whether it was getting the equipment to work or putting it away you worked at one speed, fast. It took four firemen to slip and pitch the wheeled escape ladder and three to pitch the extension ladder. We were to combine using the hook ladders with both these ladders and in order to pass-out we had to perform a "party piece." This entailed pitching the escape ladder to the fourth floor of the drill tower; tie a "first floor ladder" onto the escape to reach the fifth floor; then use a hook ladder to climb to the sixth floor and finally to haul a line of hose aloft and get it to work. If the examiner did not think you worked hard enough (or his missus had given him grief the night before) he would make you change an imaginary burst length of hose just to add some extra fun.

The pressure increased at the end of the first week of, near exhausting, appliance and ladder training, when Station Officer Rees informed us that the Training School was to be fully involved in the Brigade's Centenary Review at Brigade Headquarters in mid-November. This was to be attended by Her Majesty the Queen and His Royal Highness Prince Philip. It was non-negotiable and we would have to make up for any training time lost to the various rehearsals and the actual review. As it turned out, Dave Rees made such a fuss about how little time we could afford to lose in training that we were allocated just minor duties. In the case of Graham Holloway and myself they turned out not to be so minor.

Live rescue drills were taken very seriously indeed at the training school. Accidents had occurred previously with recruits falling to their death whilst being carried down a ladder. Ladders were always tested prior to rescue drills taking place, in addition to their normal weekly tests. Although no safety harnesses or lines were used then, they would be introduced in later years at the insistence of the Fire Brigades Union. We started with "carrying down" from a wheeled escape from the third floor of the drill tower. A new pace was established by Station Officer Rees; one of cool calmness and watchfulness. An additional instructor was in place on the third floor to watch over the mounting of the ladder. We were paired off so each person carried someone about the same height and weight, but with all our energetic training no one weighed over eleven stone anyway. On the third floor of the drill tower a set of wooden steps allowed us easy access onto the wooden sill. Carrying my partner I stepped on to the sill, grasped the top of the ladder and stepped, gingerly, on to it for my first carry down. It all went fine. Nerves got the better of one or two of the others and they had problems transferring from the sill to the ladder. Each was talked through what to do and how the carry down was to be performed. Eventually we all managed our carry down that was to be a regular feature in our weekly training schedule.

Lowering under foot was different because you were lowered from the drill tower by a line that was controlled by the friction of the line passing over the window sill then under the foot of the fireman performing the lowering. Another fireman assisted in the lower and used his foot, pressing on top of his colleague's, to act as a brake. But to perform this task the person being lowered had to climb up and out onto the sill and suspend themselves by their hands from the sill before the lower was started. There were more than one or two squeals of horror or an, "Oh shit" as forty feet up you dropped the first two or three feet before your weight was taken up on the line and the lowering was controlled. This live drill was later modified with the "live" casualty being replaced by a twelve stone dummy, but not for some years to come and certainly not before I had to do it for our pass-out drills.

In reality these "live" rescue drills did little to reflect the actual conditions found at fires especially where people had to be rescued by ladder. To start with the training drill towers had no fitted glazed windows in them and what sort of building has a convenient pair of steps placed right next to the window opening so you could climb onto the blooming ladder? Live rescue drill were then an integral part of a fireman's training so we did as we were told and got on with it. Linked to the line rescue drill were the two-man hook ladder drills. Here one of the two firemen carried the lowering line on his back in addition to working the ladder up the tower. The knack was to push the ladder swiftly upwards in a straight line to the next floor. Going too slowly or not keeping it straight meant the higher it got the more difficult it was to control. Five to ten degrees out of alignment and the weight at the top of the ladder gravity took over. You could either lose total control of the ladder and drop the damn thing or hit the guy beneath you with the extended steel hook with, possibly, tragic consequences. Hook ladder drills had taken their toll and had proved fatal to young firemen performing the drill at Wembley Fire Station during our cadet training.

A lull in our rigorous training schedule came with imminent arrival of the Centenary Review to be held on 11th November. The Fire Brigade had a strong tradition with its annual reviews and had been running them since the start of the twentieth century. This was a very special occasion though; it was to celebrate one hundred years of the London Fire Brigade. Being a Royal Review nothing was going to stop the Brigade being seen at its best, even if it had to empty the whole Training School, and it did. With over two thousand official guests on the Headquarters' balconies and hundreds of unofficial spectators watching from surrounding office windows and rooftops they waited excitedly for the Royal's arrival.

Dave Rees had secured our role as stewards so as not to interfere with our training and we were able to watch most of the "show." The review contained an impressive hook ladder display with these ladders filling every window of the double fronted nine storey drill tower as firemen formed a human chain pushing the hook ladders up ever higher whilst the excellent London Fire Brigade band played the accompanying music of "Teddy Bear's Picnic." When each of the fourteen window sills had its requisite hook ladder and fireman in position each man leant backwards, letting go with both hands, and put their faith in the hook belt that secured them to the hook ladders and safety. Fire service history was portrayed by showing the seventeenth century Insurance Companies manual hand pumps in action; The Metropolitan Fire Brigade was represented using the Brigade's historic and original horse drawn manual engines and the "steamers." A modern fire scene brought the Royals, and the cheering public, right up to date. Operational personnel did the modern drills and displays but recruits, Headquarters administration staff and Junior Fireman cadets were all thrown into the melting pot. Some were dressed as insurance firefighters and others as bystanders in period costumes. At the conclusion of the review the Queen said her thanks to the parade of 500 or so firemen and officers who marched into the yard to the sound of the Fire Brigade band.

Next the Queen was to unveil a plaque to formally open the Brigade's new control room located underneath the Headquarters complex. Enter Graham

Holloway and I dressed in our smartest uniforms. We were to be the royal door openers in the control room. Without prior training we performed this onerous task with outstanding style and grace. If we failed our pass-out we could always apply for royal pageboy duties. Whilst I am not sure if Her Majesty even noticed us whilst pulling the cord to unveil the plaque Prince Philip thought it was appropriate to talk to a minion and picked me. "Why have you a red band around your cap?" he asked. "I'm a junior fireman Your Majesty."

"You look too old to be junior," he replied. Satisfied with his own answer, and smiling, he went in search of another minion to talk to. It was my first conversation with a Royal but it was not to be my last.

Pass-out

With the Royal visit over it was back to business and the final preparations for our pass-out practical examinations. Our written exams had already been taken care of and we all passed. Now it was the last frantic rehearsals for the practical and preparation for the oral examinations just ahead of us. Although when the finals came it was almost an anti-climax. Dave Rees had been pushing us hard and had us chasing our own tails on the drill yard. We were doing combined drills back to back with only a minimal break between one drill finishing and the next starting. Despite the time of year and the winter chill we were constantly bathed in sweat and perspiration. We would sit between drills with our fire tunics undone to the waist trying to cool down before starting again, pitching ladders and throwing out hose lines in the next arduous drill session whilst Dave Rees looked on wrapped up in his thick woollen overcoat, scarf and gloves.

The night before our pass-out drills Dave Rees gathered us together in a classroom for a pep talk about the big day. He said he had taught us all he could and now it was up to us, individually and as a team. He admitted having been a little sceptical about getting a bunch of cadets after having only ever trained adult recruits but, in his book, we had proved we were adults and could hold our own against any squad in the training school. Coming from him that was praise indeed, but just to keep our feet firmly on the ground he identified individual faults or failings that each of us would have to avoid if we wanted a positive result in the pass-out drills. That man did not miss a trick.

The following day he conducted the pass-out drill set by the two Training School senior officer assessors who were officiating at the pass out. There were one or two minor slip-ups but they were quickly spotted by other crewmembers and rectified. The carry downs were undertaken at a less hectic pace but nevertheless were performed quickly and smoothly and to the satisfaction of Dave Rees who would say quietly, "Well done" or "Good carry" out of the corner of his mouth as we laid the person being carried on the ground in front of him at the conclusion of the carry. Immediately after the morning break it was knots and lines and the hook ladder drills. One assessor took the hook ladder exercises whilst the other invigilated on knots and lines and conducted the oral exam. Lastly, and through the lunch hour, we were called individually to perform the pumps and pumping drills, which involved lifting water from an open water supply, using a proper fire engine and resolving pump faults that the examiner would identify. By early afternoon it was finally all over. Anyone not passing the practical examinations would be back squadded and have to take it all over again. Fail the second time and you were out. We would have to wait until the following day to discover how we had done. Even though Dave Rees felt confident it was not the same as hearing the words, "You have passed."

The next day, immediately after parade, we were told to get into our best uniform and assemble in the cadets' classroom by 9.30 sharp. We waited excitedly and Dave Rees called us to attention as only one of the two senior officers entered the classroom exactly at 9.30. He carried a clipboard, his face giving nothing away as he took his place behind the lectern. After an agonising wait, while he studied whatever was on the clipboard, he looked up and said, "You all passed out, and as from your respective 18th birthdays you are officially firemen. You take up your individual postings the first available shift after your birthday." He then started to read out, in alphabetical order, our names followed by the station and the watch we had been allocated to. No one got a choice of where they would be posted; it was potluck if you got a busy or a quiet station. He started with the A's and Bob Adams was unable to contain his excitement at getting Croydon and such a good posting. He yelled out "Yes" before the look of disapproval from both Dave Rees and the senior officer returned him to his senses. Well not quite since he sat in his chair grinning like a Cheshire cat. Name after name was called, station after station, watch after watch, until he came to me. "Pike; Southwark, Blue watch." I could not believe my luck; here at Southwark, one of the best stations in the Brigade. It was where I would have chosen had I been given the choice. I was ecstatic. The list was finally completed and after a few well-chosen words of advice, that no one absorbed or even listened to, the senior officer left the room. Dave Rees was far more congratulatory but we were hard pressed to contain our excitement and elation as we exchanged congratulations on our postings to busy operational stations. None of us had got a quiet station, which was considered as a naff posting. Dave Rees finally managed to calm us down and told us that over the next few days we would visit our individual stations and deliver our fire kit ready to start our first shift. "You won't have far to go Pikey, make sure you don't get lost! Right you lot, you might as well have an early day, come back in here in the morning and we will see what to do with you before you take up your individual postings. Some of you will not be coming back after Christmas so I will do a kit check tomorrow afternoon. Make sure everything is marked with your name and your new station."

With excitement still filling the locker room we started to change into our civvies, ready to go home early. Dave Rees walked into the locker room and called out my name, "My office Pikey." leaving me to wonder what all this was about. No sooner had I got through the door of his office when I was told, "Sorry old lad but they made a mistake with your posting, it's not B23 Blue, its B22 Lambeth Red Watch." My heart sank. I was being sent to Lambeth, the headquarters fire station. I was not impressed one bit. Southwark was a small friendly station by all accounts and Lambeth had the largest watch in the Brigade. It did not have a reputation that made recruits eager to get posted there. But I had no choice, it was to be my posting and that was the end of it. I returned to the locker room despondent. It was now empty but the radio was still playing. It was playing the Hedgehoppers Anonymous chart-topping song "It's good news week." The very song that was playing when I walked into "B" locker-room in our first week of training in September 1965 and that seem so appropriate then. Now I was not so sure. I was fast learning to be fatalistic in what the Brigade could, and would, throw at you.

I had the penultimate eighteenth birthday date of our conversion squad, coincidently the 18th January, and I watched the others leave, one by one, to take up their new operational posts. Not only was I going to Lambeth, but I was the only one posted to the Red Watch. All the others had been posted to either the White or Blue Watch. So despite our reassurance to each other that we would stay in touch we all knew that being on different watches would make that a problem and the likelihood was very doubtful.

The week before my first shift at Lambeth I travelled from Training School on a number forty-four bus, armed with my kit bag full of fire kit and with my fire helmet tied on top, to visit the Red Watch at Lambeth. Although I had been assured that the station was expecting me, it was a different story when I arrived. "Who are you?" was my initial greeting from a leading fireman standing in the appliance room. "Fm Pike Sir. I've been posted here. I start next week."

"Well that's news to me son, and don't call me Sir, because I ain't him. You had better get yourself up to the station office and see the governor." Even finding the station office was difficult as Lambeth fire station occupied the whole of the building's expansive first floor and many separate doors ran off its central corridor. The corridor was covered in shining lino which, in the years ahead, I would get to know every square inch of as I applied the liquid polish then had to make it shine using a heavy manual floor polisher called a "bumper." Eventually I found the door marked 'office' and knocked. No reply, although I could hear voices from inside. I waited and then knocked again; still nothing! Nervously I opened the door and a tall, blonde, good-looking leading fireman with an exceptionally well-spoken voice said, "Yes?"

"I'm Fm Pike, I'm posted here."

"You're not due until next week, plus you start on nights and this is a day duty," was the polite but quizzical reply. Then a tall gangly looking officer poked his head around an inner office door. "Come on in Pikey," said the officer as I was shown into the inner sanctum.

"My name is Dick Richardson; I am the Sub Officer here but acting Station Officer because the governor got his head bashed in by a beer bottle on New Year's Eve when we answered a false alarm. We are not sure when he will be back. All three leading firemen here have just been promoted to Sub Officers and are posted. You will start together with the new office staff next shift. You're also our first junior fireman. I hope you are better than that other silly, arrogant, bastard of a junior fireman that Brixton got last year?" I thought this is going well. "I hope so too Sir," I replied, having no idea who he was talking about.

"Well get yourself a locker, no point in introducing you yet, we will wait until next week." Calling to no one in particular in the outer office he said, "Get Tom Read in here to show Fm Pike to his locker." That was it, interview over. I was back in the corridor being led by the first real friendly face of the day towards the firemen's locker room. It was the largest single room on the station. It had floor to ceiling lockers that were back-to-back and stood over eight foot tall. They separated the banks of eight bunk beds, two wide, two high and two deep, located between each set of lockers. Down the outside wall the locker room had metal-framed windows which overlooked the River Thames. The wooden parquet floor was highly polished; in fact everything seemed highly polished. "This is your locker," said Tom. "Mine is three down from you. When you come back next week ask for me, don't relieve any of the day watch and just get rigged in your fire gear ready for the six o'clock roll call." At last some advice I could follow. Travelling back on the number 44 bus I was feeling rather sorry for myself and I wondered what I had let myself in for? I wanted to go to B23 Southwark fire station, not Lambeth.

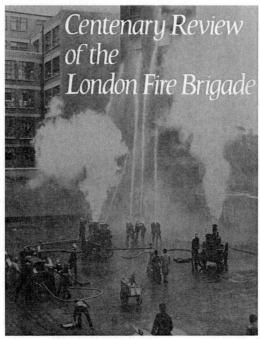

Her Royal Highness, Her Majesty the Queen accompanied by His Royal Highness Prince Philip, Duke of Edinburgh are the guests of honour at the Centenary Review of the Brigade held at the Brigade's Headquarters, Lambeth.
Copyright. *London Fire Brigade/ Mary Evans Picture Library.*

The Queen formally opening the remodeled and upgraded underground Brigade Control (M2FH) at Lambeth's Headquarters. November 1966.
Copyright. *London Fire Brigade/ Mary Evans Picture Library.*

The new B22 Lambeth Red Watch junior buck. 23rd January 1967.

Chapter 5

Probation

First night shift

Monday 23rd January 1967, I waited impatiently at home all day, wishing the hours away, and wanting to catch the afternoon train to Waterloo and start my 15-hour night duty. My very first shift as an operational "fireman." It was with a mixture of excitement and anxiety that I walked along the riverside from Waterloo railway station, passing St Thomas' Hospital and Lambeth Palace en route, before I reached Lambeth fire station on the Albert Embankment. This was now my fire station's ground. It was somewhere I would get to learn intimately. I would, eventually, know the names of all the roads, its important buildings and understand what its special risks were and how to gain access to them. But for now I was just wondering, in fact hoping, that something would catch fire tonight.

Dave Rees's words of wisdom, as I bade him farewell for the last time were, "Keep your head down Pikey, say little and listen and learn." So with his advice going around in my head I walked sheepishly through the front entrance, across the multi-bay appliance room and made my way to the first floor. Finding my locker, I changed into my blue work overalls whilst I tried to absorb the atmosphere of the station. I found this difficult, if not impossible. It was as though I was in a dream, seeing what was around me but not actually being a part of it. I felt very alone, which is strange because Lambeth has the largest watch strength of any London fire station. Suddenly these thoughts of self-doubt vanished as the house bells started ringing loudly all over the station. The din flooded my head and was immediately followed by the thud of footsteps on lino and the crashing of doors. I went into the long corridor to watch the excitement of the duty watch responded to this callout. In the centre of the long corridor, and hanging from the ceiling, was a set of appliance indicator lights (coloured light bulbs). It was these lights that the dutyman could illuminate from the watchroom to let the crews know which appliance, or appliances, were being ordered out. Another set of identical lights was mounted in the locker room whilst in the appliance room and in the main drill yard were large indicator panels, which had capital letters cut into them. The letters PE, P, TL, ET and FB could be illuminated to show which appliance(s) were being ordered to a call-out.

As I stood watching the unlit row of light bulbs, first the red bulb, then the green, followed by a yellow and blue light shining brightly, and finally the white bulb lit up. All the station's four land appliances and the fireboat were being ordered onto a shout (which is the brigade's terminology of a fire call.) All London's fire stations had the same colour code, red for pump escape; green for pump; yellow for turntable ladder and blue for an emergency tender. Only two fire stations had a fireboat attached to them and calls for the fireboat were indicated by a white bulb.

With the corridor now hushed and quiet again I went to the nearest pole house and pressed the release catch and pushed the narrow twin doors open. There in front of me was the chrome pole, shining, and rising up through a square opening in the floor and secured to the appliance room floor some twenty feet below. Lambeth had the tallest sliding poles anywhere in the brigade and I was trying to recall our one, and only, sliding pole lesson. Gripping the thick silver pole, I flipped one leg behind it whilst the other gripped in front and much too fast, I slid down to the pole mat below which is meant to stop you breaking your ankles as you hit the floor. It was not the most dignified of descents but fortunately all the crews were now on their engines and the pump escape was just pulling out of the station. They left in rapid succession, with the emergency tender bringing up the rear.

I walked over to the station watchroom to see where they were going and was welcomed by the dutyman. "You're new, aren't you?" he said. "Yes, I start tonight," I replied. "I thought so by the way you came down the pole at a rate of knots. Anyway my name is Ken, how do you do?" Ken looked smart in his undress uniform and he explained that Lambeth had a manned watchroom twenty-four hours a day because it was the Brigade Headquarters station. He said the machines had gone to Battersea Power station on Clapham's ground and that our appliances made up the initial attendance together with Clapham's pair. He spent the next twenty minutes giving me a brief tour of the watchroom and showed me the station logbook and teleprinter message book. "It's so much better now," he said before continuing, "at one time we had to write every message by hand and enter it into the log book. If you had a large make up fire you could be writing for bloody hours. Now we just paste copies of the messages in the teleprinter log book. I like progress, don't you?" As if on cue the teleprinter bell rang and the teleprinter started printing out the "stop" message from Battersea Power station that turned out to be a small fire in a basement boiler house. With the machines returning to the station Ken said it was time to make myself scarce as only the dutyman was meant to be in the watchroom, especially if his governor was about.

Tom Read came into work about 5.30pm and he found me sitting on my footlocker. "Evening young Pikey, you been here all day?" Tom changed into his overalls and told me it was time to get ready for parade and roll call. There was much activity in the appliance room with oncoming Red watch crews relieving the off-going Blue watch. Appliance lockers were being opened and the contents checked, drivers started engines and conducted their routine maintenance checks. At about 5.55 Red Watch firemen, dressed in their fire gear, started to congregate in a loose huddle at the rear of the appliance room.

Fireboots and black leggings were polished, as were their belts and axe pouches. The fireman's axe had to be worn on the left side and a carefully tied belt line hung looped on to their wide belts. Our torches were actually cycle lamps, painted black that were hooked onto our belts but with a narrow loop of webbing fixed to them that went over our heads to stop us losing them when being used in action. Although their fire tunics were brushed clean there was still a pervading smell of smoke on some of the tunics. Fire helmets were either being carried or worn on the back of the head whilst the general chatter of conversation or the laughter of a shared joke passed around the gathering.

Seconds before 6.00 pm four short rings of the house bells announced the start of my first shift and the milling crowd suddenly formed into two neat lines of men facing towards the rear of the appliances. Tom kept me at his side and in the front row. There were eighteen of us on parade that night and the acting Station Officer told his deputy to, "Detail the riders." The acting Sub Officer called us to attention and read from the duty list as he detailed the riders for the night shift. "Pump Escape. Sub O Lambert; Fm Howes; Fm Read; Fm Burns; Fm Pike." He then moved on to the Pump; followed by the Turntable Ladder; Emergency Tender and the Canteen Van. The canteen van crew also doubled as the dutymen in the watchroom, taking it in turns to cover the duty during the fifteen-hour night watch. After the riders were detailed the governor made the briefest of announcements, saying that I was joining the watch. I was now officially on duty.

With the parade over Tom introduced me to the other firemen riding the PE that night and Eric Burns said, "Thank f… you're here I'm no longer the junior buck." We were required to carefully check over the appliance we were riding, noting any equipment that was found to be missing and expected to find out if it was in for repair, or had been left at a fire somewhere.

Whilst Lambeth's PE and pump were amongst the brigade's more recently acquired appliances, most of the equipment they carried had not changed in design for years. Wartime firemen, looking over the PE or pump, would have recognised virtually all of the equipment being carried and probably had used most of it. Visually the main difference between the two appliances was the ladders they carried. The PE carried the detachable fifty-foot wheeled escape ladder, a first-floor ladder and two hook ladders. This machine was essentially a life-saving appliance. The pump carried a thirty-foot wooden extension ladder, plus two hook ladders, and was the work-horse of the Brigade. The pump also carried three oxygen breathing apparatus (BA) sets in the rear crew cab. The PE carried no breathing apparatus. Both machines were capable of pumping up to four and half tons of water a minute.

"Pikey, put your gear in the middle of the back seat," said Tom, and he then suggested that I went with Eric to check over the machine. Eric had been at Lambeth for about five months, having come from training school as a recruit. He was in his early twenties, well-built but not fat, he spoke with a slight lisp. He was clearly delighted that there was a new 'junior buck' on the watch and that he had passed on his baton to me. He was very thorough in his checks taking time to explain what he was doing and why. "Don't forget that when we go out on a shout that you and I have to wear the hook belts." These large belts were hung in the back cab and it was where the asbestos anti-flash hoods and gloves were also located together with the first aid box and two portable two-gallon fire extinguishers. "Never go into a job empty handed, make sure you always take something with you like a line, extinguisher, or large axe." After fifteen minutes of checking Eric said, "Let's go for tea."

Tea was served in the first-floor mess and TV room but because there was a staff canteen in the headquarters rear block, unlike other fire stations Lambeth did not have its own kitchen. However, it did have a small galley and an aging gas cooker on which stood a large metal kettle, simmering away, ready to make tea at any time of the day or night. It was in the mess, filled with over four hundred years of combined operational experience that my fire brigade education would take on a new meaning in the months ahead.

Just five days after my eighteenth birthday I was the youngest fireman ever to join the Red Watch, possibly on any watch on the station. I felt ill at ease having suddenly being thrown into this very adult world. I was ill-equipped, not having the life experiences or knowledge to counter the quips and comments that were rapidly being thrown in my direction. The age span of the watch was considerable with some firemen in their early fifties, the same age as my Dad. Most however were in the thirties and forties, like Tom, the remainder in their twenties, like Eric. I was bottom of the pile. Uneasily, I took my tea from Ken Thorne, the mess manager, who immediately asked for my mess money for the month. Ken had started his brigade career in 1938 and had served for twenty-eight years at Lambeth, and always on the Red Watch. He had joined prior to the outbreak of war and served during the Blitz. He had won Brigade pump escape and pump competitions in the fifties and now the watch's senior hand and only ever drove the Emergency Tender.

My first night was a catastrophe, from my point of view at least. Evening drills were interrupted with shouts for the pump and then the TL. Supper-time saw the ET get a call and each time I raced for the PE but just watched it stand there, motionless, as other appliances left the station. "Lights out" was at 11pm, although most "hands" would stay up until at least midnight, some staying down in the bar while others were in the mess having a drink, playing cards or watching TV. I had laid out my bedroll at eleven but knew tonight, of all nights, that sleep was the last thing on my mind. I waited eagerly for my first shout, the call that would send the PE out. Further calls came in the early hours of the morning for the pump and TL and soon after that even the fireboat got a call. Finally, with the station quiet about 2.00am, I lay on my bunk and pulled the rough blankets over me. I was still wearing my overall trousers and tee shirt ready for a quick reaction to the summons for help. Many of the firemen slept with their overall trousers either on the end of their bunk or folded on the floor ready to step into as they got out of bed. I finally drifted into an uneasy sleep only to be woken by the house lights coming on and the house bells ringing out breaking the silence of the sleeping station. In a flash I jumped out of my bunk, slipped on my shoes and was sliding down the pole. The clatter of feet followed me and I was sitting on the engine and pulling on my boots and leggings then slipping into my fire tunic. The sound of the fire engines starting up filled the appliance room as crewmembers mounted their various appliances. The dutyman passed out the teleprinter call slips to the officer in charge of each engine. One by one they left the station, the pump; the TL and finally the ET. I was left behind, sitting in the back of the PE on my own. Tom had at least followed me down and looking into the rear cab said, "Come on Pikey, it's not your turn yet son." Rising early, and ever the optimist, I watched the minutes pass by as the time moved up to 9.00am and the end of our shift. Finally, with only minutes to go, the house bells were dropped once again and I moved purposefully towards the PE only to see the yellow light come on indicating another shout for the TL. The whole night shift and not one bloody shout for the PE, not even a false alarm! I was gutted.

The Mess Room

It was recognised among the time-honoured firemen at any station, and Lambeth had more than its fair share, that the station mess was a hallowed haven. It was a place where freedom of speech would have been recognised by America's founding fathers in their Bill of Rights. The level of debate may not have equalled some of our nationally renowned founts of wisdom or philosophy, such as the Oxford Union, or the nearby Inns of Court, but within the confines of the mess no subject was considered too academic; to be too sacred, or profane (especially the latter) to restrict its discussion.

Now as a mere novice, and fresh from the protective environment of the College and the defensive attention of my former squad instructors, I was welcomed into the mess. Here the combined odours of cheap roll-up fags and the background smog of pipes filled with Navy Cut or Nut Brown tobacco provided a real "pea souper" that would have been a credit to a Sherlock Holmes mystery story. After only a few days exposed to that atmosphere the smoke chamber at Southwark's training school would hold no terror for me, with or without BA. It was in Lambeth's mess that my real education in "life sciences" started. It was under the combined tutelage of a worthy collection of war-time London firemen, ex-military and Royal Navy seamen and fifteen-year firemen and river "floaties" (who had seen it all and had faced their worst nemesis) that my youthful naivety was swept away in the following weeks and months. My limited knowledge in the ways of the world advanced more in my probation year than at any other time in my career.

Despite the advice of Dave Rees, I was developing the art of give and take and I laughed freely at the victim of the communal prank, even though it might be my turn next. I learned to smile when the barbed arrows flew in my direction but also took careful note of where they came from and planned a reprisal for when the time was right. In spite of my youth and inexperience, my repartee was sharp(ish) and I adjusted my vocabulary to basic English, such as was forthrightly used in station life. I had little operational experience so was unable to exaggerate tales of derring-do or "gild the lily." This did not stop others from doing so, and thereby being labelled the "utterers of terminological in-exactitudes," or plain bloody liars.

One of the station routines was to be detailed as mess assistant. This involved clearing away cups and saucers, making the early morning tea and so forth. A fire brigade tradition, on day duties, was the mid-morning "stand-easy" when a crusty roll, filled with cheese and sliced onion, was the mandatory morning snack. Earlier on I had somehow, inadvertently, mixed up the brown sauce with Camp coffee and poured the liquid coffee into the plastic brown sauce dispenser. The reaction in the mess was not couched in politest terms. Broadly translated, individuals biting into their "saucy" rolls, wanted to know how a mentally deficient illegitimate could mix up sauce and coffee and had I really passed out of training school or had I been pushed. I did not make the same mistake again.

However, the mickey taking and coarse humour also included many pearls of wisdom, timely advice as to how a probationer could learn and do his job better. This unsolicited giving of invaluable experience and practical guidance put meat on the bones of my theoretical knowledge. You would ignore it at your peril. I chose not to.

Derelicts

The tours of duty that followed my first, inactive, night shift gave me a flavour of what the future held. Rubbish fires, dust chutes, chimney fires, shut in lifts and false alarms. But for me, in the late sixties, my practical firemanship skills were mostly developed due to the unscrupulous practices of demolition contractors. Many of these were engaged in carrying out large scale clearances of the, then, back-to-back slum terraced housing and larger tenement buildings which dominated the housing stock in and around Lambeth, Waterloo and Kennington and, of course, in other large swathes of the capital. The wholesale replacement of these inadequate dwellings with high-rise flats, ill designed concrete monoliths and poorly planned local authority housing projects would, in the decades to come, bring about their own special social and community problems.

The rules and regulations then governing the tactics of these gangs of demolition contractors, employed in these mass clearances, were lax, if not quite non-existent. (This was an age before the Health and Safety at Work Act came to the fore bringing in its train the forerunners of the culture of safety regulation so familiar to us today.) But then, each day, buildings and streets would be part demolished, contents and timbers burnt on site. At going home time these derelict buildings were set alight or the site fires allowed to burn out of control, igniting the surrounding empty houses. What the contactors could not achieve the local street urchins and mischievous kids set about rectifying by setting fire to whatever they could. To a young, enthusiastic, fireman this was all heaven. It was also an excellent means of learning the art of firemanship, practical building construction, and how fire spreads and how it behaves. Some twenty-five years later the Brigade would introduce "real fire training" for recruits in the final stages of their training in order to prepare them for the real world. Our experience in those days was a forerunner to these fire houses, but to my mind far superior allowing us to learn on the job. The burning buildings were naturally hazardous but provided an ideal training aid. They also acted as a magnet to the young and those fascinated with fire, especially when it came to lighting them. The possibility that children or others might be inside these buildings was always at the forefront of our minds. This was no game.

It was extremely rare for a night shift to pass without at least two or three calls to these blazing derelict sites. As fast as you put one out, kids would light up another around the corner often using the contractors' bonfires as their ignition source. It was rare that stations would "make up" on a derelict; it was not the done thing, even if two or three buildings were blazing merrily away. Not only were these derelict fires a good training ground for us young firemen, but they also helped prospective junior officers cut their teeth on the command and control of incidents, incidents that would normally have been "made up" if it had involved an occupied house, with or without people involved.

My Station Officer finally returned from sick leave and took charge of the Red Watch again. He was a handsome chap, dark hair, in his early thirties and, although married, was said to be a ladies' man. Dick reverted to Sub Officer and would now normally ride in charge of the PE or ET. With the governor's return he brought with him more than just his personality, considerable wit and charm, Lambeth started to get busier. We had more real working jobs, fires in residential flats involving hose reel jets and BA, a make-up fire in the Myers bedding factory and a serious basement fire in a shoe shop in Lower Marsh near Waterloo station. At this job I was riding the PE and when we arrived, we found the basement was heavily smokelogged. The pump's crew were struggling to force their way through the ground floor and down the staircase to the basement. Scorching heat held them back but they persisted until some of the crew suffered blistering where their skin was exposed and they had to withdraw from the struggle whilst others took their place. Even in the street the smoke was so thick and noxious that we had to lie flat on the pavement outside of the shop just to feed the hose in to the BA crews inside, coughing as we did so. Through sheer grit and perseverance the BA crews finally got into the basement storage area and brought the fire under control; some of the crews wondered if perhaps the governor would like to go back on sick leave again!

The governor's return brought more than just an increase in the number and range of fires; it also heralded my first (double) fatal fire. Called late in the afternoon to a fire in a flat, the radio operator in Brigade Control informed the appliances, whilst they were en route, that additional calls were being received. I was starting to develop a fireman's nose for fires. Different fires generated a distinct odour or smell; rubbish fires smelt unlike burning timber, smouldering or burning rubber differed from overheating electric cables. As we drew nearer to the address there was the distinct smell of a burning mattress; a smell that gets right into your nostrils and tells you, correctly nine times out of ten, that you have a working job on your hands.

The smell of the mattress was just the prelude for what was awaiting us when we pulled up at the address in lower Kennington. The scene was one of utter despair and desperation as a young mother screamed for her children to be rescued from her second floor flat. There was a short access road at the front of these council flats and, at the rear, an enclosed grassed area that ran parallel to the main road. Looking at the rear of the flats, just before we pulled into its entrance, the affected flat was easy to identify as the oily brown smoke forced its way around metal window frames, the intensity of the heat inside was already turning the glazing black. As we jumped out of the engine and looked up, we saw that the woman was being held back by neighbours as a man on the walkway tried, in vain, to enter the open door of the flat only to be beaten back by the severe heat and the thick smoke. Even before the governor dismounted, he got his driver to send a priority message, "Make pumps four, persons reported." The Sub Officer raced to the second floor whilst we got a hose line out and the driver dropped the tank of water to fill the pump and charged off to secure the use of a hydrant. At the same time the pump's crew were running towards the stairs, putting their BA sets on as they ran; in their haste they threw the harness over their shoulders. They had no time to secure the clips that prevented their mouthpieces falling out of their mouths, which were designed to prevent deadly smoke entering their lungs. The TL crew grabbed a line from the PE locker and ran after the BA crew, with all heading for the second floor. Despite his years of experience Dick was unable to force his way into the flat without BA, and shouted down to the governor, "You need two more sets up here, the kids are at the back of the flat."

The governor was where he should have been, directing our efforts at the front of the flats, urging the two drivers to get the hose line tied to the line the TL crew had thrown over the balcony and then detailing Southwark's crew, who had just arrived, to get their sets on and to get up to the second floor and report to Dick. The next order he gave, "Get an extension ladder around the back," was given to no one in particular. But I was pulled by someone from Southwark's crew and together with Eric, we took the thirty-foot extension ladder from the pump and ran with it around the end of the flats and onto the grass area under the flat's window. The pitch was not difficult and the head of the ladder smashed the hot brittle glass as soon as it touched the window frame, releasing the pent-up heat and smoke, which rose safely above our heads. As we climbed up the ladder, an adjacent window in the same flat was being opened, releasing more heat and smoke out into the open air. Eric cleared the remainder of the glass from the frame but was initially prevented from entering because of the smoke and hot gases still forcing their way out. But the needs of the children proved too strong for Eric and he forced himself into the room; I followed not knowing what to expect.

For a couple of seconds we were both disorientated. We had fallen from the window on to a smouldering bed and then crawled on to the floor. The whole room was blackened and charred; the BA crew had hit the room with the jet, dousing the flames but dislodging plaster from the walls and ceiling, which now lay all over the room. Everything in the room had been burned and heat radiated fiercely off the walls. Initially managing to kneel, then stand, we surveyed the room and its near total destruction. Where the door had been was just some charred wood held up by two metal hinges. As our eyes adjusted to the heat and residual smoke, we noticed a strange shape, inter-twined on the single bed, which had been partially obscured by fallen plaster. Moving closer, we looked in dismay as we recognised what we had just climbed over; the charred remains of two young children, locked together in death.

We called out for the Sub Officer, but both he and the governor came into the back bedroom to check out our dreadful discovery. The remainder of the incident has for me now drifted into a blur. When we finally returned to the station it was well past the end of our watch. I left to catch my train home. That night, in the privacy and quiet of my bedroom I shed some tears for those two infants.

Watchrooms

Watchroom duties were the bane of my life. They were the blight on a young fireman's overwhelming desire to be constantly going out on the fire engines. But with the Station Officer's return there was an increased interest in moving me through the various stages of my probation, which included watchroom duties. I hated doing watchroom duties. I hated having to remain at the station whilst the PE or pump was attending calls or going out somewhere on the station's ground to undertake inspections or perform hydrant testing. I was missing out, left sitting in the watchroom and crewing the damn canteen van.

I had been under watchroom instruction since my first month at Lambeth, but I was not eager to push for my station examination, as that would get me in the "box", as it was called, on a regular basis. Besides completing the logbook when I would record any changes in the riders and note appliance movements during the shift, there were a range of other various tasks associated with the role of dutyman. Dealing with a "running call," for example, where someone would come directly to the fire station to summon the brigade; or handling secondary telephone mobilising procedures in the event of a power failure, and dealing with a range of enquiries from the general public at the Headquarters front desk, which unhappily was immediately adjacent to the watchroom by the main entrance lobby. Then, of course, you would have to report (correctly) to a visiting senior officer. But unless you were actually handling a fire call none of it was very exciting. You sat in the watchroom, on your own, and it was like watching paint dry; utterly mind-numbingly boring.

However, with all my possible excuses now exhausted the inevitable exam was arranged and I passed. I was qualified to perform watchroom duties: Oh joy. Night duties were particularly frustrating as after supper I would normally be the only person on the ground floor, with only the nuclear attack "four minute" warning signal box (always located in the station watchroom) for company. Occasionally, someone else might get bored and come down and keep me company, but only if they were very bored. Watchroom duties were split duties. You were either the primary dutyman or the relief dutyman; your other half covered the meal breaks on day duties. On nights the first shift was from 6-8 pm with the relief dutyman covering from 8-11 pm; then you would be back in from 11 pm to 7 am; a break for breakfast from 7-8 am, then the last hour until the watch changed at 9 am.

If the frustration of the watchroom duties was not enough, going out on the canteen van only added insult to injury. Whilst crews would be exceptionally grateful for a refreshing mug of tea or of Bovril during their brief respite from the rigours of battling a major fire, or dealing with a major disaster somewhere in the capital you just looked on. You were there but not part of the action. The canteen van attended all fifteen-pump fires or where the officer in charge requested its presence. This was the only appliance at Lambeth crewed by just firemen with no officer in charge. It would be two years before I went out on a shout on the "chuck wagon." It occurred Tuesday 12th August 1969 and naturally I was performing watchroom duties and doing the main shift. I had now resigned myself to the inevitability of having to take my turn in the "box." I was having a busy night. All the machines had picked up shouts in the evening and the PE and pump had picked up a couple of calls after midnight, then the TL and ET had separate calls, about an hour apart. Another sleepless night but without the satisfaction of knowing it was because I was attending calls and riding the engines.

Dawn came and the early daylight filled the watchroom and the silent appliance room. The rising sun cast long shadows over the river and the shadow of Millbank Tower, located on the north bank, almost reached the south side of the river. Standing by the open PE appliance room door. (The PE was always parked directly next to the watchroom.) I was kicking my heels and looking over towards Big Ben whilst wishing the next few hours away and an end to this bloody watchroom duty.

At 5.20 am a triangle was lit up by Brigade Control against an "E" in the main appliance indicator panel. This meant that they were dealing with a four to six pump fire in the Eastern Command, which covered East London. This was followed by the teleprinter bell sounding warning me that a message was coming through. The message said there was a four pump, BA required, fire on the S.S. Paraguay Star, a refrigerated cargo/passenger ship of ten thousand eight hundred tons, berthed in the Royal Victoria Docks. This priority message was sent as soon as the first officer in charge to arrive at the Docks saw smoke pouring from the ship's engine room skylights and ventilators aft of the funnel.

With the prompt arrival of the L Divisional Commander he made pumps fifteen immediately. As the crews were making a determined attempt to enter the engine room from the B deck, they came across two acetylene and three oxygen cylinders, already too hot for them to handle. Cooling them, the cylinders were put in improvised dams whilst a renewed attack was made on the engine room by other crews in punishing and arduous conditions. It was so hot that the crews had to be relieved frequently and their progress was painfully slow. With the canteen van now alerted, I helped get the boxes of biscuits and packets of tea from the store whilst the water boiler was lit in the back of the van.

As a refrigerated ship, the insulation that normally kept heat out of the refrigerated spaces now just as effectively kept the heat in, and made conditions particularly taxing and exhausting. Pumps were made twenty, fireboats two, and all additional pumps had to carry BA. By now ten jets were at work, six were cooling bulkheads, whilst four worked directly in the engine room.

Malcolm Roe was the relief dutyman and the driver of the canteen van. With crews fighting London's most difficult fire in years, we left Lambeth en route for the Docks with our blue lights on and the squeal of the two-tone horns easing our progress through the early morning London traffic. We arrived three hours after the very first crews had started battling the blaze and been met with the severest of conditions. The arrival of the canteen van brought a smile to the exhausted faces of crews who were taking a breather, before recharging their BA sets and going back into the burning ship.

Instructed to wait before opening up the van I got a brief opportunity to have a look at this, my first, ship fire. High derricks were located fore and aft of the seven-storey tall ship. Thick black smoke was belching out of the tall single funnel which had a big red star on a white background painted on its side. Smoke was also being forced out of the central passenger accommodation and various vents on the upper decks. Hose lines were draped over the side of the vessel like thick hawsers, as though they were securing the ship to the dock. In the distance, and on the dockside, crews with BA sets slung over their shoulders were waiting contemplatively ready to relieve their comrades who were straining with every sinew as they struggled against the effects of heat exhaustion and fatigue in the enclosed confines of the vessel. I could only stand and imagine what the conditions must have been like for the crews in those hot and humid confines. I desperately wanted to be part of it and not just an onlooker. Not realising it then I was looking at the only ship fire I would ever attend in my long career. I was witnessing, at first hand, some of the most difficult conditions any fireman could wish to face, and my part in this historic occasion was to give out cups of tea and handfuls of biscuits. What a shit! We would need no briefing as to the very real hazards of heat stroke or the dangers of fire spread due to conducted heat being transferred through the metal bulkheads. Crews chatting at the canteen van told of the hot oily dense smoke making reading a pressure gauge, only a few inches in front of a BA wearer's face, difficult if not impossible. Our brief was far more basic and straightforward, "Don't give anyone tea unless they have a grimy face, absolutely no one, do you understand?" So with tired smoke-stained crews lining up for well-deserved refreshment they were greeted by me, fresh faced and wearing my white catering coat over my overalls. The only heat and steam I had to contend with was that from a tea urn!

At 9.00 am, the change of shift, White Watch came on duty and fifteen pumps were ordered on as immediate reliefs. By the time they arrived the Brigade had been combating the fire for over six hours, under the most severe conditions. Although the blaze was still not under control it had been confined to the engine room and the adjoining machinery spaces. One of those relief pumps carried Lambeth's crew with the legendary Station Officer "Black" Jack Stacey in charge. They would see that the severe heat conditions were making deck-head plates and bulkheads buckle and internal catwalks sag.

We finally ran out of tea and biscuits at 11.30 and had to return to Lambeth to replenish stocks and, with a change of crew, the canteen van returned to the incident. Whilst I went off duty and home the crews continued their struggle all day. It was not until 6.30 pm that it was possible to enter the refrigerator compressor room, and by 9.22 pm the engine room was reported completely cool. The stop message was finally sent on Wednesday 13th at 1.30 pm. Even then the conditions in some areas of the ship were so hot that BA crews were only able to work in very short spells as they hacked away amongst the maze of pipes, valves and levers to ferret out and remove the smouldering insulation.

Red Watch

With a watch strength of twenty-four there were inevitably a considerable mix of characters; individuals with either special talents or a singular personality. I would learn that there were very few of London's fire stations that did not have their fair share of characters. Sometimes, and sadly, there were a few with unusual or unsavoury traits. But for now this was my first exposure to this mix and it made a lasting impression on me. The qualities that this group of people possessed were varied. Some were more noteworthy than others, some I would cherish, and others I avoided. The mix of personalities on a watch was largely a matter of chance. What was planned was to secure the correct balance of skills, so that the various qualifications required to crew the appliances were adequately covered. That cover also had to cater for absences caused by, for example, annual leave and sickness. Whilst each watch at Lambeth had an authorised watch strength of twenty-four none was up to strength. The Red Watch had four vacancies and, therefore, an actual strength of twenty. The Brigade had been, and still was, considerably undermanned during the sixties, this placed severe strains, at times, on our ability to crew appliances to the required level. This resulted in appliances frequently being taken "off the run" due to insufficient riders.

The Station Officer normally rode in charge of the pump; Sub Officers the PE and Leading Firemen rode in charge of specialist appliances such as the TL and ET. Qualifications dictated what appliances you could ride. Eric and I had none so we generally rode the PE. As I still had little experience, I was very much the passenger for those first few months and was led by the nose by either Dick Richardson, Eric or Tom.

Riding with a fire engine brimming with firemen was rarely a problem, unless it became defective and there were no spare machines available to replace it. So meeting the minimum rider levels was normally the focus of the office staff's attention, trying to cover all the riding positions with qualified personnel. When there were any spare firemen, especially firemen qualified to HGV standard, they would be ordered out to stand by at another fire station in the Division. Including the officer in charge and the driver, a minimum of four riders were required on a PE; three on a pump; two on the TL and five on the ET. Lambeth also had the only canteen van in the Brigade and that was crewed by two firemen.

Joining Lambeth's Red Watch only two days before me were three new Leading Firemen, all transferred in from other fire stations. They were already substantive Leading Firemen and had not just been promoted. Lambeth was not their preferred choice of posting and they were there under duress; they were Teddy, Tom and Dennis. Teddy was the only one ET qualified, having ridden the E Division's ET for a number of years. He alternated now with the Sub Officer in riding in charge of the ET, whilst one of the other two rode in charge of the TL and the other rode in rear of the pump. When there were sufficient riders a Leading Fireman was always detailed to ride BA on the back of the pump.

On Lambeth's Red Watch the Sub Officer had day-to-day responsibility for the detailing of the morning or afternoon station work routines; appliance and equipment maintenance; outside station work, or station drills. The leading firemen monitored progress though the day, especially our Tom!

It was a long-standing tradition on the watch that the very senior hands were excused certain station routines, especially station cleaning. I had no such privileges, certainly not as junior buck. I started building up an intimate relationship with the Fm's toilet and slowly progressed to the officers' toilets, both of which had to be cleaned daily. I might occasionally be extended the honour of scrubbing, then polishing, the "golden mile", Lambeth's central corridor, which ran the full length of the first floor. I certainly was not high enough in the pecking order to polish the locker room floor or, the best job of all, the recreational room floor, where the station's two full size snooker tables sat in a majestic timber panelled room. Here framed photos of Lambeth's past winners of the Brigade's Pump and Pump Escape competitions hung from the walls and a young, handsome looking, Ken Thorne; Taffy and Bill Skipsey, (both now serving on the fireboat), looked down on a room that hadn't changed in appearance since the Headquarters first opened in 1937.

The one aspect of station cleaning that was always welcome, and a real joy, was the weekly scrub-out of Lambeth's seven-bay tiled appliance room floor. Scrub-out was carried out at every London fire station on either a Friday or Saturday morning. The rota system meant that we got to scrub out twice every six weeks. Lambeth's appliance room would be cleared of its fire engines, senior officers' cars and the Brigade major control unit and all were parked in the drill yard. The metal appliance drip trays, kept under of the machines, were pulled clear and taken into the yard as well; then all the firemen would arm themselves with a bass broom. The surface of the appliance room floor would be thoroughly soaked using a jet of water, fixed to a hydrant in the station yard. Comprox (an industrial detergent and de-greaser) was poured on to the wet surface and then we scrubbed the floor. We worked in a long line across the width of the appliance room, pushing our brooms from one end to the other and mixed the Comprox with the water.

The water, Comprox and the sweeping action of our bass brooms resulted in a white soapy foam that covered the whole appliance room floor. It was incredibly slippery, especially on the grooved tiled floor of Lambeth's multi bayed appliance room. It was a great surface on which to play the brigade's own version of ice hockey. Using a large bar of carbolic soap as the puck, bass brooms as hockey sticks and our fireboots as ice skates, we had thirty minutes, or so, of unrestrained rough and tumble as we slid about trying to hit the "puck" from one end of the appliance room to the other. Junior officers often joined in this frivolity and passing senior officers would gaze in at our game, privately wishing they too could let their hair down and pick up a broom. As the suds slowly disappeared so the surface lost its slimy veneer and the game was over until the next scrub-out. Now it was just a matter of cleaning off the grime and stains by washing the appliance room clean with jets of water. This would often result in a water fight, especially on hot summer days when the temptation to give someone a thorough soaking became overpowering. Occasionally it all got out of hand, or rather the jet did, and a passing bus would get a dousing, much to the annoyance of the governor who had to mollify an irate bus inspector from the local bus depot.

Seen through my young eyes, skills qualifications gave a pecking order to the various groupings of Lambeth's Red watch. It was similar to a caste system that dictated status dependent on their qualifications. Needless to say I was one of the "unclean," the lowest of the low. But at the top came the office staff. They supervised the watch but spent little time socialising, certainly with the likes of me, during the working day. They might relax more after supper on night duty when standing down, and on Sundays, when there were no station work routines.

Next came the ET qualified firemen. The mere fact they rode the ET most of the time meant that they did not very often get involved with the shouts that our PE, pump and TL got. The ET crew would regularly attend major fires. They were seen as a specialist unit, an elite crew referred to as the Chief's Commandos, and occasionally they would let you know it.

One individual had a category all of his own, Charlie. Charlie shared Ken Thorne's crown for being Lambeth's other most senior hand. Also a pre-war joiner, Charlie was a squat rounded man, looking more than his 50 plus years. Even with his Brylcreemed hair combed back over his head he did not rate as a dashing figure. Whereas Ken only drove the ET, Charlie only drove the TL. Neither ever did a stand-by duty at another station having by now earned the right to drive only their respective appliances at Lambeth. Suffering from a weakened back, which everyone turned a blind eye to; Charlie wore a protective back support under his blue collarless uniform shirt. It hung on his bunk at night waiting to be put on when he got a shout (looking like a Victorian woman's whale-bone corset.) Charlie didn't take to me for some reason; in fact there were very few he did take to. In my first year at Lambeth Charlie never spoke to me once!

There were also the itinerant group; HGV motor drivers that drove the PE, pump and CaV. This group performed the vast majority of stand-by duties driving someone else's PE or pump. The other MDs, who were also TL qualified, would take turns to cover Charlie when he was on leave or taking "a sicky", which he did as regular as clockwork. They would also frequently drive a TL at another station to cover for deficiency of qualified personnel.

Bringing up the rear was the "cannon fodder" and I was its latest member. We were the BA and non-BA qualified firemen who rode either the PE and pump on nearly every shift, unless on watchroom duties and then we would ride the canteen van. We naturally formed a group because we interacted both on the incident ground and on the station, either cleaning or maintaining the appliances and equipment however we were occupied.

But Lambeth was also unique because it had two other groups of riders, one of which were the "floaties." Lambeth's fireboat was in fact a station within a station. The fireboat was moored alongside the pontoon directly opposite the Headquarters site. It had its own limited facilities, its own small office and watchroom combined; plus its own Station Officer, Sub Officer and Leading Fireman within its crew of seven. However, they shared Lambeth's land station facilities including the mess, locker room and dormitory.

The other Lambeth accommodation sharers were the Red Watch Brigade Headquarters staff; namely the three carpool drivers, who drove the Chief Officer and the two duty principal officers, the Brigade photographer, and the two Brigade control unit staff. All combined a grand total of thirty-six operational personnel could be found in various parts of Lambeth's extensive accommodation on night duty and made up its extended family.

Most of this last group were initially strangers, faces I would say hello to in my first few months on night duty. They were not about the station on days as they worked elsewhere in the Headquarters building. But slowly as I got to know them, and they got to know me, I discovered they were a mine of wonderful tales and stories about the Brigade, its past and many of the characters that gave it such a colourful history. As I was a fresh pair of ears, the carpool driver seemed especially pleased to relate tales that had probably been repeated ad-infinitum around the mess table but were all new to me and I loved to hear them.

On our day shifts (Monday to Saturday) it was station cleaning, equipment testing, fire prevention inspections, drilling, more cleaning and, hopefully, attending fire calls and, of course, volleyball. Volleyball was treated as an art form at Lambeth. It was something that was taken very seriously. It was also mandatory and I was utterly useless at it. It was something that the College had failed to implant in the cadet's range of necessary skills. If my successful probation was dependent on my ability to play volleyball then I was destined to fail and I had better start looking for another job. Ken and Charlie did not play and the governor rarely made an appearance. Secretly I hoped he could not play either, but sadly that proved a false hope as he was good, very good in fact. Most of the watch played well, some very well, and a few could (and did) represent the Brigade in national and international competitions. A minority played hard and I frequently found myself their target and would go flying when hit by a fast ball struck by someone determined to give me a personal lesson in the finer points of the game. Volleyball was a game that I would never master although over the years I did improve; but only slightly. I could eventually serve with a degree of skill, but hitting a winning point: that always eluded me!

What I lacked in agility on the volleyball court I made up for on the drill ground. But I was soon to learn that drills at the station were not done at the same break-neck speed as those performed at the Training School. I was told, in no uncertain terms, by some of the older hands, "To bloody well slow down," especially after the Sub Officer witnessed me running up the escape ladder to the fourth floor like a monkey climbing a tree, unhappily for me he then said that he wanted the rest of the watch to move at the same speed.

Wet Canteens

Drinking on fire stations, whilst on duty, was a way of life when I joined the Brigade. It certainly happened at Lambeth and, as I was to discover, at virtually every one of the other one hundred and twenty-six London fire stations. Drunkenness was a disciplinary offence. Drivers could face the prospect of police action, and the full weight of the law, for being found drunk or under the influence of drink whilst driving a fire engine. Yet despite all these deterrents easy access to alcoholic drink on fire stations meant that the temptation was there and, occasionally, this temptation became too great for some. For some, either with a drink problem or drink dependent, access to or the freedom to drink just made their problems worse. This was my introduction to a part of the Brigade's less publicised culture that was both pervasive and could sometimes be downright dangerous. It was something that would continue for the next decade until the ban on drinking whilst on duty was introduced.

In my first weeks and months I was far too busy keeping my head down and trying to get to grips with operational duties to notice the tell-tale signs and behavioural changes that, later, helped me identify those who had over-indulged. These changes would include staggering and falling over when running to the engine when they got a shout; looking for their fire gear on the wrong engine; trying to go out on the wrong engine; throwing up all over the crew, and passing out completely and even not going out at all! All this I would see at first hand, but not just yet.

Fire station bars were called wet canteens. All stations had one, some were elaborately kitted out, some were quite basic, whilst others were just a beer cupboard in the corner of the mess room. There was even a Brigade Order covering the establishment and local management of these wet canteens. Drinking on duty was the norm and it was not just restricted to station personnel. I would witness many senior and principal officers who were prone to over indulgence, some frequently, a couple permanently!

Divisional and Command headquarters also ran social clubs. This was a useful way of allowing the senior officers and the divisional staff to get a drink without having to visit a station. Lambeth, the Brigade Headquarters, had its own special Officers' Mess Club. It was linked to the wet canteen, located under the Brigade's bandstand, at the southern end of Lambeth's drill yard. The station's wet canteen whilst not as large, being about twenty feet by twenty feet, was a profit-making business and Charlie was its long-standing manager. He reported to a Brigade Headquarters committee that was chaired by an Assistant Chief Officer. It had formal opening hours during weekdays and weekends so as to allow the Headquarters uniformed and non-uniformed personnel access to a mid-day drink, if they did not wish to go to one of the six pubs that were within a stone's throw from the station. On duty station personnel were not allowed off the station and getting engaged in a heavy mid-day drinking session was very rare. It could, occasionally, be a different story on night duties.

The Officers' Mess had the distinct feel of a private members club, for that is what it was. Access was restricted to senior and principal officers, and their wives, who lived in Brigade Headquarters accommodation or those visiting and wishing to use the facility. The top four floors of the Brigade Headquarters building had been designed to incorporate residential accommodation for the senior and principal officers, including the Chief and the Deputy Chief. All of whom were required to live "over the shop." All senior officers had to live in Brigade accommodation as part of their conditions of service. Working an eighty-four-hour week, out of hour's operational cover was provided from their residential accommodation. With no mobile phones or pagers invented then, which would have provided greater freedom of movement, control ordered them to fires and other incidents by telephone.

Comfy armchairs arranged in an informal setting provided a relaxing and comfortable environment for those senior officers who wanted a mid-day drink, or who wished to spend some time there during the evening. Subtle table lighting made the room look warm and homely. Officers' wives dressed for the occasion in posh frocks, fashionably brimmed hats and carrying handbags, would mince in and, occasionally, stagger out, particularly if they had attended one of the regular formal evenings that were arranged in the Headquarters social calendar. A small hatchway, built in the wall between the Officers' Mess and the canteen, gave access to the bar and was where drinks could be obtained without the officers having to come into contact with the hoi polloi who frequented the canteen.

As my confidence, and ability, grew I would sometimes poke my nose into the canteen and spend an evening there. I stuck to shandy but nevertheless got intoxicated by the stories and humour that stronger drink inevitably brought out of the more affable and older members of the watch. Drinking could continue well into the early hours of the morning providing the bar steward was prepared to stay up. No one seemed to object, especially when a senior officer, who was on his way home from the pub or who had got lonely sitting on his own in the Officers' Mess, popped in for a couple of night-caps or fancied some serious drinking in the company of hardened practitioners. There existed a special bond, one that had built up over time, on each of the three watches with these particular senior officers. It was recognised that their need to lose themselves in a pint or a scotch highlighted some other personal problems affecting their lives and generally warranted some empathy. By the end of the night, or early morning, some were unable to stagger up to their accommodation, whilst others had passed out completely! In either case they would be discreetly delivered home and carried or escorted to their front door. Once the doorbell was rung a swift, tactical, withdrawal was made by the escorts leaving the unfortunate officer to face the consequences and, probably, the wrath of a nagging troublesome wife who had driven them to drink in the first place.

The canteen was not a favourite haunt of mine. Initially, as the junior buck, I would be the natural focus for those who needed to pick on someone or something. I did not see the point of intentionally putting myself in the firing line or harm's way. I was also fortunate to be invited by a small band of Red Watch firemen, who were more interested in getting on with their careers, as a new addition to their study group. I was a willing participant, feeling much safer in their company. Then, only after some study, would we take an occasional drink in the canteen after attempting to absorb some new operational note or reading through, and trying to understand, some obscure Brigade Order. Within five years however it was different story, a different bar, and a much larger me! But that was to come.

Confirmed

There was no formal training programme to get you through your probationary period. It was all very dependent on the individual standards of the watch officers, the watch, and the luck of the draw as to where you were stationed. Within the inner London divisions, (that comprised the former LCC Brigade,) there were however benchmarks which covered the areas of sickness, punctuality, smartness, watchroom duties, acquisition of technical knowledge, performance at drills and, naturally, operational capability. All these headings were used as indicators to report on an individual's progress through probation. It was these areas that had been incorporated into the enlarged Brigade and that formed the basis of information as to whether your appointment as a fireman should be confirmed or not. Based on my governors' reports it would be the Commander of the Southern Command who would determine if I was worthy to merit continued employment. This decision would be based on a six-month, mid-term report and then a final report, normally submitted after one year on station.

You had to be pretty dumb not to get through, but my Station Officer set exacting standards. I was determined to meet them or, at least, to give it my best shot. Probationary service could be extended up to two years in extenuating circumstances, such as an accident at work resulting in protracted sick leave or, sadly, problems at a station. Although such "problems" were not widely publicised, they did occur and some probationers suffered appallingly under a cruel and tyrannical regime that existed on some station watches. Stories of the offensive and intolerable actions of depraved individuals, in their attempts to dominate new entrants to their station, filtered through from time to time, especially after the movement of the unfortunate victim to a more secure and tolerant station and new watch. Initiation practices were deemed to be part of the probationer's rites of passage into station life. Some were spiteful, others were sick. I only suffered the practical jokes that just made me look foolish; like having to go to the Brigade workshop stores to ask for some fallopian tubes; or being sent up to the fourth floor to test the railway warning horns by blowing them loudly outside the door of a particularly unpleasant senior officer. I never suffered the physical or mental abuse that was handed to some less fortunate than me.

Obtaining a satisfactory probationary report after five months, but with plenty of room to improve, I was now permitted to stand by at other B divisional fire stations to cover absences or rider shortfalls. This did not happen very often since I was unqualified and the demand for a non-BA fireman was a rarity. However, my limited talents were one day required and my very first out-duty proved to be an unforgettable occasion.

Pageants Wharf

I knew something was amiss when my name was not called out on roll call to ride the PE or pump. It wasn't my turn in the watchroom either. So when the Sub Officer finally said, "Pike, out-duty to Pageants Wharf for the watch." I thought bugger and bollocks! The grins on the faces of the rest of the watch indicated they knew something I did not.

Pageants Wharf was the only one appliance station in the B Division. Its days were numbered because of the changing face of the docklands but it would not close just yet and it certainly would not shut in time to save me from this ruddy out-duty. Changed into my undress uniform, with my kit bag over my shoulder, I caught the two separate buses that would deliver me to the peculiar, out of the way, station situated in Rotherhithe Street within the Rotherhithe peninsula, located equally distant between Bermondsey and Deptford.

The station was designated a "special cover station." Its Pump Escape was not allowed to attend calls off its own ground, a ground that only had one named street; Rotherhithe Street. At both ends of this particular street was a large swing bridge, which crossed Rotherhithe Street, and when in operation allowed shipping into and out of the Surrey Commercial docks, thus closing the street to all through traffic. This also prevented other stations' fire engines attending calls on this ground if they were received whilst the bridges were in operation. The closure of Rotherhithe Street had in the past been a frequent occurrence, due to the earlier high volume of river traffic entering and exiting the docks. In such circumstances Pageants Wharfs PE provided the fire cover to the immediate vicinity. Those days had now passed so, besides being the Division's only single appliance station, it was now also the quietest. Days, sometimes weeks, could pass without a call being received and I was off to spend a whole day there as the fifth crew member. (A crew of five was always necessary at a one-appliance station.)

Pageants Wharf had not always been such a sheltered backwater. It had a spectacular past, covering the working wharfs, warehouses, barge yards and ship repair yards that lay in the twelve docks and basins of the three-hundred-acre Surrey Commercial Docks system. Rotherhithe Street, which ran from one end of the compact ground to the other, a distance of just under a mile, was narrow and winding, strung out with a rich mixture of warehouses, ancient houses and newer post war council blocks of flats, which provided homes for the local workers. In its heyday Pageants Wharf was home to the peculiarities and atmosphere of the immense dock system, with mighty ships in the Greenland Dock and humble Baltic tramp and sail ships delivering to the timber yards. Here lay vast piles of timber, mixed with an assortment of transient cargoes in the warehouses and storage areas. This made Pageants Wharf a demanding and challenging station ground which had tested the resolve of many of its firemen with the blazes they had had to face. Ancient houses, cheek by jowl with tenements swarming with children lived side by side with modern blocks of flats; where there are people, danger of fire is ever present.

The destruction wreaked during the war years, the imminent closure of the Surrey docks and the demise of the riverside wharves had seen a vast change in the area's fortunes, and those of the fire station, which now looked as run down and dishevelled as the area that surrounded it. This sad little station sat dwarfed between massive buildings that had once buzzed with the noise of warehousing and the manufacture of a wide range of products and foodstuffs such as flaked rice, tapioca flakes and cooked maize, produced for the home market and aboard.

Relieving the fireman, hanging on, on overtime, I put my fire-gear on the old Merryweather Pump Escape, which with its uniquely square shape looked as old and tired as the station itself. The station faced on Rotherhithe Street and backed directly on the riverbank, where there was still access to a disused fireboat pontoon that had once served to moor one of the Brigades' fleet of fireboats. With the then bustling Port of London the expanded river service had been necessary to tackle the warehouse fires, which in those days had ravaged riverside industry. As the river traffic and its waterfront began to change and as trade reduced, so had the number of fires. Now this rusting iron gantry served only as a reminder of the station's former glory and it, like the station, would soon become just a memory.

I do not recall much of the firemen on duty that day except for one individual, Fm Christian, the driver of the PE. With nearly forty years difference in our ages, and no invitation to call him anything else, I referred to him as Mr Christian whilst trying very hard not to sound like Charles Laughton in the *"Mutiny on the Bounty."* Mr Christian looked, and acted, older than his considerable years either moving slowly and purposefully around the station or in anything else he did, which did not appear to be much. With a full head of white hair he only needed a white beard and moustache to make a perfect Father Christmas, without the need for of too much padding either. He also sucked constantly on the pipe that was in his mouth, whether it was lit or not.

The Sub Officer in charge of the station acknowledged my presence but that was it as far as he was concerned. After looking up, but without a word, he went back to reading his paper and studying that day's racing form. I was left to continue my tour of discovery around the station, destined to spend a dull and boring day. Then to my total surprise, and everyone else's total amazement, the station bells started ringing. The violent vibrations making homeless the families of spiders that had taken shelter within. An ordering was coming over the station's teleprinter. I was already sitting on the engine, eager to go, but totally alone! In near to disbelief the other crewmembers studied the teleprinter ordering in the watchroom. Seemingly recalling what the sound of the bells and ordering meant, they finally moved more quickly toward the fire engine all except, that is, Mr Christian, who just ambled to the driver's door. He slowly climbed up into the driver's seat, his pipe still in his mouth.

With the wooden appliance room doors finally pulled open, and after what seemed an interminable delay, we were ready to move. The appliance engine at last roared into life and the Sub Officer encouraged Mr Christian to move forward. This he did and we turned left, heading in the direction of Deptford. We had gone no more than a hundred yards when the Sub Officer let out such a tirade of expletives, his face contorted with rage. Totally frustrated he turned to his driver and shouted, "You prick Christian, you have gone the wrong effing way."

Rotherhithe Street did not lend itself to three-point turns so, desperately, seeking somewhere to reverse and turn around the poor Sub Officer looked in danger of suffering severe apoplexy. I still had no idea where we were going or to what? By now even the rest of the crew were urging Christian to greater efforts to which he steadfastly refused to respond, whilst still sucking on his empty pipe. Finally, and now heading in the opposite direction, we passed the fire station but with Christian still only in second gear. Eventually we arrived at a small rubbish fire behind a block of council flats. The fire was quickly extinguished, not least because it had nearly burnt itself out anyway.

The rest of the day was spent in total silence. Returning to the station the Sub Officer stormed into the tiny office, slammed the door and was not seen again. Mr Christian shuffled around, smoking his pipe which he had now lit; I could not wait for 6.00 pm so I could catch the buses back to a normal station. When asked by the governor the next day if I enjoyed my first out-duty I could only smile and say, "Interesting!"

Moreton

Now not only was I permitted to stand-by but it also appeared I was to be allowed to attend residential courses. I found I was nominated, as a volunteer, to attend an Emergency Fire-fighting course at the Fire Service training facility in Moreton-in-Marsh, Gloucestershire. This, a time of the Cold War and the threat of an atomic or nuclear attack, was something the emergency services planned and trained for. In this event anyone with an ounce of common sense knew that the survival percentages were next to zero but, regardless, the powers that be had devised a course to bring calm to this nuclear Armageddon that might befall the nation at any moment. As no one else on the watch was prepared to go, the governor made me an offer he told me I couldn't refuse. "If you want to pass your probation Pikey, sign here." Eric Burns (who I had relieved of his "junior buck" status) had previously been on a dispatch rider's course. His job had been to ride across the Gloucestershire countryside on a BSA Bantam 125cc motorbike whilst delivering imaginary messages to imaginary columns of fire appliance fighting imaginary conflagrations in an imaginary nuclear war. He said it was all "bollocks," but he had had a most wonderful week riding the Home Office issue bike. As I could not ride a motorbike, I had to attend the "emergency" firefighting course instead.

A former RAF station, the Fire Service Technical College was a bleak and dreary expanse of wide-open space dotted with decrepit hangars and row upon row of wooden huts. It called to mind an unpleasant but close resemblance to one's image of a concentration camp. It would have provided the ideal setting for the film "The Great Escape." Only for me, there was no escape. I was lumbered for two weeks playing with Government stock Green Goddesses, green painted fire engines with which the nuclear war games were to be played out. I was an immediate star; my training at Swanley all became worthwhile, as I was the only one of twenty-four equally cynical firemen, from various parts of the country making up our particular course, who had ever used a "green" trailer pump. The former RAF hangars contained line upon line of these green fire engines, each one mothballed, but still ready for mobilisation should world peace deteriorate to such an extent that the threat of imminent hostilities became a reality. (They were actually prepared for action during the Cuban crisis, when John F. Kennedy was the US president.)

How I was meant to get to Moreton to take up my war role if the "balloon went up" was never explained to me but I was training to be part of the fire service's front line, dealing with the aftermath of nuclear annihilation. Beside the numerous "green" fire engines there were also abundant numbers of ten-ton lorries, each carrying its heavy load of six-inch pipeline, whilst others carried bridge building kits. All of which we were to get close to and intimate with in the days to come.

The wartime runways proved to be a very effective substitute for a road network over this vast site. Each day our convoy of vehicles would sally forth and we would lay furlong after furlong of pipe-work, providing an emergency water main destined to feed fire pumps quelling burning cities and towns in a post nuclear attack. We erected pipe-work bridges over the runways, to allow the free movement of traffic, whilst pumps worked in relays to maintain adequate water pressure and movement of water over distances of over a mile. And that is a lot of individual lengths of piping! No wonder no one wanted to volunteer for this bloody course. Qualified, I was now ready to return at a moment's notice to crew these machines, but welcomed my return to Lambeth fire station and comparative sanity. I would see these Green Goddesses actually mobilised into action in the years ahead, but not in a way that I would then have thought conceivable. It would be nine years before I returned to Moreton again, and in that time, it had been transformed into a world class Fire Service training facility.

Topography

In an era before the invention of "sat-nav," fire engines had to get to the address they were called to in the shortest time possible. It was not the done thing to stop en route to ask someone the way, although very occasionally this did happen. The Brigade had, over the years, developed a mapping system to break down the capital's area into quarter mile square grids. Each individual square had been given a unique identification code that comprised of two letters and two numbers, e.g. LB 41. A map, called a "route card," showed every highway and byway in that particular quarter square mile and was reproduced on a card measuring six inches by six inches. The information each card contained was based on the latest Ordnance Survey and updated by the brigade's ongoing monitoring of new roads and street closures. Every station had one set of route cards for each appliance. These route cards covered the station's ground, plus adjoining areas where the station's appliances could reasonably be expected to attend as a first reinforcing machine. Written or typed on the rear of each card was the route from the base station to that particular quarter square mile area. Marked, by a red arrow, on the front of the route card, was the entry point that the directions on the rear had led you to. From there you would locate the particular address you had been ordered to and navigate your way, using the large-scale map. Route cards were particularly important when a fire engine was standing by at another station, the ground of which the driver might not be familiar with. Every ordering gave the particular route card number and it was an integral feature of the brigade's mobilising system, be it by teleprinter, telephone, or radio. The route card numbers also mirrored the grid references in the geographic atlases that were especially printed for the brigade. These atlases covered the whole of the Greater London area and were carried on every brigade appliance and staff car.

Formal training lectures were not a regular feature of my station life, the only exception being station topography. Knowing, intimately, their station's ground was an essential part of a fire engine driver's knowledge; certainly for those who took their duties conscientiously. Learning the station's ground was also deemed to be a basic feature of a fireman's knowledge. From day one, I was not excused this requirement to learn about Lambeth's station ground, its risks and special features. In fact it formed an important part of my early education and by the end of my first half of probation I had to identify every major route on the station's ground and at least ten of the most significant risks and say what and where they were located. Both the Sub Officer and one of the leading firemen lived on Lambeth's ground. (Tom, the leading fireman, had grown up in the shadow of the Oval cricket ground.) When taking topography they would arm themselves with a blank blackboard and a piece of white chalk and then hold centre stage in the TV room, that also doubled as the station's make shift classroom. Drawing a long single horizontal or vertical line on the blackboard they would ask for the name of a primary route on the station's ground. Given a name, say Westminster Bridge Road or South Lambeth Road, we would then have to identify every street, road and turning off that thoroughfare until the whole area was covered and a new white line was then drawn on the board. Now in the second half of my probation, I was expected to learn many of these interconnecting roads between the major routes. It was not a process I found particularly easy, working just from a blackboard. My progress was slow. Memorising lists of roads was not my forte and I needed a system to aid my memory. Eric had just passed his probation and he suggested using what had worked for him; walking. I did just that and either before coming onto nights, or after finishing them, I would walk the ground, learning the routes much the same way a London cabbie learns the "*Knowledge.*" I had already become familiar with nearly every street and alleyway from Waterloo station to the fire station. In this way I soon amassed a respectable knowledge of the ground that I hoped would satisfy the governor, when the time came to be tested.

Whilst some of Lambeth's drivers had an almost photographic memory of the station's ground, Charlie's extended to the whole of south London, less gifted drivers had to rely on their route book or "*Bible*" as it was known. This personal route book was painstakingly written out by hand and listed every street, road, avenue, terrace, mews, alley and court that was on, or adjoining, Lambeth's ground. Not only were the individual locations listed, but the route from the station was contained detailing left and right turns, directions at roundabouts and traffic lights. These books were a labour of love and a cherished possession of every driver who completed one.

One of the greatest compliments you could be paid was to be handed down a driver's personal route book when he was posted to another station or perhaps was promoted. I never had such an honour but I did get to borrow one, in order to make my own out. These were not the only tomes that had to be completed, by hand, at station level. Hydrant location books were placed on every PE and pump in the Brigade. These books contained an alphabetical list of every street on the station's ground and where every hydrant could be found, street-by-street. Additionally, a spare copy was maintained in the station watchroom so that crews, standing-by to provide fire cover, could place this important information on their appliance for the duration of their stay. Their frequent use meant they had a relatively short shelf life and had to be rewritten regularly, sometimes in the most beautiful of script, other times in a barely legible scrawl. Some stations, Lambeth was one, also wrote out a "flats book" which was a useful addition to pinpoint the exact location of individually named flats in the expanding housing estates that were springing up all over London.

In December 1967 my final probationary report was prepared and sent to Divisional Headquarters with a recommendation that I was worthy of continued employment in the Brigade. I had managed to tick all the right boxes, including topography, but I was still required to attend an interview to determine if my governor's recommendation would be ratified or not. I was to be interviewed by a Deputy Assistant Chief Officer, known locally as "the Skull." He was the deputy Commander of the Southern Command and was based at Croydon Fire Station where, prior to the 1965 reorganisation, he had been the former Croydon Fire Brigade's deputy Chief Officer. Driven to Croydon in the pump, I was ushered into the DACO's office and immediately saw why he had been given his nickname. He was the thinnest man I had ever seen, almost skeletal, his skin drawn tightly over his face. He looked emaciated and with eyes that had shrunken into their sockets. His withered features gave him the impression of some ghostly apparition dressed in a fire brigade officer's uniform. I was totally mesmerised by his appearance and despite his highly educated and articulate voice posing searching questions about my probation I was unable to stop staring at his face. Eventually the interview finished and I was ushered out again convinced that this man was suffering from some terrible wasting disease. Returning to Lambeth on the pump I was recounting my ordeal to Jim, who previously served in Croydon Fire Brigade. Smiling, Jim said "That's nothing, you should have seen him before he put on all that extra weight!"

On 18th December, one month before my nineteenth birthday, and after only eleven months' probation, my appointment in the London Fire Brigade was confirmed. I was now a real fireman.

Chapter 6

Real Fireman

Let's party

Christmas 1967 saw my first Christmas on duty and it would be followed by the next nine, each year working over the Yuletide holiday – some rota system! In certain quarters of the watch there was a heightened excitement at this imminent Christmas duty. Red Watch was working Christmas Day and Boxing Day night duties and the Governor had given his approval for a party on Boxing Day night. Providing nobody went sick, the Governor also said he would let as many riders as possible go home, after any out-duties had been ordered, and we would then ride at minimum levels for the two nights, which still left seventeen of us on duty. Those without prior approved leave might be allowed home after roll call, if their name was picked out of the hat. As someone without any kids my name was not even entered, which was fine by me as I was looking forward to the entertainment.

The other two Daves were the watch "smoothies" and they had beaten considerable competition to get the title. Either one of them could have talked a nun out of her habit. Both were in their late twenties; DD the taller, over six feet tall, dark haired and swarthy with the looks of a matinee film idol. DW was shorter by a couple of inches, fair-haired and without an ounce of fat on a lithe agile frame.

Their combined forays into the Nurses homes of Westminster Hospital and St Thomas' Hospital had started in early December. They had wheedled their way in using their considerable charms, extending warm invitations to any young and available nurse foolish enough to listen, who was not wanting to spend Boxing Day evening on her own. Many on the watch hoped the evening would become the night. This was all new to me, but the others had a clear idea of what to expect as they willingly put their hands in their pockets, to make the required contribution to fund the buffet (and drinks) for the secret party.

On the evening in question assurances were given by the two Daves that the nurses would turn up, as they displayed the confidence of the con-artists they really were. With the mess and TV room now looking suitably festive, resplendent with its real Christmas tree donated by a local benefactor for the Brigade's Carol concert – but nicked from the appliance room for the occasion and now relocated on the first floor. Coloured fairy lights gave a warm feel to the normally stark mess room. Hanging decorations and lanterns added the final touches, whilst the adjacent Officers' mess had been swept and tables erected to hold the buffet that had been prepared during the afternoon by canteen staff, who were eager not to have to work on this night.

I was still very much the baby of the watch and quite naive about the expectations that most of the watch had regarding the prospect of having a dozen or so student nurses invade the station later that evening. My own inexperience and excitement was further restrained by a headache and hot flushes; a couple of earlier shouts had not helped my condition; in fact they had made it decidedly worse.

Those allowed home after roll call had long gone, free to spend an unexpected evening in the comfort of their own home with their families. Those left at the station were busy grabbing an all-important shower, fresh shave and applying liberal quantities of after-shave. Even the governor was spending an inordinate amount of time in his private shower room and trying (none to successfully) to brush his hair back and camouflage the thinning on his crown; a topic he did not like to discuss that was causing him considerable consternation.

The two Daves were starting to look increasingly anxious with each minute that passed the expected arrival time of our unauthorised visitors. Looking fresh faced, even more so because of the temperature I was running, and having a trim waist and generally pleasing features, I was warned by a few of the elder statesmen of the watch to make myself scarce if the nurses did not turn up. From some of the looks I was getting from a couple of the floaties, (whose sexual preferences we were unsure of at the best of times) I might have to hide even if the nurses did arrive!

With the threat of extreme physical violence being directed at the two nervous and now worried organisers, the two Ds were in danger, not least for taking money under false pretences. The mood was on the verge of becoming distinctly un-festive and Boxing Day taking on a literal meaning. Saved by the bell, or rather a knock at the front door, the first batch of much awaited female guests arrived. It was clear from some of the earlier comments of the watch that dancing and socialising was not the only thing on their agenda for tonight. Looks of approval went the way of the Daves as the nurses' coats were taken, revealing a fine array of the female form in fashionable and very eye-catching party dresses. Seeing that most of the nurses were closer to my own age, and despite the groggy symptoms I was experiencing, I hoped my own limited charms might work some magic during the evening and that I might just pull. The prospect of securing a "hot" body and later occupying one of the vacant bunks seemed to me to be possible. It was, but not in the way that I had hoped.

My temperature was rising as the nurses' numbers increased and they enjoyed the first of many drinks that night. I was rapidly burning up, going down with the flu, with all its accompanying shivering and total lack of energy. With the sounds of laughter and music filling the first floor I took to my bunk before midnight, covered in blankets. The only contact I would make that night came in the form of a charming young nurse who took pity on me and came to mop my extremely wet brow and left her phone number under my pillow.

The only call after midnight was around two am. I fell, more than slid, down the pole and climbed up on the engine. I had no option but to ride, as we were on minimum manning, but I would have been no good to man nor beast had there been a fire to deal with. Where we went was a blur and I have never felt more grateful to get called to a false alarm. Returning faster than we went, lest someone stole the driver's newfound companion, I returned to my bunk and drifted into a feverish sleep. I was obviously hallucinating, seeing scantily clad female figures (in bras and panties) climbing into various bunks; and hearing the coaxing words of flattery as squeals and giggles seeped into the fuzziness that filled my throbbing head.

Driven home the following morning by Teddy, who wore a large self-satisfied smile, I was dropped off. I took to my bed once again, my first Christmas at work over.

1968 brought a new face on to the Red Watch. The Sub Officer had been promoted to Station Officer and was on his way. He was now replaced by Roger, just promoted to Sub Officer and transferred in from Hammersmith fire station. Roger had a voice that sounded incredibly posh and so he was. He was also ageless, looking more like a sixth former than a fireman. Closer to thirty than twenty, he was a well-built five foot eight inches tall. But when it came to leading his crews he did so from the front. Youthful he may have looked but he brought with him considerable experience and a presence that made him very likeable.

Another newcomer was also added to the watch strength. News of the new comer from training school meant that my tenure as junior buck was over, time to hand the baton on. My joy was short lived, however, with the arrival of "Biff" on to the watch. Whilst he was a new entrant to the Brigade, he had transferred from a West Country brigade and soon let me know that he had over two years' service under his belt. Biff was a big lanky lump, with a strong slow country dialect, which exasperated the governor as he tried to interpret Biff's speech. The governor wasn't alone. I remained the junior buck.

Thames rescue

Tuesday 5th March started much as any other day shift. 9.00 am parade and roll call with the detailing of riders for that shift. I was riding the pump. After checking over the appliances the hands went for their morning tea in the mess; whilst the officers had theirs served in the station office. Station work routines started at 9.30 and I was cleaning out the toilets yet again. The station bells, ringing noisily, announced the first shout of the day at 10.12. The green light (indicating the pump) and white (for the fireboat) shone brightly from the appliance indicator panel, telling the station what had been ordered. Descending the sliding pole I mounted the pump and started to rig whilst the dutyman shouted out, "Child fallen in the river; Albert Embankment," as he read off the teleprinter ordering. The pump driver turned left out of the station and pulled across the Embankment, stopping about fifty yards up from the station. We were facing upstream towards Vauxhall Bridge, the short distance leaving me just time to rig in my fire gear.

A crowd had already gathered on the pavement and was pointing into the river at something that was floating slowly downstream. From my elevated position I saw a body, face-down in the river, about twenty or thirty feet from the south bank shoreline. Biff and I jumped down from the back of the pump even before the pump had stopped moving and we ran to the river wall with Biff carrying a line (rope). The ebbing tide was moving steadily downstream, leaving the river's foreshore exposed. A lifeless form was being carried along with the outgoing tide. I did not know if Biff could not or would not swim. But he threw the line over the parapet wall whilst anchoring one end round himself. Looks like I'm going over then, I thought, which I did, burning my hands in the process as I slid, all too rapidly, down the fifteen feet to the foreshore below, unaware of the large crowd that was now gathering, and would grow still further as the drama unfolded. Nearly every window of the Embankment's adjacent multi-storey offices, and the Brigade Headquarters building, had faces peering out, eager to watch the excitement unfold before their eyes.

I never considered myself brave, I still do not. My limited experience then, and later, was that you react to situations as you find them and do the best you can. I was the only one anywhere near the water and to do nothing was not an option, especially where a child's life was involved. Running to the water's edge I threw off my helmet and tunic, which I was told subsequently looked quite dramatic. I started to wade in still wearing my boots and leggings towards the floating body. In hindsight leaving my boots on was not the brightest thing to do! The pull of the tide was steady but not overpowering. With the river water to my shoulders I could reach out and grab hold of the limp lifeless body. It was clearly not a child's, even though it was still face down in the water. Holding on to the clothing I managed to turn the body over, hoping not to see the distorted facial features of someone who had been in the river for days on end, and who the currents had now brought up to the surface. It clearly had not, but nor were there any signs of life. Supporting the body as best I could, instinctively I started mouth to mouth, but their mouth was difficult to open and I could not bend the head back far enough to open the airway properly, but I tried to force some air in anyway.

It was now clear that keeping my fireboots on had definitely been a bad idea. I was finding it hard to maintain my balance, supporting what was now clearly a woman, and giving her resuscitation. Fortunately help was as at hand in the form of the governor. He suggested I change to mouth to nose resuscitation whilst he started to pull and manoeuvre us both back into shallow water. With the water now at chest height it was possible to get air into her lungs properly for the first time. At waist height we stopped moving her because she was getting far too low beneath us for both the resuscitation to be continued and for us to drag her out of the water. Then other members of the pump's crew joined us, including Biff, and they lifted the woman up and carried her on to the foreshore whilst I maintained the resuscitation. With her jaw loosening I was able to go back to mouth to mouth and for the first time the woman showed signs of regaining consciousness. Able to breath unaided the woman was tended by other crewmembers whilst I sat on the foreshore being violently sick. This was actually good news as it saved me from a trip to St Thomas' hospital to get my stomach pumped out. The Thames river water in the mid-sixties was still a heavily polluted and contaminated waterway. I was left sitting alone on the foreshore in a pool of vomit, the next part of this drama unfolded before an increasingly fascinated crowd of onlookers.

Lambeth's fireboat was on station and moored directly opposite the land fire station and tied up to its floating pontoon. Given how close the incident was to the pontoon, the fireboat's crew chose to use the skiff (a rowing boat) that was normally towed behind the fireboat to row the relatively short distance to the woman, ironically now safely on dry land!

Decision making means sometimes taking a chance. You can get it right or sometimes choices can be very fickle. This proved to be one of those times. My governor's choice was to put the woman in the skiff and row her back to the pontoon rather than have her carried up the foreshore to White Hart Dock, via a short tunnel and onto Albert Embankment, and a waiting ambulance. The use of the skiff was not an unreasonable decision unless you take into account Murphy's Law; which says if things can go wrong, they will.

The woman was placed on a stretcher, brought by the skiff's crew, and put in the skiff and then rowed back to the pontoon. Which was where things got tricky. The woman, still conscious, wrapped in blankets and laying on the stretcher in the rowing boat had to be lifted up on to the deck of the pontoon, which was three to four feet higher than the river level and the skiff. She was passed up, feet first, to the waiting crews on the pontoon. With the governor and another of the rowers still at her head, they attempted to lift the woman to safety but, unfortunately, at exactly the same time as those lifting the other end. A bad move, a very bad move. As they all lifted in unison the woman's feet were now four feet higher than her head and the stretcher was at a perilous forty-five-degree angle. Next, the flow of the ebbing tide caught the skiff, pulling it further away from the pontoon. Gravity, the widening distance and the tide all combined to take control of the situation and the poor woman slid rapidly, without ceremony, off the stretcher and back into the river. The governor, still gallantly holding on to the stretcher, fell out of the skiff and into the river after the woman.

It was at this exact moment that a passing London Evening News photographer took the picture that made the front page of that day's midday and evening editions. The woman hit the water like a RNLI lifeboat launched from a steep slipway before she disappeared from view. As she resurfaced, she was landed upon by one of the fireboat crew who had jumped into the river to save her. Under she went again. By this time the Brigade's senior and principal officers, who fatally were still drawn to the Headquarters windows and who had only moments ago been preening themselves because of their gallant lads' actions, were now either apoplectic or incandescent with rage. Eventually the woman was finally grabbed, and using lines and a boat hook all three were hauled unceremoniously up onto the pontoon. The poor woman was removed by ambulance to hospital and safety.

By this time, but unaware of all that had happened, I walked back, alone, to the fire station, via the tunnel, to wait for the return of the pump, nursing rope burns to both hands. I remained in the appliance room where a fireman treated and dressed my blistered hands.

News travels fast in the Brigade and bad news travels even faster. Norman Rose, a B Division senior officer, came steaming into Lambeth's yard, driven in his staff car. He was obviously livid and looking for blood. He was a large, powerful, scary looking man. He had a fearful reputation as a no-nonsense trouble-shooter. He could be an ogre. I could almost hear him humming, "Fee, fie, foe, fum," as he stormed into the station watchroom and summoned the officer in charge. The governor was still being rung out on the pontoon so poor Roger Vaughan, Lambeth's Sub Officer and deputy, had to report instead. No matter how smart Roger might have looked or how correctly he may have reported, nothing was going to save him as he walked, with considerable trepidation, into the watchroom and the beast's lair. An innocent party in all this, it made no difference to Norman, who had been dispatched by some unnamed principal officer who had witnessed the debacle, to kick arse. This was something Norman was born to do. Having made mincemeat of both Roger and the dutyman he then left the watchroom and strutted across the appliance room trailing a very submissive and pale looking Sub Officer in his wake. Seeing me with bandaged hands he summoned me over and then delivered a right royal bollocking for sliding down the line too fast and burning my hands in the process. Satisfied with taking yet another scalp, he waltzed off to the first-floor station office to lay in wait for the unfortunate governor. He left much later that day, content that the ebbing tide had been a significant factor in the poor woman's second dunking, but not before he had vented his spleen on the governor for his choice of recovery route; and anyone else who could be bollocked duly was.

The station office was off limits to all hands for the remainder of the day whilst reports were drafted, redrafted and then typed explaining the day's unhappy events. The governor was heard to be licking his wounds after the savaging from Norman but no formal disciplinary action was ever taken. The woman, who had thrown herself into the Thames from Vauxhall Bridge, made a full recovery after her ordeal and went home. Unsurprisingly no thanks were ever received. A report of my actions was sent to Divisional Headquarters.

Some weeks later both the governor and I were called to an Honours and Awards Board to consider what action, if any, was to be taken regarding the initial rescue. The Board, made up of four senior officers, was chaired by an Assistant Chief Officer. I had nothing to add other than the basic facts but the Board seemed interested in the fact that I had only recently completed my probation at the time of the incident. Don Brown was before the Board for much longer and this normally cheerful guy did not seem so cheerful when he came out of the second floor Brigade Headquarters conference room. We returned to the station in silence. It was some while later that I was called to the station office and greeted by the junior officers, all smiling at me and Roger shaking me by the hand and saying, "Well done, Pikey." I was not sure what was up but did not think my toilet cleaning merited such praise. Escorted by Roger into the governor's office, he rose from behind his desk and he shook my hand as well. Bemused I waited, starting to think this was some kind of a wind up or I was about to be posted somewhere awful. Sitting down again he picked up a copy of the latest Brigade Routine Orders that had just been delivered to the station. He read me the Honours and Awards section, which informed the Brigade that the Chief Fire Officer had commended me, and congratulated the governor, for our actions. A Chief Officer's commendation was, and still is, the highest bravery award the Brigade issues. I was chuffed, naturally, and delighted for the governor but had a worry what the reaction of the other members of the watch might be to this news. It turned out most were generally pleased, some said nothing and a few thought it was all bollocks, considering the cock-up that followed.

I was awarded the Commendation at the Brigade's Annual Review, held at Brigade Headquarters, together with seven other individuals who had received bravery Commendations during the year. This major event in the Brigades annual calendar took place on the 29th June. Field Marshall Sir Gerald Templar, The Queen's Lieutenant for Greater London, took the review and made the presentations. The review was also a demonstration of various skills and activities the Brigade was involved in, including ladder displays; recruits in training; and the build-up to a major fire. The latter was always a tricky demonstration as machine after machine dashed into the drill yard getting to grips with the simulated blaze and performing multiple rescues from the nine-storey drill tower. The review was open to the public and, despite the railway go-slow that was taking place at the time, the balconies were packed and included my very proud Mum and Dad plus my girlfriend. Following the display Sir Gerald made the presentation of the Commendation Certificates and we were called up individually to receive them. As I was handed mine Sir Gerald said a few words of congratulation and told me, "This isn't the last you will hear of this." I left the dais wondering what he had meant. I did not have to wait too long to find out.

Two weeks later on the 12th July I received a letter from the, then, Home Secretary James Callaghan to say that he felt my actions were deserving of high praise, and he had brought the matter to the attention of Her Majesty the Queen who was, "Graciously pleased to give orders for the publication of your name as having received an expression of Commendation for your services." I wondered if she said, "You know Philip, the young lad who held the door open at that unveiling thingy at their new fire control room."

I was asked to keep the information private and confidential. On the 16th July my name was published in The London Gazette as receiving the Queen's Commendation for Brave Conduct for rescuing a woman from drowning. The news brought about mixed reactions from those I worked with but some strange, yet pleasant, responses from unexpected sources. My bank manager for one, who only ever wrote about my overdraft, sent a lovely letter of congratulation. The Chief Fire Officer even wrote a personal letter addressing his opening, "Dear Pike", plus I got my very first telegram, from the staff and Junior Firemen at the Swanley College.

The final act of the saga unfolded in October with the presentation of the Queen's Silver Oak Leaf Award at County Hall. Sir Gerald was again to make the presentation and an even prouder set of parents, plus girlfriend, were there to witness the event, sitting in the front row of the elaborately panelled Council Chamber. When my name was called, I went forward to collect the award and certificate, signed by the Prime Minister Harold Wilson, from Sir Gerald. Immaculate in his Field Marshal's uniform he smiled as he handed them to me and whispered, "I told you so," and winked. Afterwards there was a posh reception where the Brigade's Principal Officers took far more interest in my girlfriend than me. I had a last brief flurry of publicity and press interest, "As local lad gets national bravery award." It was time to melt back into the watch, my moment of fame over, for now at least.

Killed on duty

Lambeth's Emergency Tender received the call in the early hours of the morning of the second night shift. Whilst some waited in the corridor until the blue light told them who was going out, others, like myself, slid eagerly down the pole to the appliance room, even before the light indicated which appliance was summoned. The ET had a shout to a four-pump fire, BA required, on Chelsea's ground. After watching the ET leave and shutting the appliance room doors a couple of us turned on the pump's radio to listen to the messages before returning to bed. An informative message said it was a fire involving a restaurant and dwellings and extra BA was required to reach the seat of the blaze. After a lull in the radio traffic a priority message flashed over the airwaves requesting ambulances for members of the Brigade at the scene of the Chelsea incident. Worried about the ET crew, but with no further information about the fire coming over the radio, we finally turned it off and returned to bed.

The ET returned sometime after 5 am that morning, and the crew went about testing and recharging their BA sets before returning them to the brackets on the tender. The crew congregated in the mess whilst Ken made them tea. They said little to each other, reflecting on the night's fire and its deadly consequences.

Introverted and brooding was how the rest of the watch found them when they started to make their way into the mess between 6.30 and 6.45. Little was said, waiting for them to open up the conversation. News of the night's tragedy had already been covered on the early morning BBC news. One of the ET crew started to relate the events to other ET qualified watch members and those nearby listened sympathetically. The two firemen from Chelsea were wearing BA sets and had got caught in a "flash-over" explosion. By the time they were reached, and pulled out, their rubber mouthpieces and goggles had welded into their faces. They later died from their injuries. One was forty-two, the other twenty-four years old. The mood was sombre and the watch went about their normal morning station routines more quietly than usual, leaving the ET crew talking things through in the mess. These were the first fatalities of on-duty firemen in the Brigade in quite a few years, made worse by the fact that this was a double fatality. Details of the tragic deaths of Colin Comber and Brian O'Connell Hutchins were circulated round the Brigade in the morning's teleprinter bulletin, which detailed all make-up fires in the previous twenty-four hours. The Union Flag was already flying at half-mast from the flagpole on top of the Headquarters building even before that message arrived at the station, put there by one of the ET crew.

The funeral took place on the 20th March at Mortlake Crematorium. As the cortege, headed by police motorcyclists passed Chelsea fire station, where both men had served on the Red Watch, officers and men from Chelsea and the surrounding stations lined the forecourt to pay a last tribute to their two fallen comrades who had died so wretchedly in the course of their duty. I joined over five hundred members of the Brigade who lined the approach to the chapel where the coffins, draped with union flags and bearing helmets and axes, were received by pallbearers from their former watch. I found the occasion, my first Brigade funeral, incredibly moving and sad. I was afraid that the emotion on my face would show me up in front of my older peers, until I looked up at the line of firemen opposite me, many with obviously vastly more experience than me and saw tears were filling their eyes and some just cried silently. My own tears rolled slowly down my cheeks as the families followed the pall bearers into the chapel where the simple, but moving, service was conducted and relayed to the mourners outside the chapel, too numerous to fit inside.

It is in the nature of a fire fighter to recognise that death may be the ultimate price that they might have to pay, for doing their job. It was something accepted but not dwelt on very publicly. So immediately following the service, there were moments of quiet reflection as we filed past the floral tributes until individuals were soon greeting old friends and comrades, brought together by the sad day's events. Stories were exchanged and knowing smiles re-lit their faces again.

Station Life

There was lot more to station life than just cleaning, more cleaning, and waiting for the inevitable fire and other emergency calls. For example, taking part in and aiming to win the Brigade's pump competition. This was a religious calling to some; especially watch governors, whose whole life seemed to centre on this one event. Lambeth's Blue Watch governor was one such animal and he would go to the most extraordinary lengths to give his team every possible advantage. Special lengths of hose would be washed and ironed, by hand, so as to make them run out smoother and faster. Fire tunics would have their linings ripped out to make them lighter, whilst standpipes were modified to make them fit on the hydrant quicker. Hose coupling lugs were dismantled and oiled to make them rotate and release faster. Every part of the pump drill underwent minute scrutiny to achieve the maximum possible time advantage.

The competition was relatively straightforward and simple. A four man pump crew had to start, sitting on their pump, dismount and set into a hydrant; run out two lines of hose; knock down two targets with jets of water; make up all the gear and return it to a marked area on the drill ground; re-mount the appliance; drive it over a finish line; all in the fastest possible time. Sounds simple? It was much more complicated than it sounds due to the time penalties that the judges would add for every technical error that any member of the team made. Drop a hose; penalty points; miss a target; penalty points. Wrong pump pressure, you miss the target; too much pump pressure and you are in danger of losing control of the branch. Months of arduous training could all be in vain because of a momentary loss of concentration. Underhand tactics were not unheard of either, pump crew's competition hose mysteriously going missing. Hose couplings were sabotaged so they would not connect properly. Strange furtive figures, lurking around the back gates, could be seen spying on the opposition practising their drills, making copious notes and looking remarkably like the team trainer from the fire station down the road.

Divisional watch related elimination rounds would start the competition season, followed by the Divisional finals where the fastest three crews ran off against each other. With one winning team from each of the eleven Divisions selected, the Brigade pump competition finals were held in autumn in Lambeth's yard, the Brigade Headquarters. Supporters filled the balconies, cheering on their particular crew. Competition was keen with the team's own enthusiasm spurred on by the chanting of their supporters that would have done credit to any London football derby.

I was picked and despite our best efforts, although winners in the 1967 Red Watch run offs, our team never reached the Brigade finals. Our chances were not helped especially after our prized hose went missing and our fanatical rivals, at the next station, wanted to know, "If we wanted to borrow any." We fared no better the following year when a new Brigade record time was set by Edmonton's Blue Watch, of one minute 47 seconds, from dismounting to passing over the finish line; a truly incredible time. It was a record that was to remain unbeaten. Lambeth's Blue Watch, with their bellowing governor, urging them on, gave an excellent account of these themselves, being only 1.8 seconds behind the winners.

When our governor was not trying to encourage us to enter the Pump competition, he was putting us in for the Brigade's technical quiz, another annual event. Being the junior buck it seemed I had an automatic pass into everything that others had to volunteer for. The technical quiz competition led to national finals. London's winning team would represent the Brigade in the southern counties district, covering some ten different surrounding Brigades. The questions were drawn from any of the Manuals of Firemanship, which ran to eleven books; thousands of pages; and tens of thousands of potential questions. Learn all the answers to all the questions, and there was not one promotion examination you could not pass. Tom, Eric Grant, "Boots" and myself once again managed not to get kicked out in the first round but got nowhere near the Brigade finals, which was won by an exceedingly knowledgeable Battersea team. They later went on only to be narrowly defeated by Bournemouth Fire Brigade in the District finals, held at the Junior Fireman's College.

Volunteering, sometimes, got you out of station work but there was still plenty it would not exclude you from. These included dealing with mundane calls, which were unlike those shouts that gave you such an adrenalin rush, like a house fire or something potentially larger. Attending a rubbish fire or a burning dust chute just did not engender the same feelings of nervous excitement. Knowing that you would be first damping down then shovelling up someone else's shit and rubbish could be soul-destroying work, especially when you knew in a couple of hours you could be back doing it all again. But it had to be done and, occasionally, it would catch the unwary out. A stack of rubbish burning against a doorway might start a more serious blaze; a dust chute rubbish bin, containing nearly half a ton of household rubbish alight may smoke-log the enclosed lobby of a block of flats, perhaps trapping people on the upper floors. Suddenly your lackadaisical and half-hearted actions of dealing with a rubbish fire would take on a whole new meaning and you would find yourself rushing around like a "blue-arsed fly", fighting something totally unexpected. It could be a salutary and valuable lesson, prompting future junior officers never ever to take things at face value and to always be prepared for the unexpected.

Lambeth fire station had its own dustbin and rubbish area located next to the station's drill tower. My lesson in being prepared for the unexpected came literally in our own back yard and for Graham Orange, the pump driver, a highly embarrassing blemish on his previously clean vehicle accident record. Having had drills just before lunch the yard around the tower was still very wet. After lunch we all gathered in the appliance room waiting for the afternoon's work detail when someone noticed smoke coming up from the dustbin area. The bins were kept behind an eight-foot high brick wall that separated the bin area from the drill yard. A leading fireman told Graham to take the pump and get a hose reel jet on to the burning dustbin. Reversing out of the appliance bay Graham told me to climb aboard the pump, which I did, sitting myself in the governor's seat. The smoke from the burning dustbins was by now attracting considerable attention from those crossing the yard. Graham tells me to "give the bell a ring" as he sets off across the yard like a dragster from a standing start. If my vigorous bell ringing spurred him on to even greater speed, he never admitted to it at the subsequent inquiry. What was certain is that when he finally decided to brake there was insufficient space left on the wet surface for him to stop. He hit the very solid brick wall, hard. The angle of the wall meant that the engine hit it on the driver's side, totally smashing the fibre glass right-hand corner of the cab, causing considerable damage to the fire engine and even more damage to Graham's pride and the station's reputation. There was hell to pay after, especially as was it was witnessed by so many senior officers walking through the yard. The governor, whose attention was first drawn by the ringing engine bell, then the awful crunching sound coming up from the yard, came onto the first-floor balcony to investigate. He looked on in total disbelief at what had just happened. If looks could kill there would have been a whip round for Graham's wreath there and then. It transpired, despite considerable damage to the appliance (which was in the workshops for weeks), plus the reams of paperwork to cover the statements and accident reports. No formal action was ever taken against Graham. (Strangely enough, not one of the Red Watch personnel saw a thing, as they had all been facing the other way at the time of the accident!)

Waiting for the next recruit to get posted to the station was like waiting for a bus; you wait for ages and ages and then three come along all at once! With Dave (the smoothy) granted a year's unpaid leave to travel to South Africa and a driver posted to Clapham, the Red Watch was considerably undermanned. In as many weeks three new entrants joined the watch. The last one to arrive in the batch being another Dave, a junior fireman who had just completed his training. I did not know him from College; he was new and the squads did not mix much socially beyond their own intakes. Dave was tall, but seemed to look even taller because of his thin gangly appearance. He suffered badly from acne and had a beaky nose. He was self-conscious about his physical appearance, which combined with an initial shyness gave the impression of someone who was rather nervous. Aware of my own first tentative days at the station I tried to offer the advice Dave Rees had given us and that had been so useful to me in settling into the watch. For whatever reason, whilst Dave was not rude, it was evident he was not as nervous as he made out and was determined to find his own way. This attitude made his probation more problematic than it might have been as it turned out. He did eventually pass but was drawn towards the wet canteen culture. On night duties he would be seen holding his own with the more hardened and determined drinkers on the watch, thus we were to become even more distant, just nodding acquaintances if we were not actually working together on the incident ground.

M2FH

M2FH was the call sign of the Brigade's central control room, located beneath Brigade Headquarters. It was one of the four control rooms that came into being with the enlarged Brigade on the formation of the GLC. There were three other mobilising control rooms located at Wembley (Northern Command), Stratford (Eastern Command) and Croydon (Southern Command).

Lambeth's new, state of the art control room was officially opened by the Queen in November 1966 (remember I opened the door for the Royal personage) but the control had been operational since that summer. Its function was mobilising the central London area as well as being the general communications and co-ordination centre for the whole Brigade.

The new control room was in fact a total refurbishment of the former wartime underground control room, which had been answering emergency calls since 1939, where in view of the impending hostilities, an underground site had been considered prudent. If you needed the fire brigade then you dialled the operator (0) or two-two-two-two. Yet despite more than the quarter of a century that had elapsed, many of the original wartime mobilising features reappeared in the new design, just updated. The philosophy being, I guess, "If it ain't broke, don't fix it."

So now equipped with modern telephone switchboards, the control answered ninety-nine per cent (now, nine-nine-nine) of calls, the other one per cent being received via direct lines. Orderings to stations were sent out by teleprinter. Magnetic boards showed appliance availability and dispositions, plus senior officer availability. A message board listed make-ups and informative messages. A pneumatic dispatch system transferred messages from the officer of the watch's desk to the radio officer's position and the display board officer's position, and vice versa. At the rear of the control room the VIP area was a magnet for me on a quiet night duty, to see what else was happening in the Brigade. Tucked safely away behind the soundproof glass screen I could watch the nine-nine-nine calls being received and processed. The call would be monitored by the card index operator, whilst the address was checked against the twenty-two thousand address cards that covered the mobilising area. The ordering details then being passed to the fire situation board control officer. If the shout happened to be on our ground, I still had time to run up from the basement and catch the fire engine on the call I had seen just come in.

Plus, from the viewing platform, there was the added attraction of looking at the young female control officers who made up at least forty per cent of the control officers' complement. Mostly in their mid-twenties, some were already spoken for. At least one or two of them partnered watch personnel at Lambeth; but just looking did not hurt anyone. I too was to get involved, enticed by the witty charms of an attractive young control officer. But not yet and not at Lambeth.

The VIP viewing area was fitted with a one-way radio receiver, allowing visitors to hear the control room activity but without being heard. It was a testimony to the control officers' thorough training how calm and collected they remained, even under the most distressing of circumstances. Nine-nine-nine calls were dealt with in a cool and composed fashion although the caller might be ringing under the most stressful of conditions, occasionally fighting for their very lives. The radio operator, speaking in a collected and unruffled manner, dealt with the most hectic of radio traffic, taking the messages in turn, and telling "All stations wait" when a priority message flashed over the air waves. The exception to this efficient yet calm atmosphere was when a message came in indicating an injury, or worse, to an operational member of the Brigade. All the control staff were inextricably linked to the front-line troops and they shared in the concern and pain that such events bring, some even more so when their own partners were operational personnel.

As my face became more familiar, looking in from behind the glass, providing there were no senior officers present I would be invited in to the control room to learn more about its operation. The control staff matched our own watches and the Red Watch control staff at Lambeth had a mix of former firemen, retired on injury pension, and male and female control staff, all under the control of a Station Officer, Sid Snell. He already had over twenty-five years' service and would receive the BEM for distinguished service in 1970. He would turn a kindly blind eye as the control staff let me monitor the incoming calls and look up the attendances, using the Rotadex street index cards. Occasionally I would be able to monitor an incoming call for Lambeth's appliances and see the shout from beginning to end. I even turned this to my financial advantage from time to time, when dealing with a nine-nine-nine call made by a child that you could be ninety-nine per cent certain would turn out to be a false alarm. Running up to the appliance room and going out on the engine I would bet the other crew members five or ten bob (twenty-five and fifty pence in today's money) that it was a false alarm. Many liked a flutter and could not resist the chance of picking up what they thought would be some easy money.

My time spent down in the control was both enjoyable and a useful investment for the future. It helped us, in later years, to avoid the graveyard shift on horrible turning-over relief orderings and conversely picking up orderings to the good jobs that stations were clamouring to go to; reducing my crew to wonder, "How do you do that?"

River training

One aspect of station life I hated, besides doing watchroom duties, riding the canteen van, driving the divisional lorry (in fact, anything that stopped me riding either the PE or pump) was the possibility of standing by on Lambeth's fireboat. So far, my stand-bys had only been to other land fire stations, but now I was eligible to attend a River Service Training Course, which in essence was a familiarisation course that guaranteed I would stand by on that damned boat.

Lambeth's fireboat was a purpose-built craft named *The Firebrace*. It had been commissioned in 1961. An all steel vessel, it was sixty-five feet long, had a beam of thirteen feet and a draft of three feet eight inches. Its two powerful diesel engines provided the boat with a maximum speed of nearly twelve knots. All the engine room controls were operated from the forward wheelhouse, which had a connecting door leading to the crew's accommodation and a small galley. Access to this area was also provided from the stern of the boat. *The Firebrace* had two sets of pumps, each capable of pumping two thousand gallons of water per minute. Mounted on the deck, immediately behind the wheelhouse, was the boat's sole monitor, its three-inch nozzle capable of throwing a solid stream of water hundreds of feet into the air. More importantly, it could reach the tops of any riverside wharf or warehouse standing on the banks of the Thames, delivering tons of water per minute in the process. With its distinctive livery of red and black bodywork, and white painted pump outlets and fittings, it made an impressive sight as it patrolled the upper reaches of the Thames, from Wapping to Teddington weir. Woolwich's fireboat covered the lower reaches, although if one fireboat was unavailable the other would cover the whole length of London's River Thames. The normal crew was seven but they could ride four as a minimum plus a river service trained (RST) fireman, making five. If the crew was below minimum anyone in the Brigade who was fireboat qualified could be ordered to stand-by on the boat.

Eric had already done his RST training and I knew my turn was next, although I did everything I could to put off the inevitable. Finally caught, like a rat in a trap, I went like a petulant child over to the pontoon to undertake my familiarisation. The training would last two weeks but I could not be considered to be a crew member during that time.

I soon had to eat humble pie for it was far more interesting than I had thought possible. Being taken out training on the river, every day duty, was an eye-opening experience. I learnt about the drills and manoeuvres required of *The Firebrace* and its crew. The boat required a qualified coxswain and an engineer at all times, plus, if he was not the coxswain, an officer in charge. Station Officer "Dodger" Long was the Red Watch's fireboat governor; he loved the river and was a fount of knowledge regarding all things riparian. His knowledge was encyclopaedic. He was also a good trainer and made the course interesting and varied. Days were filled by man overboard drills, rowing the skiff to pulling hose ashore; pumping vast quantities of water out of the river and putting it back in again. If only the fireboat got some working jobs it would be much more interesting; as this happened only rarely you can see why I did not want this qualification. Fortunately it fell off my list of qualifications some time later, when I typed out new watch personnel cards.

On the last night duty of my training course I was to see just how hard the fireboat's crew would have to work when called upon to do so. Although a couple of shouts came in for the fireboat during those two weeks we never once arrived, being returned to base, unwanted and unloved. In the late evening on my last night duty the station bells rang and the white light came up, a shout for the boat. Leaving the land station and running across Albert Embankment we all trotted down the gangway on to the pontoon. Whilst the experienced hands cast off the mooring lines I went to the bridge and waited for an opportunity to ask where we were heading. I knew we were going downstream on an ebbing tide, so not all the two weeks' training had been wasted on me. The Station Officer told the crew that we were ordered to Battle Bridge Lane, Tooley Street, adjacent to Tower Bridge, on the south side of the river. The shout was on Dockhead's ground and the call was to a fire in a warehouse. Even with the tide behind us the fireboat was not renowned for its rapid arrival at an incident. We were just approaching the Charing Cross railway bridge when Bravo two-four-two (Dockhead's pump) sent a priority message over the radio, making pumps a straight ten. Calmly, Station Officer Long announced, "We've got a job, lads," which I thought amusing; given that the youngest full-time crew member was at least twenty years older than me. There were still four bridges to pass under, Waterloo, Blackfriars, Southwark and London before we saw Tower Bridge and the blazing warehouse on its southern approach. The tide had run its course and the Thames was at its low water mark by the time we reached Southwark Bridge. "It means bloody hose ashore by skiff," came from the galley below, from one of the old floaties busy making a brew. It was the first and only time I've had a cup of tea going to a shout.

Clearing the next bridge another priority message came over the radio, this time from Bravo one zero (B Division BA control van) making pumps fifteen and requesting the ETA of the fireboat. (It would eventually become a thirty-pump fire). "Blimey we're wanted," mused the coxswain whilst trying to get the maximum revs out of the engines. Even from the wheelhouse we could see the glow illuminating the night sky on the far side of London Bridge. Charts were pulled from the wheelhouse drawers as the Station Officer and the coxswain looked for anchorages and low water lines. A message was dispatched to Brigade Control giving our ETA as five minutes and requesting instructions from the fireground as to what was required of us.

We were now passing Hays Wharf head offices, its clean white stonework making it a distinctive feature of the riverside façade, alongside the old and dirty buildings that surrounded it. Three large sculptured reliefs, symbolising Capital, Labour and Commerce, fill the centre of the building's river frontage. It was this company's warehouses that totally dominated the vast warehouse and wharfages that run between London and Tower Bridges, these included Chamberlains, Cotton, and Wilson's wharves. Many were now lying idle or empty, their former days of hectic trading and unloading goods from all over the globe consigned to the history books, when London had been the Port of the Empire. Gaps in the riverscape told the story of those already lost to the ravages of fire; others would follow before developers would once again bring life and wealth back into the area, not least with the creation of London Bridge City and the conversion of warehouses to prestigious inner-city apartments and flats.

The fireboat was detailed to lay offshore and supply water to the quayside, to feed the pumps that would redirect the water to crews fighting the fire. The large, ugly, brick warehouse was well alight by the time the fireboat stood by at its station, laying about fifty yards from the exposed shoreline. The quayside stood thirty feet above the shoreline; here the river frontage (that included Mark Browns Wharf) had enormous baulks of timber sunk into the riverbed. This timber had been used to construct a wooden jetty where once famous ships, like the Baltic Trader, would have moored to discharge their valuable cargos of goods and commodities. Now it was just rotting and derelict, providing yet another obstacle to getting the hose, and much needed water ashore.

The fireboat crew had been busy getting long lengths of flaked three-and-a-half-inch hose ready, coiling lengths of grass line that would be used to pull the heavy lengths of hose ashore. The Station Officer had already decided it was too dangerous to use the rocket line from the boat but his crew could use it from the shore to fire over the boat. It would trail a line that would be connected ultimately to a grass line that would haul the hose through the water, and on to the shore. I was seeing at first hand the methodical workings of the boat's crew. On land firemen were frequently like sprinters, going for the quick all out physical assault required for a snatch rescue, or the speedy attack on a blaze. But here they were like marathon runners, maintaining a steady powerful rhythm, preparing for the long haul.

The skiff, which had been towed, was now pulled to the side of the fireboat, two hundred feet of flaked hose line was placed aft, the rocket line box placed forward, and wearing lifejackets for the first time four of the crew prepared to row ashore. With the end of the hose line connected to the pump outlet they rowed and trailed the hose line out behind them. Crews who were waiting on top of the jetty had lines thrown down to pull up the hose, and deliver the desperately needed water. I was watching all this activity, detailed to remain on the fireboat. As the skiff crew reached the shore the first man jumped clear, immediately sinking into slimy ooze that came up to his knees. It took the combined efforts of all four men to haul the single line of hose though the mud to the jetty wall where it was hauled aloft and connected to the first pump. Giving the water-on signal the hose was charged with water. It took on the image of a giant python as the hose was slowly engorged with water as it snaked a path through the mud-filled foreshore, then slithered up the jetty wall.

The skiff's crew moved on to their next task. Still wading through mud, two found a vertical iron ladder and climbed to the quayside with the rocket line in its special carrying box. Positioning themselves opposite the fireboat they opened the box and removed the hand held rocket launcher, which looked like a large flare gun. In the box, made up on a special 'former' was the thin nylon line that would be fixed to the rocket. Taking the former out and turning it upside down, the line fell out in a criss-crossed free running pile on the ground. With one end tied to a fixing on the rocket and the other secured to the ground, the crew member took careful aim and fired the rocket over the wheelhouse of the fireboat. With a whoosh the rocket passed overhead and fell into the river, its line now lying across the fireboat. Pulling the free end in, it was secured to a long line that was pulled back to the shore by the two crew still waiting by the skiff. Tied to that long line were two two-inch grass lines. Grass lines were special ropes that floated on the water; these were used to pull the next lengths of hose ashore. Finally, to each grass line was secured a length of three-and-a-half-inch hose. With all four crew now back on the foreshore and joined by other land crews, the process of trudging the hose lines through the mud, up the jetty and connecting to another pump was repeated and completed. It had taken nearly an hour to connect the final hose to its pump, but now an endless supply of water was available to the fireground. The crew rowing back from the shore were almost unrecognisable; even their helmets were caked in black slime and mud and they stank to high heaven. Smiling, the Station Officer shouted, "Don't even think of going below until that lot's washed off," before he returned to the warmth of the wheelhouse to monitor the pump controls.

We pumped water all night. There was little hope in saving the warehouse, its empty floors rapidly collapsed leaving high walls dangerously exposed and unsupported. Crews were withdrawn and reluctantly the fire was fought from the outside, not the London way. With the roof finally gone the building was just a shell when the first rays of light brought a new day. Crews had protected the surrounding property but had just unfortunately provided National Car Parks with a new site, once the building was demolished and the land cleared. But for now, crews would be here for two or three days, putting out the last remnants of flame and make the site safe for the demolition crews to move in. With the White Watch crew delivered by a brigade personnel carrier we were finally relieved at about ten that morning and made our weary way back to Lambeth. The fireboat would remain on station for the whole of that shift but now moored on the jetty until the tide changed again. My two weeks had ended in style. I now had a greater appreciation of the role of the fireboat and even greater admiration for the crews, who were, in the main long-serving land-based fireman who had transferred their skills to the fireboat. They might not have to use them very often, but when called upon, they won my respect and admiration every time.

BA Course

I was never what the older hands would call a smoke-eater. Whilst attending a smoky job I would be on my hands and knees, grovelling around on the floor, trying to sniff up some fresh air that hugged the floor. Coming across a pair of fireboots and looking up I would see some old lag from a surrounding station, seemingly oblivious to the smoke and fumes, his eyes streaming but looking down in total disdain at my feeble efforts to handle the conditions. I always got stuck in, just at a lower level than these men with lungs made of cobalt steel. "Get the eff up and fight the fire like a man," would sum up the majority of their comments as they continued to wander around apparently impervious to the smoke. To top it all, as soon as they came out of the job the very first thing that they would want to do was get the "baccy tin" out and light a roll up. Maybe that is what was required but I never ever smoked cigarettes and I had no intention of starting. I also found working in such smoky conditions for more than an hour, which happened far more than you would think, that I would get a blinding headache that would last for hours. Sod being a smoke-eater!

So when the course nomination came through for my BA course at Croydon I was delighted and relieved. All firemen must pass their BA course and you usually attended it near your two-year service point. I got to go early for some reason but was not about to argue; the sooner I could get one of those bloody sets on the better, even if the "smoke-eaters" thought I was a softy.

There was still an incredible macho image in the sixties about the need to wear BA, no doubt perpetuated by the very smoke-eaters who seemed to have their very own internal BA set. Unless there were rescues to be carried out, or smoke so thick you could cut it with a knife, these guys would rather cough up soot for a week than wear a sissy BA set. For over a year I had listened to the sound of firemen waking up in the locker room each morning, coughing and spitting up phlegm before they lit up their first ciggy of the day. Whilst smoking was the norm on the watch, and call me a smart-arse if you like, to my young mind smoking was definitely not good for your health. Given that the average life span of a fireman after retirement was only sixty-three to sixty-five years of age (they had to retire at fifty-five) what more proof was needed?

A small training room at Croydon fire station equipped with basic desks and uncomfortable chairs provided the classroom for the two-week course. We were to learn about, and wear, the Siebe-Gorman Mark V self-contained oxygen breathing apparatus set. Although modified and updated, this was the same type of set that had given such service and protection, to London firemen since the 1920s. Leather harnesses and canvas bags had been replaced by nylon. Safety features, such as the BA tally and the distress signal unit, had been added after firemen died wearing BA in major underground fires, such as the Smithfield Market of 1952, but the concept of the set remained the same.

Our instructor was a Sub Officer, and for the first few days we were taught how the set was constructed, the names of its component parts, how they fitted together, how the set was checked over prior to use, how to don it, turn it on, turn it off, take it off, take it apart, clean it and test it, then put it all back together again.

This BA set used pure oxygen and it was re-circulated through an absorbent filter to provide a breathable oxygen supply, lasting about an hour under most conditions. The small oxygen cylinder was mounted horizontally in the set's harness and carried so the cylinder fitted in the small of the wearer's back. With the harness placed over the wearer's shoulders, the main part of the set was at the front on the wearer's chest, with the on/off valve located by the left hip. The breathing bag was made of vulcanised rubber, with connections for the various components on the top, plus a clamp across the main opening to close the breathing bag making it airtight, when assembled. It was placed in a protective carrying bag that formed an integral part of the harness. A brass air cooler (painted black) was located on the outside of the carrying bag as were the breathing tubes and rubber mouthpiece. A pressure release valve was fitted to the top on the rubber breathing bag at one end and the small diameter oxygen supply tube to the other. The inhalation tube was connected to the bag and the exhalation tube to the cooler. The complete set also had a spark-proof torch; pressure gauge (fitted with a low cylinder pressure warning whistle); a distress signal unit (DSU) and an individual BA tally (with a key that turned off the DSU permanently attached) clipped to the carrying bag. We had to learn, word perfect, the circulation of oxygen through the various parts of the set, where it went and why. We learnt the set's safety features and practised the essential art of fault finding, how to rectify them and how to maximise our oxygen supply in the event of a problem whilst working in the set. The safety modifications mentioned above had come about due to hard-earned past experiences that in many cases had cost the lives of firemen, either getting separated or lost in fires and then running out of oxygen.

Towards the end of the first week we were able to assemble, don, start-up, close-down, clean, test, and maintain the sets, recognising faults and take remedial action. We were not permitted to call the oxygen cylinder a bottle! This was something I did regularly because of my Scuba diving where the air tanks were commonly called air bottles. This was a particular pet hate of the Sub Officer and the punishment for perpetrating this horrendous crime was to run around Croydon's expansive drill yard carrying an oxygen cylinder above your head whilst saying out loud, "This is not a bottle." A couple of laps and the message sank in.

Essentially the BA set worked by using a two-stage reducer that allowed low-pressure oxygen into the breathing bag. High pressure oxygen was first reduced in pressure as it left the cylinder and then passed through a second stage reducer to provide a continuous low-pressure supply into the breathing bag. Part of the high-pressure side was fed off to the pressure gauge which recorded the contents of the cylinder and told the wearer how much of the supply was left. Also, as part of the pressure gauge tube, was a warning whistle which sounded when the contents of the cylinder got to a predetermined pressure, letting the wearer know the oxygen supply was getting low. A pressure gauge valve, located at the second stage reducer, could isolate the pressure gauge in the event of a high-pressure leak so as to conserve the oxygen supply if there was a failure in the gauge.

The breathing bag was separated into two compartments by a central rubber curtain that went from the top to within an inch of the base. Into the bag was poured a white granular, absorbent substance, which filled the space at the bottom of the bag and extracted the carbon dioxide from the wearer's exhaled breath. To reduce the heat from the exhaled breath, exhaled breath passed over baffles in the brass cooler, which contained a central core containing a crystallised agent that absorbed some of the heat from the wearer's breath. With the bag clamped closed, and connections made, the action of inhaling through the rubber mouthpiece drew oxygen from the front of the bag. The breathing tubes (fitted to the top back and front connections of the sectionalised breathing bag) had non-return valves. Inhalation through one tube, exhalation through the other. The action of breathing caused a circulation within the bag. This drew the exhaled breath through the absorbent (Protosorb) thus removing the exhaled carbon dioxide, replenishing it with low-pressure oxygen and back to the wearer's lungs.

With donning and starting up and closing down all under our belts the class of ten, from various stations south of the Thames, were about to get a dancing lesson. We were to learn the BA shuffle. With our personal issue BA head harness placed on our heads and connected to the securing clips of the rubber mouthpiece (that would now prevent speaking) we were given frosted glass goggles to wear instead of the normal goggles fitted with laminated glass. Finally doing up the chin straps of our helmets, our sets started up, we were led out in crocodile file, each man holding on to the cylinder of the man in front, into the drill yard. The shuffle consisted of keeping your weight on your rear leg and probing with your foot and the back of one hand. We were working in pairs, groping our way around the various obstacles in the yard, unable to see because of the obscured vision caused by the training goggles. We were moving slowly, two abreast, keeping to the perimeter walls and sweeping the area in front of us with our leading foot and moving our free hand up and down, remembering the Sub Officer's catch phrase of, "Spectacles, testicles and wallet." It was this movement that would take you through an unknown building, full of smoke and potential hazards, whilst you blindly felt your way around, searching for those trapped inside or probing for the seat of fire somewhere within.

Week two saw us in Croydon's Smoke Chamber. It was in essence a three-dimensional maze contained in a single storey brick building about twelve feet high and with thirty-foot sides. Interconnected galleries, trap doors, hatches and openings passed through three levels, transferring you from crawling on the floor to scurrying along the upper gallery below the ceiling line. In twos or threes we were set tasks that required us to find our way in and out of this adjustable obstacle course. Electric heaters built up the internal temperatures to over one hundred degrees Fahrenheit, whilst smoke canisters generated a visually impenetrable environment. A powerful extractor fan was ready for activation in the event of one of the trainee BA crews getting into difficulty and requiring rapid evacuation. The galleries where made increasingly more difficult and arduous with each passing exercise. Heavy dummies had to be recovered and charged hose lines taken through the "rat run" as it was lovingly called. With our task still incomplete, a low cylinder warning whistle would often sound, indicating that we had not read our pressure gauges frequently enough.

This would not only endanger ourselves but others too, who would have to be sent in to rescue us from our self-inflicted difficulties.

We learnt and practised procedures using personal and BA guidelines, and communications equipment, which we exercised to enforce the classroom theory and technical instruction. Every aspect of the course had to be committed to memory and be demonstrable by practical application. Q and A round ups, each day, prepared us for the BA examinations conducted on the last day.

Before that, however, there was one more all-important lesson to be covered. This was entrapped procedure. The very serious looking Sub Officer said, "This may be the only thing that saves you if you become separated from your crew or become trapped by fallen timbers in a smoke-filled building." First, he ran through the procedure in the classroom but soon followed it with real thing in the BA chamber. Back went on the frosted goggles as we were sat in twos on the solid floor, sets started up and one crew member's foot over the other, in constant contact.

"Right, do exactly as you have been told," said the Sub. We made ourselves as comfortable as we could on the hard floor. One CEAG torch was turned off, not that we could see anything anyway, and the DSU activated by pressing its spark proof rubber button. The DSU looked exactly like a 6-inch rubber torch only without a reflector and bulb. Then its continuous warning noise started, its monotonous loud tone hopefully summoning our rescuers if this had been for real. The noise completely blanked out the reassuring regular plip-plop sound of the mica valves lifting and seating in the breathing tubes.

Unable to speak we carefully thought through the rehearsed procedure. Relax, stay calm; finger on the bypass valve and inflate the bag; turn off the main cylinder valve; wait for the warning whistle to sound and then turn off the pressure gauge; hand goes back on the main cylinder valve and keep your hand on the cylinder wheel; re-inflate the bag when the bag's nearly empty.

Already the DSU's droning sound was filling our heads with its samey high-pitched wailing, making concentration increasingly difficult. We were safe, being watched in the safety of the chamber. What must the heat and humidity of a real fire be like, fearful of running out of air before help arrives? Turn on, operate bypass, re-inflate and turn off. The Sub Officer kept us in the chamber for nearly an hour before he was satisfied that we had the procedure in our heads and had experienced something he hoped we would never carry out in action. Turning on the main valve and reverting to normal use, we were told to shut down our sets.

The last day saw an unknown ADO arrive to conduct our BA examinations. Jointly we went through donning and starting up, performing a simple exercise in the chamber, closing down and then were closely observed whilst we did the required testing and set maintenance. Finally, taken one by one, we faced the Q and A session and performed the required party piece, the circulation of oxygen. I never understood why this was so important. I did not want to know the passage of petrol when I started my car and even if I did it did not make me a better driver. Anyway, we all passed. Now I would return to Lambeth a BA fireman. I would even get to ride the pump, even if I was the only one in the back.

"Ginger" Crittenden

The backdrop for my first BA job is also a reminder of the premature and painful ending of "Ginger" Crittenden's operational career. Station Officer Harry Crittenden was Brixton's Red Watch long standing governor. A tall, lean powerful man with a gruff south London accent, he had a fearful reputation as a no-nonsense governor as well as an exceptional and gifted fire officer. His head of thick red hair was now mixed with grey and silver but it had given him his nickname early in his career, although few said it to his face now.

Just after the chimes of Big Ben had sounded a new day, Lambeth's pump was ordered to a "fire in a fish and chip shop, Wandsworth Road, SW4." The call was on Clapham's ground and we joined their PE and pump to make up the initial attendance, and as Brigade Control had received multiple calls to the same address, Brixton's pump was also ordered on. When our pump pulled into Wandsworth Road from Vauxhall, we could see a serious fire ahead of us. Flames were shooting horizontally out of the shop front, like a blow torch, and reaching almost the centre of the roadway. Set back from the projecting shop front were the upper two floors of the terraced building and smoke was already billowing from the second-floor windows.

Although this fire was on Clapham's ground its location was almost equally distant from the three stations attending. As my 'acting' governor shouted above the sound of the engine noise for the two of us in the back, to "get your Proto sets on," the pump driver pulled up safely short of the fire. Brixton's pump arrived just behind us and was parking in our wake. As we stood on the pavement, donning our sets, the noise of the flames sounded like an express train as they continued their avid consumption of the contents of the shop, its radiated heat reaching our exposed faces some thirty feet away. Clapham's crew had got a jet to work and it was brought to bear on the flames through what had been the glazed shop front. The water generated an angry hissing sound and crackled as it turned to steam when making contact with the super-heated interior. Our 'acting' governor now came hurrying back to grab his own BA set telling us, "People were reported to be trapped in the accommodation above the shop." As we were making ready our entry into the upper accommodation, by the separate front door, the iconic figure of "Ginger" strolled purposely around the incident. As the substantive Station Officer he was now in charge and his natural authority and presence provided, even for the older hands, a sense of assurance and moral support.

Climbing the staircase, the wall separating us from the shop was warm and the heat was discolouring the wallpaper. Moving up on to the first floor the accommodation was extremely hot. Thick smoke continued to permeate up through the shop's now non-existent ceiling and was filling the flat. No fire had broken through but the smoke was so thick and acrid that no one on this or the top floor would be able to make their way out unaided, if at all. We searched quickly and thoroughly, covering both floors, ventilating as we went. Despite the residual heat we saw the smoke clearing as the crews fighting the fire brought it under control. The shop was utterly gutted but a small fire had now spread to the first floor which a hose reel jet promptly dealt with. We had only taken fifteen minutes to enter, search and leave the building yet we were bathed in perspiration and our clothing beneath the fire gear was wet through. The occupants, a family of four, had escaped when the explosive force of the fire blew out the shop front. It had taken time to confirm their safe location and, if in any doubt, the assumption is someone's there and a search must be made.

That would be the last operation incident where I would witness Station Officer Crittenden in action. However, it wasn't his last "shout." Not long afterwards he was attending another blaze on Clapham's ground that, for him, would have dire consequences and for the occupant of a terraced house, prove fatal. Clapham's pair were ordered to a fire in Garfield Road, Battersea and on their arrival found a serious fire engulfing a three-storey private house. The fire had taken such a firm hold that Clapham's Station Officer had no hesitation in making "pumps four-persons reported." Brixton's pump, with "Ginger" in charge, was ordered on to this incident in support. (The blaze was caused by the owner of the house trying to carry a lighted paraffin oil heater, then falling over and starting a blaze in which he received fatal burns.)

When Brixton's pump arrived Station Officer Crittenden jumped down from the still moving appliance onto the pavement. While his left foot found solid ground, his right foot missed, catching the edge of the granite kerbstone. His foot, forced by his own momentum, slipped off the kerb into the path of the still moving front wheel of the appliance. Even above the roar of the fire the sound of the single excruciating cry of agonised pain filled the air. His foot, pinned by the moving wheel and the kerbstone, was trapped and twisted as the combined forward movement and weight of the appliance crushed and shattered his foot and ankle. The machine stopped, but too late to avoid his crippling injury. Whilst Brixton's crew, realising his plight, rushed to his aid, Clapham's crews battled to contain the fire in the house and search for missing persons. Station Officer Crittenden was carried carefully away from the engine and remained conscious throughout, despite unbelievable pain. He was reported to have said to his crew, "Don't worry about me lads, get on with your job." It seemed so typical of what was said about him; that in spite of his enormous strength, his "rough diamond" and brash character, he always put the "job" first.

Although I had only stood by at Brixton a couple of times, I had only ever called him "Station Officer Crittenden." I did not even call him "guv"; he was that type of figure to a young fireman. His foot was irreparably damaged and he never walked properly again. Garfield Road was his last shout. After hearing of the sad news of his serious accident, and laying on my bunk at Lambeth on night duty but unable to sleep, I thought about this man's untimely and unfortunate accident and his legendary fire service story. He was an old school "smoke-eater", something anyone with a sense of self-preservation would not contest – unless they wished to lose some of their front teeth. He was a super fire officer but not unhappily immune from the prejudice and racism that was prevalent in much of British society during the mid-1960s.

Brixton was a popular relocation area for a vast number of Afro-Caribbean families, and there were many house fires involving them in Brixton and its environs. His attitude towards, and treatment of, them at these incidents was sometimes said to be less than friendly; unless they were attractive women. Young or old, married or single, it made no difference to him. His size and strength meant that he had little or no problem dealing with the protestations of husbands or boyfriends who took exception to his overly friendly advances. If his expletives did not resolve the problem then the occasional slap would.

It was not unknown that when such fires occurred in their frequently poor and run-down accommodation, adults, but especially the men, gave preference to their personal possessions over the safety of their own children. Instances occurred where a child was left inside a house or flat on fire whilst the TV or some other "irreplaceable" item, was brought out first. "Ginger" was alleged to have, on more than one occasion, punched anyone doing so full in the face before dragging them back in, nursing a broken nose, with whatever they were taking out, to search for, and retrieve the child.

As a lowly probationer fireman you did not mess with this man. In fact I would not even consider speaking to him unless it was to answer some question or query he had just barked out. Thus it was during my early probation that a serious house fire occurred in a four-storey terraced Victorian property, just off the Camberwell Road. The terrace had once obviously enjoyed a more prosperous era but now it, and the surrounding vicinity, had fallen on harder times. Nevertheless the owners of this particular property had tried hard to maintain it and the contents. So when a fire broke out on the first floor and quickly involved the second floor, Brixton's governor made pumps four on his arrival and our PE and pump were ordered on to the incident. It was a "good working job" with both pumps committing BA crews to tackle the fire and the PE crews getting stuck in as best they could but without the added protection of any breathing apparatus. The Brigade remained considerably undermanned and it was not unusual for fire engines to ride with only minimum crews; four on a PE and three on a pump. Both stations were doing so on this day, so even though it was a four-pump fire there were only fourteen firemen to deal with the incident. There was, of course, the option of making pumps more but hell would freeze over first before most governors would make any house fire more than four pumps (unless it was some exceptionally large mansion). So six men were in BA; Station Officer Crittenden in charge; one BA control officer; four tackling the first-floor fire without BA; a pump operator and yours truly. Normally, when there were sufficient numbers, I would be taken under a more experienced fireman's wing and taught the art of firemanship. Not today; this was not the time or the place to teach and fight a fire at the same time, if the property was to be saved from more serious damage. So there I was, a spare prick at a wedding, unable to get stuck in with the lads above and having been told by my Sub Officer, "Do something useful downstairs," before he crawled into the smoke on the first floor and disappeared, not having given any indication of what useful was.

The ground floor had two large reception rooms, a wide hallway that led to the back of the house and another rear room that, so far, was completely unaffected. The two large rooms reminded me of my grandmother's own home; large sofas or settees in the front and polished table and chairs in the other. Both had pictures and paintings hanging from the walls and with mantel shelf ornaments and bric-a-brac placed on occasional tables. Already water was coming through the central ornate plaster ceiling rose in the front room and water was making the ceiling bulge in the other. I found what useful meant and made myself busy doing some salvage work. Having collected all four large salvage sheets from the engines I threw one over each pile of furniture I had gathered together in each of the two rooms. The black plastic or canvas salvage sheets were about twelve feet by twelve feet and afforded a fair amount of protection from the dripping water. I rolled the carpets and folded and placed them under these sheets, together with the paintings and prints from the walls, making two large black parcels, if somewhat untidily wrapped. The ceiling in the back room was bulging badly and looked in danger of collapse under the weight of water above. Using a salvage sheet and securing it to the various picture hooks hanging from the wooden picture rail that ran around the room, I secured three sides of the sheet and fed the unsecured lower end out through the bottom of the window that I had opened. The sheet was to act as a funnel and, hopefully, would catch most of the water and direct it outside. Next, using a long-spiked pole, called a ceiling hook, I punctured the ceiling allowing the accumulated water to cascade into the sheet and away outside.

With the situation above now coming under control, Brixton's Station Officer came to look around the ground floor and assess the damage. I was still working in the back room, protecting the furniture, keeping the water directed towards the open window and trying my best to minimise any further water damage. He looked carefully around at my efforts before he spoke in a rasping voice that was due to the effects of the smoke. "Who told you to do this?" Immediately from the tone of his voice I thought I had done wrong; his was not so much a question, it was a demand. Nervously I said, "No one sir. I was told to stay downstairs and saw water coming through the ceilings." He inspected the salvage sheet draped out of the window, turned and said, "Come with me," as he headed for the front room. "What's your name, where are you from?" His voice still grating and severe. "Pike sir, I'm stationed at Lambeth and riding the PE." He studied the front room, furniture piled high and covered in salvage sheets, and with galvanised buckets collecting the water dripping from the ceiling. "Good job lad, there is more to fighting fires than just squirting water, so have a look around upstairs before you go and see what you can learn up there." He left the room and I started to climb the stairs as Lambeth's PE crew were coming down, grimy faces, bloodshot eyes but with the satisfied smile that getting stuck into a "good working job" seems to bring out. "Come on Pikey, time to go." Disappointed, I turned around, not even having seen where all the action had been. "Brixton's governor said you did a bloody good job downstairs, sheeting up and your salvage efforts," said my Sub Officer. "Coming from him that's praise indeed, it's more than we bloody got."

The Rotunda

How the propane cylinder became dislodged and fell down the shaft was never established at the subsequent Coroner's inquest. What was beyond doubt was that it had. Hitting the concrete floor the normally robust cylinder ruptured, releasing a devastating flammable vapour cloud. It was looking for an ignition source. It found one, causing severe consequences.

Pulling up outside the three multi-storey towers of the Government offices in Marsham Street, Westminster, there was no immediate sign of the fire and explosion that we had been called to. Nor was there any sign of Westminster's appliances. Lambeth's pump and ET had formed part of the augmented attendance, together with Westminster's pair and Soho's TL. The vast office complex ran the full length of Marsham Street and it was on the riverside that the main entrances to each of the towers were located. As the governor said, "Take a drive around the block," two things happened simultaneously. A security guard came running out of the building and pointed up the street as Westminster's pump sent a priority message from Great Peter Street (at the east end of the complex), "Make pumps 4 BA required, persons reported." The driver did not need telling twice as he moved off at speed towards the end of street and Westminster's crews.

With both the leading hand and me rigging in our BA sets we turned into Great Peter Street to see Westminster's crew laying out hose lines and setting into a hydrant. Smoke was coming from the wide vehicle entrance leading to the car park beneath the building. There was considerable confusion around the garage entrance with construction vehicles randomly parked, making access difficult. Building workers were running, some coughing and spluttering up the vehicle ramp, some having to be assisted by Westminster's crew.

I could see down the ramp into the car park from street level. The smoke was hugging the car park's ceiling line and rolling up the side of the building, leaving quite a gap near the floor free of smoke. Taking a quick glance down the ramp there were no obvious signs of fire, just a continuous stream of smoke coming from a set of doors to one side. There was a rapid exchange of words between Westminster's governor and someone that clearly looked like a foreman or site manager. Whoever he was, he was making lots of movements with his hands and pointing into the car park. Our own governor was listening into the conversation and then waved us over towards the entrance, where we joined two of Westminster's crew, also in BA and ready to go. The discussion over, the four of us were called closer. Whilst our governor was charged to do a head count with the site manager, Westminster's governor made pumps six. As we were starting up our Proto sets, Westminster's governor said that possibly four workers were still unaccounted for. It seemed that they had been working in the Rotunda at the time of the explosion. I had absolutely no idea what a Rotunda was and by the look on the face of the leading fireman neither did he. "There's a government war-time tunnel system under the building, it's under refurbishment and about three levels (floors) down," continued Westminster's governor. "It's a bloody big circular construction and the entrance is over there," he said pointing into the car park far wall from where we saw the smoke emanating. "Start searching; the ET crew will back you up with a hose line, there's no report of any serious fire down there yet, so get moving."

Starting up and leaving our BA tallies at the entry point we made our way easily towards the lift shaft and the staircase that surrounded it. The stairs would lead us down into the circular tunnel complex. Conditions on the staircase were tolerable with the smoke the density of a very foggy day but the heat was increasing as each flight of steps took us further below ground level. It was the equivalent of working in a very warm oven but at least the heat levels were not increasing. The sight of the ruptured propane cylinder and the double doors hanging by their hinges at contorted angles told us we were at the base level. Small spot fires were still burning in and around the corridor where the force of the blast had blown smaller doors clean off their hinges. Scorch marks had blackened and stained the concrete walls. Unable to talk properly because of our mouthpieces, the leading fireman spoke a garbled instruction, which was almost impossible to understand, but his hand signals let Westminster's crews know we would search to the right and they should go to the left. If it really was a big circle, we should meet up somewhere on the other side, providing we had sufficient oxygen in our sets.

Some of the bulkhead lights had withstood the force of the blast and still gave out diffused light through the smoke, which made the searching easier. The arc of corridor disappeared into a haze of smoke and the light created strange shadows as it filtered through the array of construction materials now littering up the passageway, making progress more difficult. Rooms ran off the only corridor and the first few, without a door to force open, were easy to search. The next room was seemingly a plant room, its space filled with an assortment of lagged and un-lagged pipework running horizontally and vertically. Wedged between two of the thigh-high, six-inch, heating pipes was the crooked shape of a partially clothed and severely burnt man, thrust between the pipe work by the power of the blast. He still had a weak pulse so, as carefully and quickly as we could, we lifted him free and the leading hand hoisted him on to my shoulders. There was no time for the BA shuffle now; it was the quickest route possible up to ground level, which meant the staircase. Looking around to make sure none of the other missing construction workers were in the same vicinity we started to retrace our steps, passing our ET crew at the base of the stairs.

Once again in muffled speech, grunts and sign language, my leading fireman told the ET crew how far we'd got with the search and where the other crew had gone. The conditions were easing all the time, except for the casualty who was drifting deeper into shock with every passing moment. I had only ever done a carry-down, now the reverse was required. I started the climb, flight by flight, with the leading fireman following close behind, supporting the casualty. By the second landing my leg muscles were protesting against the effort of carrying my load, each step harder than the last, my lungs burning, as they demanded more oxygen. With this weight increasing, finally willing hands took the casualty from me and rushed him to a waiting stretcher. One more injured worker was brought to safety, but the third missing employee remained where he was found. Once the police surgeon had done his duty he too would be brought up, but this time in a body bag. Thankfully the last missing worker had made his own way up but had been miscounted in all the confusion.

The adrenalin had done its work. Now, having collected my tally from the BA entry control point, my legs were like jelly and my hands shook uncontrollably. With a pat on the back, and with a smile that said nice one, the leading fireman led me back to the pump to return our sets and then to help make up the gear before returning home.

Bag-pipes

When I was told to collect the "bag-pipes" just before going out on hydrant inspection I thought, "You're joking!" But my reluctance to rise to the bait was clearly irritating Dennis, the eldest of our three leading firemen, who had been detailed to ride in charge of the pump whilst we went out on hydrants. Telling someone else to collect them he waited, then upon his return he said, "These are bag-pipes," and another piece of my formative station education fell into place.

Hydrants were a regular feature of our weekly outside work schedules. The bag-pipes (a simple yet effective device) cleaned the hydrant pit out if it had been flooded by water leaking from a defective hydrant. A clever bit of physics, called a venturi action, occurred when the bag-pipes were screwed on to the hydrant outlet. When the hydrant was turned on the force of the water lifted the contaminated water out of the pit.

Testing and inspecting hydrants was an all-important task. These strategically placed connections to the water mains augmented the limited supply carried in each PE and pump's one-hundred-gallon tank. (Later appliance design would increase this capacity to three hundred gallons per appliance.)

Despite the fact that every hydrant should have been tested and inspected regularly, lifting up a hydrant cover could tell a very different story. Perhaps years of accumulated soil would stare back up at you filling the pit to pavement level, making finding the hydrant outlet in an emergency an almost impossible task. Sadly, hydrant duties were seen by some as a necessary evil; a monthly target to be met by filling in false test details in the hydrant book. Hydrant testing was used by the less conscientious as a good skive, taking the pump to some out of the way pub and having a few pints whilst the hydrant book was completed, regardless of the condition of hydrants. Clearly, bar room hydrant inspections occurred at Lambeth given the state of a number of the hydrants that were found in need of some desperately needed TLC.

Looking after, and testing, water pipes was not just restricted to pipes laying under the ground. There were also dry rising mains, which were tested annually. They were either a four- or six-inch pipe, leading from the ground floor, vertically, to the top floor. The fire brigade could thereby connect to the ground floor inlet and pump water to all the outlets on each floor, in the event of fire. Most tall buildings, certainly those built since the mid-fifties, had these rising mains installed. These buildings included council and private flats, trade and industrial properties, such as warehouse and riverside wharves, and office blocks. Wherever these mains were to be found, for someone in the pump's crew these tests involved a lot of walking; climbing every step of every staircase that contained the dry riser outlets, checking that all the outlets were strapped closed, and then walking down every flight again to look for possible leaks. Going out on these tests as a junior buck you would not be surprised to learn who this particular task was assigned to, time after time.

Generally speaking, the tests were straightforward and un-noteworthy. Very occasionally some wag, or the local kids bunking off school, would add a little excitement to the affair by opening an outlet (sometimes two or three) after they had been checked to see if they in fact were closed. The result? Given that the main was tested under pressure, hundreds of gallons of water, sometimes thousands, would cascade down the staircase, flooding anywhere the water was able to run. Proving that the damage was the product of vandalism, and not the consequence of the brigade's incompetence, was an area that challenged the Council's legal team in fighting off claims for damages following these sometimes-unfortunate visits.

It was our job to constantly watch what was happening on our station's ground and to keep the watch abreast of changes. Developments meant new firefighting methods had to be considered and adopted, especially during the late sixties and early seventies. The rapid growth of new building materials and techniques may have benefited an occupier but they could also create a potential death trap for an unsuspecting fire crew member. Our lifeline was the knowledge of what could happen and how. Those who could not be bothered to learn did so at their peril. Tragically, events would prove that some would disregard or flout these basic doctrines of our trade.

Observing and interpreting information is essential to be a successful fireman, or a fire officer for that matter. If you forgot or ignored these basic rules your folly could result in a very public display of ineptitude!

I watched Lambeth's pump turn right out of the station on its way up Lambeth Palace Road to the Westminster Bridge Road roundabout responding to an early morning call to flooding. I never saw the resultant crater that the thirty-six-inch bursting water main blew out of Westminster Bridge Road, just south of Westminster Bridge. The ruptured main threw tons of debris high into the air whilst discharging tens of thousands of gallons of water into the surrounding network of pedestrian subways and underpasses. My governor was totally taken aback by the sheer volume and speed of the water coming out of the fractured main and immediately requested six further pumps to the scene.

Our PE was not ordered on but we heard Westminster's pump coming over Lambeth Bridge followed by Clapham's pump passing the station. Its two-tone horns, even though there was virtually no traffic at that time of day, a reminder to the senior officers sleeping above that the lads were out and about. Before the Metropolitan Water Board turncock could isolate the supply and shut down the main a massive expanse of water now lay, in places many feet deep, from County Hall to St Thomas's Hospital, and from Westminster Brigade to Waterloo Station's taxi access road. The area resembled a boating lake rather than one of the capital's busiest road junctions and roundabouts.

Finally the PE was ordered to deliver the station's light portable pump and then return to station. Our arrival coincided with one of life's nicer ironies. One of the pumps sent on to the incident was Deptford's. Its governor was a wholly miserable man whose sole ambition in life seemed to be to make himself as unpopular as possible; a task that he had excelled at. He was not only disliked by his own watch but also by anyone unfortunate enough to have to stand by. His trademark arrogance and superciliousness was evident on his face as he waded through the water, along what he thought was the pavement line. Now everyone, but him, had read the signs and had therefore avoided the area between the parallel galvanised railings (that ran close to the where the kerb line would have been). His mind clearly focused elsewhere he continued, everyone else watching intently as he progressed. He moved two more steps forward and then disappeared totally from view, just as one of Old Kent Road's crew said in such a soft whisper as to be almost inaudible, "Mind the underpass governor." The only indication of his presence was his cork fire helmet floating on the surface of the water, marking the location of a sign which read "Will pedestrians please use the underpasses."

It was a testament to the man's reputation, and to the high esteem in which he was held, that no one moved forward to his immediate aid. The general consensus was that if he was not up soon, lots would have to be drawn to see who went in after him. Coughing and spluttering, he finally emerged from the depths and with all the aplomb he could muster put his helmet back on, spilling its contents over his head. This final act was just too much for the appreciative audience, hilarious laughter greeted the return of Neptune and even his fellow officers could be seen trying to contain their mirth at this entertaining interlude to the morning's proceedings.

Lolly sticks

By now I had a regular part-time job for the Victoria Wine Company and delivered wine to the rich and famous around Victoria, Pimlico and Chelsea, working between my night duties and on my first leave day. On the 24th April, parking along Millbank for a sandwich at lunchtime, I watched Lambeth's three appliances, the PE, pump and TL, turn right out of the station and head along the river on a shout that had obviously interrupted their lunch break. The appliances continued over Lambeth Brigade roundabout and disappeared, heading down towards County Hall. Looking further I followed the line of the river and saw the tell-tale sign of a column of smoke rising skyward in the distance and, whilst I finished my sandwich, it was growing ever higher and thicker as each minute passed.

Frustrated at not knowing what was happening or where, although it looked close, I returned to my wine deliveries around Westminster. In the early afternoon the distinctive taint of smoke that only comes from a serious fire filled the air and I knew Lambeth had a working job on its hands. Rushing to finish my round I left the shop and walked from Victoria Street to the fire station, eager to learn more. Arriving at about 4.30 I saw that a stand-by pump was in the station, covering Lambeth's ground, so whatever had happened was still going on.

Changing quickly into my work overalls, I went to the watchroom to catch up on the teleprinter messages and information from the fire-ground. Multiple calls had been received at 1.02 pm to Eldorardo's ice cream factory, Stamford Street, SE1. It was established later that most of the employees were in the first-floor canteen. A man walking from the canteen across the main storage area towards the staircase saw fire among a stack of corrugated cardboard cartons. Raising the alarm, the canteen was quickly evacuated and a few of the employees attempted to tackle the fire with extinguishers. However, the speed and intensity at which the fire was developing trapped two of the men in the canteen because of the dense smoke, which had now filled the first floor, preventing them from reaching the staircase, and their escape to safety. They ran to the windows, their only possible escape route, or so they hoped.

The call was on Southwark's ground and their pair, plus Lambeth's machines, supported by Cannon Street, made up the augmented attendance. When the first appliance arrived smoke was pouring from the windows along the whole of the first floor and a man was seen shouting for help. Make pumps four persons reported was sent as a priority radio message. Whilst crews attempted to rescue the man via an extension ladder, they found the window opening too small for the trapped man to climb through, and as the smoke in the building appeared to be impenetrable the crews set to work with hand tools to cut their way in.

Lambeth's turntable ladder crew saw a man shouting for help at the first-floor window. For quickly and decisively siting the ladder and rescuing the man the driver and the officer in charge of the TL were, later, to be congratulated for their actions. It was not the first time a one-hundred-foot turntable ladder had been used to rescue a person from the first floor but it was unusual.

Southwark's governor, Station Officer Arthur Money, found a building of one, two and seven floors about one hundred and fifty feet by one hundred and twenty feet (fire brigade speak), with the whole of the first floor smoked-logged. Rescues were being carried out on the front and side of the building. Making pumps eight, BA required, he gave instructions for BA crews to enter the first and second floors to carry out a search, as it seemed likely that other employees might well be trapped in the building. A few minutes later the first senior officer to arrive ordered three more BA pumps. With the arrival of more pumps, ladders were pitched to the windows on the Stamford Street frontage and crews entered with hose lines.

Difficulty was experienced in penetrating the fire area. The build-up of heat was now considerable because of the combustible nature of the storage, the area involved, low ceilings and the lack of direct ventilation. Even those working on the external iron staircase were subjected to extremely punishing conditions. The smoke was hot, dense, black and extremely difficult to work in. It was obvious that this was going to be a prolonged and difficult BA job, which would necessitate relays of BA crews gradually forcing their jets further into the building until the seat of the fire was reached and extinguished. More BA pumps were requested and by 2.30 p.m. the BA incident box was requested, together with one hundred extra oxygen cylinders.

For the next few hours relays of BA men slowly and painfully worked their way further into the building, foot by foot, many recharging their sets and returning to the fray. Appliances were summoned to relieve the original crews and more BA pumps arrived to enable crews who had been at work to recharge their sets. So it was that Lambeth's PE and pump returned to the station with exhausted crews. The pump was to exchange crews and, with a Red Watch crew, including me, we returned, even before the 6 p.m. change of shift, to continue the battle. Our crew wearing proto BA sets were committed twice. I experienced at first hand the extreme heat conditions that other crews had been facing all afternoon.

When the stop message was finally sent by the Deputy Chief Officer, fifty pumping appliances, four emergency tenders, two turntable ladders, plus Lambeth's canteen van attended the fire. The last one was a very necessary appliance in those trying conditions, although no ice cream was served! We worked into the night, and when eventually relieved, to return the following morning. We came back the following night as well, still damping down and finally we saw the full intensity of the fire. Concrete had spalled off beams, exposing the steel reinforcements; large sections of the lower surface of the floor had spalled off completely. Hundreds of thousands of lolly sticks were destroyed, the major fuel of this extraordinary blaze.

Flood procedure

Getting to work was decidedly tricky on Saturday 14th September 1968, for the first of our two night duties. It had been an incredibly wet day, the heavens opened and stayed open. I had got a lift to work with Teddy, one of our leading firemen, in his flashy little sports car. We seemed in danger of flooding ourselves, as Teddy tried to negotiate the rising level of rainwater as the drainage system started to fail under the volume of rain pouring down. Getting through Catford and Lewisham became increasingly difficult as road after road became impassable due to flooding. Teddy had to use all his considerable knowledge of South London's topography to get us through, using the back-doubles that by-passed the affected routes and to get us to Lambeth fire station; and still the rain kept coming down.

A white star shone brightly against a capital S in the headquarters appliance indicator board as we finally drove into Lambeth's yard, signifying that the Brigade was experiencing major mobilising procedures in the Southern Command, which covered all of London south of the River Thames. Saturday evening, I was riding the pump and we were pumping out, in and around south London, dealing with just a few of the one-hundred and fourteen calls to flooding. But this was just a dress rehearsal for what was to come. Just when we thought it could not rain any harder, in the early hours of Sunday morning it did just that. With no spare capacity in the sewage and drainage systems, when the rain came deluging down, the calls went up, to an incredible one thousand seven hundred and seventy-three. Of those, one thousand six hundred and sixty came from the worst hit South London areas where two rivers, normally hardly known or noticed, came into prominence. In particular the River Ravensbourne burst its banks sending millions upon millions of gallons of muddy water into the surrounding streets, houses and anything else it could find.

With over six-hundred and fifty calls attended, most between midnight to the change of watch at 9.00 a.m., we went out armed with a list of affected premises to see what we could do. Priority was given to old people's homes, hospitals, public utility services and food storage plants. The disabled and those trapped on upper floors were rescued. We were running out of sand bags and the local authorities were establishing emergency supplies at selected depots.

At its peak over one hundred major pumping appliances were in use whilst we were out and about, and one hundred and eighteen light portable pumps were deployed. Crews were drafted in from the less affected areas into the hot spots. Lewisham was particularly hard hit with the town centre resembling Venice. Shops, department stores, garages and, of course, people's homes were all flooded. Other areas affected included Tooting, where over four hundred houses and fifty industrial sites were flooded. Armed with Thermos flasks we took refreshment when we could whilst travelling from one call to the next. Because the drains and storm sewers could not cope with the overpowering volume of water, contaminated water filled with sewer sludge and debris made a horrible, repugnant cocktail, tainting and polluting everything it came into contact with. Our pumps were relatively easy to decontaminate. Sadly, many of those involved were not so fortunate, losing stock, goods and precious personal possessions and belongings. It was at times heart-breaking to see the havoc that nature had caused and the distress it left behind as householders started to get to grips with clearing up the mess. It would take days and would eventually lead to new major flood defence programmes for the two rivers concerned. For me that night, it meant the first time I worked the whole fifteen-hour shift without even touching my bedroll. Compared to the suffering of others affected by this exceptional deluge I had no real cause to complain.

A Black Year

In the summer of 1969 news of an unfolding tragedy came in the most unlikely of settings. I was delivering wine to a flat in Dolphin Square, Chelsea. The owner was one of the shop's regular customers and was really extremely 'nice' but a decidedly gay, single, middle-aged, man. (The term was 'queer' then, gay still predominately having happy connotations.) Immaculately dressed and well spoken, his mannerisms clearly betrayed his sexual preferences. Opening the door to his elegantly appointed flat and inviting me in as usual he said, "Oh you poor boy, you must be so sad." It was obvious from the confused look on my face that he could see I had no idea what he was talking about. "I'm so sorry, you have not heard the news; five of your fellows have been killed in an explosion in east London."

I had built up a rapport with this particular customer over time as I dropped off his regular weekly cases of wine at his posh London flat. He knew I was a fireman serving somewhere in central London. He loved to chat and as I liked the generous tip he always gave me, I would normally accept his kind offer and stop for tea. Today his devastating news hit me like a hammer blow and the sudden change in my mood reflected the awful sadness I now felt. "Here, please take this and put it in the widows' collection box," he said as he thrust two ten-pound notes into my hand. This was an exceptionally generous gesture and one I had not experienced before or since. Twenty pounds was then a great deal of money, as much as I earned in a week.

The mood was very sombre when I went into Lambeth fire station later that day for my night duty. The vacant bays that normally housed the principal officer's staff cars and the Brigade's Control Unit indicated, if it were needed, the severity of the afternoon's events. Details of the explosion, which had killed five East London firemen, were on the teleprinter and announced with the deepest of regret etc… These deaths seemed even more poignant by the fact that they died at an incident which appeared, at the outset, to be almost trivial.

A Headquarters staff driver added grim details to the briefest of information given out on the official teleprinter messages and he told of his part in the extraction of some of the bodies from the oil laden sludge in the partly demolished oil tank farm at Dudgeons Wharf.

There was much debate and speculation about the incident, no doubt across all watches around the Brigade that night, and the asking of many questions raised by this wasteful loss of lives. The who, how, what, where and why was speculated about endlessly; emotions and anger generating some ill-founded assumptions and accusations. What was known is that the Dudgeons Wharf disaster was caused by a workman hot cutting away an old oil tank that had contained flammable substances. Although the affected tank was marked "light oil and linseed oil" the lettering was indistinct. There was certainly no warning of the potential dangers to firemen having to deal with a fire within them. The papers the following day gave fitting tributes and reported, "They died simply doing the day-to-day job of a London fireman."

(Their deaths did eventually bring about change and the "Hazchem" code was introduced in the 1970s. This simple code provided all the emergency services, but especially the fire service, with information and actions to be taken in the first minutes of an incident involving chemicals without the need to refer to text books. It told crews what fire-fighting media was to be used, what personal protection was required and if there was any risk of a violent reaction e.g. explosion.)

It was a bright sunny July day when hundreds of members of the Brigade gathered, unified in grief, to pay a personal farewell to five "good firemen." Sub Officer Michael Gamble, Firemen John Appleby, Alfred Smee, Trevor Carvosso and Terence Breem were carried on their last journey on five gleaming scarlet turntable ladders. Each fire engine bearing a flag draped coffin. A blaze of floral tributes were mounted on both sides of each turntable ladder. A requiem mass for Fireman Breem had already been held and a funeral service at West Ham Parish Church held for the other four, when the procession reunited the five comrades on their final journey to the City of London Crematorium and Cemetery in Manor Park. As moving as the turn-out of the Brigade's Honour Guard was, an outstanding feature of this sad day was the presence of the people of East London who came out in their droves to pay homage to five firemen they probably would not have recognised as they sped by on their engine, responding to some call or other. Any feelings that the public took us for granted were totally dispelled that day as the "Eastenders" lined the route; either in small groups of neighbours, or as they added their considerable weight to the single file of firemen who stood to attention, under the hot sun along the kerbside.

As the pallbearers moved with solemn gravity through the quiet cemetery, along its narrow pathway to the grey stone chapel, standing shoulder to shoulder, covering every yard of the route, was the Honour Guard. Unmoving we were bound together in common tribute, but each thinking our own thoughts. My own position just happened to be near the chapel entrance and with the modest dignity the occasion demanded the pallbearers gently carried the coffins into the chapel one by one. They were followed in by the chief mourners, whose own private grief had been shielded from public gaze by the dark windowed limousines.

After the brief sermon, relayed outside to the very many unable to get into the packed chapel, there was a particularly poignant moment when the muted sobs of a woman, broken in grief, overshadowed the words of the committal and the music...then it was over...and the mourners eventually, almost reluctantly, left the cemetery. But not before an astonishing act of personal courage was displayed by one of the newly widowed wives. As they were preparing to finally leave the cemetery one of the wives got her limousine to stop and stepped out of the vehicle. A beautiful and graceful young woman, she walked over to some of the Honour Guard to thank them for their attendance and then moved to the other side of the car to repeat her personal thanks before returning to her car. This simple act of gratitude, yet delivered with such sincerity and displaying such resolve and fortitude, was just too much for some of those receiving it. I was crying just watching. Many overcome with emotion we broke the continuous line that had seen our fallen comrades arrive but would never see them depart.

Within months of Dudgeons Wharf occurring a further tragedy hit the Brigade with the death of Michael (Mickey) Lee. He died during a fire at Goswell Road. The derelict building he was working in collapsed and he died from his injuries at the scene. If a graphic account of these last moments was necessary it was provided by the front cover of the London Fireman magazine, which showed the frantic efforts of his rescuers desperately trying to reach "Mickey" under the debris. His own Divisional Commander's gaze, as he led the rescue operation, conveyed the dreadful urgency of their task. The unity which such misfortune brings out in the emergency services was self-evident by looking at the images of the combined efforts of firemen and policemen hauling on lines, in their frantic efforts to pull away wreckage from the collapse.

Mickey's death was practically poignant for me. First he was a former junior fireman and only a year separated our ages. The death of any fireman was naturally painful; this was like losing someone who you went to school with, and it was personal.

He was carried to Rainham Parish Church on his own station's turntable ladder, C21 Shoreditch, again equipped to provide him full Brigade burial honours. The stations of East Ham and Barking bid their own farewell as the turntable ladder slowed to a crawl as it passed them en-route to the memorial service and committal.

It would have been just another insignificant fire had it not have had such deadly consequences. In its obituary to Michael Lee the London Fireman magazine printed the last reported words of Michael at the incident, "Kids started this; come on they might still be in there." The editor challenged anyone to come up with a better definition of what a fireman's job means. No one did.

A grumbling appendix

I needed the next night shift off, desperately. My fiancée had made arrangements for us to go out and I had wrongly assumed that getting the leave would not be a problem; big mistake! Two of the more senior hands, (in fact everybody was more senior to me) had already requested leave that morning and now all the available leave allocation was taken. I had promised her I could make it and she had paid for the evening on the strength of my undertaking. I was in deep shit.

I confided in Tom, then my mentor and guide into the unofficial workings of the brigade. Tom originally came from Somerset and still retained a strong West Country accent. He just met the brigade's height requirement to join but what he lacked in height he made up for in an incredible sense of humour, fun and wisdom. Tom was no skate, in fact quite the reverse. He took his job seriously. He had been around a fair time and knew how to work the system when necessary. This was just such an occasion in my book. Taking me aside he said, "Pikey, you will have to lay-in for the watch; go sick tomorrow night." Laying-in was a way of life for some members of the watch, taking a "sicky" to cover some covert meeting with the opposite sex, normally not their wife, or just because it was their turn to lay-in. I had not had a day sick since joining the Brigade, other than the one day when I could not face my driving instructor and fabricated an upset stomach. I certainly did not want to go sick now but Tom convinced me that I had no other option unless I wanted to incur the wrath of a seriously pissed off girlfriend. I was enjoying a good sex life at the time so I was not keen to jeopardise that part of our relationship. Still going sick did not rest easy with me. "The governor will know I'm pulling a flanker," I told Tom. "I appear fine today."

"That's your answer," Tom suggested. "Complain of feeling unwell today and it won't look suspicious when you ring in sick tomorrow night." We schemed and at Tom's prompting I had lunch in the Headquarters staff canteen whose reputation for culinary expertise was dubious at the best of times. During my lunch I was to ask, to nobody in particular but hopefully someone from the office staff, if the meat tasted alright? Later in the afternoon I was to complain of a stomach ache or even a case of the trots.

All went to plan. At lunch I ended up sitting next to one of the leading firemen and duly asked, "Does the meat taste alright?"

"No worse than usual," came his reply. By mid-afternoon I had built up sufficient courage to walk into the station office and complain about my bogus upset stomach. Nervous about the obvious lie that I was about to spew forth I must have looked somewhat pale and I was actually sweating slightly, if for no other reason than my own deceit. Rather than say I had an upset stomach, as I had rehearsed with Tom, it came out as "My stomach is hurting." The combination of my pallor and my apparent complaint rang alarm bells for the office staff, who promptly escorted me to the first aid room whilst an ambulance was summoned to the station. Things were not going to plan!

Now I really did feel pale. The situation only got worse when the ambulance crewman asked, "Where does it hurt?" I pointed to some imaginary pain in my stomach. Convinced I was a genuine emergency he assisted me into the ambulance waiting in the drill yard, where a curious Headquarters crowd had now gathered which meant I had to maintain my phantom illness. With blue lights flashing and two-tone horns blaring their warning I was transported the short distance to St Thomas' Hospital A&E department and wheeled in on a stretcher.

Thing were getting totally out of hand now. I only wanted the night off and had got myself stuck in A&E, waiting to see a doctor who would immediately see through my scam and I would get the sack for a falsehood. The continuing combination of increasing panic and nerves must have culminated in an incredibly convincing image, when the doctor finally arrived to conduct his examination, of someone "genuinely" unwell. When asked to indicate where it hurt, I pointed to somewhere on my abdomen. "Does this hurt?" he asked as he pressed his fingers into different areas of my lower stomach. I was hardly going to tell him, "Not really Doc, this is all an act." So I continued with the performance. "Hum," was his only comment as he asked me to turn over on the examination bed and expose my bare back through the full-length slit in the hospital examination gown in which I was now wrapped. First he tapped my back with his fingers then, listening to my breathing through his stethoscope, finally said, "This may hurt a bit." I fully expected him to push his fingers harder into my lower back. I certainly did not expect, nor was I prepared for, what came next.

Armed with a lubricated latex covered finger he stuck his digit, but what felt like an enormous appendage, without any further warning straight up my arse. I thought I was being raped by some escaped sexual deviant posing as a doctor. Nobody had ever stuck anything up my bum before and certainly never another man! Any previous fictitious shock was now totally real as the finger started its strange exploration and it felt as if it might be joined by others. To make matters worse, satisfied grunts were coming from the direction of the doctor. What went in must come out. The traumatic experience was repeated as the finger was extricated in what felt like slow motion. My dignity in tatters, I hoped that people could not tell I had been the subjected to anal abuse. I felt I would never again be able to walk properly.

"OK," said the deviant, "You can turn back over." Happier now that my back passage had protection from any further surprise assaults I listened as the doctor told me, "I think you have a grumbling appendicitis and it is better to keep you in for a few days for observation." I only want a bloody night off I thought. Wait until I see Tom, which, as it turned out, was not too long. A concerned pump's crew, including the governor, came to check on my progress. Tom, who came with them, could hardly contain himself at the dilemma I now found myself in. Whilst the crew made polite conversation Tom kept in the background wearing a knowing smile. As a footnote to this sorry tale of deception, I stayed in hospital for three days and sustained no further anal examinations. My girlfriend was full of sympathy and got a full refund because I was in hospital. I chose never to repeat Tom's advice; it just was not worth the hassle or anal interrogation.

Precarious carry-down

Grant was a fellow fireman on Lambeth's Red Watch. Six years my senior, he was married and lived with his wife and baby daughter in fire brigade accommodation, in a little cottage at Purley fire station. With just over five years' service under his belt he recently became Lambeth's latest HGV driver and was desperate to get promoted. He loved his work and was dedicated to the Brigade. Grant had taken me under his wing in recent months and we were becoming close friends as well as work colleagues. Grant was not part of the womanising fraternity that frequented the watch and was encouraging me to become interested in promotion myself.

Grant and I were of similar size and weight; both about five feet eleven inches high and weighing eleven stone. We would normally partner each other when doing hook ladder drills, but particularly when performing carry-downs. On the ill-fated day we were due to practise carry-downs during the afternoon drill session in preparation for a VIP drill to be held later in the month. During the lunch hour Grant mentioned, in passing, of feeling sick or rather nauseous but he did not think it was much and would pass. After lunch he drove the PE into the yard and we got busy testing the escape ladder and then pitched it to the fourth-floor window in readiness for the carry-down. We all climbed the ladder, entered the drill tower and I waited for my turn to carry-down. Everyone had to perform at least one carry-down and with fifteen of us to perform the drill we waited our turn patiently. Grant's go came after the fourth or fifth carry-down was completed. As normal we teamed up and Grant lifted me on to his shoulder and got ready to mount the ladder. It was necessary to have one junior officer in the tower, at the head of the ladder, whilst the Sub officer conducted the drill from below. Between them they ensured that all was safe for the carry-down to be undertaken. Whilst they conferred, in preparation for Grant's carry-down, he spoke quietly into my ear that he was getting a bad headache. I told him to put me down before we were called forward to the ladder and I would carry him. He refused, saying that we would be down in a moment and he was sure it would pass once we started to descend. He mounted the ladder and started his descent with me draped across his shoulders. Straightaway I noticed he was not moving as smoothly as normal, not unsafely but not with the steady strong rhythm he always managed to produce.

As Grant reached the middle section of the ladder, he told me he could not see. He would not stop and told me to hang on whilst he proceeded to cover the last fifteen feet to the bottom of the ladder blind! He was becoming distressed and I was getting concerned for our safety. I tried to remain calm, not wishing to make matters worse by making any sudden grab for the ladder in an attempt to pre-empt a fall. Clearly things were not right and his movement was faltering but he sought to reassure me. Others saw there was a problem too and they were waiting at the bottom of the ladder to support Grant and lift me from his shoulders. Willing hands came to our aid, lifting me one way and Grant the other. Without speaking another word Grant collapsed in the arms of his helpers and had to be carried to the first aid room. An ambulance was ordered and anxious moments passed as we waited for news of Grant's condition. He was now being violently sick and it was assumed that he had suffered a violent migraine attack. As the ambulance crew carried Grant to the ambulance their faces seemed to indicate something more serious and their haste and their rapid exit from the station seemed to support this worry. Something must have been said by the ambulance crew to the governor because he followed the ambulance to the hospital in the pump.

The pump later returned to the station but without the governor. He had remained at the hospital awaiting news of Grant's condition. News filtering back during the afternoon told us that Grant was seriously ill and that a team of doctors were fighting to save his life. No one went home when the shift ended at 6 pm. Instead, we all remained at the station to await further news. This came shortly after 7pm, when the pump collected an emotional governor who informed us Grant had suffered a massive cerebral haemorrhage and was not expected to last the night. We were devastated and went home our separate ways with heavy hearts whilst Grant's wife was rushed to his bedside in a fire brigade staff car. Most of us spent a fretful, if not sleepless, night. Grant's wife certainly did.

Grant did not die then, but he would never again return to the fire service. Paralysed down one side of his body, his speech lost, it would take months of intensive therapy and specialist care for him to regain the power of verbal communication and the partial use of one leg and arm. His condition brought about a serious personality change in him and a deep sense of frustration that would drive a permanent wedge between his wife and himself. They would later separate and divorce. I was reassured that regardless of whether Grant had carried me down or not it would not have saved Grant from the devastating and life changing stroke. It said so much about the man I knew as my friend and who told me to hang on whilst, unable to see, he carried me safely to the bottom of the ladder.

Fond farewells

Ken and Charlie both retired in 1969. In recognition of their long service (both joined in 1938) they accepted the invitation of the Chief Officer to have separate fond farewell chats with him in his Headquarters office. The Chief himself was preparing for his own retirement so we were not really sure who was saying goodbye to whom. Ken and Charlie had served over thirty years together on the same Watch, at the same station, but they did not come across as bosom buddies. They were, in fact, opposites in so many things, not least their attitude to sickness. Ken had not had a day's sickness in all his service, a truly remarkable record. Charlie on the other hand had always taken his full "quota" of sickness whether it was needed or not.

Their interviews were programmed for the same afternoon. Ken went first and after about forty-five minutes returned to the mess preening himself like a peacock, eager to relate the pleasant things that the Chief had told him and how much the Brigade had valued his service. His return was Charlie's cue to head on up to the Chief's office. Dressed in his best number ones he cut a dumpy little figure striding out of the mess room. He too returned after the requisite time for any farewell chat given by the Chief and came back into the mess with a satisfied smile on his face. Eager to compare notes Ken immediately wanted to know what the Chief had said to Charlie and went over to conduct his interrogation. So Charlie told him all, blow by blow, and as he did so Ken's face visibly fell. "That's what he told me," Ken said, irritation clearly etched into his voice. "What have I always told you, they don't give a shit. You have never had a day's sick and I bucked the system. End result we both get told the same thing and what good boys we have been. Wake up Ken!" Bored of being in his undress uniform Charlie returned to the locker room to change leaving Ken to ruminate over the day's events. The fire brigade was in Ken's blood and with his retirement he went into the Brigade workshops to be re-employed as a storeman (something he enjoyed until he retired again, 10 years later.) Charlie rode out of the station on his last day, as he did every shift, on his trusty but ageing bicycle. He was never seen back on the watch again.

Getting down to it in 'Proto' BA at a smokey job in 1967.

Copyright. *N/A. Photograph by permission of Clive Skippins.*

Author and Fm Ken Thorne (Lambeth-Red Watch) giving presents at Lambeth fire station annual Christmas party to local OAP's. 1967.

A woman slips back into the River Thames having already been rescued once!
5th March 1968.

The 1968 Annual Review and the presentation of eight bravery awards to London Firemen.

Field Marshall Sir Gerald Templer. KG. GCB. GCMG. KBE. DSO. presenting a Chief Officer's Commendation to the author at the Brigade's Annual Review in 1968.

A typical 'working job' in a large North London house in 1967.

Chapter 7

New Era

Change at the top

My coming of age in 1970 heralded the start of a new era within the London Fire Brigade. The Chief Officer, Mr Leslie Leete, had announced his intention to retire in May, the same month that I was to get married at the grand old age of twenty-one. I, and my fiancée, had already bought our house, a small two storey terraced property with three bedrooms, a lounge and separate dining room, plus a ground floor kitchen and bathroom, located in the London Borough of Bromley.

A sea change was coming to the Brigade in the form of a new Chief Officer, Joseph Milner; aged forty-seven. He was the current Director of the Hong Kong Fire Service. Many would soon discover him to be a forthright man who did not mince his words. He was in stark contrast to the outgoing Chief who gave the impression of being particular uncomfortable in the company of the lower ranks. In fact he came across as rather a snob. As Chief he was rarely on the fireground unless it was politically expedient for him to be seen there. To his credit, he had brought together the amalgamation of the Brigades that made up the enlarged London Fire Brigade in 1965. He was nevertheless old school, distant from those riding the engines, certainly from the "shop floor's" perspective. He was a toff and his look as he walked occasionally across Lambeth's yard let you know it.

Joe, as he was to be affectionately called, was not tall and was slightly built. He had the appearance of a marathon runner although he was in fact an avid walker. On nights, when on duty in the watchroom, you might see him leaving the Headquarters' front lobby around 5 am for his regular six-mile constitutional with his favourite pipe in his mouth. He would return some ninety minutes later, occasionally popping into the watchroom to chat with the dutyman. A practice that would have been a complete anathema to the previous post holder.

In the profile produced for the in-house magazine, Joe's war record was akin to something taken from of the Boy's Own Annual. Joining the Army before the outbreak of the war, aged seventeen, he ended up in the King's Regiment and in 1942 became one of Wingate's Special Forces. He served in Burma and China until the end of the Japanese war. During his time with the Chindits Joe Milner fought in some of the war's most hazardous operations such as the crucial blocking of the Mandalay railway. His unit flew into Burma in gliders of which only half reached their objective.

His UK Fire Service career had started in 1946 but five years later he transferred to Hong Kong as a Station Officer. He rose through the ranks serving in all branches of the Brigade and as its Chief brought forward radical changes to the Force, including introducing its Search and Rescue Division, which comprised about ten per cent of the total force manpower.

Asked to highlight some of his priorities on taking up his new post, he was quoted as saying he believed, that although helmets and clothing were some insurance against injury, not enough attention had been given to preventing the damage done to firemen's lungs. Well the man certainly got my vote for not just believing that but actually saying it. As the Chief in Hong Kong he had ensured that there was one breathing apparatus set for every two men on duty. We were lucky to be riding one BA set between four. Joe Milner was to start in the Brigade in mid-June. I for one, could not wait.

Chief Officer Leete retired on 10th May, a week after I tied the knot and was now enjoying my honeymoon in the West Country, reflecting on a "Red Watch" wedding. Our simple wedding service took place in the picturesque local parish church. It was delayed somewhat by my Dad who had naively asked the invited members of the watch if they would like to come in for a "quick" drink, at the nearby family home before the wedding. Silly Daddy! I was having mega butterflies inside the church with my bride-to-be waiting increasingly impatiently outside. Red Watch duly arrived, late, looking flush faced but not as flushed as the bride's mother who was almost incandescent with rage. They shuffled their way noisily into their pews, with Dad in tow. Dad's arrival finally allowed the ceremony to start. But not before one Red Watch wag, emboldened by my Dad's generous measures of drink and who was sitting directly behind the governor said, "Here guv you really are getting thin on top." It was the only sound to fill the church as the bride waited for the organ to start playing in the hushed packed church. Well it would have been hushed except for the wave of sniggers and muffled giggling that spread out like a ripple to the surrounding pews, much to the continuing annoyance of the almost mother-in-law who was mouthing to the bride's father, "I told you it was a mistake inviting that lot!"

My mortgage repayments were a good incentive to prompt my preparations to seriously consider starting my ascent up the promotion ladder. I had not yet even got a foot on the bottom rung. With my monthly take home pay just over seventy pounds and with a mortgage of thirty-four pounds there was not a great deal over to pay the rates, electric and gas without my new wife's wage as a secretary to a national magazine executive.

Having passed the Leading Fireman's written examination at my second attempt (a common theme for all my written examinations up to Station Officer). I was now eligible to "act up" as a Leading Fireman. At Lambeth acting up was a highly competitive business, even getting a sniff of temporary promotion was the equivalent of winning the pools. At least eight other members of the watch were better qualified; some having passed both the L.Fm's written and practical whilst others had passed their Sub Officer's written exam as well. One individual had even passed his Station Officer's exam. Fortunately for me he was all brains and little common sense, possessing an incredibly supercilious attitude, which made him scornful of his peers. This pompous attitude and his stuck-up manner made him a very difficult individual to get on with let alone like. He was the former junior fireman (one of the originals) that Dick Richardson had referred to when I first came to the station. Originally posted to Brixton, he was in grave danger of meeting an untimely and unpleasant accident because the watch there just could not cope with him any longer. He was posted to Lambeth and was not winning friends here either. His only saving grace was that he bought my old Vauxhall Victor car from me as I could not afford to run it anymore.

Whether I was still running on the euphoria of the honeymoon I was not sure but my practical examination in late May presented no great obstacle in securing the next hurdle towards my first possible promotion. Whilst I struggled with the written work I excelled on the practical side. I passed the practical at the first attempt and with that under my belt I moved up the station ranking and soon became an acting Leading Fireman for the very first time. It was only for two weeks but it was two weeks of no station cleaning. It gave me an enticing taster of what being a junior officer was like and I loved it (even if my typing was crap). I rode in charge of the turntable ladder, never getting to use it, and had my first make up in charge of the PE. I could become addicted to riding in the number One's seat and learning to ring the engine's bell.

The new Chief quickly established his authority; but anyone thinking that the new broom was going to sweep away the practices of the past overnight, with a programme of rapid reforms, was disappointed. Although he was spreading himself around with considerable energy and enthusiasm, he made it clear it would be rashly premature to set out, even in the broadest principles, any of his development proposals. He displayed a keen sense of humour that, sadly, had been all too lacking in the previous incumbent. Given his Hong Kong pedigree he had to confirm (tongue-in-cheek) that there was no truth in the rumours that he was replacing senior officers' cars with rickshaws or that pump-escapes were going to be converted to junk-escapes.

Chief Officer Milner was rapidly establishing himself as a regular feature on the fireground. He was attending make-up incidents whenever possible and not just attending incidents where he might be expected to take command. He was also gaining a hands-on perspective as to how the Brigade was managed locally within the eleven Divisions. I would later learn that he was putting into practice "MBWA" (managing by walking about) as he looked at fireground command and operational practices at incidents. He was also speaking widely to the crews, not just a quick, "Hello, how are you?" either.

After observing the hectic activity of combating whatever blaze he had gone on to, rigged in his fire-gear minus his helmet but with his now familiar pipe in hand, he could be seen talking to firefighters, sometimes standing in a loose huddle or sitting on the kerb-side alongside his men who were covered in grime, hair wet with sweat. He was learning what was going on, whilst they drank their well-earned cups of tea. It was on such an occasion that I first met him.

He was not only talking, he was listening too. Some told him of the day-to-day gripes that any gathering might put forward to a sympathetic ear, like the wrong uniform issue or no bloody sandwiches on the canteen van. Other concerns had real substance, such as not being issued with lightweight hose instead of the heavy canvas hose we still had to work with; or abolishing station cleaning by firemen and getting them involved in greater fire inspection work; or dealing with the serious under-manning within the Brigade and even possible revisions to the duty system.

Whatever his thoughts were on what he heard, he was to reflect on them, but it was clear that changes were a coming. Some senior officers thought the prospect of a major change in principal management style and direction too much to take. They chose retirement, rather than manage the changes that the Brigade was destined to take. Not least amongst these was the then Deputy Chief who left shortly after the new Chief started.

Remember, remember

Remember, remember the fifth of November. Well I certainly did on the night of the 5th November 1970, which turned out to be the Brigade's busiest night in over thirty-five years. Fires raged in north, south and east London. The following day national papers said "London's firemen passed their greatest test since the Blitz last night." I was one of one hundred and thirty fireman who had agreed to do voluntary overtime. I rode with the Blue Watch at Lambeth.

Six weeks of uncollected refuse had accumulated in hundreds of London's streets and city squares. These piles of rubbish were the residue of the council dustmen's strike and were now seen as additional ready-made bonfires. Calls trebled, beating the normal busy nights associated with previous year's bonfire nights. Lambeth's Pump and Pump Escape were answering calls continuously until the early hours of the 6th, dealing with out-of-control thirty-foot-high bonfires and the burning piles of uncollected household and trade rubbish. In Vauxhall, as quick as we doused one blazing pyre of rubbish and the street filled with acrid steam, another was started up just around the next corner. The youngsters and teenagers were brazen in their determination to fire as much as they could find (which was not hard). A young boy, probably still at junior school, turned the air blue with English his teacher certainly did not teach him. More repeatable comments included, "When you bastards have gone, we will light them up again, we have plenty of paraffin."

As if the bonfires and multitude of rubbish fires were not enough, in Battersea a church was destroyed by a major fire and needed seventy-five firemen to confine the fire to the church. In Stratford, East London, another one hundred firemen fought a massive blaze on the Broadway that required one hundred and fifty residents of nearby flats to be evacuated. It was always disappointing to miss out on a big fire but that night we did not have time to think about what we could have been doing, we were too busy chasing our tails around Lambeth, Westminster and Southwark going from call to call. Listening to the appliance radio we could imagine the Brigade Control staff, working under extreme pressure yet with the radio operator's calm and controlled voice ordering appliances to new blazes as well as responding to the "priority" messages from serious incidents. Such were the messages sent from Islington crews who came under attack from local residents, disgruntled because their dangerous bonfire was doused before it set surrounding property alight.

Fires were not just restricted to the bonfires and the tons of refuse the street urchins and older teenage delinquents made the most of. More daring (or malicious) individuals were igniting piles stacked against or near to derelict and vacant premises. All too quickly the blaze would spread and ignite its real target, the adjoining building. Still supper-less, stinking of smoke and our faces thick with street grime and dirt we were ordered to a rubbish fire in Kennington Lane. We saw the flames licking high above Black Prince Road even before we arrived. A derelict house sealed off by corrugated steel sheets was blazing like a torch and children had been seen running away just before the bangers had been lobbed into the pile of rubbish outside. Glass showered into the street as the walls cracked and we got a jet to work, soon to be supported by Southwark's crews coming to reinforce us. With a strange, if pleasant quirk of fate, despite being the busiest bonfire night on record the number of serious casualties caused by fireworks was, that night, at an all-time low.

Dear Editor

The London Fireman was the in-house magazine of the London Fire Brigade. Its new editor Gordon White, for whom I would later work, was a young bright twenty-five-year-old former newspaper reporter. He had already re-formatted the magazine, giving it a new look, and was now asking from members of the Brigade for a greater involvement in the form of articles and letters. After the weeks of dealing with the resultant fires caused by the dustmen's strike, I had a real bee in my bonnet so wrote to the magazine under Dear Editor. Much to my surprise, whilst on day duty at Lambeth, I was summoned to get my best togs on and have a photograph taken, by the Brigade photographer to accompany my letter, which was to be published in the December edition.

An even greater surprise was the fact that my letter entitled "Where is the justice?" prompted a full-page editorial. It seemed that my article had put into a nutshell the feelings of many members of the Brigade at the unbalanced (and the injustice) of the national and local press coverage of the dustmen's strike (which ran to column after column of newsprint and picture coverage). Meanwhile firemen, left with the task of putting out hundreds of rubbish fires and crawling over stinking piles of refuse, got scant praise from the Press. In recognising that my criticisms were valid in many respects (because it was unarguable that only the non-stop efforts of crews prevented a fire problem of massive proportions breaking out in many parts of London) the editorial also sought to make a valid defence of the actions of the Brigade's Press Office. It could not dictate to newspapers what they should or should not print.

It was my first incursion into seeking "social" justice for what was so patently a wrong. It was also a valuable lesson in what the press, nationally or locally, considered newsworthy. I had a few "Well done Pikey" comments from the watch and surrounding station crews for expressing a commonly felt point of view, and for being prepared to put my head above the parapet and challenge an apparent management failing. What I did not expect was the number of senior officers who just dropped me a short note, or rang to say that it was pleasing to see a responsible approach (in raising the concerns of so many disgruntled members of the Brigade) seeking to right an obvious injustice. It was too early to recognise it then, but making a political stand (with a small "p") for something that I believed in, even if it was against Brigade policy, wouldn't necessarily make one a pariah. There were senior officers who would (perhaps) welcome such action, even if they could not publicly support it.

ET Course

With over four years operational experience behind me I considered putting in for an Emergency Tender (ET) course. It was something I had not wanted to rush into as I felt it was necessary to get some decent BA jobs behind me before making such a move. The ET crews were held in high esteem and expected to deliver the goods at difficult BA incidents and at special operations requiring BA work, in addition to their wider rescue role. This was not a view held by everyone at Lambeth. On other watches some (equally young) firemen put in for this course as soon as they had passed out in BA arguing that they would gain the experience by being ET trained. The truth was they were initially just passengers, diluting the overall expertise of the crew because they had to be babysat until sufficiently competent to add value to the crew, not detracting from it.

The role of the ET crew was occasionally extremely demanding and even dangerous. The ET crew were seen by many senior officers as "Leete's commandos." These crews would have to combat their individual fears of hot confined spaces, face the risk of a sudden unexpected explosion of flammable gases or liquids whilst still working as an elite crew. They supported and contributed to the combined effort that would give the fireground crews synergy. Their skill was something that could be the difference between life and death in the rescue of a trapped BA fireman. In these situations it required every ounce of the ET crews' combined expertise and was not the place for a mere novice. This was the widely held view of those that rode Lambeth's Red Watch ET. It was with their blessing that I put in for the next possible course nomination.

The course came almost immediately supported by my governor's endorsement, but not before our monthly salary slips changed from pounds, shillings and pence (£. s. d) to pounds and pence. Monday 15th February 1971 was Decimal Day and with it came years of confusion, with converting new money back into old money and the spread of metrication into all aspects of fire service work including examinations. It left many of the pre-decimal hands scratching their heads when post-decimal recruits came to stations talking in millimetres, litres, kilograms, and kilometres per hour!

I would be at Southwark Training School for three weeks attending my ET course. Southwark was the centre for all the Brigades ET training and serviced the seven ET stations qualification needs. As well as incorporating intensive BA training, the course covered the rigorous and demanding roles expected of its crews including visits to specialist installations and premises. One of these was London's sewer system.

Taken to Cornwell Road, adjacent to the South Bank, we were greeted by the Ganger of one of the GLC's sewer crews and we were introduced to their subterranean world. The sweaty brickwork of the tunnel was closing in on us almost as soon as we descended the metal ladder that took us thirty feet below London's streets, the hot and humid smell of detergent contrasting with the cold water flowing around our feet. This first visit was without BA, a familiarisation of the strange and at times, amazing place sewer men spent their working day. With each step the dull turgid screen of mist parted to allow us through. Shafts of light from our torches picked out the glistening highlights of geometrical lines of brickwork, creating their own claustrophobic *son-et-lumiere* with every move we made. Vast distorted shadows transformed us into phantoms wandering in an aquatic maze.

We were wading through the tunnel in single file. Cold greyish water, flowing eastwards, knee height pushed against the backs of our waders urging us on. We could not walk upright, the egg-shaped tunnel being only five foot high. Cramped, we moved in a stoop, the shadows mirroring our movements on the brickwork. After a while the Ganger at the head of the file turned around. "Keep in your place," he said, "and if you get lost, then don't start doing anything clever like trying to find us. Just stay where you are, we'll find you."

The Ganger was the head of a team of five flushers who spent their working hours cleaning the bowels of London. He had on heavy waders that came up to his waist. Beneath them he wore thick thigh length woollen socks like leg warmers. Above the waders and the leg warmers he was garbed in a blue jacket, kept in place by a belt and the all-important safety harness. Although the tunnel we trudged through was egg-shaped the sewer bed was flat covered by a layer of sediment that felt like sand and shingle; our boots sank into it with every step. "That's what we call muck down here," the Ganger said. "It's full of little pockets of gas, waiting to overpower the unsuspecting worker. That's why if you ever get called to get us out of one of these tunnels only ever come down in your breathing apparatus, otherwise we will all be in the shit, literally."

From that simple inconspicuous manhole cover we had entered just one of the many lifelines of the metropolis, twisting and turning beneath the roadways;

fifteen hundred miles of neo-gothic sewers. Some were much smaller than the one we visited that day, others were almost like caverns; the storm relief sewers that direct away millions of gallons of water, thus protecting the capital from flood damage, during torrential rains.

We returned for our second visit, this time wearing breathing apparatus and entered a tunnel no taller than four foot. Our backs started to ache within the first one hundred yards as the bottoms of our breathing bags were dragged through the sewer water. We negotiated the subterranean waterway conscious that a rain cloud bursting some miles away might quickly fill these tunnels with torrents of water, taking with it the unwary worker towards a storm-flow sewer, then out into the Thames. The only protection against this possibility was the two-way radio that gave the top-man regular weather forecast updates, which for those working below can mean the difference between life and death.

We practised the rescue techniques necessary to lift, carry and raise an injured sewer worker. Later in the comfort of the classroom we supplemented our practical experience by learning of the health and biological hazards such rescues can expose the rescuer too. These include Weil's disease, spread by rats' urine, the virus of which can get into the body through cuts and scratches and end up in the brain and in most cases leading to an unpleasant death. Hepatitis is more common but is not the only organic peril since other bacteria will cause a range of potentially life-threatening conditions. It is therefore vital that the washing and decontamination procedures are rigorously followed, after the crews return to street level. Just as potentially lethal are the reaction of different chemicals mixing in the sewer system possibly producing a cocktail of toxic gases. Hence the importance of the sewer safety lamp which has been designed to warn of its presence.

The ET course is very "hands on." We lift, pull, cut, spread with the full range of rescue equipment the vehicle carries. We visit various lift installations and learn how to recognise the differences between electrical, mechanical and hydraulic systems, how to shut them down and hand-wind the lifts, how to open or remove lift doors and release the "dead" brakes so that we can move a lift either up or down…

Our explorations covered the London Underground system; we learned the lifting points on varied rolling stock, and how to isolate the power supply to the tracks. We go beneath escalators; we enter cold store refrigeration plants (where the hairs in our nostrils freeze solid within seconds). We performed drills wearing the full protective clothing only the ETs carry, and which will be the fireman's only protection when dealing with serious leakages of toxic gases and refrigerants such as ammonia.

At the end of all this the course participants, consisting of Sub Officers, Leading Firemen and Firemen are extensively examined by Training School senior officers. All aspects of the course are covered. Attendance alone is no guarantee to gaining a pass on this demanding course. A genuine camaraderie was established between us, this helped ensure that the high standards expected were met. Finally, armed with our new skills and knowledge, we returned to our respective stations to put it all into practice. Or so I hoped.

Old Kent Road

With not so much as a four pump BA fire or some dramatic extrication on which to exercise my newfound qualification, the first couple of shifts were decidedly uneventful. Oh, the ET got a few shouts but we were "returned to base" because the crews attending were more than capable of handling the situation, and anyway they did not want the ET crew stealing all their glory.

I had already sat my first and only Leading Fireman's promotion board interview. I had been told by the Governor that I had been recommended, so success at the interview rested with me. I had to explain any one of a multitude of office and operational procedures selected by the Promotion Board and that I would be required to know if I were to be a substantive Leading Fireman. It had always seemed strange to me, however, that anyone could ride in charge of an engine without this knowledge. When it came to keeping appliances on the run almost anyone, usually the senior (in years served) fireman was put in charge and amongst them there were a few real "plonkers." Anyway, the interview was now behind me; those coming at the top of the list were immediately promoted to fill the vacancies. The remainder were placed on a panel, which was published. The knack (or rather hope) was to get promoted before the next round of promotion interviews took place. Not enough vacancies before the next interviews and you would have to retake the interview.

I knew the panel had been published in routine orders just by the look on Eric's face and the way he said, "Well done" through gritted teeth. Half a dozen candidates had been promoted immediately, and around thirty-five others of us were placed on the promotion panel. Only me, and the obnoxious brainbox were considered suitable on the watch, much to the displeasure of the other unsuccessful candidates. One particular individual who vented his considerable disappointment concluded, "It's only because you got that bloody gong that you got on the panel Pikey and that job was an effing cock-up." There may have been some truth in this but, regardless, I was on the panel and I was cock-a-hoop.

So without even getting my seat warm on the ET I was given three months temporary promotion at the Old Kent Road fire station. The station was completely new having replaced the Victorian era station that now stood empty on the far side of the Old Kent Road. It was placed next to the "Thomas a Becket", one of south London's most famous boxing pubs and where Henry Cooper used to train. The station was one of a new breed of fire station design; bright, airy and with a proper firemen's dormitory, something we had not previously enjoyed. On older type stations we had had to find a space anywhere there was room enough to put up an iron bed frame and then bung a mattress on top.

The station still had its two appliances, a PE and pump. So if I was not riding BA on the back of the pump I would be in charge of the PE. I had stood by at Old Kent Road a few times so I was not a total stranger to the lads who made up the Red Watch. Old Kent Road's pump had a formidable reputation of being one of the busiest in the Brigade due to the station's strategic location. Its "ground" was a mixture of residential, light industry, commercial property, the vast Bricklayers Arms Goods Depot and great swathes of now dilapidated, decaying housing stock. Acres of these slum dwellings had been under on-going demolition, to make way for the new housing estates and the GLC's much heralded open green space which was meant to be south London's equivalent of Hyde Park. So far, the only green to be seen was to be found in the former Surrey canal that had been part drained in preparation for the open space project.

Next to the deliberate fire-raiser, and the malicious caller, the demolition workers were now becoming a right "pain in the bum." To save time and money, they would deliberately set fire to the buildings they were demolishing. These irresponsible actions led to firemen being injured unnecessarily. They were a good bet for a high score in any fireman's unpopularity poll. That the "knock'em down" brigade had a really poor reputation with fire station crews was not difficult to understand. Calls to rubbish burning on demolition sites were now totalling many hundreds every year. Sometimes we were going out to the same sites so often, that we were on first name terms with the demolition crews. However, when confronting these downright dangerous contractors, as opposed to just the inconsiderate, these names were best described as sexually explicit!

The local Boroughs, in conjunction with the GLC, were finally starting to try to come down heavily on these demolition men. So many of their fires were lit with both a flagrant disregard of common sense, and for the safety of the firemen who had to respond to the call. They were becoming a public nuisance. They would go to any lengths to get the job completed in as shorter as time as possible, frequently torching the building and knocking down what was left afterwards. A "good derelict" had been the bread and butter of teaching new hands their craft. However, large areas of London were subject to wholesale clearance and the chances of more serious fires were raising genuine concerns, within communities and "the powers that be." Despite tighter regulations being introduced the cowboy crews would continue to keep us busy for some years to come. Their handy work also provided me with my first opportunity to "make pumps" at the Old Kent Road.

The Red Watch had the usual watch strength to serve a two-appliance station. On the night in question there were just seven of us on duty. There were originally nine but the Sub Officer and one driver had been ordered out to stand by at other stations. Our couple of early shouts were of little consequence; a rubbish fire and an elderly lady shut in a lift. Sam, the senior hand, was also the mess manager and his supper of sausage, beans, eggs and chips had been prepared with the care that a master chef would dedicate to some gastronomic delight. Sadly it had been stuffed in the oven to keep warm, whilst we attended a call in a waste paper merchants on Deptford's ground. An hour later, the shrivelled remains of our supper were removed from the too warm oven. With only the sausages considered salvageable, we ate them between slices of bread spread with margarine. At midnight the pump was sent to stand by at Whitechapel, whilst their crews were attending a four pumper on Shoreditch's ground.

I was enjoying the luxury of having my own room for the first time; no one farting or the sound of snoring, just me. The station bells summoned us sometime after 1.00 am; the pump had still not returned. The dutyman told me it was a fire off Neate Street, on our own ground. On route the staccato sound of our two-tone horns disturbed the peace of the deserted south London streets. Then, as our speeding appliance turned a corner off the Old Kent Road, there was a glow so bright it could have been mistaken for a magnesium flare. A disused two storey warehouse was ablaze from end to end; the heat of the fire had already started to blister the dilapidated paintwork and brickwork of the adjacent derelict buildings which were separated only by a narrow-cobbled alley.

With only four of us on the PE, no BA; the next few minutes sped by like seconds. As I told the driver to, "Make pumps four" I sent another fireman to set into the hydrant shouting (unnecessarily), "Twin it," whilst I and the last fireman got off two hose lines. I directed my jet into the blazing building whilst he covered the surrounding property, so as to prevent the fire spreading over the alleyway to the adjacent buildings. My hoarsely shouted commands filled the air competing with the cracking of timber in the heat of the flames.

Our feverish activity continued as Peckham's appliances, with horns blaring, arrived and I then handed over command to their Sub Officer. They were followed by Lambeth's pump and TL. Slowly, the deep red glow of the fire started to dim. Lengths of hose snaked down the street and into the building and water poured from the head of the TL directed through the void that had once been the roof, prior to its collapse on to the burning interior. We had worked our socks off and I was thanking my crew for their efforts when a voice behind me said, "Trying to make a name for yourself Pikey?" I turned to see my governor from Lambeth giving me a satisfied smile. "It's a shame you can't type otherwise you might make someone a decent Leading Hand! Now bugger off and start getting the details for the fire report, then come and tell me what you've got."

Later, leaving the two pumps at the scene to damp down, we returned to the station to the jeers of the pump's crew who were sitting drinking tea in the watchroom. "The crew did well," I told the Temporary Station Officer, trying to look nonchalant but failing abysmally. "OK smart-arse, let's see how good your fire report is. See you in the morning." Chuckling, he went to bed, leaving the six of us to re-stow the appliance and me to type up the fire report.

Times were changing. Whilst I was at the Old Kent Road news circulated around the Brigade that the Chief was being as good as his word. The Brigade was to introduce the Siebe Gorman Airmaster compressed air BA set; in fact some had already been on trial. The days of the Proto (oxygen) sets were numbered and the new BA sets would be placed on both the PE and pump, in the not too distant future. Not all the news coming out was so well received, our firemen's black helmets were to become yellow! "He just wants us to look like those *chinks* when he was Chief in Hong Kong," said a disgruntled Sam. These were not the only things that were to change and with change came uncertainty and unrest at station level.

My return to Lambeth with the temporary promotion concluded also saw my return to more station cleaning, although with so many new faces on the watch, I had now achieved sufficient status to polish the locker room, instead of bleaching the urinals. A spate of retirements had hit the Brigade with a great number of those who had joined the Brigade at the end of the war now coming up to the age when they could leave on a full pension. This affected both senior and lower ranks. Although sad to see friends leave the Brigade, this was the natural order of things and it provided a wealth of opportunity for promotion aspirants. Many on the promotion panel had attained their new rank and my name was moving up the list.

Fifty pumper

One of the fiercest and most difficult fires that the post-war Brigade ever had to face, lasting nearly thirty hours and involving all three watches occurred during early August 1971. The location was Wilson's Wharf, Battle Bridge Lane, Tooley Street. It was ironic that this should be the same location that cost the life of the Brigade's very first Chief Officer, James Braidwood, when in 1861 he was buried under a collapsed wall in a warehouse blaze that took several days to bring under control. (The Brigade was then called the London Fire Engine Establishment.)

Wilson's Wharf was built on the site of that first devastating fire, part of the Hays Wharf Companies great rebuilding scheme, and had opened in 1868. Starting life as a coffee and cocoa wharf it later became the company's first wine and spirit bottling department. Just over a century later it now lay unoccupied, having previously undergone conversion to a refrigerated warehouse and major cold store.

For the day watch afternoon routines had been underway for nearly an hour; some stations performing drills, others considerably extending their lunchtime game of volleyball. At some stations the pump was unavailable for calls, either engaged in outside inspections or "off the run" waiting for a mechanical defect to be repaired at Lambeth workshops. So when the bells went down at Dockhead, Southwark and Cannon Street fire stations only the pump escapes were available to attend the call that would eventually summon another one hundred fire engine crews to the scene.

Those three machines responded at 2.48 pm and were joined by a TL from Barbican fire station. But already the blaze was drawing considerable attention as it rapidly gained a hold in the warehouse's interior. With the second of many subsequent calls received, Brigade control sent on Whitechapel's pump and Lambeth's fireboat.

The six-storey warehouse had an irregular shape and sat tightly wedged between other wharfs. On the riverside was a wide vehicular jetty where previously goods and products had been delivered to its one hundred and fifty-foot-wide riverside access. It was also one hundred and fifty feet from this side of the building to the far side, which faced Tooley Street. Various raised open and covered iron bridges were connected to surrounding wharves.

Unable to stem the rapidly developing fire with an extinguisher, contractors beat a hasty retreat from the building leaving their oxy-acetylene cutting plant in situ. It was sparks from their hot cutting that had ignited combustible tape on the pipe-work insulation. It had spread to the building's insulation material itself, four-inch thick very flammable expanded rubber. Even as the contractors were running out of Wilson's Wharf and as our crews drew closer, the hot and smoky atmosphere was being trapped inside this now disued cold store. The windows and loopholes had been bricked up, making the building a veritable fortress, turning large parts of the complex into a vast brick oven, superheating the interior.

Five minutes after the first call was made the officer in charge made pumps four, BA required. With crews unable to make an easy entry into the building and with the smoke thickening by the minute, pumps were made eight, two minutes after 3 pm. (The new style BA guide lines were about to get their "baptism by fire", if the crews could actually penetrate into the warehouse that is.) These modified guide lines had pieces of string bound into the line. Placed at regular intervals were two sets of tags, set six inches apart, two long tags and two knotted tags. Getting "knotted" was the clue to finding your way out.

Concerted efforts were being made to enter the building despite the heavy smoke pouring from all the available openings on the third and fourth floors. After thirty minutes of fruitless searching by BA teams, probing in the hot but accessible areas of the warehouse there was still no sign of fire, just the constant build-up of intense heat. As more appliances arrived, sweating men laid out more lines of hose to increase the number of jets available. Other men were using the interconnecting bridges to direct jets into the conflagration, they themselves being protected by water spray from other jets from the TL and from pumps.

In the space of forty-five minutes pumps went from fifteen, to twenty, and then thirty. Command of the fire changed hands so quickly that no single plan of action could be properly implemented until the Chief Officer finally took command at 16.16 pm. He faced daunting problems, taxing even his considerable know-how of commanding major incidents from his time in Hong

Kong. He had all his Headquarters' principal officers at his disposal, including the Deputy Chief. It would take their combined experience and expertise to direct operations at this incident, which was now extremely serious, due to the complex layout of the building, the thickness of the walls and lack of access points. The heat build-up, deep inside the structure, was likened to a potter's kiln operating at its maximum temperature.

Despite the tenacity and doggedness of the firemen, this tremendous heat and smoke posed major problems for any of the crews fighting to establish a bridgehead to counter the blaze. Contractors working alongside firemen tried to break open some of the bricked-up windows at third floor level with elementary breaking-in gear, club hammers and cold chisels, but little or no progress was made. Meanwhile those BA crews that had made exploratory forays into the building were slowly being forced back out by conditions so severe that their exposed skin blistered.

Two workmen came forward with pneumatic drills in an attempt to break through the bricked-up windows. They assisted our firemen and worked in the most difficult conditions for nearly thirty minutes before they had to be withdrawn for their own safety as precarious and unstable cracks appeared in the walls above them.

The smell of the fire was ever present anywhere in the vicinity of London Bridge that late summer afternoon. Travelling to work by train I sat mesmerised as we came into London Bridge station, the vast pall of smoke blocking out the sun. I ran to work from Waterloo station, and found an unfamiliar stand-by pump at the station, from some place I was not even sure was in London. Except for this one strange "silver" fire engine the place was deserted; not a staff car to be seen, no control unit, no canteen van. The watchroom teleprinter messages conveyed the story in stiff fire brigade speak. What the messages could not convey was the true extent of the gruelling and arduous conditions that the crews and officers were having to struggle against. In truth they were fighting a battle that would be near impossible to win. The teleprinter messages showed that Lambeth's ET went on after the first make up message, the station then emptying with consecutive make ups, the PE finally going on at "make pumps thirty."

With no one there to relieve I changed and went down to the viewing gallery in Brigade control. I was not the only curious visitor; the place was packed, day duty fire prevention officers, even some admin staff, all keen to connect with this breaking news story that was only two station grounds away. The activity within the control was composed yet the control staff appeared tense, not because they were being watched, but because they knew the fireground messages conveyed far more meaning and drama than the simple wording that the informative messages portrayed.

The whole control room became hushed as the priority message from the Brigade control unit was received by the control room radio operator. All eyes turned to him as he told the control unit to go ahead with its priority message. "From the Chief Officer at Wilson's Wharf, Battle Bridge Lane, make pumps fifty." The radio operator repeated the message back and timed the message at 5.12 pm. Gasps of surprise filled the viewing gallery except for one white-haired Rumpole-like inspecting officer who could only utter the words "Effing hell!" A grinning (fire prevention) colleague said, "Didn't you inspect that warehouse last week and pass it as OK?" He got a mouthed profanity plus a sneering smile as the only reply.

The officer of the watch organised the mobilisation of the next twenty pumps, then set about the task of arranging stand by appliances to cover empty stations. The special cover stations retained their pump escapes but there were lots of empty stations all over central London. Restricted mobilising (where reduced attendances were sent to all calls) had been in operation since the make pumps thirty but another large make up could see the fire cover in London reach desperate, possibly dangerous, levels.

With the change of shift coming up it was time to return to the appliance room and parade, even though there was nothing to ride. Station routines were cancelled and early suppers ordered in anticipation of reliefs being ordered to the fire. There was excited chatter amongst the glut of newcomers to the station as they hoped to be ordered on.

As roll call was being taken a violent flashover occurred in the warehouse; whether it was the acetylene cylinders exploding or the massive build-up of flammable gases from the insulation igniting was never determined. Nonetheless three BA firemen working from a covered bridgeway connecting two warehouses were injured. One was rushed to hospital suffering serious burns to his hands and face.

The fire was now so severe that crews were concentrated on confining the spread of the fire to an area bounded by Battle Bridge Lane, English Lane and the river. Several floors of the building had collapsed and fire was finally breaking through the building's face at ground, first and second floor levels. After the change of watch the organisation of getting the day shift crews returned to their stations and exchanging them with the night shift personnel added to the pressures on the control unit staff. Maintaining the attack on the fire was vital, any weakness in the containment now being put in place would allow it to quickly spread to surrounding property.

By 7.00 pm large cracks had opened up in the eastern and southern walls of the warehouse. Whilst belching flame and smoke the release of pent-up heat enabling crews to make better progress with the assault on the fire in the surrounding sections of the complex. These were the scenes that greeted us when the pump, then Lambeth's ET, returned to the scene.

Parked fire engines filled Tooley Street. Others were arriving, some preparing to return weary crews to their station, to exchange crews and immediately return. Some crews, tired, wet, grimy and smoke stained were cradling cups of tea in their hands. Others, clearly exhausted, sat in the street, some dunking biscuits, whilst many were having a well-earned drag on a cigarette or pulling their trusty pipe from an inside tunic pocket. Senior officers, looking equally weary, mixed freely with the firemen, unified in battling a common foe.

Detailed to relieve a day shift crew, I carried my BA set over my shoulder as our crew negotiated its way over a multitude of hose lines that filled the narrow access lane. It was a tribute to the accuracy of the, hand drawn, fireground plan displayed on the control unit that we found the crew working in the general area indicated. As we neared our position, passing under the connecting bridges, we looked up as two white helmeted figures emerged from the swirling smoke. The Deputy Chief, accompanied by his staff officer (wearing a walkie-talkie on his back), crawled out from the smoky second floor, leaned over the iron bridge, retched violently, then turned and crawled back in.

Reporting to the senior officer directing operations in our sector we had to start up our BA sets just to direct our jet from the outside of the building through a second-floor loophole and towards the glow of flame inside. So intense was the fire at this stage that complaints of smoke drifts were received as far away as Bethnal Green and there were reports of smoke drifting into some underground stations in the City.

The mixed cacophony of sound was even punishing our hearing. The loud cracking of timbers, the crashing of internal walls, the humming of pumps working at high pressure, combined with the thud of the jets hitting brick walls. The echo of these sounds reverberated in the confined spaces we were working in. It seemed to be trying to drown out the frightening noise of the fire (but failing), which rose above the sound of everything else. This fire truly was a whole-body experience affecting every one of the five senses.

Our attention was drawn to movement on the overhead connecting bridges as men ran away from the fire then, dropping one level, ran back into the building. A Sub Officer, who had been moving in the smoke across the sagging floor had suddenly stumbled, overbalanced and fallen through the already weakened floor on to the debris laying on the floor below. What we saw was the prompt actions of his crew, retracing their steps and gaining access to the first floor. They crawled their way through the debris to comfort him as he was placed on an improvised stretcher and carried, in considerable pain, to safety and the first aid area.

Just before 9.00 pm the situation seemed to have improved and the "fire surrounded" message was sent. Crews were re-deployed at this stage to prevent the fire from "jumping" across the narrow Battle Bridge Lane to adjoining premises. We left the fireground just after midnight but were back again at five in the morning, this time with the Sub Officer in charge of us instead of the governor.

The new arrivals who had come to Lambeth's Red Watch in my three months away, riding the pump escape, had looked forlorn, frustrated and despondent as the pump had been ordered to the fifty pumper whilst they remained at the station. My own early days came flooding back as I knew the frustration they must have been feeling at missing the "big one." So letting as many as possible ride the pump, and with me covering the BA position, we returned, this time deployed on radial branches. The radial branches, looking like military mortars, were throwing vast quantities of water on to the burning building and, as flame was reduced, like skirmishing troops the crews moved forward consolidating the bridgeheads gained earlier. The building, once red with anger, was now obscured by dense smoke as the cooling water dampened the flames. The choking smoke blinded the weary men but still they moved ever closer for the final kill.

By the time we were again relieved, the fire in the complex had been subdued and was now confined to the top three floors of a warehouse in the corner of the site. Crews continued to be exchanged throughout the 11th and 12th August, extinguishing pockets of fire. Relief crews continued the work until only the smouldering ruins, tall, gaunt and with dangerously cracked walls, belched only steam. The last pumps left the scene at 5.00 pm on the 12th. The damage to the complex consisted of three quarters of all the floors being severely damaged by fire, heat, smoke and water, half the roof was destroyed. Twenty jets, eight radial branches and two hundred Proto BA sets had been used to quell the blaze.

National news reports covering the fire said that three hundred firemen had fought the blaze of the century on the banks of the Thames and that three firemen were injured. There was little or no follow up news. The incident was not considered sufficiently newsworthy despite the fact that the effort of containing the conflagration took three days and only the actions of London's firemen prevented a blaze of catastrophic proportions.

Fond Farewell

On the 6th October 1971 I received a memorandum from the Chief Officer (a rubber stamp signature, not a real one!) saying he was "Pleased to inform me" that he had approved my promotion to Leading Fireman with effect from Monday 18th October. He was pleased? I was effing ecstatic. I was to be posted to B23 Southwark, White Watch. It was Christmas and my birthday all rolled into one. Many changes had taken place on Lambeth's Red Watch in the four years I had been there; retirements, promotions, postings and new arrivals. I had made some surprising friends; Roger Vaughan remained a loyal colleague for many years to come. I had managed to antagonise others. Regardless, we all had one thing in common; we were cohorts together and when the "chips" were down. It was these people you could depend on, banding together, working as a team, ready to tackle any emergency. So, as it transpired, this was more than just a farewell to those serving at Lambeth, it was a permanent departure from the Red Watch. I would never serve on the Red Watch again.

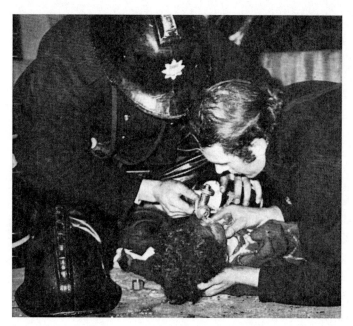

Two Old Kent Road firemen performing resuscitation on a young child rescued from a flat fire near the Elephant and Castle. South London.

Serious flooding in Lewisham during 1969 and Lambeth's pump wades in.

***London's Chief Officer Joe Milner, with trademark pipe, listening to
firemen's concerns at a North London major fire.***

Copyright. *London Fire Brigade/Mary Evans Picture Library.*

Fireboat 'Firebrace' showing her pumping prowess.

Copyright. *London Fire Brigade/Mary Evans Picture Library.*

Five turntable ladders carry the flag draped coffins of the firefighters killed at Dudgeons Wharf, through East London streets enroute to the Crematorium. September 1969.

Divisional Commander 'Charlie' Clisby leads the desperate efforts to rescue, and save the life of, Leading Fireman Michael Lee (Shoreditch). Alas it is too late. 29ᵗʰ September 1969.

Copyright. *London Fire Brigade/Mary Evans Picture Library.*

Scene of the fifty-pump fire-Tooley Street in1971.

Copyright. *London Fire Brigade/Mary Evans Picture Library.*

Thames-side warehouse blaze in Southwark in the early 1970's

Chapter 8

Leading Hand

New Family

Each of the Brigade's three individual watches were like separate extended families. Move station but retain the same watch you remained in the extended family. Change watches and you were in a totally different family, an outsider within a familiar world. That pretty well sums up what it was like for me moving from Lambeth's Red Watch on to Southwark's White Watch. I also had, unfortunately, an exceptionally hard act to follow. The previous White Watch Leading Fireman, who had just been promoted to Sub Officer, was not only an excellent station administrator but he could also type using all his fingers! More importantly his typing spelt all the words correctly. I, sadly, was still only able to use two fingers and spent an inordinate amount of time with my nose stuck in the office dictionary looking up the correct spelling of the words the damn antiquated typewriter kept getting wrong.

Southwark was an old rambling station. It had been added on to the nineteenth century Brigade headquarters' complex in 1911. An extension to the original three appliance bays that had housed the horse drawn steamers. Now with at least seven of the new-fangled motorised fire engines to house, four new bays were required, plus the necessary accommodation to cater for the extra firemen to man them. Southwark's accommodation had changed very little over the years. It had just been adapted to reflect the fact that its firemen no longer lived and worked at the station, on duty, twenty-four hours a day.

The station accommodation could, at best, be described as gloomily basic. On the first floor there was one small station office shared by all three office staff. Only two dormitories were provided, one for the governor and the other shared by the Sub Officer and myself. The firemen had to sleep anywhere they could find a space, the mess room, snooker-room, locker-room or in the tiny TV room, located over Southwark Training School's entrance arch. The ground floor gear room, where all our fire kit hung, doubled as the BA maintenance room (not the most ideal or hygienic of situations given the danger of possible contamination to the BA sets). The station's rambling basement covered the whole area on which the station stood. It had had numerous coke cellars that were once required to feed the two huge boilers that heated the station and the four floors of accommodation above. They also provided the whole building with a continuous supply of hot water. (The boilers were called "apparatuses" (or "appy" for short). A fireman on roll call would be detailed as the "appy" man. God help the poor sod who let the boiler/appy go out.) These boilers had eventually been replaced by a gas fed system, but the majority of the confusing collection of interconnected former cellars and storerooms remained unused, just blackened and dust filled by over half a century of regular coke deliveries. Now the only utilised areas were the boiler room itself and the stations dead record store that was located right at the far end of the basement. It was rumoured that a trapdoor once led into the beer cellar of the Goldsmiths public house, next door. Yet despite repeated attempts to find it, it was never located, if it ever existed at all.

Behind a solid brick wall that ran along the back of the station's basement was the largest of the Brigade's smoke chamber training complexes and its most testing facility. The sound of the BA crews, some under tuition, could be heard scurrying and clambering through the smoke chamber's "rat run" and filled Southwark's basement with an eerie and haunting sound. The combination of this darkened maze-like basement, the peculiar scraping noises, and my fear of the dark made having to go to the dead record store a hateful task. I would break out in a cold sweat as I tried, unsuccessfully, to tell myself the noise only came from the chamber. But I was never really sure. Part of this dirty old basement would soon come into its own and find a very special new role. It would also start a mystery that would have senior officers at Divisional Headquarters scratching their heads in puzzlement. A puzzle they were determined to solve regardless of how long it took.

But for now I was the new kid on the block. I was both new to the office staff and new to the watch. It was similar, in many ways, to starting all over again, building new relationships and establishing a rapport with this unfamiliar family, the head of which was "the governor." He was relatively newly promoted himself. Yet despite his considerable intelligence, a well-developed sense of humour and reputation as a good fireground officer, he was a troubled soul for reasons that we never really understood. He went from considerable highs into morose lows and a more astute diagnosis may well have concluded that he suffered bouts of depression. Years later he may have been described as being bi-polar but for now we thought he was just plain moody. His solution to combat these moods was to drink and this occasionally made station life very tricky, to say the least. I was also a new face to crews of the surrounding stations, an unknown quantity, and whose trust I had yet to win. The oldest member on the watch was my new Station Officer. He was only in his mid-thirties and, depending on his demeanour or consumption of alcohol before coming to work, he was not always very approachable.

The rest of the watch were all under thirty, including the Sub Officer. I was the babe of the watch at twenty-two. The closest thing there was to a senior hand, with ten years' experience, was a quiet Irishman. He was never flustered, never ever rising to take the bait of some wind up or other. He just drifted around the station like a spectre. There was always a folded-up copy of that day's Daily Mirror in the back pocket of his overall trousers. He never once objected to cleaning the firemen's toilets where he would sit, in tranquil solitude, on one of the two thrones reading his paper cover to cover. He was also exceptionally bright and academically gifted. Although he had passed his Station Officer's written examination, he had also failed to pass the Leading Fireman's interview, despite his extensive acting up and temporary promotion. It was widely believed his failure was due to no one on the promotion board being able to understand his broad Southern Irish brogue. He eventually transferred to an Eire fire brigade and rose to become its Chief Fire Officer. It was always an amusing notion to imagine him strutting around in his Chief Officer's uniform, still with the folded-up copy of the daily paper in his back pocket, as he headed off to the loo.

So there was no real "senior" fireman on the watch. No father figure, whose wisdom and insight could be relied upon to mediate between firemen working closely within this tight family unit. We were eating, sleeping and working together, sometimes seeing more of each other than our own families. Without this elder statesman, whose good judgement could help relieve the stresses and strains of apparently innocuous problems, anxieties inevitably built and leached out into the workplace. This could affect not only an individual's performance, but that of the team. When these situations erupted from time to time, the first warning sign was normally tension around the mess-table. These would be followed by raised voices in the firemen's locker room and finally the sound of metal lockers crashing together as tension spilled over into pushing and shoving, with the occasional fist thrown in for good measure. Serious damage was usually avoided as other firemen stepped in, before a member of the office staff had to read the riot act.

It took me a few months to fathom out that when these pressure build-ups erupted it seemed to coincide with the governor's "black dog" phases. It appeared that these times were when his eye was clearly off the ball and the consistency of his own behaviour was, at best, questionable. In these circumstances I started to appreciate the art of managing people. I learnt early on how important it was to defuse a problem before it got out of hand and to be consistent in my running of a watch, or in my case helping the governor run his watch. Not reading the signs properly or, worse still, ignoring them could lead to tensions getting completely out of control. On Southwark's Red Watch, George and another fireman had had a needle match going on for a couple of months, but without any intervention by their governor to resolve the matter. One day George was pushed too far by the veiled threats and insinuations of his antagonist. During that afternoon's drill session, and whilst in the main training yard (and in front of at least two squads of recruits), one comment too many was mouthed and George lost the plot. Whilst the rest of the crew stood in line George calmly walked over to the appliance that was parked just behind them, and removed a shovel from the small gear locker. He walked back towards the line and struck his unaware adversary with such a powerful blow that it lifted him clear off the ground before he collapsed unconscious. George then slowly returned the shovel, just as calmly, to the locker before retaking his place in the line.

Needless to say the s--- hit the fan. Ambulances and police cars filled the training school drill yard. All training for the recruits was temporarily suspended. George was arrested and the injured party carted off to Guy's Hospital. Brigade senior officers were summoned who then went on to Borough police station to negotiate with the station Superintendent. Once the full extent of the provocations were made known, George was released without charge, especially as the other guy was none the worse for wear other than a shovel shaped bruise on his back. George never returned to Southwark. He was posted immediately to West Norwood fire station instead (where we would meet again in a few years' time). Whilst the incident became a topical mess room yarn, the lesson was not lost on me. The importance of picking up on tensions within a watch was well made. Spending time listening to the concerns, or feelings, of individuals was an investment I knew was well worth making.

An addition to the White Watch's little family group was someone I had not previously come across. She was the station cook. Ours was named Lily and what she managed to concoct from the meagre provisions provided by some of the mess managers, was inspirational. A slightly built, modest, almost shy woman, in her late fifties, she was a born and bred South Londoner. She was employed only to cook the station personnel's breakfasts and lunches. The suppers were left to the somewhat doubtful talents of the mess managers. Occasionally Lily would prepare a pie or a stew during the day and leave it to be consumed by the ravenous night watch, who were grateful not to have to eat sausage, egg and baked beans yet again. She was the longest serving member at the station and, encouraged by a lunchtime tipple, she would relate a tale or two about some of the station personnel's past antics that made our displays of high jinks seem like pure kindergarten.

Not least amongst her many tales was that of a former Southwark Leading Fireman who was awarded a national bravery medal for an incredible, almost implausible, rescue performed during a serious fire in a nearby four storey tenement building. He was watched in stunned silence by the bystanders, as he shinned thirty feet up via a drainpipe to the third storey. He then balanced across two window sills to gain entry to a smoke filled flat and single handily rescued the trapped occupant. A sharp-eyed policeman, standing in the crowd, watched in increasing amazement as this acrobatic and heroic performance was played out in front of his eyes. Unfortunately, this policeman was even more curious than he was amazed and wondered if there could be any connection between the spate of cat burglaries in the vicinity and this nimble footed gallant fireman. There was. He was nicked and given a custodial sentence. It was inside prison walls (and now sacked from the fire brigade) that he received his bravery medal.

My promotion and transfer also introduced me to the wider White Watch family. I not only met them on the fireground but I was now carrying out an increasing number of out-duties to cover officer shortfalls at surrounding stations. I was beginning to wonder if I was the only spare Leading Fireman in the whole Division. However, it did have a positive side in that whenever I went out to stand-by it was to ride in charge of an engine. Besides going back to Lambeth to ride in charge of the ET, I was now becoming a regular at Dockhead, Old Kent Road and Peckham fire stations, in charge of their pump escapes. Pageant's Wharf had finally closed so I was excused that particular pleasure. I was, however, being assessed by each of those station's governors and I was beginning to discover that I was being requested to remain at a station, if the duty covered more than one shift. Whilst this was gratifying, I do not think my typing skills had anything to do with the request. I just put it down to my outstanding charm! This enforced mobility also gave me a valuable insight into the performance of the other stations' crews. These insights would help me to decide when to make up or not; were the take crews up to it, or not? Invaluable information in either case. The White Watch was coming across as a pretty good watch to be on, which was just as well, since it would be the only watch I would serve on from now on.

Old Southwark

Only a few miles separated Southwark and Lambeth fire stations. Yet Southwark's ground was quite different from that of Lambeth's. This was strange as the two grounds shared a common boundary, from the river down to the Elephant and Castle. Southwark had some heavy industry mixed amongst the decaying, but occupied, riverside warehouses. New modern office developments had sprung up along Southwark Street, including a vast Government department, plus a high security banking complex and a range of commercial buildings. Guy's Hospital, itself the size of a small town, was further to the East. Its state-of-the-art multi-storey tower (still under construction) would be topped off by its distinctive cantilever lecture theatre overlooking the Thames and St Paul's Cathedral. The other hospital on our ground was the Evelina Children's Hospital that was directly opposite the fire station. The gargantuan brick-built structure of Bankside Power station directly faced St Paul's Cathedral, whilst our own, more modest, Southwark Cathedral was hidden from the river by St Mary Olave's Wharf. It could be found amongst the narrow-cobbled roads that formed Bankside and Clink Street (site of the original Clink debtor's prison). Clink Street led into the famous Borough fruit and vegetable market, with its plethora of stalls and adjoining warehouses, supplying produce to swanky West End restaurants and South London street markets traders alike.

However, the most surprising and noticeable aspect of the immediate area surrounding the fire station was the range and quantity of impoverished housing. These included drab little terraces, tenement buildings (run by charities), poorly maintained pre-war council flats (none of which had its own inside bathroom) and the former artisan's dwellings. Peeling paintwork and brickwork deprived of mortar combined to tell of the community's own sad hard-up story.

Add to this canvas the proliferation of dingy and grubby little public houses, with their bare wooden floors and simple tables and chairs and you could be forgiven for believing you were still in the very streets that Charles Dickens had brought to a wider public's attention when highlighting the most appalling social deprivations that Southwark's inhabitants had then to endure. Things had improved in this rundown area since those Victorian times, but I was still bemused by the level of squalidness, meagreness and scarcity that I had not realised still existed in the 1970s. Parts of this area, to my impressionable eye, looked reminiscent of the harsh poverty-stricken living conditions in the works of Dickens. Especially so when the rows of smoking chimney pots added their own exhaust fumes to the frequent autumn fogs that still occurred (despite the implementation of the Clean Air Act). Yet despite the physical appearance of the surrounding streets, the local population came across as cheerful with a remarkable toughness and resilience. Most local inhabitants also worked within the immediate area and were either costermongers, local factory workers or other blue-collar workers. These workers could bring home only a meagre wage so seemed imprisoned in these conditions. It appeared to me that this was evidence enough of an enduring class system that would keep them in their place; the bottom. I also could not help but notice that for many of them social justice was just an ever-present dream.

Unsurprisingly it was these very conditions which provided the fire station with a fair chunk of its considerable operational workload. Candles were still regularly used to supplement, or provide the only, lighting; poorly maintained property meant electrical systems became incapacitated, overheated and started fires. Careless smokers, often fuelled by too much drink, discarded lit cigarettes with insufficient care. These, when falling onto armchairs or beds, led to smoky, sometimes fatal, smouldering fires. Young children, left unattended, discovered the sometimes-lethal attraction of playing with lighted matches. Yet around this time the most frequent and potentially serious cause of a house fire was the portable paraffin heater. These devices (sometimes bought second-hand and generally poorly maintained, if at all) when knocked over, whilst lit, provided a ready cause of fire. Tragically, and in increasing numbers, they were the cause of frequent fires including many where lives were lost. The headline, "Children die in oil heater blaze" became an all too commonplace winter feature in our daily newspapers. The London Fire Brigade was the very first UK Fire Brigade to take a fire prevention initiative and bought prime time on commercial television to back up its public awareness campaign in an attempt to reduce the number of these often-fatal fires.

Southwark's less than prosperous neighbourhood and its resultant fires was not unique. Many of London's fire stations were located in areas that had similar problems of social deprivation and who saw increased operational workloads because of it. Some stations, such as in the East End of London, far exceeded the number of calls that Southwark had to deal with. But regardless of wherever these areas were located the fires tested the crews' teamwork and fireground skills. In those early months at Southwark, I helped pitch the escape ladder at more fires than in all the previous four and a half years I had served at Lambeth. "Small fire flat/house, hose reel, BA" may well have been one of the most frequent stop messages sent from our run-of-the-mill "domestic" incidents. However, those few words simply could not portray the reality of these dramas nor the intense effort that went into resolving them. Neither could that simple message portray the plight of the occupants. Often these heart-rending scenes would also involve the human and social predicaments that the impoverished found themselves facing. There might be child welfare dilemmas that had to be passed onto Social Services, or in the case of careless or uncaring parents the Police. Lastly, unscrupulous landlords of neglected and run-down properties left their tenants exposed to serious fire and other health hazards. Southwark fire station's ground provided a valuable schooling for a new Leading Fireman. Some of the lessons, for this twenty-two-year-old were much harder to absorb, or understand, than others.

The Broom Cupboard

Anyone going down the station stairs leading into the basement had a simple choice, they could turn left and enter the labyrinth of darkened storerooms that surrounded the boiler room or turn right and enter the relocated gear room where the off-duty firemen's uniforms hung on their individual pegs. Here the white-washed walls were in stark contrast to the roughly cut timber cupboard, grey with age, that was mounted in the bare brick alcove that was just inside the gear room entrance doorway. This inconspicuous open cupboard just had two bass brooms and a shovel hanging from simple wooden pegs that had themselves started life as a broom handle. Nothing about this open cupboard looked new. In fact it looked as though it had always been there, part of the fabric of the station. Only the most inquisitive (and knowing) eyes would have seen the one thing that seemed so out of place, the small new black hook and eye that was fixed to the outside edge of the cupboard and to the back wall. Even when you released the hook nothing actually happened. So what purpose could the hook and eye possibly serve? Anyone holding on to the side of the cupboard that had been invisibly hinged to the wall would still believe the floor to ceiling structure to be an integral fixture. However, a slight tug on the hook and eye side and the cupboard would swing towards them in an effortless arc, on its concealed hinges, thus revealing its secret.

The broom cupboard (mock circa 1911) was in fact the very latest addition to the station's unofficial inventory. It had been constructed with painstaking care and with such artistry that it looked every one of its alleged sixty years of age. Rumours had circulated at B Divisional Headquarters that Southwark fire station was operating an illicit bar. Although drinking on duty was not banned then, the opening of any new bars, or wet canteens as they were called, was actively discouraged. Divisional senior officers called at the station for accommodation inspections or unusual impromptu visits, to investigate what truth there was in these "reliable" whisperings but failed to discover anything. No matter how hard they searched they could not find a room big enough to accommodate the alleged full-size bar, beer pumps, coolers and the other accoutrements that were alleged to exist on the station. The concealed location of the bar remained a closely guarded secret. The disguised entrance passed even the closest of inspections and its secret would remain undetected, for now, at least. Southwark was the proud owner of its own *speakeasy* and it was not long before surrounding stations asked to come and pay homage to the broom cupboard.

The idea to build a station bar emanated from Southwark's Red Watch but was unanimously supported across all three watches. A station planning meeting was held, attended by a representative from a famous south London brewery who undertook to supply and fit the necessary equipment, providing the bar was constructed to agreed standards. The water and electricity supply was diverted to provide the necessary power and washing facilities. The covert building project highlighted the raft of skills and expertise that individuals had brought with them to the fire brigade. Carpenters, electricians, plumbers, ventilation installers, upholsterers and carpet fitters all came forward (seemingly out of the station woodwork) to slave away on their night duties to complete the works. The outcome would have been the envy of any professional construction company. The piece-de-resistance turned out to be the ex-telecommunications engineer. He not only extended the station teleprinter and house bells into the bar-room but also fitted a mute facility, so that they could be isolated, when the bar was not being used.

Under the pretext of an inter-watch volleyball competition station personnel gathered for the grand opening. Sponsored for the opening night by the brewery the inaugural evening was an outstanding success. Rather than cutting a ribbon to declare the bar well and truly in business a toast was made to its silent guardian, the broom cupboard. The station was committed to taking delivery of two barrels of beer a week, which after the first night seemed wholly inadequate.

Whilst there was an agreed station policy that no drivers on duty would over-indulge, it was not long before others did. None with greater frequency than my own governor. On night duty, depending on his mood, he could be found opening up the bar even before suppertime. On one particular night duty he had started drinking early; even earlier than usual, and was propping up the bar, on his own, until the evening meal. During supper we received a shout to a warehouse blaze, off Tooley Street. Southwark's pair and Dockhead's pump responded to the initial call and on arrival found a narrow fronted two storey warehouse blazing away, a real "go'er."

The governor had just managed to get himself onto the pump. I was riding BA in the back. It became clear en route to the shout, that he was totally pissed. To make matters even worse Dockhead's governor arrived in the same condition. In normal circumstances there would have been no hesitation in making, "Pumps four." But with the two governors hugging each other in a drunken embrace and starting to serenade one another, these were not normal circumstances. My Sub Officer could not risk the possibility of a senior officer being ordered on so he made the best of it. We all got stuck in leaving the drunken duo sitting, and singing, on the kerbside. Fireground messages were sent in the governor's name and the Gods looked kindly on us that evening. There was no fire spread to the surrounding property and some three hours later we left the sodden remains of the warehouse behind us, our incapacitated governor sprawled out in the rear of the pump. I helped put him to bed when we got back to the station and he was, "Taken off the run", feeling very unwell!

The governor's compulsion to drink heavily and not being able to control the craving whilst at work was raising considerable worries amongst the watch. Sadly, none of us was prepared to take the bull by the horns and bring the matter out into the open. He was genuinely respected and it was not the sort of thing that you did, so we all continued to cover for him. In doing so we incriminated ourselves should it ever, "All go pear shaped" and it came pretty close on more than one occasion. After another late night in the bar, and with the governor the last to go to bed, a fire-call to a flat alight had us scrambling for the engines in the early hours of the morning. The call was on our own ground and the pump escape swiftly left the station expecting the pump to follow immediately behind. It did not. I was on my own riding in the back of the pump and something was clearly wrong. The pump driver and I were both looking at each other through the gaps between the BA sets. I said, "Where's the effing governor?" Leaving the pump's engine running we both got off the engine and a quick glance down the basement stairs confirmed that the broom cupboard was closed from the outside. Racing upstairs to the governor's room we found him, still fully dressed, prostrate across his bed in a drunken stupor. No amount of shouting or shaking would rouse him. So leaving him snoring loudly, we ran back to the appliance room, jumped in the pump and nervously gave chase; just the two of us and with no governor!

By the time we arrived smoke was coming from a second floor flat of a tenement building. The escape crew already had a hose reel to work and a pump's crew from the "take" station, wearing BA, were backing them up. Whilst this small fire was quickly extinguished, concealing the governor's obvious absence was not so straightforward. Although the Sub Officer had managed to cover for the governor's non-appearance it was clear that the situation was putting a considerable strain on their relationship. Raised voices coming from the station office the following morning indicated that things were coming to a head. A strained silence accompanied breakfast that day and the normally boisterous watch was very subdued. I was angry that the governor's drinking was getting out of hand. I also shared the watch's concern (and pity) that the governor could not come to terms with his drink problem. The broom cupboard might be disguising the fact that we had a bar but it could no longer hide the governor's drink dependency. This had to be addressed if he was not to bring about his own destruction and possibly do harm to those covering for him. His embarrassment at missing that shout seemed to strengthen his resolve to beat his addiction. I don't know if he ever won the war but he did win that particular battle; he never missed another shout, at least not whilst I served with him.

The Salvage Corps

Southwark's northern boundary is the River Thames. Beyond that lies the City of London, the home to the then London Salvage Corps. Around three thousand five hundred times a year the appliance room doors at their Headquarters in Aldersgate would crash open to allow the salvagemen to speed their way to a call within the capital. Southwark's close proximity to the City meant it was one of the inner London fire stations to get a salvage tender on the first response to all fire calls involving higher risk properties, such as riverside wharfs, hospitals, high-rise office buildings, factories and commercial sites.

The Corps had only one hundred and twelve uniformed personnel, comprising both salvage men and their senior officers. The salvagemen operated a two-shift system, twenty-four hours on and twenty-four hours off duty (with additional leave days on a rota basis). The senior officers lived in the flats above the multi-bayed purpose-built station. A senior officer was designated as the "Officer of the day;" a duty which lasted the twenty-four-hour shift and during which time he controlled the attendance of the Corps to the Brigades outer Divisions (on a discretionary basis). However, a salvage tender was automatically sent to all 4-pump fires in the Brigade's area and additional tenders requested, as required, by either service. The Corps also attended incidents in the Home Counties, taking account of the value of the insurance cover, or in a case such as Windsor Castle the national prominence.

Originally formed in 1865, the Corps had been set up and funded by Insurance Companies. These companies continued to finance the Corps until it was finally disbanded in the late 1980s; the Brigade then took over the salvage role. This function had been enshrined in law since the passing of the 1947 Fire Services Act but within London however, little attention had been paid to these responsibilities; the Corps carried them out for us.

Their joint headquarters and station was opened in 1961. Its appliance room housed the Corps' nine salvage tenders each designed to carry a crew of six. A casual passer-by seeing a salvage tender answering a call could easily mistake their red appliance for a fire engine, complete with its alloy ladders, blue flashing lights and chrome warning bell. Only the London Salvage Corps sign, on either side of the tender, would tell the more discerning observer of its true identity and purpose. The equipment carried on the tenders was comprehensive and allowed the crew to cover every aspect of their work. Among the salvagemen's considerable armoury were salvage sheets, temporary roof covering, pumps, deodorising apparatus (for clearing the smell of smoke), heaters, brooms and squeegees, tools and padlocks, used for securing property.

Whilst the salvageman wore an almost identical fire tunic, their black waders and distinctive "Braidwood" style helmet clearly set them apart from a fireman. Rightly or wrongly, there was not the camaraderie between the average salvageman and fireman that you might have expected. Despite frequently working in the same environment, salvagemen were viewed by firemen as second-class citizens. Not good enough to be a real fireman, they had joined the Salvage Corps instead. In truth, the Brigade was not always as good at salvage work as it should have been. We did not always give sufficient importance or priority to these duties despite the fact that sometimes our water caused as much damage (if not more) as the fire itself. Mitigating this water damage was a primary responsibility for the Corps. They were not helped by the occasionally overly enthusiastic fireman directing his jet into smoke, without sight of actual flame. Nonetheless occasions did arise where the Corps and Brigade worked side by side in perfect harmony determined to avoid any unnecessary damage. A "make-up" at Guy's Hospital was one of those instances and (whilst I am sure that there were many other examples) it was one I attended and witnessed at first hand.

Late one spring afternoon I was waiting impatiently for the change of watch and the possibility of a mutual exchange so that I might leave work a bit earlier, after a particularly tedious day. Southwark's White Watch had had no fire calls during the day shift; worse the continuous heavy rain had prevented any volleyball, which for the watch meant that there had been nothing to break the regular monotony of dull and tiresome station work. The governor was again in one of his darker moods so the station office was a place to avoid, if at all possible, which was not easy for either the Sub Officer or me.

Two minutes before 5 pm, the vigorous ringing of the station bells broke the gloom that had, unusually, hung over the station all day. The appliance room was now filled with the sound of controlled excitement, as the teleprinter spewed forth it first message of the day. Multiple calls were being received by the fire control to Guy's Hospital laundry. Accordingly the four machines dispatched to all calls to Guy's were now supplemented by an additional pump from the Old Kent Road.

Guy's Hospital fills a massive site. It is a collection of old three, four and five-storey brick-built buildings used as hospital wards, teaching blocks and research wings and the more recent (post-war) nurses' accommodation. In addition there was a major new high-rise tower and various other buildings (many of nineteenth century construction) to meet the needs of a pre-eminent teaching hospital. One of these older buildings, on the outskirts of the site, was a commercial sized laundry. The site had a network of inter-connected roadways and alleyways that eased traffic flow around the site and facilitated emergency vehicular access, principally ambulances. Additionally, other goods and services the hospital needed had to be moved from one place to another. Dotted around this maze of routes were parked cars belonging to medical and hospital staff. Whilst most parked in their allotted places some opportunist parking presented real problems and regularly restricted the already narrow access routes.

A shout could always be guaranteed to concentrate the governor's mind and for now he reverted to the sharp minded and experienced fire officer that had won him the respect of the watch and the benefit of the doubt when the "Black dog" took hold. The short travel distance to the hospital laundry, which was located just off Borough High Street, took less than two minutes and from Southwark Street onwards the strong smell of acrid smoke was very noticeable. Southbound traffic coming over London Bridge was bumper to bumper, as Southwark's two appliance drivers fought their way through the rush hour congestion and then veered southwards themselves towards the laundry's main access point in, White Hart Yard.

With the sound of multiple two-tone horns in the distance, Southwark's machines were forced to park in Borough High Street. The narrowness of White Hart Yard and parked cars blocked our entry to the laundry's entrance. Thick brown smoke was pouring from the open, elevated, loading bay that led to the laundry's ground floor. Whilst the laundry was on the extremity of the hospital site it was, nevertheless a wide three-storey building, although happily not connected to any of the other outlying wards or research buildings.

Met in the street by the laundry's manager the governor was informed that all the staff had been safely evacuated when the alarm had been first raised. Their own gallant attempts to quell the blaze had proved fruitless, as the overpowering smoke had forced the staff to escape to fresh air. The governor was now issuing curt precise orders, framed in his favourite language (in the best traditions of the fire service!). The Sub Officer, now lying flat on his stomach on the loading bay floor, was trying to get a feel for the situation inside and glean an insight into the general layout of the floor area. "Make pumps six." was sent immediately soon to be followed by "Make pumps eight." Water was secured from the nearest hydrant, which was, unfortunately, on the other side of Borough High Street. The twin "seventy-millimetre" hose lines snaking their way across the street brought the already slow-moving rush hour traffic to a complete standstill. (Placing ramps over the hose would come later.) The injurious and pungent smoke was a major concern, not only within the laundry building but also in the narrow confines of the access yard.

Ordered to don breathing apparatus, I led the first crew in with the governor's simple instruction ringing in my ears, "Find that effing fire and quickly." We were picking up our charged hose line as the first of two salvage tenders, ordered on with our initial call, was approaching the north side of London Bridge. Their swift arrival would prove crucial to the successful outcome of this incident. The fire, had started in an industrial hot air dryer. It is probable that accumulated fluff had ignited perhaps because someone had forgotten to clean the filters properly. This was something nobody was going to own up to. It then had spread to densely packed stacks of hospital linen, bedding and other clothing all piled on timber racking and shelving. This combination of materials resulted in a hot, smouldering and very smoky fire.

Although the laundry was distant from the main hospital buildings it was linked to the backs of the three-storey High Street shops and dwellings together with some other adjacent small lock-up factory units. Failure to contain this fire quickly could easily lead to a far more serious fire spreading to one or more of these properties. Whilst we made our initial entry, via the loading bay backed up by a second BA crew, extension ladders were being pitched and BA crews were entering the upper floors suitably armed with charged hose line. Clouds of smoke were pouring from these upper access points, which were impeding the progress of the crews as well as filling White Hart Yard. The senior salvageman off the first tender to arrive told the governor (who had not yet been relieved by a more senior officer) that he, "Could help move the smoke and so ease the conditions inside, providing the seat of the fire was sufficiently covered by jets." Mine and possibly too many other jets were now at work inside the laundry building. The main fire area appeared to be at least surrounded, if not contained. Salvage crews, braving the very smoky conditions and working under the direction of their senior salvageman, strategically placed large extractor fans just inside the loading bays. Other extractor units pushed the smoke out of White Hart Yard and away from the hospital. Soon conditions inside the laundry building improved considerably and, with the effects of the smoke-logging greatly reduced, the attack on the fire could be pushed home more easily.

Naturally, our attack on the blaze had involved copious amounts of water. This water had to be removed, or at least diverted, if we were not to replace fire damage with severe flooding. The second wave of salvagemen, now reinforced by the arrival of a third salvage tender, set to, to minimise the water damage. They constructed channels and dams, using rolled up salvage sheets and lengths of sand filled canvas hose, to direct the water out of the building. With the main seat of fire all but out, and only small pockets of fire remaining, the salvage boys swung fully into action continuing to ventilate the premises and even starting to dry out parts that had been affected only by water. Armed with their scoops, buckets, mops and squeegees, it appeared that they were able to push water out of the building almost as fast as we pushed it in.

The Brigade's senior officer (who finally arrived and took control) and the Corp's senior officer appeared well pleased with this unusual level of close co-operation between their respective crews. So much so, that correspondence was exchanged with each side praising the other for their endeavours. (Although ours appeared not to be so noteworthy on this occasion.) Sadly, this was not always the case but when it did happen it certainly appeared to be effective and worked really well. But things never got to such an intimate friendship that the salvagemen were invited to see the secrets of the "broom cupboard." Co-operation was one thing, trusting them with such a "state" secret was something else entirely.

Many people, when informed that the Corps was independent of the brigade and paid for by the insurance companies believed, mistakenly, that the salvagemen would only set out to work at insured risks. Time and time again the Corps showed that there was no such discrimination, and that they carried out their salvage work without regard to insurance cover. Thus, much of our contact with them was in this "public service" role, particularly with regard to calls such as hospitals. At Guy's Hospital it was to the salvagemen's credit, that largely due to their sterling work, the laundry was fully operational again, in a relatively short period of time following the fire.

You don't get me I'm part of the Union

I wanted my fireman's tale to cover much more than just an interesting or unusual incident or even a particularly memorable event. I've tried to convey a sense of the wider social and political factors that influenced the Brigade during my service and how it impacted on the lives of ordinary people, who made up the London Fire Brigade. During my four decades of service possibly no single time span was more momentous or significant than the 1970s. Whilst the sixties gave us The Beatles, what the seventies brought forth (either because of political or social pressures) affected millions in their everyday lives, including those in the Brigade. This decade, the seventies, introduced both major internal changes within the Brigade and furthermore national legislation dramatically affected the way individuals thought about their role and, for some even, the future direction of the Brigade. Some law making was thought, by some, not to have any great significance to the workings of the Brigade. However, in many instances the impact of these changes would remain, frequently combine and ultimately influence, in one way or another, the remainder of my fire service career. Health and Safety law and Equal Opportunities legislation are but just two examples that changed the way we had previously worked and who we worked with.

The early seventies maintained the momentum of the late sixties with growing political and industrial unrest. It was making its presence felt in every part of everyday life. Widespread national dock strikes (that were to sound the death knell of London's docks) gave rise to dire economic effects. The then Labour government lashed out in response at its traditional stronghold of support, the Unions. Inflation had risen sharply by the end of the previous decade as the reduced buying power of our (meagre) monthly wage demonstrated. This new decade saw an increasingly powerful trade union movement sweeping the nation (it also saw the removal of Labour's Harold Wilson and the arrival of the Tory's Ted Heath as Britain's Prime Minister).

This increased power and the demands by the Unions for better working conditions was felt within the fire service too. A Royal Commission (into local authority employee working conditions) was published in 1969. The Holroyd Report, which looked into the efficiency of the fire service, was presented in May 1971 and this was followed by the Cunningham Report in November 1971 (which looked into fire service pay and conditions). These were brought about by the increasing influence of the Fire Brigades Union, led nationally by its General Secretary Terence Parry. All these reports were used by both the Local Authority employers and the Union to seek to influence policy and bring about change. From the national employers' perspective, modernisation and productivity were the key justifications to increase our fire service pay. This view was also in accord with the Fire Brigades Union's desire to improve the pay and conditions of its operational members in the fire service. However, events did not turn out in the way either side hoped. The fire service was at this time relatively small fry in the wider national scheme of things. There were much bigger fish to fry and more troubling issues to worry a fragile government.

Change was a key to the seventies. The Irish problem, whatever its origins, brought demands for unification. Hostility to Catholicism in Ulster lead to barbaric acts of terrorism (that would all too quickly transfer to mainland Britain), was all about change. What had started as a protest about unfairness, bigotry and political corruption, brought indiscriminate bombings (by the IRA) to London's streets and put London's firemen back on the front line against these "acts of war." It was the first time in over thirty years, since the London Blitz in fact, that we had been put in such danger because of politically based terrorist violence.

Not only were the Unions extremely powerful, there were a lot of them (over six-hundred altogether) of which the Fire Brigades Union was but one small voice. 1972/3 was a time of considerable political militancy within the Unions and the London Regional Committee of the Fire Brigades Union was no exception. A 1973 hit song from the rock band The Strawbs (which stayed in the top ten for many weeks) was titled *"Part of the Union."* Its chorus ran, *"Oh you don't get me, I'm part of the union"*, whilst a verse commented, *"And I always get my way...If I strike for higher pay...So though I'm a working man... I can ruin the government's plan."* This song would prove to be almost visionary. The removal of our fifty-four-pound London under-manning allowance annual payment in 1972, combined with the start of four-year qualified fireman's undertaking the Brigade's industrial relations on a rocky road that was to last for the next five years. (A fireman was not deemed "qualified" until he had served four years and successfully completed a prescribed training module for each of those years.)

The relentless rise in union power also tested the new Heath government to the full and this was in addition to its other major problems. Such pressures, combined with huge rises in the world prices of crude oil and other essential commodities, put increased stress on family budgets. It made housekeeping, on an average fireman's monthly take home pay, increasingly difficult, especially, given our below average national wage. It was a very sore point with firemen nationally that a fireman's level of pay was not commensurate with the risk and demands of the job.

Following on from another major dock strike the country faced yet a further local authority dustmen's strike. Once again, we and London's communities were up to the knees in tons of uncollected refuse. The direct results of this action was not lost on much of London's inner-city population, or the Brigade, who were having to cope with the health and fire hazards caused by the consequences of the continuing battle for better pay and conditions demanded by the dustmen's unions. Employers resisted these demands supported by the Government's unseen controlling hand. Rubbish rapidly accumulated all over again in the capital's designated dumping areas. Night after night we either travelled around many of central London fire stations' grounds dealing with these fires or standing-by whilst the home station's crews were dousing putrefying rubbish fires piled ten feet high in some cases. Leicester Square became a notorious "emergency" rubbish dump and the stench, after just a few days, was almost overpowering. South of the river much less salubrious locations were used to pile the uncollected garbage. But regardless of location, clambering over this mixture of rotting and smelly household and commercial waste was equally unpleasant regardless.

The power workers struck next which lead to severe power cuts followed by a national postal workers' strike. Most prominent amongst this spate of national strikes was the first countrywide strike by the National Union of Mineworkers at the beginning of 1972. It showed union activists (and the nation) what the flexing of serious industrial muscle could achieve when an independent inquiry, headed by Lord Wilberforce, came out in favour of the miners' claim and the NUM settled. This was to be followed (now that the sweet smell of success was savoured by the NUM leadership) by a second national miners' strike the following year. This further strike was also successful for the miners, in part, because of the marked hike in oil prices caused by the short (six day) war between Egypt and Israel. The severe impact of this particular miners' strike lead to the introduction of the three-day working week and scheduled power cuts across the nation. It also saw the introduction of emergency electrical generators to fire stations to enable mobilising to function adequately. Candle lit dinners took on a whole new meaning – certainly not the romantic image normally associated with such occasions.

The seventies was an extreme decade as regards its industrial relations record. The extreme left dominated many Unions, including the Fire Brigades Union. Progress and proposed changes in the London Fire Brigade's working practices were challenged and obstructed, not necessarily supported by the whole of the London union membership. But in a show of hands, union activists (many of whom would happily be described as "militant") would carry the day. The first in a series of "emergency only disputes" hit the Brigade during the middle of this era. London firemen answered just nine-nine-nine calls and at some of the more militant stations appliances were taken "Off the run" for the most trivial of reasons. This new type of fire brigade "industrial" action grew incrementally until, finally, the first national strike involving firemen started in November 1977. It was to last for sixty-nine days.

It was argued by some political commentators at the time that the firemen's national strike was the catalyst for the subsequent infamous (and selective) quote by James Callaghan, the then Prime Minister *"winter of discontent"* (a line from Shakespeare's play *Richard III* – "Now is the winter of our discontent") to describe the industrial and social chaos of 1978/79. But the national firemen's strike was some while off yet. However, the seeds of dissent and dissatisfaction at our continuing low pay and the firemen's perceived poor status had been firmly planted. The returning Labour government's new (enforced) pay policy guaranteed those seeds would grow into an unstoppable energy that would eventually bring the majority of firemen out on to the streets.

Chapter 9

Special Services

Back to Lambeth

My Emergency Tender qualification finally caught up with me in April 1973. I got posted, unwillingly, back to Lambeth's White Watch to ride in charge of the ET. Recent promotions within Lambeth's office staff had brought about a shortfall of ET qualified junior officers and my name was top of the Divisional list for recall. So it was farewell to Southwark, for now at least. I was set to follow in the footsteps of many other ET junior officers, gaining valuable experience and expertise from the hand-me-down know-how of the longer serving crew members. I benefited greatly from their wealth of knowledge and operational skills, which they had gained from attending a wide variety of major breathing apparatus fires and special service calls.

As well as attending many of London's major fires, or where extra breathing apparatus was required, Lambeth's ET, like the Brigade's six other ET's, dealt with a wide range of special service calls. So this seems a good place to relate some of those incidents; not only whilst I rode in charge of Lambeth's ET but some others of note I encountered during my two decades of riding the engines.

The Hither Green train crash, the Moorgate tube disaster, the Marchioness river tragedy and Clapham rail crash are all part of the Brigade's major incident history and I missed every one! Although disappointing from a personal perspective it is not so surprising. Actually getting to attend such tragic events was very much a matter of chance. With three watches I had only a one in three chance of being on duty when a significant or catastrophic happening occurred. A disaster that could test London's emergency services and pushed their combined skill and co-ordination sometimes to the limit. Then programme in annual leave, possible sickness, attending training courses and the odds of getting to attend a major incident was reduced to about a twenty-five per cent chance. So I always felt I missed out. I was unable to test my fireman's skills and powerless to help alleviate the pain and distress of those involved. I also wanted, selfishly, to test and measure my own resolve in dealing with the challenges that such an incident invariably places on individuals and on those leading their teams. It was not from any ghoulish desire to witness, at first hand, the death and carnage that these incidents brought but, rather a desperate wish to bring my training and previous experience to bear. I wanted to be there, to help those involved and hopefully to contribute in whatever way, no matter how small, to the incident's successful conclusion.

Within the average fireman there exists an enormous amount of humanity. I am sure, in fact I know, this still applies today, it is part of the job. So not being part of such high profile, yet thankfully, infrequent events gave me a unique sense of frustration and disappointment. Knowing that people are in urgent need of assistance and not able to be part of the action is like not being picked to play for your team. As fate conspires to bring the rescuer and the rescued together, so fate (or rather the duty system) determines whether an individual firefighter will be part of any particular story. Tragically, it is not only the rescue of the living that tests the expertise and endurance of fire crews at incidents. The extrication and recovery of the dead is equally demanding but with the sense of urgency, sadly, removed. Crews have to demonstrate sensitivity as well as skill in the recovery of bodies or occasionally the remains of someone's loved one. Compassion and respect in such situations are not only demanded but have to be shown.

A special service call was (and still is) anything the Brigade attended that was not a fire. Sometimes they might be combined but in the main they were normally stand-alone incidents. Special service calls could involve the mundane, even the trivial, to incidents involving a serious risk to life and limb and, sadly, loss of life. Floodings, building collapses, lift incidents, road traffic accidents and chemical incidents were but a few of the many and varied activities that involve the use of an ET. So despite the fact that I never attended, "the big one" my career inevitably exposed me, and my crews, to an enormous number and variety of special service calls. Many were challenging, some with tragic consequences, whilst others were amusing and occasionally downright funny. In the many years I rode in charge of front-line appliances, including Lambeth's ET, special services calls grew in number. Their growth and diversity would eventually demand additional training and the provision of specialist equipment and kit in particular to deal with the increase in road traffic accidents and chemical incidents.

However, in my early career, during the late sixties, Pump escapes and pumps carried no equipment dedicated to dealing with special service calls that might require the extrication of people from car crashes, structural collapses or industrial accidents. The Brigade's fleet of Emergency Tenders and their crews were the primary means of handling the more demanding special service calls. Their crews gained a wealth of experience by virtue of this lack of equipment provision on PEs and pumps. In later years (and by the time I moved to senior rank) appliance design had dramatically improved. Front-line appliances later carried a wide range of specialist equipment (and protective clothing) that these situations (and Health and Safety legislation) now demanded.

A serious car crash in 1968 would find station crews making do with crow-bars, hacksaws and even the appliance jack if a person was trapped in a vehicle (whilst praying for the swift arrival of the ET and its specialist crew and equipment.) Twenty years on, and every London station had at least one front-line appliance with equipment that could be used to cut into most cars. We also had spreading equipment to open up compacted or twisted car chassis and their internal components, sometimes even before the ET arrived.

Special service calls were varied and diverse, for example a simple job involving just one appliance crew that was required to gain entry in to a locked flat or deal with an overflowing toilet. Another might be a large-scale flooding incident involving many appliances and their crews, pumping out for hours at a time. Many calls turned out to be not as straightforward as they initially seemed. A nine-nine-nine call to gain entry into a property might result in the discovery of the near mummified remains of an unfortunate occupant who had died, alone, some months earlier; or occasionally the discovery of a body found in suspicious circumstances which would start the Police off on a murder investigation. Having to gaining access into someone's premises, or home, did on occasions provide a unique insight into the darker side of people's lifestyles, shedding light on the unusual, or unsavoury, behaviour that went on behind the privacy of closed curtains. These revelations were sometimes quite bizarre and something you might read about in the more lurid tabloid newspapers. Other discoveries were occasionally much sadder and could even be tragic. Undernourished or impoverished children might be found left alone by the parents, or a single mother who's out drinking or on the "game," or both. The antics of hoarders (individuals who would fill every available bit of floor space in their home with years of accumulated rubbish, newspapers and magazines) was distinctly odd; worse were other individuals who would rather defecate on the floor or in the bath rather than use a toilet. One particular man converted the rooms of his innocuous semi-detached house to cater for his unusual sexual practices; he was found stuck in the manacles that were suspended from the ceiling! In many of these cases just getting in was only the first part of a continuing story involving either the police, ambulance crews, social services; or sometimes all of them, as they had to deal with the consequences of our special service discovery.

People got themselves stuck in the strangest of places too. There was the "plump" woman who got her toe stuck in a bath tap whilst bathing. Sadly, she was no nubile beauty but rather a hefty wench who had bad teeth and the breath to match. Her choice, and range, of language made even some of our most hardened firemen blush. When I was told to delicately remove her toe from the tap, she refused to cover herself up and just cursed instead, telling the crew and me in particular to, "Stop looking at my fanny." In a swift riposte my governor replied, "Look at it, madam? We would need spreading equipment to even find it!" She was not the only heavyweight. Another individual, an enormous man, who had eaten himself into his fourth-floor council flat, literally, had become unwell and needed hospital care. The ambulance service was summoned but its crew were unable to lift him on to the stretcher and so get him out of his flat. Weighing nearly thirty stones, it took six of us to lift and carry him on the stretcher, but only after having first removed the front door, its frame and two feet of the surrounding brickwork to deliver him to the waiting ambulance.

Very occasionally special service incidents came to us. Whilst I was at Southwark a woman, whose toddler had got his head stuck firmly in a saucepan, brought him into the station. She then promptly disappeared for some inexplicable reason, only to return some hours later to collect her now saucepan free child. By then the police were waiting to hear her explanation and they all left in a police car.

Heads in railings, fingers in holes, and even a pair of feet stuck in a bucket of concrete were all part of this very special service. The troubled guy with his feet in a bucket of quick setting concrete had originally intended to throw himself into the River Thames; but the concrete set too quickly and was then far too heavy and prevented him from moving anywhere. He was discovered by a passing police patrol car and we spent the next hour chipping away at what was meant to have finished him off but had in fact, ironically, saved his life.

Finding body parts, with their owner still attached, stuck in peculiar places was not a normal run-of-the-mill call. However, infrequently these incidents occurred I was amazed at what some men chose to stick their penises into. I attended two such "erotic" incidents, one at Guy's Hospital and the other at King's College hospital. On both occasions we were called by the duty staff in the respective A&E departments. At Guy's, a middle-aged, tubby man had used a stainless-steel ball-race (what else!) to give himself some form of sexual gratification. With his penis erect the steel ring became firmly stuck around the shaft of his "dick." This had occurred some hours earlier and despite the strenuous efforts of the man to remove the ring it had refused to budge. With his manhood turning, first, an unpleasant reddish purple and then an ugly blue he (and his still erect swollen lump of flesh) finally arrived at Guy's A&E where he with considerable embarrassment explained the nature of his *pre-dick-ament*! In spite of the best efforts of the A&E team, they were unable to remove the ring and the duty doctors decided to call the fire brigade. Together with my pump's crew, and still unaware of the exact nature of this call for assistance, I duly arrived from Southwark fire station.

Briefed by the A&E's duty doctor I went to assess the situation. A look of horror and total disbelief filled the man's face as I, with four burly firemen, appeared from behind the screens, which shielded him from the wider public's glaze. The end of his penis, above the ring, was terribly swollen and discoloured. If prompt action was not taken, he was in imminent danger of having his penis amputated. His embarrassment was adding to his already raised stress levels, and although we felt we could remove the ring we thought it was better that he was not part of the audience. As we prepared our equipment the man was given a general anaesthetic and drifted into oblivion. We were not sure, but thought we noticed a sudden increase in the number of nurses present as all this was taking place. In particular we saw an increase in the number of nurses carrying cameras?

I and another crew '*member*' were scrubbed up whilst our saws and clamp were disinfected. Now, with our fire tunics removed, we were ready to operate. I had called for ice packs to reduce the swelling, and whilst these were applied the screens were pulled back to reveal half a dozen or so giggling nurses. They were standing on chairs, cameras at the ready, waiting to record this unfortunate man's encounter with a ring. To the clicking of camera shutters, and the amused chortling of the A&E staff, a clamp was placed on the ring to prevent any unfortunate or disastrous movement. Then the first of two cuts was made in to the ring. Holding this man's dick (even in a gloved hand) was not the highlight of my day but it did prevent the hacksaw blade from cutting too far thereby turning him into a latter-day soprano. I thought to myself, "Well they never covered this in Training School!" Eventually, and with both sides of the ring cut through and with a minimum of grazing to his engorged penis, we beat a hasty retreat back to the safety and normality of the fire station, not relishing the prospect of sausages on the menu for a while.

Some years later, whilst a Station Officer at Brixton, I got a second taste of this bizarre practice. This time we were called to, "Assist with the removal of a ring," at King's College A&E. It was custom that crew members never went into any situation empty handed. So they took with them what they considered useful and appropriate gear.

We were directed to the emergency treatment area. This time, we were confronted by a very handsome and virile-looking young white man, in his mid-twenties and who could easily have been a male model. Stripped from the waist down he displayed three bronze rings firmly constricting the base of his penis. Despite the painful-looking discolouration and bruising, it was clear that this guy had not been short changed when it came to the size of his manhood. He was enormous! His own desperate efforts to remove the rings having ended in failure, he too had sought professional help. Whilst attempting to maintain his composure, he ignored the comments and wide-eyed glances of the buxom, black, staff nurse who told him, "I see why you needed three." He eyed our arrival with a look of consternation. As the last of my crew arrived at his bedside, I saw the blood drain rapidly from his face as his complexion turned a whiter shade of pale. Seeing this, the last crewmember uttered, "Don't worry mate, we'll soon have it off," forgetting that over his shoulder he was carrying a large pair of metal bolt croppers. This was all too much for this poor young man, who slipped into a dead faint. Whilst the nurses clearly enjoyed our sense of humour and the poor man's reaction to the prospect of those bolt cutters coming anywhere near his dick, a po-faced A&E doctor did not; he was unable to see the funny side and even threatened to make an official complaint. Harmonious relations were eventually restored with the doctor but only after we regained our professionalism with the rapid and skilful removal of the offending hardware. Not, however, before yet more nurses appeared armed with their cameras allegedly taking photos for "training purposes!" That was my last experience of such extreme special services that required a personal "hands-on" touch. It was but a taste of the weird and peculiar dilemmas some people got themselves into and the Brigade's efforts to get them out of it.

Sadly, death and serious injury are an all too familiar part of dealing with special services. Despite the circumstances, absurdity was found in some of these tragic situations. Firemen's "black" or "gallows humour" is an essential element in helping firemen, of all ranks, to deal with the aftermath of these fatal events. It helped us keep our role in perspective. Although this might sound crude, possibly even cruel, I never witnessed (nor would I have tolerated) any insensitivity from personnel when confronting or resolving distressing situations. But after the event, back in the confines of the station, if there was any possible amusement to be found in how a life or death situation was resolved you may rely on firemen to find it. So although I did not personally attend this next incident, I did witness it, first hand, from a window on Lambeth's first floor.

Responding to people falling or jumping into the River Thames was a fairly common occurrence for Lambeth's fireboat crew. On this particular day one of the "floaties" saw the event unfold before his very eyes. A man had climbed over the side of Lambeth Bridge and was now standing on the edge of the bridge. He was facing the fireboat's pontoon, preparing to throw himself into the murky water flowing below. The fireboat was tethered to the pontoon and this crew member, seeing the man on the outside of the bridge's side, raised the alarm. Whether his shouting prompted the man to jump or whether he would have jumped anyway nobody ever bothered to ask! But the man hurled himself outwards and fell, feet first, towards the fast-flowing discoloured water of the Thames some forty feet below.

So as to make the most speedy rescue attempt, four members of the fireboat crew took to the skiff (that was kept tied behind the fireboat) and, having untied it, were presently rowing for all they were worth towards the flailing man, meanwhile the fireboat got underway with the remainder of the crew. Since the skiff's crew were rowing with the tide, they were rapidly shortening the distance between themselves and the apparently drowning man. The sound of Lambeth's house bells ringing, and the white light indicating that the fireboat had a shout, brought me to a front window that provided a clear view of the river and Lambeth Bridge. The fireboat had by now cast off its mooring lines but was still on station. The skiff was going hell-for-leather towards the north side of the Bridge. The combination of the skill and strength of the skiff crew made the craft guide effortlessly across the surface of the river. I could not actually see what they were aiming for, but my guess was someone had gone in the river.

Sadly for the suicidal man not everything had gone to plan. Not only had he chosen to jump off a bridge in front of the fireboat station but he had not selected his position on the bridge very carefully either. Lambeth Bridge, in common with many of London's bridges, had foundations and stonework that extended out some eight to ten feet from the bridge's edge over the river. Our unfortunate jumper was not privy to this information and had chosen to position himself directly over one of the very solid foundation buttresses, before taking his desperate leap to his intended watery grave. Had he jumped just a few minutes later he would have seen what he was jumping on to, instead of in to! The murky Thames water obscured the projecting stonework that he was hurtling down towards at thirty-three feet per second. Imagine his utter shock and surprise as he expected to disappear under the water only to hit something extremely hard, and solid, instead. The impact immediately broke both his legs. Fortunately for him, the strength of the tide held him against the bridge's buttresses just long enough for the skiff's crew to cover the last remaining yards and grab hold of him before the current could sweep him into the river's flow. As one of the crew held the man firmly, it was later related, he looked up pitifully towards his unwanted rescuers and said, "Nothing ever goes right for me!"

People can, and do, choose some horrible ways to die. In most circumstances I feel that a suicide is an incredibly selfish act. Not only does it leave friends and family to face the consequences of these actions, in most cases some poor soul has to clean up their mess. The lack of any normal rationale of these desperate people cannot be more painfully illustrated than of those throwing themselves into the path of an on-coming underground train. Yet people do make that choice and very few of them live to tell the tale. Genuine accidents do occur on the rail network, with individuals attempting to get on or off a moving train or misjudging distances and stumbling or falling onto the tracks. Occasionally they may be caught or trapped by the train. Lambeth, Southwark and Brixton fire stations all had both mainline and underground stations on their grounds. I attended both fatal and non-fatal incidents at these locations, plus some much further afield as a member of Lambeth's ET. Sadly, all too often, there was little we could do other than pick up the pieces or wait until the train was moved and then recover the body. In most of these cases of a suicide my thoughts went to the distraught train driver who would be haunted by the images of the person they knew they had no chance of avoiding. Incredibly some did survive the experience of getting into an argument with a moving, multi-ton, train. One such incident occurred on the Northern Line at Lambeth North underground station, where a young lady slipped in front of a moving train as it came into the platform. Shocked, and rather dirty she got up to walk away with just superficial cuts and bruises after she was assisted from beneath the carriage and lifted back onto the platform. I could not believe her incredible luck at not being either killed or seriously maimed.

British Rail rolling stock is incredibly heavy, the engines alone weighing hundreds of tons in some cases. As a Leading Fireman at Southwark I attended a call to Waterloo mainline station. We were called to a, "Man under train" at a given platform number. With the power to the track already isolated by British Rail staff the ambulance crew attending had already established that the man was dead but he remained trapped beneath the train. They now withdrew since the British Transport Police were responsible for the removal of the body, once it had been released. I was in charge of Southwark's PE and with my governor remaining in charge on the platform it fell to me to go under the train to assess the situation. How it had happened was uncertain but the well-dressed "city gent" had fallen beneath the slow-moving train as it entered Waterloo Station. His head was now firmly wedged between a wheel of the leading carriage and the large electric motor housing located beneath the carriage. The man had been dragged along under the train before his head was finally caught by the wheel's motion. It first moved and then trapped his head against the motor housing whilst stretching his neck to its physical limits without actually decapitating the man. Any slight movement of the carriage wheel would finish the task and with the train already touching the platform buffers there was no chance of securing any possible forward movement, which might release his trapped head unaided. I told the governor the situation and offered a possible solution as to how to extricate the body. He considered it and gave his approval. I was given the requested equipment.

Working conditions beneath the train were extremely cramped and restricting. It afforded only sufficient room for myself and one other member of Southwark's crew to work. The heat from the train's motors made the space very warm and the smell of excrement from the unfortunate man made it even more unpleasant. My solution, if we were to remove the body intact, was to carefully tap the man's head out of its trapped position and so releasing the body. Then the train could be moved backwards and the body recovered. Now armed with a four-pound club hammer, a narrow wooden block and some unwrapped triangular bandages I proceeded to set about my task. My companion was clearly very unhappy about my chosen course of action but since he did not have a better solution, and British Rail was putting considerable pressure on us to move the train, a series of blows on to the block (that was placed on the unwrapped bandages placed on the man's head) slowly released it from the vice like grip. With the head now free the train could be moved. We were now able to remove the body in a dignified manner, behind the protection of raised salvage sheets. My colleague (a sensitive chap at the best of times) considered my methods barbaric! He really got out of his pram and was having a considerable rant about how I had released the dead man. I challenged him as to whether any possible family would have preferred the man's body intact (something I had achieved), compared to the horrific injuries that would have been done to his face (besides pulling his bloody head off). He could offer no alternative solution other than the action I had taken. But he sulked away mumbling his disapproval. So sometimes there is no correct answer. You just have to do your very best in whatever conditions that are presented to you. Always remember though that someone, somewhere, gets the task of identifying the dead; anything that can be done to minimise the distress of that task is worth a try.

In central London, during the late sixties and seventies, major road traffic accidents were an infrequent event. They happened, but multi car pile-ups involving high-speed impacts, that led to protracted cutting out of the dead and injured were noteworthy, because of their rarity.

At the end of the sixties Nine Elms Goods Yard was still an enormous British Rail marshalling area and an industrial site housing, then, London's largest cold store and giving rail access to Battersea Power station. Goods wagons and trucks were pulled or pushed by small, but powerful, shunting locomotives that crossed Nine Elms Lane from one side of the marshalling yard to the other. Although there were crossing traffic lights in Nine Elms Lane there were no level crossing gates to stop the flow of traffic when goods wagons were shunted across the main road. One impetuous and impatient driver tried to jump these lights at red but either misjudged his timing or did not see the goods wagon, or both. The sheer weight of the wagon being shunted across the road and its momentum made it unstoppable. The goods wagon caught the car and carried it before it until the car hit a large brick pillar on the other side of the crossing. Trapped between pillar and wagon, a second goods truck following slammed into the rear of the first wagon crushing the car still further. Their combined weight had compacted the car to about one-third of its original size. When I pulled up on the first machine to arrive, I looked on in total disbelief at the cars and occupant's plight. The car was concertinaed between the brick wall and the wagons, crushed almost beyond recognition. There was no way anyone could have survived such an impact, or so I thought. On closer inspection, and to my Governor's total amazement, the driver of the car had his feet over the passenger's seat and was laying sideways across the vehicle. He had miraculously survived, totally uninjured, but was now entombed within the twisted metal of his former car. Lambeth's ET was part of the initial attendance and arrived immediately behind our PE and pump. With the goods wagon removed the ET crew cut away at what no longer resembled a car. Given an opening, the driver even managed to slide himself out. Although clearly shocked and shaken he walked to the waiting ambulance, no doubt counting his blessings. A policeman who accompanied him to hospital, just to make sure he was all right, probably thought he was just arsehole lucky.

Rubber suits!

Chemical incidents were increasing in frequency due to the growth in the use, and transportation, of hazardous substances. It was to become a regular feature of our work. We would often have to work in unpleasant and stressful conditions. In the early seventies it was only the ETs that carried Draeger suits. These suits afforded the full body protection that many of these incidents demanded. They were an all in-one rubber suit (identical to a diver's dry suit) with gas tight collar and cuffs. They were designed to protect the wearer when dealing with the release of refrigerants, especially ammonia, used in cold stores. Such leakages were particularly unpleasant because of ammonia's affinity for water. Any unprotected moist or wet part of a body would be subjected to its corrosive attack. Working in these suits, particularly in warm or hot weather, was very demanding. Dehydration could be a real problem if you worked too long particularly whilst undertaking strenuous tasks. As each ET only carried four suits, larger chemical spillages or leakages would normally require the attendance of two or more ETs. In this way crews were not over-exposed to these undesirable side effects.

At an incident in West Norwood two very attractive young women found that the suits had quite a titillating and magnetic effect. Responding to a call to a spillage of cleaning fluid in a dry-cleaning store in Norwood High Street, Norwood's crews, protected by their BA sets, were already dealing with the spillage. Norwood's governor had asked the ET crew to stand-by just in case of a problem. With a fellow crew member I had rigged in my Draeger suit en route and we now stood encased in rubber with just our faces exposed waiting casually on the pavement near to the affected premises. The two young ladies in question lived over the shop. They had been evacuated and were waiting in the street for the situation to be resolved. Both in their early twenties, slim, and very good-looking one was dressed in a mini skirt and the other in (very) hot pants. They were both in a playful mood and, apparently fascinated by the suits, came over to chat with the two of us. After some flirtatious small talk they got down to serious business, and asked if we would like to come back to their flat after we finished work. They left us in no doubt that they were not just interested in the conversation and we were definitely on a promise. Our mutual excitement was obvious as we anticipated how the evening might pan out. Their sexy whispered tones were combined with them gently touching our rubber suits. They caressed the rubber, sensing its smoothness and traced their delicate fingers along the welded joints at the arms and wrists. We were getting excited too and promised them we would return later, meanwhile what would we tell our respective wives? Probably another overtime shout when we would eventually arrive home later that night.

With all the arrangements made for our rendezvous, in passing the girls said, "Please don't forget your rubber suits."

"Sorry love, can't do that." I replied, "The suits have to stay on the engine." The gleam in their eyes vanished, as their hoped-for excitement at fulfilling their rubber fetish vaporised. So did our promiscuous evening. *Eh enfin, c'est la vie.*

All in the mind!

Wearing full protective clothing not only had the occasional strange effect on others, it affected us as well. Attending a major chemical spillage in an industrial estate in East London I was riding in charge of Lambeth's ET leading a four-man crew. We were working to neutralise a toxic leakage from damaged forty-gallon steel drums that had fallen from a freight container. The crews attending were working under the direction of the Brigade's Scientific Advisor. He had instructed us to mix a special ash in with the noxious fuming substance and thereby make it safe. Essentially it was like mixing cement.

However, the weather was really warm and the four-hundred-pound drums had to be manhandled away from the contaminated area. Then the fifty-pound bags of ash could be poured around the spillage, initially to contain it and then mix with it to counteract its effect. The gooey mix was then shovelled into bags to be taken away for safe disposal at a landfill site. All this was hot work and we probably worked longer than we should have done even though there was a second ET crew, in full protective clothing, standing by in case of an emergency. With the task completed we were decontaminated and finally got out of our suits after possibly forty-five minutes' strenuous work. Although tired we felt no immediate ill effects and, now released from the incident, I told the driver to take us home.

It was en route back to Lambeth that I started to feel headachy and generally unwell. As I was not feeling too good, I asked the other three guys how they were feeling. All said they had similar symptoms and so, not wanting to take a chance, I told the driver to take us to the nearest hospital, which happened to be St Bartholomew's. This was not a good move in the opinion of the senior officer who had been in charge of the incident. For although we were all considered to be suffering from the effects of dehydration due to working very hard in the enclosed suits, none of us had required any medical treatment other than to be given some saline drinks, which tasted foul. But it was not as bad as the taste I had in my mouth after receiving a severe bollocking, over the phone, from that very same officer. It seemed he felt we had dropped him in the mire with my unannounced detour to St Bart's. The inquiry was not over yet either. Separate accident reports had to be completed for each of us and an investigation carried out, because of our hospital visit. Maybe I would have been better off just coming back to Lambeth with the crew and then collapsing! It would certainly have resulted in much less paperwork. Just to add insult to injury, the Red Watch Station Officer, a certain "Bill" Butler, and our Governor had a lively, if not heated, exchange of views as Bill was of the very strong opinion that we had only suffered psychosomatic effects (which I had to look up in the dictionary) and I had grossly over-reacted. Bless him, our Governor, Dave Aldrich, was not having any of that, nor would he allow Bill to demean anyone on his watch; so their row continued to reverberate along Lambeth's first floor, even as I was going home at the end of this "win some-lose some" day shift!

Terrorists Attacks

The "Troubles" as they were known came to London in October 1971 when the Post Office Tower (now called the BT Tower) was an IRA terrorist target. The bombing, although not resulting in any fatalities, did cause the closure of the building to the general public for many years to come. Like so many others I watched these events unfold on national and local news. However, the threat of becoming caught up in this new breed of incident was not only promoting discussion and speculation amongst station personnel, it was also increasing the concerns of our wives, partners and families. As it seemed the IRA could make an attack on any high-profile London landmark, most of us when on duty were far more concerned about our other halves, many of them worked in the capital and could become an innocent victim of this hate campaign.

The bombing of Old Bailey law courts, the heart of the British justice system in March 1973, marked a dramatic shift in the tactics of the IRA in their attempts to bomb their way to achieve their political ends. The IRA exploded two car bombs in the heart of London and injured over two hundred innocents. Sadly, one man died, although not through the direct impact of the bombing but from a fatal heart attack. The bombers had callously chosen a day when thousands of commuters were forced to drive into central London because strikes had hit the capital's public transport services.

It was to be St Bart's that bore the brunt of the one hundred and sixty or so patients that were either taken there or who made their own way to the hospital's emergency treatment department. The hospital had had no warning of the bombing or of the impending arrival of so many patients. Accordingly its procedures for implementing a major accident plan could not be used. Most of the walking wounded required treatment for cuts and abrasions, but nineteen individuals were admitted and nine required surgery.

The following year the IRA attacked Earls Court whilst the Ideal Home Exhibition was being held. Placing a large explosive device under an escalator, they succeeded in injuring seventy people who were either working or visiting Earls Court. Four of them lost limbs in this explosion. The IRA brought nine separate bombings to the capital during the whole of the 1970s. But only a year would pass before I would personally witness the devastation that these evil people could wreak. I would thus become involved in the fight to save one of the world's most recognised buildings.

Chapter 10

Promotion Ladder

Sub Officer

The birth of my first child, Liam, in January 1974 was, and remains, an incredibly moving and memorable event. I watched him come into the world, whilst my wife tried to crush my hand in hers as she was encouraged by the hospital midwife to make that final life-giving push. After the initial euphoria the responsibility of parenthood soon hit home, as did the fact that with my wife bringing up a baby, the meagre wage of a Leading Fireman was not going to go very far. I was still working part-time, now as a removal man to make ends meet, but the two pounds fifty pence per day, for eight hours, was close to slave labour and it was not something I wished to make a career of.

I had secured my Sub Officer's written exam at my second attempt the previous year. I then passed the practical examination, despite having stage fright when it came to reciting, word-prefect the flow of oxygen through a Proto BA set to the examiner! Also, the practical exam required a high degree of understanding when it came to conducting "Squad drill" and an in-depth knowledge when giving a lecture on an item of equipment chosen from a list prepared by the examiners. With both these examinations under my belt I was ready to apply for the promotion interview, which I did with a fair degree of confidence because of the excellent report that I had received both from my Watch Governor at Lambeth and the Watch ADO, both of whom had recommended me for promotion to Sub Officer.

The interview went well, at least from my point of view, and this time there was no waiting. As soon as the results were published, I was promoted and on my way back to Southwark. I was beginning to feel like a yo-yo, my only two permanent stations having been Lambeth and Southwark. Now I was bouncing my way back there again. Bouncing in more ways than one too. I had put on considerable weight, in fact three and a half stone since passing out of training school. I was becoming a fatty and I decided enough was enough so started to jog. I would keep up the jogging until I retired. But I wouldn't see eleven stone again!

Most of the "old" Southwark White Watch had now moved on to pastures new. The Sub Officer had been promoted to Station Officer and my old Governor, who still had drinking issues, was transferred to Clapham, the Divisional Headquarters, so senior officers could keep an eye on him. Only three firemen from the original White Watch remained. They now had a Station

Officer transferred in from the White Watch at Old Kent Road; a rather old and tired Leading Fireman; and some new blood, recruits who had been posted to the station during the time I was at Lambeth.

When I went to the Divisional Headquarters for the presentation of my new rank markings, I was told by the senior officer making the presentation that I had been selected for Southwark for a special reason. He left me to determine what that reason was. It didn't take too long for me to find out. My new Governor had had some problems running the watch at the Old Kent Road. In fact the watch, it appeared, was running him. The firemen there were nearly all old hands, at least ten-year service men, and they took great delight in finding new ways to wind up their Governor. The last straw came when they saw a helicopter go past the station, heading down the Old Kent Road, on a low loader. Taking note of the telephone contact number on the side of the "chopper" they made arrangements for the company to ring their Governor in the belief that he was the Brigade's "chopper" supremo, and that the Brigade was going to start up a Helicopter Division for Search and Rescue. Pretending to be the Governor, one of the wags asked if the Company Chairman would contact him to discuss the viability of the Company tendering for this innovative contract work. When this Station Officer was next on duty the Chairman duly rang the station and asked for the Station Officer by name. The poor Station Officer immediately thought that the Chairman was just another fireman from a local station and told him in no uncertain terms exactly what he could do with his helicopter, with or without the rotor blades turning. The Chairman angrily threatened to do exactly the same to the now bewildered Station Officer before hanging up and making an official complaint to the Brigade. The watch stayed put but he was posted to Southwark, with, hopefully, a more manageable watch. I was sent there to support him, starting on 1st June 1974.

End of an era

The shutters came down on Lambeth's control room after thirty years of continuous mobilising. It was the main control room for central London throughout my service. It had enlivened many a quiet night duty at Lambeth when everything was going out except the fire engine I was riding and I would go down to see what was going on elsewhere. From 1939 this subterranean control room was at the forefront of dispatching fire engines to nine-nine-nine calls. The original wartime control was totally remodelled and rebuilt in 1965 with the creation of the Greater London Council. I was there in 1966 as a door opener for Her Majesty the Queen when she formally reopened the Control Room at the Brigade's Centenary Review.

During my early service in the brigade Lambeth control had mobilised all central London stations and co-ordinated major incidents anywhere in the Brigade area. I had enjoyed the privilege of being taken under the wing of retired firemen, now turned control officers, who had allowed me, in less stressful times, into their sanctum to learn a little of their job. I had also witnessed from the visitors' gallery large scale mobilising to major fires and the professionalism and calm demeanour that control officers displayed in, sometimes, the most distressing of circumstances.

Now its staff were to be dispersed to the three remaining control rooms, with Lambeth control's mobilising area being absorbed by them. Southwark would in future be mobilised by the Control staff at the Croydon control room, who were responsible for mobilising all stations south of the River Thames. The other two control rooms were located at Wembley, the old Middlesex Fire Brigade control room, and Stratford, the former West Ham Fire Brigade control. Wembley covered the west of London whilst Stratford mobilised the east. A central mobilising control would eventually return to Lambeth and, once again, I would play a small part in its opening ceremony. But for now it was an end of an era as the other three controls started to mobilise their additional new charges.

Palace of Westminster

The prolonged and concerted efforts by the Provisional IRA to bomb their way towards a political settlement revolving around the Irish "troubles" had deadly effect. Their actions brought the emergency services into the capital's front line because of their continuing and indiscriminate bombing of high profile or high value targets. Attacks on The Old Bailey, New Scotland Yard and the Hyde Park terrorist attack (where both troopers and horses from the Blues and Royals Regiment were killed and maimed) all brought about heightened tension within the Capital city and beyond. Accordingly London's security precautions were increased and these would become a part of everyday life for years to come. In fact they would remain in place, and evolve, right up to the present day and will no doubt continue into the foreseeable future.

On the 17th June 1974 and 17 days after my arrival at Southwark the IRA made an audacious terrorist attack on the seat of British government. Just before 9am a powerful twenty-pound explosive device shattered the normal tranquillity of the Westminster Hall, in the Palace of Westminster, and brought additional chaos to the morning rush hour. The national press was to describe the attack as, "One of the deadliest bombings of the IRA's mainland campaign."

Despite the reverberating sound of the explosion through Parliament and Parliament Square's surrounding area there was no indication of the drama that was unfolding for us, until Southwark's station bells rang out their alarm some ten minutes later. Westminster, Soho and Lambeth's appliances, totalling eight in all, had made up the initial attendance to this historic and national heritage site. It was, alongside Buckingham Palace, one of the Brigade's most high-profile special risks. Westminster and Lambeth fire station crews both heard the sound of the deafening explosion. They knew it sounded close and were impatiently waiting to find out to just where they would be ordered. Adrenaline was pumping through the veins of these crews as they tried to imagine the carnage that the terrorists had unleashed on the capital this time. The ringing of station alarm bells and the teleprinter ordering soon brought the answer;

Westminster Hall had been the terrorists' target and the crews now had to deal with the consequences of those vicious actions. Suddenly the dominant sound pervading Westminster was the cacophony of emergency vehicle two-tone horns filling the air with their characteristic warning sound as they raced to the scene. Fire engines, ambulances and police cars were all converging on a common destination and one of the world's most famous landmarks. Smoke was already rising into the morning sky as Westminster's appliances headed to the scene via Victoria Street, Lambeth's machines crossing Lambeth Brigade and Soho's crews speeding down Whitehall.

The scale of the explosion and the first signs of the resultant fire left the officer in charge of Westminster fire station in no doubt that without immediate reinforcements he would not be able to contain the blaze. Even before his arrival he made "Pumps twelve BA required." Pulling into the Palace of Westminster courtyard he was confronted by a serious blaze that had taken hold in the north-east wing of Westminster Hall. Smoke was billowing from the gothic windows and the massive roof timbers were already alight. The great hall was filled with the dust of centuries together with smoke drifting in from the side annexe to the hall where the device had been planted. Among the organised chaos of the early stages of evacuation, the task of assessing the situation and liaising with other emergency services the officer in charge's plan of attack started to unfold. His initial plan of attack was put into action as Westminster and Lambeth's crews started to pitch their wheeled escapes to the upper floors. Soho crews donned their breathing apparatus sets, water supplies were secured and jets of water were got ready to bring into play. Liaison with the police responsible for the security of the Palace of Westminster tried to establish whether people were still inside the Great Hall and, if so, who and where?

Southwark's PE and pump formed part of the make-up and joined the second wave of attack. Our engines raced through the Elephant and Castle and on towards Westminster, eager to join in the fray. Traffic had been brought to a standstill around County Hall and Waterloo station as the police closed Westminster Bridge to all traffic. Our appliances weaved their way through the traffic in the heavy congestion, that was rapidly getting worse by the minute, by making use of whatever clear stretches of the opposite side of the road the drivers could find. The sound of me ringing the fire engine bell marking our progress.

Only fourteen minutes after the initial call we passed through the police cordon on the south side of Westminster Brigade. We had a strange but uninterrupted view of Big Ben and the Palaces of Westminster and not of the dramatic scenes that were being played out behind them. We could only see the vast column of smoke rising skyward, immediately behind the House of Commons. Westminster Bridge was completely closed to all but emergency vehicles and it was completely empty save for our two engines. Reaching the north side, and to our left, we saw the concerted attack that had already been made by the first crews to arrive. Escape and extension ladders had been pitched to the upper floor windows, firemen were dragging the heavy hose lines, crews in BA were entering the smoke-logged Great Hall's northern corner. Turntable ladders were positioned; ready to direct their monitors on to the roof, as thick brown smoke was giving way to flames breaking through the ancient slate roof and shattered windows.

Westminster's Station Officer was still in charge and could be seen standing in front of the Great Hall's historic wooden main entrance doors directing operations and dealing with the multitude of tasks that befalls any officer in this type of situation. The fire was being fought both from the inside together with jets directed into the burning building from vantage points on ladders outside. I reported and was told to make an attack internally, via the corner turret, with our PE crew backing us up. We were also to search the offices off the stone spiral staircase that led to an access door into the roof void where fire had been seen to be taking a strong hold. Wearing our Proto oxygen sets we started to climb the stone spiral steps with the PE crew feeding our hose line in as far as they could without the aid of BA. The first few feet were relatively smoke-free and progress was swift especially as the PE crew was lightening the hose-line and feeding it through. From the first-floor level we met the heat barrier and proceeded more cautiously, our exposed ears starting to tingle under the effects of the heat and hot gases. The smoke was still not thick and dense and it was rather like navigating through fog. Off the staircase were small storerooms and offices; each had to be checked as we passed, a chalk mark left on the door to indicate it had been searched. The distance between floors was unusual. Each ceiling was about fifteen feet from the floor. By the second floor, some thirty feet up the staircase, the heat now combined with thick smoke. We could feel the heat reflected off the walls and, even more worryingly, the stairs. Stone staircases that are involved in fire where cooling water is applied may result in severe spalling of the stonework. In certain circumstances this can lead to chronic structural weakening, and ultimately its collapse. We did not know if these were the conditions here as this was only something we had read about in the Manuals of Firemanship. This was our first experience of meeting such conditions and we were, to say the least, concerned. The fact that stonework was falling off the walls did little to boost our confidence but we maintained our progress upward. At the third floor level we started ventilating as we went and both the heat and the smoke eased to more tolerable levels but the strain of pulling and manoeuvring the heavy hose-line up forty-five feet of winding staircase was taking its toll, despite the best efforts of the PE crew to lessen our load.

The oxygen levels in our BA sets were now getting low and, even if we made the top floor, we would not have sufficient oxygen supply to make it back to fresh air. Leaving the hose line on the staircase we made our way to the top, and final level to see what access into the roof void was possible. There was none but neither had the fire broken through into the turret. The heat we experienced was from the hot gases being forced through ventilation ducts, which had also allowed the smoke to fill the turret. With one of the crew's oxygen supply now really low we retraced our steps back down the staircase, his low cylinder pressure-warning whistle starting to sound as we reached the first floor. Exiting, with only minutes to spare, we collected our tallies from the BA control point and reported our findings.

Although the fire was now contained the crews were still working hard to minimise further damage from fire spread. Fire had broken out in the roof void and, after removing our BA sets, we were set to get to work on the outside of the Great Hall's roof. The early frantic activity had now given way to a more steady pace. Crews were isolating and investigating hot spots and cutting away and tackling pockets of fire within the vaulted ceiling space and areas of the roof void.

With an escape ladder pitched to the north wall, under the watchful gaze of Oliver Cromwell's statue, our crew of four climbed over the parapet before pitching hook ladders that would enable us to work on the slated roof. The individual slates were enormous, nearly two feet wide, three feet long and each weighing about seventy-five pounds. Smoke was percolating from between the slates and the orange glow of smouldering timber could be seen near the ridge of the roof. The slates had to be removed and handled carefully. Not only were they original and therefore valuable, but if one fell from the roof its weight could smash into the escape ladder and break it or, worse, hit poor old Oliver and do to him what he did to Charles the First; knock his block off! With openings made into the roof, exposing the timbers, steady progress was made extinguishing the small fires which had started in the years of accumulated debris laying between the slate battens and that had now spread to the timber roof trusses. Four hours after arriving at the scene, with our task still unfinished, we were relieved by another crew and told to make our way back to Southwark. Waiting on Southwark's teleprinter was the "stop" message from the fire at Westminster Hall; twelve jets and two turntable ladder monitors had been needed to extinguish the blaze and a total of forty BA sets were used. Another job done and dusted – or so we thought?

On the 13 February 1975 I received a telephone call from Brigade Headquarters to confirm I had led my crews at the Westminster Hall fire and were any of the crews on duty that day? I said, "Yes" to both and was told to get the pump over to Brigade Headquarters by lunchtime. When I asked why I was told, "You and your crew are to be presented to the Queen." "OK," I said, thinking that this was a wind up. I rang Division and asked what they knew about the afternoon's excursion and they confirmed that we and Lambeth's pump crew were on this Royal duty. Practical jokes were a way of life in the Brigade and the lads were as sceptical, as me, especially as it called for some rapid "bull" to press our uniforms and shine our shoes. Only after they saw me getting out my best uniform and buffing my parade shoes did the penny finally drop; this is for real.

That February day the Queen was to tour the headquarters of the Metropolitan Police, London Ambulance Service and the Brigade to personally pay tribute to the emergency services involved in dealing with the aftermath of the recent terrorist bombing campaign. We were to be one of eight London Fire Brigade crews that were to represent all those who had been involved with terrorist incidents. Although we felt honoured to be selected, we were also conscious that we had not, so far had, to deal with the horror and human misery that some of the Brigade's crews had had to face. I had not had to confront the dreadfulness of mass or individual slaughter and confront the fear of knowing that my crew might be next, drawn into a trap, targeted by a secondary device (and thus pay the ultimate sacrifice of death or maiming) all in the line of duty. Whilst I had not seen first-hand the awful injuries inflicted by one human on another I was naturally appalled at the possibility. I knew I was lucky and wanted it to stay that way.

Like four bright new pins we arrived at Brigade Headquarters at the allotted time and joined the other seven crews for a briefing in the Officers' Club (a hallowed haven at Brigade Headquarters) where mere mortals like ourselves were normally denied access. The Deputy Chief gave the briefing so we knew this was high profile stuff. After a warm and genuine welcome he told us that we would stand informally in individual crews. The Chief would introduce the Queen, in turn, to each group and she would spend a short time with each crew before moving onto the next. He said, or rather insisted, "You will address the Queen as *Your Majesty* when she first speaks to you and after you will call her Mam. That's Mam as in Spam. You do not speak to her unless she speaks to you. Clear?"

Eight crews from London central divisions, those that had first-hand personal dealings with the bombing, waited in anticipation for the royal guest. Paddington, Knightsbridge, Chelsea and Westminster crews represented the A Division. Clerkenwell and Barbican from the C Division, whilst Lambeth and Southwark represented the B Division. Precisely at the allotted time the Queen's car arrived at the Headquarters main entrance and was welcomed by the Chief Officer, Joe Milner. Lambeth fire station's crews, dressed in their fire gear, formed a guard of honour that directed the Queen towards the reception area and the waiting gathering. Her Majesty looked vibrant and chirpy as she entered the Officers' Club smiling and cheerful. It was not a sombre occasion but whilst we were naturally nervous, she moved from group to group putting us at ease with well-informed questions. Dressed in a shapely coat with mink fur collar and fur lined cuffs, smart hat and carrying, of course, her trademark handbag, she moved effortlessly between the various crews with the Chief acting as host and escort. He introduced each station represented and then remained in the background whilst those present savoured the moment of having this special audience with the Queen.

No doubt her question format was probably the same for all three visits she was making that day, meeting London's emergency service crews. Nevertheless she possessed a remarkable gift and demonstrated a presence of being genuinely interested in what stories each group had to tell and enjoying the humour that makes dealing with such incidents possible. She left all of us with a warm and friendly smile before moving on to repeat the process all over again. With no formal speeches, forty-five minutes later the Chief escorted Her Majesty back to the Royal car and she was gone, to the next gathering of emergency crews, eager to tell their stories and, hopefully, to cherish the occasion of her visit.

Reliefs

A relief ordering to a fire or other incident was generally the bane of any fireman's life. It was, however, a necessary part of the job, if a lot less exciting and exhilarating than actually attending an incident from its start, or as it grew and demanded ever-greater resources to deal with it. Reliefs might last for days, and in some cases weeks, as crews continued damping down until it was certain that every vestige of fire or possible source of re-ignition was properly extinguished. It was normal practice that relief orderings only involved pumps and would last from three to four hours at a time, until (you yourself were relieved or) the incident was finally closed down. It was also very common that the deputy would be ordered to ride the pump whilst the officer in charge of the station remained behind to ride the Pump Escape. The graveyard shift was normally after 2am when, on a cold winter's night, you had the unenviable task of pouring water onto some pile of smouldering waste paper, or the steaming remains of a warehouse that had collapsed in on itself after a serious fire. But it was a job that had to be done, even though crews from some stations would just stay put in the comfort of their engine, hoping nothing would ignite whilst they were there and wait for the next relief pump to arrive in a few hours' time!

Some relief orderings could be far more interesting and informative and they allowed me to study the anatomy of a fire at a controlled and more leisurely pace. One came within my first couple of months back at Southwark and had occurred in a flat in the back streets of Bermondsey not far from Tower Bridge. It had been a fatal fire in a tenement block, a building that had changed little since it was built some eighty years earlier. The incident had occurred before the change of watch and now the day watch crews wanted a relief pump in attendance rather than them having to wait for the police surgeon to arrive. I was ordered with Southwark's pump as an immediate relief about thirty minutes into my night shift.

The red brick tenement building gave no clues as to what had happened earlier in the afternoon. Nor did the few people passing by take any interest in the fire engines that were frequent visitors to this street. Climbing up the four floors to the top floor and entering the flat I met the off going Station Officer whose crews had two hours ago crawled along a dark hallway and into a small, sparsely furnished living room. In the room, which was lit only by the flickering light of the smouldering mattress, they saw the body.

I knew the Red Watch Station Officer from standing-by at his station. He told me that the Brigade photographer had taken all the photographs required for the coroner but the Police surgeon was delayed dealing with another death elsewhere. "There is some stuff to learn here Pikey boy, have a look around while you're waiting and give me a ring tomorrow when you come back on duty and we will compare notes." With that he left with his crew.

The flat was squalid and smelt of dried human waste. The odour in the room was only marginally better. Food decaying in the hallway and the smell of urine added a sharp, unpleasant character to the smell of death in the room. The remains of the man lay across a stained, burned double mattress on the floor. Water from the hose reel jet, used to extinguish the fire and the man, still marked the bare timber floor, but the tell-tale charring of a burnt wire lead back to an electrical socket that was probably the same one installed when electricity was first put into the flats. Food stains formed a small circle on the floor near the mattress and in the debris outside the front door was a single ring electric fire, plus a stained saucepan next to a raised metal grill. In the room were numerous empty bottles of cheap "wino" port. The single naked light bulb in the room was still intact but was stained black and had melted, forming a strange hanging globule. A look at the old fuse box showed that the fuses had been removed and replaced by strong wire wound around contact points. The worst charring on the mattress was on the side nearest the round mark on the floor and the man was laying on his back facing the ceiling. One half of his body was badly burned whilst the other side was undamaged, consistent with the burning on the mattress. The remains of a plug were still in the socket with its charred exposed bare wires hanging down to the skirting board below it. I concluded that the man had used an electric fire as his cooking stove and put the grill over it to support the saucepan. He had probably been cooking, having been drinking or was already drunk. The flex leading to the fire had got caught under the mattress and had most likely overheated. Not having any fuses meant that the cable would continue to overheat, allowing the mattress to smoulder and then ignite. The light bulb indicated that a slow build-up of heat had occurred and this was supported by the staining on the closed windows in the flat. The man was either overcome by the smoke or too drunk to get off the burning mattress.

The next evening I rang the Station Officer and was told, "Nice job, except for one thing? You didn't notice the remains of the man's pipe still in his burned left hand, but not bad all the same." It was a valuable lesson for me. In the future I must consider every possibility and carefully study the evidence for all possible clues and not just focus on the obvious.

Station closure

The decision to close Southwark fire station had been taken some years earlier when the approval to relocate Cannon Street fire station to Dowgate, in Upper Thames Street, was given full Council approval after being agreed by the GLC's Fire Brigade Committee. Even the Fire Brigades Union had not lodged objections, taking at face value the case put forward by the Brigade's principal management.

I had only just got there and this decision could not be right, could it? I became a man on a mission. Not only was I disappointed by the decision I was angry too. I liked Southwark fire station but my feelings were based on far more than just sentimentality or emotion alone. The case to close Southwark was clearly flawed. But my problem was proving it and not only convincing the Brigade's principal management that they had got it wrong but to get the policy, approved by the GLC's parliament, changed. I also had to get the Fire Brigades Union back on our side and to fight to keep Southwark fire station open. The decision had been on the stocks for a few years but nobody had ever thought to fight the pronouncement. I only had until the middle of next year (1975) before Southwark's appliance doors would shut forever. The case for closing the station was that the surrounding fire stations would adequately cover Southwark's fire station ground without any detrimental effect. Many had uttered mumblings that they felt this to be untrue but no one had put their head above the parapet to say so publicly, until now.

My first port of call was to challenge the Fire Brigades Unions' agreement on the closure. I was already the station Union representative and had built up a good rapport with both our Divisional Secretary and many of the other station representatives. I got a more than sympathetic hearing at the next Divisional committee meeting and the Executive member who attended was left in no doubt at the level of concern at the Council's decision to close Southwark, but of even greater concern was the Regional Committee's lack of opposition to fight this proposal. A motion was unanimously passed condemning the decision and demanding an urgent review by the London Regional Committee. In private, and after the meeting, the executive member told me that there would have to be considerable public and political support if there was to be the remotest chance of reversing the closure decision. However, and unusually, I was invited to attend the next full meeting of the Regional Committee and allowed to put the case for retaining the station. I had no hard evidence then, just a strong conviction that the decision was flawed. I, apparently, spoke eloquently and with considerable passion. I was asked to leave the room whilst the topic was debated. I returned to be told that, subject to detailed evidence being provided which showed there was reasonable doubt about the Council's decision, the London Region would oppose the closure of Southwark. So no pressure there then!

I called for a station branch meeting the following week and was amazed by the turnout. Normally it was hard getting even the on-duty watch to attend these meetings. There was now universal agreement that station personnel would actively fight the closure, but how? The three watch Station Officers at Southwark were all in the National Association of Fire Officers (NAFO) and although sympathetic they were not going to get actively involved fighting alongside the Union; sad but true. It was the way with NAFO members, especially when it came to the national firemen's strike a couple of years later. They would happily accept the wage increase that the strike brought about whilst actually doing nothing to win it.

I was studying for my Station Officer's examinations at this time, not doing very well but having a go. By chance the day release course had recently covered the national Standards of Fire Cover. These standards are applied by all UK fire brigades to determine how many fire engines are required to attend the different risk categories, which were graded A (highest) to D (lowest) and how long each engine must take to arrive at the scene of a fire. (These standards only applied to fire calls and not to special service calls.) Ninety-five per cent of Southwark's ground had been categorised by the Brigade as A risk. All calls to an A risk required two appliances to arrive in five minutes and the third within eight, three appliances in total from the time that a "999" call is made.

Southwark had the smallest station ground in the whole of the B division, in fact one of the smallest in the whole brigade. But it was in the top ten busiest stations in the Greater London area, attending nearly two thousand calls the previous year. The proposal was that Dowgate's new station ground, even though the station was north of the river, would take about one-third of Southwark's existing ground. Revised station boundaries would see the remainder of the ground divided between Lambeth, Dockhead and Old Kent Road stations. It was difficult to see the logic of closing the two stations, on opposite sides of the Thames, and replacing them with just one new station on the northern shore. Southwark and London bridges were heavily used both am and pm and they were the most direct routes to get to Southwark's area on the south of the river by Dowgate's fire engine crew.

I approached both the local press and our nearby community groups and they gave unswerving support for retaining the station. Tenant and trade associations were also mobilised to add their considerable weight in applying local political pressure. But it was our closest neighbours, operating out of a former corner shop, where the campaign really got its first big break. They were the recently formed North Southwark Community Development Group, and were in the main former graduates and left-wing political activists. (They would describe themselves as "radical" but militant would be a far more apt description.) This group was looking to make waves in what they saw as the political "status quo." Southwark fire station's closure provided them with an ideal platform on which to get some local "cred" whilst at the same time fighting what they saw as the oppressive Tory GLC regime. I could not care less about their politics. They were willing to help and that was fine by me. They took our campaign to their hearts and some of their activist ideas were a real tour-de-force. Their wide network of local political connections reached right into the heart of Southwark Borough Council and other London-wide Labour pressure groups.

My own contacts with scores of local publicans, through distributing the Benevolent Fund collecting boxes, brought about an amazing publicity campaign that covered over one hundred pubs in the immediate Southwark area. The public was getting increasingly vocal, some quite forcibly. The fight was gaining momentum but was still playing the emotion card, and not utilising the hard facts that would be necessary, if the Brigade's principal management would even contemplate a change of policy.

In September I wrote to the in-house magazine with a hard-hitting letter questioning the closure. The editor, Gordon White, placed the letter as the lead article in the Dear Editor column. It was printed in full and I expressed the feelings of the "condemned man" requesting my last few words, or in my case, questions. The letter found favour in a number of surprising quarters and again a number of senior officers came out of the woodwork to voice their support for the campaign, albeit privately. Or so I thought.

There is much truth in the saying; "It's not what you know, it's who you know." I found that after my letter appeared in the magazine that I had a willing ally ("a mole") in the Brigade's card index section, the group responsible for ensuring that the standards of fire cover were monitored and maintained. It had been their original work that meant that the proposals for the revision of Southwark's station boundaries met with high-level approval. The phone call, when it came through, suggested I might like to go for a drink after work and learn something to my, or rather the station's, advantage. So over a couple of pints I met this new found friend in a quiet corner of a pub in Lower Marsh, near Waterloo station. I was told that some of the planning for the station closure was not as detailed as was thought. It could be, in fact, seriously flawed. Then to my amazement he produced a copy of a map showing Southwark and its surrounding stations and passed it to me in a copy of that day's *Evening News*. I was unable to retain the map but it was clear that there were central parts of Southwark's ground that had not been subject to detailed "timed runs." It was left to someone's judgement, using other timed data on the map, if attendance to a particular street or road could be met within the criteria or not. My own thoughts were, that they did not. I was then told exactly how the Brigade conducts its timed runs in order to determine its level of fire cover. Contrary to widely held belief, including mine, fire engines were not used to test and time routes. Cars were used driving to the different locations. I reluctantly returned the map but not before I made a mental note of the questionable areas that needed further exploration.

Armed with this invaluable data I set about conducting our own timed runs. Over a weekend duty, when the roads were quieter, my Station Officer allowed me and another fireman out of the station on our clandestine quest. Using the Dowgate construction site, where the new station was being built, as our starting point we conducted separate timed runs to over thirty locations on Southwark's ground. This process was then repeated from Lambeth, Dockhead and some from Old Kent Road, the most distant of the three stations. According to the Brigade's own rules a car is driven at thirty miles per hour from a fire station to a determined point and the time recorded on an "accurate" stopwatch. (My mole had sent me two such stopwatches from their store.) The second stopwatch is used to record any delay because of traffic lights set on red. (Although fire engines are allowed to pass red lights on emergency calls.) The stopping time was subtracted from the running time and the end result was the attendance time. It was that simple. Our timed runs took the whole of Saturday and Sunday and quite a considerable amount of petrol, paid for by a whip round on the watch. But the results were worth all the effort and also very encouraging.

Other sources of information were coming from the most surprising of places. Unsigned papers, sent from the GLC's Traffic Management Division at County Hall, provided detailed traffic flows on all the major routes into our station's ground, plus highlighting the congestion hot spots that surrounding stations would have problems with. The "lefties" on the corner had not been sitting on their laurels either. Both the national press and the local BBC and ITV television news were showing an interest in our plight and providing coverage. So had the Editor of the *"London Fireman"* who had come to the station with a photographer and wrote his own story for the magazine. It was a two-page spread under the banner headline "Southwark shutdown puzzles firemen." It was published in the December issue of the magazine, diplomatically however not under his name. He had either got himself into hot water for printing the story or someone higher had approved its publication!

Southwark fire station also had a vast building fire safety inspection programme under the London Building Acts. (This was fire safety legislation that existed then in the former London County Council area and which the Brigade had responsibility for policing and reporting upon, particularly any infringements.) It was so large that other stations regularly had to assist in our inspection process to complete the annual programme on time. These and other tests and inspections, such as "dry riser tests", all added to the considerable weight of information and data that appeared not to have been previously considered, but now made a powerful argument for reviewing the decision, if not overturning it completely. But the real thrust of our case rested on the fact that whilst some of the ground could indeed be covered by the surrounding stations there remained a considerable central core where the surrounding appliances could not meet the required attendance standards if Southwark was closed.

It was then that those nights I had spent in Lambeth's control room helped deliver the "coup-de-grace" to the Brigade's case for Southwark's closure. When the original decision to close Southwark was made both it and Cannon Street (Dowgate) were mobilised by Lambeth control. Lambeth had now closed and Croydon control mobilised Southwark and Stratford would mobilise Dowgate. But all nine-nine-nine calls made on Southwark's ground were routed through BT's "South Bank" exchange to Croydon for actioning. If Southwark closed this would still be the case but Croydon would have to pass the call to Stratford in order that Dowgate could be mobilised to a nine-nine-nine call on its own ground, but south of the river! Where this happens the Brigade policy was that one minute must be added to the attendance time for "call handling and transfer time." An Area Controller at Croydon, who became a close friend when I was at Lambeth, told me of this "fly in the ointment" and this policy shot the

Brigade's case out of the water. The timed runs I had seen on the "secret" map did not take account of this fact and the timed runs that we had recorded from Dowgate that just made five minutes now became six minutes. They did not meet the required standards. The Brigade clearly could not meet its own attendance times if Southwark closed.

I was feeling pleased with myself but from my own Divisional senior officers' point of view I was becoming persona non grata! I was seen as a "lefty" troublemaker as far as they were concerned, at least that was the impression they gave. They also thought that I was fighting a lost cause, and said so, publicly at least.

Having now accumulated all this valuable data it had to be presented in the form of a comprehensive and detailed report. This was something that was new to me and took me totally out of my comfort zone. However, with a few pointers from the tutors at Southwark College and the "lefties" my two digits worked away on the obsolete office typewriter and only after much midnight oil was burned, I completed my fifty-page report. I had not thought to use carbon paper in order to make a copy and naively left the completed tome in our watch drawer when I went off duty on my two days leave. When I returned to duty my report had been confiscated. A Divisional senior officer just happened to be visiting, our drawer apparently flew open and the report fell into his hands. I was so angry, not least because my typing skills were still all fingers and thumbs, well two fingers anyway and that report had been such a labour of love.

However, I had an ace up my sleeve or rather a guardian angel. It was the Chief Whip of the Labour Party. The previous week I had been to see our local Bermondsey MP, whose constituency covered Southwark Fire Station. He was Bob Mellish, the Labour MP who was the Party's current Chief Whip. He was a powerful man within the Labour Party but still in touch with his South London roots, having been born in Deptford over sixty years before. He held his surgeries in the Labour Party offices in Walworth Road, just a stone's throw from the Elephant and Castle. He clearly knew of the proposal to close the station and of the groundswell of public opinion against the closure. He also knew who I was, even though I had made no prior appointment or told him my name. He was a very astute political operator and showed considerable interest in the findings of my report and made notes, particularly on the "black spots" where fire cover was dubious if Southwark fire station was to close. I knew little of this man but was impressed by his ability to absorb the detail and throw penetrating questions at me about the validity of my research and how I had arrived at my conclusions. Seemingly satisfied, he said he would make some inquiries and, without making any promises, said he would be in touch.

I later discovered that Bob Mellish had been appointed by Harold Wilson to be the Parliamentary Secretary to the Treasury before holding other various senior government posts. He certainly came across as a tough, no nonsense cookie, but I didn't realise just how tough. In that week's edition of the *South London Press* the leading headline was "Local MP opposes fire station closure" and a message was left at the station asking me to contact Bob Mellish at his parliamentary office in the House of Commons. When I got through, he asked me to meet him again to discuss some further points from the report. Embarrassingly, I had to tell him that it had been confiscated and it was the only copy. He asked about the circumstance and told me not to worry.

I cannot say what Bob Mellish did or did not do, if anything. But the following day the Divisional Commander arrived at the station, and after the Station Officer went to report to him the Commander came alone into the office and shut the door. He was holding the confiscated report in his hand and after telling me that the information it contained should be restricted to the Brigade he left without another word, clearly irritated at being someone else's messenger.

I did not see Bob Mellish again and he later (1976) fell out of favour with his constituency party, because it had become dominated by left-wingers including many of those from the North Southwark Development Group.

Things moved fast now. I was told by John Lewis, the London Region's national executive officer, that I was to attend Brigade Headquarters the following week to meet with Brigade principal officers at an informal meeting. It may well have been informal for them but it was daunting for me. Three uniformed, high-ranking officers, were seated in an office for what clearly was not meant to be a cosy chat over a nice cup of afternoon tea! It was actually a very short meeting. I was asked by the most senior of the three to outline my objections to the closure, which centred on the standards of fire cover and the Brigade's own questionable data on attendance times, which I said was flawed. Their look said it all, "Who the bloody hell are you to tell us how to do our job?" but they did not actually say so. They thanked me for my attendance and dismissed me with a wave of the hand. John Lewis winked at me as I left the room. He was holding my report in his hands.

No news did not seem good news because the closure deadline was drawing ever closer. Then at the end of the year (1974) the decision was announced that the closure of Southwark Fire Station was to be reviewed. In the following March a further reprieve was given by the Fire Brigades Committee who had postponed any decision on the station until not less than twelve months after the opening of the new Dowgate station.

It had been a very intense few months. At times I doubted my own ability to see the fight through to the end and probably I would not have, had there not been such a genuine and overwhelming desire from the local population to see their fire station retained. Most did not know or care about attendance times; their fire station was part of their community and they did not want to lose it, even if we were noisy occasionally in the wee hours as we turned out, or put out their bonfires on November the fifth because they were just too big! Southwark fire station stayed open. It still remains open today, despite the many subsequent reviews of London's fire cover and the closure of other fire stations. It is an accomplishment that I am very proud of, hopefully for all the right reasons.

In August 1975 Southwark fire station threw open its doors to the local community for an Open Day to celebrate the station's reprieve. It was an outstanding success and various sections of Southwark's neighbourhood came to say, "Thank you" to the firemen for the work they did in saving their fire station. It was reciprocal and I knew it probably better than most. We had some very special guests too that day, the children from the Evelina and Guy's Hospitals. Woolworth had donated toys and other suitable gifts for the children who seemed overawed by the whole occasion. Inevitably we also had the local little "herberts" whose sole purpose was to drive us all mad by continually ringing the appliance bells and sounding the two-tone horns, but it was their fire station after all.

Southwark College

 With the arrival of my second child, Abby, in September 1975 and a take home wage of only two hundred and forty pounds per month, which included overtime and an under-manning allowance, things were getting a bit tight, especially as we had recently moved from Bromley to a newish house in Orpington. I really needed to concentrate on getting my Station Officer's examination under my belt, which was easier said than done.

Since the early 1960s Southwark College, located in the shadows of the Imperial War Museum, had been helping fire brigade personnel get through their statutory fire service examinations and I had benefited previously from the tutors' teaching skills. The college was formally Kennington College before it re-invented itself and began preparing students nationwide for a range of learning in relation to Fire and Health & Safety courses.

I managed to get a place on the Sub Officer's day release course, which only took sixty students a year, and have no doubt that it got me through the written examination. Now I was benefiting again, having secured a place on the Station Officer's written examination course. But despite the best efforts of the experienced tutorial team I failed to pass the examination at my first attempt. The examination was a full one-day affair made up of separate papers covering the four subject areas. Whilst I could at least understand two of the papers, sciences/hydraulics and legislation/fire prevention were way out of my league. I had struggled all year to get to grips with calculating formulae to determine specific gravity, whilst vapour density had me scratching my head. When it came to the periodic table and the reaction of substances expressed in their chemical formulae a mist would come down before my eyes. The reaction of water on hot magnesium may well be represented by the equation;

$$Mg + H_2O = MgO + H_2 \text{ and } 8,555 \text{ B.Th.U}$$

But it meant nothing to me! So I was not surprised when my Station Officer's examination results dropped through the letter box and the notification started "We are sorry to inform you…" etc.

Determined to try again I signed up for the College's correspondence course that year. It was still designed by the College but allowed students to work through it at their own pace. At home our dining room became my study for the next ten months as the table became piled higher and higher with manuals, study notes and assignments. But chemistry was the bane of my life, I just could not "get it" until my neighbour came to my rescue. Ken was a doctor, not the medical kind, but a PhD in Applied Physics. He also had the patience of a saint. Each Sunday morning, for two hours, he would talk me through what I was required to learn. I even got to understand atomic weights, radicals and valency. Before the examination I was selected for the one-week intensive revision course the college ran for those who had worked their way all through the correspondence course and I even managed to understand at least some of the chemistry input. I took the exam that year in a more hopeful mood. Now I had to wait for the results.

False alarm at St Paul's

The call to a fire alarm actuating within St Paul's Cathedral came in the early hours of an incredibly stormy night. The house bells were ringing in unison at the four fire stations, summoning the crews of Southwark, Barbican, Soho and Cannon Street, on whose ground St Paul's was situated. As the eight fire engines were leaving their respective stations, central London's night sky turned into daylight as enormous flashes of lightning followed the rolling thunder moving from west to east down the length of the River Thames. Torrential rain was falling from the sky and the empty streets glistened under the weight of the torrent.

St Paul's, like many national heritage sites within London, attracted a special attendance. Two pump escapes, four pumps, two turntable ladders and an emergency tender were ordered to all calls by the mobilising Control. Whilst one pump and a turntable ladder went to a designated point on the cathedral's west side, the remainder of the attendance responded to the South side. Cannon Street's machines were first to arrive and as we pulled alongside them no obvious signs of fire were evident. Utilising the special keys that Cannon Street carried, their crew was preparing to enter the cathedral via a small access door that lead directly into the crypt.

Standing in the pouring rain and with the thunder still rolling above our heads I found myself in charge as Cannon Street only had a Sub Officer in charge and I was "acting up" as Station Officer, since mine was on leave. It was necessary to enter the cathedral in order to inspect the fire alarm panel and determine in which part of the cathedral a sensor device had activated, if at all. (Violent thunderstorms can cause fire alarms to go off.) Whilst detailing the crews remaining outside to set into street hydrants and prepare the dry rising main, my pump crew and Cannon Street's entered the darkened crypt. I did not know where the fire alarm panel was actually located. This was my first shout here and I had to rely on the Cannon Street crew's local knowledge. Making our way around by torch light, because nobody from Cannon Street could find the damn light switch, I had no great confidence that they knew the way to the alarm panel either, especially as we had just passed the same tomb for the second time!

Moving through the dark eerie crypt in single file, our torch beams cast haunting shadows in the arched bowels of the cathedral, as well as making the marble and granite faces on the various statues and memorials look remarkably lifelike. The fact that these works of art, erected to the nation's rich and famous, covered the mortal remains of those interred in the crypt was not lost on me either. Bright flashes of lightning filled the main cathedral as sheets of it passed overhead. The sound of the thunder was reaching a crescendo and it echoed in the cavernous space of the empty cathedral. Some of the flashes from the lightning filtered down a stone spiral staircase directing us toward the main cathedral floor and hopefully the alarm panel? Things were not getting any better as I next discovered that Cannon Street's Sub Officer was a stand-by himself and it was his first shout to St Paul's too. This motley crew of firemen were not looking particularly comfortable wandering round in the dark, in a crypt, on a stormy night. It was like something from an Ealing horror movie. All we needed was a bat or two and probably the lot of us would have legged it. But at least no one from the outside crews was shouting, "The dome's alight and going like a bastard!"

As we climbed the spiral staircase into the cathedral, we thought that the storm was abating and the strange feeling of calm and silence was almost palpable. Moving towards the vestibule, which housed the alarm panel, (thankfully one of Cannon Street's crew finally got his bearings) a sudden violent flash of lighting illuminated our faces as an enormous crack of thunder broke immediately overhead and seemed to shake the cathedral to its very foundations. The combination of our setting, the lightning through the stained-glass windows and the atmosphere in the cathedral was making this brave little band of souls very jumpy.

Plunged back into intense darkness after the brilliant white light of the lightning there was a terrified scream of shock, and gasps of surprise from the crews, as suddenly and without warning the cathedral's massive organ burst into life. The sound from its bellowing pipes reverberated throughout the nave, filling our minds with un-godly thoughts, each of us sure that it was time for our past sins to be atoned for and a prelude for the arrival of some dark angel who would smite us down with a burning sword!

Normality was restored when one of Cannon Street's crew saw a distant dim light revealing a figure sat in the organ gallery. "What the eff are you doing?" shouted the clearly agitated fireman, clearly forgetting just whose house we were in. A small but highly educated and well-spoken voice replied, "Awfully sorry old chap, I'm tuning the organ and this is the only time I can get in to do it. Who exactly are you?" Explanations were offered, the fire alarm panel finally examined (which had been actuated by the storm) and a "stop" message, indicating that the alarm was caused by an automatic fire alarm fault, was sent. Although an "Act of God" seemed far more appropriate.

The Biker

This was one disturbing shout too many for my Station Officer now back from his leave. Despite his sharp mind, keen intellect and not inconsiderable time spent at fire stations, he could and did easily become agitated when it came to stressful situations. He generally managed to cope but his demeanour did not always inspire confidence in those he was trying to command. This particular incident seemed to tip him over the edge.

The pump was already off the run when we came on duty at 6pm. With no spare appliances available anywhere in the Brigade, something that was becoming increasingly common, six of us rode the PE whilst the remaining firemen were sent to stand-by at other surrounding fire stations. It was my very first time riding the back of the PE as a Sub Officer and I was looking forward to the novel experience. With the Station Officer and I in the office, the mess manager preparing supper, the three spare hands, after checking over the PE and having a general tidy round ended up in the office, and we all had a bit of a yarn.

The call to the RTA (road traffic accident) in Waterloo Road came in just before suppertime. It was reported to be located outside the Old Vic Theatre. Our single engine turned right out of the station and then right again at the traffic lights into Webber Street, which leads directly to the Old Vic.

En route control informed Bravo Two-three-one (our radio call sign) that additional calls were being received. The tone of the Station Officer's voice rose an octave or two as he relayed the information to myself and the remainder of the crew in the back of the PE.

In the back of the PE, with the BA sets hanging directly in front of our faces, it was impossible to get a clear view of what was ahead of us. The machine drove past the front of the Old Vic and then sharp left into Waterloo Road, running down the side of the theatre. All we heard then was the Station Officer shout out, in almost a scream, "Oh my God, my God no." Peering through the gap between the sets I saw the cause of this outburst and the Station Officer's sudden alarm. A powerful motorcycle was laying on its side. The motorcyclist had been thrown from it and was laying in the road. His feet were pointing towards our fire engine, which was now only yards from him. A car that was in front of him had not stopped before it hit the motorcyclist or the motorcyclist had hit it. Whichever way it was the motorcyclist now had his head caught under the front of the car, trapped by the weight of the car on his full-face visor helmet. The petrol tank of the motor bike had split or ruptured and its petrol had spilled on to the road, completely engulfing the motor biker. On finding an ignition source it ignited just as we turned the corner. Blazing petrol completely surrounded the unfortunate man and his screams of sheer agony were the only sounds filling the busy street as the fire engine drove as close as the PE driver dared.

The Station Officer appeared riveted to his seat as I shouted my instructions to the crew in the back of the cab. We jumped from the PE even before it came to a halt, two getting out one side while I and the other crew member dismounted closest to the Old Vic. The next sixty seconds passed in an instant as hose reels were taken from either side of the engine, the tank was dropped, the pump engaged and one hundred and fifty pound per square inch set as the pump pressure. With the hose reel jets set to high-pressure spray we moved forward in two pairs at the run. Whilst the other pair pushed the still blazing petrol away from the motorcyclist with water spray, I and my crew mate doused the burning man from head to toe. The burning petrol was still generating considerable heat when I shouted, "NOW." I and two others moved to the front of the car, taking whatever grip we could find and lifted the car off the man's head. The PE driver, who had jumped down from the engine, helped the remaining fireman ease the man clear of the car and the blazing petrol that had also ignited the motorbike.

Both the police and the ambulance service were now on scene, the ambulance coming from across the street from the LAS Headquarters building in Waterloo Road. It was obvious that the poor man was critically burned and the ambulance crew were making strenuous efforts to stabilise their casualty before removing him rapidly to hospital, which they did under police escort, heading off in the direction of Guy's Hospital. With only the burning bike to extinguish I left the crew to it whilst I returned to the PE. The Station Officer had not left the appliance. He had remained there, transfixed, seemingly unable to comprehend all that had just happened.

With the police now conducting their accident investigation our PE returned to the station. It was a surreal journey, unlike anything I had experienced before. There was none of the usual banter; in fact no one said anything, not knowing what to say. Although each of us had questions going around in our heads, we were most concerned with what had just happened with the Station Officer? I know I was.

It was a silent supper. The Station Officer was sitting in his usual place at the head of the mess table. After supper I went to the office to start the fire report and to contact the hospital to check on the man's condition and the extent of his injuries. Things were not looking good. He had received almost seventy per cent second degree burns to his body and was not expected to survive the night. Starting to draft a statement for the police I was joined by the Station Officer who closed the office door behind him. "Thank you for what you did this evening," he said as he sat behind his desk, still looking drained and shaken. I did not know what to say to him. I had never come across this situation before and did not feel it was my place to criticise his actions, or rather lack of them. All I could think of saying was, "Do you want to talk about it?" To which I got a very short "no" before he rose and went to his room.

The remaining shouts on that shift were of little consequence and we did not speak again until the morning. Shouts or no shouts, I got very little sleep that night, too busy reflecting on the events of the previous evening. When I was not thinking about the motorcyclist with his agonising screams still ringing in my ears, I went back to the image of the Station Officer unable to get out of the PE. I just laid on my bed considering what action I should take or, at least, who I should talk to about it.

I rang the hospital again in the morning only to be told the man had died in the early hours. Forty per cent burns to the body render the chances of a recovery pretty slim, due to the effects of shock and loss of body fluid. But it did not make the news of the poor guy's death any less painful. Before going home I pondered about speaking to the Station Officer again concerning his reaction on seeing the motorcyclist but with two days leave ahead of us I decided to think about it and follow it up when we came back on day duty. As it turned out he confronted me as soon as we completed parade on our first day duty. He then faced the whole watch. "I've put in for a transfer to a day related post. I think it is for the best," he told everyone. There was no further debate about the events outside the Old Vic, no gossip, nor were there any rumours of "Did you hear about old so and so outside the Vic?" It was not talked about again. I felt it was a good decision on his part, not least because there is no room for passengers when the chips are down and it might be my neck on the line next time if I needed help and I would like to think I would get it.

He moved very soon and he never rode a fire engine again. We were told that a new Station Officer was to transfer in from north of the river. Somewhere vague, Finchley, Hornsey or some other equally obscure fire station up that way. But in the meantime, I was to be the acting Station Officer until he arrived. Don't hurry I thought.

Men wanted: apply here

For the past few months the brigade had embarked on its most intensive recruiting drive ever. You could not look anywhere without seeing advertising space taken up in the national and local press and even on commercial television and radio encouraging men to join the London Fire. Brigade recruitment posters were even pasted on to the sides of fire engines! Apparently, the last time such a campaign had been run was to recruit auxiliary firemen at the outbreak of the last world war. But we were told that desperate times called for desperate measures.

We knew things were getting bad. Staff shortages were getting worse with appliances being taken off the run at an increasing rate because there were not enough men to man them. Where there was normal manning it was quickly reduced to minimum levels and the firemen were constantly sent to other stations to make up the shortfalls. Some firemen were spending more time riding engines at the surrounding stations than at their own.

Why this sudden urge to get people to join? Men (still no women yet!) were needed for the introduction of the forty-eight-hour week, a reduction of eight hours from our present fifty-six-hour week. But the fire brigade was operating in a very competitive market place. The Post Office, London Transport and the Metropolitan Police were all wanting extra staff and just as urgently. But the brigade remained almost totally a white dominated operational work force and the desire to see a reflection of the multiracial society that London was rapidly becoming was not part of its recruitment campaign. But many non-white applicants did apply and "times they were a changing."

The brigade's training school was overflowing with new recruits. It was so hectic that we were not allowed to use the drill towers during our day shifts but had to drill on nights. Southwark's recruits were taken by their instructors to the surrounding stations just to get access to a drill tower. Satellite training stations were springing up all around the brigade at stations with a large enough drill yards to accommodate the Portakabins that would be the twelve-man squad's classroom, locker room and eating space for the twelve weeks of basic training, and at some locations the training was very basic. Rumours were circulating that recruits were being sent to stations well below par. (Some sadly were?)

The recruitment drive was so intense that someone who made an application to join, but did not turn up for the interview found a fire engine on their doorstep with someone asking, "why?" I did not support this policy one bit. My thinking was if they cannot be bothered to turn up for the job interview, are they really interested in joining? Rightly or wrongly my annotation on the required paperwork was "No reply" or "Not at home." It soon changed to, "No longer interested" because we were sent back again to inquire when they were not in on the first visit.

There were minimum entry requirements into the Brigade; height being one of them and it was blatantly obvious that some of this vast new intake had their height measured whilst standing on tip-toe. Southwark's White Watch got two "pint sized" recruits and they were like chalk and cheese. Both were the product of satellite training and were, shall we say, not tall. But however they did it, they were accepted into the brigade and who were we to argue. Whilst one of them got stuck into adjusting to life on a fire station the other had come from a privileged background and found station life, its humour and basic living conditions obviously difficult to adjust to, and he made little or no attempt to try. He was extremely well educated but was also extremely arrogant, conceited and self-important, all the qualities needed to blend in on the watch!

Both were now in their probationary training and whilst one was progressing well at the six-month reporting stage, warning signs were ever present that the other would be likely to have an extended probation if he did not make greater efforts. Our arrogant probationer was no less arrogant when members of the watch took time out to help him through some of the areas of training he was clearly having difficulties with. He was his own worst enemy. When the other probationer passed his probation and he did not he added truculence to the list of qualities that endeared him to the watch. He was even argumentative with the senior officer who now had to extend his probation and told him he was to be placed on monthly progress reports. Then one day he did not come to work anymore, eventually sending in a letter saying he was considering other career options.

The Coroners' Court

Southwark Coroners' Court, located in Tennis Street, is just off Long Lane and was one of the capital's busiest coroners' courts. Maybe it was a reflection of the unforgiving conditions that some of the inhabitants of a deprived inner London borough had to contend with and that had helped bring about their demise? I don't really know. What was certain was it had a considerable workload, in processing the numbers of post-mortems that came before its team of coroners, under the direction of its principal coroner.

Violent, unnatural, sudden or cause unknown deaths fell to the coroner to investigate. The coroner was one of the UK's oldest "law officers" whose origins can be dated back to the days of William the Conqueror. Fire deaths were always heard before a coroner and whilst it was customary for firemen's statements generally to be accepted by the coroner it was not uncommon for junior offers to have to appear in court. They were required to give first hand evidence and to state what had occurred at a fatal fire and face questioning from the coroner, and in some cases the solicitor or barrister representing the interests of one party or another. Although far less formal than presenting evidence in the Criminal or High Court, nevertheless you were on oath and the coroners (who were generally qualified as both a medical doctor and a lawyer) would give no quarter if your evidence was less than precise, unambiguous and professional. The death toll across the three watches from fatal fires had run well into double figures in my time at Southwark and I had given evidence at a coroner's inquiry.

I had previously taken both probationers and prospective junior officers to visit Southwark's combined coroner's court and its adjoining mortuary. Probationers, so that they might see a dead body in the least stressful of circumstances and so prepare themselves for seeing one in a fire situation. (Handling the dead was part of our job but something not covered in the recruit-training syllabus.) The "would-be" junior officers on the other hand might have to give evidence in court, so these visits were arranged to the local court where we would sit with the public and listen to a typical case or two.

I had four leading firemen promotion candidates under my wing on Southwark's White Watch at this time and one probationer. Arrangements were made with the coroner's officer (actually a serving police officer but not wearing a uniform) for us to visit both the mortuary and the court. The visit took place on a Friday morning and the mortuary was full to capacity. The mortuary attendants were happily preparing the bodies ready for the pathologist who would conduct that day's post-mortems. Various organs were removed, weighed and samples taken before the bodies were stitched back up again. Before the intervention of more recent graphic portrayals of post-mortems in film or on television many people thought a post-mortem to be like an operation on the dead instead of the living. It is not, I assure you. For example very large openings are made and the scalp is pulled over the corpse's face whilst the top of the skull is removed and the brain taken out and examined.

Taffy was one of the four leading firemen hopefuls, having been at Southwark since he moved from the Old Kent Road some years prior. He had failed his leading firemen's written exam more times than he cared to remember. But this year he passed, followed by success at his practical. In all his time at Southwark he had not attended a coroners' court and never witnessed a post-mortem. My crew seemingly took the mortuary experience in their stride as we filed into the court to listen to the morning's cases.

The coroners' court had a court feel but without the pomp and ceremony of a Crown Court. It had space for a jury if the case required one, a witness box or stand, and the coroner, wearing a suit, sat behind the raised desk overlooking the court. I never saw a female coroner at this particular court. The officials, witnesses and the deceased's families sat in the body of the court and in Southwark's case that meant sitting on tiered pews, with the highest tier at the back of the court. We sat ourselves in the back row to keep a low profile and so as not to interfere with the movement of people as one case finished and the next started.

As the first case concluded the court emptied except for the coroner, the coroner's officer and ourselves. There were no witnesses for the next case, just the report of the pathologist that he would read to the coroner, involving the case of a sudden death of a vagrant found under the arches of London Bridge station. Before this case there was a brief exchange as the coroner asked me what we were doing in court and he seemed genuinely interested that it involved training for possible future brigade junior officers. As the pathologist stood in the witness box to read his statement out under oath, the impact of what Taffy had seen in the mortuary took full effect. He fell into a dead faint, then slid off the bench and proceeded to slide effortlessly and gracefully under each of the benches in front, only stopping when his feet hit the coroner's desk with a resounding thud! He was as white as a ghost and still in a dead faint as we looked on in disbelief, whilst the coroner, peering over his spectacles, said, "Do you think you could take him outside for some air?" Shuffling out, somewhat embarrassed we collected Taffy and carried him into the fresh air where he soon recovered and we tried, and failed, to hide our amusement at his predicament. The coroner's officer, who came out to see if Taffy was Okay, was far more understanding. "Don't worry old chum you are not the first and won't be the last to react that way to a post-mortem." Never a truer word…

Wapping Wall; Thirty pump fire

There was always a special buzz of excitement when you knew that you were being ordered to a large make-up fire. The realisation that you were to be part of the struggle to bring a huge blaze under control was exhilarating, like waging battle on an unforgiving foe. Such fires brought with them their own particular dangers and special care was necessary and woe betide anyone who was foolish enough to ignore the rules of engagement.

So when ordered to Wapping Wall on the "Make pumps twenty," our PE and pump soon left the station behind us as we rapidly covered the distance through Bermondsey's bustling streets; over Tower Bridge; into Shadwell and then on to Wapping itself. Even from Bermondsey we could see the vast pall of smoke that would guide us to our destination, a six-storey large early Victorian dockside warehouse whose stacked goods were fuelling the blaze.

In the mid-sixties the decline of the London docks was relentless. They were not able to compete with the expanding container ports of the Continent and other modernised ports around Britain, and unwilling to encompass the new radical techniques in cargo handling. (This was also driving commercial shipping from the upper reaches of the Thames.) Their total demise was now inevitable. The closure of London's seven-dock system had already begun in 1967. The riverside wharves were now going the same way. Yet the buildings thrown up by the trade lingered on, some empty, many unloved, but a considerable few still commercially active in the handling of a multitude of imported goods. The area, once densely urban and confused, now had more space as demolition or previous disastrous fires left wide-open spaces causing unsightly gaps in the river frontage.

We arrived at the Brigade's control unit and booked-in. I noticed volumes of smoke pouring out of every opening on the upper floors. Window openings and loopholes all provided a limited escape route for the hot gases and smoke as the fire contained within continued its relentless consumption of everything in its path. The fire was so serious that when the first officer in charge arrived, he sent a message, "Make pumps ten," followed later by his, "Make pumps twenty." This fire would reach thirty pumps before it was contained successfully and extinguished.

Water was in short supply to deal adequately with the demands of combating the blaze so I was ordered, together with two other reinforcing appliance crews, to set in two of our pumps to lift water from the Thames, via the adjacent dock. This would provide an additional unlimited water supply. The heavy lengths of 8-foot hard suction hose were taken from every available appliance close at hand. They were added to our own complement of two lengths per engine to cover the distance to the river, some forty-five feet away. The maximum height a fire engine's pump could lift water was between twenty-four and twenty-eight feet (three lengths of suction hose) but here seven lengths of suction were needed from each pump (passing over the quayside wall) to reach the river water. The tide was now "flooding," which was good news. The river level would rise and make the pumping easier, also providing a guaranteed source of water for twelve hours at least.

Getting this water was a priority and the crews worked quickly and tirelessly at their task, connecting couplings, tying lines on the suction hose and getting it into the water whilst other crews connected hoselines to the pumps, leading them away towards the warehouse frontage and, once charged with water, into the warehouse itself.

Each individual pump outlet had a wooden painted tally to indicate which hose it was feeding. This tally was secured to the jet at the end of the hose lines, sometimes many hundreds of feet away, so the crew using the jet would know which pump was supplying their water and who to contact if they wanted more or less pressure or if there was a catastrophic burst length. Our initial task now complete, my pump driver was left to operate his pump, whilst I and my crew reported back to the control unit for re-deployment. "Get your BA sets Acting Station Officer, and relieve Poplar's crew working on the rear of the ground floor," said the senior staff officer in charge of the control unit.

Hose lines filled the narrow street, inter-twined and snaking their way from the pumps, carrying its vital water to the crews working at the other end within the burning warehouse. It was one of these tangled hose lines that we had to follow to find the right crew and relieve the lads who had been inching their way forward into the smoke-filled ground floor.

Stacked goods filled the ground and first floors, with less storage on the upper floors. Baled paper products were stacked almost to the ceiling on the ground floor and boxed fancy goods from Asia were said to be located on the first floor, again filling it to capacity. We followed our chosen hose line in, having first booked in with BA control at our designated entry point. As we passed through the tall double doors our vision immediately became obscured due to the mixture of smoke and steam emitting from the opening. Feeling our way in, with the hose line between our feet, we followed it up and over the bales and boxes, which stopped eighteen inches short of the ceiling level. Now we were crawling across the top of the goods on our bellies with the compressed air cylinders on our backs, forcing our bodies down as they brushed against the ceiling. In front of us we heard their coughing and spluttering even before we saw them. Poplar's crew leader was trying to gauge the effectiveness of the jet he had at work. Without BA they could go no further but they had achieved a remarkable feat just reaching as far as they had. Obviously delighted to be going back out into the fresh air they passed us their jet. With their eyes streaming from the effects of the smoke and fumes they offered us brief encouragement as we pushed further forward, whilst they lifted the hose line and lightened our load as they made their way out.

We had still not found any fire but the heat levels were rapidly increasing. With the aid of the outgoing crew and dragging our hose line with us we moved steadily forward. We managed to penetrate a further thirty to forty feet into the warehouse, moving over the stacks of boxes, seeking the all-elusive fire. Hot water was percolating through the timber flooring on to our exposed necks, so at least some of the water was finding its target on the upper floors. In these hot and humid conditions, the guy behind me tapped my foot. He shouted, in muffled tones through his facemask, that he saw an orange glow and the flicker of flame over to his left. Dragging our hose line, we slowly and painstakingly made our way in the direction he had indicated. As we did so the heat intensified further, the orange glow becoming visible through the smoke. The gap between the ceiling and the storage was getting less and less, impeding our progress. Directing the jet of water into the glow we were rewarded for our efforts by a sudden blast of very hot steam hitting us full on. It was like taking a Turkish bath with all your clothes on whilst carrying forty pounds on your back – not pleasant. But we had struck gold or at least a small vein of it in the fight to eradicate this fire.

Unlike the old oxygen Proto sets, the harder you worked in a compressed air set the quicker you used up your air supply. The combination of the extreme heat and the exertion of dragging the hose in was taking its toll. We should have had at least forty minutes of working time but now, checking our pressure gauges, we were all getting close to where the low cylinder pressure warning whistle would tell us we should be back outside. No relief crew was behind us, ready to take over our jet so we secured it to a pillar using a personnel line and left it aimed at the glow which was almost obliterated by the continuing wall of steam that reduced our visibility to just a few inches.

I gave the instruction to withdraw back the way we came in. We now exited in reverse order. I was the last man in the crew. Whilst making our way in we had pulled the hose line tight and it no longer lay along its original path, at least we assumed so, because the space between the stacked stock and the ceiling was smaller. Clearly, we were not taking the same route back. The hose would lead us back out but we did not know just how safe or dangerous this route might be. The fire could have spread and burned its way under the stock, leaving just a thin crust of material, which would give no warning or indication of the dangers that lay below. But it was not this problem which gave me an unwelcome sense of my own mortality.

Large timber ceiling beams ran the width of the warehouse, supported on cast iron columns that rose up through the piles of stock. Negotiating these beams meant twisting and turning your head from side to side whilst your facemask was scraping the stock below you. This frequent movement had the unfortunate (and undesirable) effect of dislodging my demand valve from the front of my facemask. My next breath consisted of a lungful of smoke and steam. The smoke in my facemask was making my eyes water, but what was of more concern was that I should not be breathing in smoke at all. Instinctively my hands went to my facemask, which was made all the more difficult by the restricted space and almost claustrophobic conditions. One, and then another breath, and I was still breathing in smoke and crap. Then the coughing started. I was telling myself to remain calm. My hand had found the hole in the facemask where the demand valve should be, but it was not!

I was the tail-end Charlie and the crew, worried about their own whistle time, were not hanging about, despite our BA procedures which said we had to be in close personal contact at all times. Through my smoke-filled visor I could just see the man in front of me moving further and further away. Another lungful of smoke and I would be sounding my distress signal unit, then the s--t would really hit the fan! Emergency BA crews and everyone else wearing a BA set would be committed to searching for the poor soul in distress, possibly in life threatening danger. I did not want that person to be me.

I struggled to calm myself and groped for the air supply tube that lead to my demand valve. Still coughing, I found it and started to reconnect it to the facemask. This time I had a mixture of air and smoke as I breathed in and tightened the connection. With no regular tapping of his foot the guy in front finally stopped the crew to check all was well. Having re-established my air flow, I indicated it was and said, "Let's get out." We saw the outside light filtering its way into the warehouse just as our whistles started their continuous shrill. With only minutes to spare we collected our BA tallies and were directed to the BA tables and told to change our cylinders in preparation for going back in.

I decided not to mention my BA set failure, just too much paperwork. As we changed our cylinders and tested our sets, I noticed the change in the colour of the smoke coming from the warehouse. It was becoming lighter, whiter and less dense. Crews were finally getting to grips with the blaze. It was not out, but was beaten. It would take some days before it was finally extinguished, which took many hours of laborious slow turning over, cutting away and damping down. Fifteen jets and over eighty BA sets had been used to quell the blaze that had started on the first floor and then spread outwards and downwards.

The new Governor

Finally, the new governor arrived. I had had only a few weeks as the acting Station Officer of Southwark's White Watch but had loved every minute of it and knew that I could enjoy this job on a permanent basis. The replacement Station Officer was a tall lean man with a wide moustache. He seemed friendly, almost jovial, and wanted to settle in as quickly as possible, but maybe it was that I was resentful he had turned up at all because there was an atmosphere between us almost from day one. Maybe we just had to get to know each other better?

As Sub Officer watch training was my brief. The new governor would come out and take the occasional drill, which I would join in, but generally drill sessions were my responsibility. On day duties, training school recruits would look on in total amazement as I got my crews hauling a 30ft extension ladder up one side of the drill tower and then lowering it down the other, whilst wearing BA sets, rescuing a dummy casualty and then bringing it back via the same route to safety. My natural enthusiasm and zeal rubbed off on my crews and they would play to the enthralled watching trainees by moving with speed and accuracy, completing the task with great aplomb as though this type of rescue was an everyday occurrence at a station, which of course it was not.

One of the things that both the new governor and I were in total accord with was the cooking ability of the new station cook. Lily had retired and advertisements in the local rag had brought forth a range of candidates for the job. The other Station Officers left it to my governor to conduct the selection interviews and he was assisted by a non-uniformed manager from the Brigade's personnel section. One particular candidate stood out head and shoulders above the rest, a Nigerian lady who had excellent references and qualifications in nutrition and catering hygiene. She got the job but within a very short space of time it was self-evident that there was a serious problem, as she could not actually cook! If an army marches on its stomach, the harmony of a station can rest on the ability of the station cook. Serious rumblings were spreading around the watches about spoilt breakfasts and inedible meals prepared for lunch. Still the union rep, I was charged with doing something about it and formally raised it with my governor, who was already seeking to get her dismissed. Meals became more hazardous as she became aware of her imminent demise. On her last day at the station I was accosted by her as she placed a voodoo curse on me. I laughed it off until I found the chicken's head pinned to my locker at the end of the shift! But if her curse was as good as her cooking it probably would not work either.

When news of my success at the Station Officer written examination came through in February 1977, I was euphoric. My first port of call was to Ken, across the road, with a case of wine for getting me to understand chemistry sufficiently for me to pass that damn examination. I would not have done so without his assistance and help. It was very difficult trying to be nonchalant when telling my governor the news when really I just wanted to jump with joy. Strangely my examination result brought about a change in our relationship, a change for the better I might add. Maybe he was pleased at the prospect of being able to run his own watch without me being around. In any event he was genuinely delighted for me and immediately set about preparing me for the Station Officer interview, which was scheduled to take place in the next couple of months. He indicated that he would be recommending me for promotion and told me that I would be getting the support of my watch ADO as well. Things were looking up.

They improved even further when a letter sent to the Divisional Commander by a neighbour arrived at the station with a covering memo from him giving me a pat on the back for a bit of off-duty firefighting. Having a lay in, I was awoken by the frantic knocking and shouting of a neighbour from across the road. The silly woman had been using her hair dryer whilst at the same time getting her two kids ready for school. She left the dryer still running on her bed, which had then caught alight and was blazing merrily by the time she realised what she had done. Her children were still on the path, where she had left them, when I ran back with her wearing my "boxers" and trainers, shouting to my wife to dial 999 and summon the brigade.

The first floor of their two-storey house was completely smoked-logged, her double-glazed windows were closed thus not allowing any of the acrid smoke to escape. The fire was getting a hold now, having ignited the mattress as well as the bedding. Armed with saucepans of water from the kitchen downstairs I subdued the fire but without completely extinguishing it. The smoke was now filling the ground floor as well and I had to beat a hasty retreat out of the back door whilst Orpington's crews, who had just arrived, entered through the front. Thinking that the lads could deal with it I now sauntered home via the pathway that ran along the back of these houses, not knowing that my wife was standing out the front with our two young children in tow waiting for me to emerge. Anxiously she asked Orpington's Sub Officer, "Where is my husband? He went inside." Now it was an anxious Sub Officer who shouted out to his BA crew inside, "There's someone in there, lads." Unaware of the frantic activity I had sparked off I re-joined my family and got rather a disapproving look from the Sub Officer as I told him I was okay and he then called off the search.

The family had to move out of their home temporarily due to the severe smoke damage that left them without any usable clothing. It would be weeks before they were able to move back home again. The husband wrote in glowing terms to the brigade of his appreciation of the efforts of Orpington's crew and my own efforts. His letter did not reflect the little I actually did and I read with considerable embarrassment the Divisional Commander's commendation when he wrote, "You acted in the best traditions of the service and are to be commended for your prompt and decisive actions." If only he knew, but I was not going to tell him with an interview pending! I might need all the help I could get.

National Theatre

Lastly, I thought it impossible for me to leave my recollections of Southwark fire station without making reference to something, or rather somewhere, that whilst only having the most tenuous link with my career in the Brigade brought so much into my life. It was the new National Theatre, built in King's Reach on the South Bank. I was familiar with the National Theatre company because it had been performing at the Old Vic, its temporary home since 1963, and we had made regular visits to the Old Vic to familiarise ourselves with its layout in the event of a fire there. Now a permanent National Theatre site had been acquired near the Royal Festival Hall on the South Bank. The site had been cleared and work commenced in 1969. My first contact with the NT, as it came to be known, was when we had a few small fires on its construction site. I became a more regular visitor as a leading fireman at Southwark when we made familiarisation visits to monitor the progress of the building works and the site's development. As the construction moved into the fitting out phase the visits were made on a much more frequent basis with each watch at Southwark making at least one visit per quarter.

The NT complex incorporated three theatres in the one building. First to open in March 1976 was the Lyttleton, which was built in the traditional proscenium style. Next came the Olivier theatre, which was a contemporary "open" stage and lastly came the studio theatre, called the Cottesloe, which officially opened in November 1977. The Cottesloe was a small oblong space that was exceptionally versatile, as the audience could be seated at either end or all around the stage. The building was entered from several levels, from Waterloo Road, the concert-hall terrace or from the riverside walk. A new feature came into view as the vast fly tower of the Olivier stage thrust up into the South Bank's skyline from the monolithic grey concrete fabric of the NT. It was to be officially opened by the Queen on 25 October 1976 but that was some way off yet.

All the watches at Southwark had built up a good rapport with the NT's Fire and Safety manager, but especially the Red Watch that had responsibility for liaison and monitoring of the theatre's development at a local level. Despite the multitude of things that this vast national project of this scale required and which had to completed before the complex could open to the public in early 1976, all seemed to be going to plan. Until, that is, it was discovered that one small but vital, ingredient was missing. The NT did not have its own theatre "fireman" and without this legal requirement public performances could not be undertaken. Discreet negotiations took place between the Red Watch Station Officer and the F&S Manager to overcome this awkward hurdle. The theatre agreed to pay Southwark's off duty firemen to cover its public performances, including matinees, cash in hand. The Red Watch agreed provided that only firemen from Southwark fire station could undertake the work and gave a "cast iron" guarantee that every performance would always be covered, with the "uniformed" fireman that was required. A deal was struck and a fireman on the Red Watch became the "unofficial" theatre fireman co-ordinator. All three watches covered the NT rota and there was never a missed performance nor any quibbling over the allocation of the duties, democracy at its best. As each of the three theatres opened in turn the fireman just had a larger area to cover and it was only when special effects, involving real flame, were used that two firemen would be required to cover the performances.

I loved going to the NT. It started a love affair with live theatre that has lasted a lifetime. I had the privilege of seeing some of the best actors and actresses of a generation, witnessing jaw dropping performances and peeking at the hilarious and occasionally stressful back-stage antics that both the cast and production crews would get up to. Also, I was paid for the opportunity of doing so. How good was that? There were just so many stories, but some stand head and shoulders above the rest. Perhaps you will indulge this slight (but hopefully interesting!) digression as I recall just a few.

My introduction into this new found part-time role was in March 1976 when I was covering a production of Hamlet, the NT's inaugural Shakespearean performance in its newly commissioned Lyttleton theatre. What an introduction. Albert Finney was playing Hamlet, Denis Quilley was the King of Demark and an actor unknown to me, Phillip Locke, was Horatio. I was spellbound and would have willingly given back the "little brown envelope" with my night's wages for just being allowed to see the performance. It was truly outstanding and made the hairs on the back of my neck stand up as the cast brought the characters to life. Phillip Locke won that year's best supporting actor's national award for his role and it was easy to see why. I was made to read Shakespeare at school but could neither understand it nor get into it in the confines of a classroom. That first night at the NT a light switch was turned on in my head that brought magic and illumination to the words and phrases that were so hard to grasp from the page of a school textbook. I was hooked. Equally so when the play later moved to the Olivier in the October of the same year.

Sir Ralph Richardson and Sir John Gielgud had transferred with Harold Pinter's highly acclaimed play No Man's Land from The Old Vic to the NT. Directed by Peter Hall, it was a master class of a production. Sir Ralph was a frail elderly man even then. On one occasion I was sitting in the wings of the Lyttleton, doing my theatre fireman bit, when I became conscious of the sound of Sir Ralph moving along the back-stage corridor, wearing his soft carpet slippers as he shuffled towards the stage. His arm was supported by his personal dresser, who was also carrying Sir Ralph's stage shoes. With hunched shoulders he came into the wings and, painfully lowered himself, with the dresser's assistance, on to the chair next to mine. The dresser removed the slippers and put Sir Ralph's shoes on for him. He was an incredibly courteous gentleman and said, "Good evening young man" as he sat next to me. Then on his cue, stood up, erect and transformed, and strode tall and purposefully through the wings and on to the stage to give a wonderful performance. He exited the stage on the same side as he had entered. With his dresser waiting, slippers in hand, Sir Ralph marched off the stage as upright as he had walked on, yet in the darkened sanctuary of the wings he instantly reverted to his former frail self, bent over as his shoes were exchanged for slippers and he shuffled back towards his dressing room assisted by his loyal and trusted dresser.

As each new theatre opened, I moved from production to production, through the labyrinth of corridors that interconnected the various stages, to see what was going on. I was becoming increasingly familiar with the layout of the maze-like complex and could move from the Lyttleton's fly tower to the Olivier's swiftly and silently. The NT's scene dock, back stage, was enormous and the artists that created the scenery there were incredibly talented. Electricians, stagehands, special effects people, wardrobe staff and costume makers, the place was a hive of industry, each creating their piece of the enchantment that was brought together on the stage. Nothing was allowed to break the illusions that had been created as the actors brought their own special talents to the audience.

Blithe Spirit was another early production performed in the Lyttleton. This Noel Coward play, a highly amusing farce, was sometimes too amusing. I adored this play and would watch it from a vantage point high above the stage. I became so involved in watching it one night, anticipating the script, that I got an uncontrollable attack of the giggles. It was just as the ghostly spectre of the deceased wife, Elvira played by Maria Aitken, made her entrance on stage. Madam Arcarti the medium (Elizabeth Spriggs), who was trying to communicate with Elvira's spirit, looked up in my direction and ad-libbing to the audience said, "I can hear her laughing now" as I beat a hasty retreat along the fly gantry.

Between night duties I even joined the paying audience and would take in the occasional afternoon matinee. A circle ticket was two pounds then, which included VAT naturally! Albert Finney was again the leading actor, in October 76, only this time starring in the mammoth production of Marlowe's Tamburlaine the Great, which was performed in the Olivier. Not only was it an incredible and demanding performance but he was alternating this performance with the still running Hamlet on selected dates. If that was not enough to challenge Mr Finney, he had to contend with the practical jokes of the other actors too. In Hamlet there was a scene where Hamlet has to address his soldiers. Maria Aitken, from Blithe Spirit, dressed up one night as one of the soldiers and went on stage for a bit of fun. Although there was a "double take" when Hamlet confronted the unexpected face before him, as the consummate professional he continued unabashed – that was until he got off stage and he and Maria Aitken fell about in fits of laughter.

Although the Cottesloe did not officially open until November 1977 it was used for some experimental productions that were way out of my league. "New Age" work I think it was called and a young Bob Hoskins was clearly at home with radical theatre, far more than I was or would ever become.

Playboy of the Western World was staged in the Olivier with Stephen Rea in the lead role and the irascible J.G. Devlin supporting along with a first-rate cast. The play had rave reviews for its laughter and pathos and poetry and sympathy. I could not wish to spend a happier few hours, pay or no pay, absorbing acting at its finest. I even got friendly with a particular young actor who played one of the two peasant boys. It was only a very small role, but he was destined for much greater things. Michael Keating would go on to play a lead role in the BBC's hit series Blake's 7.

The Night of a Thousand Stars was a break from the norm for the NT. The theatre was to host an evening televised charity extravaganza with many well-known actors and showbiz names taking part. With a separate matinee performance to cover that afternoon I had to do an extended shift covering both the afternoon's play and the evening's special performance.

The stars of the show started to arrive during the late morning, some to grab a rehearsal on stage, others to get a couple of hours drinking in the Green Room (bar) before the curtain went up. I was checking the dressing room corridor (part of my duties) and my curiosity was drawn to the sound of music coming from one of these rooms. The door was open and inside were three musical jazz legends – Stéphane Grappelli, Acker Bilk and Kenny Ball "jamming." They were to perform that evening but had yet to decide just what to play. This was as close as they got to rehearsing! They saw me listening by the door and I expected a flea in my ear and to be told to b----- off! Instead I was invited in and asked to listen to a couple of numbers which they had "knocked" together. "What do you think?" I was asked. I thought it sounded incredible and said so. The three looked at each other and Mr Ball said, "Okay that's what we'll play", and they did, and it was great. My brush with the late Les Dawson, however, was not so memorable. His diminutive figure had probably spent just a little too long in the Green Room before going on stage and it seemed I was standing in the very spot in the corridor where he wished to stand! Maybe he just wanted to pick on someone, anybody, and I was handy. His suggestion involved me taking up sex and travel, so I did, thinking, "bloody thespians!"

I always took my station officer's study material with me to the NT during 1975 and 76. When not checking fire precautions or watching a new play I was trying to cram in some extra study and would sit quietly in the wings going through my notes. I was always ready to cover an extra shift for someone else at short notice and was becoming quite a familiar face as the NT theatre fireman. Having now taken the written exam in February 77 I had a brief break from my study material. When I heard that I had passed the exam my nose was stuck in different notes preparing for the interview. That March, Shakespeare's Julius Caesar went on in the Olivier. Sir John Gielgud was to play the role of Caesar with Brian Cox as Brutus. As the Olivier was an open stage, actors would enter from access points both sides of the auditorium as well from the wings. I had found a quiet little study spot in one of these auditorium entry points, the one Sir John entered by before his assassination scene. He had arrived earlier than usual this evening and as he waited to make his entry, he started up a conversation, as you do! He asked who I was and what had I been studying for. I was taken aback that he had even noticed me, let alone noticed that I had my head in a book most times when he saw me. I explained what I had been doing, the fact that I had passed the first stage and now had to buff up for my interview. He was genuinely interested but all the time listening to the action on stage. As his cue approached, he rose and wished me luck, then went on stage, fully into his role as Caesar, and got stabbed to death.

Sir John had a special place in the history of twentieth century British theatre. He had a career that spanned almost eighty years on stage and screen, radio and television. He was arrested for homosexual soliciting in 1953, an incident which helped to eventually change the law in Britain. He was one of the most-loved actors of the twentieth century, although he was reported to have hated the new National Theatre, comparing it to an aircraft hangar, its only decent theatre being the Cottesloe, and even that he thought was like a coffin. He thought the dressing rooms uncomfortable but loved its people, that quality alone spoke volumes about the man. His brief conversation was both genuinely warm and friendly and remains, to this day, a treasured memory.

My interview done and dusted, my promotion in the bag, I had to say goodbye to Southwark. I also had to say goodbye to the National. Now no longer one of Southwark's number, I was out of the loop. My days as a theatre fireman had come to an end but my time as a Station Officer was just beginning.

The IRA terrorist bombing of the Palace of Westminster in June 1974.

Copyright. *London Fire Brigade/Mary Evans Picture Library.*

Mrs. Lily Jones at Southwark fire station, a lovely cook and mother hen.

Station drills and a hook ladder from the head of the escape ladder will get them to the top of the drill tower. 1970's.

My son. Liam, seeing me off on my last night duty at Southwark fire station at our Orpington home. August 1976.

Author presenting gifts to children from Guy's hospital during the Open-day that celebrated the reprieve of Southwark fire station from closure. 1976.

A Station Officer

On 15 August 1977, after only ten years' service, and at the relatively young age of twenty-eight I was promoted to Station Officer and posted to West Norwood fire station, in charge of its White Watch. If little green men from space landed on this planet and asked to see a typical inner London suburb, they could do no worse than take a tour of West Norwood in South London. The decaying Victorian terraces contrasted starkly with the growing expanse of pre-cast and modular dwellings that some architect, who did not have to live in them, called homes! The early 70s had seen much of the area in the grip of both private and municipal renovators and developers. It was rather typical of much of the inner London suburban scene, a hotchpotch of housing with its industry in decline. The fire station was a local landmark and still stands in the busy Norwood Road, a sturdy memorial to the men who built it back in 1916.

Despite its imposing frontage the station has only a tiny drill yard and the drill tower, or rather training windows, are actually incorporated into the rear of the building on the building's' communal staircase. The inside of the two-appliance station was an absolute warren of small rooms and passages which told of the stations history when the accommodation was used to house the firemen who were on duty twenty-four hours a day and where their families lived. Sadly, all this posed a familiar problem faced by most stations built in those early days when the requirements were so very different from those needed now. The small rooms, wrongly shaped, tested the ingenuity of the station's firemen in housing the three thirteen strong watches and meeting their accommodation needs. None was more testing than the miniscule ground floor office, which was shared by the respective watch officers, and not the place to be if curry was on the menu!

The station's ground borders Brixton, Norbury, Tooting and Peckham and had a regular tally of over one thousand calls a year, involving a variety of incidents associated with the characteristics of mixed commercial property and the surrounding residential area. Typical of many such areas of London in the 1970s, a considerable number of these properties were of multiple occupancy, and of those many involved immigrant families. Despite the workings of the then Race Relations Regulations, they presented particular problems when it came to preventing and tackling fires, which involved these dwellings. At the other end of the social scale was Dulwich Village, containing Dulwich College and the famous Dulwich Art Gallery. The ground's most concentrated life risk was centred in numerous old people's homes. Whilst most were new and purpose built there were a few much older ones which posed special problems, should a serious fire occur.

This was my first time at West Norwood, ever. I had not even stood-by at this station, the only station in the B Division I had not been to at some time or other. Southwark's ground was predominately a risk and you hardly had time to rig before you arrived at an incident on your own ground. Norwood was predominately B risk and some C risk. My first impression of the station when getting a shout was just how far you travelled to get to the calls on the circumference of the station's ground. I was beginning to feel that I needed to take a packed lunch when we headed off in the direction of Crystal Palace and Streatham. The other noticeable impression was how long you were on your own before the next "take" stations engines actually arrived to give you, quite often, much needed support and occasionally vital backup. But this was my watch now and I relished the opportunity I had been given.

Very Temporary

Shortly after my promotion to Station Officer a rather strange thing happened. The Brigade was having a bit of an ageism crisis, certainly in respect of its senior officer corps. It was considered, by someone high up, that the senior officer ranks were becoming too old! Assistant Divisional Officers who wanted to progress further in the Brigade and who were over forty-five were deemed to be too old for further advancement, at least that was the belief of many who were of senior rank and were being seen as over the hill! As you might imagine this really p----- off quite a few of them, not least my own watch related ADO who, on a visit to the station, spewed forth his clear displeasure at this proposed policy. His concern was self-evident and despite the fact he came to the station on another important matter entirely, his only topic of conversation was that any possible further advancement was stymied because of his apparent "old" age! After venting his spleen, he completely forgot why he originally came, drank his tea and b------- off in his staff car, still grumbling to himself as he drove away from the station. Although he was twenty years my senior, I understood his frustration and the feeling he had of being let down by the service he had committed his working life to. There was a belief, held by some, that "time in" as in seniority was sufficient to get them promoted. As I was later to witness the ability to hold one rank did not on its own qualify someone for the next. But for now, I listened sympathetically to his ranting about the proposed changes, before saying that the idea was ill-conceived, whilst privately thinking this would not have any impact on me. How wrong I was.

Within days of that conversation our acting Divisional Commander ordered me up to the Divisional Headquarters at Clapham for a private interview. I was given no indication as to what the subject matter was, only told to get on my pump and get myself up there pronto. The Divisional Commander was "old school." He was a highly respected senior officer, held in esteem by both his peer group and firemen alike. Having spent most of his service in the East End of London, he was a smoke eater by reputation and considered a good fireground officer. Whilst he could give you the impression of being a favourite uncle with his gentle and kind demeanour, he was certainly no fool when it came to managing one of the toughest Divisions in the Brigade. Now in the twilight of his career, he had accepted this temporary promotion as our Divisional Commander to give a boost to his pension and a considerable increase over his substantive DO1's salary.

This wily old bird was well aware of the unhappiness of his "older" ADOs and the problems facing them. His solution was to send a message to the Brigade Headquarters principal officers engaged in formulating this flawed policy. However, I did not know that when I walked into his office that morning. A short-term vacancy had occurred for a watch related ADO, on my own watch, the White Watch. His pleasant small talk quickly put me at my ease; in fact, it was more like a fireside chat (but without the fire). He had obviously memorised the recent entries in my personnel file as he recounted my progress from Sub Officer to Station Officer without any reference to notes. He was complimentary but without being overly flattering. It also became clear that he was fully conversant with the conversation that had taken place between myself and my ADO earlier in the week and the fact that I was more than sympathetic to the plight of my particular watch ADO.

Without warning he suddenly said, "I am offering you temporary promotion to Assistant Divisional Officer. You would cover the White Watch." The mood of the interview changed, no more fireside chat, that vaporised as my mind started to race through the implications of his offer. We were now playing a poker game and I was a mere novice compared to his experienced card sharp mind. I did not need reminding that I was the newest and youngest Station Officer in the Division and the least experienced in that substantive rank. I knew the reaction of my watch peers, in fact all the Station Officers in the Division, to seeing a third pip on my very new epaulettes, indicating Assistant Divisional Officer rank. It would seriously p--- some of them off. I might even need a stab proof vest before visiting them at their stations if I was not to befall the fate of Caesar in the company of such "honourable" men. Despite my ego kicking in with this offer of temporary promotion, my initial reaction was to decline, stating that there were other far more suited and deserving officers for this temporary promotion.

The Commander seemed to read my thoughts when he said, "You have a reputation for standing up for what is right even if it requires a personal sacrifice or risk." He then went to repeat what I had said to my ADO about "promotion should be based on the ability to do the job. Someone's age should not be the only determining factor." This guy was holding a full house. I now realised where he was coming from. I was to be his message. "You want youth, you got youth!"

Still clearly tuned into my thought processes he reverted back to his fatherly figure and said, "I know this isn't an easy decision, ring me tomorrow to give me your answer. I am sure you will come to the right choice. I wouldn't be asking you to consider this if I didn't think you could handle it." Then bidding me farewell with a reassuring smile and a firm handshake I was on my way back to West Norwood, my mind already made up.

My few tours of duty as a senior officer were operationally insignificant, a few four pumpers, the occasional persons reported fire (thankfully no fatalities) and a six-pump fire in a waste paper merchants on Deptford's ground. My dealings with my peer group officers on the incident ground was informative if nothing else. The older in service they were, generally the more respectful and helpful they were, genuinely seeking to help and assist in the process of fireground command. Fortunately, none of the incidents were that challenging, which sounds rather immodest, but with the considerable experience of the particular officers I came into contact with, it was a unique opportunity to watch and observe their operational command skills, which were both considerable and impressive.

Visits to actual fire stations were far more … shall we say spirited and sometimes animated. None were more so than a particular visit to Lambeth and the meeting with my former White Watch governor. Having developed a "mischievous" sense of humour, the necessity of calling on Lambeth fire station to investigate some apparently missing equipment seemed too good an opportunity to pass up. Having gone to the station watchroom to book in attendance, the dutyman reported correctly and when instructed to summon the officer in charge he did so with a wistful grin on his face.

I could see the officer in charge walking down the central staircase at the rear of the large appliance room. He had no idea what senior officer had summoned him and he was busy adjusting his uniform jacket as he approached the watchroom to report. The look of disbelief on the poor man's face was only surpassed by the uncontrollable flushing on his face, a condition that haunted him whenever he was annoyed. As he tried, in vain, to control his obvious irritation at having to report to me, the dutyman was trying hard to stem his sniggering and started coughing instead to camouflage his obvious amusement at his governor's dilemma. The officer curtly reported and my pleasant and friendly manner did not seem to make the situation any better. Telling him, "Let's go to your office shall we," in order to deal with the reason for the visit, we never got into the normal polite pre-amble and small talk that usually precedes the business in hand. He was very eager to pursue his own career and advance to the next rank and it was self-evident that my presence was not making his day. With the business concluded, and without even the offer of a cup of tea, I made to leave, saying, "I'll see myself out." Leaving him in his inner office I said farewell to the junior officers and I walked back towards the central staircase, passing the alternative door to the Station Officer's room, which immediately adjoined the governor's inner office. The door was not a very effective sound barrier and the poor soul was in full flow, issuing an angry rant full of expletives. "I only recommended him for Sub Officer yesterday, now I have to effing salute him." The rant and the intensity of it increased as I descended the staircase and made my way back to the station watchroom. The dutyman was an old fellow ET fireman and we had been good friends whilst I was on the watch. As I entered the watchroom he said, "I wish you told me you were coming – I could have sold tickets! You realise that he will have us drilling all afternoon until he calms down again." I just smiled, thinking he will get over it and I have no doubt he will enjoy returning the honours when he's next temporary, so we will be even. (He did and we were, both later serving together harmoniously in senior rank.)

At the conclusion of this first taste of temporary senior rank I was thanked privately by the Divisional Commander for accepting his offer. It alone had not changed the "too old" policy proposals but other Divisional Commanders had made similar moves or were more openly challenging this dubious strategy. Anyway, there were soon far more pressing problems on the horizon. A national strike was looming. It would divide watches, stations and even long-standing friendships, so this young whippersnapper seemingly chasing promotion was very small fry in the greater scheme of things.

Firemen's National Strike

Since 1961 the fire service had suffered badly because of last minute interventions caused by government pay policies. Although in 1971 a qualified fireman's (someone with four years' service) pay was two pound fifty pence above the average male earnings, now it was almost thirteen pounds per week below the same comparative pay position. The Labour government had insisted that from the 7 November 1977 any pay award to the fire service must be within their ten per cent guidelines. This position was unacceptable to our Union's demand for a twenty pounds per week increase for qualified firemen. My own salary had only recently increased by twenty pounds from being a Sub Officer at Southwark to now a Station Officer at West Norwood. It stood at the princely sum of three hundred and three pounds per month, for a forty-eight-hour week, and that included the seventeen pounds thirty-nine pence monthly under-manning allowance.

Accordingly, the pressure building for the first ever national firemen's strike was increasing exponentially. Neither the employers' side nor the Fire Brigades Union were giving any ground in their respective positions. Certainly not the employers, who were totally constrained by the Labour government's then pay policy. The mass meetings of firemen around the country had signified a considerable weight of opinion in favour of strike action. In London each Division held its own mass meeting. The B Division's was held in the drill yard of the Brigade Headquarters building at Lambeth. It was filled to capacity as hundreds of firemen milled around whilst union officials spelt out the grim current position of the employers and the Union executive's recommended course of action, which was for strike action. There were many there that had a heavy heart, not wanting to strike but knowing that they were left with little or no alternative. I was one of them. The vote was by show of hands, which whilst overwhelmingly in favour of strike action remained questionable because of the very large number of unfamiliar faces, all wearing fire tunics, who were the most vocal supporters but nobody seemed to know them. They were thought to be from militant non-fire brigade groups, such as the Socialist Workers Party whose London office at Clapham had orchestrated similar infiltrations around the Brigade.

I was increasingly uncomfortable about the prospect of going on strike. I had voted for it but passionately hoped that it would be settled and a deal struck. I did not want this strike to happen because we were putting our own families on the line too. It was inconceivable to me, and so many others, that the government would allow the fire service to strike, the consequences were all too horrid to contemplate. I was increasingly anxious as each day the strike drew nearer and no positive news of a solution to the situation came. I wrote letters to MPs and GLC elected councillors. I wrote to my own local MP, Norwood's sitting MP and even Willie Whitelaw, Shadow Home Secretary setting out what I thought was the firemen's justified pay claim. All replied, but along party lines. The Conservative MPs were most supportive but John Fraser, Norwood's Labour MP, who had been born in a fire station and whose own father had spent most of his lifetime in the London Fire Brigade, would have none of it. He totally rejected any special case for the firemen's claim. Things were not looking good.

Coming onto duty the night before the strike started was strange to say the least. There was a hush that hung over the normally vocal faces that made up Norwood's White Watch. Conversations were stilted and the gung-ho feelings that some had expressed weeks before had completely disappeared. The clock was ticking, in fact the time had already run out. Battle lines were drawn and neither side had moved their position, the government insisting that its pay policy remained intact whilst at the same time saying that it took no part whatsoever in the pay negotiations!

The night duty passed without notable incident, just an increase in the number of false alarms, which we assumed were the public still checking to see if we would come out. The strike was to start at exactly 9am, the normal time of the watch change, but there would be no change of watch today. At nine o'clock on 14 November the station house bells rang out signalling the end of our shift. They also signalled the start of the strike. The on-coming watch were already gathered on the station forecourt, with members of the off-duty watch coming in also to show their solidarity. As we left the station and joined them the engines remained unmanned in the appliance room. Most of us still believed the strike would be settled in days if not hours. I certainly did. We listened intently to a portable radio one of the lads had brought in, keeping silent whenever a news broadcast was made, waiting for news of fires burning out of control, conflagrations around the country that the Army, whose poorly trained troops had been mobilised to replace us, failed to bring under control. No such news came; it never did.

The army soldiers now thrown into a new front line had only been given the most basic of firefighting training. I think I covered more when I did my fire-fighter's badge in the Boy Scouts. They were to man the Green Goddess fire engines and operated out of army barracks or TA centres around the country. The origins of the Green Goddesses was a throwback to the Cold War and the heightened tension in the West's relations with the Soviet Union, with the next possible war being nuclear! All built on a Bedford chassis, some three thousand two hundred vehicles were put into the Civil Defence fleet and the Green Goddesses were utilised mainly by the Auxiliary Fire Service until it was disbanded in the late 1960s. Painted "deep bronze green" they were never intended as emergency response vehicles since their original function was to travel in mobile columns of around one hundred and forty vehicles at speeds of twenty to forty miles per hour, depending on traffic and the state of the roads, if any remained that is.

In November 1977 "Operation Burberry" swung into action, putting these stored Home Office appliances on the streets of the UK and perhaps for the very first time exposing the British public to these Green Goddesses, on a nationwide scale. But some of us recalled the slow and cumbersome machines from the days of the AFS and I even rode one for a couple of nights at Lambeth fire station because it was put on the run as a spare. It was a pig, uncomfortable and unreliable. It did not stay there long either. An irate principal officer ordered this "green" monstrosity removed from his Headquarters fire station and demanded a red engine be put there instead, and it was.

The news reports, both in the national press and on television, in those first few days gave considerable coverage to the firemen's strike. It told of the efforts of the army in trying to come to grips with their newfound profession. It also gave prominent coverage to the bravery of the firemen in leaving their picket lines, putting BA sets in their own cars, as they went off to rescue people reportedly trapped in fires. Public opinion, which had always been supportive of firemen, continued to be so. The "hoot if you support us" campaign was giving us an audible affirmation of the public feeling as car after car drove past not only our station at Norwood, but cars and vehicles passing stations all over London hooted and tooted their support.

Our engines stood, in impeccable readiness, behind Norwood's large red appliance room doors unthinkingly obstructed by the parked cars and motor bikes of the lads standing on the bleak station forecourt. We were now standing around a fire blazing away in an old cut down oil drum, still with many of us thinking that we could not really be standing here, on strike. Our pay claim had turned into a poker game. News of the emergency debate, taking place in Parliament was filtering through the grapevine. Some firemen from the next station had gone to the public gallery to listen to the discussions taking place in the House of Commons. MP after MP rose to speak in support of the firemen until, that is, Merlyn Rees (Home Secretary) rose to speak and it was blatantly obvious that he was not bothered about the firemen striking or their case for a reasonable living wage. In fact, a report in the press the next day concluded that the Labour government believed our strike was inevitable. It could see no way of meeting our demands without threatening their most important piece of current government thinking, its pay policy. The Prime Minister, Jim Callaghan and his cabinet were convinced our strike would not last long. Our Union was not strong enough and could not carry its members with it and our loyalty to the job would drive us back to work. But they were wrong. The public was showing an unparalleled degree of support towards the firemen who were on below average wages.

However, bitterness was growing elsewhere, particularly between ourselves and our own senior officers who were not striking and were members of the National Association of Fire Officers. These officers were not even following their own Association's guidelines about not getting involved in active firefighting. Our Divisional senior officers were based in a TA Centre in Camberwell. I was the Union's Divisional officer's representative and had led a flying picket to ask these officers to abide by their own rules and not to cross our picket line. An ugly exchange ensued with the officers refusing to accept the picket line was properly constituted. Any feeling of mutual respect that had existed between the temporary Divisional Commander (who had promoted me to an acting ADO only a couple of months earlier) and myself vaporised that day. It was not the only friendship or relationship to suffer because of the strike.

My Sub Officer at Southwark, when I was the Leading Fireman, and I had forged a firm and strong friendship in the ensuing years. We met up socially and visited each other's homes on a regular basis with our young families. He had been promoted to Station Officer before me and had been my mentor in preparing me for my own Station Officer's interview. He was very committed to his views and so was I. We would enjoy bouts of sparring at retirement or other "dos" about the politics of the day in a friendly and enjoyable fashion. When he got promoted, he had joined NAFO whilst I had remained in the Union. He was not striking and I was. We stopped speaking to one another and even when we unavoidably bumped into each other you could cut the atmosphere with a knife. We never talked during the strike and made new friends. Even after the strike the innocence in our relationship had gone. It was no longer a friendship. It became a working relationship. Meeting on the fireground or at a "do" we both only ever managed an "ay up." I regret it now. We were both the same, firemen, but we were both so stubborn. The strike divided people, and for some this division lasted years.

The talks of Friday 18 November failed and they were to be followed by others. It was the first real indication that the strike was turning into a lengthy affair. No better sign of the entrenched determination of Norwood's firemen to see it through to the bitter end appeared when I returned to the station forecourt's picket line after my two leave days. Yes, we even picketed in watches at Norwood! On the forecourt stood a "shanty" hut, complete with door, a window and a chimney flue for the brazier now burning merrily inside the hut. The Red Watch had constructed a none too pretty but effective barrier from the winter weather. It was not the only hut they built either, the first one actually catching fire and burning down. But a replacement soon sprang up and was occupied once again.

Saturday 26 November saw firemen, and many of their families, take to the streets as they marched through London. Abby, my daughter, was pictured in

The Sunday Times the following day sitting on my shoulders in the middle of the throng as the paper reported, "toddler gets a grandstand view." Over ten thousand protesting firemen and officers, all within the Union, walked from the Thames Embankment to Whitehall calling the now time worn battle cry of "What do we want? More money. When do we want it? Now."

Although no negotiations had taken place for a week the local authorities' organisation, representing the employers, were suggesting productivity deals, but our Union leadership remained dubious of the proposals. Sadly, or fortunately depending on your point of view, the troops had been spared the kind of fire disaster that might have forced the Government's hand. Yet the troops' continued enthusiasm held, despite the poor conditions in which they were billeted. But their inexperience and lack of equipment was providing serious concerns, even if the Government was not expressing then publicly.

Some NAFO officers were voicing concern in the national press that the troops might drown with the amount of water they were putting on fires. "All they do is smash a window, put a jet in and hope that's where the fire is." NAFO was also considering its own industrial action at this point in pursuing their own independent pay claim. Its four thousand members nationally had been balloted and its result would be announced next week. I for one was very sceptical that they would ever strike. I was right; they did not.

There was no ill feeling towards the troops from the striking firemen; in fact, there was considerable sympathy and understanding for the unenviable task that had been foisted upon them by the Government. As the Divisional Officers' rep, I travelled around the stations frequently speaking with other union officers on the picket lines. When Green Goddesses were spotted going to "shouts" I and the Divisional FBU secretary, who travelled together would often give chase and see how our "understudies" were performing. We followed one such engine to a small car fire in Rotherhithe; well it was when it started. Normally with such a small car fire, an extinguisher applied quickly, would have dealt with it. But not here, the car burnt out completely before our eyes and the troops'. First, they could not get the pump to work whilst the small fire in the engine quickly spread to the car's interior. As thick black smoke rose high into the air, the intense heat caused the car tyres to explode and sent the troops scurrying for safety behind the engine. When they finally did get the pump engaged and got a jet to work the pressure was so great that the two squaddies could not control it and drenched the crowd of onlookers who had gathered to watch the performance. I thought ruefully that I would probably shoot myself in the foot if I had to assemble, load and fire a rifle given the same amount of training these young boys had.

This was not the only tale of "must try harder" either. My immediate neighbour was a policeman working in Bromley. His role during the strike was to escort the soldiers on their Green Goddesses to the shouts as the military drivers did not know the area very well, if at all. He was working from the Bromley TA Centre and told me with considerable glee of the shout he had attended the day before. Called to a fire in a hut on an allotment site, they eventually found it on land adjacent to the Orpington to Victoria railway line somewhere near Beckenham. By the time the troops arrived the hut was blazing fiercely. Using the water in the four-hundred-gallon tank the engine carried, the troops hit the blazing hut so hard with the jet of water that it disintegrated before their eyes and sent burning debris in every possible direction, and set light to the surrounding allotment huts close by. Now over half a dozen of these huts were alight. Bereft of any more water the unfortunate troops had to search for a water supply before eventually being able to extinguish the various fires that they had inadvertently started. By this time some of the allotment holders had seen the smoke rising and had come to investigate. They thought they had been the victims of a concerted and particularly vicious arson attack as they surveyed the smouldering remains of the huts that were now totally destroyed. They thanked the troops profusely for their gallant efforts in preventing any further damage and the troops said nothing to dispel this arson theory as they made a hasty retreat back to the safety of their barracks.

The pool of HGV drivers from the Royal Navy, Army and RAF fire services were gradually used up and non-HGV service personnel were put behind the wheel and, in good faith responding to an emergency, threw the engines around and with sometimes disastrous, even fatal results. During the strike many service personnel were sent on two-week HGV courses to improve the worryingly low standard of driving and to reduce the number of accidents.

I had previously been requested by the London Regional Committee to accompany them when they went to the House of Commons and lobbied the shadow Home Office team. Seated in a Commons committee room, where we were given a polite hearing but no promises of anything, I apparently spoke with honesty, considerable commitment and conviction about the firemen's pay claim and the validity of their case. My eloquence did little to improve the course of the strike, but I was surprised when I was contacted again and asked to appear on television. Thames Television wanted two firemen's families to appear on the *"After Noon"* programme and I was asked if I and my family would do the interviews. My wife agreed, and (leaving our daughter, who was too young) we went along with my three-year-old son Liam (who actually stole the show). The production team gave him a soft cuddly toy dog and he sat quietly throughout the whole live broadcast just smiling, angelically at the television camera whilst playing with his toy dog. We found the experience far more daunting, but were given a warm reception by the show's presenter, Mavis Nicholson. She ran through the question areas but clearly did not want anything rehearsed. She did not get it. Although charming, she was searching with her questioning and my interview went well, according to the show's producer Catherine Freeman. Possibly too well, in fact, as my emotion spilled over as a quivering lip and moist eyes expressed my innermost feelings as I spoke of the hardships, which firemen faced and the poor financial rewards they got in return. "Close up on the face." instructed the producer to the cameraman. It was good television apparently.

Christmas was now fast approaching – my first Christmas leave since joining the fire brigade, so I thought. Democracy was ruling the picket line at Norwood and it was decided that the fairest way was to draw lots. Needless to say, I drew the short straw and spent Christmas Eve night on the 10pm–6am shift in the hut in the company of three other holders of the short straws. However, we were not alone as many of the local community continued to visit into the early hours dropping off bottles of drink and Christmas nibbles. There was enough drink in the hut to open an off-licence by the time I got on my motorbike to ride home to see my family on Christmas Day morning.

I had been concerned that Christmas would be a difficult and stressful time with no money coming in since the strike started. There was no strike pay from the union and what little savings we had was paying the mortgage interest. My family and friends had already been exceptionally kind and generous ensuring that we did not go hungry. They now gave us a Christmas to remember as they provided for our every need, including presents for the children and a completely decorated tree and Christmas dinner. This kindness and generosity was repeated across thousands of firemen's homes that Christmas as communities showed in very real terms the high regard which they held their firemen in.

The impact of the strike reached my own doorstep with the frantic knocking on our front door in the middle of Boxing Day morning. I opened the front door to an anxious neighbour who said, "Help, my house is on fire." He had dialled nine-nine-nine but knew that the army had to come from Bromley, eight miles away. Grabbing the two-gallon fire extinguisher from my garage I ran back to his home just around the corner. Smoke had filled his two-storey town house and his kitchen was ablaze, fortunately the flames had not spread any further, yet. Crawling in, keeping low to the floor, I used the extinguisher to good effect but was unable to quell the fire completely. The smoke was acrid, burning my eyes and making my throat raw. Other neighbours were bringing their fire extinguishers, which were passed to me still inside the house. The kitchen window suddenly exploded inwards as two soldiers resplendent in their tin hats directed their hose into the smouldering kitchen. The sergeant in charge of the troops fortunately told them to wait before opening the jet and washing me and the remains of the kitchen out of the house. A quick exchange and he understood that I was a fireman and told his men to get the smaller hose reel jet instead. A NAFO officer who had also turned up to monitor the army's efforts saw me and left, without saying a word.

Early January 1978 brought the possibility of progress in the pay negotiations. Rumours of a deal being struck were now circulating in the press. The intervention of the TUC leadership and faceless government intermediaries may or may not have had anything to do with it, I do not know. But a recall conference to consider the FBU's executive council's recommendation was held on January 12 and the advice to accept was passed by twenty-eight thousand to eleven thousand votes. We were going back to work, returning on January 16, two days before my 29th birthday. It was the best present I could have wished for. The upper quartile pay agreement (that put the fire service finally in the skilled manual workers' pay bracket) proved to be a fair and just pay settlement that prevented a repetition of any further pay strikes for the rest of my career.

Norwood's firemen returned to normal duties. We had stayed on the picket line throughout the dispute whilst some stations stood empty and with only the occasional token presence on their forecourt. There were none of the recriminations and bitter feelings of resentment experienced at other stations between strikers and non-strikers. We had stayed unified throughout and it was now time just to get back to work.

The Control Officer

A new tenant had arrived at West Norwood fire station and occupied a flat on the second floor, directly above the station's own accommodation. This new arrival took the form of a young and attractive control room officer and she had moved into her flat immediately prior to the national firemen's strike. As nearly all the control room staff were working normally throughout the strike, she had very wisely kept a low profile when entering or leaving the station. The station had six residential flats on its upper floors, which were rented out to members of the brigade either as family accommodation or, as in this case, single person accommodation. Now with the strike over and us back at work she felt far more comfortable smiling as she passed by the station office on her way in or out of the front door that was used by the station personnel, residents and visitors alike.

She really was a pretty little thing, short auburn hair, a cute but healthy figure, smiling brown eyes and a lovely engaging smile, which I always seemed to receive as we passed each other on the common staircase or when meeting in the entrance corridor. As a single female, seemingly unattached, she was a natural focus of much attention by the various watch personnel. It was something she clearly enjoyed but seemed more than capable of dealing with.

I soon discovered that she did have an interest in someone particular on the station but did not realise it was actually me. My curiosity aroused I became increasingly more aware of her presence, especially as she would look into the station office as she passed through the station entrance. Our initial "hellos" quickly grew into polite small talk, followed by my suggestion to talk on the phone when we were both on night duty. I now found myself waiting for a glimpse of her as she either left for work or returning home to her flat. Her night duty shift finished at 8am, whilst mine finished at 9am. She could travel from the Control at Croydon and be back at the station by the time I was going off duty. So after a particularly long conversation on the phone when we were both on the same night shift, it only seemed natural to accept her invitation to come up for a coffee in her flat when she got home in the following morning. We had enjoyed our telephone chats and talked about work, ourselves and our various interests. It was obvious that we were flirting, I certainly was, and eagerly looking forward to meeting privately for coffee....

Having finished my night shift, I got a strange look from the oncoming Station Officer as I walked upstairs from the Station Officer's room to the tenant's flats instead of downstairs to the rear car park and home! I got an even stranger and disapproving look from her immediate neighbour (a Station Officer who was a bit of a prude) as I stopped and rang her doorbell. She opened the door still wearing her uniform, less shoes and her tie. She stepped back from the open door into the small entrance lobby. She leaned against the wall, standing there in her black skirt and stockings, with her white shirt opened wide at the neck and revealing a delicate cleavage. She looked radiant, a shy smile greeted me and her eyes sparkled with anticipation. Sexual tension filled the air as we both said, "Hi" and I stepped into the lobby and pushed the door closed behind me. We never got past the lobby as we fell into a passionate embrace. It was clear we had made a connection, but I was not prepared for how strong, or how complicated, that connection would soon become.

I eventually went home later that morning and started to build the web of deceit by which I would attempt to cover the continuing deeds of an unfaithful husband. It became an intense and powerful relationship, even more so for her because, at the tender age of twenty-one, she had been saving herself for "Mr Right" and she believed that I was he.

One of those strange quirks of fate happened in those heady days after our first encounter. Whether it was lust or infatuation, it does not really matter, but whilst at home, and with my wife out shopping, I was desperate to speak with her again, so I rang her at her flat. I dialled her number and ended up with a crossed line. An unfamiliar female voice was talking, and asked the question, "Well come on, what was he like?" My interest aroused, I put a hand over the mouthpiece and listened, now curious about this interesting girl-talk. I could not believe my ears when the answer was given and I immediately recognised the other person's voice. It was her. I hung on her every word as she gave a pretty accurate assessment of our "coffee morning." Modesty prevents a more detailed account of that conversation, but whatever her criterion was of what she wanted in a man, it seemed I had passed with flying colours. What was also very clear was that she did not want this to be a "one-morning" stand or a quick fling. Silently, I put the phone back on the receiver and thought about what were the chances of that crossed line happening at that exact moment in the conversation and thinking what happens now?

I soon got the answer and a much better appreciation of the saying "Having your cake and eating it too," as the affair rapidly intensified and I spent many a night in the company of the "upstairs tenant," who would sneak downstairs, to the privacy of my station officer's room. My wife was beginning to think that West Norwood must be one of the Brigade's busiest stations because of the increasing number of times I returned home after night duty, tired and exhausted.

Our relationship grew and strengthened. I was leading a double life. I made excuses for not getting home or having to spend time at work between night duties because of "welfare work" or "charity fundraising." I took leave at short notice when I had left for work as normal and should have been on duty. We were enjoying each other's company more and more. She centred her life around the time we could spend together and began to have expectations that I could not deliver. Despite my very strong feelings for this remarkable person, I was not willing, or prepared, to give up my life with my young children to start a new life with her.

Despite every attempt to be discreet, the watch was well-aware of my affair with the young control officer and it was to their considerable credit that they never tried to capitalise on their knowledge of my dubious comings and goings. Her natural beauty and charm also helped to keep them sweet, amply aided by her outward fun-loving personality. But two separate and unrelated events almost catapulted our affair into the open. First was a rumour that our pump was visiting Control Room all too often, especially when she happened to be on duty! The rumour was a complete fabrication and any simple check of the station logbook would show that no machine had left the station to attend the Control Room. But then the truth never was known to stand in the way of a good rumour. So armed with only the rumour, a senior officer was dispatched to the station, arriving after supper on a night duty to check the story out. He arrived and went to the watchroom and rang one bell, which summoned the officer in charge of the station, yours truly. As was our regular practice now, my little "indiscretion" was with me in my room. Slipping my uniform jacket on and picking up my cap I left her there whilst I went to report to the watchroom on the ground floor, curious about a visit at such an unusual hour. I tried to usher the senior officer into the station office but he would have none of it. I was told, "No this is rather private, so let's go to your room." I was left with no option but to escort him upstairs and show him into my room, which was empty!

Trying hard to cover my relief, and surprise, I offered him the only chair in the room, but he declined and sat on the footlocker of my personal locker. I had known this particular officer ever since he had been a Staff Sub Officer and we had a mutually good regard for each other. He came straight to the point and said he had been sent to check out a rumour of the station's pump, with me on it, was spending too much time at Croydon Control room on night duties. He had already checked the station log and was satisfied that such visits had not taken place. After a short chat about nothing in particular he strolled around the station looking for evidence of any "unauthorised" personnel lurking. But with nothing found he returned to my room and delivered a mild bollocking for not padlocking shut my locker. "How do you expect the watch to follow correct security measures if you leave your locker unsecured?" With that he replaced the padlock and snapped it shut and prepared to leave, so I escorted him to the watchroom and said goodbye.

After watching him drive up Norwood Road I quickly returned to my room and phoned the flat upstairs, intending to thank her for making such a swift exit. I dialled her number but got no reply. Whilst muttering to myself "bugger" as I put down the phone, I heard the sound of tapping coming from inside my locker. Opening the locker door, a hot and flushed face looked out as she said, "I almost peed myself when he touched the locker door." We were both grinning wildly as I helped her out of the locker. It was another "busy" night by the time I got home the following day.

The perceptive power of a woman is a truly remarkable thing. Only it does not always come from the direction that you most expect. My second close call was at an inter-divisional dance (a disco then!) held at the "Cats Whiskers" in Streatham High Road, once a famous Mecca ballroom. All the watch were planning to go and I had invited some non-Brigade friends to join us. She was there too but in the company of her friends from the Control Room, most of whom already knew what was going on between us. Trying to avoid her all evening was just not going to happen and after getting on the dance floor with my wife and some of the watch's other halves, the opportunity presented itself when we "innocently" bumped into each other and managed a couple of dances together. Unfortunately after the very first dance a couple of slow romantic numbers followed. We danced close and tried our hardest to get lost in the mass of bodies on the expansive dance floor and as far as possible away from the people I was sitting with. Afterwards I danced with my wife and then the wife of the friend we had brought with us. Jayne had had designs on me for quite some time but I considered this to be much too close to home. Our first dance was a slow number and she snuggled closer to me and whispered into my ear, "You are having an affair with that young thing you danced with earlier, aren't you?"

"Which one?" I replied, which was a stupid remark as I was the youngest guy on the watch and their wives were all much older than me.

"Do you think I should tell your wife?"

"Please yourself; I have nothing to hide." I lied with all the confidence that I could muster. But it obviously was not enough since she asked my wife later on if she thought I was having an affair with that, "girl from the control." Even if my wife had thought it, she would never have admitted it to Jayne since she had disliked her ever since they had been at school together. But the seeds of doubt were now sown and were just waiting for me to allow them to germinate.

My young Control Officer was an incredible person to be with. She had just chosen to fall in love with the wrong guy, me. I knew I was causing her immense pain. I also knew that I had fallen in love with her too. We had a doomed relationship because, regardless of my powerful feelings for her, I realised that I could not turn my back on my own young family to start the new life that she so desperately wanted.

My imminent transfer to Brixton Fire Station saved the day and for me, provided me with the excuse I needed to put some distance between us. My reaction to her unexpected visit when she turned up at Brixton was both cruel and unkind. So why does this love affair find space in my story? Simply this, she deserved better, her first love turned out to be a bastard and the pain I caused her remains one of my life's regrets.

Bogged down

Some days things just do not go right, or so it seems. In this case it happened to be an evening, an evening that I would have preferred to forget!

Each watch, at every station, was meant to organise a small-scale training exercise once a year. The location was to be a building or an installation on the station's ground which was considered to be a significant risk. A local convent was thought to be such a risk, as well as providing an added attraction because of the numerous young ladies that were boarded there. I had previously organised some very successful exercises whilst at Southwark and I had no reason to believe this exercise would be any different. How wrong could I be.

A pre-planning visit had been arranged for this particular evening to the expansive four-storey gothic style building that stood in its own extensive grounds. A private asphalt road led from the main highway and gave limited access to the rear of the building. The convent itself once lay in the wooded confines of Beulah Hill, a salubrious area of Crystal Palace. It would have previously dominated the open landscape but now its high boundary walls were surrounded by extensive council flats and less than respectable housing. The main building had lost its original lustre and now showed little sign of its former glory. Its occupants nevertheless provided a significant life risk, being the older teenage ladies who were the boarders and who the lads were hoping to get a glimpse of.

The Mother Superior was a polite but no-nonsense nun who had on a previous visit already given outline approval for the exercise to take place. She had also given permission for this evening's return visit to plan a possible scenario that would give the exercise the appropriate level of realism. God certainly moves in mysterious ways. Whether it was the impure thoughts of my crews towards the many attractive older girls who were taking such an active interest in our presence I will never know, but as that evening unfolded it became clear that the inexplicable hand of fate was at work.

My plan was to arrange a BA exercise that required the rescue of some trapped boarders and staff from an upper floor of the convent because of a serious fire on the ground floor. Rescues would be undertaken internally by a BA team and externally by ladder. Because of the height of the premises I thought it a good idea to secure the attendance of a turntable ladder for the external rescue and my old governor at Lambeth (who was now actually talking to me again!) willingly allowed his TL to attend this evening familiarisation visit. My pump's crew and Lambeth's TL crew met outside the convent and I explained to them what was planned and what I expected of them from this visit. It is important to point out here that Lambeth's TL was not just any old TL, oh no. It was the London Fire Brigade's latest, and most expensive, acquisition to its vehicle fleet. It was the most technically advanced aerial ladder that the Brigade had ever purchased and it had only just been commissioned and put into front line service.

Both appliances drove the short distance down the private drive to the main front entrance of the convent. Having said hello to the Mother Superior she gazed in awe at the large shining new turntable ladder and seemed genuinely excited that it was going to be used at the exercise. Young girls also looked down from the upstairs windows at the firemen below, also excited, but probably for a different reason from the Mother Superior.

I knew the TL crew very well from my own time at Lambeth and I reiterated what I wanted from them in terms of performing a ladder rescue from the third or fourth floors. They did not see any difficulty and said they would do a couple of trial pitches along the front aspect of the convent. Whilst they were getting ready, I told my pump's crew to follow the service road around the perimeter of the convent and to check for general access and the private water supplies. As the pump drove off around the right-hand side of the convent, I was feeling quite pleased with myself at this point, and a clearly impressed Mother Superior went off to sort out the girls still ogling out of the upper windows. I watched as the new TL was positioned and the operator got ready to extend the ladder to some of the upper floor windows.

Looking to my left I saw a member of my own crew walking towards me with a worried look on his face! "You had better come and see Guv," were the only words he spoke. "What's up?" I inquired. Silence at first then a very sheepish reply came out of his mouth, "There is a bit of a problem with the pump, it's got a bit…er stuck." Following him around the corner towards where the pump apparently was, I noticed my fire engine at a rather strange and unfamiliar angle and the crew, less the driver, gathered at the rear of the vehicle. I also noticed that the asphalt road was not on this side of the building, only a gravel track. Rather than stop and turn back the pump driver (bless him!) had followed my instructions to the letter and attempted to drive right around the building. To make matters worse, and for reasons only known to himself, he had veered from the gravel track and the rear wheels of the pump had spun on to soft ground whilst at the same time digging themselves deeper into the ground. A number of expletives went through my mind as I immediately realised that this appliance was not going anywhere without some serious help. Getting a fire engine bogged down was definitely a big fire brigade no-no! The driver offered no real excuse and I could not believe how stupid he was to get himself, and me, in this predicament. I had no option but to send a message saying my appliance was bogged down and requesting the attendance of the Brigade's breakdown lorry from Clapham. I also knew that a senior officer would be summoned to attend and investigate the situation.

As I stood looking at my pump, wallowing in its mud bath, I felt a tap on my shoulder and the Leading Fireman from the TL crew uttered an unbelievable phrase, "You'd better come back around the front, it gets worse." It was and it did!

Although standing on the asphalt road, the extending of the ladder towards the upper floors had put considerable pressure and weight on the nearside TL jacks that are meant to stabilise the appliance when working with the ladder raised. These hydraulic jacks had sunk into the asphalt, causing the extended ladder to lean even further into the building, thus putting greater pressure onto the sinking jacks, making the appliance even more unstable. Only the quick thinking of the TL operator and his expert handling of the controls brought the ladder back into the vertical above the appliance but not before substantial cracks broke up the road surface causing the appliance wheels to sink as well. The whole TL was in danger of toppling into the semi-basement area adjacent to where the TL operator had stopped to make his pitches. Having one fire engine stuck was bad enough, having two was a bloody disaster and it was to get still worse.

The Deputy Chief Officer is responsible for the day-to-day overall operations of the brigade. When my "second" message was received by Control concerning the TL it was duly relayed to him. He, apparently, went ballistic. Lambeth's TL was his new toy, his showpiece as regards the front line's latest capability and it was in real danger of doing a "roly-poly" without even ever getting to work operationally. The London Fire Brigade was built upon many Royal Navy traditions and if the Deputy had got his hands on me, then it was highly probable I would have been keel-hauled under the fireboat.

The crew of the breakdown lorry did eventually haul my pump from its hole but specialist heavy vehicle recovery crews had to be hired to stabilise and recover the TL, then tow it back to Lambeth workshops for detailed examination and testing. I knew, like my pump, that I was in deep shit! Reports were written and statements taken, extending into the early hours of the following day. Extensive damage was caused to the asphalt roadway by the TL and its subsequent recovery. I was banned from making any contact with the convent, not even to apologise to the Mother Superior, something I wanted to do. I knew as I shaved that morning that only one man was going to carry the can and I was looking at his reflection in the mirror.

The sound of one bell summoned me to the watchroom on my next day shift. The Divisional Officer tasked to investigate the "crime" had arrived at the station. I was taken off the run and asked to reiterate my statement concerning the happenings at the convent. No sooner had I confirmed that I had instructed both my pump and TL crews into the convent grounds, I was formally cautioned. I was to be put on a "fizzer," a charge that would lead to a disciplinary tribunal. If the Deputy heard the case, I would undoubtedly receive the maximum penalty, given the circumstances, and reduced in rank back to Leading Fireman. Although if the Deputy had his way, I would be lucky to hold a job as a station cleaner. I had only just made Station Officer and it was all to come to an ignominious end, or so I thought.

The Divisional Officer completed his discipline investigation and I waited for my charge sheet to be issued and my case heard at Brigade Headquarters. Lambeth's TL suffered no damage and was returned to the station. I waited weeks, then months. Nothing happened. Life carried on at Norwood and another exercise was planned and carried out without incident. I never knew what actually happened. Maybe the discipline papers never got sent, maybe they got lost in Brigade Headquarters? Nearly a year on and I now had a new Divisional Commander, one destined to be future Chief Officer. My first contact with him was to receive a memo, stating that the caution was lifted and no further action was to be taken.

Make 'em four!

What someone thinks you mean and what you actually meant can sometimes be easily misunderstood, leaving each party thinking that the message was clear and unequivocal but inevitably leading to unintended consequences. So it was after an average supper, but above-average mess-table banter that the sharp and playful repartee was brought to a sudden halt by the call bells summoning us all to the appliance room. Nine of us were on duty that night, five riding the PE and myself and three others riding the pump.

The rhythmic tapping of the teleprinter keys was forming the words that would very soon send us on our way. The Control had received a 999 call to a fire in a block of flats in a council estate in Christchurch Road, near the boundary of our station's ground. Whilst both drivers were already in their respective machines, only the sound of the pump's engine rose above the sound of the teleprinter. The PE remained uncharacteristically silent. It had failed to start and refused to respond to the driver's strenuous efforts to get the engine to fire up. With the ordering completed there could be no delay; lives might depend on our speed of response. I knew that the Leading Fireman in charge of the PE would send a priority message stating that the PE failed to start and could not attend this call. The mobilising control would then order a second appliance to complete the initial attendance of two appliances, the minimum attendance for any property fire in London.

I heard his priority message whilst en route and therefore knew my crew would be on their own in those first few minutes. As we moved rapidly along Christchurch Road the tell-tale smell of smoke told me that we had a job on our hands. I did not know that the PE driver had finally coaxed the engine into life, and with the appliance room now full of exhaust fumes, and the engine revving unmercifully, the appliance pulled on to the station forecourt and into Norwood Road, heading towards the fire.

The council flats were typical of so very many built after the Second World War and into the early fifties. Four stories high and with a common balcony serving each floor, separate flats fed off the balcony. A courtyard that would have once been spacious was now filled with the vehicles of residents and other cars left abandoned by inconsiderate drivers or car thieves. As my driver tried to drive into the courtyard, I saw thick brown smoke coming from an open doorway on the fourth floor and the frantic waving of the woman on the same balcony only boosted our already adrenaline-charged bodies. Finally pulling into the centre of the courtyard the pump stopped and we leapt into action. With only one machine in attendance I instructed my crew in the back to don their BA sets whilst at the same time laying out a forty-five-millimetre hose line, ready to be hauled aloft. Taking a long line from the crew I ran towards the staircase whilst I shouted to my driver to watch for my signal. He had already engaged the pump and "dropped the tank" and was now running in the opposite direction armed with a standpipe, key and bar searching for the nearest hydrant. Having got to the fourth-floor balcony by the stairs (there were no lifts) the distressed owner of the flat, who was almost incoherent with sobbing, assured me that no one was inside the flat and that her husband had only just left for work. The blackened line on the inside of the balcony windows, plus the force of the smoke coming from the flat, told me that a serious fire involved at least one of the four rooms of the flat, maybe more. Getting low and looking down the passageway from the open front door only about twelve inches of relatively clear air was visible above floor level, whilst above it a lethal concoction of noxious and poisonous gases were spewing out into the night sky. A deep orange glow filtered through the smoke and with it the signs of rapidly rising temperatures.

Throwing the line over the balcony I looked for the BA crew and my driver. The BA crew were nowhere to be seen but the driver was ready to tie the line on to the laid-out hose line with the nozzle already attached. Without our rapid intervention this fire had every chance of getting out of control and spreading into the roof void and then involving the extensive pitched roof and adjoining flats. Hand-held radios had been promised but were yet to be issued universally to front line appliances. Only senior officers at major fires came equipped with walkie-talkie radios and they were notoriously unreliable. In theory my driver should have run up the four flights of stairs, taken my message, run down again and then sent it. But not here, and not tonight, given the situation we found ourselves confronting. As he finished tying the line, and before I started to pull up the hose, I sought to catch my driver's attention. Although I shouted down to him, he could not hear me clearly above the sound of the pump's loud engine noise. So as well as shouting I extended my arm over the balcony wall as I shouted down, "Make pumps four," and held my hand out showing four separated fingers. The driver waved back in acknowledgement as I started to haul on the line, pulling the hose up the forty or so feet to the fire floor.

As the hose reached the fire floor so did the BA crew, their sets already started up and ready for action. The sound of their breathing was greatly exaggerated through their facemasks and told of the strenuous effort of running up the stairs whilst wearing these heavy BA sets. In the distance the sound of two-tone horns was filtering through the background noise of surrounding London streets, the fire itself and the high revving engine below. The glass panes in the flat's windows, already blackened, were starting to crack under the effects of the heat generated by the still unchecked fire as it continued to grow in intensity. As I watched the BA crew moving along the hallway, hugging the floor because of the heat, I saw the first wisps of smoke starting to seep through the pitched roof tiles. I shouted to my crew not to bring the ceiling down with the force of the jet. This would have allowed the fire free access into the roof space.

The sound of the two-tone horns was very close now but appeared to have an echo. The sounds were coming from opposite directions so maybe the extra pumps were finally coming to assist? But then four appliances were unlikely to contain the blaze if it broke through into the roof space. Temperatures were already many hundreds of degrees centigrade within the flat and my BA crew were struggling to move forward despite their best and determined efforts. Reinforcements were required and urgently. In my mind I was preparing to send a further priority message, the question then would be making pumps eight... or ten. (At the very first sign of the fire breaking through.)

The Station Officer from Norbury, with his BA crew, had arrived on the balcony. Explanations were not necessary when I told him to break into the roof void to check for fire spread. He got his crew to work immediately, extra hose was hauled aloft, a short extension ladder brought up and the roof hatch located. "Your PE is around the back and they are pitching the escape to the rear of the flat," he shouted between encouraging his own crew to greater efforts. The PE crew was making up for lost time. They had pitched the escape, having driven the appliance on to the grassed area between the flats and the roadway. Armed with a small jet they had broken through the rear window allowing the pent-up heat to vent above their heads. This had made progress deeper into the flat easier for my BA crew and they were now able to enter the rear rooms. I had committed my available crews and was getting concerned that the remaining reinforcing appliance had still not arrived. Norbury's crew had now got into the roof space and whilst they had experienced considerable heat no fire spread had been detected.

It is all too easy to lose all sense of time when dealing with an unfolding drama. Time seems to go into overdrive in the initial hectic moments of a live incident. We were now at least twenty minutes into the fire and it was expected, in fact necessary, to send an informative message about the incident to Control saying what was involved and what was being done about it. My driver finally joined me on the balcony armed with his message pad and his pencil at the ready, whilst Norbury's driver had taken over the control of his pump. So when I asked him, "What time did you send the 'Make pumps four' message?" Peter, the pump driver, (who was a London taxi driver on his days off) and a man never normally lost for words, fell uncharacteristically silent. "Well?" I asked, now somewhat irritated.

"I didn't send that message Guv," he replied, clearly embarrassed and looking very uncomfortable.

"I shouted down to you and showed you four fingers, what did you think I was saying?"

"I thought you said, 'I got this floor,' and you waved to indicate that all was okay; so I went back to check the pump controls," he replied. Frustrated, I made a mental note to always brief any driver in future as to just what my signals meant before I gave them. (A Sub Officer – I forgot his name – on Southwark's Blue Watch was cursed with a stutter. He is alleged to have said, "Make pumps f-f-f-f-f-oh effing ell, six.")

The crews worked their socks off and they were justifiably proud of containing the fire just to one flat, which was not much consolation for the poor, and now homeless, flat owners. Others would pick up their pieces, the Council and Social Services. It was not part of our brief, thank God. The stop message was eventually sent, rather late, but its wording "Four room flat on fourth floor, fifty per cent damaged by fire, one jet, one hose reel, BA," did not quite tell the whole story, but the Station Officer from Norbury did put his slant on it when he came up to me afterwards, as the crews were making up the gear, and said, "You sailed pretty close to the wind there Pikey boy, I would have made them four personally." Little did he know!

Abandoned calls

In the main these were nuisance calls, normally false alarms made from a public call box or a telephone in the home by a child or a drunk who hung up before the call was completed. The control could either check on the location of the call box or get sufficient information to identify the address for an attendance to be made. In either case appliances would always be ordered. The crew's mind-set was this was either a waste of time or that whilst they were attending a malicious call another genuine call could be received. Fire engines from further afield would have to respond, adding irreplaceable minutes to the attendance time and turning a small fire, into a bigger fire or even a fatal one.

Not all abandoned calls were malicious however; some were anything but false alarms. Called in the early hours of a cold winter's night to an abandoned call in the Knolly's Road area of Norwood the two machines had to climb up Leigham Court Road before dropping down over the crest of the hill to the address. As we neared the address, control informed us that further calls were being received and two additional machines had been ordered. As we looked ahead, we could see why. A large semi-detached house was well alight. Flames were engulfing the open front door and were licking up the face of the building through the ground floor windows, which had been blown out by the ferocity of the fire. The occupants of the house had all escaped relatively unharmed and the owner had even managed to call the fire brigade using the house phone, well almost. Laying half way up the front path to the house was the phone; the receiver still off the hook. Trailing away from the phone and into the house was the telephone cable, only it did not go into the house any more. The cable had been burned through whilst the man had been making his "999" call.

Another not so typical abandoned call was to Dulwich village. The call was to a fire in a flat but the call had ended abruptly with the address, not being given. The caller had stopped talking but had not replaced the receiver. Control had been able to trace the address and I responded with Norwood's pump. From the outside nothing looked untoward in the elegant Georgian house, which had been converted into self-contained flats. Going to the flat in question, there was still nothing to raise our suspicions as we knocked on the door and waited for a reply. None was forthcoming. We lifted the letterbox and detected a slight smell of smoke, or rather burnt cooking. I told the crew to force an entry through the door with the fireman's favourite breaking in tool, a size eleven fireboot. In the kitchen we found the burnt out remains of a chip pan that had flashed over and ignited. In the adjoining room was the unfortunate occupant still with the telephone receiver in his old and wrinkled hand, dead. The line to the control was still open and I spoke to the control officer telling her what we had found and requested the attendance of the police. The poor soul had discovered the fire and thrown a wet tea towel over the blazing chip pan and then called the fire brigade. It was a call he would never finish. Either from the shock of discovering the fire or for some other reason, he suffered a fatal heart attack and it was the coroner's officer who later informed us, "He was dead before he hit the floor."

Canine rescue

Brixton's and Norwood's crews combined forces at a serious fire at the bottom end of Tulse Hill, early one evening, when multiple calls were received to a fire in a three-storey terrace of shops with flats above. In fact, so many calls were being received that Control had included four appliances on the initial ordering. Norwood's pair, plus Brixton's pair and turntable ladder, turned out of their respective stations, already knowing that they had a real job on their hands.

The fire was so severe in the ground floor shop that flames were blasting out on to and across the street. The severity of the fire had brought the traffic to a halt with motorists too frightened to drive near the burning shop. The flames were so fierce that they were curling up the face of the building. Although the "shout" was on Brixton's ground, the resultant traffic congestion had delayed Brixton's machines and on this occasion all five fire engines arrived within seconds of each other.

With skill and precision that would have done justice to a drill display at Brigade Headquarters, our combined crews got to work in a co-ordinated attack on the fire. Both crews pulled up short of the incident, jets were quickly brought to bear on the flames and water supplies secured from the adjacent hydrant. The crews hit the fire from both the front and back of the premises simultaneously. But it remained uncertain at this stage just how far the fire had spread into the flats above, although there was plenty of evidence to suggest it had, as dense smoke was coming from all the first-floor windows.

Brixton's Station Officer had established that the owner of the shop had escaped and that it was he who raised the initial alarm. He had also shouted warnings to the occupant of the first-floor flat who had managed to jump to safety, out of the rear first floor window. He was certain that the occupier of the second-floor flat was still out at work. She was but had now returned home, making a dramatic entrance. "My dogs, my dogs," she screamed as she saw the scene of devastation that was unfolding before her very eyes. Her considerable distress and protestations were such that she was clearly going into shock. "Where is your dog?" asked Brixton's leading fireman, the officer in charge of Brixton's turntable ladder. "Dogs," she shouted. "Dogs, and they are both up there," pointing to the second-floor front window.

With most of the crews already committed and the staircase burnt away between the ground and first floor I gathered the few available spare hands together and we quickly slipped Norwood's wheeled escape ladder pitching it to the front second floor sash window. The leading fireman, who had spoken to the woman, dashed up the escape to try to rescue her animals. He was followed by one of my escape's crew.

The flat was filled with smoke but no fire could be seen as he pushed the bottom window up and prepared to enter the room. Just as he was about to climb in a bloody great Alsatian (that clearly could have doubled in The Hound of the Baskervilles) jumped up on to the sill and barked. Just the once. The leading fireman was so taken aback, not expecting this canine greeting, that he let go of the ladder with his hands and may have fallen from the escape had he not taken a leg lock. Then the dog suddenly disappeared, collapsing on to the floor overcome by the smoke. Which, with hindsight, was quite fortunate, as I have no idea how he would have got the bloody dog out and down the ladder if it had not been in that sedated state?

Now assisted by the second fireman, who had entered the smoke-filled room, they also found the second animal and prepared to bring them both back down the ladder. It was a "f------ heavy dog" commented the leading fireman who carried down the first Alsatian. "I ain't rescued one of them before." he said getting off the ladder. It was not the only thing he, and the other fireman got as they stepped from the ladder. The crowd, that had gathered to watch all the excitement, broke in to spontaneous applause. "Shame we don't bloody get that when we rescue people," he mumbled as he carried the still unconscious animal towards a waiting ambulance crew that had been standing-by. (This applause was the only time I ever heard it happen anywhere at any incident!)

The two dogs were in a pretty sorry state. The ambulance service was trying to revive them by administering oxygen. Brixton's Station Officer had, by now, requested the attendance of the RSPCA to care for the animals. The woman reunited with her pets kept them calm as they slowly regained consciousness yet still very bemused and groggy after their unusual exit from the flat.

With the fire out and our gear made up we returned to Norwood leaving Brixton's pump crew damping down and turning over. We were all feeling rather pleased with the outcome, especially for the young woman, who obviously cared so much about her dogs. The following week there were a couple of lines in the local paper about, "Dogs rescued from blaze," and that was that or so we thought.

Much to our surprise, and delight, the actions of the crews at the fire were brought to the attention of the managing body of the Royal Society for the Prevention of Cruelty to Animals by the Inspector who attended the incident. In recognition of the actions taken, particularly by my escape crew and Brixton's leading fireman two RSPCA bravery awards were issued to the White Watches of both fire stations. The framed certificates were hung, in pride of place, in the respective station offices, and the dogs? They made a full and complete recovery.

Green Watch

Someone obviously had a sense of fun because the Green Watch, the Brigade's fourth watch, was created on April Fool's Day 1979. The date chosen had much more to do with the start of the new financial year than anything else, but why let the truth get in the way of a good story. There was little or no fanfare about the start of the Green Watch. But behind the scenes there was an enormous workload required of Divisional Commanders and their management teams, to organise and co-ordinate the moves of the twenty-five per cent of the front-line workforce that was necessary to be transferred, voluntarily or compulsorily, to bring the Green Watch into being. It was the biggest re-organisation in the movement of personnel in the brigade since the creation of the Greater London Council. Not only were station personnel being posted but appliances were moving too. The Chief Officer had put forward proposals to reduce the overall number of appliances in the brigade as well as a review of the location of specialist appliances. The Fire Brigade Committee of the GLC endorsed these ideas and the whole package was brought into the agreement to reduce our working hours from forty-eight hours per week to forty-two hours. This duty system change meant instead of working two-day duties, followed by two-night duties then two leave days, the new system would be two days, two nights then four leave days. To some, such a radical change in duty system spelled the end of the brigade as they knew it. Others saw it as an opportunity to increase their availability for part-time work. Time would tell if it was a move for the better.

Turning three watches into four required a reduction in the overall existing watch strengths; the creation of new single appliance stations, that had previously had two appliances and the transfer of surplus personnel. Personnel in the main selected to go to the newly created Green Watch, rather than leave their home station. There was much heated discussion, and some occasional violence, on watches about who was to stay and who was to go. Officer postings and transfers were sorted out at Divisional level and much to my surprise and considerable delight, I was to be transferred to Brixton White Watch as their new Station Officer.

Not everyone was delighted with their proposed move. A fireman from Lambeth, somewhat the worse for wear due to drink, took it upon himself to discuss his imminent transfer personally with the Divisional Commander at the Divisional Headquarters, Clapham. Having barged into the staff floor he demanded to see the Divisional Commander. The Commander, hearing the commotion in the corridor, came out of his office to investigate, whereupon the fireman produced a knife and told the Commander in no uncertain terms that he was going nowhere. Sadly, the fireman had not anticipated the speed of the Divisional Commander's reaction. He moved swiftly towards the fireman and pushed, very hard, two fingers up the fireman's nose. He fell backwards, dropping the knife, and was ushered from the building by the staff officers and told to sober up, whilst the Commander walked calmly back to his office. The fireman's transfer to the Green Watch stood but he remained at his home station, Lambeth.

Norwood's pump was one of the many pumps that ceased to be. Instead Norwood got Brixton's TL. I was still going to be in charge of a two-appliance station and personally I could not wait for my transfer.

HOUSE OF COMMONS
LONDON SW1A 0AA

19th October, 1977

Dear Mr Pike,

Thank you for your letter of 12th
October about fire officers' pay.

The police of course are very much
in the public eye just now because of the
very serious increases in crime. I can
assure you that equally we appreicate the enor-
mouse importance of the Fire Service's work,
and of course a future Conservative Government
would wish to ensure that their remuneration
was consistent with their value to the
community.

Yours sincerely,

D C Pike Esq
West Norwood Fire Station
445 Norwood Road
London SE27

First morning of the first national Firemen's Strike in November 1977 at Lambeth Fire Station.

FIRE BRIGADES UNION
Why Firemen are on strike

THE national strike of Firemen is the first in the union's history. **WHY** did they strike and why is the strike so solid? **Gross pay of a Recruit Fireman is £52.53 per week.**

For a Qualified Fireman after four years' training and experience it is £65.70 per week. This, for a married man with two young children, means, after tax and pension deductions, a take home pay of £46.71. There are no additional allowances on top of pay.

Time after time since 1961 the Fire Service has suffered badly because of last minute intervention caused by governmental pay policies. Arising from the Cunningham Inquiry in 1971, a Qualified Fireman was placed on a rate of pay which was £2.58 above average male earnings. Today, his weekly pay is £12.90 below average earnings: a total worsening in his comparative pay position of £15.48 per week.

The Government insists that any increase for Firemen from November 7, 1977, must be within their 10 per cent guideline and that any further pay increase coming from the National Joint Council negotiations on a pay formula would have to be considered in the circumstances prevailing at the time.

A working group of the NJC under the independent chairmanship of Lord McCarthy finalised a series of job-evaluation exercises by recommending that the value of a Fireman's job should be compared with the generality of jobs in the Community.

Based on this recommendation, the pay formula sought by the union is:

> To set the Qualified Fireman's Rate at an annual salary calculated from the current average male weekly earnings plus 10 per cent to take account of the special skills required by Firemen and for the many hazards they face.

This in effect would mean an increase of about £20 per week or 30 per cent on the Qualified Fireman's Rate for a 48-hour-week which now stands at £65.70 per week.

FIREMEN BELIEVE THIS CLAIM TO BE FULLY JUSTIFIED. THEY HOPE THE PUBLIC, THE GOVERNMENT, AND THE EMPLOYERS WILL RECOGNISE THE JUSTICE OF THE CLAIM.

The Government's offer of reduced hours in the autumn of 1978 and the recruiting of the necessary additional men is a totally separate issue and in any case the move to the 42-hour-week is long overdue.

***The then Home Secretary, Mervin Rees, became the focus of the striking
firemen's increasing frustration about the Labour Government's stance to
their pay claim. November 1977.***

Copyright. *London Fire Brigade/ Mary Evans Picture Library.*

***Firemen picket the rear entrance to Brigade headquarters at Lambeth.
December 1977.***

Union officers and firemen in a protest march through central London en-route to Parliament to lobby MP's. December 1977.

FBU members lobby the TUC General Council at Congress House, London on 21 December 1977 calling for a TUC campaign against the government's pay guidelines. Although the TUC opposed the pay policy, it refused to launch a campaign in support of the firemen.

Copyright. *London Fire Brigade/Mary Evans Picture Library.*

Firemen George Perrin and Micky Meech giving a rendition of Chas and Dave's "Gercha" after pulling a 5-ton fire engine over 12 of London's bridges.

The 1918 vintage fire engine driving through northern France en-route to Paris. June 1978.

George Perrin greeting his French counterpart after the vintage fire engine reaches the Paris fire brigade headquarters. June 1978.

Chapter 11

Brixton

Below par

Why write a chapter dedicated to just one station? Well the answer is very simple; it was the most enjoyable and challenging period I spent in any single posting in a career spanning more than thirty-one years. Naturally there were highs and lows. But the combination of serving at London's busiest fire station, the good fortune of running a watch with such a diverse collection of characters who were mostly both proficient and professional; even in the most harrowing and volatile of situations – and who possessed the ability to bond effectively, as a team, brought its own very special reward. I acquired an enormous sense of job satisfaction and personal pride whilst serving at Brixton fire station. I did on occasions get it not quite right. But nobody ever suffered because of my, albeit infrequent, lapse in vigilance, other than my own temporary loss of pride. Afterwards I was always determined not to be caught wanting again.

Firefighting is not an exact science. The reactions of people involved in a fire or emergency situation cannot be predicted with any certainty. Brixton fire station's ground was certainly not unique. There were no large industrial complexes dealing with highly volatile substances; no international airports; no high concentrations of high-rise dwellings; none of the increasing number of main arterial routes bringing ever greater volumes of traffic into the capital that some other London fire stations had. What gave Brixton the "edge" was covering large parts of a deprived inner-city area. Much of its old slum housing stock had been replaced with large modern concrete urban housing estates, which brought with them their own special problems. Added to which was a combination of considerable social deprivation and inadequate local and Government funding. A significant minority of the local population also displayed anti-social behaviour and a general carelessness of attitude. All this provided Brixton's firefighters with one of the highest workloads anywhere in the capital.

Following my transfer to Brixton from West Norwood it is true to say that my first year was challenging, at times extremely so. I was the new boss on an established close-knit watch. Nearly every member of the watch, with the exception of only one fireman, was older than me. Taff, the mess manager, was old enough to be my dad and Jim, another senior hand, was not far behind him. Most were experienced Brixton hands. Taff and Jim had served all their twenty years plus service at the same station. They had been at Brixton through the sixties when many West Indian families were frequently involved in fatal house fires. Many of those involved poorly maintained paraffin portable heaters and cookers. On occasion petrol, either misused or mis-sold, contributed to these mostly avoidable deaths. Three or four large families were often confined in a single house and tragically it was often their children who became the innocent victims. At the time these families were exploited by ruthless "Rachman" style landlords who packed these families into tiny flats. Worse they were also charged extortionate rents as the then "colour bar" prevented them from renting anywhere else. Social change had brought about some improvements to the housing stock for these families and their offspring, but Brixton retained a very high ethnic mix. The area boarded by Railton Road, Effra Road and Coldharbour Lane contained the highest concentration of Black Caribbean population in south London.

Having this young, "new" and enthusiastic Station Officer thrust upon them did not fare well with some of the older hands or any of my junior officers. They were fearful I would upset the status quo of work hard and playing harder. Volleyball was something I had never excelled at but it had been a major part of the previous governor's working day. Restricting volleyball and replacing it with daily training and appliance drills went down like a lead balloon with the watch, but this was not a popularity contest. I had been sent to Brixton to do a job and I was intent on discharging my brief.

My transfer to Brixton had not been without a degree of personal pain because of my affair, which had ended whilst at Norwood. It had been an intense relationship, something that we both thought we had gone into with our eyes wide open. Leaving my young children for her eventually became a major issue. My young children won. It left me feeling very guilty, however, and she was very hurt. Whilst her flat at West Norwood fire station had been a wonderfully convenient and safe bolthole, her popping down to Brixton when I was on duty, especially nights, was just not going to happen – not if I was to bring about the changes that were expected of me. Whilst the watch at West Norwood knew of the affair, I managed it in my own time. Her coming to Brixton, to take up where we left off, would undermine both my role and authority. Having their volleyball time reduced was more than enough incentive for the watch to drop me in the mire and get me posted to some out-of-the-way fire station. So for now, I had to play strictly above board and I did.

On my first couple of shifts we had some good working jobs. This gave me a chance to see the watch in action at close quarters so I was able to assess their individual and combined abilities. Some of the watch were clearly below par as regards the level of firemanship I expected of them. I loved my job and took the incident ground extremely seriously. Those that would not, or could not, pull their weight were putting an extra burden on the others. Worse they were potentially putting lives at risk because of their lackadaisical approach to their work.

The long-standing Sub Officer was a possible hurdle to me making the required changes. He was an established member of the watch and I saw him as running both with the hare and the hounds and it was time for that to stop. He was my deputy and I expected him to lead by example and that did not include a poor example. Then there was Taff. He was both the mess manager and the station Union representative. I had worked with Taff previously as an FBU station rep myself. We had built up a good working relationship then and I hoped I could maintain this relationship now. I explained my disappointment to him, in private, in the poor performance I had noted on the incident ground. I told him what my approach would be and the reasons for it. I told him I would be speaking to the watch collectively later on the same subject. He listened and indicated that whilst he had no problem with what I had covered told me it would not go down well in some quarters

I held my first watch meeting as an open forum, where I gave an assessment of the performances I had seen and asked for the watch's comments and opinions. I had not highlighted any particular individual as under-performing, but the spotlight soon came to bear on those concerned who drew attention to themselves by their lame excuses and passing the buck on to others saying they were equally at fault. This was a bad tactic on their part. Had they had the wit to remain silent it would have been just me giving a group bollocking and they could have retained their normal watch solidarity. Now it was one of their own who, in particular, was saying the rest were at fault too. The gloves came off and a build-up of past frustrations at individuals getting away with an easy ride was now out in the open. I explained only what they already knew, that we worked best as a team and that was exactly how we would be working in the future. I said I had a simple perspective when measuring my expectations of their performance on the incident ground. This was from the point of view of the general public, because when the public dialled nine-nine-nine and needed us in an emergency they had an expectation that, not only would we turn up; but we would be professional and competent. Everyone was left in no doubt that there was no room for passengers on the watch, and that we would all train together to ensure that we were an effective team and capable of delivering the range of skills expected of us. I could not prevent individuals from requesting a transfer out of Brixton now I was there but I did not believe in passing on my problems to someone else. I let them know that they moved when I thought them ready.

It was some days later when dealing with a minor incident that Taff came over to me to have a quiet word. He said the chat had gone down well generally on the watch, especially with the older hands. They did not like "skates" either but were not always in a position to deal with them effectively. I felt then that I could make this work and bring about the necessary changes.

My "inherited" leading fireman found these new changes just too much and transferred out for a quieter life at a station in the suburbs. A mature and level-headed fireman on the watch accepted my offer of temporary promotion to cover this long-term vacancy. He was much more in tune with the proper running of a watch and helped me deliver the goods.

Taff, as the mess manager, was allowed to be excused certain station routines but not generally station training as Brixton also had a cook who prepared the watch's meals during the day shifts. Taff only cooked on night duty, where normal routines lasted from 6pm until stand down for supper at 8pm; this stand down lasted until 6.45am the following morning, unless essential work was required. Taff now joined the rest of the watch in daily station training, which was now a far more regular feature of my station routines than had been the case previously. There was no doubting the watch's general level of fitness. In fact, some were exceptionally fit and both Bunny and Wally were very powerful individuals indeed but in their own way.

Basic appliance drills were the norm at many stations, but they soon became repetitive and boring, lacking imagination and the requirement for crews to think about problems and resolve them. After the initial series of elementary ladder handling and pump operations, I expanded drills to replicate incidents using a wide range of equipment. However, I had to guard against emptying the appliances, which would have delayed our response time should a call have been received. The initial reluctance to this training was slowly eroded as the drills required greater thought and effort to complete the tasks set. Much to the watch's delight a fire call would frequently curtail the drill as one or both of Brixton's fire engines responded to some incident or other. It was the nature of our job to be ready at a moment's notice but they also knew that the drill would not be lost and at the next available opportunity the aborted drill would be renewed and completed.

"Jumper" was one of the firemen who had been performing under par. He was a professional skate and would work harder at avoiding work than if he had actually done the job required. He was an individual who would always take short cuts and required monitoring to ensure that the task he was set was completed properly. He was a Jack-the-lad and that combined with a keen sense of humour saved him, in large part, from the onslaught of the rest of the watch, even though they had to make up for his missed or unsatisfactory work. He was now fully engaged in station routines. Pushed together with the rest of the watch at station training and with his individual tasks more closely monitored he had been told clearly what was expected of him. Yet he still tried to push the boundaries in his endless efforts to buck the system. Sadly for him, they were becoming less and less effective as the watch gelled more and more together taking a greater pride in their work and in themselves. Jumper took the path of many who found themselves in a similar position, rather than make the effort he took the "sicky" route and was eventually pensioned off. He never returned to work and I certainly was not on his Christmas card list. His departure left a vacancy on the watch and it was to be filled by someone who wanted to be at Brixton and would work for the privilege of being there. Others were also to leave, as first Taff retired later that first year, and Jim followed soon after. Both had served the brigade loyally and were talented and valued operational firemen.

I also got through quite a few Sub Officers during my initial period, as Brixton was seen as a good development station for junior officers. My temporary leading fireman had now been promoted but remained with me on the watch and he became a constant companion and a trusted colleague. Some of my early Sub Officer deputies were less than enthusiastic about how the watch was managed and others arrived with their own personal issues. In either case they did not stay too long before they were either moved out or chose to move on elsewhere.

Ron Burton was my fifth Sub Officer to arrive at Brixton. Once considerably overweight he had shed a few stone and was now once again a tall and elegant man. He was also an exceptionally gifted junior officer who was both loyal and totally trustworthy. I had at last a motivated and enthused officer who fully supported what had to be done and was willing to achieve it. I was blessed!

All change...

Major changes were underway within the brigade in the early eighties. The Greater London Council had brought forward policy proposals to reduce the number of fire engines at twenty-eight stations, and downsize the aerial fleet from twenty-six to eighteen appliances, and to reduce the brigade's fireboats from two to one. New compressed air sets had been issued to all front-line fire appliances providing essential protection to firemen and hopefully saying farewell to the old days of the smoke-eaters.

The previous twelve months had seen a dramatic increase in the number of chemical and hazardous incidents with over five hundred firemen having to be decontaminated and sixty-two of them attend hospital. Now the fifty-foot wheeled escape ladder was to be phased out with the introduction of the forty-five-foot aluminium Lacon extension ladder. For many, the demise of the wheeled escape ladder was just one change too many. It was for them a retrograde step that they believed affected both their own personal safety and that of the public. The wheeled escape was considered by many in the brigade to be the principal rescue ladder, although statistics might have proved otherwise.

Fierce debates and arguments took place between senior officers mandated to sell the new Lacon ladder concept and the traditionalists who wanted to retain the escape ladder. As with the earlier withdrawal of hook ladders the decision was a case of pure economics in the end. The cost of repairing and rebuilding the wheeled wooden ladders had become prohibitive, even though they were built and maintained in-house at the brigade's own workshops at Lambeth. Our acting Divisional Commander, Gerry Clarkson, had volunteered the B Division to be the first Division to be trained in the use of the "new" ladder. On completion, our appliances would be modified to enable the ladder to be carried, turning the Pump escapes into Pump ladders (PL).

Firemen were trained to be proficient with ladders or at least were meant to be! But quite a few of these new aluminium ladders found their way to the scrap yard because they either fell (or were dropped) by reticent crews during the initial phases of training. There were however some genuine problems with the ladder that had to be overcome. The ladder "walking" was one of them. In order to support and stabilise the ladder two handling props were fitted to the underside of the main (lower) ladder. Once the ladder had been carried into position for pitching, two of the crew at the base of the ladder removed the hinged poles to help raise the ladder whilst the other two crew members walked under the length of the ladder pushing it up vertically as they went. Now upright it was pulled up to the required height by a rope fitted to a pulley, and the top of the ladder could then be lowered into the window opening. The poles were now used as stabilisers with one on each side of the ladder. So far so good! But when these poles were left out of their holders and standing on the ground, crews running up the ladder (which we always did) caused the props to move inwards towards the ladder. This resulted in the top of the ladder pushing away from the building or the window sill it was meant to be resting on. Needless to say, this made the ladder very unstable and it could, and did, move unexpectedly. Fortunately, there were no serious injuries to any firemen but the same cannot be said for many of the bent ladders sent back to workshops for repair.

With the drill revised, we did eventually get it right and the new ladders were introduced right across the brigade where they remain in use today. The wheeled escape became a distant memory and for those traditionalists with a nostalgic temperament they would be seen again, very occasionally, at fire displays depicting over a hundred years of the wheeled escape's use in London Fire Brigade's history.

Brixton's White Watch was still under strength and I needed suitable candidates to fill the gaps. George (he with shovel from Southwark!) and then Peter (the cabbie) transferred in from my former watch at West Norwood. Both were HGV drivers and replaced Jumper and Taff to maintain our driver complement at its normal level of four. George was one of life's true characters and although small in stature he was larger than life. He knew the system and how to work it, never doing too much but never shirking his duties either. If you were ever in a tight corner it would be someone like George who you would want at your side. George's love was driving, besides women that is, and he was a fast and an excellent driver. Getting to a fire with George at the wheel could be an exhilarating experience in itself as he negotiated the traffic at speed and getting me to wherever we were heading in the shortest time possible.

Peter was a London "black-cab" driver as well as a fireman. Slightly rotund, but not too overweight, he too had a wonderful sense of humour and one of the sharpest wits you could come up against. Meal times would often end in tears of laughter as the banter flowed around the mess-table and Peter would parry any mickey taking and return it tenfold. Peter was still the Divisional Fire Brigades Union official and undertook these duties conscientiously. We had enjoyed an excellent rapport at West Norwood and he, like George, had responded to my suggestion that they fill the vacancies at Brixton. Despite Peter's other job as a cabbie he was passionate about his role as a fireman and about the working conditions of his members. He was not a "political" animal in the radical sense and enjoyed the wide support of his Divisional Committee. He was a fireman's fireman, fair minded and not easily manipulated by the Regional Committee's more left of Lenin radical members.

I had previously used charity events to bond my watches together and with considerable success. This seemed a good time and place to try the tactic again here. In June 1980 I arranged a London to Brighton Fire engine pull and used the talents of our own watch and members of Brixton's Blue and Green Watches too. The Red Watch still weren't playing ball but three out of four was good and the station, well three-quarters of it, was gelling together nicely.

Greater Divisional station supervision was also being introduced by our keen-to-impress Divisional Commander, especially in the early mornings when crews should normally be up and ready for station routines by 6.45am. However, part of my personal give and take with the watch was that everyone was up by 7.30 and had their morning tea and the appliances were cleaned out and washed off by breakfast at 8am. Roger, who had been my Sub Officer when I was a fireman at Lambeth, was now Brixton's group supervisory senior officer and held the rank of Assistant Divisional Officer. We had stayed friends and enjoyed a first-rate working relationship. Roger lived outside the greater London area and therefore had to pay for "camping out" at Clapham (which was the privilege of using the brigade's accommodation) in order to provide the brigade with operational cover. He could have stayed at one of his numerous girlfriends' but either their husbands or his latest wife might have taken umbrage. Anyway, Roger did as he was told by the Divisional Commander and would come down in the morning to check up on us. Being Roger, he arrived at around 6.45 am just in case he was being watched, put the kettle on in the mess-room kitchen and about 7am knocked on my door and brought me in a cup of early morning tea. I never had the heart to tell him I only drank coffee. On his second or third early morning visit at 7.15am we received a call to a fire in a basement in Wiltshire Road, Brixton, about a quarter of a mile away from the station.

Leaving Roger behind at the fire station, our two appliances turned out and on arrival I found that the fire in the basement of a wide four-storey terraced house was confined to a foam filled sofa. Although not a fierce fire it had nevertheless produced a great deal of acrid toxic smoke. This had spread throughout the whole of the house, which was in multiple occupation and had trapped everybody on the upper floors. Hearing the many loud cries for help I ordered a priority message be sent to Control indicating "person reported." With the fire in the basement being dealt with by two BA firemen using a hose reel jet everyone else set about rescuing those trapped by the smoke above the fire. A total of twelve people, including three children, were either assisted or carried out of the house by my crews and myself, some of whom were wearing BA. Roger, still at the station, had been told of the incident by control and had naturally responded. He arrived as the last person was being carried out of the building. Four of those rescued, including two children, had to be removed to hospital suffering from smoke inhalation. Seeing all was in order he stopped for a brief chat about the incident before going on his way. This was the last shout of our second night duty, and feeling rather pleased with our efforts, we all went off duty onto our four days rota leave.

On my first day back on duty I was ordered up to Clapham to see the Divisional Commander. I, together with other Station Officers, had been critical of his early morning visit policy saying it undermined our authority to run our stations properly. Called into Mr Clarkson's office he asked me my views of his policy, which I reiterated. In reply he said, "That they were an effective management tool to identify good as well as poor station management practices." Apparently at random he pulled a completed station visit report form from the file lying on his desk and started to read from it. "Attended the station at 6.45am and was reported to correctly by the dutyman. Station personnel had finished their tea and were preparing to start station work and appliance maintenance. The office staff were completing the night's fire reports and the officer in charge reported promptly and in the correct manner." I was thinking where is this station? Surely it cannot be one of ours.

Divisional Commander Clarkson continued. "At 7.15am a fire call was received and the crews responded speedily and an excellent turn out. This call was subsequently made 'persons reported' which I attended. Upon arrival I found all the crews assisting twelve residents from the affected property. Although the fire was confined to the front of the semi-basement the whole building was severely affected by smoke and ventilation of the house was being undertaken. Two children and two adults were removed to hospital. A good effort by all the crews with proper procedures in place and directed by a diligent officer in charge. Signed R Vaughan."

Placing the report down on his desk the Divisional Commander looked up and said, "I don't know what your concerns are Mr Pike? An excellent report that lets me know just how my stations are being run." Random my arse I thought. I had been hoisted by my own petard. I left remembering I owed Roger a drink.

That was my penultimate meeting with our Divisional Commander who was about to be posted back to Brigade Headquarters. (He would eventually rise to become London's Chief Fire Officer in a few years' time.) A short stocky powerful looking man he had a clear belief in his own destiny. He had just been promoted to the substantive rank of Assistant Chief Officer and was now off to pastures new. We had crossed swords a few times, yet it was his decision to send me to Brixton. On his departure tour of the B Division he made a point of calling in at Brixton to see me. It was not an emotional farewell as he marched straight into the station office unannounced and simply said that before he went, he wanted to tell me he thought me "devious." He then turned and left. I wasn't sure what devious really meant so I had to look it up in the office dictionary; "not sincere or candid; deceitful; underhand; going away from a proper or accepted way." Now my wife might want to call me that, but this was the pot calling the kettle black. I had not been his willing lapdog nor was I intellectual enough to beat him at his own game (something that he greatly admired in others). In the future there would always be an atmosphere of mutual mistrust and suspicion between us whenever we met.

Mr Clarkson was a complex character. He was "Machiavellian", a schemer and someone who had clearly marked out his own career path, whilst delivering the widespread changes that the then Chief Officer was imposing on the Brigade. Whilst he was our Divisional Commander it was something at which he was very successful. However, given his "alleged" personal behaviour (or rather misbehaviour) and the dubious activities that were attributed to him, he could have made a very successful and "notorious" London crime boss had he chosen such a walk of life. Towards the end of his career, when he was fighting to extend his own term of office as Chief, this was how the now almost obese individual looked, surrounded by his gang of henchmen he seemed every inch the Mafioso godfather. But he also had a passionate vision for the future role of the Fire Service and in particular London Fire Brigade's place as the capital's most progressive and responsive emergency service. It was largely due to his determination and his forceful character (and to his lasting credit) that he delivered a large part of what he set out to achieve. But for now, it was "au revoir" Gerry and "bonjour" to Brian Butler, our new acting Divisional Commander. Brian Butler was to have a strong influence on my career over the next few years; only I didn't know it then.

Early midlife crisis!

The transition from three watches to four, adding the Green Watch to the existing Red, White, and Blue Watches had settled in well. Certainly everyone at Brixton had got accustomed to their regular four days leave. I know I had. But the four watch Station Officers still had to ensure that the watches worked effectively together and had to make sure that the day to day routines and tasks were completed, and that both the appliances and operational equipment were tested and correctly maintained. This was sometimes easier said than done with inter-watch conflict and occasional poor management of a strong watch that could undermined the overall effectiveness of the station. Brixton's Red Watch had some very forceful characters and, sadly, the first two of its Station Officers when I was posted to Brixton lacked the personal authority and drive (plus the total lack of support of their office staff) to bring the watch to heel. The Blue Watch's officer in charge also had his fair share of problems but largely of his own making. A brash and outspoken Yorkshireman; a former prison officer he tried to run his watch along the same lines as in his previous employment. He was also a tad vindictive especially when it came to getting new probationers to perform unreasonable tasks. This did not bode well for good station management and it was not too long before they were transferred out and replacements sent in.

The White Watch's main change of watch contacts were with the Red Watch when I came on to night duty and the Green Watch as they came on to their nights. The Blue Watch were on duty whilst we had our four days off. Building up and maintaining a good relationship with my opposite numbers was an important ingredient in helping to run an efficient and effective station. Eventually with four like-minded Station Officers at Brixton things would run well at the station, but the same could not be said for me! By the end of 1980 I was having a bit of a personal crisis.

The New Year did not see things improve any. In January 1981 I was thirty-two and coping with the fallout of yet another affair. The emotional aftereffects of the recent national firemen's strike finally came home to roost. Despite the fact that the firemen's strike had delivered a very good pay formula and considerably improved the previously low wage levels, making ends meet with two young children and a heavy mortgage was taking its toll on my income. I had also considered the fire service to be a vocation prior to the strike and the act of walking out on strike had taken that strong feeling away. I was grieving and despite my natural enthusiasm and commitment things were now just not the same as it were before the strike.

On my days off I was having to work part time to make ends meet but I could not rely on that permanently. I was still better paid than the three lower ranks at Brixton and I wondered how they managed? Some of my watch had partners who worked part-time, a couple worked full-time. Two of my firemen had incredibly lucrative part-time jobs and their fire brigade wage was just a second income to them.

Two close friends were both serving constables in the Metropolitan Police. A frequent topic of conversation was our respective jobs, in particular the disparity in our take-home pay. One of them, Dave, also happened to be my immediate neighbour and he took great delight in constantly winding me up about this disparity, some four thousand to five thousand pounds per year in his favour. As I held the equivalent rank of a police Inspector, and they earned far more than he did, it made the disparity even worse. Besides his regular chiding he also suggested that I should seriously consider changing jobs and join the Met. Even as raw police recruit, I would get a substantial and instant pay rise. Discussion with my family, and other non-fire-brigade friends, added weight to the argument and my wife was keen to see our standard of living rise to that of our policemen friends.

Persuaded, I sent off for an application form to join the Police. The form completed and returned, I was surprised to be called for their selection tests and interview only a few weeks later in early March 1981. The selection took place at the Metropolitan Police Training College in Hendon, London. I had no doubt that I would pass the eyesight test this time and passed both the medical and selection tests with ease. The subsequent interview was conducted by two senior uniformed police officers and they almost bit my arm off to have me join the police force. They were naturally curious why I wanted to leave, but after explaining my reasons and commitment to public service they expressed the view that the fire brigade's loss would be their gain. Unusually, they told me that, subject to the references, there was no reason why I could not start my training before that summer. Events moved swiftly, for shortly after I received formal confirmation of what those officers had told me. I had been accepted as a potential police constable and was told to report to the Training College in June to start my basic training.

I kept this news to myself and tried my best to carry on normally at work. We were preparing for a major fundraising event later in the year and it involved me in quite a lot of work. I felt guilty about opting out but felt confident that those involved would complete the task regardless. Station personnel moving on was an occupational hazard of the job and you just made the best of it. However, the grapevine works in mysterious ways, or the Masonic grapevine in my case. Dave was an active freemason and under interrogation I had told him of the letter from the police inviting me to join that June. What I did not know was that my Divisional Commander's best mate was also a freemason and in the same lodge in Penge as Dave. For whatever reason Dave spilled the beans and it got back to my Commander.

Unaware of any of this I was called up to Divisional Headquarters to see the Divisional Commander, Brian Butler. I naturally thought it was something to do with the charity event as we had had a number of meetings already. Sitting in his office he asked, "You got anything you want to tell me?" Thinking it had to do with the event I said I could think of nothing new to report since we last spoke. "This has nothing to with that, it is about a change you are considering." My mind was racing. How the hell had he found out? I tried to compose myself. Maybe the police had contacted the fire brigade? But they had said any contact would be kept confidential. Anyway, who at Brigade Headquarters would care what I did? It quickly became apparent that the Commander did and he spent the next hour talking me through my options and trying to convince me to change my mind. I felt flattered that he had taken time out to talk to me but nothing was going to change my mind, or so I thought. Asking me to seriously reconsider he sent me on my way back to Brixton.

My contact with the police was to get even closer when I reported for duty on Wednesday 11th March, a day duty. We were called during the afternoon to assist the police gain entry to a house in Hayter Road, Brixton. When I arrived on our pump, I was met by two uniformed police officers, who told me a suspected burglary had taken place and it was believed the burglars were still inside the three-storey house. They explained they did not want to break down the door and would we provide access for them by using our ladder to get through an upper floor window. I did not have a problem with that and got the crew to pitch the ladder to a second-floor window, which our thirty-foot extension ladder just reached.

An embarrassed policeman came over to quietly tell me that he did not like ladders at all and could we go in, open the front door and they would then search the house. Fine by me. So Bunny and I climbed the ladder and gained entry into the house through the window. Now an important fact here is Bunny. He had two part-time jobs, one as a bare fist back street boxer and the other as a bouncer in a Beckenham nightclub. Just the sort of guy I wanted with me at a time like this. As we moved towards the staircase, we heard movement in the loft space above us and saw a pair of feet about to disappear through the loft hatch. Bunny grabbed a foot and quickly pulled the miscreant out and on to the floor. The scuffle was short-lived as we quickly overpowered the man, well Bunny did and I supervised! Taking him in tow we started towards the ground floor when rushing out of the front first floor room the second unauthorised occupant came to the rescue of his companion. Charging at us he fought to release his partner in crime. This time Bunny supervised as he was not letting go of his villain. After a very short struggle, where I got in a lucky blow or two, we marched the two miscreants out into the street and into the waiting arms of two very surprised policemen. We handed them over and went to make up our ladder. Now despite Bunny's considerable strength and size he was a gentle and fair-minded man. The police were giving the two housebreakers a slap before they put them in the police car. Bunny was having none of it and told them so in no uncertain terms. The police desisted and bundled the two into their car. They appeared less than pleased that we should criticise them and drove off without a thank you. We went back to station and Bunny made capital of his story of derring-do soon to be forgotten as the next shout came in.

A week later a letter was sent to the station via Brigade Headquarters. It was from the Chief Superintendent at Brixton Police Station addressed to the Chief Fire Officer praising us for the co-operation in the arrest of the two burglars. Fortunately for us it did not tell the tale as it happened. Otherwise, I could have been in deep trouble, since it was Brigade policy only to pitch a ladder for the police, and not do their work for them. Even so we were subject to an internal inquiry to check that my version of the events matched the police's. Thankfully the police officers concerned were not going to admit they did not like heights or ladders.

Because of the letter sent from the Police I also received a letter from the Chair of the Brigade's Honours and Awards Board, Assistant Chief Officer Cliff Colenutt, but in a most unorthodox fashion – he delivered it personally. ACO Cliff Colenutt was a true gentleman. Possessing a gifted mind and a keen sportsman he no doubt cut a handsome figure in his younger days. He lived and breathed the fire brigade. It ran in his blood. A former Divisional Commander of the A Division (which covered London's West End) he was a highly respected officer both for his firemanship and management skills. It was nevertheless all somewhat embarrassing, since I was getting the Board's congratulatory letter but I could not let the cat out of the bag. We sat in my office and had tea over a very pleasant chat. Then, as he was departing, he asked me to reconsider my decision to leave the brigade for the police. I felt my own Commander's hand at work in getting ACO Colenutt to come to the station. After he left, I called Bunny into my office and showed him the letter telling him, "This is for you too."

This was not the only pressure put upon me to remain in the brigade and this came from yet another totally unexpected source. At the end of March, the brigade was inspected and assessed by Her Majesty's Inspector of Fire Services. A high-ranking team of Inspectors, all holding (ex)Chief Officer rank, were visiting stations and Divisional HQs to assess operational readiness and to view the level of proficiency of the workforce. My Divisional Commander had selected Brixton fire station and my watch to be included in the afternoon's inspection itinerary. We were expected to perform drills and then be questioned by senior members of the Inspectorate. At 2pm we were turned out for station fire drill, which even I thought was impressive and by the smile on our Commander's face so did he. The appliances were then driven into the station drill yard. The Inspector asked for a situation drill to be performed, which we had been warned of previously (and had practised many times) the shift before.

My drill had ladders flying all over the place, the pump was twinned into the hydrant and jets of water were quickly got to work from the upper floors of the drill tower. Simulated rescues were effected by a BA crew whilst a second BA crew removed a gas cylinder from the tower's basement and immersed it in an improvised dam. The whole thing went like clockwork and the lads worked their socks off. I could see the pleasure on the crew's faces and the look of relief on the Divisional Commander's when, with the drill completed, we lined up to be inspected and questioned on operational topics.

The HM Inspector was a former brigade principal officer and an old drinking partner of the Commander's. I was asked by the Inspector to show him around the station whilst his inspection team quizzed the rest of the watch outside. When we got into the station, he asked me to find somewhere quiet to sit for us to have a talk. This was highly irregular since it was normally all very formal and a tea for two session was not on their regular agenda. Now sitting in the station's TV room in two easy chairs he asked me about my decision to leave the brigade for the Met police. I was taken aback but guessed the link as this officer did not know me from Adam! But he came across as genuine and very sincere as he advised against such a move, saying that I was well regarded and destined for higher things.

I had received good annual appraisals but this was the first time an HM Inspector took time out to give me any career advice. I was flattered that he had taken the time to speak to me and assumed that he owed Brian Butler a big favour or wanted one? Returning to the yard the Inspector swept up his entourage and, thanking the crews, made his departure for his next port of call in the Division. The Commander also thanked the crews and said it was only what he would expect of his Division. He smiled as he asked me if the Inspector had had anything interesting to say. I told him nothing that he did not already know and said I would think about it. The decision as to whether to stay in the brigade or join the police was made for me over the weekend of Saturday 11th April and the days that immediately followed it. It was made by the very people I was planning to join.

Late on that fateful Saturday afternoon the Brixton riots started. Their impact would have implications felt right across the capital and subsequently brought about both limited social change and heated political debate. It certainly changed my own perception of the Metropolitan Police and its culture of racism that was sadly demonstrated so forcibly by the officers involved in dealing with and quelling the rioters. During that Saturday morning I was riding the pump through the very streets that would later be illuminated by the many fires started, deliberately and burning out of control, destroying pubs, local shops and numerous overturned cars.

Something was definitely in the air, it was palpable. Lines of police "tactical support" vehicles (transit vans) were parked in the side roads and there was a strong presence of uniformed policemen everywhere; many standing on street corners and looking tense waiting for something to happen.

A fierce exchange had already taken place the previous evening involving the police and black "punters" who frequented the clubs and back street bars of Railton Road, which resulted in a number of arrests. I tried repeatedly to speak to the duty officer at Brixton Police Station that Saturday trying to gain an assessment of the situation but no information was forthcoming. It seemed obvious to us looking out from the relative safety of our fire engine cab, as we drove the same route again, that all it needed was another spark to ignite the blue touch paper. The police appeared to be more than happy to supply the matches.

I passed on my concerns to the duty senior officer at Divisional Headquarters suggesting that local stations be advised of the potential for serious trouble in the Railton and Mayall Road area of Brixton. He came back to me at 1.30pm saying that the police were of the opinion that no flare-up was likely to occur before nightfall. He had obviously spoken to the wrong policemen since those we saw were planning to get the action going long before then.

Despite my fears about the possibility of a flare-up that seemed likely at any time, I was required to leave the fire station in the early afternoon to attend a meeting elsewhere, leaving my Sub Officer, Ron Burton, in charge. I never got back to the station that day, prevented from doing so by the police cordons and the serious rioting already taking place near the fire station. So much for nothing until nightfall. Meanwhile Ron and Brixton's fire crews caught their very first taste of the civil disturbance when at 5.30pm they were ordered to a house ablaze in Railton Road. They never reached the incident, prevented from doing so by brick throwing mobs involved in street-to-street fighting with shield wielding police officers. The mob was filling Coldharbour Lane and Railton Road. Ron's attempt to get a police escort to take him towards the pall of smoke clearly visible in the distance failed. The senior police officer present on the ground was not committing his officers and told Ron to forget it because of the volatile crowds and the danger they posed. Ron had by now been joined by the crew of West Norwood's pump-escape. They had just made it down Railton Road to deal with a separate car fire but not before the appliance was badly damaged by the rioters and their driver seriously injured.

What was happening before the eyes of my crews was a completely new and unprecedented experience for them. They were unable to attend the incident not knowing if lives were in danger or not. With the situation in Railton Road deteriorating rapidly both firefighters and police officers were now in considerable danger from the constant hail of bricks, bottles and sharpened lengths of wood being hurled at them by the hordes now gathering in numbers and charging at the police lines. Unable to return to the fire station lest it be attacked, Brixton and Norwood crews were ordered to a temporary mobilising point just outside the immediate danger area. Widespread damage and looting had spread as far as central Brixton and Ron attended further calls to Brixton Road, including Burtons the men's clothes shop, where the looters had fired the shop as they left with their arms filled with their swag. Other fire station crews had been ordered to the numerous nine-nine-nine calls that the mobilising control was now receiving continuously. Their fire appliances had become a regular target for ferocious attacks.

As the evening moved into night White Watch crews were slowly relieved and Green Watch crews took over. They would face a night of increasing violence, running street battles and having to deal with several major fires that were seriously under-resourced. This was the country's most serious public disorder in modern times and radicals and extremists from various parts of London were willing and eager to join in the violent assault on public order, coming out of the ground like rats from Brixton and Stockwell tube stations.

The Divisional Commander took overall command of the mobilisation within the area of the civil disorder. He set up a forward command post in Jebb Avenue, adjacent to Brixton Prison and established a safe marshalling area for his appliances and crews. His were new operational tactics and were being developed on the hoof. It was the first time that the deployment of a forward control point had been used in the British fire service. His vast operational experience as a command officer and his intuitive and decisive decision making, together with an intimate knowledge of the affected area, served to provide a comprehensive and effective plan of attack that the fluid and rapidly changing situation demanded. He made sorties into the area to make a personal assessment of the situation and ensured the best use was made of his personnel and the resources available. (Brian Butler's officership was later recognised when he was awarded the MBE for his actions during the Brixton riots.)

Others also faced severe challenges that night. The acting governor of Brixton's Green Watch had to fight a most serious fire in a three-storey public house with only two appliances and eight firemen, which in the normal course of events would have demanded eight fire engines plus special supporting crews. Needless to say the pub in question, which was well alight even when the crews arrived, was a burnt-out shell by the early hours of the Sunday morning.

Sunday was our second day duty. A surreal calm had befallen the very streets that only hours earlier had erupted in such destructive violence. With the PE crew remaining at the station, and many other fire station crews damping damp what were now mere smoldering ruins, the smell of burning and smoke filled the air. Voids had been created in what, twenty-four hours before, had been continuous lines of property. I was charged with obtaining all the details for the multitude of fire reports that had to be collated and completed. A task that took many days to obtain the necessary addresses, names of owners and to assess the, near total, fire and related damage. Television and news reporters mingled with the inquisitive onlookers who had come to view the scenes of carnage. Some were curious, the locals clearly concerned. Owners of the burnt-out cars and affected buildings looked on forlornly. Some wept, others angry. All the while the numerous policemen, not now carrying riot shields, looked on from every street corner, watching and waiting.

However, Sunday night did not see a repeat of Saturday. Only skirmishes that the overwhelming police presence contained, if not exactly controlling. Monday's Red Watch day shift was quiet. When we came back on duty Monday night, we still hoped to be part of the story and not just onlookers. I had taken charge of Brixton at 5pm, then at 5.54pm I took a phone call from the Divisional Commander. He ordered me to evacuate the station immediately. To say I was unhappy about his decision would be an understatement. But it was blatantly obvious that this was not an issue for debate as far he was concerned. Ten minutes later the station was secured and empty.

Whilst the pump and driver headed off to West Norwood and the Pump Ladder was driving towards Clapham fire station. We would have to cover our station's ground from these two adjoining fire stations. It was clear that fire engines remained a legitimate target as far as the rioters were concerned, who were starting their hostility and aggression for a third night but without the same mass destruction that had taken place previously. That night the tension and running street battles were confined to the rioters and the police, who now presented a massive presence in the affected area. None of the numerous arson attacks that materialised Saturday night were repeated. I spent a boring night at West Norwood waiting for calls that never came.

Tuesday, the 14th, was our second night duty and we expected the same evacuation drill as nightfall came. None came and we remained at Brixton. Before supper our first shout of the night was to a house alight in Mayall Road and new tactics were in place to ensure better crew safety in case of an attack. Driving as close to the incident as possible the drivers were told to reverse the fire engines down the cul-de-sac to provide a quick exit if necessary. Working direct from the street hydrant, the derelict house fire was soon extinguished.

At 9.30pm both appliances were ordered to a car alight in Railton Road and we were rapidly learning the tactics that the situation demanded. The car was blazing fiercely and as we approached, we stopped and again turned the appliances around and reversed the last one hundred and fifty yards towards the incident. The street was illuminated by the light of the burning car and the air was heavy with the acrid smoke of burning rubber and the car's interior. With water used directly from the street hydrant, and not put through the pump, the street filled with clouds of steam as the jet made contact with the white-hot metal of the car. It was so hot that the car now lay flat on the road with all its tyres completely burnt away. We had no police escort despite their ever-strong presence. But these were not local Brixton coppers. They had little or no knowledge of the vicinity. Small groups of stone throwing black and white youths were playing cat and mouse with the police and causing a great deal of confusion as they attacked, waited for the inevitable chase, then disappeared amongst the narrow alleys and pathways leaving the police increasingly frustrated and angry.

That was the last fire that was attributed directly to the riots. However, fourteen brigade personnel sustained injuries from bricks and other missiles and eight fire engines and one staff car were damaged. The triangular area most affected by the arson attacks at the height of the rioting looked like a war zone. Damage to buildings and property was on an unprecedented scale for peacetime in London. Many fires, that crews were unable to attend, spread and involved other surrounding premises. In one particular case five buildings were destroyed after the initial blaze spread out of control. Having been tasked to co-ordinate the compilation of all the Home Office fire report data over the coming weeks, I became more closely aware of the prevailing attitude of many of the police officers still patrolling the affected area. It was this that finally made up my mind about my desire to join the Metropolitan Police.

It is easy to say, "I am not racist," but I never have been and, I hope, I never will be. I do not judge people by their skin colour or cultural differences. That's not to say there are not people or groups of people I don't get on with or actively dislike. I do not relish the company of people who smell regardless of their colour or creed. I dislike intensely the National Front and what it stands for and the individuals that make up its membership. I cherish my liberal views and our freedoms. I love living in a democratic society. So I found the prevailing attitude of so very many of the police officers now swamping the surrounding streets of central Brixton made me feel increasingly uncomfortable. Their personal beliefs and feelings were adversely impacting on the public order task that they were meant to be performing. It was blatantly obvious that the vast majority I came into contact with were extremely racist and bigoted. They were itching for a fight with anyone of a skin colour different from their own, which was universally white. This was a feeling that they seemed to expect anyone who was white and in uniform to share. They distorted values of racial harmony and in some instances practiced outright race hatred.

Maybe I had been naïve but I found this discovery extremely worrying and it made me feel very uncomfortable. I took time to speak to as many police officers as I could. They came from all over London and not just from local South London stations; being bussed into Brixton to police the area while it slowly reverted to normal. If there were individual officers who did not agree with the majority of their colleagues' racist attitudes they were not indicating it publicly. This was the very organisation that I was signing up for. Even if I got through the recruit training there was no way that my beliefs or values of tolerance towards others would match the culture pervading so openly within the Met and demonstrated by these "bobbies" on the beat in and around Brixton. I pushed my own police friends further over the prevailing attitudes to be found in their workplace. It was obvious that black people were always destined to get a raw deal when compared to a white person.

"Sooties," as some of the police referred to them, were more likely to be targeted and challenged in ways that would not be applied to white "British" folk. Whilst I expected that there must be police officers that did not share this point of view, I was finding it very hard to find any. In the days and weeks following the riots much was reported nationally of the causes and implications of the civil unrest and disturbances in Brixton. But it would take future public inquiries to recognise the "pernicious and institutional racism" that prevailed throughout the Metropolitan Police Force. The Stephen Lawrence inquiry conducted by Sir William Macpherson, and published in 1990, highlighted these very attitudes and the organisational racism that I had witnessed first-hand in 1981.

This unacceptable face of London's police force that I had been exposed to had made up my mind. Money was not the be-all and end-all. I would not last five minutes in the Police if I wanted to keep to, and practise, my personal beliefs. I withdrew my application to join. I would stick with my lesser paid, but far more racially tolerant, career in the London Fire Brigade.

Paddy

Paddy was a former governor of Brixton's White Watch having served there for many years before being promoted to Assistant Divisional Officer, although now he was a temporary Divisional Officer attached to B Division's Clapham HQ. We had crossed swords (big time!) during the firemen's strike. He was a NAFO (officer's) rep and we were not what you would call bosom buddies. So when he came to visit the station the atmosphere was somewhat strained as I had to report to him and he asked to inspect the station. There were strong moves afoot to disband all bars on fire stations, in particular those stations, which still kept stocks of barrelled beer. Brixton had its barrel, shared between the watches, and Paddy knew it because he had been one of the instigators of installing

Brixton's small bar room, affectionately called the quiet room, that was located just off the snooker room on the first floor.

So when challenged by Paddy, "Does this station have a bar?" I told him that if anyone knew the answer to his own question, it was him. Now it might well be possible that Paddy lived in some sort of parallel universe, a place where his time at the station existed in some other dimension, because he acted as if he knew nothing of the station or its history regarding its bar. I was losing patience with his inability to just come out with it and say, "I know that there is a bar here and the barrels have got to go. Now." He was getting equally irritated by my surly attitude, which said, "Bar, what bar?" Demanding to inspect the store cupboard under the stairs, where he knew the barrels were stored, he got the key and opened the store whilst I looked on, now concerned. With a sneer he pulled the door back and stepped inside ready to point at the irrefutable evidence. However, the store only contained teleprinter rolls, toilet paper and piles of boxes of pre-war carbolic soap that no one had ever bothered to throw away. Now with the bit well and truly between his teeth he scoured the station like a terrier after a rat in search of the offending barrels but he found absolutely nothing! Trying unsuccessfully to contain his anger I had to follow him to the watchroom where he told me in no uncertain terms, "This is not over." before he left the station.

Now I was as bemused as Paddy as to where the bloody barrels of beer were because that was where I last saw them, in the store under the stairs when I went there during the previous shift. Enter Bruce, the keeper of the barrels on the White Watch. "We moved them last night shift because we got a whisper that senior officers were checking up. I forgot to mention it."

"Where are they?" I enquired. "In the BA chamber under the tower and at the end of the sewer pipe," he said with considerable pride. "Well they have got to go now," I said, "as Paddy is after my blood and he is determined to get me one way or another."

"Can we empty the barrel first?" asked Bruce clearly anxious about the possibility of wasting a few gallons of his precious ale. So a deal was struck. Once this supply was run down no more barrels on the station and I for one was not upset to see them go. Beer remained on the station, however, but in cans kept in the welfare cupboard, where else!

Paddy had a long memory and during that summer on a particularly hot and sultry day Brixton had been in and out all morning. A couple of little house jobs, a car alight and lots of dust chutes set alight. At lunchtime we had our 6th or 7th shout of the day so far, another "shit" chute in a block of flats at the bottom of Brixton Hill. There were a couple of very large refuse bins alight and full to the brim with burning household rubbish. Having put the fires out the bins were turned over and the rubbish tipped out. Now hosed down we were in the processing of putting it all back into the bins and trying to leave the place reasonably tidy. I had told my pump's crew that, due to the hot weather, they could remove their fire tunics providing they all had their issue T-shirts on, which they had. I had my white shirt on which is how Paddy found us as he mysteriously turned the corner in his staff car and got out and told me to tell the crew to put their tunics back on. Now if anyone was prone to cut corners it was Paddy when he was a Station Officer at Brixton. I had attended shouts on Brixton's ground when Paddy had sent a "stop" message, "Small fire house hose reel," and we had stripped all the machines bare of hose, and jets were everywhere putting out a couple of blazing derelict houses.

Maintaining my calm, I asked Paddy to move away from my crew as I would like a quiet word. Out of earshot I told Paddy to "eff off" and if he did not, I would stuff him in one of the dustbins. He did go but ran straight back to the Divisional Commander. I could almost hear him whingeing, *Please sir, please sir, Pike swore at me.*" No sooner had I got back to Brixton than I was ordered immediately up to Divisional headquarters. Having just had time to change into my best uniform I was marched straight into the Commander's office when I arrived. The Commander was sat behind his desk with Paddy hovering close at hand, looking for all the world like Uriah Heep from Charles Dickens' David Copperfield.

A stern-faced Commander said, "I understand that this officer," pointing to Paddy, "happened to be passing and saw you and your crew improperly dressed and when challenged you swore at him and threatened him with violence. This is a very serious accusation. What have you to say for yourself?" Without a moment's hesitation I said, "It was a momentary lapse Sir and I realise that I was totally out of order and for that I profusely apologise to the officer concerned." With the Commander's only words, "Don't let it happen again." I was dismissed and returned to Brixton. I have no idea what the Commander said to Paddy, but Paddy never visited Brixton when I was on duty nor did we ever speak to each other again.

New Pin

Much against my better judgement I agreed to a request from a fireman at Lambeth to fill a vacancy that had occurred on the watch by the premature retirement of George on medical grounds. Although not a motor driver (I still had four HGV drivers on the watch and therefore sufficient to cover the drivers normal leave requirements) I preferred to run with a full watch strength. This particular fireman also happened to be the cousin of one of my watch and I thought that if he was as competent as his cousin what could I lose. Finally, checking with my opposite number at Lambeth regarding this guy's background I was told he would fit in just fine. So he duly arrived and during the 'initial honeymoon' period he seemed all right, then things changed.

I think, with hindsight, that this young man would have agreed that he was a bit wayward, uncertain of what he actually wanted out of life other than to enjoy it in every way possible, regardless of the consequences. It was difficult not to like him, however, even though he possessed a natural stubborn streak and that may have had something thing to do with his Irish background and family name.

It soon became all too evident that it was necessary to keep a watchful eye on him around the station, as he could be easily distracted from the task in hand. Although not actually lazy he did, shall we say, have a short attention span unless, of course, it was something that actually interested him. It also became apparent that Brixton was not his cup of tea or maybe it was because I now kept him on a short rein. Whatever the cause, once again he put himself on the monthly transfer list seeking a mutual swap with another equally qualified BA fireman. However, this was not before he had yet another party trick up his sleeve and came into work on a night duty with a little surprise for us all, but especially for me.

He had naturally fair hair and had tried a couple of punk style haircuts but the wearing of the fire helmet made short work of his coiffeur. Taking the 6pm parade that evening I knew something was up just by the line of silly grins on the faces of the watch as they were detailed for that night's shift. But whatever it was they were not sharing it with me, yet. Parade completed we all went to put our firegear on the engines and as he removed his fire helmet, I saw the reason for the watch's mirth. In fact, how could I possibly miss it. The top of this fireman's hair had been dyed a shocking pink! With his punk cut he obviously thought he looked cool, with his spiky hair looking like an effeminate hedgehog. "It's flamingo pink," he proudly proclaimed in response to my open-mouthed disbelieving gaze, unable to look away at his latest display of immaturity.

Whatever he thought he looked like the watch were willing participants in his desire to see what he could get away with. There was no specific Brigade Order prohibiting "punk" hairstyles so it required a bit of stealth to resolve this issue and it was the watch who I was going to get to deliver it for me.

After tea the watch gathered in the station office for the normal detailing of station routines or evening drills. Gathering everyone on duty including Bunny, the mess manager, I told them that hair colour was a matter of personal choice but that pink might be seen as contrary to maintaining acceptable standards when it came to an individual's "appearance and bearing." Therefore at any time any of the watch were outside the four walls of the fire station they would be properly rigged at all times in strict accordance with Brigade Orders. This meant either wearing their uniform cap or their fire helmet. Caps were in fact rarely worn when on outside work, a concession I was happy to apply providing the watch were smart and tidy in every other respect. Now instead of the grins that had occupied the faces on roll call there were looks of considerable unhappiness directed at the owner of the pink hair sitting in their midst. Bunny, who hated wearing his cap full-stop, said, "You mean we got to wear caps even if we are in the station yard or on the station forecourt guv?"

"Yes, hydrants, drills, returning from shouts, your head will be covered at all times," I replied. "Drills in five minutes, I suggest you all go and get your caps,"

I said before turning away and walking into my office. I could hear the mumblings right across the appliance room as they went reluctantly to collect their headgear. "Do you think this will work?" asked the leading fireman, sticking his head around my door. "I hope so because there is no plan B," I replied.

There was no normal early supper that night, everyone working outside until 8pm and all wearing their caps. Cleaning the appliances on the forecourt in the morning it was caps on again. Bunny, who had to empty the kitchen waste bin into the yard dustbin after breakfast, had difficulty containing his resentment as he was made to wear his cap to perform this duty. Upon his return to the mess he summoned a mess meeting from which the office staff were excluded, although from the whispers that filtered down later a "kangaroo court" better describes what transpired. The case for the prosecution was forcefully put without any defence on their agenda. A vote was taken and the verdict delivered on the accused, "Lose the pink hair or we will do it for you." Business quickly returned to normal the following evening with all trace of the vibrant colour removed, replaced by a more conservative brownish hue!

This was his last act of rebellion before his transfer was approved with my blessing to the A Division. His exchange arrived at Brixton even before his first actual duty. Andy was a fresh faced, fair-haired young man who looked much younger than his twenty-two years. If the junior fireman scheme had still been running, I would have expected his cap to carry the distinctive red band. He introduced himself and immediately created a good impression by his appearance and bearing which was simply immaculate. He had started life in the E Division and after his probation had put in for a transfer to the A Division, seeking greater operational experience and excitement. Sadly, Manchester Square was a poor choice from his perspective as it delivered neither. He couldn't believe his luck when the opportunity for a transfer to Brixton came up. So eager was he to start that he had asked his Station Officer if he could bring his gear over on days in preparation for starting on nights and here he was.

He paraded on his first night duty at Brixton with the rest of the watch and lined up between the Pump ladder and Pump where we always took parade, only he was not like the rest. If he looked smart before, now he outshone every other member of the watch, including myself, as he stood at the end of the line. His firegear was spick and span and the looks of the others on parade told its own story as they surveyed our newest member, neat as a new pin. Then followed the asides as some said in very flowery terms, "We will see what you look like after a night at Brixton." Chided by these remarks his cheeks flushed up in embarrassment, glowing bright scarlet which only added to the barbed comments directed his way.

It was exceptionally rare for Brixton to have a quiet night but nothing prepared our transferee for that particular first night shift at Brixton. We didn't stop, shout after shout, and it wasn't long before our new pin was looking more than somewhat tarnished with his firegear covered in soot, grime and water stained. His wide smile let everybody know that he did not care, letting slip his sheer delight at having such an incredibly busy night. But he was still not given any quarter from his new comrades in arms as they asked him, "How are you going to cope when we really get busy?"

His second night duty and 6pm parade time again. Despite the fifteen calls the previous shift our new boy repeated his immaculate turn out. You might be forgiven for thinking he never got stuck in on the rubbish fires, burning derelicts and the two more serious fires, one involving a high-rise flat and the other an underground car park blaze. His second night was calmer but only marginally, and I do not recall any occasion that he did not maintain this high standard in personal appearance regardless of what was thrown at him.

Taking charge

Four of my watch were keen to progress their careers. The Leading Fireman was waiting on his Sub Officer's practical examinations and much to the dismay of the watch he had them drilling each shift from the Fire Service drill book until he got his promotion drills word perfect. I and my Sub Officer had been running promotion classes in addition to providing the Leading Fireman with free access to the drill yard. The other three firemen, having passed both the leading fireman's written and practical examination, had not been successful at interview for the leading fireman's promotion panel. They had to take turns in "acting up" at the station, as they were excluded from being offered temporary promotion at other stations, until there were no other "panellists" left on the current list.

These three "junior" contenders would help out in the station office, to learn the procedures and to acquire the general administrative knowledge required of any junior officer. But the opportunity to ride regularly in charge of an engine was sadly lacking, not least because I had an incredibly conscientious substantive office staff and the thought of going sick was anathema to both of them. I wanted to be able to help these three out so I put a suggestion to them that might enhance their operational skills as potential leading firemen. The idea also needed the support of the watch generally to work, but one thing at a time.

The proposal was that when they rode in the back of the pump with me in charge and we were ordered to a shout, providing it was not a make-up, I would pass them the teleprinter ordering slip. Then the fireground decision-making would be theirs, and I would only step in should I consider their actions hazardous or that they might get me the sack! They would cover a whole shift, a day or night duty, and the messages and the gathering of incident information would fall to them. I would, as far as possible, just watch. Having considered the implications, two said they wished to give it a try, the third (who had transferred in from Mitcham) wanted to see how the other two got on first. Having already discussed the idea with my two junior officers they agreed to play along, as did the watch.

Our "new pin" turned out to be the first guinea pig. I told him on day duties that on nights he would ride the back of the pump and the ordering slips would be passed back to him. Although enthusiastic he said he had never heard of this type of thing being done before. As that night shift started, he admitted to being somewhat apprehensive, realising that what he wanted to send as a radio message, in my name, I would actually let him send. "What if I cock it all up?" he asked as we were putting our firegear on the pump. "Well, I guess I will get a bollocking for getting it wrong," I replied, just a little concerned myself now about the wisdom of this "on the job" training scheme.

The first call came before supper, an inconsequential shout to a shut in a lift, followed soon after to a car alight in Brixton Road. I passed the ordering slips behind me to this young "apprentice" sitting in the back of the pump who clearly took his role seriously. These types of calls were run of the mill and my experienced crews took them in their stride, following through the procedures required of them. With regard to the lift incident, they established that the occupants of the lift were alright before ensuring that the power supply was isolated to the affected lift. My unofficial "junior officer" was required to ensure that the hand winding gear was correctly fitted before (and not after) the lift brake was released; then the lift was wound in the correct direction whilst the occupants were reassured. Once the occupants had been released it was necessary to ensure that the lift doors were closed and that the scene was left secure. Plus, he was also responsible for sending the correct messages to control. It was one thing being part of the crew, but he was rapidly learning it was something else directing them. For their part the crew went along with this role-play in very accommodating fashion; it was that type of watch.

In the months that followed the others benefited from my unorthodox delegated authority, the first two (thankfully) not getting into too much trouble. I only got the occasional bollocking for a message that some senior officer considered poorly worded or not quite appropriate. But what do they say about, "You cannot make an omelette if you do not first break some eggs." Not only were these promotion students gaining operational command skills but they were also learning a lot about themselves and what judgement calls to make. Often it would be necessary to relieve them of this unofficial command role when we arrived at a fire and people were reported trapped inside the building or where we attended calls on another station's ground and their crews were also in attendance. Even then I would let then talk me through their decision-making process and ask them to justify their proposed course of action.

Towards the end of a pretty hectic day duty during the school holidays, when the local kids were keeping us busy with lighting fires (and then relighting almost as soon as we left the scene) a call came in to a fire in an unoccupied house in Stockwell Road. "Unoccupied" meant very little in Brixton, because if somewhere was not legally occupied it was inevitably occupied illegally by either squatters or vagrants, or both! With our pump ordered from the station and the Pump ladder (returning from another call) ordered via the radio, I passed the teleprinter call slip behind me as it was a nominated training day.

I arrived first on the pump but I could hear the Pump ladder in the distance. The fire was in an extensive four-storey terraced house in a very poor state of repair. In its heyday it would have accommodated a well-to-do family with a cook, a nanny and probably housemaids too. Now it was just lying vacant, a shadow of its former self, giving refuge to the homeless or drug addicts that sought its sanctuary. Whoever started the blaze had long departed, but a serious fire was now in progress involving the ground floor back room, presently spreading up the wide timber staircase to the first floor above. We were riding five and five and had been for quite some while now, so extra pairs of hands were becoming increasingly available at shouts. Seeing the fire situation confronting him today's "student" prepared to return the call slip, which I declined. "No, this is yours," I said. "What are you going to do about it?" He had by now ridden in charge of the Pump ladder on a number of occasions so being in charge of a one appliance shout was not unfamiliar to him. He could see the intensity of the fire developing, the heat and flames making their way to the first floor, the crackling of burning timber and sound of falling plaster emanating from the back of the building. "I think I should make this up," he said, seeking reassurance. "I think I should make 'em four, don't you?"

"Get some water on it first," I suggested "and see what happens." The rest of the crew were not interested in our little debate as a jet was speedily set into the pump and a very convenient hydrant augmented our own limited water supply. Flames in the ground floor were starting to lick their way along the ceiling towards the entrance door as the first jet was coming up the front steps leading into the house.

With the Pump ladder crew now in attendance a second line of hose was taken through the adjoining unoccupied house to cover the back of the burning building. As they were going in a motley collection of unwashed and rag-tag individuals were making a hasty exit. Using a combination of a jet and spray the pump's crew started their attack on the fire and were immediately engulfed in a wall of steam! (In those first few seconds, water hitting the fire instantly vaporises as its cooling effect begins to take hold.) The scene was far more dramatic-looking than it was in reality. The whole house filled with smoke and steam before it made its escape to open air, via the various broken windows above us. The sound of the Pump ladder crew's jet could now be heard coming through the back window and striking at the heart of the blaze. "Still want to make it up?" I asked. "It's your decision." But he could clearly see the effect the combined impact that the two crews were having and he said, "No we've got this one," as I sent him in to support the pump's crew. I, on the other hand, made my way around the back to see how the PL's crew were doing but not before waving home Clapham's PL and pump that had been ordered due to additional calls that had been received. The initial attack on the fire took about ninety seconds. Making sure it was out, took the next two hours as we cut away and damped down potential hot spots, ripping down lathe and plaster walls and ceilings to check for further fire spread. It would not have been the first time a crew went away too early without making sufficient checks only to be recalled to the very same incident hours later. Often, hidden smouldering had built up sufficient heat to rekindle a flame and thus start another fire.

A slightly crest fallen "student" said in a lull in the damping down, "I didn't need to make it up, did I?"

"The decision was all yours to make." I countered. "Others might see the incident and think this is not much of a four pumper when they arrive, but they did not have to make the call on what you saw when you first turned up. If in doubt make up. No one will think any the less of you. I wanted you to see the difference that a quick and concerted attack on a fire can make and the factors that can influence your decision-making. You had a good water supply, enough crew to get two jets to work without the added complications of rescues or trying to gain access to a boarded-up building. Experience will help you develop your skills. Sessions like this will hopefully give you that experience sooner rather than later."

I related to him my own very first make up as a young acting Leading Fireman, riding in charge of Lambeth's PE in the late 1960s. All of Lambeth's other appliances were already out on a shout and only the PE was available at the station. My early evening fire call was to a similar incident except the terraced house in Kennington Lane had three floors not four. There were only four of us riding the PE that night and the ground floor seemed (to me at least) well alight when we pulled up outside the house. Brixton and Southwark's PEs were the rest of the initial attendance but for now I was there on my own and any decision to make was mine.

The lightweight seventy-millimetre hose we now carried had yet to be issued and forty-five-millimetre hose was only carried on the ETs. Heavy canvas hose had to be used where a fire was more serious than just a hose reel jet could handle. Only one hundred gallons of water was carried then in the PE's tank and a jet would only last a few seconds without a hydrant being set in and supplementing the limited water supply. I reacted far too quickly to what I saw as we pulled up, even before any hose came off the engine. Smoke was coming out the door in considerable quantities and a wall of flame was clearly visible though the soot-stained front windows of the ground floor. I made pumps four on the appliance radio whilst the driver ran for the nearest hydrant and the two crew members got a jet to work. Although I was the acting leading fireman, I was also the least experienced member of the whole crew, my Station Officer having made sure that I had support on this, my inaugural tour in charge of Lambeth's PE.

As the water pulsed up the canvas hose, forcing the air before it out of the spray branch (jet) with a loud hissing noise, the two-man crew were ready and waiting to enter the building. With the water spray of the hand control branch on a wide cone and the central jet open wide they made very short work of the accumulation of burning rubbish filling the hallway before the three of us dragged the heavy lengths of hose into the house and directed our efforts on the main body of the fire in the front room. It was out almost as soon as we hit it with the water. We had put the bloody fire out and not even the first attendance appliances had arrived, let alone the "make pumps four" appliance and the Divisional BA van which attended all four-pump fires. I felt incredibly foolish and then embarrassed as Brixton's Station Officer, himself an acting Station Officer, took control of the incident. After a suitable time delay, he sent the radio "stop" message and saved me even further ignominy. All the other appliances had been returned to their stations leaving only my crew and Brixton's pump at the incident. "There is no disgrace in making jobs up young Pikey, this is your first and there will be plenty more." said the acting Station Officer as he took me to one side, out of earshot of the others. "You will get a bit of stick and ribbing but it goes with the territory if you want to ride in charge; there will always be someone who will think you should have done this or that differently. The disgrace is doing nothing, not reacting when you should have done, having too many fire engines is far less dangerous than having too few. Remember that." I did.

Dancing with death

Not all fatal fires are the result of the wholesale destruction of someone's home or even the room in which the body or bodies are discovered. Sadly, it was on the fifteenth floor of a high-rise council owned block of flats that an elderly gentleman met his untimely demise. He was apparently overcome by smoke from a small smouldering fire in his flat as he died alone in his bedroom.

There was no apparent sign of any fire on our arrival at the tower block to our call to, "A smell of burning, flat number 49 Cornwall Towers." This grey, unattractive, concrete and brick structure was typical of the high-rise flats that Lambeth had erected in the seventies as a solution to its social housing problems. It was still much better than some as we did not have to endure the overpowering stench of urine as we entered the lobby where we activated the fireman's switch. This would summon the fire lift and return it to the ground floor and give us access to the upper floors, under our sole control. Whilst some of my crew made ready the dry rising fire main, just in case, I, with three of Brixton's crew, went up in the fireman's lift, taking with us a branch, hose, BA sets and extinguishers to investigate the fifteenth floor. A pervasive smell of burning greeted us as we stepped out of the lift into the common lobby. Wisps of thin smoke could be seen seeping around the doorjamb of number 49. Neighbours said the man, who lived there on his own, was normally little trouble except when he had a drink and left his cooking on the stove to burn.

With no reply from No 49 we quickly made entry with two size ten fireboots shattering the door lock, sending the door flying inwards on its hinges. Whilst the flat was full of smoke there was neither the volume nor intensity, despite it being extremely acrid, to indicate a serious fire within the flat. The two wearing BA sets soon discovered the charred remains of the man's cooking left on the lighted gas cooker. With the windows opened the smoke quickly thinned. The BA now crew made a search of the flat, despite the reassurances of the neighbour who said that the man had been seen going out earlier in the evening. He said the man, who lived alone, liked spending his time in the pub where he got some company and conversation.

The BA crew found him, clearly dead, lying face down fully clothed across his bed. His left leg was towards the floor, his right arm extended towards his pillow and left arm bent at his side. It was evident he had been dead for a while. The appropriate messages were sent, saying I had a fatality and requesting the presence of the Police and the Brigade photographer for inquest purposes. There was little to do now other than wait. The fire had been extinguished and the evidence was soaking in the sink. The flat, whilst still reeking of the acrid smell of burnt food, was clear of smoke and the man's body remained in its final prone position on his bed.

The police with the duty Inspector duly arrived and we all awaited the arrival of the police surgeon to confirm the man's death. Photographs were taken of the deceased; the seat of the fire; the offending saucepan and the empty bottle of cheap whisky that lay by his side on the bedroom floor, and the empty glass by his hand on the bed. Arrangements were made by the police for the undertakers to collect the body and remove it to the local mortuary. All this would take some time and we were left, four of us and one very young and inexperienced policeman, with the corpse who would require the skills of the pathologist to determine his cause of death.

One hour turned into two before the "private ambulance" carrying the brown plastic coffin arrived and a worried looking undertaker poked his head around the door and said to nobody in particular, "The coffin won't fit in the bloody lift!" Obviously people were not meant to die in tower blocks. It was all too much for the poor young police officer who looked totally bemused. The lifts did not seem that small to us but the undertaker was quite insistent, "It ain't going to fit so what are we going to do?" Where did this "we" suddenly come from?

We had been at the flat for nearly three hours and past tales of who did what and where had dried up some time ago. Also the corpse had got bored stiff waiting for his ride to the mortuary, literally. Rigor-mortis had set in and he was firmly fixed in his deathly position on the bed. It was seeing him lying in that position that gave me the idea of how to move him down to the ground floor.

Telling one of my lads to take control of the fireman's lift again, and with the young policeman told to guard the lobby and not to let anyone out of their flats, I and my driver raised the completely rigid body off the bed into an upright position and stood him on the floor. His stance was that of a dancer doing the waltz with one of his arms raised and the other crooked at the elbow pointing down. I told the other member of the crew to put the dead man's feet on my fireboots and whilst I held his elevated arm with my left hand, I gripped his elbow with my right. In this dancing position and with the deceased man facing me I walked him to the lift, carrying him on my feet. Checking that the landing was clear I saw the astonished policeman watch us enter the lift and then disappear downwards. Passing our charge over to the undertakers, who now had the difficult task of fitting the extended body into the temporary coffin, we beat a hasty retreat back to the station and a long hot shower for me. The result of the post mortem found that the man died from natural causes, not from smoke inhalation thus saving me much report writing and my attendance at the coroner's court.

Snapshots of 1982/3

As you may have gathered Brixton was a busy station, one of the London Fire Brigade's busiest, and it was never out of the top four stations for the five years that I was the White Watch's Station Officer. 1982 saw the station top the league of "make ups" on its own ground with thirty-six four pump fires or above and with an annual total of two thousand one hundred and ten calls just on Brixton's ground alone. With another fourteen hundred calls off its ground Brixton beat the next highest station by a significant margin.

During this period there was considerable emphasis on fire station personnel getting more closely involved with community work. Delivering fire safety was one thing but this involved attending fêtes and church bazaars just so that we could get closer to the public. It was becoming a bit of a chore each weekend but watches had little choice as the era of meeting targets was upon us. In fact, they had been around for some while but had been measuring the number of hydrants tested or premises inspected under fire precautions law or regulations. Now much greater accountability of our time spent in productive work was under the microscope and it was not being received too well at stations.

But Brixton's White Watch was a happy band of men and none more so than Bruce. Bruce was a chunky, shortish chap with a cheery round face, rosy cheeks and with a little moustache that always seemed to need to grow just a bit more to actually look manly. He was a true character and someone who was very funny, often unintentionally. Yet he worked hard as a fireman and devoted considerable energy to voluntary duties as the station benevolent and welfare representative. He didn't drive, which was fortunate as he liked a drink, and this would occasionally expose his only flaw. If he had too much to drink his personality could change and he could become argumentative and even aggressive which lead him into getting in a few scraps now and then. But he had a heart of gold when he was sober and was every inch a fireman's fireman. He came to Brixton straight from training school and had a bit of a rocky start during his probation, which concluded before I joined the watch. However, his antics were still the stuff of station legend. He once managed to get his foot caught up in the hose reel tubing as it was being made up after a fire and was dragged, mumbling "Get this off me," as he was pulled along the street by the two firemen who were feeding the hose reel on to the power-assisted drum and wondering why it was slower than normal. Then at a chimney fire he poured two gallons of water, from a bucket he carried up a turntable ladder, down the wrong chimney pot and wondered why two very blackened faces were shouting up at him after a "ton" of soot suddenly, and unexpectedly, fell into their grate and exploded in their faces. Needless to say, much report writing followed after that whilst Bruce kept a low profile and wondered if he still had a job. Well he did and made a valuable contribution to the watch. His was the only watch wedding I ever attended and where we did the full guard of honour thing with crossed axes held over the bride and groom as they left the church when he got married the following year. It goes without saying that Bruce had one hell of a reception, even inviting the Divisional Commander, who secretly had a soft spot for Brixton but would not admit to it publicly.

Meanwhile the much-heralded central mobilising system, promoted with such a fanfare in 1980, remained firmly stuck in the design stage. However, firemen's personal safety improved considerably in 1982 with the introduction of the positive pressure facemask fitted to our BA sets. This meant if a fireman could not achieve a completely air tight seal around the rim of his BA face mask, the slight positive pressure of air inside the mask leaked out and thus prevented toxic or poisonous gases seeping in and then possibly being inhaled. Face seals could be impaired by facial hair such as long sideburns or beards. The foolhardy could thereby endanger themselves and others whilst in BA. Fortunately, none of the White Watch were into facial hair and even the unshaven were sent off to shave if their seven o'clock shadow was considered to be pushing their luck. But there were those who persisted and they then were subjected to a facemask seal test and if they failed and refused to remove their facial growth were pushed down the discipline route until they conformed.

The UK was shot (literally) on to the world stage that year when Argentina invaded the Falklands on 2nd April. The successful outcome of the war in Britain's favour was cited by many as the reason behind the return of Margaret Thatcher for a second term the following year. At home the cost of petrol was one pound fifty-nine pence per gallon (that was thirty-one pence a litre!). The average house price was around twenty-three and a half thousand pounds according to the statisticians who clearly were not trying to buy a house in London, where the prices were significantly higher and the bank rate stood at ten percent. For those of us with a mortgage we were well aware of the financial pain that those rates brought; they would get even worse. Channel Four was launched this year and Dutch Elm disease hit the UK with such vengeance that up to twenty million elms would perish and change the face of the English countryside. The wearing of seat belts also became mandatory although it would take years before the practice was widely enforced in the brigade.

The previous year (1981) was the last time the Greater London Council would go to the polls. A Labour controlled GLC was returned but in a clever coup Ken Livingstone, dubbed Red Ken by the right-wing press, managed to oust the elected Labour leader in a behind closed doors coup, and was elected its new leader. This was seen as treachery by some – it was certainly undemocratic, but he remained its leader right until the GLC was abolished a few years later. In the interim the so-called "Looney left" was directing GLC policy and many of their policies actually proved highly successful. Others had more questionable results. This Labour controlled GLC was a thorn in the side of the Conservative government. Its famous banner strung up across the front of County Hall, in full view of the Palace of Westminster, reminding the government just how many people were unemployed. Mrs Thatcher would wreak her revenge on the GLC eventually and bring about its abolition albeit with the narrowest of parliamentary majorities.

Local authorities in London, including the Brigade, were falling over each other to be the one that did not discriminate against the largest number of groups in their job ads. "We are an equal opportunities employer," became the by-word in their job adverts. Disabilities prevented many from employment as a fireman, now termed firefighter. But homophobia was still rife in our macho working environment. If any were gay, and there must have been plenty in the brigade, they remained firmly locked in the closet. Lambeth Council, which covered the whole of the Brixton area, openly elected a black lesbian as its council leader, something that would have been unheard of a few years previously. Some used this as an extreme example of political correctness, something that was also making its presence felt in brigade policy and language.

The Brigade was governed by and answerable to this Labour controlled GLC. If it actually existed, any reluctance to recruit female firefighters was finally shattered in 1982 when Sue Batten completed her training and was posted to the E Division. She would later transfer to Old Kent Road fire station, serving on the Red Watch. I never met her but she proved to be an excellent ambassador for the introduction of women into the fire service. She was not the first nationally but was within London. She did not open the floodgates but certainly breached the dam. Others would follow and a very small minority (with their own feminist political agenda) did little to endear themselves, or sister firefighters, into this male dominated environment.

Brixton's watches were not put to the test with the posting of a female firefighter, but others were and some clearly failed. Here, sexist prejudice and active harassment, including sexual, made the life of this new breed of firefighter, in a few cases, completely unbearable. Training in equality helped to provide a workable system for the introduction of more women firefighters. Those stations where adequate facilities existed for washing and changing, plus a separate dormitory area, were identified. But considerable resistance to change and prejudice continued. Change was slow but came as more and more women joined the brigade. Eventually full integration would be achieved even if the percentage of female firefighters remained disappointingly low when compared the number of male firefighters and which GLC recruitment policies set out to achieve. One of Sue Batten's later contemporaries would eventually rise to principal rank but that would not be until the 21st century.

The last snapshot from this period was a near disaster, at least from the point of view of the tenant of a nearby council flat. Fire can hold such a terror for many people, its raw power, its destructive forces and unforgiving nature making rational thought and actions impossible. Brixton's pump was at the far end of the ground, engaged in hydrant inspection, and I had swapped with the Sub Officer and was now riding in charge of the pump ladder and made up its crew of four.

Nothing had interrupted the day shift, in the way of shouts, until our first call came in the early afternoon. We were called to a fire in a maisonette just off Millbrook Road, a couple of streets away from the station. We arrived in under a minute and saw smoke forcing its way round the second-floor level flat door and windows. The low-rise block of maisonettes had garages along the whole length of the ground floor. The two-storey maisonettes were one on top of the other with a common balcony running the length of the first and third floor level, which provided access to the individual maisonettes.

Unable to drive down the vehicle access side of the building because of obstructions, the pump ladder remained at the end of the block whilst the hose reel tubing was run out ready to be hauled aloft. It was common practice at Brixton (and many other stations) for the crews to rig in BA en route, but this call was so close to the station that the lads grabbed their sets and rigged whilst running up to the second level access balcony (three floors up). The front door was firmly shut when we got to the affected flat but a fire was clearly evident inside. Armed with the hose reel the crew kicked the door in and an entry was made, leaving me with their BA tallies outside, pulling up extra tubing as they made their way in.

The rush of air through the open door revived the smouldering fire and an armchair suddenly burst into flames considerably increasing the choking smoke already filling the flat. From somewhere above me came a shout, more of a wailing actually, as the occupant trapped upstairs in the maisonette, alarmed by either the sound of the door being kicked in or the smell of the smoke, or both, realised that he was trapped in his upstairs room. He had opened the sliding window and was already in the process of climbing out four floors up with absolutely no alternative practical escape route. Looking up over the balcony I tried to tell him to stay calm and stay put and someone would bring him down safely. But his pitiful cries for help in some Caribbean tongue meant whatever I was saying was clearly not getting through, as he was by now half in and half out of the open window.

Unable to shout to my BA crew I jumped up on the balcony wall and positioned myself directly under the man and pushed my arms up above my head, wedging myself between the top of the balcony wall and the ceiling above. Our black, and very scared, friend had by now climbed completely out of the window. He was suspended by his arms whilst hanging from the window frame by his fingers. Luckily his feet found my shoulders and I was praying for the swift arrival of the pump's crew (or anyone else!) to help. My thoughts were that I could at least support the man until I had some more help and then we might be able to pull him to safety. He, however, clearly had other ideas and staying there standing on my shoulders was not one of them. How he managed to do what happened next, I still have absolutely no idea because he just let go of the window frame and dropped! His feet went either side of my head and in front of my shoulders, stopping below my chest as he made a grab for my head with both his hands. My own desire for self-survival kicked in as I pushed upwards for all I was worth in an effort not to be pulled backwards and fall to the ground, some thirty feet below. Even with him to cushion my landing I did not fancy my chances of surviving the fall. He was, however, extremely nimble and agile and was already moving his weight in front of me, sufficiently so that I could now lower one arm as he swung around in front of me and jumped to the safety of the balcony floor. I followed him down.

Finally the pump's crew arrived just as one of the BA crew returned to tell me that he had searched upstairs and found no one. I said, "I know I just helped him out!" Our friend was clearly grateful, but no one could understand exactly what he was saying. My messages seemed a bit of an anti-climax now but with the pump ladder driver able to leave his engine under guard with one of the pump's crew, I told him to send "Small fire flat, hose reel." How to word the escape from the fourth-floor window, and who would believe it anyway?

BBC Shouts

The BBC wanted to make a documentary about the brigade's front-line crews and life at a typical station. The show's producer, Fisher Dilke, approached the brigade and, whether it was his choice or the powers that be, Brixton's pole position as regards its operational workload made it the subject of this hour-long national television documentary. Two watches were short listed to portray life at London's busiest fire station. Station Officer Lou Gill, Blue Watch's governor, and myself with the White, were nominated to host the producer's research visits, prior to the actual filming starting.

Fisher Dilke was a tall, athletic, bespectacled man, highly educated and very well spoken, but incredibly laid back. Both watches were to host him for a complete shift (two days and two nights) and as the White and Blue Watches worked back to back, he would come and go (at the station) over an eight-day period. He asked to be treated as though he was just a shadow, an observer noting how the station worked and how the watches reacted and were run. Whatever he was looking for he didn't actually say. In a highly unusual agreement no senior officers chaperoned our visitor and he had the run of the station, mixing freely whilst acting as a detached spectator, yet all the time planning his film in his head.

With more free time on night duties he spent time sitting around the mess-table absorbing the stories and tales of incidents he might have wished he had witnessed at first hand. Humour came through in most of the stories and we were not too convinced that he shared or understood our "black" humour. He requested a further final visit to both watches prior to making his decision about which to film. A little more excitement accompanied this visit as we had an exceptionally busy day and he seemed to genuinely enjoy the experience.

His mind made up, he called me personally to say he would be filming the Blue Watch. Although naturally disappointed I was not surprised given some of the characters on the Blue Watch and the charisma of its Station Officer. Lou and I got on just fine in the atmosphere of friendly rivalry that existed between us, each of us thinking we had the better watch; but I knew I had and he just had difficulty accepting the fact!

Lou had a natural flair and a pleasing personality. He was an excellent choice to front a programme not just about Brixton fire station but to project a good and truthful image of life at station level. Tall, well-built and confident he acquitted himself well when talking on camera and most annoyingly, came across as photogenic and articulate as he stood in the station watchroom to give the viewing public an insight into the station and its ground. His stomach appeared wash-board flat beneath his crisp white uniform shirt and completing the look were his intelligent eyes and short dark hair. He had a "polished" south London accent which could charm the birds from the trees and frequently did. But bringing a film crew on to a station with the expectation that the call rate, or make-ups, they will match statistics can be a big disappointment. Whilst all the other Brixton watches were maintaining the near normal call rate, near doom and gloom befell the poor Blue Watch. Burning rubbish in the grotty back streets of Brixton, a car alight and a couple of small flat fires were the mainstay of their operational input. However, the watch made a very good fist of it all and Lou sought Equity membership, once his face was plastered across the nation's television screens.

Fire Investigation

The concoction in the firebomb was thicker than water and therefore had more surface tension. It flung outward and dripped and ran and burned fiercely. It set fire to the wall immediately. The dry old wood panelling burned with no hesitation at all. Blue flames crept upwards and sideways and the faded cream paint of the saloon bar bubbled and peeled ahead of them. Hungry tongues of flame found any vertical seams between the panels and raced up them.

When the flames reached the ceiling, they paused momentarily and then curved horizontally and spread outwards. The air in the long bar area stirred to feed the fledging inferno. The flames were blue and smooth and curled and liquid. They glowed with a mysterious inner light as the flames released gas and vapour from anything flammable with which it came into contact. Flakes of burning paint were drifting on the hot currents and landing randomly. They set fire to whatever was not already alight. Now the fire was creeping clockwise towards the bar itself and the long array of spirit bottles held captive in the chromed optics. The fire was now moving fast, very fast. The original accelerant was all but consumed but there was plenty more to fuel the blaze.

The flames had found the bottles of brandy, whisky and vodka stacked on the mirrored shelves, which were already cracked by the intense heat. Pressure within the bar was rising. Superheated smoke was in the hundreds of degrees centigrade. Smoke was layering at the ceiling and crowding down in layers. The first of the spirit bottles either cracked or burst; either way it released its contents that erupted into a fireball leading to a domino effect as the other spirit bottles followed suit, consuming the stacked shelves in a waterfall of flowing iridescent flames.

Naturally none of this I saw at the time. I only witnessed the result as my two fire engines pulled up outside the blazing public house in Mostyn Road. We were soon to be joined by the crews of Peckham and Lambeth PLs who had been ordered on to the blaze to which Control was now receiving multiple nine-nine-nine calls.

Even as my first BA crew made their forced entry into the burning ground floor interior of the saloon bar it was possible to detect the distinct odour of an accelerant. It was a smell that seemed to be petroleum based. That and the fact that one of the windows was clearly smashed inward, and not blown out, meant it did not need Sherlock Holmes to deduce that this fire was clearly deliberate.

The Brigade had introduced a Fire Investigation Teams some years earlier. They had since been expanded due largely to their success at improving causation rates and now each of the brigade's eleven divisions had their own dedicated fire investigation teams. Each team consisted of a watch related Station Officer and Leading Fireman with specialist fire investigation training. Their role was to assist the officer in charge of a fire to accurately determine the cause of every fire they attended. They also worked closely with police forensic teams where fires were deemed "suspicious," although in all known crimes involving fire or arson, the police always remained the lead agency.

Having made pumps four I knew I would get such a fire investigation team as part of the "make up" response. However, it was clear to me that this was an obvious case of arson, a criminal offence. So immediately after the informative message I requested the attendance of the police "To assist in fire investigation." The Brigade remained very prescriptive in the formation of its fireground messages and even when the most obvious crime had been committed, that necessitate the attendance of the CID, woe betide any officer who tried to request them directly. So I waited for PC "Plod" to arrive, then outline the circumstances and my suspicions and he, or she, would duly summon the CID.

In the meantime, the fire investigation team from Clapham had arrived and using their Gas-tech device they confirmed the presence of a petrol-based accelerant. This had seeped into the thick bar carpet covering the saloon floor.

Despite the fierce intensity of the fire the heat had risen upwards leaving the foam underside of the carpet virtually undamaged. The foam had absorbed the un-burnt arsonist cocktail and left its tell-tale trace signature in the residue.

Both Brixton and Stockwell were busy areas for the local police station to cover so it was not unusual for there to be a delay before the police arrived on scene, especially for just "fire investigation." Serious assault, rape and robbery including street muggings warranted a far more urgent response time particularly in this part of South West London. So with no policeman on scene and the FIT's Station Officer sifting the debris I crossed the road towards the adjacent housing estate in search of a potential witness to what might have happened. I had already given instructions that the immediate area of the saloon bar under the broken window should remain undisturbed. It was a crime scene and could yield possible evidence when the police's Scene of Crime officers (SOCOs) finally arrived. It was even taped off to ensure that no over-enthusiastic firefighter shovelled the evidence out the door!

At its height the fire had attracted quite an audience. Even at this late, now early, hour there was always someone about on Brixton's streets. Some of the adjacent estate's residents had just gone to their windows to look at all the excitement, others had ventured out on to their balconies, whilst quite a few had even got dressed, drawn to the street by their curiosity. Some did not bother dressing but stood in the street in just their night clothes passing a critical eye over the proceedings on what, for them, was a far from infrequent event on their doorsteps.

However, my attention was drawn to a young dishevelled black man who stood alone in the shadows of the underground car park entrance. I thought I had seen the same man as we were pulling up but I could not be sure, being preoccupied with the unfolding drama on the other side of the road, rather than its audience. But he looked the same nevertheless.

I half expected the man to turn tail and disappear into the murk of the sparsely lit car park but he stood his ground. He was probably in his early twenties, ebony black and scruffily dressed. Some little distance behind him was a rolled up sleeping bag, held together with a "bungee" strap and a black bin bag possibly containing all his worldly possessions.

I was still a few feet away when he said, *"What you gonna do mon?"*

The glazed look in his eyes and the difficulty he was having forming his Creole-English words said he was possibly high or drunk, but either way he seemed willing to talk. "Have you been here long?" I asked. *"Ya mon, I say I see every-ding."*

"What exactly did you see?" I continued.

"Dere mon in da moto car. It stop mon, he got out with a bottle din his hand, lit de bottle he brith wit him and trow it in de window. Dat's how the

world be mon – next big whoosh and fire. Moto car drive off real slow, no problem."

"Can I take your name?" I enquired. *"Don't try nah tricks on me mon. Day find me, day hurt me. Ya'll be okay but I won't. I say no more."* He did not and when I told the first policeman to arrive of this eyewitness he had already disappeared into the night.

This was not the only policeman to arrive as he was followed by others and the duty inspector. A succession of CID officers arrived, each one out-ranking the preceding one until finally a Detective Superintendent arrived. He was a giant of a man, at least six feet six inches tall with the face of a hardened rugby player. Mine was the only appliance left at the scene by now apart from the FIT team's mobile unit. My crew were shovelling the unrecognisable burned debris out through a now glassless window frame and damping down the remains as it landed in the street outside.

As the Superintendent took me gently aside, he said, "You were the first officer on the scene." It was not a question but a statement of fact. "I hear you let our eyewitness go," he said with a smile, but it could easily have been a sneer! "Anyway we think we know who he is. How did you spot him?" I explained but it was of little interest to him. The "Super's" presence here indicated that this was not just a one-off arson attack and he was clearly reading my mind when he said that a "turf-war" had broken out between rival gangs that ran South London protection rackets. He told me, "This is the sixth such attack in as many weeks. Oh, and by the way, an excellent job of preserving the crime scene. We have recovered most of the remains of the bottle that came through the window. Makes a pleasant change because you lot normally throw our evidence out with the rest of the crap." This time he really was smiling. "Someone will call at the station to take your statement." With that he turned and left and with the fire now totally extinguished we left too. The FIT crew remained to work alongside the SOCOs and the pub remained under police guard until their forensic team could make a minute search for any further evidence.

As so often happened we were just part of a continuing story. Although my statement was given to the police there was no subsequent follow up or any appearance at a criminal court case. The local "rag" covered the story and concluded the article with the well-worn phrase, "The police are continuing with their investigations." Finding the cause of a fire was one thing, finding the culprit was very often a very different tale. The words of my missing witness came back to me, *"Dat's how the world be; Ja mon!"*

The Good, the bad and the ugly

The Good. You would not think that in the space of twenty-four hours that you would see such a dramatic change in a watch's performance. But over two consecutive night duties that proved to be exactly the case. The first night duty was on a Sunday. After parade and with the regular appliance checks completed, the crews stood down, as they were free from normal work routines on a Sunday evening. Wally was now the mess manager and he was an accomplished cook. We were all looking forward to tonight's creation. Brixton's regular "dinner parties" were quite an event. Wally was fast becoming a bit of a "cause-célèbre" with his special three course meals and we occasionally invited our watch ADOs along as paying guests. They loved these evenings as once again they enjoyed the cut and thrust of mess-table banter whilst enjoying a glass of Chateau plonk with their meal. Tonight, it was just the watch however and our supper was cut short as the station bells' sudden ringing saw dinner plates hastily shoved into the kitchen hotplate, prior to the crews running to the pole house and sliding down to the appliance room below.

"Fire at Tulse Hill junction of Brixton Water Lane," was the only information on the ordering slip as both machines turned right out of the station and headed up towards Coldharbour Lane. Our suppers would not be seen again for many hours as additional calls to a warehouse alight were received and Clapham's pair were sent on additionally. If it was possible to have a text book fire where everything fell into place at the right time and crews responded without hesitation and demonstrated the art of firemanship (firefightingship never sounded right!) this was it.

The warehouse, I subsequently discovered, was owned by Forte (the hotel chain) and it stood on a site that was surrounded by residential property. Although a single-storey structure the pitched roof was about fifty feet high and had twenty feet high surrounding brick walls. It was forty feet wide and sixty feet deep and was set back from the main road. The force with which the dense smoke was being driven through the roof vents and the deep red glow that could be seen through the barred and reinforced glazing indicated a serious fire within the warehouse. The warehouse was extremely well secured, with its thick security padlocks, fitted to the double corrugated metal front doors, which would prevent any speedy access into the building.

I knew this location very well, including the position of the surrounding hydrants. I did not need a prompt from a crewmember shouting out the hydrant's position found in the hydrant location book maintained in the back of the machine. (I remembered them from a previous serious fire directly across the road, where the dogs were rescued, when I was at West Norwood.) Even if we made a quick entry into the building, which was looking extremely doubtful, three or four BA crews would be called for. With the PL pulling past the incident and the pump stopping before it at the road junction, I instructed my driver to radio a priority message, "Make pumps eight," before telling the crew to twin the supply from the double hydrant on the corner. As hose lines and jets were made ready the PL crew tried to force an entry into the warehouse via the front entrance. I made a quick reconnaissance of the side of the building to assess the potential for further spread and returned to the front to direct the reinforcing crews. Even through the frosted wired glazing along the side of the warehouse fire could be seen involving a large proportion of the building. Within less than a minute of our arrival three jets were charged and ready with one being directed to cool the side of the warehouse, but still the crews had not been able to force their way in past the padlocks and security arrangements that were in place.

Clapham had a Sub Officer in charge that night and he reported to me at the front of the warehouse. I ordered him and directed his crews into the next street, behind the warehouse, to make an attack on the back via the private houses' back gardens. Ensuring he had his hand-held (EVAC) radio with him I told him to let me know what the situation was when he got there. With the sound of two-tone horns moving ever closer, Lambeth's and West Norwood's appliances were deployed to cover the Brixton Water Lane side of the fire. The divisional BA control van had arrived from Clapham and the Sub Officer in charge had established his control point just the other side of the junction and was preparing for the arrival of the Brigade's major control unit. Making pumps eight not only gets you eight fire engines, control automatically orders on other supporting appliances as well. They had ordered two ETs, one hose laying lorry and the Brigade control unit. Additional senior officers were also sent on to take control of the fire since a Station Officer can only remain in charge of a four-pump fire. But I was in charge for now and would be until I was relieved

Peckham and Forest Hill's crews made up the balance of the make-up. With the exception of Forest Hill, I knew all the surrounding B division officers in charge very well and had a good rapport with each of them. Giving them a clear brief of what I wanted, and communicating via the hand-held radios, a formidable attack was waged on the blaze that had by now broken through part of the roof and had blown out some of the side windows. Finally, the front doors gave up the struggle and succumbed to the combined physical assault made on them by large axes and sledgehammers to allow access into the building by BA crews armed with jets.

I had in my head where all my resources were deployed and was satisfied that I had sufficient water supplies available to feed the six jets now in use. The two ET crews would back up the BA crews, if needed, when they arrived. The BACV Sub Officer was now picking my brains to draw up the fireground map. This would be duplicated on the Brigade Control unit, when it arrived, showing a simple plan of the fireground and listing what crews were working and where. The Sub Officer had sent his leading fireman to collect the appliance nominal roll boards from every appliance in attendance and place them in the dedicated holders on the BA van. This was an essential procedure in case of an emergency evacuation of all crews. A roll call would then be made to identify if anyone was missing, possibly trapped.

Roger Vaughan was now a temporary Divisional Officer and he beat the duty ADO, who was somewhere else in the Division, to the scene of this fire. Roger booked in with the BA van and found me at the front of the warehouse monitoring the fire situation and checking on the progress of the crews.

Although the blaze looked dramatic, with flames now seventy to eighty feet reaching up into the night sky, it was going nowhere other than eventually out. Roger formally took over command and I briefed him on what I had done and who was where. It was still a serious fire and Roger was now in charge. I didn't know it then but Roger thought further assistance was necessary and made pumps ten, only to hand over command to the duty ACO upon his arrival. With the Brigade control unit now the control point, its crew was monitoring and recording the fireground activity and I was free to re-join my crews.

After about another hour the "fire surrounded" was sent which indicated that the fire was under control and the stop message followed some little while afterwards. With the blaze totally under control I was left in charge of the four pumps tasked with continuing to damp down and turn over the considerable debris, quenching hot spots and ripping down false partitions searching for any remaining signs of fire. With the details gathered to complete the fire report and a senior fire prevention officer tasked to investigate the cause of the blaze my pump's crew made our way back to the station in the early hours having handed over to the two pump crews that would continue to damp down the fire until satisfied it was completely extinguished. Arriving back at the station the only other charred debris I had to contend with was dispatching the congealed and dried up remains of my dinner to the dustbin.

The Bad. 24 hours later who would guess that things could be so utterly different? The call came in after supper and we were able to eat in peace for once. We were attending a call to a disused synagogue at the bottom end of Brixton Hill. The former synagogue was recognised as a well-known "squat" for vagrants or other local "street" people. What might have been a good little jet job, handled by just Brixton's crew, turned into a nightmare! The problems started when the PL driver parked on top of the nearest available street hydrant. While the two fire engine drivers ran up and down Brixton Hill frantically looking for a hydrant, first the three hundred gallons of water in the pump's water tank and then the three hundred gallons in the PL's tank ran out. The blaze inside the semi-derelict building, still not under control, regained a strong foothold in the ramshackle interior of the once house of Jewish worship.

Then, with a hydrant finally located seven lengths of hose away and my stop message already overdue, a very drunk vagrant came staggering out from the undergrowth asking for his pal. Seeing the blaze inside the building, or rather the considerable smoke coming out of the door, which now had a jet and a hose reel directed on to the fire burning inside, he started to shout for his pal saying, "He's in the building, he's in the building." With considerable irritation I interrogated this poor soul somewhat harshly but he held his drunken ground insisting that his pal must be in the building.

I was stuffed! Instead of sending my considerably overdue stop message I had no choice but to send a priority message, "Make pumps four persons reported." My crew could not search the building for the drunk's pal and fight the fire at the same time. I followed the make-up message with my informative message, "Disused synagogue of 1 floor (it was actually two!) thirty feet by forty feet. Ten per cent of ground floor alight. One person believed involved search by BA crew in progress." The fire was not yet contained but a thorough search had to be made to locate the man's alleged missing friend. Nobody was found but that did not stop that night's duty Divisional Officer from telling me my dubious future when he arrived because of the delayed "persons reported" message and commenting on my lack of officership. There was no defence to offer so I did not try. I was duly bollocked and he left. As the crew was making up the gear, after eventually extinguishing the blaze, a bag of rubbish laying against a street wall outside the building got kicked away revealing a hydrant tablet. Seeing it I followed the hydrant marking and found the hydrant cover under the front wheel of the PL!

The atmosphere, when we returned to the station, was strained as I vented my spleen that the hydrant location book had not been used and then parking on the bloody thing just added to my already short temper. Silence reigned as we all took to our beds and I reflected on the uncharacteristic under performance of us all.

My mood was not improved when at about 5am the following morning we got another shout. When I read the teleprinter ordering to my horror it was to exactly the same premises as the previous evening's debacle. This time the fire had managed to get a considerable hold before our arrival and I reluctantly had to "make pumps four" immediately. Now with every member of the crew knowing exactly where the hydrant was located there was no delay in getting a couple of jets to work and my BA crews got stuck in.

Now I say reluctantly because having to make pumps four at the same location in the space of a shift always raises alarm bells with senior management, none more so than my own Divisional Commander and very little got past Brian Butler. I wondered, "Did we put the first one out properly or not?" I thought we had but there was no denying the evidence before my eyes. This bloody building was alight yet again. This was the very question the same Divisional Officer put to me as he returned for the second time. But until I could get back in the building to investigate, I could not reassure him otherwise. I was not the only one having these doubts for my crews looked very crestfallen as we started to turn over the debris after bringing the blaze under control. Small pockets of fire can continue to smoulder for considerable periods under debris and can re-ignite whatever surrounds it. Although I know I made a thorough search and examination before leaving the night before I was feeling more and more uncomfortable and thinking, how could I have missed the signs?

Out of sheer bloody mindedness I had made the crews stay working longer than was necessary because I was so miffed about that damn hydrant. However, now the seats of this fire were concentrated in separate areas but this still did not discount the possibility that we allowed the fire to spread or left a "bull's-eye" (a small core of burning material that can be found in timber joints and beams) to re-ignite.

Before the Divisional Officer departed, he warned me, "You haven't heard the last of this Station Officer Pike." But my own self-doubt was brought to an end by the arrival of a police patrol car. I had requested the attendance of the police "to assist in fire investigation," more to cover my back than for any hard evidence I had discovered. The police constable came over and said, "No need to investigate; a guy was seen running away from the fire this morning and he was nicked up Brixton Hill. He has put his hands up to starting the blaze this morning and the one last night too." Feeling very relieved, no one was more pleased than me when that particular night duty was over.

The Ugly. Myatts Field estate and Angel Town estate represented the worst of 1980s inner city housing development solutions. Large swathes of back-to-back brick-built terraces went under wholesale demolition in the late seventies and early eighties for the construction of new inner-city estates. Brixton and Stockwell were not immune from these housing development programmes and acre upon acre of land either side of Brixton Road was swept up to become part of Lambeth Council's urban regeneration policy.

Sadly, what might have looked innovative and pleasing to the eye on the drawing board did not transfer into reality. These vast multi-layered flats, maisonettes and extensive underground car parks and lock-up garages all too soon identified the social problems that their very construction brought about. What seemed a characteristic of British municipal housing designers in this period was their belief that, at least where the poor and less privileged were concerned, aesthetics did not matter. Having just moved from what the planners deemed a slum, why should those being relocated care about greenery? Open pleasant spaces in which to meet or a garden in which to sit were deemed unnecessary when the occupants are housed in new centrally heated flats, built in modern elevated unfriendly designs and, not to mention, cheap materials. With the elevated "streets in the sky" there existed a criss-cross of pedestrian access paths, providing an escape route for those that wished to avoid contact with the world below.

The result of this planning and development was the construction of scores of similar estates across the Greater London area, concrete wildernesses, brutal in their utilitarianism. The Myatts Field estate in Mostyn Road was not even completed before the first phase started falling apart, the underground garages rarely used for legitimately parked cars, the lock ups used for other illegal or offensive purposes and a safe location to "torch" a stolen car without prying eyes seeing what was going on, until that is thick black smoke filled the whole space and left its tell-tale signs up the grey concrete walls above the entrances.

In later years this new concept in housing would itself be replaced and more conventional housing schemes erected. They returned to the sense of community and not the former feeling of isolation of these designs. But for now, the estates would continue to add to the station's operational workload. Sadly, for many people that had to live there, add to their misery.

New Year's party

It was to be my last Christmas and New Year at Brixton, only I did not know it then. Another duty over Christmas spent at a fire station also meant we would pick up the New Year's Eve duty too. The watch had asked permission to hold a party at the station on one of our night duties and I had said fine, providing there was no drinking and driving for the two drivers. With only nine of us on duty it was not going to be reminiscent of the big parties at Lambeth but nevertheless every effort was made to make it a memorable occasion. Two of the watch had used their resourcefulness and had invited some local female company. Some "friends" they had said and these friends brought along their girl friends too and a very pleasant evening started to unfold with only a couple of interruptions before midnight (and the New Year) with uneventful calls.

What the drivers were not drinking was more than made up for by the way the "girls" could put their drink away as they circulated freely with the watch in the station snooker room. (It was the only decent sized room on the station.) The two "friends" were off limits as far as the instigators of the evening were concerned but their friends were fair game with those that wished to chance their luck.

As the New Year arrived and kisses were exchanged (mainly with the girls!) the dimmed lights of the snooker room suddenly shone brightly as they came on in unison with the station call bells ringing. With whispers of "see you in a minute" the crews mounted the two engines and we were on our way out to a fire call on our own ground. It was a fire in a public house between Stockwell and Brixton Road and even before we cleared the end of Gresham Road, the home of Brixton fire station, further calls were being received and Peckham's PL was ordered additionally in support.

A serious fire involving the pub's ground floor bar area was self-evident as I pulled up in the pump behind the PL, whose crew was already making a grab for the forty-five-foot Lacon extension ladder. As a matter of course my driver had left sufficient space for them to pull the ladder off the PL. Frightened faces were up at the third (top) floor windows and calling for urgent help. I made "Pumps four persons reported" whilst the crew ran across the road with the ladder. It was pitched and extended to one of the top windows. Meanwhile a jet was brought to bear on the ground floor fire via the shattered remains of the side door, which had come worst off after an argument with Bunny wielding a sledgehammer. With the staircase heavily smoke logged and the occupants in no mind to stay within the building, while one of Brixton's crew remained on the third floor to reassure the frightened residents, three people were quickly assisted down the ladder one after the other and all were brought to safety. Peckham's arrival added greater weight to the rescues and the attack on the fire and when the fourth pump arrived, I set the crew to work in BA searching the remainder of the building and ventilating it.

The casualties were all shocked and one had suffered considerably from smoke inhalation and was removed to King's College Hospital by ambulance as a precautionary measure. As the ambulance was departing, the duty ADO arrived having been informed of the incident by control. He was Brixton's current Red Watch Station Officer and had been "acting up" in his first temporary promotion to higher rank. I was just about to start my investigation to try to determine the cause of the fire when I was told by one of the reinforcing pump's crew that I was wanted by the ADO at the BA control van.

The lads had worked extremely well and carried out the rescues in an exemplary fashion. It was a testament to their training and a fine example of good old-fashioned team work and mutual support. The fire was confined to the ground floor but heat and smoke had caused extensive damage elsewhere in the building because the severity of the heat and the thick smoke that had mushroomed up into the stairwell and into the first-floor rooms.

Wishing my opposite number (whilst at Brixton) a "Happy New Year" I was taken aback by his first words that were, "Where is your belt and axe?"

"On the appliance," I replied. I had forgotten to put it on when we arrived as I had other things on my mind at the time and afterwards simply forgot as I got involved in the rescues and taking control of the fire. It was clear my "temporary" superior wanted to make an issue of my lax dress code and proceeded to deliver a lecture on the importance of being correctly dressed at all times. I listened politely but was inwardly seething. I waited until he had finished and said, "You done?" In a level-controlled tone, I said, "Listen you eff! You turn up here where three rescues have been carried out and not even inquired about the job; how it went; or are the crews alright and was anyone even injured? All you can find to comment on is that I am not wearing my effing belt and axe. Get your arse back in your staff car and eff off back to Clapham. If you want to carry on this conversation later, I am happy to do so in front of the DC (Divisional Commander)." Which is exactly what he did. He left in his staff car and I waited for the flack. It never came.

I stayed at the incident with my pump's crew and another pump's crew turning over and I continued with my fire investigation. I sent the other crews back to their stations. None were in a greater hurry than my own PL crew concerned that the stand-by pump sent into Brixton to cover the station's ground would abscond with the guests, or worse, back at the station.

A thorough search of debris and the pattern of burning on a wall in the bar indicated the probable area where the fire had originated. A chat with the landlord, who had not had to go the hospital, confirmed that that was the location where a rubbish bin was normally kept. He thought it possible that after closing up one of the ash trays which were emptied into the bin may have contained a cigarette that was still alight. He thought it possible. I thought it highly probable.

The New Year was two hours old when I returned to Brixton with my pumps crew. What happened next was something I only ever imagined happened in a movie. It is the scene were the good guy walks into the room after dispensing with all the baddies and gets the girl! You know the type of thing? So I was not exactly sure what "bullshit" or acts of derring-do the PL crew had been trying to impress our lady visitors with but as I walked back into the snooker room wearing my rather sweaty, now off-white, shirt smelling of smoke, one particular, not unattractive, young "filly" with an obvious sparkle in her eye moved over to me. The smell of the smoke seemed only to add to her sense of excited anticipation as she moved closer and whispered softly into my ear. The New Year was looking decidedly rosy as we walked back out into the corridor together and made our way to my room to discuss her proposal further.

Royal Tournament

The appointment was made for the afternoon. A Divisional Officer Franklin was coming to the station to ask for our help. It was my first meeting with "Barney" whose short compact stature and facial features bore an uncanny resemblance to that of Barney Rubble from the iconic television series "The Flintstones." He was given Barney as a nickname when he first went to a fire station and it just stuck, he was simply known as Barney to his brigade colleagues. He worked in Brigade Headquarters within Press and Public Relations. (A place I would get to know intimately, but for now was just another headquarters department.)

He arrived promptly at 2pm and cut straight to the chase. "We (meaning Brigade Headquarters) would like you to represent the Brigade at this year's Royal Tournament at Earls Court." I thought it best just to listen for now before committing myself but clearly my frown gave my thoughts away as he continued. "Don't worry, you only have to do one afternoon and evening performance as this year's guest Emergency Service's appearance."

In the 1970s and 80s The Royal Tournament was a regular feature on BBC television. The tournament had always provided a very special opportunity for promoting the Armed Services to the wider general public. It had a long history going back over one hundred years and was held each year in London, firstly at Olympia and then more recently transferring to Earls Court. It comprised a mixture of music from the massed or regimental bands and demonstrations of military skills. These practical demonstrations (which cleverly combined strength and fitness) gave the public a flavour of the requirements of the modern British Armed Services as well as projecting the very best of our British military heritage that was portrayed both through pageant and military ceremonial. Some of the all-time favourites were the Musical Drive by the King's Troop; The Royal Naval field gun competition and the Royal Marine Commando assault course. As a young child I was a frequent visitor to Olympia and the Royal Tournament and I loved every minute of it. I never once thought I would get to be part of it.

But it was not to be all plain sailing as my visitor began to explain. "There are some strict conditions put down by the Tournament organisers." Barney was just about to explain further when his wristwatch began to start bleeping loudly. "I set my watch alarm for thirty-minute intervals so I manage my day better," he said. "I want to finish our chat by the time it goes off again if that's okay with you." Greatly amused, I waited for him to continue. "Firstly, you only have a twenty-minute slot, no more. Secondly, you cannot use any water. Thirdly, as you are only there for one day there can be no special scenery or portable drill tower for you to use. Lastly, there isn't any budget for this except to cover your crew's sundry expenses. But I will provide you with what support I can." I thought, "You are having a laugh, aren't you?" But I just smiled instead. There was a popular television series in the eighties where a team of television celebrities were set "impossible" challenges they had to perform against the clock. I was beginning to understand just how they must have been feeling. "Okay," I said, "I will give it some thought and come back to you after I have spoken to the watch." I had no clear idea of what to do but am a sucker for a challenge! Barney left before the next bleeps came from his watch but sought reassurances that I would try to come up with something. He got them.

That afternoon's technical lecture in the TV room was what to do for the Tournament? Everyone was clearly eager to get involved but the restrictions on what we could do or use was greatly limiting our available options. With little or no money for special effects we clearly weren't going to be able to deliver any jaw-dropping spectacular. Without water there was no point involving a dramatic fire scene and in any case the prospect of getting any scenery was remote if not totally non-existent. Ours was a small "fill in" slot in the Tournament's two-week schedule. Whatever we came up with needed to be simple, slick and (hopefully) informative whilst at the same time exciting and entertaining.

Exciting was the biggest challenge. What can you do with just two fire engines and their crews? Water was out! A snatch rescue from a burning building was definitely out! Visions of us pitching the forty-five-foot Lacon ladder vertically in the centre of the arena whilst we all held it upright with Wally climbing up and performing a one-armed handstand on the top was mooted and quickly kicked into touch. Whatever we did needed a visual impact that could be seen by all the audience. We had only been given a short time to do our stuff and there is an enormous difference between how quickly the public expects us to do something, like rescuing someone trapped in a car, and how long it actually takes in reality. Just to stabilise a casualty, cut open a car or remove its roof, then remove the casualty may take at least thirty minutes. So whatever we came up with needed to be choreographed and we needed to cheat!

We would have to represent an incident but not in a normal time frame. So what could we "cheat" at that would still look credible? We needed some inspiration and at the end of the shift, with still with no firm ideas coming forward it was hoped the local pub and a few pints would help. It didn't.

The next shift it was back to the drawing board and finally some viable options were coming forward. We settled on one that we all thought both feasible and credible. It needed some planning and refinement but it could work if we could beg, borrow or steal the necessary props and get the support of the Brigade's scientific advisor. It also needed more manpower than we had available since all of my crews would be required to ride the two fire engines. Enter "Mad Mick" and Woody from Brixton's Blue Watch. I had worked closely with both of them in fund raising events I had arranged at Brixton and both were always willing to get involved especially if they thought they could get some extra leave by joining in.

"Mad" Mick did not get this nickname lightly. He was ex-military and a former soldier. Now in his late-thirties he was losing his hair and to compensate for what hair he had it was worn long at the back and he had cultivated exceptionally long sideburns. Added to which he also wore a Mexican style drooping moustache that would have done credit to any "spaghetti western" that were all the vogue at the time. Mick had been stationed at Brixton throughout his considerable service. It was "alleged" that he once had a tendency to be hyperactive and so excitable that he was required to take pills to calm him down. Sadly the pills did not mix well with alcohol. Having partaken of both on night duties, and in the early hours of the morning, Mick would regularly perform military rifle and squad drill in the firemen's locker room. As this doubled as the firemen's dormitory it was much to the annoyance of those trying to grab some sleep.

Mick could, and would, play up on his excitable nature as the new station cook soon discovered. In her first days at the station Mick had been seriously falling out with another member of his watch. As this particular day duty wore on the exchanges in the mess-room became more and more heated with raised voices and veiled threats of what Mick would do to his adversary if he did not back off. By the time the cook finished her duties that day there was a sense of impending doom because of the intense friction that was being generated between these two so called work colleagues. The following day, with the cook in the kitchen, the two of them are still at it, bickering and antagonising each other. By the mid-morning stand-easy and with the whole watch sitting around the mess-table the atmosphere could be cut with a knife. The poor cook was beginning to wonder what she had let herself in for. She was soon to find out.

After yet another pointed barb directed at Mick by his antagonist Mick suddenly jumps up from his chair and storms out of the mess room. He returns a few moments later armed with a gun! He told his opponent that he had had enough and that he had just made his last barbed comment; ever! Now a very frightened and shocked opponent was also standing and was moving slowly away from the mess-table whilst the rest of the watch were pleading with Mick to put the gun down and just calm down. Being calm or sensible was not high on Mick's agenda as he raised the gun and without aiming shot the defenceless individual in the chest. A loud scream went up from the cook before she fell lifeless to the kitchen floor in a dead faint having witnessed the whole shooting through the doorway of the kitchen. She saw the large blood red stain spread across the poor man's chest as he spun towards her before her own lights went suddenly out. She never heard the subsequent explosion of laughter erupting from the mess-room.

Mick's antagonist was in fact his co-conspirator and the blood was no more than sachets of tomato sauce concealed beneath his shirt, which he burst when his hands hit his chest. For the watch this was all a "jolly jape" but to the prostrate cook laying ashen on the kitchen floor it was her initiation into the extremes of station "humour." Fortunately for the watch, but especially for Mick, once seated and being fussed over by the practical jokers and recovering from her initial shock she showed that she was made of sterner stuff and told them they were all "effing" mad. She remained Brixton's station cook for many years to come.

Mick's medication had now, it seems, finally worked or maybe his increasing years had calmed him down. Although he still had his moments like when he nearly blew the top off Brixton's drill tower in an over enthusiastic demonstration of his pyrotechnic skills during a station open day and display. He was however an exceptional firefighter and worked tirelessly to raise money for charity. A talented marathon runner he devoted his considerable energy these days to doing good rather than pretending to shoot people and practising the "changing of the guard" in the wee-wee hours of the morning whilst on night duty.

Barney Franklin had given the "green light" to our proposal and it now meant getting the necessary hardware to make it all work. I had to secure the loan of a twenty-ton flat back lorry that we were going to "crash" into a car in the arena of Earls Court. That was to be the starting point of our little display or demonstration of skills as Barney liked to call it. I had chosen Mick to drive the lorry and Woody was the poor unfortunate driver of the car. Our near neighbours in Gresham Road (the location of Brixton fire station) were a well-known London wide scaffolding firm. Their Director kindly agreed to the loan of a lorry (a new lorry in fact) which proudly carried the company logo. I omitted to tell the Director about the crashing bit, just that the lorry would be seen by thousands of people at the Royal Tournament. A car was also required and a very dodgy car breaker in Stockwell agreed to the loan providing we took our fire engines to his kids' local school. It seemed a fair exchange and a deal was struck, especially as he agreed to deliver and pick up the car we wanted to use. Even the Brigade's scientific advisor was intrigued by our idea and promised to provide our special effects and to give the necessary technical back-up for the performances. This, particularly, was a considerable relief as it kept Mick well away from things that went bang, although it would not stop him from creating his own!

Having talked and then walked through our idea for the display with Barney at Brixton, (who was our only audience) he seemed pleased with what he saw but delivered some very disappointing news, for me at least. I was not to take part in the arena activities as he wanted me to sit with the distinctive voice of the Royal Tournament, its commentator of many years, Basil Weitz. Ron would now lead the crews whilst I acted as a technical advisor stuck up in the commentary box!

After yet more rehearsals at Brixton and taking delivery of the list of equipment I requested, the scene was finally set for our departure to Earls Court. The Brigade had sent to Brixton two new(ish) appliances that were temporarily put on the run at Brixton. Everyone was the under the threat of death not to break them or damage them in any way and much to my surprise they didn't. Fully equipped with our own gear that shone like new pins we departed in convoy heading for Earls Court. Rehearsals had been a problem because Brixton's yard in no way represented the size of the Earls Court arena but we were to be given one limited rehearsal slot before we, or rather they, went "live" on stage. It was all a bit stressful as I still had to rely on the car breaker to deliver the car that we had to make some necessary adjustments to, to make it safe, like removing the petrol tank and all the engine oil. Our merry band, along with the lorry complete with its prepared props bringing up the rear, set off from Brixton Fire Station. On arrival at Earls Court we were directed to the marshalling area, which was situated immediately behind the main arena. If you think that the arena is large then the waiting area behind the scenes was vast. Much to my relief the car was there waiting for us. As you might expect with a show of this nature it was run with typical military precision. That said, we were welcomed incredible warmly by all the services taking part and almost immediately built up a rapport with the army lads that we were parked next to. They were as fascinated about our display as we were with all the military hardware that completely surrounded us.

I was introduced to Basil by Barney who had also secured the assistance of the Tournament's chief lighting technician. He was the key to us being able to set the scene effectively for our display. I had already prepared a script for Basil and he said it was fine but he would rely on me giving him prompts and the answers to his questions as our display got under way. Talking to Basil it was easy to see why he was the voice of the Tournament. He had a melodic voice that was deep and mellow and with perfect diction that generated authority and confidence. "Okay just get up here with me five minutes before your boys are going on." Behind him sat the sound and lighting technicians with their enormous array of control panels containing knobs, switches and dials. Wires led everywhere and it looked like multi-coloured spaghetti. I was feeling more confident now as the rehearsal had gone well although none of the special effects were actually used. Just as we were all gathered together back in the waiting area Barney announced that the Chief Officer was coming over to watch the evening performance. No pressure then lads, get it wrong in front of the public and they just won't clap. Get in wrong in front of the Chief and we are all in the mire, especially me!

The sound of the public entering and filling the tiered seating surrounding the arena was filtering through to the waiting area. An air of anticipation was getting stronger as the buzz of excitement from the audience was getting louder and louder. Military musicians were tuning instruments, uniforms were being brushed and buttons straightened. Stern looking sergeant majors were making last minute inspections and leaving no one in any doubt what would happen if anyone did not come up to muster. We were thankful that they only looked at us whilst smiling a knowing smile and shook their heads from side to side to indicate that we clearly were not up to their military standards. I wished my crews good luck as I made my way to the commentary area. It was clear that their adrenalin was already kicking in as the time for them to perform came ever closer.

Our particular slot was midway during the performance. The earlier massed bands, the gun carriage crews and the mind-boggling sheer speed, excitement and precision of all the military displays set an exacting standard. It was one that for us was very difficult to follow. Basil gave us a most generous introduction saying that the London Fire Brigade was the special guest act for today (there was a guest act every day during the tournament) and that the crews demonstrating just some of the skills of a firefighter that were to be seen today were from Brixton Fire Station. Then the arena floor darkened, which was the cue to push the car into position whilst Basil told the audience of the increasing problems the Brigade had to face because of the transportation of chemicals and hazardous substances. He continued that the London Fire Brigade had been at the forefront of bringing into being the now national Hazchem code; a means by which all the emergency services could identify what initial action was required to deal with chemicals involved in a fire or a spillage.

With the car and Woody waiting inside it, the previously unrehearsed special lighting effects were primed as Mad Mick started up the lorry. The two enormous arena entry doors opened and the lorry made its entrance. I had devised a simulated road crash involving a chemical lorry and a car. The car was stationary, but as yet unseen, in the darkened arena. Strobe lighting picked out the slowly moving lorry (which Mick had been told firmly by me to drive at no more than twenty miles per hour). The intensely bright flashing lights created the illusion of the lorry moving much faster than it was as it headed directly towards the car. Strobe lights or no strobe lights I was sure that Mick really was moving faster. The sound effect of a road crash boomed through the arena loudspeakers in what was meant to replicate an actual collision. But the wisdom of putting Mick behind the wheel was now very questionable as he struck the car with considerable force (instead of stopping the lorry before he actually hit the car) with a distinct "crunching" sound! Basil, covering his microphone, said, "Your stunt team are very authentic." I was far too busy thinking what to tell the scaffold firm Director about their dented lorry than to respond to Basil.

The arena lighting technicians were making the make-believe incident almost credible. By the clever use of spot lights on the lorry and car, and most of the arena still darkened, Basil talked through the accident scene and drew the attention of the audience to the forty-five gallon chemical drums that were carried on the rear of the lorry and which had now tipped over causing some of the prepared contents to spill on to the back of the lorry. Thanks to the efforts of our Scientific Advisor the special effects worked perfectly. The audience jumped in surprise as a loud explosion erupted from one of the large drums and the purple smoke started to rise and quickly shroud the lorry and car.

To the soundtrack of a nine-nine-nine call being made to the scene of the arena crash site, once again the arena doors swung open and Brixton's two appliances entered noisily with their two-tone horns blaring and the blue lights flashing. With only their headlights on full beam for illumination they completed a circuit of the arena whilst Basil let the public know a little more about the Hazchem code that was clearly visible on the sides and rear of the lorry and what it would tell the firefighters when they arrived.

As the two appliances drew up in front of the crash site, and stopping a short distance from it, the PL's crew were already rigged in their BA sets and jumped down eager to rescue the two injured drivers. Thanks to the kindness and co-operation of the London Ambulance Service and a friend at Brixton Ambulance station the ambulance that was also part of our display arrived on cue. Mick and Woody were carefully eased from their respective vehicles looking suitably wounded, but in Woody's case he may not have been acting since Mick had already knocked him for six after hitting the car! As Basil read out the Hazchem code of 4X he explained what this meant to the crews and that the firefighters must wear chemical suits and fight any fire with a dry agent. He also said that the spillage must be contained and kept on the back of the lorry.

Finding a suitable chemical that fitted in with our display had not been an easy task, especially as we had to give the public a very visual display whilst not using any water, not even water spray. But the Scientific Advisor had come up trumps again. So for all the "boffins" in the audience Basil was able to say with authority exactly what the chemical was, and what the audience was now witnessing was how it would be dealt with in reality. This reality did not, however, extend to a real time frame since the Pump's crew was already fully rigged in their yellow chemical protection suits and wearing their BA sets as they jumped out of their fire engine. Whilst Mick and Woody were administered first aid near the ambulance by the combined ambulance and PL's crew, the Pumps' crew moved purposefully towards the lorry with their dry powder extinguishers at the ready. Basil was doing a wonderful job of narration and covered every aspect of what the crews were doing by reading the notes that I was passing to him.

Ron had clearly missed his true vocation, as he should have been on the stage. As the officer in charge he moved with authority as he directed his crews. Pointing here and looking there he demonstrated the obvious thespian skills he had kept hidden so well. With a dramatic wave of his arm he encouraged the yellow suited BA crews to deal with the incident on the back of the lorry. As they climbed aboard and used the dry powder extinguishers, the steel drums were quickly engulfed in a cloud of white talcum powder. Having dealt with any possible fire threat, bags of dry sand were passed up by the BA crew to make a containment dam of sand around the affected drums whilst the ambulance carrying the two casualties drove off and out of the arena.

On Basil's cue Ron indicated that all was well and the crews returned to their fire engines. The incident was dealt with and the two engines did a lap of honour before driving out the arena. Now with the arena lights darkened again the lorry and car were removed. The lads had received warm and generous applause from the public. I would like to say that it was rapturous but it was not. Our efforts were never going to replicate the massed jets demonstration or the major fire scene of Lambeth's public displays. In fact, our two fire engines were rather dwarfed by the size of the arena. But the lads gave an excellent account of themselves and improved even further on the next showing. However, Woody told Mick that if he hit the car again Mick would not need make-up for his injuries as Woody would ensure his injuries looked totally authentic without it.

We never saw the Chief but he sent a polite note to the station about maintaining the "finest traditions of the service." I was just grateful we got through the performances without a serious glitch and were not all going to be posted. The lorry was returned with a rather dented front bumper that I blamed on a poorly driven army tank! Barney went happily back to Headquarters although we would work together again but not for a couple of years and under a totally different regime. I would meet Basil again too. This time his intoxicating voice would bring life and meaning to one of the most poignant public displays the London Fire Brigade had devised for many years, but that too was for later. For now, it was back to normal station life, if life was ever normal at a station like Brixton.

Final Days

The buzz of turning out to a rubbish fire or a blazing dustbin at 3am had lost its edge. It was no longer exciting. Although I still longed for the much-needed adrenalin rush that a real "working" job always provided (in fact I craved it) the mundane was just that, mundane. I needed new challenges. I needed new things to learn. The Division Commander's phone call seemed to fit the bill perfectly. His offer of giving me temporary promotion at Brigade Headquarters came at just the right time. He seemed to know me better than I knew myself? Maybe I would see Brixton fire station again, but somehow I doubted it.

Brixton's Pump Escape stands in readiness for the next call. August 1979.

Brixton's Pump Escape and Pump-two of the London Fire Brigade's busiest fire engines during the late 1970's and early 1980's. March 1980.

A shared joke over breakfast in Brixton's mess room. 1980.

Being the 'Guvnor' of Brixton's White Watch remains one of the highlights of my operational career. Summer 1983.

Damping-down in the aftermath of the Brixton riots. 12th April 1981.

Divisional Commander Brian Butler took charge of the Brigade's response to the Brixton riots on Saturday 11th April 1981. His innovative tactics and decisive command skills, in the face of unprecedented public disorder on British streets, were subsequently recognised when he was awarded the MBE for his actions. 1981.

Sunday morning after the Saturday night riots and the full extent of the devastation becomes apparent. 12th April 1981.

Chapter 12

Raising Money

It would be nice if I could admit that my involvement in charity work started for purely altruistic reasons. It did not: I was volunteered. I was asked (which was the fire brigade's way for being told!) to help Malcolm Roe. Malcolm was Lambeth fire station's Fire Services National Benevolent Fund representative serving on Lambeth's Red Watch. The "Ben Fund", as it was then called, aimed to give financial and practical assistance to the dependants of firemen killed on duty and to provide restorative and respite care to those who were injured in the course of their duties as firefighters. This practical and financial help also included access to the Fund's convalescent home and assistance to the widows with raising dependent children and similar assistance in funding their children's higher education. (It has since been re-branded and called The Fire Fighters Charity.)

This "help" involved me walking to all the various locations on Lambeth's fire station ground and emptying the Ben Fund's little plastic collecting boxes. Most were placed in pubs but some were also distributed to small corner shops, and a few of the larger High Street outlets. Not every pub landlord on the station's ground actually wanted one of our collecting boxes but nevertheless the station still had over two hundred boxes scattered about, mostly at its numerous public houses. I very soon got the measure of my job, doing this benevolent work! Whilst I collected the money from the shops Malcolm would only collect from the pubs. An incredibly sociable chap he liked (loved would be a better description) going from pub to pub, passing the time of day whilst being offered the occasional pint (or two) from each one. So besides collecting the money from the shop's boxes, my main task actually was to make sure that Malcolm got back to the station in one piece after his "hard day's" collecting. This was frequently easier said than done especially when generous landlords had been supplying him with free beer since opening time.

Lambeth's Red Watch also had a long history of arranging the station's annual Christmas children's party and organising a community old people's Christmas bash (in association with a local Lambeth church). Many of the elderly came from an almshouse located on the Duchy of Cornwall's estate, just off Black Prince Road, close to the fire station. Funding for these two events came from local companies and the gifts for both parties were generously donated by Freemans, the mail order company located in Brixton Road. Items that had been returned to Freemans (because of some slight damage/defect or that were just unwanted) were stockpiled during the year in their warehouse and around each October we would collect a lorry load of goodies that required sorting and repairing.

In the basement of Brigade Headquarters, Lambeth were range of storerooms and two of them easily resembled Aladdin's cave. The various items were first inspected, then repaired if necessary and the toys allotted to the firemen's children's party and more practical gifts set aside for the elderly folks. Having made such a good job of always getting Malcolm back to the station in one piece (but not necessarily sober!) I was promoted to be Jim Connolly's assistant in getting this recycled stock ready for the two annual events. It seemed there was not much Jim could not repair or cannibalise to make fully functional gifts. This seasonal work got me out of the mundane station cleaning so I really did not mind too much being volunteered yet again. Both these annual gatherings were great successes in their own way, but it was the old people's party that left a lasting impression.

The congregation of the local C of E church donated foodstuff, which we made up into individual hampers, one for each invited pensioner and they also received a special Christmas floral decoration. These special gatherings had been running for over ten years, starting in 1954, and in that time nearly three hundred needy pensioners had benefited from this festive get-together. Although it was clear that some were frequent returnees as they eagerly scanned their food parcels and commented, "I had tinned salmon last year, got anything else ducks?" After their tea party, given in the smart surroundings of the Headquarters officers' club, the pensioners were given an escorted tour of the Christmas lights hanging in the West End's Oxford and Regent Streets. Two or three of us acted as escorts to our elderly guests as they were divided between the personnel carriers that were especially laid on to transport, what for many, was clearly a real treat. It was also an extremely hazardous duty since after a sherry or two in the officers' club some of the elderly women would become very frisky. With or without mistletoe they were not shy when it came to grabbing a fireman and demanding a festive kiss. So for this young nineteen-year-old, obliging those senior ladies (especially without their teeth in,) made it an unforgettable experience. One that was above and beyond the call of duty.

My promotion to Leading Fireman, and transfer to Southwark fire station, did not curtail my collecting for the Ben Fund. In fact, as Southwark did not have a Benevolent Fund representative (and had not had one for some time) I took on the role. Southwark had even more public houses on its ground than Lambeth had. Many of the boxes had not been collected in years and lots were found full to the brim. Unlike Malcolm I had no minder and when the offer of a free pint came my way, I made sure I could get back to the station unaided. With empty replacement boxes in situ and regular collections once again taking place the public's generosity towards our firemen's charity was clearly demonstrated by the increasing amounts that were being collected. Southwark fire station was moving up the collecting league table and after the first year topped the whole Division with the most amount of money collected from these boxes.

Later and upon my return to Southwark, but now as a Sub Officer, my venture into organising a fund-raising event met with considerable success. First an Open Day was arranged and this was followed by a Half Marathon road race from Tower Bridge to Wandsworth Bridge. The race had as its theme crisscrossing London's bridges, the runners crossing each one alternatively from the south and north sides of the Thames. It was very well attended and everyone, myself included, made a tremendous effort in securing sponsorship for each mile covered. With over fifty entrants and the average individual sponsorship in excess of forty pounds (nearly a week's wages) over two thousand pounds was raised by this one event. The race was won by a fireman from Brixton called Wally. I did not really know him then but would do so in the years to come. Wally, a serious runner, was also the double of Manuel from the BBC's famous television series Fawlty Towers. He cut a comic figure as he lightly, but speedily, raced across the ten bridges to be the first to the finish line and those of us in his wake would hear the comments of the public delighted at seeing such a well-known personality running on London's streets and exactly in the same style of his television persona! The race was at the time the biggest earner of that year within the B Division and once again Southwark won the Ben Fund's Divisional shield which was proudly displayed in the station office.

Raising money was becoming contagious at Southwark as both the other two watches came up with their own schemes to pour extra funds into the Fund's hungry coffers. I also learned that other benefits came from these fund-raising activities. They were excellent team building activities and added to the general camaraderie that existed both on the watch and across the station as a whole.

My subsequent transfer to West Norwood as a Station Officer meant my days of walking the streets collecting money from boxes were at an end. But now in charge of a watch things went full circle as I "volunteered" one of my new watch into the role of the Ben Fund rep. Cliff was a former Royal Navy seaman and liked his pint. So he was an easy convert to the job of distributing new collecting boxes to Norwood's hostelries and talking the landlords into placing the fund's boxes on their respective pub bars.

However, in 1977 and with the national firemen's strike now behind us (and with a steady stream of money coming in via the boxes) it was time to consider another money-spinner that could involve all the watch in doing their bit to raise some money for the fund. It was not to be the only 6-ton fire engine I was to pull but it was the first. Much to my surprise the idea of pulling this great lump of a fire engine over London's bridges, from Tower Bridge to Albert Bridge, went down well on the watch. Too well in fact as first Norwood's Blue Watch wanted to join in and then my old watch at Southwark asked to take part as well. Who was I to refuse? It meant more bodies to pull the bloody heavy engine and more to drag in sponsorship money through their efforts.

On a dry, but overcast, late spring Sunday morning we all assembled at Tower Bridge for the start of the London bridges pull. Not only was our

Divisional Commander there to start us off, but Brenda (from Croydon Control) had rounded up some other very attractive Control Officers and they joined the gathering for the 10am start. We first headed northward to the loud "crack" of the Commanders starting pistol being fired. It was much louder than we had anticipated and as we took the strain and pulled the engine towards the Tower of London, the Commander was left trying to explain to a concerned City of London police officer what he was doing discharging a firearm in such a public place!

Trundling around the Tower amazed tourists stood gaping at us "mad English." But the charms and feminine wiles of our Control girls managed to raise the odd dollar and franc for our collecting boxes. By Southwark Bridge we realise that this was not the easy Sunday morning stroll that we all thought it would be, the strain was beginning to tell. However, we pushed and pulled onwards and I was surprised that we had managed to reach Trafalgar Square before 12am, ahead of schedule. As we first did one circuit, then two, our accompanying Pearly King and Queen from Lewisham played and sang to a very surprised coach-load of American tourists whilst the Control girls once again separated them from their hard-earned tourist dollars.

As the sweat and the procession ran (it was more of a fast walk actually) down Whitehall we were all reminded of a previous march, not too long ago, when thousands of firemen and their families took their case for a just outcome to the national strike to the very seat of Government. But this time everyone was enjoying themselves, although we were still crying out for more money, only this time it was from the bemused passers-by and innocent, if not rather naïve, tourists who some of the lads conned into believing that they had to give money as it was a requirement, not an option.

With Westminster and then Lambeth Bridge under our belts it was the long haul up towards Chelsea. The procession went extremely quiet as the flat ground gave the team the incentive to stride it out ever faster. Chelsea Bridge came and went and finally Albert Bridge was in sight. My estimate had been for a 2pm finish but we crossed the final bridge with almost an hour to spare. So it was decided to refresh ourselves in the Earl of Spencer pub at Battersea, which proved to be one of the highlights of the day. With impromptu entertainment supplied by the Pearly King and Queen and their banjos, two of our number provided a musical distraction from aching limbs and sore feet by giving an excellent impersonation of Frank (Sinatra) and Dean (Martin), with the drink in hand naturally.

This party spirit continued back at the station where the station cook and the on-duty Red Watch laid on a banquet for all of the participants of the day. The afternoon passed all too quickly, especially for the Pearly Queen, who emboldened by a few too many tipples was last seen chasing a good-looking member of the Blue Watch around the station. In fact a good time was had by all and nearly one thousand pounds was raised by sponsorship and the girls with the boxes, although, due to a quirk in the Ben Fund collecting rules, all the money was officially collected only on the south side of the river lest those firemen on the north side accused us of poaching! God forbid that we would ever do such a thing.

The Invasion of France 1978

To infer that all of my fund raising was done for the purest of motives would be stretching the truth too far. What I originally suggested as a watch outing grew, as an afterthought, into something that just might earn a few bobs for the Benevolent Fund along the way. Paris seemed rather a fun destination and the whole watch warmed to the idea. It was a destination that we could reach to and from in our newly acquired regular four leave days. The question was how to get there and at minimal cost to ourselves? A possible answer seemed to present itself when I saw in a fire journal that the contract to supply the Brigade with its latest fleet of fire appliances had been awarded to Hestair Dennis; a commercial vehicle manufacture based at Guildford in Surrey. They had been in the fire engine business for a very long time and I wrote to their Managing Director to see if they had an old fire engine we could borrow for a sponsored trip to Paris. Much to my surprise, and delight, the Managing Director actually wrote back personally and said yes. The engine turned out to be a truly magnificent beast, a 1914 open topped fire engine that was first supplied to the then Coventry City Fire Brigade. After a bit of a mixed history and an absence of forty-four years it was finally returned to its birthplace at Guildford, where it was kept and lovingly maintained in full working order by a small group of enthusiasts from within the company, one of whom would join us on the trip as mechanic, driver and the machine's guardian.

Having scrounged the fire engine, we still had the Channel to cross. I also had to come up with some additional transport to carry the lads when not taking it in turns riding the fire engine to Paris and back. Some clever marketing (known within the Brigade as "bullshit") resulted in me securing three major sponsors that resolved all the remaining problems and our associated costs. Townsend Thorensen, the car ferry company, pledged free return cross Channel travel for us, the engine and the support vehicle (which was secured from the Ford Motor Company's Bristol Street Motors in Bromley). Finally, Courage Brewery met all associated fuel and insurance costs plus a generous donation to our Fire Service charity for the completed journey. We had only to pay for our accommodation and food, or so I thought.

The Fire Service probably is the least known, but best served, private club on the planet. The common dangers that firefighters face creates a unique bond and a willingness to assist fellow firefighters wherever possible. So, with the valued assistance of a neighbour, who could write fluent French, I wrote (dictated actually) to the Paris Fire Service requesting basic accommodation for an overnight stop in their city. A reply was duly received, written in French naturally, which nobody at the station could read. Later translated by the same kind neighbour, it said we could stay at one of their stations and would just have to make a nominal contribution for our meals. The letter was signed by the Chief Fire Officer of the Paris "Sapeurs Pompier." With all the necessary elements in position I was feeling guilty that the fundraising side was not so well organised. Companies in and around West Norwood fire station resolved that problem by responding to the excellent local press coverage of the proposed trip and requests for financial support all in aid of our Firemen's charity. They made firm pledges that easily exceeded one thousand pounds. Now with only a tongue-in-cheek bollocking for having the audacity to write to Paris's Chief, my own senior officers sanctioned our fund-raising trip.

On 10 September 1979, with the fire engine gleaming and support vehicles ready plus the four-man crew wearing Victorian firemen's uniforms, including original brass helmets, we all congregated at Brigade Headquarters, Lambeth, for the 3am start. The vintage fire engine looked immaculate, its red bodywork highly polished and brass fittings shining brightly. Carried on the top of the engine was its wooden ladder and secured to that ladder we had placed an elevated sign, written in French and English, saying what the trip was in aid of. Secured to the very front of the ladder was a large golden cockerel, standing nearly two feet tall. It was the Courage brewery's logo and we had to place it on the engine as a condition of their support of the event. We were soon to discover that this bird was far more than just a logo. Also fixed to one of the ladder supports, and hanging limply, was the French tricolour just waiting for the speed of the engine to show it in its full glory. I and the remaining lads, not riding the engine on the first leg, waited impatiently for the arranged signal for the start of our trip.

Despite the early hour, both Lambeth fire station crews and many Brigade HQ senior officers were there to see us off. The station bells rang loudly and as the station teleprinter typed out its ordering for West Norwood's vintage pump to stand-by at Brigade HQ – Brigade de Sapeurs Pompiers de Paris. Lambeth's large wooden appliance room doors swung open and to the sound of the engine's brass bell ringing out loudly, and echoing across the Thames, the vintage engine pulled on to Albert Embankment on the first mile of the two hundred- and seventy-three-mile journey to Paris. The outward route to Dover was via the A2 and M2 and the sixty-four-year-old fire engine made good progress and it maintained a steady speed of about thirty miles per hour. Although for the crew on board the speed seemed much faster and their journey southward, under a clear star filled sky, was later described as exhilarating.

Our arrival at Dover harbour and the boarding on to the 4.50 am ferry was trouble free. We were greeted by the ship's First Officer and given VIP treatment. Escorted to the restaurant we were afforded a lavish breakfast (at no cost to us). Much to the steward's surprise we managed to keep it down in spite of the very choppy crossing, although one or two were definitely turning a deeper shade of green with every mouthful. Still a free meal was a free meal and these lads were not going to part with any of it easily.

My first planning cock-up came with the dawn and our arrival at the Port of Calais. French energy-saving time was one hour in advance of our own, something that I had overlooked! This meant that our planned lunch break would either have to be cut short or forgotten completely if we were to meet our planned arrival time in Paris. The route to Paris was via the N1 to Abbeville, Poix and Beauvais and then into the capital. Full of enthusiasm we started off across the open countryside of northern France and were immediately accompanied by a constant companion, a very strong head wind. Then, just when you think all is going well, it doesn't. The first of many enforced stops occurred whilst coming down a particularly steep hill. Our driver from Dennis's, Roy, noticed the oil pressure drop to zero and he had to pull off the road. Our mechanics, in the guise of George and Roy, soon located the problem, a broken fuel pipe, which fortunately was located near a joint section. They set to work. With drills and soldering irons, they lengthened the damaged section of pipe and fixed the problem, but it took fifty minutes of valuable time; time we could ill-afford to lose.

At 11am Abbeville was in view in the distance and none of us had slept in the last twenty-eight hours. Our planned meal stop here was very short-lived as the café's prices were way out of our limited budget. You needed a bank loan just for their sausage and frites! Cheaper cups of coffee were consumed instead and a phone call, using very poor pigeon French, advised our hosts of a revised arrival time of around 4.30 pm, providing the fire engine behaved itself.

For this 1914 fire engine maybe there was something symbolic about this section of the journey, which was through the northern battlefields of the First World War. We were not sure but the fire engine obviously thought so as it advanced then stopped, over and over again, just like those courageous warriors on both sides of that terrible conflict so long ago. During those sixty miles it overheated, slipped a leather fan belt and finally lost a gasket bolt! Eventually, and with the sun breaking through for the first time that day, the appliance seemed to warm up too and we joined the road from Beauvais to Paris and became the focus of lots of curious French drivers.

The large cockerel on top of the fire engine was causing a considerable amount of interest and I was not sure why? What was far more worrying was the number of French drivers who, whilst whizzing along at speed, would take both hands off the steering wheel and point at the bird whilst waving at us. I discovered later that this golden bird is an iconic cultural emblem of the French. Little did they realise that this one was far more famous for its links to Courage's beer. But judging by the standard of French driving they appeared to have had far too much of their own beers already.

We were now running late, but the sky was blue and we were receiving considerable applause and encouragement from French motorists and bystanders alike. They clearly appeared to be very impressed by our old machine as we headed into Paris. We were too, or would have been, until we reached the auto-route that circles Paris. It was suffering its worst traffic congestion for a decade.

In the best traditions of the fire service (and chancing our luck) some excellent driving forced our way through, aided by the fire engine's bell clanging away loudly. Causing only the minimum of disruption (but no accidents) and now two and a half hours behind schedule we finally arrived at our destination, the Brigade de Sapeurs Pompiers Headquarters in Place Jules Renard. It was now 6pm and, including the enforced stops, we had been travelling for thirty-five hours continuously. We all looked as though we had too.

The Champagne reception put on by the Paris senior officers and a small detachment of their firemen was both a surprise and overwhelming. Thankfully one of their officers acted as our translator, but it was self-evident that the French clearly appreciated our pitiful attempts to speak to them in their own tongue. During the reception I made a presentation of a pewter figurine of a London fireman to our hosts together with a framed signed cartoon print of a 1914 Pump Escape as a reminder of our escapade. In return we were given a short tour of their Headquarters before being given a Brigade motorcycle escort to our overnight accommodation that was located nearby.

Unlike the United Kingdom fire service, selected French major cities, like Paris, have their fire brigades run as part of the French armed services and where conscription is still the norm. Conscripted individuals can opt to serve in the fire brigade and many of its officers and firemen then decide to make this their long-term career. The full extent of this para-military style service became much clearer to us as we arrived at our overnight accommodation. Somehow I thought it would mirror a typical London fire station and whose facilities can, at best, be described as basic. But not so and certainly not here in the French capital. We had been escorted to the No 1 Battalion HQ at Messena in southern Paris. This building had to be seen to be believed. I thought we had arrived at a large smart modern hotel. As I turned into the private entrance road, I was confronted by the new looking ten doubled-bayed appliance room. The frontage of the building was some two-hundred metres wide and went back over three-hundred metres deep. I was to learn that this vast complex not only housed the two-hundred and fifty operational personnel but also included a training establishment and barracks for other Pompiers. After being shown to our accommodation (that not even the most modern of London stations could match) we had a most welcome shower and changed into fresh clothes. Still with our French translator helping with our conversation we were wined and dined by our French hosts who were now the Pompiers serving at Messena. A common bond, helped by the firemen's universal sense of humour, was very quickly established and stories were exchanged about shared dangers and operational problems that make firemen want to do what they do the world over.

After the meal, which was more like a feast compared to our station fare, two of the French lads invited us to see some of their city and they kindly offered to act as our guides. Naturally not wishing to offend we accepted especially as we guessed where we were heading, the Pigalle, Paris's red-light district. It was the most informative of excursions and where we received some extraordinary offers of companionship, some of which were accepted by the more adventurous of our number in exchange for remarkably few francs. One got far more than he bargained for. Disappearing into the seedy entrance of a brothel with a stunning looking blonde, who had legs right up to her pelmet of a skirt, he returned far too quickly and looked very shaken and shocked, babbling, "That bloody she is a he!"

It was 3am when we arrived back at the barracks. Bed came as a most welcome sight and a chance to finally catch up on some much-needed sleep. By 9am everyone was shaved, showered and fed and we were on the move again, ready for our return journey. Our departure was originally to be preceded by a photocall with the engine and crew at the Arc de Triomphe and then the Eiffel Tower. "Was" being the operative word since the fire engine had other ideas. It did not want to start. Roy was back with his tool box, only this time he had an abundance of willing helpers in the form of the pompier mechanics who just could not wait to get their hands on this historic engine. So, whilst the engine was undergoing surgery, our hosts gave us the opportunity to see a little more of their capital. For most, including myself, this was a first visit to Paris. We were given a lightning tour of the major tourist attractions. However, it was a tour with a difference because our hosts had a universal pass that clearly took no heed of the signs, "Queue here" or, "No parking." The Pompiers in Paris obviously enjoyed a far greater rapport with their police counterparts than we did in London. The local police took no notice of our hosts parking on the central island of the Arc de Triomphe, then driving right up to the Eiffel Tower and Notre Dame whilst we looked around and took our snaps.

All too soon our tour ended. By 2 pm it was time for us to depart if we were to connect with our 9 pm Calais to Dover ferry. Remembering the outward delays, I was preparing myself for at least a public flogging for causing all of us to be AWOL. As we were about to depart, our hosts at Messena, continued to surprise and overwhelm us with their generosity and their willingness to assist us. The French mechanics had ensured the fire engine was given a clean bill of health whilst the Pompiers brought out an enormous food hamper. It was filled to the brim with goodies for our return journey. It surely would have won a Michelin star had we given anyone the time to judge its contents. Finally with the crew mounted up and farewells said, the next surprise came into view. It would stay with us to the very outskirts of Paris's suburbs. The Pompiers had provided a blue flashing light motorcycle escort and our two outriders cleared our path right to the city limits. We continued on unaccompanied via the N1 to Calais and the cross-channel ferry.

I am sure everyone making that trip has their own personal highlight. For me it was the one hundred- and eighty-five-mile drive back to Calais. Roy, the official driver, was near exhaustion and he handed his precious cargo over to George who looked like he had just inherited a fortune. With George driving and me riding shotgun, the pair of us had the most incredible and exhilarating ride across northern France. The wind was in our hair, the weather was warm and dry and the roads were clear of any hold-ups. George was one of the finest, fastest and safest, Brigade drivers it has been my good fortune to have driven me on the "bell" to fire calls. This "old" fire engine must have recognised George's driving skills because it went like a dream. Not a hint of any of the previous troubles, just a carefree drive, plus the pure enjoyment of witnessing and absorbing the French landscape as we passed through picturesque villages, historic towns and were captivated by France's wide-open northern countryside.

With us all safely back on the ferry and the vehicles secure on the car deck, the exertion of the previous sixty-eight hours was rapidly taking its toll. We were keen to get home now. We had hoped for a speedy passage through Customs until some wag told them there were fifty cases of whisky stashed in the fire engine. Customs didn't see the joke and kept us there another hour while they checked and emptied every locker on the fire engine. Finally smiling they said, "Bugger off." How the driver got us the final seventy-nine miles back into London no one really knows for the rest of us were comatose in the rear of the transit, the fire engine having been driven back to Guildford from Dover. Home, in the form of West Norwood, came into view about 3am on Tuesday. Most reported being in a state of complete limbo when we reported back for duty on that Wednesday morning.

All our sponsors were extremely pleased with their publicity and the positive coverage the trip received. No damage was done to the fire engine and a special commemorative plaque was placed on the Hestair Dennis engine in recognition of the trip. We raised over twelve hundred pounds for the Benevolent Fund on our watch outing. So where next?

London to Brighton Fire Engine Pull 1980

I had now been posted to Brixton fire station and after a few tentative months of getting to know my new watch thought it time to deliver a new fund-raising scheme. So it was, around 6pm, on Saturday 7th June the participants for my ridiculous idea began to arrive at Brixton Fire Station for their final briefing. Stowing personal gear and food bags on the support vehicles some were looking around to find out who else was sufficiently crackers to take part in this event. Myself and Ron, my Sub Officer, were doing our utmost to contain the almost schoolboy like excitement that seemed to affect everyone. The idea had been simple, three teams of ten were to pull (and occasionally push) a fully loaded six-ton modern fire engine from Westminster Bridge to Brighton seafront. A distance of fifty-five miles and without stopping once! Some forty-five minutes later we were all in position on Westminster Bridge and the specially constructed pulling harness was secured to the front of the fire engine. Final safety checks were made and the obligatory group photo was taken with the more vain pullers elbowing each other out of the way to gain the best possible vantage point in the front row.

As Big Ben started to chime 7pm I and nine other members of Brixton's White Watch were the first of the three teams undertaking this hare-brained venture to pull the engine. Wearing the harnesses and taking up the strain we resembled a very strange looking human "dog-sledge" team. As Big Ben rang-out its seventh chime our Divisional Commander, who had forgone an evening in front of the television, officially started the pull. The appliance, which was facing down a slight slope of the bridge lurched away as George, one of the two nominated drivers, released the hand brake. Under the terms of our own self-imposed sponsorship we were not allowed to engage the engine or allow it to stop. Traffic at County Hall roundabout was brought to a complete halt by our support vehicles, who were blocking the road, and allowed us free passage over the traffic lights. Very soon we settled into a smooth and steady pace, much better in fact than our rather limited practice pulls in the back streets of Brixton.

Our route was the same as for the famous London to Brighton vintage car rally, brought to the "silver screen" by the British classic film Genevieve. We progressed steadily along Brixton Road towards Gresham Road, the first of eighteen change over points along the chosen route. This was achieved smoothly by the second crew outside Brixton police station by ten lads from West Norwood fire station, the attendant police officers being totally ignored least they prevented us from stopping the traffic as we passed through the junction without altering pace. The first three miles were completed in just forty-six minutes, which was good going. But now the crews met the first of the many testing hurdles, Brixton Hill! As the effects of the hill were felt the other two teams sprang into action pushing as well as pulling and the first hill quickly disappeared behind us.

Right from the off those not actively pulling or pushing were out with red plastic buckets collecting coin of the realm from the generous passers-by who, in the main, simply stared in blank amazement at the odd sight presented to them. Some were heard to say, "I've heard of service cuts, but this is ridiculous." But they kindly donated money anyway. Bruce, Brixton's FSNBF representative, had provided a dozen specially marked collecting buckets and it says much for the persuasive powers of the collectors that nobody escaped the pull of these magnetic buckets as more and more coins (plus the odd note or two) clattered noisily in.

With Streatham Hill quickly overcome the next change over team takes over the harness and hands out derogatory comments about the puffing and panting of their relieved colleagues. It is 8.30pm and nearly six miles have been covered. Team three was a mixture of lads from Lambeth and Tooting Fire stations. They are noisily confident as they whiz along at a remarkable pace. This motley crew encourage the six-ton monster past Streatham Police station where one of the helpful coppers hands Ron Cunningham, who has relieved George, a motor vehicle defects sheet along with an ardent plea to get off his patch as soon as possible. Great fellows those boys in blue!

With the six-mile marker now behind us we approach a set of traffic lights where a car has broken down and threatens our rate of progress. With great presence of mind, the car is gathered up by the pullers and pushed along ahead of them, much to the astonishment of the lady driver who is now being instructed to put the car into gear so that they can bump start her car. The lady eventually gathers her wits but not before about fifty yards have been covered and the lads are now wondering whether she is going to Brighton as well? As the car starts with a splutter and she drives off with a smile and blowing her saviours a friendly and grateful kiss.

With Norbury police station in sight we see lots of coppers waiting on their forecourt, the local police jungle drums clearly advising them of our imminent arrival. They wish us well and advise us to seek professional help from a psychiatrist should we ever get to Brighton. In response they are given the vehicle defects sheet provided by the previous police station and some choice asides that could have got us all arrested. Moving swiftly on through Norbury and with Croydon in view we have eight miles on the clock and are ahead of time. Bruce and I confer and decide on a slight change to our original route. With the public showing such generosity it was felt prudent to head for the heart of Croydon to catch the night crowds thus swelling our coffers. The word was passed that Croydon is going to be honoured with our presence. With the fresh team going like the clappers someone notices a police car parked in a side road. The car contains a male and female police officer who are approached for a contribution. As they only produce a small handful of bronze coins and drop them in a bucket, they are encouraged to give more by the collector who tells them in no uncertain terms that unless they increase their donation considerably, they will be reported for "necking" on duty. Several silver coins now hit the buckets before the pair make a hasty retreat probably calling for reinforcements to have us taken in for highway robbery.

Croydon proved to be a lucrative diversion with late night revellers giving generously, probably assisted by the feel-good factor of a drink or two. Clearing central Croydon, we are still managing to keep ahead of schedule. Changeovers are going smoothly and the fire engine continuously moving forward without stopping. Purley and Coulsdon slip past us and a road sign advises us we are thirteen miles away from Crawley. At 11.45pm the pullers surge over the Surrey border at a cracking pace. Now with very few poor unsuspecting souls around, from whom we can extract a few more coins, the teams settle down to resting between changeovers and getting some well-earned recovery time and refreshment. The support vehicles continue their vital role of protecting the pullers and engine as they pass through the various road junctions. The pace is adjusted to get through traffic lights at green if possible and the fire engine's blue flashing lights switched on and support vehicles positioned strategically to ease the passage through red lights attempting to halt our progress.

Saturday moves into Sunday and there is thirty miles to go to the finish line. Redhill railway bridge is in sight at the top of a monstrous hill that stretches up for about a mile. Cracks are starting to show with Tony and "Bunny", two of Brixton's more macho lads, walking hand in hand at the front of our team pulling the engine. The rest are actively discussing furtive plans to lynch Bruce and me for dreaming up such a daft idea. The East Surrey Water Company is passed at 1.05am as we slip unnoticed into Redhill. Three of the lads are drawing lots to see who gets to punch Bruce in the face. He persists in being cheerful and giggling almost continuously.

The road leading out of Redhill is a vicious and gruelling hill that seems to be endless. All three teams have been pressed into service to help at both ends of the fire engine. As we slowly and painfully trudge up the hill two very attractive female police officers suggest that there are easier ways of raising money. The answers provided by the lads are best left to your imagination, suffice to say the ladies could have considerably increased their night's earnings had they agreed to the lewd suggestions of the lads.

With the hill a painful memory, another change-over point is reached and many of the lads put on warmer clothes in the hope that they will rest easier and in more comfort in the support vehicles. Spirits remain high and good humour is ever present even though most of the lads have had little or no sleep in over thirty hours, many having been on night duty on Friday. I avoid the threatened lynching by shifting the whole of the blame for this silly journey on to Bruce. Bruce is smiling as he thinks he has successfully put the blame on me.

Gatwick Airport is uncharacteristically silent and even appears deserted as our party trundles past it. Just at the end of the dual carriageway which bisects Gatwick Airport from the adjacent railway line we are hailed by the public address system of a passing police car with the suggestion that we turn back as Brighton has burned down. With the Europa Hotel in sight the ninth changeover takes place just before 3am and twenty-six miles are on the clock. However, our earlier gains in the schedule have been lost due to the arduous steep hills over the last forty minutes that kept us to a crawl. At 3.40am the first sign of daylight start to show as the darkness begins to recede in the east and the birds start their dawn chorus. The air is keen and smells sweet as the darkness moves slowly into twilight and finally full daylight giving every indication of a clear sunny day. This new daylight finds Brixton's team back in the harness and trudging purposefully onwards towards Brighton some twenty-seven miles in the distance. We are almost half way.

With daylight established all the lads reverted to the official rig for the pull, specially monogrammed T-shirts advertising the event, shorts and trainers or walking boots. Bob was especially fetching in his royal blue shorts displaying to such advantage his funny looking legs with bulging muscles and geometrically opposed knee bones. Our support crew was busily running around the whole group with plastic bowls containing cornflakes and milk and liberally sprinkled with sugar for energy. This was much needed for conquering the next monstrous hill that stretched into the distance and where the next changeover point was located. Our early lead slowly dips away as each consecutive hill takes its toll both on our time and our strength. But with this changeover comes the opportunity to regain time lost on the last hill. The road ahead of us is straight as far as the eye can see, which also unfortunately allows us to see the next series of hills that confronts us.

From my reconnaissance trip I knew this was a particularly arduous part of the journey that would require all hands on many occasions and robbing the crews of their well-earned rest periods. Ahead and crouching in the distant verge is noticed a furtive figure waiting at the roadside. It is soon recognised as a photographer apparently waiting for our passing to take a photo for a national newspaper. The rustle and noise of make up being applied and coiffeurs being adjusted is deafening as the more vain members of the party get ready for their moment of fame. John finally stops holding Tony's hand and leaves the team at the next village to place his order for fifty copies of *The Times* for whom the photographer worked. (Our photo made the front page of that Monday's edition.) Thankfully the hills went down too and the route towards Hickstead was a great fillip for the hard-working lads on this part of the journey. As the fire engine gently rolled unaided forward, George used the brakes to prevent the engine driving over the team ahead, but he constantly threatened to do just that if they did not move bloody faster! Everybody was once again in great spirits and noisily confident as the miles slipped by and Brighton got closer by the minute.

The arrival of a cruel hill leading up to Hickstead puts the dampers on the team's boisterous noise and jollity. Hickstead was holding a major dog show that morning and I felt a little guilty that we were slowing the traffic to a painful crawl as drivers made their way around us to the showground. Getting the collecting buckets out here did not seem such a good idea. However, nearly all these drivers and their passengers gave us a smile and words of goodwill so we did not feel such a nuisance. That particular hill took almost fifty minutes to climb, thus cancelling out much of our hard-earned lead. The South Downs were to prove even more challenging for us all.

The fourteenth changeover was made at Sayers Common with almost forty-four miles of amazing and considerable effort behind us. As we closed in upon the final ten miles into Brighton the hills of the South Downs appeared to rise almost purposefully to prevent us from achieving our goal and reaching Brighton seafront. Word quickly spread that the worst was still to come. The longest and most painful hill of all lay directly in front of us and we drew on our reserves for the effort that would be required to get us into Brighton. For those with a knowledge of that approach into Brighton you will be familiar with the hill that guards it. It took on a mocking presence against the teams lumbering forward hauling their heavy fire engine towards it. Every team member was pressed into service with our heads bent in effort and muscles protesting strongly with each step taken. Even the support vehicle crews were co-opted, parking their vehicles some distance ahead and running back to give much valued help at this crucial stage including poor Roger Vaughan (our watch ADO) who had only signed up to be the event's adjudicator. The hill in question is exactly two miles long and at this point in the journey it was overcome only by the sheer determination, grit and bloody mindedness of a group of firemen who were not going to give in or be defeated having got so close to the finish. At last the brow was reached and the going became a little easier. The problem I faced now was that all the lads were engaged in the Herculean task of climbing that damn hill. There was no fresh team to take over at the next changeover point. It was resolved by the lads themselves who stayed at the engine, pulling. With no one seeking a rest the support vehicles stayed empty save their drivers.

By 10.50am we were on the very outskirts of Brighton. With far more people around the collection buckets made a welcome return and taken up by the most persuasive of the lads so that the maximum donations could be secured. George secured himself aloft precariously on the lead support vehicle so he could get donations from passing motorists. Tony actually hi-jacked a passing coach and was seen going seat to seat gathering funds as he headed off in the direction of the town. This tactic established, others hi-jacked passing coaches and boosted the takings as they did so. The famous Brighton pillars were passed at 11.30am exactly. The support crew were busy handing out water and saline tablets to those that needed them and preparing us all for the final lap. The collections increased as the crowds grew significantly as we hit the town proper. People were now throwing money; from first floor balconies and shop windows as the lads scurried in and out of the traffic deftly scooping coins off the road and dropping them into the buckets. The whole team found new energy and a lease of life as a carnival spirit grips the teams. As we pass Brighton's main fire station the fire appliances and crews line the forecourt giving us a rousing cheer. They are joined by the team's friends and families who have travelled to Brighton to see if we actually got there and it is not just yet another, "boys only night out."

Even in these final few moments we are not without some hilarity and a little drama. One over-zealous traffic policeman told us to start the engine and drive the fire engine the last few hundred yards to the sea front. I was later credited with a far more diplomatic reply than the officer actually got when the incident was reported in that day's edition of the *Brighton Evening Argus* under the banner headline "Police in marathon protests." We received a very good press from that paper for our efforts, which was far more than that particular "*jobsworth*" of a police officer got. As we approached the Palace Pier roundabout five attendant policemen stared at us then burst suddenly into life, stopping and starting traffic and clearing a route to allow our fire engine to cruise majestically the few final yards before coming to a halt on the seafront close to the pier, its first since leaving Westminster Bridge yesterday.

It was now 12.58pm and only two minutes before my estimated arrival time. We had fifty-four and a half miles on the clock and hundreds of pounds collected in the buckets. With the appliance at a stately halt the lads could rest to the loud cheers and rightful applause of an amazed, if not bemused, public for what had been a superb achievement of endurance and stamina. Whilst the teams went off to join families and friends Bruce and I went to soak our sore and tired feet in the cool and inviting sea. We chatted on the beach about the venture giving each other words of congratulation and denying that either of us had tried to blame the other for this hare-brained scheme.

Fate was still to play its hand however. With almost all of the group already returned to Brighton Fire Station for some refreshment and the small reception that had been arranged for us, John Halford and I got ready to drive the fire engine back there and to re-join them all. John pressed the starter and nothing, pushed it again and still nothing. After the third attempt he declared, "The bloody batteries flat." With disbelief and considerable frustration showing on my face I managed to round up the few remaining stragglers and got them to push the appliance a final time to bump start the reluctant engine. It fired up and back at the station the lads would not believe a bump start was called for until the stragglers confirmed our story and laughter again filled the air.

Our hosts were thanked for their kindness by Roger Vaughan and it was time to return to London. £3,711.59 was raised from the rattling buckets and by individual sponsorship clear of all costs. Not bad for just eighteen hours work.

Paris to London Marathon Row, August 1981

Just how this idea actually came about was lost in the smoky haze of the Gresham public house. Sometime in late January, after a particularly harrowing day duty, most of the watch went for a couple of pints at the Gresham and the germ of an idea was formed. The following evening and after supper on our first night duty, Wally, the instigator of anything involving a whaler, was still throwing ideas into the melting pot about what we could do to combine some fun with fitness? I kept my head well down knowing that whatever scheme they came up with was going to involve me in convincing the powers that be that we could actually do whatever "it" turned out to be? Discarding the ridiculous and frivolous they ended up with a short list of three choices, all involving that blooming boat. One was rowing around the coast of Britain; two was rowing the Danube River through Germany; or three undertaking the fastest crossing of the English Channel. By our second night duty those interested in the project were tasked to come back with the pros and cons of the three possible options by our next tour of duty. Wally, who was slightly built and looked like Manuel from Fawlty Towers, was a total fitness fanatic. Austrian by birth, speaking poor English he had managed to join the Fire Brigade somehow and fell totally in love with the physical aspect of the work. Doing one hundred one handed press ups was his idea of fun. However, not everybody on the watch shared his enthusiasm for burning the maximum number of calories in the minimum amount of time. Some were less than enthusiastic with the prospect of playing about in one of his bloody boats. But it was a very close-knit watch and I knew they would all agreed to provide moral support to whatever was decided and would assist in the necessary preparation, albeit given some gentle persuasion.

Over a greatly extended morning break at the start of the next tour Wally was quizzed about what was possible and what was not? Those interested, including myself, had already set self-imposed criteria that it would be a fundraiser and we would try to complete whatever was agreed over our normal four days leave. The Round Britain row was considered much too long. The Danube posed too many logistical problems, which left the Channel crossing. This was something Wally was really keen about and confident of achieving. The consensus was it did not have the necessary "wow" factor that could pull in money or sufficiently interest sponsors. The event needed a prominent starting point and ideally to finish in London. Having already undertaken a fundraiser to Paris I floated the idea of a Paris to London event that incorporated the channel crossing. After a short discussion it was agreed we would try and row the 400 miles from the centre of Paris to Tower Bridge in London. Wally assured us with training that the row was do-able, but he failed to mention just how hard it would be and how much actual training it would take.

Now I had to try and sell the idea to my Divisional Commander, Brian Butler, and get him to sanction our outline scheme, which was all pretty vague at this point. So nothing ventured, nothing gained and, armed with more bullshit than facts, I requested an interview with him at the Divisional Headquarters, Clapham. It turned out to be an interrogation more than an interview. The bullshit got me nowhere. However, I did have proven track record of making the seemingly ridiculous work and had demonstrated both commitment and enthusiasm in seeing my projects through. I got his provisional approval providing I came back with a detailed plan within four weeks. It was now mid-February.

Early on our next day shift Brixton's pump, with me in charge, was ordered to report to Brigade Headquarters, Lambeth and meet with the Divisional Commander. This was not the normal way Brian Butler did things. He always got his minions to report to him on his own turf at Clapham. Wearing my best uniform, I pulled into Lambeth's appliance yard on Brixton's pump. Deputy Assistant Chief Officer Butler was already waiting, impatiently, by his car. As I got down from the pump, I noticed he looked unusually nervous. Looking immaculate in his uniform, with his tall lean figure, he was carrying his officer's leather gloves, which senior officers do for some inexplicable reason? I reported and he told me we had an appointment to see the Chief Fire Officer at 10.30am. Suddenly I was feeling nervous too.

The London Fire Brigade has a well-established history of helping other charities as well as its own Benevolent fund. This year was no different and the Brigade was supporting The International Year of the Disabled, which was being promoted by the United Nations worldwide. During the lift ride up to the Chief's suite of offices on the seventh floor, Brian Butler told me he had mentioned our scheme to the Chief and the Chief had wanted to hear about it at first hand. Ron Bullers had been the former Chief Officer of Greater Manchester and had only recently arrived in London to take up post as our Chief Fire Officer. At forty-nine years old, the same age as Brian Butler, he had risen to Chief Officer rank in under twenty-five years, which was exceptionally quick then. Although Brian Butler had met the Chief, I had not and it was me that had to sell the idea to the Chief, which was why Brian looked, and still was, nervous.

The meeting turned out to be very informal, with coffees and sitting around the coffee table in easy chairs. It was not at all what I had been expecting. When I was being interviewed, I normally have to stand to attention when in front of a senior officer's desk, let alone the Chief's. Brian Butler did the introductions and briefed the Chief of my past escapades. I told the Chief what was envisaged and he listened politely. When I finished my pitch, he asked if I could pull this thing off. I said I believed so and the guys were very positive about the whole venture. Returning his coffee cup to the table he said my scheme had his personal support and he wished us well, "Mr Butler will keep me updated on progress." Turning to me he said, "This will be the London Fire Brigade's major fund-raising event of the year in aid of the International Year of the Disabled." The interview was over. Travelling back down in the lift, Brian Butler said, "That went well." Without any major sponsorship promises I might have just sold the Chief a very dodgy deal. No pressure then, I thought.

Returning to Brixton fire station it was time for a crisis meeting. Gathered around the mess-table to discuss the morning's events I told the watch, "I have just told the Chief we can do this so it is time to put up or shut up before this all gets out of hand." I had enormous belief in my watch's ability to pull together and their determination to carry things through once they were committed to something. Once again, they did not disappoint me. I had already started mentally preparing a list of must haves and prioritizing what needed to be done post-haste if we were to get this project moving. Explaining what was required there was soon a delegation of tasks to those on the watch who were taking an active part in the extensive planning for this event.

Brixton fire station was the busiest operational station in the London Fire Brigade during 1981, and there was still the day to day running of the station to consider as well as the additional burden of this self-imposed extravaganza to deal with. I was extremely fortunate in having two of the most competent and hardest working junior officers anyone could wish for. Sub Officer Ron Burton was my deputy and Peter Hall my leading hand. Ron agreed to share the event's organisational workload with me and Peter would ensure the normal routines were not missed and would keep day to day office administration to a manageable level.

It was unanimously agreed by those taking part that the sponsorship monies would be shared equally between our own Benevolent Fund and the International Year of the Disabled. Wally was tasked with getting the necessary rowers together who were willing to undertake the event and draw up a training programme. Ron and another member of the watch would review our proposed route and come up with a shopping list of what was needed to be sourced or actively scrounged. It was a very hectic tour of duty. Despite the many fire calls we had to deal with, by the end of our second night duty we had our professional looking headed letter paper printed and the first batch of our many "begging letters" ready to post. Letters were sent to targeted major sponsors such as cross channel ferry operators, vehicle hire firms; insurance companies, translator services and camping equipment suppliers. Now I had to wait for the replies.

Not Wally, he already had his training programme up and running and we all had to get used to his programme too. The Brigade had a long-standing arrangement with the London Division of the Royal Naval Volunteer Reserve to use its naval whalers. These heavy wooden boats were moored at HMS President, its London headquarters that was located on the Thames near the Palace of Westminster. These traditional whalers were used by rowers from the Royal Naval reserve, Royal Marines, The City of London Police and the Brigade in the annual Whaler Race that took place on the Thames between Vauxhall and Blackfriars. The Metropolitan Police also took part in these races but had their own whalers moored at Wapping, headquarters of London's river Police. Each whaler was over twenty-one feet in length and built on a "clinker built" design and weighed one and half tons. They were the type of boat that Captain Ahab might have chased Moby Dick around the southern Atlantic. Each whaler was rowed by a crew of five using long heavy wooden oars and the coxswain sat at the rear (aft) steering the boat using the tiller, which directed the rudder. Gaining access to these boats for our training was not a difficultly. However, we had to borrow one of the whalers for the actual event and transport the damn thing overland to Paris.

Our first training session took place after a busy night duty in early March. The weather was grey and bloody cold. It got even colder sitting on the Thames in an open boat with no protection against the wind's cutting chill. Eight of the watch had originally declared an interest in rowing. Wally had found himself about thirty other firemen from surrounding stations that wished to be considered for the trip, four of whom were in that year's winning whaler crew. After the third cold and sometimes wet training session three of the watch came to the decision that rowing was definitely not for them. They were willing to assist in other ways and would make a valuable contribution to the event in the weeks ahead.

Mid-March and there was still no feedback to any of my letters. Other aspects of the plan were coming together however and a comprehensive list of our requirements had been formulated together with the number of personnel required. Wally had proposed three five-man teams to undertake the actual rowing with two coxswains and three reserve rowers. I had deemed it necessary to include a support team that included a cook, first-aider, mechanic, two translators, four drivers, plus one or two general dogsbodies to do the hundred and one things that might (and inevitably would) crop up. It amounted to a grand total of thirty personnel.

Ron, Wally and I had undertaken some detailed research of the route and what the row would entail. We found that the total distance, via the canals, from Paris to London was estimated to be three hundred and fifty-five miles. A total of thirty-six locks, many industrial size, had to be negotiated on the French side before arriving at Calais. Then thirty-four hours of non-stop rowing from Dover to reach Tower Bridge in London. In addition, there was the "little" problem of crossing the English Channel, one of the busiest sea routes in the world in our rowing boat. It was becoming evidently very clear that we were not going to complete this journey in just four days!

Finally, good news arrived and it came twofold. First was an invitation from British Rail's Sealink ferry operator to meet with their Marketing Director and his team. Second was an offer from the Ford Motor Company for the loan (free of charge) of two Transit support vehicles. Bruce and I took ourselves off to Euston Road on Brixton's pump one afternoon to meet with the Sealink Directors at their Euston based London headquarters. They seemed very keen to assist but insisted that the whaler be painted in Sealink's corporate colours. I had not even got the promise of the whaler yet but it seemed only polite to say, "Of course, no problem at all." I also agreed that Sealink would be our principal sponsor. In return they promised free return passage for all concerned plus two reconnaissance trips prior to the event. They also agreed to fund the team's customised sweatshirts, T-shirts and to sponsor all our advertising costs. Bruce, who was a talented artist, said he would prepare a poster design and promised to come up with the artwork for both the official poster and our clothing logo. Which is exactly what he did and when presented to Sealink they loved it and so did we.

My Divisional Commander was hankering for a briefing on our progress and I wanted to do some arm-twisting, his. I now had a clear idea of what the event was going to take in terms of time, effort and resources. I still had quite a few problems to overcome but this meeting could solve at least some of them. The row was clearly going to exceed our four days off and all of us would have to combine a mixture of leave days and days when we should have been on duty if we were complete the event as planned. I also needed a minimum of three support vehicles (but ideally four) in order to provide the necessary support and backup transport. After explaining to Brian Butler Sealink's positive involvement, I got down to the nitty-gritty of getting all those involved the necessary time off to complete the event. He was sympathetic to my request but we were a rapid response emergency service after all. The fire brigade is a twenty-four-hour service and sufficient bums had to be on seats to provide the necessary level of operational cover. So it was blatantly obvious that we could not just all shoot off on some French jolly. I proposed that those involved would use annual leave to cover fifty per cent of their scheduled duty absence and in return would be granted special leave to cover the other fifty per cent providing sufficient volunteers were found who would ride in place of the individuals taking part and at no cost to the Brigade. He was considering this whilst I told him that we needed four support vehicles and would he agree to the Brigade providing two if we secured the other two? I forgot to mention that we already had two. It was not actually misleading but what the hell. I had my answer the following day and it was all positive. It was time to call all the team together and have our first formal meeting.

Everyone involved congregated at Brixton Fire Station one evening in April. There were twenty-six gathered around the snooker table in the recreation room, which was the largest meeting area available at the station. Wally provided an up-date on the training, which had been going remarkably well and he was able to indicate just who the rowing crews would be. Ron and Monty (who coxed the Brigade's whaler crew) had agreed to be the joint coxswains and five of Brixton's Blue and Green Watches had volunteered to form the support crew together with Bruce as the gofer. News of Sealink's involvement had already spread around but securing all the necessary support vehicles was hot off the press and was well received.

Filling most of the top of the station's full-size snooker table was a large-scale detailed map of northern France. (It was four maps actually, all joined together with tape.) Using a snooker cue as a pointer I ran though the proposed route, detailing the selected staring point on the Seine and charting the various canals to the Port of Calais. The thirty-six locks presented a formidable barrier to our proposed continuous non-stop journey through France. I was not sure at this point what the locks' operating hours were. Wally had estimated daily rowing targets and said it would be necessary to locate suitable campsites for the first three nights if rowing could not be maintained through the night.

The ability of firemen to just get on with dealing with problems or seeking solutions to them never ceased to amaze me. The lads took the briefing in their stride and light-hearted banter filled the room, mainly about who was going to sleep with whom or not in the case of Bruce! It was clear that reconnaissance trips would be required to provide the information and local knowledge we were still sadly lacking. It was agreed that two trips should suffice.

There was genuine eagerness amongst those present to get the event on the road. Getting them to part with their money was a different matter however. There was a sharp intake of breath as I detailed Ron and my estimated costings to cover food, camp fees and meeting at least part of the fuel costs. We would have to put in about one hundred pounds each to cover these expenses with the proviso that anyone raising over five hundred pounds in personal sponsorship would get a fifty-pound refund. This hundred pounds had to be paid up front, four weeks prior to the departure date which I said was Tuesday 25th August. A buzz of excitement filled the room with this news. Wally explained the rationale behind this particular date, "*Zit is all to doo wit zee tide times*" he explained in his strong Austrian accent. "*I haf vorked bok to front.*" "Typical Kraut logic." came a muttering from one of Wally's whaler cohorts. "*If we get zee Channel crossing right, zen ve catch the flood tide zat will help us up zee Thames. We don't want to do zee last fifty or sixty kilometres* (he still had not converted to miles!) *rowing against an ebbing tide.*" Pausing for comments Wally continued, "*You will haf at least four months training to be able to complete zee row. Aulsoo using this time of year it will give us zee best advantage of gitting a neap tide as opposed to a strong spring tide.*" Wally clearly assumed that everyone was conversant with the Channel tide tables. But no one had a problem if it meant less hard work, they were all far too busy working out how to tell their wives and girlfriends they had to cough up one-hundred pounds and at least five days leave so they could bugger off for a week in France at the height of their kid's school holidays.

On the 31st March the Greater London Council and the London Fire Brigade's press office issued a press release about the "Channel Charity Row." It came without warning and so did the inquiries from the national and local press. Somewhere along the line a reporter got it into their head that this must be some sort of a new record attempt and published it. Sealink was delighted with the news report. I was dismayed as it was the first I heard of it. I managed to hide my surprise until the Marketing Director told me that they had been in touch with *The Guinness Book of Records* to check what was required of them. Get yourself another bloody team to do it I thought, but managed to say, "Oh great." The team were also surprised, but not overly fussed, again taking it all in their stride. Many thought that if they did not end up getting divorced after taking part in yet another hare-brained charity scheme that really would be a record. Boxed into a corner I contacted *The Guinness Book of Records* to find out what was actually required of us. A very polite young lady said, "You must either establish a new record or break an existing one, plus it must be authenticated by two noteworthy independent adjudicators and a formal record of the event presented for the Records Books consideration." The adjudicators were not allowed to come from the Fire Brigade or any of the sponsor organisations. I tried to envisage my advert for the job;

Adjudicator wanted for free 6-day trip from Paris to London.

Must enjoy cramped small boats, camping and canned food.

Swimming may be necessary.

Sense of humour and unlimited patience essential.

Apply Brixton Fire Station.

However, fate can move in unexpected ways. A neighbour read the press coverage and came to have a chat about the event. As it turned out, the neighbour, David Bruce, worked for the International Maritime Safety Organisation located next door to Brigade Headquarters at Lambeth. David was a fully-fledged merchant navy Captain and a Master Mariner. Although only in his mid-forties he had suffered from heart problems but was on the mend or so he said! I could not believe our luck when he said he wanted to volunteer to be one of the two adjudicators. He was also a Scot and wanted assurances that the trip was actually free? With a reminder to myself that I must make sure we read up on CPR, David's offer was accepted. He proved to be a most valuable asset and a door opener when it came to getting clearances for the Channel crossing in the whaler. One down, one to go.

The time had come to see if I could secure the whaler to use for the event? In early April I made an appointment to see the Commander of the Royal Naval Volunteer Reserve on board HMS President. The ship was then permanently moored alongside the Thames Embankment, opposite the Royal Festival Hall. The Commander greeted me in the uniform of a senior Royal Naval Captain. Although now retired from active sea duty he looked every inch the part with a smartly trimmed neat grey beard and a ruddy sea weathered face. Despite being in his sixties he looked remarkably fit and had piercing intelligent eyes. This was clearly not a time for any bullshit. I just gave him the facts and what the aims of the event were. As the London Fire Brigade had previously thrashed his team in the annual Thames Whaler race, I was hoping he was not one to hold a grudge. He did not and he came up trumps on all counts, even granting permission for the painting of the whaler in Sealink's livery, providing it reverted to its normal battleship grey by the time it was returned to HMS President. I had to arrange for transport of the whaler overland to Paris and show proof of insurance for damage or loss to the whaler prior to collection. The loss part sounded ominous but with a firm handshake the deal was done. The Commander then promised to post a notice about the need for the second adjudicator in the Ship's routine orders. We finally had the boat to row from Paris to London and just might pull this thing off.

Saturday 11 April and the shit hit the fan. The Brixton riots erupted. They were to last three days and nights. I have mentioned elsewhere what happened during that time but the after-effects of the riots knocked our training programme to tilt for a few weeks, together with impacting on the general organisation and planning for this event. However, from the point of view of the Fire Service, gaining excellent publicity and engaging both public sympathy and support for our role in dealing with consequences of the rioting and the widespread arson attacks immediately around Brixton fire station, it turned out to be a Godsend.

What happens in life can sometimes be a matter of luck and timing. Both were on our side immediately following the extensive news coverage of the Brixton riots. Freemans, the national mail order company, was located on our station's ground and they pledged to cover fuel costs for the whole event and to meet all postal charges. Hot on their heels, an Underwriting firm from Lloyds of London arranged free comprehensive insurance cover for all aspects of the proposed trip including, thankfully, the loss of the whaler. Personal insurance cover for the participants was arranged by the Fire Services Benevolent Fund as we were raising money for them. Lastly, Black's Camping Company arranged the free loan of all the required camping equipment inclusive of tents and cooking equipment.

Towards the end of the month a telephone call to the station resulted in finding an interpreter in the delightful and shapely form of Henrietta Sullivan, aged twenty-three and single. She was, for some inexplicable reason, prepared to put her honour in our hands and act as one of our interpreters. Having completed university, she was a voluntary French tutor at a local Brixton business centre before starting her paid career elsewhere later in the year. A concerned Mr Sullivan, her dad, contacted me to check us out and to make sure everything was kosher and above-board. Although in getting to know Henrietta better, she was obviously a young lady who clearly knew her own mind and could take very good care of herself. She possessed a bubbly personality, was highly intelligent, articulate and full of confidence.

Finally we got two for the price of one in the form of Lieutenant Commander Mike Bidwell from the London Division of the Royal Naval Reserve. He rang me and asked for more details about the event, having read the Ship's notice on HMS President. He sounded an incredibly posh sort of chap and I really doubted if he would, in truth, enjoy slumming it on our little adventure? He said he was prepared to act as an adjudicator and spoke French like a native. So who was I to try to dissuade him that he did not really want to go. He was in.

With the training back on track, by late May it was time for the first of the two reconnaissance trips. Alan Pryke and myself had managed to talk our respective other halves into spending a few days in France and with the promise of a quick look at Paris, they agreed. With my two young children in tow and Alan's wife seven months pregnant we spent our four leave days in a cold, wet and windy northern France getting to grips with checking through the route and available campsites for the first 100 miles from Paris. Seeing the canals for the first time we saw the locks, how could we miss them. The locks were huge, some truly enormous, and operated by vast hydraulic rams that moved the thick steel reinforced lock gates. Without the close co-operation of the French lock keepers our row would be in serious trouble. An address was obtained of the Canal Authority with a mental note to write to each lock keeper personally, seeking their help and assistance when the time came. Paris in the spring did not live up to the wife's expectations. My wife felt sick and dizzy looking down from the top of the Eiffel Tower and Jackie Pryke was doubting her own sanity after a second night stuck in a tent coping with her very obvious and protruding bump. However, much valuable information was obtained and important contacts were made with the Paris Fire Brigade, the French Water Authority and the Port of Calais Harbour Master's office.

The second trip in June covered the lower reaches of the canal system and the access into the port of Calais as well as other possible camping locations. For this trip six of the support team made up the recon group and it included Bruce Manser and Roger Vaughan. Roger was now a Divisional Officer, still working in the B Division, and had been invited to join us, as he had been such a loyal supporter of previous undertakings. Bruce was a good fireman and a lovely guy but had a tendency not to know when to say no as far as having a drink was concerned. Sadly, this was to be yet another of those occasions, although I did not know it then. The team returned, having met all its objectives, but not before Bruce had had an over indulgence of liberally consumed French wine and ended up having a drunken bust up with Roger Vaughan. I only got the good news on their return and no mention of Bruce's drinking or the fracas. That was until the Divisional Commander rang me to tell me the sorry tale of woe as related by Roger. I had to listen to this one-way conversation as Brian Butler berated Bruce and concluded that he should be removed from the team, as he would jeopardise the whole venture with any repeat of his unacceptable behaviour. I was disappointed that no one had thought to warn me, but even more disappointed in Bruce letting the project down. After calming down I ordered Bruce to the station office and told him in no uncertain terms that he had been ordered off the trip as a result of his drinking. I also told him who goes or does not go is not a decision that the Divisional Commander can make, but if Bruce so much as looked at a bottle of wine during the trip that he will be left with it, wherever he is, and he can make his own way home.

Bruce had special talents, besides his ability to drink and although he could not drive, row or speak French he could bring a very valuable commodity to the undertaking, an incredible sense of fun and ability to make others laugh, which might prove to be a precious asset on this trip. Much to my surprise and relief the Divisional Commander did not challenge my decision. To underline my faith in Bruce's ability to behave himself I suggested to the Commander that he join us as a support team member and see for himself. He accepted my invitation without a moment's hesitation. Now I had to tell the others of his involvement. I managed to slip this news in during a feedback session on the very positive sponsorship progress, without too much fuss or disagreement from the others.

Despite the success in getting many of the various elements put in place there was still much to do. Not least was obtaining the necessary approvals and giving the required notifications to HM Coastguard and Dover Port Authority regarding the actual Channel Crossing.

As for the whaler we still had to get it out of the River Thames and transported to Paris. The idea of rowing it there had crossed my mind but only in a fleeting moment of desperation. The Metropolitan Police kindly offered their services and a means of getting the whaler out of the water or rather the Workshop Manager of their boat repair facility at Wapping did. A keen rower himself, he had read of our proposed venture in the press and had frequently seen the team's training on his stretch of the river between Tower Brigade and Greenwich. We had been actively looking for somewhere to get the boat out, when during a training session, we noticed at the police's elevated riverside workshop a police-boat being raised out of the river and onto their large workshop on a boat hoist. It was a boatlift really. The boat was manoeuvred into it and whilst held in a cradle, raised into the workshop or lowered back into the water. When asked for help the Manager readily agreed saying he just needed a phone call when we were ready to take the whaler out of the water.

July was upon us and Wally had ensured our training had gone ahead at a respectable pace. Respectable by Wally's standards that is. It was daunting for us. From the original one- or two-hour sessions once a week it was now at least twice a week with required minimum mileage targets. His shorter five to ten-mile sessions were designed to row against the tide for at least fifty per cent of the time. We were also doing a whole day's rowing each week, putting in around forty miles to the river's upper reaches near Teddington and back to Lambeth's fireboat pontoon where the loaned whaler was now moored.

Two regional newspapers, *The Kentish Times* and *South London Press*, were following our training and fundraising and were giving us extensive coverage. This was in addition to the continuing snippets in the national press. All this exposure helped bring in the promises of sponsorship but also help solve one of the last remaining hurdles, providing an escort craft for the Channel crossing and seaward row from Dover to the Thames estuary. David Bruce had lived up to his job title as a maritime safety expert and he had advised us of the need to have a safety boat for the crossing. It was very sound advice and he pointed us in the direction of where we might find suitable craft. I had contacted a number of the firms David had suggested but most could find much better things to spend their money on than us. Then with less than six weeks to go the Alexandra Towing Company, working out of Gravesend, came up with the goods. They promised a chartered thirty-foot fishing boat for the actual Channel crossing and, if that was successful, provide an escort craft for the final stages from Dover to Tower Bridge. It was to be some escort craft. They had allocated one of their ocean-going firefighting tugs, the Sun XXVI. This powerful and well-equipped tug could accommodate all the rowing crews' needs, cater for the two adjudicators and even some of the support crew as well.

The very last problem of transporting the whaler was solved when we were returning from a fire call somewhere in Stockwell. Driving along Stockwell Road, but in the opposite direction to us, was an AA recovery vehicle towing a trailer. This was no ordinary trailer, it was long, very long. It could carry our whaler easily. I told my driver to, "Follow that trailer." Turning our fire engine immediately around we were now in hot pursuit. We caught sight of the AA vehicle again near Vauxhall Bridge. Being stuck some distance behind the trailer it looked as though we might lose it in the increasingly heavy traffic. I told the driver to turn on the blue flashing lights whilst I sounded the two-tone horns and we rapidly gained on the AA vehicle and pulling in front of the driver brought him to a halt. The poor driver's obvious concern was that his vehicle was on fire. It turned to surprised relief when I asked him, "Who do I contact to borrow your trailer?" Giving me the AA contact name, the begging letter was in the post that evening. The reply was equally as quick. The AA's Regional Director promised us use of the trailer plus the cost of fitting the necessary tow bar so it could be towed by one of our loaned support vehicles.

The list was now complete. Everything that I and the team had considered necessary had now been begged, borrowed or stolen. We didn't actually steal anything but we might have done if the trailer had not been spotted.

It was nearly time for the off. Months of planning, organisation and hard training were now coming altogether. There was not an individual involved, either in the rowing crews or support teams, who had not pulled their weight. Volunteers had been found (or blackmailed) into covering our temporary absence from duty on the days when we could not take leave. Bob Erwin and Brian Edwards, both Brixton lads, had taken on the demanding roles of quartermaster and cook. They had also made a very efficient job of collecting all the one thousand pound plus expenses money and promised not to disappear with some ladies of the night as soon as we arrived in Paris. The whaler was finally delivered to Brixton fire station, on the AA trailer, having been given a complete repaint. It looked resplendent in its blue and white livery and with the Sealink logo painted on either side and a Union Flag flying from its prow.

July saw an increase in the amount of press interest, particularly in Henrietta. They were not the only ones very interested. Many of the wives were now asking some very searching questions of their other halves about this linguistic Goddess who would be alone with us for six days and, of greater concern, six nights! This flurry of pre-launch publicity did have a very positive outcome with nearly five thousand pounds being pledged should we complete the row. This sum was only a fraction of the actual cost of delivering our six-day expedition, whose costs were in excess of thirty-five thousand pounds and met by the major sponsors in providing the various elements required to bring the whole thing together.

During our last tour of duty before departure Brixton's drill yard resembled the marshalling yard for a major expedition to some faraway land. Bob and Brian had fitted out one of the vehicles as a chuck wagon and it was full to the brim with provisions. All four vehicles carried extra-large roof racks that were straining under the weight of camping equipment, spare oars, wooden paddles, safety equipment plus our personal baggage that had to last us though the coming week. On either side of the roof racks were mounted large painted signs, written in French, informing likely bewildered French onlookers what the event was all about.

LE MARATHON WHALER ROW DE SAPEURS-POMPIERS DE BRIXTON (LONDRES) E PARIS A LONDRES 1981

Nous remercions nos amis Francais pour leur hospitalité et nous espererons qu-ils nous souhaitent un Bon Voyage

With the long trailer hitched up and secure and vehicles fuelled, the last-minute checks were completed. This event had been planned like a military operation. All the important locations identified, daily targets scheduled, potential hazards planned for and alternative courses of action considered. Now it was all down to our ability to work together as a team. It would also require all our combined strength of character and determination to see this thing through to the end.

During that evening of 22 August those that lived a long distance away from Brixton fire station arrived earlier and tried the best they could to find somewhere to get a few hours rest prior to the departure. In no particular order, places were allocated in the three twelve-seater mini buses, except for Capt David Bruce, Lt Cmdr Mike Bedwell and Henrietta who were all put together so they could get to know one another on the journey down to Dover. Ron Burton, Wally and I divided ourselves between the three vehicles to deal with any last-minute questions and Bob Irwin and Brian Edwards took charge of their chuck wagon.

Mike Bedwell arrived at the fire station mid-evening. Although we had talked on the phone a few times it was our first actual meeting. He was dressed casually, spoke with a soft but upper-class accent and looked every inch the dapper gentleman I had conjured up in my mind's eye. He was in his late-thirties, of average height and clean-shaven. He seemed immediately relaxed in the company of all these strangers. He was later to publish a report of our rowing marathon. One was printed in his own in-house newspaper and repeated in the Brigade's *London Fireman* magazine. His opening paragraph provides a flavour of his first impression of what he had let himself in for:

"Your sleeping space is a bit primitive but it's all been swept out" I had to take Stn O Dave Pike's word for the swept bit, for the primitiveness of the penthouse area of Brixton fire station extends to the wiring which makes a gallant but vain attempt to bring amps to dark places. I did a blind pilotage into my sleeping bag after sampling Saturday Night Fever in a Brixton chippy. I was telling myself that I should never have joined.

We were booked onto the 6.30 am Sealink ferry from Dover to Calais. At 2 am on the 24th August with the teams assembling, the early morning banter had already started. Mike and David Bruce had their first taste of firemen's coffee and humour, which they would become all too familiar with in the succeeding days. A worried father delivered a radiant looking Henrietta insisting that I gave a personal undertaking to look after his daughter. Everyone was clearly excited except possibly Mike who was still looking for an opt-out clause and trying to get the taste of the coffee out of his mouth. The rain of the previous evening had disappeared and we all gathered, wearing our sponsorship blue and white sweatshirts, for the obligatory group photo in front of the whaler. Morale was exceptionally high as we boarded the ferry on time and were escorted into the restaurant for a sumptuous complimentary breakfast. With the French Tricolour now firmly fixed to the front of the whaler we disembarked the ferry and drove into France.

The journey to Paris went like clockwork, some aspects even exceeding my own expectations. Much to my surprise and to the obvious delight of all, we were met at Calais by a police motorcycle outrider escort that saw us on our way to Paris. There they were later replaced by our opposite numbers from the Paris fire service who escorted us to our overnight stop at Messena, the largest barracks of the Sapeurs Pompiers in Paris. Brian Butler just loved all this special treatment and with a beaming smile asked, "How the effing hell did you arrange that?" Knowing it was solely down to the kindness of some French official who took pity on us when I wrote to tell them of our undertaking, I told him, "Put it down to good planning."

Late afternoon and we are off again. This time to put the whaler into the River Seine. The starting point of the adventure was to be Pont Notre Dame, in the centre of Paris, but the boat's overnight berth was at a Paris fire service's fireboat station where they would watch over our craft until the early hours of the following morning. However, trying to get the boat into the Seine was easier said than done. A narrow slipway (that was the width of the trailer) first had to be negotiated and then we had to physically lift and pull the one and a half ton craft into the water. After much huffing and puffing, with the odd expletive thrown in for good measure, the whaler flying the French Tricolour was finally afloat on the river. With the boat secured for the night it was back to the barracks. Our hosts had laid on a magnificent reception and provided a stunning meal. Brian Butler was still wearing a huge grin that went from ear to ear and was clearly wondering how I managed all this? Mike Bedwell considered our Parisian feast light years away from that Brixton chippy. Our planned early night turned out to be not so early as the wine and conversation flowed, highlighting the natural kinship that exists between firefighters everywhere but especially when there is a glass or two of wine to share and stories to exchange largely due to our overworked interpreters.

The rowers and the support team were up by 4.30am the following morning, some not so jauntily, after our "Entente-Cordiale", ready to catch the first morning light and start the row. Our travel distances had been checked and re-checked, estimated daily rowing distances (based on training times) set, crew change-over locations identified and the fall-back positions made known if crews were too quick or had been delayed for some reason. Good communications were vital but sadly restricted to just our two-way radios that were notoriously unreliable and which in any event only had a one to two-mile signal strength. Whilst the whaler crew navigated first the river then the canals, one support vehicle carried the relief crew and the other two leapfrogged between the locks attempting to speed the passage of the whaler through them. The chuck wagon would assist during the morning shift but made its own way in the afternoon to establish that day's base camp and start a much need hot meal.

Our Brixton White Watch crew was the first team at the oars, our coxswain (Ron Burton) was ready and Capt David Bruce, the adjudicator, was seated in the back of the whaler with the official logbook lying on his lap. For many, memories of the rest of the week became increasingly blurred as the marathon progressed. For now, our crew savoured the unique experience of rowing majestically down the Seine, passing Notre Dame Cathedral on the Ile de la Cite then on down to the entrance of the Canal du Nord. It would much later continue into the Canal de Calais that would lead directly into Calais harbour. But for now, the river traffic was light, the sky was clear and it had the making of a hot summer's day. Raw details of our course were recorded in the log by David and Mike in their alternating turns as witnesses to this marathon attempt. The weather remained kind, which apart from dense early morning mists and some slight headwinds, provided a sun filled week.

The French canal system is far more important for the movement of goods on their waterways than its English counterpart. In fact, what seemed like super-tanker barges were all too soon starting their day, moving goods and cargoes around the French countryside and from city to city. These big barges required equally big locks and we were soon dwarfed against the side of these craft as we vied for space in the locks, waiting for the water levels to equalize and for the massive hydraulic lock doors to be opened. Advisory letters to the French lock keepers played a part but so did the considerable talents of the interpreters and support crews who had to sweet talk them into allowing us priority over other craft. A task that was made easier by the French tolerance of the "crazy English." The day's alternated between hard rowing and then resting as bridges were passed and locks cleared until 11pm when the lock system closed down for the night. The first crew were always ready and waiting at 5am the next morning when the lock keepers returned. The Canal du Nord also had its fair share of tunnels, one of which was over two miles long. One of these tunnels only allowed one boat at a time and that had to be paddled, not rowed. The others in contrast were so wide that the whaler could be rowed properly. It was passing though the canals that I discovered the reason for Mike Bedwell's presence. He was a canal enthusiast. The chance to travel the routes through northern France was an opportunity too good to miss even it if did mean travelling with us!

The scenery was usually interesting, although never stupendous and sometimes monotonous. The first two days found us struggling through the very disturbed waters of the Canal du Nord under an unkind sun. Here we nearly all came to grief when one particularly large houseboat, filled with curious French spectators, passed far too close and almost overturned the boat. The third and fourth days were spent toiling through the Canal de Calais, whose neglected, weed-infested water had the consistency of undercooked packet minestrone. Here the locks reverted to do-it-yourself style and some were even inaccessible to the support crews, and the whaler crew nervously operated the mechanism on the overgrown footpath whilst reading the signs. **Warning vipers!** Still the relentless sun bore down and the evening hordes of mosquitoes feasted on our bodies. It seemed, at times, very reminiscent of Humphrey Bogart's African Queen.

The support crews were working magnificently and it was rarely necessary for the rowers to have to wait to get through a lock because they were not at the right place and there was always a "fresh" crew waiting at the designated changeover point. Bob and Brian became a tour-de-force, working incredibly well as a team, mothering the rowers and chasing the support team up when necessary, thus ensuring the campsites were set up under their watchful eye. Despite seeking the best advice from the chief nutritionist at King's College Hospital regarding the most appropriate diet for the venture, sadly our budget could not match her shopping list. So under these expedition conditions, where sleep was often short, our food (despite the best efforts of Bob, the chef) was notable more for its carbohydrate than its protein. Minor tensions were inevitable but these were released in an unremitting earthy and stoical humour that was designed to sting but never injure.

My most treasured memory was whilst rowing with our Brixton crew and arriving at a small village near Noyon. It was towards evening and we had been rowing hard to make up some lost time in the schedule. Waiting by the lock were the local part-time Pompiers, all standing in line and dressed in their very best bib and tucker and accompanied by the Mayor and other village elders. It would have been churlish to have refused the Champagne that, after the obligatory mayoral words, awaited us. Fortunately, Mike was on hand to make an appropriate response and gifts were exchanged before we were back on our way. This was not the only official welcome either. In the town of Thourotte we were given a formal civic reception and made honorary Freemen of the town. Once again Brian Butler was found smiling like a Cheshire cat.

Mike, David Bruce and Henrietta were all of a similar view when it came down to commenting on the whole undertaking. It was the people rather than the place that made the event. They considered that there can be no occupation that transcends nationality more than that of the fireman and the camaraderie that was so evident between the Londoners and their French opposite numbers and it was enough to melt even Mike's chauvinistic heart. More than once when they were in the escorting vans, they found themselves outside a fire station, in fact towards the end of the week they suspected it was not always a coincidence. Within minutes of their arrival they would have their feet under the table with people they had never met before, helmets would be exchanged, equipment would be demonstrated, corks would be drawn, phone calls made and perhaps most welcome to Henrietta, a very reluctant camper, a hot shower could be taken. It was their belief that you could cross Europe for free equipped with just a fire engine and enough cheek.

The timing of our arrival at Calais was crucial. The inner harbour is a tidal basin and the lock gates are only open at high tide so to mis-time our arrival could mean a painful delay. It was a tribute to the whole team that we arrived one minute ahead of our planned arrival time. Brian Butler now believed anything was possible and half expected us to walk across the Channel. Pre-planning had secured a pre-allotted berth arranged by the Harbour master in the outer harbour and there, waiting for us, was our escort craft, the fishing boat FE 22 ready to accompany the crew for tomorrow's Channel crossing attempt.

Day 5 saw a division of labour. Whilst the vehicles and the drivers made ready to board the morning Sealink ferry for the return trip to Dover, the crew selected to row the Channel made their way to the whaler with its Union flag now back in pride of place. The adjudicator and as many of the support crew the fishing boat could carry made ready to add their encouragement to the Channel crew's efforts. David Bruce would adjudicate the crossing whilst Mike joined the two remaining crews on the ferry. Monty Banks was the coxswain for the Channel crossing and almost ended the whole venture when he strayed into the path of an incoming Sealink ferry. Avoiding a David and Goliath confrontation the whaler made a dive to the seaward side of the half-mile concrete pier for protection against the ferry's giant wash. Take two, and this time the whaler got away without incident. Now the biggest challenge faced us, the crossing of the Channel and the tidal Thames.

For those of us on the ferry we were once again treated to a wholesome meal and made the most of the offer of steak for breakfast with considerable relish. The ferry departed after the whaler but mid-crossing the Captain of the ferry invited the crews on to the ship's bridge to cheer on their companions in the whaler. He had steered a course as close to the whaler as safety would allow and with the ship horn sounding a series of mighty blasts, we saw just how hard the lads had to work against the swell and the pull of the tide. Just in case the passengers thought it was the signal to abandon ship the Captain made a special announcement about our row and Sealink's involvement. Crowds filled the side of the ferry adding their voices to our calls of encouragement. Whilst on the bridge a photo was taken of poor Henrietta. Our fresh-faced young goddess looked like she had been to hell and back, looking tired and worn out, but she nevertheless managed a smile and a wave for the camera.

After landing at Dover and clearing Customs we went to the harbour's East Wall to witness the whaler's anticipated arrival. Waiting there for us was the Sun XXVI tug and I was greeted by the skipper and crew, all of whom thought us quite barmy but they were genuinely delighted to be involved with our efforts. We placed our gear on the tug but were getting concerned that the whaler was now overdue. In fact, the strong off-shore current was pulling the whaler eastwards up the coastline under the famous White Cliffs of Dover. It was only by a tremendous effort and dogged determination that the crew battled against the prevailing currents and were finally seen entering the harbour entrance. They were welcomed enthusiastically by a small flotilla of local boats, canoeists and the Dover lifeboat. They were exhausted but jubilant, but with the minimum of celebration and fuss it was a change of crew and, with the tug now as escort, the final phase of this marathon was under way. It was already late afternoon and with a clear sky and the weather very warm I and my fellow rowers made our way back out through the harbour entrance and steered eastwards towards the River Thames.

Whilst we were making our way easterly in the whaler, the Channel crew and David Bruce were brought out to the Sun tug by the fishing boat. Mike was already aboard the tug recording locations and crew changes in the official log. All the whaler crews now rowed for three hours then rested till it was their turn to return to the oars. The reserve rowers had taken the places of the Channel crew, allowing them to recover before they re-joined their normal crews. We finished our three-hour stint at about 8 pm and after a hot meal slept in pairs, head to toe in shared bunks. We were woken by Bob Irwin at around 1.30 am to get ready to row again at 2 am. It was incredibly dark. The darkness made the distant lights of the Kentish shoreline shine like a string of white Christmas lights. The lights disappeared into the distance and marked out the coastline that lay ahead of us. With a strong fresh headwind blowing hard the crew in the whaler looked very relieved to be getting on to the tug. The coxswains were now alternating between crews and only getting three hours break before getting back in the whaler.

The tide was turning and we picked up a most unwelcome adverse current. For the next three hours we pulled on those five oars with all our might and the whaler did not seem to move at all, the same shore lights always appearing to remain level with our boat. We were to discover they were. In the thirty-four hours of non-stop rowing from Dover to Tower Bridge this was the most demoralising session of rowing anyone had to contend with. When our three-hour stint was up, we climbed back into the tug exhausted only to be told in our worst hour we covered less than half a mile!

With all three crews on the tug, the land support teams still had their own tasks to perform and made their return to London and prepared the surprise ending to the row. The first rays of daylight found the rowers in the lower reaches of the Thames estuary and the early morning BBC shipping and weather forecast said we were in for a scorcher of a day. Being on the Thames gave us all a boost and we made very good headway as we made our way progressively up the Thames. Passing boat crews would shout encouragement and gave blasts on their array of different sounding horns. As we passed the Sun tug's depot at Gravesend, we were treated to a grand water display by the moored tug's fire monitors and a passable rendition of the *"Drunken Sailor"* played in concert on their ships' horns. The earlier tiredness had all by now evaporated and was replaced by considerable excitement now we knew that the finishing line was soon approaching.

Our crew's last scheduled row was from 11.00 am until 2 pm. We were now back in London and the fire stations that bordered the Thames on both sides of the river turned out to cheer us on. We raced through the Thames Barrier and as we approached the Royal Naval College at Greenwich the last piece of my organisational jigsaw fell into place and I couldn't help feeling a sense of achievement. Prior to our departure I had arranged for the fireboat's crew to bring down to Greenwich two other whalers. All three crews would now row from Greenwich to Tower Bridge for a combined joint finish. What we were not to know was that the Chief Fire Officer, Ron Bullers, and senior GLC politicians were also there to greet us. Thankfully with a swift "well done" they understood we had a marathon to finish and stayed on the fireboat to see us complete it.

With a "fresh" crew in the Sealink whaler the other two crews got in their whalers to form an escort party. As we pulled away from Greenwich pier, we were bending the oars with an inner strength most of us would not have thought possible during the previous night.

The last five hundred yards seemed to pass in slow motion despite the fair old speed we were all managing to maintain whilst still keeping in a tight arrowhead formation. Above and ahead of us lining the downstream side of Tower Bridge were hundreds of eagerly waving and shouting well-wishers. We had just expected some family and friends to turn up plus the support team of course, but not the large numbers who were now sending up such a hue and cry of excitement and jubilation at seeing us pulling strongly the final last yards towards Tower Bridge. This support not only came from the riverbanks, it was on the river too. The Sun's fire-fighting monitor was sending a vast plume of water hundreds of feet in the air. Police launches and the Port of London craft added their weight to the private and other commercial river craft who turned out to see these "crazy English" complete the Paris to London marathon row. The total time from start to finish was six days fourteen hours and one minute. The footnote by Mike Bedwell in the Official Log sent to The Guinness book of Records probably best sums up the week.

"Their unconventional style and technique might raise an eyebrow on the least anchor-like of naval faces, but for sheer guts, stamina and determination no praise is too high."

Sadly we did not make it into the record books this time! We did raise over **£10,000** for charity and gave true value for money to our sponsors. I even got a very nice letter from Brian Butler congratulating me on the organisation of the event, but his praise did not last long as I soon got a bollocking for some minor misdemeanour or other, but it was nice while it lasted.

Some things I did not get right. Well not in the eyes of the Brigade's principal management at least. The presentation of the cheques from the money raised was held later in the year, on the 7th November in fact. The venue was HMS President and we had by then returned all their whalers to the RNR and repainted the Sealink boat in its original colour of "battleship" grey. Our principal guest of honour for that evening was the Brigade's former Chief Officer Joe Milner, who although retired (many of us thought he was actually forced out) was still highly regarded as a fireman's Chief Officer and he had maintained very strong links with the Benevolent fund. However, the fact that I had the sheer "audacity" to invite him was relayed to me via Brian Butler on behalf of the principal officers who considered Joe to be "persona non grata." Brian got a swift and none too polite reply saying that this was a private reception and if the Brigade did not like Joe attending then we would find another charity to donate the 50% that was intended for the Brigade's nominated charity. Apparently the threat of not getting the money concentrated the minds of those whingeing about Joe attending and an Assistant Chief Officer was dispatched to collect the cheque for the International Year of the Disabled.

What a record

"At precisely 6.26am on Saturday 7ʰ May 1983, six firemen from Brixton, dog tired but still rowing strongly pulled their whaler level with the end of Southend pier to ensure a place for themselves in the Guinness Book of Records."

That was the press release of our sponsor, which for me was my last major fund-raising adventure. Otis Elevator plc had its head office in Clapham Road, on Brixton's fire station's ground. They had responded almost immediately to the inevitable "begging letter" that the station typewriter could now type by itself. I was asked to attend a meeting with the company Chairman and his Marketing Director and it soon became very clear that they wanted in and to be fully involved. In fact, they not only promised to give financial support they wanted to provide help in a physical way too. Our success in the previous Paris to London row had proved to them that we were able to deliver the goods. They wished to involve some of their staff, from their offices and branches located along the Thames Valley and Southend (Essex), in a supporting role. In doing so gain some valuable PR for the Otis Company, but also to use our row as a useful team building exercise for their London and regional staff.

Our disappointment at not getting into the Guinness Book of Records, the previous year, was still grating on some of us, but especially Wally. Prior to my posting to Brixton he and other members of the watch had attempted a Thames row, which had ended in failure. He still had a bee in his bonnet about this particular marathon and now felt he had access to a crew who he thought could succeed and an organiser who could bring the whole event together, me. I was a willing conscript to his crew and so were two other members of the White Watch. Determined not to fail again Wally co-opted two other members of Brixton's personnel, that just happened to be in the Brigade's winning whaler crew. But there was also a novice, John Yaxley. Tall, with a head of bright ginger hair and a matching moustache, he was a born and bred Londoner who, in his twenty-five years, had never stepped a foot outside of the Capital.

One of my first ports of call in putting the row together was to write to the editor of the "sports, games and pastimes" section of *The Guinness Book of Records*. A Beverley Waites wrote back. She was the assistant sports editor and she set out the criteria that had to be followed if we were stand any chance of setting a record and making an entry into their 1984 edition. She also told us that the fastest record held by them for a River Thames row was set in 1974 when a team from Guy's Hospital, in London, rowed an "eight" from Oxford's Folly Bridge to Westminster, a distance of one hundred and twelve miles (one-hundred and eighty kilometres) in fourteen hours thirty-five minutes. However, we had a more pressing target to beat, that set by some firemen from the F Division who had completed this very row in fifty-three hours two minutes in 1981 and were the current holders of the published record. Wally believed that we could achieve a time of fifty hours (given some luck and a following wind) even though we would be using a much heavier rowing boat. The clinker-built wooden whaler was a ton heavier than the lighter (and faster) fibreglass boat used by the F Divisional crew.

With Otis covering all of our expenditure for the event I could concentrate on securing the necessary transportation, which the AA willingly provided yet again plus the whaler from the RNR, which retained its battleship grey colour. As for the sponsorship monies, that was to be divided between the Ben Fund and the Guild Dogs for the Blind. My support crew were the stalwarts of the previous escapade who said they would willingly swing into action at the drop of a hat.

Approvals were sought and received from the two authorities covering the Thames from Lechlade Bridge in Gloucestershire to the pier head at Southend. Thames Water controlled the upper reaches of the Thames whilst the Port of London Authority had jurisdiction on the lower reaches. The total distance to be rowed was stated to be, "**185.88 miles**."

Only Wally had attempted this row before and had never reached Southend. Whilst he excelled in physical prowess it was the lack of detailed planning on the previous attempt that had seen its downfall. It was not going to happen this time. Our strength and determination might let us down but I was determined to ensure that the planning would not be the cause of any under achievement.

Every one of the Thames's forty-five locks, from the first one at St John's, near Lechlade, to the last at Richmond, were visited. Each lock keeper was written to personally advising them of our record attempt and seeking their co-operation and help with our endeavour. The support crews drove and practised opening and shutting the locks and the routes were checked and rechecked to see which lock was best supported by land or by our support craft.

Whilst I was happy to leave the details of our feeding and lock opening in the more than capable hands of my support teams, Wally was putting us through our paces. In yet another rigorous training programme, during the early months of 1983, he was making us face the cold winter days, insisting that we would get warmer if we all rowed faster. John Yaxley was beginning to think that travelling outside of London was not such a good idea if this is what he had to do to get to see Gloucestershire. But spring was much kinder that year and our thirty to fifty-mile training sessions became far more pleasurable as the weather got warmer and the days grew longer.

The event was planned for early May. Based on our training times, and the high/low water times for the tidal stretch of the Thames, Friday 5th May was chosen as the designated day to start our record attempt. All the rowers, and the support crew, had taken leave in order to compete in this event. They all gathered at Brixton fire station on the 4th May for a briefing prior to the "photo-shoot" at Otis's Headquarters. Resplendent in our sponsorship strip of red tracksuits and matching sweatshirts, promoting the event, both rowers and the twelve-man support crew congregated on the entrance steps to the Otis building.

With the whaler, parked on its trailer taking centre stage, we were joined by the senior management of Otis whilst the press took their pictures. The only one from the Brigade not all in red was our uniformed Commander, who looking as immaculate as ever, had come to see the show get on the road.

He had been most supportive of our event and had even secured the use of two brigade personnel carriers. In fact, senior officers from the Division had not only been supportive but some had volunteered to take an active part in our support teams, none more so than Roger Vaughan and the deputy Commander, Bob Fielder. Roger's association with Brixton and some of its more recent fund-raising schemes had made him a natural choice to be asked to be one of the two adjudicators required by the *Guinness Book of Records* (Bruce Manser was the other). However, Bob Fielder's request to be involved had come as a welcome surprise. The best way to describe him is to conjure up an image of Desperate Dan. Bob was a big powerful man and an accomplished and highly respected senior officer. His background within the Royal Navy, first as a boy seaman and then as an Able seaman working as a naval "frogman" may have given him an affinity towards our Royal Naval whaler.

He was someone we were delighted to have on the team not least for his legendary determination and ability to get the job done no matter what he had to undertake. He had been one of the very few London firemen to get a national bravery award (BEM) for performing a hook ladder rescue. In June of 1969 a fierce fire was raging at the front of a Pimlico hotel. After climbing a ten-foot high spiked gate and straddling along the ridged roof of an annexe building, Bob Fielder and a fellow fireman climbed up floor by floor to the rear of the sixth-floor, some sixty feet high. Projecting brickwork under several of the windows made the climb particularly difficult and dangerous. Entering the hotel, the pair found an elderly man who was trapped and was suffering from the heat and smoke rising up from the fire below. Using a sling they lifted the man out of the window and lowered him safely to the ground and a subsequent full recovery. Bob's rescue was photographed by a passing member of the public and made the national press. An immensely modest man, he nevertheless wore his medal ribbon with great pride but rarely went into any detail as to how he actually came by his gallantry award, batting away enquires from those curious enough to ask, "It was just some job where I happened to be in the wrong place at the right time." We would be grateful of this unpretentious man's considerable strength of character before our row was over.

Leaving the Commander hobnobbing with Otis's Chairman and his board of directors we headed west, driving up the M4 and swinging right at Swindon towards the A361 that would take us to our destination. Lechlade is considered to be the upper limit of the navigable length of the River Thames and it was the starting point of our venture. But first we had to get that bloody whaler into the water again! The narrow slipway into the Thames was meant for the small little rowing boats that visitors to this quaint little Gloucester village could hire by the hour for a meander on the river. It certainly was not meant for our whaler which dwarfed the little boats that were tied up and waiting for the summer season to get under way. Even with our AA driver carefully reversing the 30ft trailer, on which the whaler had been carried from London, down the slipway, so its wheels were almost in the water, there was still not a sufficient angle for the whaler to slide easily into the water under its own steam. It did not budge an inch, just sat there, all one and a half tons of it, a dead weight. Rowers and support crew gathered around the static craft and braced themselves to push, pull, drag or heave the damn thing down the length of the trailer and into the water. A young chubby mother, out walking her toddler, beat a hasty retreat least she too was recruited to add her not inconsiderable weight to the task as some of the lads shouted, "Give us a hand missus."

After about twenty minutes of huffing and puffing the whaler finally, but none to gracefully, entered the water and was tethered for the night next to Lechlade Bridge, the starting point of our 185.88 miles row the following morning. Our support boat was the proud possession of Reg Ball, a fireman from West Norwood, who got in on the act simply because he offered the use of his aluminium flat-bottomed boat which resembled a miniature landing craft. He had no difficulty getting his boat into the water, not least because the driver was reversing the trailer back into the river much too fast. Realising his error, he braked suddenly coming to an instant stop. Reg's boat was by now unsecured on the trailer and had no option than to follow the natural laws of physics and shot off the rear of the trailer at the same speed the driver had been moving backwards. It hit the water like a launched RNLI lifeboat from a steep slipway. It was just such a shame that no one had thought to hold on to the securing line tied to Reg's boat as it floated majestically away downstream and Reg was wondering what he had signed up for?

Thanks to the generosity of Otis I had booked all the available bed and breakfast accommodation in the village for that night. It consisted of The Bull public house and a nearby farmhouse. Putting up nineteen burly firemen for the night had put a severe strain on the obtainable bed space at these two locations. It put and even greater strain on some of us who found ourselves having to share a bed with someone who you hoped would not snore or fart all night. But first we had to actually get to bed, something that the owner of The Bull seemed reluctant to let us do and who seemed happy and willing to serve drinks well after closing time. However, common sense prevailed in the end and just before midnight everybody hit the sack, some with a partner they had not expected to spend the night with.

For those staying at The Bull, myself included, we rose after only five hours sleep to a not so chirpy and rather hung-over owner of the pub who dished up our fortifying "full English" breakfast. The others staying at the farmhouse had a far more cheery start to their day as the farmer's wife already had an hour's start on them and was full of the joys of spring as she served them their breakfasts. Afterwards everyone congregated at the riverbank around 5.45am to make the final preparations. We rowers checked over the whaler whilst Reg and the boat's crew, wrapped up warm against the early morning chill, checked over the "tin bath" as the boat was now affectionately called. The two personnel carriers were fuelled up and ready to move off and some of the many Otis staff who would be on hand over the two days had turned up to see us on our way. Their presence added considerable weight to the much-needed land support that would be necessary to clear all the locks speedily if we stood any chance of setting a new record.

One other small contingent was also getting ready. The Brigade had sent its in-house film crew to capture the row from beginning to end and to record our success or not. One cameraman would be travelling on the water in the "tin bath" whilst the other one would stick with the land support crews. As for us we were now eager to get under way. My pre-planning could make or break this event but it was too late now to worry about what I should or could have done better. The minutes were ticking down to 6.30am, the start of our attempt.

Slowly rowing upstream, we passed under the ancient arched stone bridge that crosses over the Thames at Lechlade. We could feel the power of the river surging downstream as we rowed against the flow. We hoped that power would be our constant companion for at least the next thirty hours or so. Planning this row for early May had been no happenchance. Not only were we wanting to gain the extended length of daylight hours but also wanted to gain the maximum benefit from the spring fed flows. The River Thames catchment area is estimated to be about 3,845 square miles and this year's late winter and early spring, above average seasonal rainfall meant that the river was above its normal levels. This excess flow of water downstream, and its greater than expected rate, would increase our speed for every hour we were rowing. Whereas rowing against the current on the tidal section of the Thames speaks for itself!

A van or boat's crew had been allocated to every lock. They were responsible for making sure that the upstream lock gates were open when we arrived at them. They would then immediately close them, wind open the sluice gates before opening the downstream gates to allow us to move swiftly into the next lower stretch of river. This task had to be performed forty-five times and our own time trials with two separate locks found that from opening the one set of lock's gates, operating the sluices, waiting for the water level to equalise then opening the other sets of lock gates averaged out at about five minutes. Some lock had enormous bulks of timber either side of the lock, which had to be pushed or pulled to open the pair of lock gates, others had hand-cranked winches, (still one either side of the lock) and it required at least four people to pull/push or wind to get the job done in the time allowed. Even allowing for only five minutes per lock it meant three hours and forty-five minutes would be spent just getting through the locks. Every extra minute spent at each of the locks added another three-quarter of an hour to our overall time that could be much better spent rowing.

The two-way radios allowed the crew in the "tin bath" and the vans to talk to each other. Details of every lock keeper's telephone number were listed and during normal working hours they would be contacted and requested to give us priority. The lock keepers were exceptionally tolerant of our requests as were the other river craft waiting to use the locks. Detailed maps showed the routes to every lock but many of the small, un-signposted, country lanes that led to them challenged even the navigation skills of the most competent of our map-readers.

Getting refreshments to us could only be done at the locks and other physical (bathroom!) requirements had to be accommodated in the time it took to get into the lock and out again. A poo or a sandwich? The choice was ours to make but if the former took longer than five minutes the individual concerned would be in the "s---!" in more ways than one! We were to take turns in coxing the whaler, changing over every two hours. I had thought it best to draw lots, which we did. I pulled the short straw and would be the last to cox in the first round of this shared duty. Ten hours of rowing before my turn came around. But with fifty hours rowing ahead of us (all being well) it worked out the same for everyone.

With Wally first at the tiller we headed back downstream and cleared the Lechlade stone bridge. Our record attempt had officially started and with the boisterous shouts of encouragement from the Otis staff, waking up the few remaining residents of Lechlade we had not already woken, we were pulling away strongly and heading to the first lock, St John's, which was only half a mile away.

In less than six minutes we reached St John's lock, already ahead of schedule, a good omen! Standing on either side of the open lock entrance were big powerful looking men wearing the distinctive blue overalls of the Otis Company. They made easy work of shifting the two large elongated wooden levers that were the only means of opening the substantial lock gates. The levers were twice the width of the actual lock, which was only fourteen feet wide. This was our first test of upping oars! As we drew closer to the open lock Wally called, "Oars" and we all lifted our heavy oars out of the rowlocks and into a vertical position and then laid them down the centre of the whaler, for and aft. Whilst Wally steered for the entrance four of us grabbed the wooden paddles and propelled the whaler through the narrow entrance into the lock whilst John Yaxley, who rowed in the prow, got ready to throw a line to the waiting land crew. The moment the stern of the whaler cleared the upstream gates the Otis boys pushed back on the wooden levers and closed the lock gates behind us. Seeing the lock gates closed our own support crew opened up the downstream sluices that allowed the water in the lock to drain out as both the support boat (which was in front of us) and the whaler steadily dropped down three feet to the level of the next stretch of river. With both the Otis team and our own guys leaning on the downstream levers, the moment the water level equalised the lock gates were pushed open and we were on our way again. This was a process that was to be repeated time and time again as we moved further and further down the river during the day.

Rapidly leaving St John's lock behind us the dominant sound was that of the enormous outboard engine that was powering the support boat on towards Buscot, the next lock. As it moved further and further away, I was able to enjoy, for the first time that day, the scenic beauty of the upper reaches of the River Thames. The river seemed so incredibly narrow. This was the river that I had grown up knowing since a child but was only used to seeing it as a wide expanse of water as it wound its snakelike path through London and then onwards towards the sea getting ever wider. Now here in the tranquil and serene upper reaches of this majestic river our oars were almost brushing the banks on either side of the whaler. They were touching the overhanging branches of the numerous willows as they fought for space in this crowded tree lined aquatic avenue.

The distance between the locks varied. Some were just under two miles apart; most were separated by three or four miles of river. As the day progressed the lock drill was honed to perfection by both ourselves and more importantly the support crews. The Otis people were incredibly supportive and on isolated bridges that crossed the river, and seemed miles from anywhere, shouts from smiling faces would encourage us on to even greater efforts and there seemed a genuine pride in seeing the large blue and white Otis flag (we had designed and made) fluttering from the bow of the whaler as we continued onward along the fast moving river. By lunchtime of that first day we were over an hour ahead of schedule as we continued downstream though Oxfordshire. By late afternoon we had increased that lead still further. There was considerable excitement in the team and expectations were high that this progress could be maintained. Sandford lock was number 14 on our list and it also had the greatest fall of any of the Thames' locks, almost nine feet. The greater the fall, the more water to be discharged. The greater the amount of water the longer we were stuck in a lock not rowing. So despite our good progress it was a concerned Roger Vaughan who said that we could ill afford to waste the nine minutes it took us to clear the bigger locks. Roger, as well as being an adjudicator had taken on the role of team manager and was making an excellent job of it. It allowed me to just concentrate on rowing knowing that Roger would have no deviation from my game plan and whatever problems might arise he would get sorted.

Along with high morale came the banter, it was infectious. Reg was getting considerable stick about his "tin bath" and decided to show those in it what his boat was capable of. Gunning the throttle, he shot off at an alarming rate of knots that took the crew totally by surprise and two were in danger of having an unexpected dip before it was agreed that Reg and his boat maybe deserved a little more respect. Reg just smiled as the wake from his shiny metal boat washed over the notice warning river users about excessive speed!

As twilight moved into darkness the physical effort of rowing almost non-stop was starting to be felt by all of us. Each rower had had a turn of coxing for at least one two-hour spell, but that still left you pulling on an oar for fifteen out of the eighteen hours we had been on the water. There was a noticeable change in the mood of the support crews too. The Otis people had called it a day but had been wonderfully supportive and committed since the early morning and promising to send more supporters the following day. The boat and land crews now hunkered down for the serious business of getting us through the night and safely through the next six or seven locks before sunrise on the 6th May.

Unlike our epic row from Paris to London, where the industrial sized locks of Northern France close during the hours of darkness, the locks on the Thames remain open for public use even though the lock keepers are snuggled up warm in bed. Although the locks are usable, they are also unlit! Torches held by the support team guided us to the lock entrances. Our own measly little light on the prow of the whaler just managed to give a warning of our position on the river. Operating each of the locks in the dark was an arduous task for the support team especially as four of them were some of the longest locks in the system. Goring Lock was one hundred and eighty feet long and Mapledurham was over two hundred feet long. They also had falls of between five and seven feet of water to discharge and that is a lot of water when you are in hurry.

Dawn found us with Oxfordshire on one bank and Buckinghamshire on the other. We had put on warmer clothing during the night and the chatter in the boat was minimal with each of us lost in our own thoughts and concentrating on maintaining the stoke rate. At some point during the night, I have no idea when, I fell asleep at my oar. How long I slept for I have no idea, it was probably no more than seconds although it seemed like several minutes. I tried desperately to keep my eyes open but my eyelids felt so heavy I just could not keep them open any longer. Pandemonium never broke out on the boat, with the resultant crashing of oars because I had stopped rowing, so maybe I did not stop, I do not know? But when I woke, I felt strangely reinvigorated and determined not to let it happen again. It didn't. The river was very much wider now, a size you more readily associate with the Thames. The weariness we were feeling was equally shared by the support teams but especially the support boat crew. At least we had the rowing to keep us warm. They were just sitting in the open boat. Now chilled to the bone, despite the flotation jackets that were meant to insulate them against the fresh night air as well as acting a life-jacket lest the boat capsized or they fell in. The first shards of daylight saw them huddled up and looking uncharacteristically miserable. We no doubt looked the same but we would argue that we were simply concentrating on our rowing.

Our sprits rose in direct proportion to the rise in the temperature as the sun's rays burnt off the chilling river mist and dried the moisture lining the river's banks. We flew passed Windsor Castle pulling strongly. Sadly there was no Royal Standard flying so the prospect of some Royal personage popping down to the river bank to have their valet or footman shout for them, "Come on Brixton, put your backs into it" was clearly a non-starter! As we moved steadily though the next eight locks (that would bring us to Teddington lock) we were joined again not only by the staff from Otis but senior officers of our own division. How they managed to smuggle themselves outside the boundary of

Greater London no one asked, but it was both pleasing and rewarding to know that they were putting themselves out to support our undertaking. In fact we were beginning to wonder just who was looking after the Brigade's B Division, as Brian Butler (the Divisional Commander), his deputy and most of his management team seemed to be scurrying around the locks as we waited impatiently for the water to drop whilst they wished us well and encouraged us to even greater efforts. Brian Butler even jumped into the support boat and travelled downstream for a couple of locks, occasionally ordering us to pull harder. Mumblings were heard from within the whaler, "What the eff does he know about rowing, the only thing he has ever pulled is crumpet!" But the fact that he was there was not lost on us either, although it would be his deputy Bob Fielder that would be truly inspirational as the row progressed further.

The roar of aircraft engines overhead, clearly visible in the day's clear blue skies, let us know we were under the flight path into Heathrow that crosses over Sunbury lock. Despite the expertise with which the Otis staff and our own support crew now operated each lock in turn it was a concerned Roger Vaughan who told me, "You lost nine minutes on the last lock so we want to push you through faster on this one." True to his word he smooth-talked us ahead of the other waiting craft in the lock to get us out first and away.

Teddington lock was an important milestone. It is where the River Thames changes from flowing just downstream to tidal. The last few locks had seen us paddling in and out like native warriors. The sun was beating down and we were all shirtless, sweating profusely and grateful of the locks enforced stop so we could take on more fluids. Having a pee was no longer an issue since we were perspiring so much there was no excess liquid going to our bladders.

Fast flowing brown mucky water warned of Teddington's weir ahead. We were facing upstream so it was only the coxswain that was watching the angry water as it roared through the weir. As we drew closer the pull of the river towards the weir was tangible but we were steered safely past through to the open lock and got a friendly wave from the owner of a luxury private cruiser, which was one of many, moored alongside this stretch of the river. In contrast a graceful swan gave no more than a bemused look as it continued effortlessly upstream against the current and continued its feeding. The whole scene, as it moved further and further away, looked idyllic and peaceful with even the graceful willows, in early leaf, moving gently in the morning's warm breeze. (In fact, it was getting increasingly hot.)

Still well ahead of schedule, things were going to plan. Well they were until the support boat disappeared! At the time we had no idea why it was not with us any longer? For some reason the two-way radio in their boat would not work either. So for us it was a case of "out-brain, in-cabbage" and just keep rowing onto the next scheduled stop; Lambeth's fireboat pontoon. Even the support van was no longer visible as we first passed Chiswick then Hammersmith and Putney. With one and a half hours of slack water we still had the advantage of no incoming tide impeding our progress downstream even if it did seem that all our support teams had simply disappeared?

By Chelsea Embankment the familiar sight of the film crew pointing their video camera out the window of the support van came into view as they tried, and failed, to get a shot of us whilst they negotiated Friday afternoon's busy traffic. At 3.30pm we pulled alongside Lambeth's fireboat pontoon hours ahead of schedule. (We had not been expected until midnight). We had been rowing for thirty-three hours and it was beginning to feel like it. But we were on familiar ground now and, whilst not quite the last lap, our spirits were incredibly high as were the reception parties that greeted us. A mixture of London's Otis staff, our support crew and Lambeth's land and fireboat crews, their general consensus was that they all thought us all quite mad. Finally, the mystery of the support boat was solved, its outboard engine had conked out. A replacement was being sought and all being well they would catch us up somewhere near Greenwich. With a quick comfort break for those that wanted it, a change of coxswain and we set off again to the loud cheers of our gallant band of supporters and the rather feeble hooter blaring from the fireboat.

Passing the Houses of Parliament, we had that stretch of river between Lambeth and Westminster Bridges totally to ourselves. The photograph that was taken of us pulling strongly down river at this point became a favourite of the crew when we saw it but something else was grabbing our attention at the time it was being taken. The tide was turning and not in our favour.

The row was planned to minimise the effects of the incoming spring tides. We had plenty of experience rowing against the Thames' tides, it was never easy. Not getting into the right position on the river, to reduce the effect of the tide, makes it so much harder especially if you get your line all wrong. Twice a day the tides rises and fall. The Thames' tidal velocity varies considerably in different parts of the river. The rates above London Bridge may be between one to three knots but can be high as seven! Below London Brigade and as far as Woolwich the norm is around two knots on a flood tide. Someone had put the brake on the whaler and the advantage of rowing with the tide evaporated as we were now pulling against the power of the river's incoming tide. It would run for the next five hours before the next slack water and ebbing tide.

Despite the very many times we had rowed against the tide in training now it seemed different. Nature was flexing its muscles and saying, "You want your record, well you earn it." It was like rowing in treacle. For all the effort and strength you put into pulling that damn oar, you got such a small return. We were rowing in slow motion. Well that's not quite true because our row rate was still well over thirty strokes per minute. It was the whaler that was moving in slow motion. We hugged the shoreline to reduce the full impact of the tide, sliding in between HMS Belfast and Hays Wharf before passing under London's iconic Tower Bridge (our finishing line in the Paris to London row). But Southend was still many miles ahead and we would have to endure another flood tide before we reached it, and we still had to row through this one.

A fillip to our spirits came in the form of the Brigade's fireboat crew. Booking "mobile" they became our unofficial escort down to Greenwich before making their way home again for the change of watch at 6pm. With its departure a familiar sound was heard in the distance and for the five rowers facing up river we saw the low, but distinct, outline of our own "little" support craft. It seemed dwarfed in the wide expanse of the river that fronted the old Millwall Docks that was already under massive redevelopment and would be eventually transformed into the now famous Canary Wharf.

We were getting hungry, very hungry, having not stopped (except to change coxswains and grabbing a quick snack at Lambeth's pontoon) for proper food since the early morning. We were expending a massive amount of calories (over one thousand an hour) and our energy reserves were in need of some serious recharging. Passing a message to the support boat's crew they sped off in search of some sustenance. We continued downstream a little further and moored up on the north bank by a derelict wharf that towered above us. We sat like fledgling chicks, stuck in a riverside nest, waiting for the parent birds to bring us a meal. When it came it was wrapped in paper. Fish and chips! "Sorry lads, it was all we could find." But it had retained a modicum of warmth and we consumed it hungrily. People probably underestimate the rejuvenating power of "greasy" fish and chips, but to us it was a feast and fortified, we were ready for the night ahead.

With slack water once again our companion we were moving steadily along the north shore at an impressive forty strokes a minute. Ahead of us was the Thames Barrier whose pillars looked like alien sentinels strung across the width of the Thames. Joining us was the night shift on the Brigade's fireboat. They had come to bid us farewell as we followed the green arrows that directed us to the gap between the downstream piers of the Barrier, which was the extent of the fireboat's lower Thames patrol area. With its monitor sending a column of water high into the evening air we left the barrier behind us. The mood in the whaler was again very positive.

Bob Fielder had now taken up his position in the support boat. His large frame dominating the "tin bath's" crew whilst his powerful voice boomed out over the water as he called out the stroke. *"Onea, twooo, free, fourr"* and repeating this cry until he was satisfied that we got the message. If we did not hear him those standing on either the north and south banks surely must have done as his echo occasionally bounced back towards the river.

The London Fire Brigade's Operations Room was monitoring our progress and at 10.30pm circulated at message around the Brigade that we had passed the Ford Motor Company at Dagenham. With twilight now reducing visibility considerably we (or rather the coxswain) had to be ever more conscious about the danger of driftwood or debris floating in the river, but it is what they cannot see that presented the greatest danger. Large bulks of broken timber, whose jagged edges, could cause considerable damage to either the whaler or the support boat's outboard engine. Collecting a large piece of tarpaulin on the end of one of the oars is not much fun either as the sudden and unexpected resistance could pull unsuspecting muscles or even rip an oar right out of your hands.

Nighttime on the river was dark; very dark. Our small navigation light provided little illumination nor did the quarter moon clearly visible in the star lit sky. We could hear rather than see the support boat whose still noisy outboard engine took on a surprisingly reassuring sound. Even "big" Bob had gone quiet, unable to see if we were pulling the oars to his demanding stroke rate. However, I knew that we had reached Gravesend as an important piece of my organisation came into play. Thankfully once again a Tug Company had responded to my sponsorship request and the "Hurricane", a seagoing tug, would now be our constant companion on the final haul to Southend, its VHF radio and radar providing an important safety function and informing other shipping of our position and its radar warning us of any unseen hazards in our path in the near total darkness.

With us now rowing the wide expanse of the lower Thames Estuary there was little for the land-based support crews to do. So with the van drivers taking the vans onto the finish at Southend pier, the remainder of the support team hitched a lift on the tug to catch a well-deserved rest and give us their verbal support as soon as the morning light allowed.

Darkness brought with it a change of tide. Although we could not see it, we certainly could feel it. We were getting tired and had to follow in the wake of the tug that was navigating us through the estuary via Shell Haven and passed Canvey Island on towards that elusive pier! Breaking light did little to ease our load as instead of helpful currents we were facing strong incoming sea tides that were trying to sweep us back up the Estuary. It was also a bitterly cold morning and our coxswain was wrapped up warmly to protect himself from the chilling breeze. The tug, festooned with support banners promoting the row, was silhouetted against the creeping light whilst the Essex coastline seemed shrouded in opaque "Clingfilm."

A whaler was made to be rowed at sea. It was on home ground but the conditions were not conducive to our record attempt. Not only were these adverse currents stronger than on the upper Thames, the prevailing breeze was not helping much either. Bob was once again standing proud at the front of our small support boat. He looked extremely precarious in the swell, as he faced us and started his distinctive call. "*Onea, twooo, free, fourr. Come on, lift that boat.*" Clearly noting our waning strength after almost two full days rowing virtually non-stop he added, "*Well done lads, keep it up. I promise you I can see the pier.*" Whether he could or not we could not tell as we were facing the other way. If our coxswain did or did not see it, he was not about to contradict Bob.

Bob's voice was sounding increasingly hoarse and raw as he continued almost non-stop to drive us forward. Now Roger (our adjudicator) was standing by his side, the pair looking like Little and Large. With the end clearly in sight their commitment to this event, and to us, was plainly and unmistakably evident.

Waiting on the end of Southend's bleak and lengthy pier (it's the world's longest pier) were a loyal band of supporters including wives and family plus a very chilly and bleary-eyed Brian Butler huddled up in his civvies. They had all seen the light from the halogen lamp on the front of the whaler, although it was rumoured that they heard Bob's voice first shouting at us, "***Pull your fingers out.***" At 6.10am the tug moved off from our stern and darted ahead and turned its prow pointing to the end of the pier as a marker. The last sixteen minutes seemed agonisingly slow as we drew nearer and near the pier but never seemed to bloody arrive. Then at 6.26am our one-and-a-half-ton whaler drew passed the marker with us still pulling strongly and setting a new national record time of forty-seven hours and fifty-six minutes. We alighted the whaler jubilant, euphoric even, but exhausted. I was wondering why I had chosen the end of the damn pier for now we had over a mile walk to get to the support vans and a much welcome long hot shower at Southend Fire Station.

Otis continued to deliver the goods. Later that same morning they organised a civic reception for the rowers (and support team) at a nearby leisure centre attended by the Mayoress of Southend. This smiling squat and portly lady wearing her Chain of Office round her neck and a none-too-fashionable floral dress and matching hat (with feather!), was greeted by a uniformed Brian Butler who had to apologise to her that we were all a bit dozy and were not actually drunk (we sounded drunk because of our extreme tiredness that was now rapidly consuming us). Exhaustion had already got the better of Andy Snazall who was already sound asleep and oblivious to the Mayoress' speech and subsequent questions. He gave an excellent impersonation of the dormouse from the Mad Hatter's tea party until wakened with a swift kick. Aroused from his slumber but totally bemused he said to the Mayoress, "Who are you?" before recalling where he was and why. Bob Fielder could say nothing by now, his voice completely spent. It was Roger Vaughan who paid an emotional but fitting tribute whilst he rolled his fag as we sat, totally spent, on the end of Southend pier.

"I have known these blokes for years and I can honestly say I have never felt prouder than today at seeing them, with fatigue literally running through each one, finish this with such resolve and a determination that displayed such grit."

I could not put it better myself regarding my fellow rowers. This time *The Guinness Book of Records* had no hesitation in accepting our record-breaking achievement that knocked over five hours off the previous best time. It would not be the last time someone attempted to set a new Thames record, but it was for us. No one has since tried to smash that record in the "beast" of a naval whaler. With £10,000 divided equally between the Guide Dogs for the Blind and the firemen's Benevolent Fund it was my swan song as regards organising major fund-raising events. But what a way to finish.

A sour note

Despite the very many years of collecting money for the Benevolent Fund and then actively engaged in raising funds for it, when the time came to seek its assistance it sadly let me (or rather members of my family) down. Since Southwark, then West Norwood and latterly Brixton, many thousands of pounds had been placed in the coffers of the fund, if not by my efforts alone then by my organisational skills in bringing a series of major fundraisers successfully together.

Later, and whilst in senior rank, my grown-up son, who now had a partner, had to face the traumatising discovery of a horrendous and protracted abuse that his partner had endured during her teenage years (and into early womanhood) at the hands of her own father. My wife and I were initially unaware of the full details of what the problems were or what the father had done, but the change that came over my son in trying to come to terms with unearthing this devastating secret was seriously affecting his own physical and mental wellbeing. Once my wife and I were conversant with the enormity of the full facts we extended our own home as a safe haven to my son's partner for her own protection. With details passed to the police they started their detailed investigations into the serious allegations that had surfaced.

It was not a simple or a swift process and both my son and his girlfriend were in need of some professional counselling. My son did not get on with it, largely because of the anger and loathing he felt for his partner's father. The pair had a very strong relationship but the lack of any admissible evidence, despite the best endeavours and active support of the police, made the prospect of any successful prosecution and the delivery of justice through the criminal courts unlikely in the opinion of the Crown Prosecution Service. This news was a devastating blow for us all but especially so for my son and his partner who was now, for all intents and purposes, a fully-fledged member of our family. The pair clearly needed some respite from all the harrowing soul searching that had taken place and the stress and anxiety of pursuing justice against her cruel and even wicked so-called parent. This person's despicable actions would ultimately lead to a slow, and sadly, inevitable path of self-destruction for my son's partner. Despite them having, and raising a daughter of their own they later separated because she tried, unsuccessfully, to hide from her past in a cocktail of drinking and drugs. My son became the legal guardian of his daughter and remains a caring and devoted father. His partner tried hard to rehabilitate herself but the damage was too great for her small and now frail body and she died in hospital barely thirty years old and weighing less than her primary school age daughter.

But now they needed to get away and the Fund's convalescence home on the south coast provided an ideal setting to find some space and a period of recuperation. It was what the home was intended for, to facilitate the aid of emotional and physical recovery for individuals or families within a peaceful environment. I had only ever contributed to the Fund and in the previous twenty years of my service had never taken anything out. I applied for my son and his partner to attend for one week with evidence to support their case from doctors and the police. My application was rejected since my son's partner was not his lawful wife! Although not married (and never did marry) she changed her name legally to Pike. The Fund's bureaucratic rules prevented them gaining access to a facility that I had devoted both sweat and occasional tears to help maintain and improve with the not inconsiderable amount of money that I (and others) had managed to raise. All the work I put into the Fund counted for nothing. No offer of help to my family was ever forthcoming. I was angry, very angry. But anger was not going to change their decision. I felt let down and hurt, it was a kick in the face as far as I was concerned and I walked away from the Fund, never again to put myself out to raise money or support their fundraising activities. It may appear churlish or an immature reaction but at the time it seemed the only course of action to this officious judgement in my son's hour of need. On reflection I have no regrets about walking away from the Fund; it had provided so many things, just such a pity it ended on such a sour note.

The non-stop fire engine pull from London to Brighton reaches the South-Downs in Sussex. 8th June 1980.

One of the three rowing teams on the Canal du Nord heading into Calais during the Paris to London marathon row in August 1981.

The Sun tug-boat escorts the rowers to the finish line at Tower Bridge after their marathon row from Paris-France. August 1981.

Copyright. *London Fire Brigade/Mary Evans Picture Library.*

Bob 'Bruce' Manser presenting one of two £5.000.00 cheques to London's former Chief Fire Officer, Joe Milner CBE QFSM who accepts on behalf of the Fireman's Benevolent Fund. November 1981.

Rowing into the Guinness Book of Records during our marathon non-stop row of the length of the River Thames-Lechlade to Southend Pier. May 1983.

Chapter 13

Senior Rank

Up the ladder!

Despite my brief foray into senior rank whilst at West Norwood my time at Brixton was far too enjoyable to bother about seeking any further promotion, temporary or otherwise. There was simply just too much going on. But in the November of 1984, I was given an offer I could not refuse. The phone call, when it came, was totally out of the blue. The staff officer said, "I have the Divisional Commander for you, hold the line please." I sat in my office and waited for him to transfer the call. "Hello David," he said as he came on to the line. That was always a worrying start to an unexpected call from my Commander. After a brief exchange of small talk, that led nowhere, he finally came to the point. "Brigade Headquarters is looking for a suitable, experienced, Station Officer to join an implementation team for the introduction of Station Commanders. (This turned out to be news for the Head of the Implementation team, but that's senior management for you!) The Commander continued, "I have put your name forward already, are you interested? It will mean temporary promotion for you while you are at Brigade Headquarters and you'll be there about three months."

I enjoyed my work at a fire station and was never shy in saying so. I had been at station level for nearly eighteen years and, in recent months, had been thinking seriously of trying my hand at securing promotion to higher rank and moving up the pecking order. So, if this was a way of getting my foot in the door who was I to argue – especially if it meant the possibility of influencing the Station Commanders' role. It was an opportunity too good to pass up. I told the Commander I would be delighted to accept and would try not to let him down in my temporary rank of Assistant Divisional Officer. "You had better not effing well let me down because you are not promoted by one rank, it's two. You are going to Headquarters as a Divisional Officer."

How I got to be short-listed for this role was never explained. My annual appraisals had recorded me as promotable but the actual role of a Station Commander was still a very foggy concept, to say the least. But I had learnt to stand out from the crowd at station level and had managed this, in part, by re-organising the station's outside working routines. Every station had its outside work schedule, hydrant inspections; fire prevention inspections and associated tests plus regular familiarisation visits to special risks. I had reviewed and re-structured Brixton's workload so as to maximise the station's annual inspection schedule. With the aid of a wall-mounted year planner I had introduced an effective "bring forward" and monitoring system. I had spent weeks of night duties analysing every aspect of the station's outside work and drawing up a hitherto unwritten annual schedule. It provided an even distribution of work spread over the four watches, which could then be rotated, and listed the high-profile life and special risks that each watch should target for regular six-monthly visits.

This unsolicited work, and my report requesting its formal adoption at station level, not only found favour with my immediate bosses but my bosses' bosses. I had trialled the system unofficially at Brixton and my fellow officers considered it both workable and advantageous. The planner was then professionally drawn up and mounted behind a Perspex covering that could be written on with dry marker. It was not rocket science, but it was a first within the Division. Not only did the planner make planning or rescheduling inspections easier to monitor but it also caught the eye of visiting senior officers who could see for themselves how the station was maintaining its inspection rate and testing programme. The loyalty of my fellow watch officers was truly commendable as they admitted, when asked by senior officers, where it came from, "Pikey did it."

It no doubt sounds rather pompous but as a watch Station Officer I had got to know my job rather well. It seems I did it well too, as in the opinion of my peer group as I was able to demonstrate these abilities consistently both on and off the fireground. The hard part was trying to make sure nobody knew just how bloody hard I had to work to do it so well. I did much of my learning in private only just did not say so. I was also supremely fortunate in having some excellent tutors. They showed me the value, and importance, of looking calm and efficient whilst being on top of everything and totally in control. But never forgetting that I must always be totally proficient at my job, an operational firefighting officer.

Central Operations

As the name implied Central Operations advised, oversaw and monitored the Brigade's operational policies and considered the implications of new and revised operational practices resulting from, for example, Home Office directives and Fire Service Circulars. Its head was my former Divisional Commander Gerry Clarkson who had now been promoted, the previous year, to the rank of Deputy Chief Officer. He had four Assistant Chief Officers reporting to him, each with a defined area of responsibility. Central Operations occupied nearly the whole of Brigade Headquarters' second floor and included the Brigade's Operations room. My new boss was one of these four Assistant Chief officers, a former junior fireman himself although not from London. The same age as me (thirty-five) but looking younger he was also five ranks above me! He had travelled from his original Brigade in Hampshire to surrounding Brigades, progressively gathering higher rank as he went. Clearly ambitious, talented and driven, London was yet another stepping-stone on his career path to achieve his goal of becoming a Chief Officer. Something he was to secure in a few years' time by becoming Kent's Chief Fire Officer. He would later oversee, amongst other things, the fire safety arrangements of the Channel Tunnel and help devise new operational procedures for tackling incidents in a tunnel system that was over 31 miles in length.

Jerry Beech was a slim fair-haired man. He tended to the skinny rather than muscular but enjoyed youthful (some said boyish) looks that gave him the appearance of someone in their early twenties. Given his very elevated rank this caused considerable consternation among his more elderly, but subordinate, senior officers who were clearly envious of his rapid progress within the service. Jerry's youthful looks were not without its problems however. His body still clearly thought he was going through adolescence as he suffered from constant facial acne. Much to the consternation of his small team, and despite his razor-sharp mind, he would sit idly picking at the latest eruption on his face whilst delivering a brief on his latest policy imperative that required detailed investigation. As head of the Policy, Performance and Review group (PPR) he led a team of handpicked officers whose task was to review and report on national and Home Office directives and identify their Brigade-wide implications. It was into this elite team that I had been dispatched from Brixton, in the rank of Divisional Officer, albeit temporary. I was already feeling way out of my depth!

Some might say the Brigade's principal management and organisational structure was a little sycophantic. It seemed the philosophy was to mirror whatever direction the Greater London Council took in its policy initiatives and particularly the structuring of their various policy departments. The GLC had created a Programme Office (to enact the council's Labour controlled policies) so the Brigade set up a Programme Office. The GLC had a Policy, Performance and Review Group so the Brigade again followed suit. The work this group did was identical to the former operational policy team it replaced but the change of title kept the GLC politicians happy and was the 'in' management thing of the time.

I was not the only newcomer to the PPR team that first day. I was to share a second-floor office, overlooking the Thames, with another newly promoted Divisional Officer, only he was a real DO. Two other senior officers were already in situ and we were PPR. The ACO's small team also included a Sub Officer who acted as his "bat-man" and general runner. He was, however, much better staffed than the two territorial ACOs (one covering the North of the river and the other South). They had to share a none too spacious office and even the same staff officer.

This new Brigade headquarters world was all very alien to me. Having come from an environment where I only had one principal officer to contend with, I was now working on the same floor as the Deputy Chief Officer, four Assistant Chief Officers and where there was more gold braid and laurel leaves than you could shake a stick at. But to them I was a relatively low form of life in the headquarters pond. However, my presence had not gone unnoticed and certainly not by the headquarters ADOs and Station Officers (who were would-be ADOs). I was being treated with equal amounts of curiosity, suspicion and envy. "How come he got promoted two ranks?" was the, not so silent, whisper circulating around the second floor from ADOs struggling to prepare for an imminent promotion round to Divisional Officer. (I was excluded from that promotion round as I did not hold the substantive rank of Assistant Divisional Officer.)

I was not, however, totally alone. I was befriended by a former Station Officer from the B Division who was now a Divisional Officer. He was determined not to see me flounder in my first few days adrift in these strange and intimidating surroundings. "OK Pikey, come in here" he said as he welcomed me into the box room of an office he shared with another senior officer. (He was rarely there because he was the Fire Brigades Union national Officer's representative and if he was not negotiating this or that then he was taking his compensatory leave).

Clearing away a pile of grey headquarters policy files from the only available spare chair I was invited to sit whilst he gave me a more practical induction into Brigade Headquarters' life than my earlier formal welcome by my youthful, but spotty, ACO. "First we've got to get you some transport, a staff car from the car pool in Newport Street." (Which was in fact a series of railway arches behind the rear of the headquarters complex.) "Next, once you get your car, you will have to fight to get a parking space on the rear block forecourt. It's a first come, first served policy. Senior officers had been seen to squabble over their parking spaces much to the amusement of everyone else who had already secured a space for the day. Your time here will be all the more enjoyable if you find a parking space and manage to keep it." This benevolent man was Geoff Townley. He was in his late-forties, had a good head of greying hair and looked every inch the Justice of the Peace (which he was) as he peered over his half-moon reading glasses, observing, listening and offering sound advice. "Off you go and get your transport. We will cover your next lesson or two when you return and I will tell you the secrets of the typing pool and get you on the operational rota." With a regal wave of his hand he dismissed me, sending me on my way as he returned to the pile of grey folders he was trying to wade through.

Bedecked in my senior officer's uniform and braided cap, (borrowed from Roger Vaughan) I walked to Newport Street and made my way to the backstreet car pool. The car pool occupied two very deep railway arches, leased from British Rail, and served as a garage for principal and senior officers' cars, a refuelling point and a rest area for the Headquarters drivers, when not out driving their principal officers. (All senior officers drove themselves.) Here I discovered that my time spent at Lambeth fire station had not been wasted because Newport Street was managed by the very staff car drivers I had befriended when I was stationed there and who were now rapidly approaching their own retirement. I was welcomed like a long-lost son and given the pick of a very dubious selection of white Cortina saloon cars. Issued with my magnetic blue flashing light, that went on top of the car on "shouts," I now had my own personal transport to emergency incidents. The car was in fact my transport everywhere, to and from home, around the Brigade, anywhere in fact. I was beginning to like this job.

That first evening my children looked on in awe as this slightly dented and off-white staff car arrived home and Dad parked his fire car on the drive. My son checked and then rechecked that the blue flashing light went round and round when he stuck the light's fitting into the cigarette lighter attachment whilst he let his younger sister sound the two-tone horns, least he got in to trouble.

Day two, and my parking place was secured due to my early arrival. (I was so early in fact that I had the pick of the whole bloody car park!) Once again, I was ensconced among the grey files, in the box room, with my newfound mentor. My induction course continued with an introduction to the "policy" files. They were the sacred scrolls of Brigade operational policy. There were also similar policy files for the other three main Headquarters' departments: Technical Services, Fire Prevention and Personnel (before it reinvented itself and became Human Resources). These policy files were listed A to Y (there was nothing beginning with Z) and they covered every possible aspect of operational policy. Each individual policy file provided a unique insight into how operational policy was arrived at, how its changes were determined and by whom. The guardian of this wealth of policy information was a small and slightly built non-uniformed administrator who wore an ill-fitting toupee. What he lacked in stature he made up for in his total and almost obsessive commitment to his task of guarding the "scrolls." To aid him in this important task he had a small team of equally committed administrators who ensured that every file was signed in and out. Its progress from officer to officer was monitored as it passed up and down the chain of command.

My wise mentor rose from behind his desk and squeezed himself between the limited available space and moved towards the door saying, "Follow me." He led me back into the central corridor and towards a small alcove. I had not previously noticed the opening but he disappeared into it. Following, I found a narrow spiral staircase that went up and came out in the middle of the third floor. "Where are we going?" I asked. "Probably the one place that will determine just how successful your stay in Operations is," he replied. Opening a door, he ushered me in. It was a large open plan office with maybe ten to fifteen desks arranged in rows filling almost the whole room. I say almost because at the front and in the centre was a desk standing on its own facing the other desks. On each desk was a typewriter and behind it was a woman, some young, some older, some pretty and some definitely not! They all had one thing in common, a talent I marvelled at; they were tapping away at the typewriter keys without even looking at them, just reading the script by the side of their respective typewriters. My attention was only broken from this feat of sheer wonder by a woman's voice asking, "Can I help you?"

The voice came from the woman behind the solitary desk. As she rose she had the build of a legendary Amazon. She dominated the room with her presence. Considerably above average height she was not overweight at all. Her physique was well proportioned and more than amply provided for, height, build and cleavage! You would not call her beautiful but there was nevertheless an attractiveness about her that was immediately noticeable. "This is Dave Pike," my minder said as I moved forward to shake her hand with every expectation that she could crush it without even trying. "He has just joined Operations and I brought him up so you could meet him and tell him how things work up here." I was getting the same visual inspection that I had given her and the smile on her face seemed to indicate that I passed muster. "Please call me Shirley," was her introduction as she briefed me on what was expected of me when presenting any work to be typed in the "pool." There was a definite pecking order as to who got their work pushed to the top of the list if it was urgent, or if you were trying to impress your boss with a quick turnaround. Only the Deputy Chief Officer had his own PA, so even the Assistant Chiefs had to get their general typing sent up to the pool (although we prepared nearly everything for them). Confidential reports required by the Assistant Chief Officers would either be undertaken by the Deputy's PA or Shirley herself. Fully appraised, I left the typing pool with my escort whispering in my ear, "She likes you Pikey. You can take my typing up there in future."

Finally returning to my own office I was confronted by the long-standing Divisional Officer (who occupied the biggest desk in the room). He wanted to know what I had been up to over the last day and a bit. "Sorting out my transport, my operational rota, learning about policy files and instructed by Shirley about the typing pool protocols," I said defending myself and waiting for the inevitable frown of disapproval he appeared to give everyone. "Good," was his only reply as he looked back down at his daily newspaper and once again left me to my own devices.

At Brixton fire station I had only ridden on fire engines. Now I drove a staff car with a blue flashing light and a two tone that sounded that it had a bad attack of asthma. Without any formal command training (or an assessment as to my suitability to command a major fire) I was now expected to take command of multi-pump fires. I waited excitedly for the opportunity to do just that. I waited and waited. My moment of glory eluded me for now at least. I had no midnight summons to take charge of a dockside warehouse blaze or some other large industrial complex burning out of control. For now, my role was to assist in the implementation of the new Station Commanders. However, too many cooks were already spoiling the broth. Another review group was striving away on the implementation process and yet another was considering the issues of factoring in the Divisional ADOs to be relocated to stations as Station Commanders. Even from my lowly position in the Headquarters food chain I could see that this was a classic case of over-kill and fire brigade belt and braces management style. I would learn much later that it was typical of Clarkson to send "several ferrets down one rabbit hole" and then compare their findings.

As the most recent arrival from a fire station my opinions were sought (occasionally eagerly) but, at best, the Policy, Performance and Review team were only duplicating what others had already discovered or determined. Shaping the role of this new breed of officer in London was one thing, determining and providing the necessary resources that would make it all work was another thing entirely. (Other UK Fire Brigades already had Station Commanders in post.) Questions such as; "how are we actually going to make this work in practice" were considered not to be part of the brief! It was worrying to say the least. I would soon get to see just how worrying, but why spoil a good idea with mere practicalities.

My temporary elevated position brought with it new responsibilities. I was now rostered, among other duties, as the duty officer for the Brigade's Operations Room when on 24-hour call. The Operations Room was located at the eastern end of the second floor and was a large open plan office that ran from the front to the back of the building. Staffed by both operational personnel and a small team of dedicated control room officers, its rostered Operations Room personnel manned the Brigade's major control unit (that was based at Lambeth) at large or serious incidents. The Operations Room team provided a number of important Brigade wide functions not least amongst these were: Monitoring make-up incidents or incidents (involving chemicals) other than the norm: maintaining and providing a wide range of information on chemical/radiological and biological hazards to fireground crews: maintaining liaison with Water Authorities in respect of water supplies throughout the greater London area and, although a separate function, running the Brigade's "transport desk" which monitored the availability of the whole appliance fleet and the disposition, and status, of all spare appliances.

The Senior Divisional Officer in Central Operations was Bill Williams. He had been a Junior Firemen instructor at Swanley. Although not my instructor we nevertheless remembered each other from those early, happy, days. When promoted to Station Officer he was posted to Cannon Street fire station whilst I was the Sub Officer at Southwark and with both of us on the same watch, we frequently met up on the fireground. Although he started his fire service career at Plumstead he later transferred to Clerkenwell and established a formidable reputation as an excellent fireman. He rose through the ranks, serving more north of the river than south before reaching senior rank as an ADO and then DO in the "H" Division (based at Croydon) before being posted to Brigade Headquarters, where he had remained ever since. Bill possessed a special quality, which whilst not unique, was nevertheless rare amongst his contemporaries. This was especially so when compared to those colleagues, who unlike him, had not fought during the Second World War. Bill Williams had the ability to remain incredibly calm in even the most stressful of situations. Not only was he calm, but he had the ability to instil that calmness in those around him and to focus on the important decisions necessary to resolve the problems at hand. To see Bill in the street you probably would not give him a second glance. An average sort of chap, he was neither overly tall nor well built. His hair was thinning by now and "Brylcreemed" back in the style so popular in the fifties and his face inevitably carried a smile. It was his eyes that told you he had something different; something that inspired confidence in those that met him. Clear and searching, his eyes appeared to both absorb and understand what they were seeing whilst reflecting a coolness and self-reliance. This, combined with his composure and unruffled nature, reassured those he was dealing with.

Bill's military background was with the 3rd Battalion, Parachute Regiment. He, along with so many others, were part of the "airborne carpet" that was the thrust of Operation Market Garden, an assault on Arnhem in September 1944. It was considered to be, by many notable historians, one of the boldest plans of World War II. Although the plan was unsuccessful and the airborne assault forces were overwhelmed by powerful German forces who, after being significantly reinforced, repulsed the attack.

The defiance of the British forces in holding their positions, whilst a tactical withdrawal was planned and executed, won the praise and admiration of both the British and Dutch nations that lasts to this day. The British (and allied) casualties were very heavy with, in many cases, only twenty per cent of Company numbers returning to their barracks after the failed assault. The remainder were either killed in action or, to a much lesser extent, taken enemy prisoner, including Bill. Bill's Battalion fought with extreme courage against tanks from the German armoured Divisions with far inferior armament and ammunition under the most dire of circumstances. After the war, Bill was repatriated and continued to serve in the 3rd Battalion. Later promoted to sergeant he remained in the army until 1954, before leaving and joining the fire brigade the following year.

An extremely modest man about his war exploits he nevertheless brought a very realistic sense of perspective to his role as a senior fire officer. Something not all of his fellow officers were able to do. Others were of a similar ilk to Bill, however, and some had even gained bravery awards for their outstanding valour during the war, but they were not serving alongside Bill, whilst I had the opportunity of witnessing this man in action at first hand. It was, for so many of my generation, something that we had no appreciation of and certainly no exposure to. The petty day-to-day dramas of Brigade Headquarters must have paled into insignificance in comparison and Bill would simply take them in his stride. The knowing smile he wore on his face as he carried the latest "urgent and vitally important" missive from some principal officer or other (and hot off-the-press) was maybe not so vitally important after all. However, when coping with a genuine disaster or some major incident that called for his attention, whilst others might be getting excitable, or even overawed, Bill's presence would soon settle things down. His rational and thoughtful decision-making was the order of the day for those under the watchful gaze of his intelligent eyes. For me he was an excellent tutor. My exposure to the Operations Room "drama" was greatly aided by either his presence (in the background) or his debriefing after the event. It was a very positive learning curve for me and his guidance was something I was always grateful for in the years that followed. (The following year, in 1985, Bill was awarded the Queen's Fire Service Medal for distinguished service in the New Year's Honours List.)

Fifth Columnist

I thought that the phone call from my Divisional Commander, Brian Butler, was touching. He asked how I was doing and how was life at Brigade Headquarters? Almost in passing he asked me to call in at Clapham to see him at the end of my day. Although friendly, his tone indicated that this was not so much a suggestion as a requirement.

Arriving well after the 6pm change of watch, I made my way along the top floor of Clapham fire station and the B Divisional Headquarters, towards the open door of the Commander's office. I knocked and was welcomed in with a friendly smile as he sat behind his desk contemplating the nearly empty glass of whiskey he held in his hand. "Get yourself a glass and pour me another one," he said in his cockney, and highly individual, tone of voice. Please and thank you were never high on his list of interpersonal skills. After some small talk he got down to the business in hand.

He had been short-listed for promotion to Assistant Chief Officer, but the decision on who had been successful in the final promotion interviews was still pending. He did not indicate how the interview had gone, but his obvious confidence about the possible outcome would have led anyone astute enough to believe he had it in the bag. However, I was not that astute since I was far too preoccupied wondering why the hell I had been called up here to have this unofficial chat?

It had, in fact, been a very successful year for Brian Butler. That June's Queen's Birthday Honour List saw him awarded an MBE for his outstanding officership during the Brixton riots. (It was a sign of the times that a 'B' Divisional fireman had also received Birthday honours on that particular list, but his long and honourable service to the Brigade's welfare fund only merited the British Empire Medal (BEM). Sadly, unless it was a much higher bravery award, there was very much an officers and lower ranks distinction when it came to getting Birthday Honours, certainly within the Brigade. Officers would be awarded the MBE and other ranks the lesser BEM. It was a form of snobbery that, thankfully, was later abandoned when the BEM was discontinued and everyone, who meet the criteria, was awarded the MBE regardless of rank.)

"You got any idea why you are here?" he asked. I had absolutely no idea! My temporary promotion so far had, if anything, been totally underwhelming. If I had been meant to ignite Brigade Headquarters with my wealth of experience and depth of understanding about the complexities of the new Station Commanders' role then I had clearly forgotten to take any matches with me. If anything, the work had, largely, been completed before I even arrived and it was now a case of dotting the *i*'s and crossing the *t*'s. (Although I might take some small credit for crossing a couple of *t*'s, but that was all.)

"Tell me about the miners' strike?" he asked, apparently pulling the question out of thin air. "What do you want to know?" I replied wondering just how much whiskey he had drunk before I arrived. "I want to know about your involvement in the miners' strike." he demanded, his tone now much less friendly and with a hint of menace about it. This guy has clearly lost the plot I thought, the promotion board to ACO had all been too much for him and he had become delusional. But he was the least delusional man you could ever wish to meet. He clearly knew where his line of questioning was going but he was not about to share it with me.

"Shut the door." he said, clearly an instruction and not a request. He had risen from behind his desk and moved over to one of the easy chairs in his office, whiskey still in hand. "Sit down." Again an instruction, not a request. In a serious, yet strangely concerned way, he said that what he was about to divulge I was not to tell another living soul! Now I was really worried. Was he now about to declare his, so far undeclared, love for me? But given his heterosexual track record I thought this highly unlikely.

Without pause he continued, "Scotland Yard's Special Branch have been taking a special interest in you and your involvement on the picket lines of the NUM's national miners' strike." Now I was delusional, not believing what I was hearing coming from my own Commander's mouth. "I have no idea what you are talking about," I managed to mutter in a state of shock as my mouth finally caught up with my brain. Miners' strike; flying pickets; political activist and Special Branch! Are you having a laugh? I for one did not think it funny. But it was self-evident he was not. "A report has been sent to the Chief Officer and you have been identified. You are being watched." he said as he finally started to react to my increasing sense of agitation and growing anger.

"Who can I see to sort this out?" I demanded. "This is utter nonsense." (Which it was.) "You cannot talk to anybody because you do not know about it. I have not told you anything because you are not even here. I just thought you should be aware that's all." Thanks a bunch Brian, I thought, tell me something that I can do nothing about. There was not much more to say. I drove home a troubled soul. It was a condition that did not improve much when I told my wife of the "non-existent" conversation. "The Americans will not let you in." she said. "You won't be let into the United States if you are on some Special Branch watch list. That man (Brian Butler) is a bloody shit. He must know this is all wrong." This was one of the few occasions in my career when I had no idea how to deal with a situation and, worse, had nobody to turn to for advice or guidance. One sleepless night turned into two, then three as the consequences of this obvious case of mistaken identity took on a life of its own.

My strongly held beliefs regarding seeking the truth, at all costs, were tempered by my (almost) unswerving loyalty to my Commander and the necessity of breaking his confidence. My wife only added to my feelings of discomfort by reminding me, frequently, that we had promised to take our teenage children to Florida the following summer. In desperation I contacted a close friend, a detective Inspector working in the serious crimes unit at New Scotland Yard in Victoria, to ask him for help. His initial and immediate reaction was, "This is a load of old bollocks or a silly wind-up." But nevertheless, he promised to make some inquires before saying that the next two curry nights were on me. Despite efforts to hide my anxiety about the allegation (even though I knew it had no foundation whatsoever) I was clearly not making a very good job of it. "Everything okay?" was a frequent comment from colleagues as the week slowly progressed and I got no news from my man at the "Yard."

I was on twenty-four hour call that weekend and, as usual, I went into Brigade Headquarters to work my normal daytime office hours. The headquarters second floor resembled the Mary Celeste. A ghostly quiet filled our normally hectic second floor offices that were now apparently deserted. There were some senior officers working elsewhere in the building, but other rostered officers chose to ride from home at the weekend, arguing they did enough extra hours during the week. I was a "temporary" and thought it better to be at my desk rather than cite such a dubious reason not to be where I was expected to be.

I looked up as another uniformed officer entered my office. Saturdays and Sundays at Brigade headquarters could be very boring and it was not uncommon for a fellow officer to seek out some company, grab a coffee and have a chinwag. However, it was not any fellow officer. It was my ACO. It was Jerry Beech. Although I did not ask him, I was thinking, "What the hell are you doing in here on a Saturday?" ACOs do not normally come in at weekends unless there is a major incident, and I would have known if there was; or if the Chief Officer had set him a special task then he would certainly not waste time visiting a minion. But with problems of my own to contend with I was not about to waste time wondering what my ACO wanted with me. In hindsight that was a big mistake.

"Can I help you Sir?" I inquired. "No, I just wandered down the corridor for a chat." Curiouser and curiouser! Alarm bells should have sounded then because he had never before "just wandered down for a chat!"

"Would you like a cup of coffee?" he asked, "I was just going to make one" I would have been shocked if he had done so for such comments were in fact principal officer code for, "Get off your fat arse and make the coffee," which is exactly what I did. What followed was a master-class of cleverly contrived questioning as my ACO conducted a skilful and subtle interrogation that would have done credit to John le Carré character George Smiley. Jerry Beech first got me to open up about the problem troubling me and then to "spill the beans" as to the name of the informant. Way too late to be of any use a warning light finally came on in my head. This was not caused by anything that was said but by the change in the demeanour of my "friendly" interrogator. His apparent empathy and contrived concern vaporised as the fact that it was my Divisional Commander who had passed on this sensitive information came to light. There was a glint in his eyes that I had not seen there before. He was like a predator sensing a kill whilst in search of its prey. Now his time seemed at a premium as he made an untidy and hasty retreat back down the corridor with a half-hearted comment that was meant to reassure me. "I'm sure this will all pan out." It did and much to the displeasure of Brian Butler.

With confirmation from my "man at the Yard" that his source could not find any substance to the possibility that my name had ever been held on a Special Branch watch list I felt much relieved. I was convinced that something funny was going on but I was not in on the joke! Then by pure coincidence both Brian Butler and I attended a Metropolitan Police "Do" at their Hayes (Bromley) Social Club and Sports Centre the following Saturday evening. Asked by Brian for a word, he found a quiet corner where I was verbally torn to shreds by a very disgruntled man and who was clearly agitated that I had broken a bond of trust (regardless of the circumstance I found myself in). There was no defence that he was prepared to accept and we parted company plainly not on the best of terms. Thankfully I was not working within the Division at this time so could avoid the worst of his wrath.

It was never confirmed but I had been an unwitting pawn in a trap set to test the credibility of Brian Butler. It was known that there was a connection between us and he had been my sponsor to get me into Brigade Headquarters. Either the Chief Officer or the Deputy, or both, wanted to check the loyalty of someone who was about to be promoted to Assistant Chief Officer. Jerry Beech provided the conduit back to one or other of them to say (as far as this insensitive and vindictive plot went) he had failed! But Brian Butler was promoted anyway and within a few weeks was walking the second-floor corridor of Central Operations; its latest Assistant Chief Officer.

Down the snake!

My temporary reign as a Divisional Officer came to an abrupt end shortly after I had been subjected to that interrogation. Station Commanders were about to take up post; this concept was to be one of the most significant changes to the Brigade's management structure for a number of years. There had long been recognised a need to establish better continuity between station watches and to see that stations functioned as a unit rather than four separate entities. I had contributed little to this process other than to remind those who would listen, that a plan is no good without the means to deliver and then support it. It seemed to me the sole criterion was implementation regardless of the ability to support and resource the Station Commanders in post.

I was expecting to be kicked back to Brixton, my role in exposing a weakness in Brian Butler having been used to the full. Much to my surprise, and amazement, I was not sent back but was asked to stay on in Central Operations. Jerry Beech never again mentioned that Saturday but stated that my promotion by two ranks had been to perform specialist duties. (Dropping your Divisional Commander in the mire counted for specialist duties I guess!) But it appeared my work on matters other than Station Commanders had been well received and I seemed to be getting typing done by the typing pool quicker than the other officers in the team. So only dropping one rank, I remained in situ as a day duty ADO. (I would have willingly stayed at Brigade Headquarters as a Station Officer since the work I was now doing was both stimulating and rewarding.)

The one, and lasting, contribution I made whilst in Central Operations was to review and update the first aid equipment carried on all London's fire appliances. A Fire Service Circular and a Health and Safety directive had been issued regarding the range and standard expected of first aid equipment provided to front line appliances. The Brigade was falling well short of the standard required. What was carried, and how it was carried, had long been a bone of contention with fire engine crews. Yet despite all their protestations and promises of improvements nothing was ever done. In fact, the Brigade's general attitude towards first aid was dire and totally unprofessional. A recruit fireman, to pass out of training, had to obtain his St John first aid certificate. That certificate was valid for only three years. When the certificate lapsed there was never any re-certification. Over 90% of fire engine crews did not hold a current first aid certificate!

What first aid equipment that was carried on appliances was basic. It would have been familiar to our wartime counterparts. So was the manner in which the first aid equipment was carried. Placed in a metal box, it was far from user friendly and had on a considerable number of occasions actually caused an accident rather than aiding in the treatment of one. I had got hit by the bloody thing once when the fire engine I was riding in the rear of stopped suddenly and the first aid box shot off the shelf and hit me in the back. (That very accident would, in later years, be cited in my own medical discharge from the Brigade).

It was discovered (in fact it was already known!) that we were not carrying the recommended equipment. Much of what we currently carried was outdated or wholly inappropriate, or both. I was given the brief to consider the implications of the Fire Service Circular and report back to my ACO. I relished the task and produced a hard-hitting report that highlighted the Brigade's failings and the need to replace that metal first aid box with a more versatile first aid bag. I knew the station superintendent at Brixton ambulance station and he agreed to loan me a London Ambulance Service (LAS) first aid bag, by way of an example as to the type of design that should be carried by fire crews. With my recommendations approved at the highest level, at last, bags were to replace those damn boxes. However, there was just one remaining glitch, our own Brigade's workshops.

The LAS bought their first aid bags off the shelf, custom-made, and they were ideal for the Brigade's needs too. But why buy one when you can make your own! That seemed to be the philosophy of the Brigade's workshop manager who had a job lot of yellow plasticised canvas that had been purchased to make carrying bags for long and lowering lines. Anything that could be made with this bloody yellow stuff was and workshops had it coming out of their ears. So, much to my displeasure, it was decided that the first aid bags would be made in-house and after quite a few attempts, one finally arrived on my desk that all the required and updated first aid equipment actually fitted in. A rolling programme would be introduced to replace all the boxes after the prototypes were trialled at a busy inner London fire station. Naturally I selected Brixton and without any undue influence from me the bag got rave reviews from the crews. It was with a sense of pride that whenever I saw crews using the bags, I thought that my time in Central Operations achieved something.

The end of 1984 was memorable for two reasons. First was that the Deputy Chief had invited all the Central Operations staff to his luxurious offices for an after-work Christmas drink. Naturally all the officers were expected to contribute to the cost of the gathering, which included both uniformed and non-uniformed colleagues. It was, in fact, a very pleasant affair with the Deputy holding court and all the "wannabe" promotees particularly noticeable as they nodded enthusiastically to his every utterance. (He could actually tell a very good joke.)

As was his right, the head of Central Operations administration (the guardian of the policy files) was also there, having clearly done the rounds of every headquarters bash he had been invited to (and a few he had not). He arrived the worse for wear and needed a convenient wall to give himself the necessary support whilst he downed his umpteenth sherry of the afternoon. Sadly it was just one sherry too many and he started to slide down the wall. As he did so his toupee was pushed over his forehead and onto his face with the poor man totally oblivious to his predicament.

Fascinated by this spectacle I did not notice Shirley sidle up to me and obviously, from the colour of her cheeks, she too had indulged freely of the sherry or whatever else. She was dressed for the occasion and her ample bosom was getting ever closer to my face as she tried to manoeuvre me into a quiet corner of the room. The mere fact that there was no quiet corner of the room did not seem to worry her one little bit. She evidently was intent on getting some payback for all the special treatment I had received with my typing requests. The woman was charming but she could, I was sure, crack walnuts between the cheeks of her arse and she was much too much woman for me to handle. I beat a hasty retreat to Waterloo Station and my train home for the Christmas break.

Second was the unofficial promise of new doors opening for me in 1985. I for one could not wait.

Station Commander

I was returning to the B Division. Bill Williams was now the acting Divisional Commander and wanted someone to fill a Station Commander vacancy at Deptford Fire Station. Asked if I was interested my answer was, "Yes please!" Interviewed later at Clapham, Bill said that it was necessary for me to "Camp-out at Clapham when performing my twenty-four-hour duties." Living at Orpington put me too far outside the B Divisional boundary to meet the attendance times to incidents occurring within the Division. So like all senior officers in a similar position, alternative accommodation had to found. Senior fire officers were also divided into one of four rota groups so as to provide "out of hours" operational cover. In theory any officer could be ordered to an incident when on a nine-hour day duty (8am-5pm), but only officers rostered for twenty-four hour duty provided an immediate response from 5pm until 8am the following day, or until the end of their twenty-four hour duties when they covered more than one day.

I was required to pay for this privilege of "camping-out" in accommodation provided by the Brigade. I could have rented somewhere within the Divisional area but the cost would have been prohibitive. So my twenty-four-hour base was a former senior officers' flat adjoining Clapham fire station. Although the rent was not exorbitant it was not value for money either. The place had not seen a lick of paint in years, its kitchen was worse than basic and creature comforts were non-existent. However, I only needed a place to write up reports in the evening, get my head down between calls and boil a kettle to make an occasional cup of coffee so it would do. It would have to if I wanted the job and I really wanted the job so no pain, no gain.

Deptford fire station was typical of the early twentieth century red brick London County Council fire stations where station personnel lived above the fire station and where the firemen were on twenty-four-hour call. Whatever Clapham's accommodation had to offer it was palatial compared to the Station Commanders office at Deptford fire station, which was dire. It was located in a former third floor flat, above the fire station. With the creation of shifts, firemen were no longer required to live and work at the same fire station (although some still did). Over time, and with considerable improvements to working conditions in post war years, station accommodation was rented out to Brigade personnel. Now very few flats existed at fire stations and all of Deptford's residential accommodation had been vacant for some time. However, the former occupant of this particular flat had had a peculiar (nasty) taste in floral wallpaper, which still adorned the Station Commander's office walls. The office furniture consisted of a second or third hand office desk, a chair, a filing cabinet and a metal personnel locker, which the previous Station Commanders had managed to scrounge or purloin.

Finding sufficient finances to provide Station Commanders with some semblance of adequate, and appropriate, office accommodation and office furniture was proving problematic. Putting Station Commanders in post was being done on a shoestring budget. (Some would argue even that was managed by "sleight of hand.") But in fairness there were conflicting priorities for the Brigade's limited financial resources. Approving the introduction of the Station Commanders was one of the last major decisions of the Greater London Council's Fire Brigade Committee. The GLC was in its death throes. It would be totally abolished by the following March. In 1986 Margaret Thatcher was determined to see the back of the GLC and its leader, Ken Livingstone.

(Thatcher remained in power until 1990 when she was challenged in a leadership contest and lost. Ken Livingstone would eventually return to power as London's very first elected Mayor in 2000. He went on to win a second term until losing to the Conservative, Boris Johnson in May 2008.)

It is a matter of debate if the then elected Members of the GLC's Fire Brigade Committee had been advised of the true cost of implementing Station Commanders whether the scheme would have been approved? The report sent to Members had used clever "weaselly" words, which talked in terms of utilising "existing resources," except that there were not many of those resources available. Given my drab looking, poorly appointed, office (in need of a coat of paint) there was very little evidence of anything "existing." Getting anything done to it was a far cry on anyone's must-do list, unless of course, I did it myself. Which is exactly what I did.

Station Commanders were, among other things, meant to be the "interface" between the local fire station and members of the local community or other local officials. What a pathetic message I would send out if these visitors were to be invited to attend the station and I was to show them in to a semi-derelict flat! So having requested, and been given approval to spend, no more than one hundred pounds (about one tenth of the redecoration costs) I set to over my first forty-eight-hour weekend duty. Working through both days, and most of the nights armed with roller and paintbrushes and an ample supply of magnolia emulsion and white paint (with only a couple of operational interruptions) by Monday morning the office looked more business-like. It was a great improvement on the questionable ambience of the former faded wallpapered room and its yellowing and chipped paintwork.

In addition to managing the operational readiness and performance of their own stations, Station Commanders also inherited a raft of duties performed by the previously Divisional based ADOs (now termed Station Commanders, but with the same rank). These tasks could frequently remove you from your own station to investigate accidents to other stations' personnel, appliance accidents or complaints against the Brigade. Covering Station Commanders, who were unavailable because of leave, sickness or attending training courses generated considerable additional paperwork. Also health and safety investigations and enquiries that required the taking of statements and writing up the subsequent reports were becoming a growth industry. Some of this investigative thrust was to counter the substantial increase in compensation claims, for alleged work-related injuries. Substantial sums were being won by the Fire Brigades Union's highly accomplished firm of solicitors in the Courts. This claim culture would, however, be eventually countered by the Brigade utilising selected officers working in "secret" surveillance teams. These officers monitored (and filmed) claimants who were listed as being on sick leave but believed to be working part-time. Some cases involved personnel engaged in strenuous sports having been placed sick after a due to service injury. One such long-term absentee turned out to be a successful weight lifter.

Conducting and monitoring divisional training programmes, including BA training at Southwark's BA chamber also ate into our available time at station level. It detracted from one of the most demanding and time-consuming challenges; that of transforming the concept of Station Commanders into a reality at station level. There was a resistance from some to having senior officers working on fire stations. It was something that many at station level considered a retrograde step, one which diminished the responsibility of the four watch officers.

In many instances the incoming Station Commander did not help this integration process. Problems arose when station accommodation was seconded for the Station Commander's use with little or no consultation with the station's watch officers. It was a difficult transition. In many instances, within those first two years, the "them and us" mentality was clearly exacerbated by a number of contributing factors, not least amongst these was the legacy from the national firemen's strike. There was still hostility towards non-striking officers, especially as they had willingly taken the financial benefits gained from a strike they did not support.

Further complications arose from the nature of some of those officers who were now Station Commanders. These were the former Divisional or Headquarters based ADOs. Some felt demoted, others demoralised at being returned to fire stations. Sadly, a few of these ADOs found themselves totally out of their depth on return to a fire station. Although very few in number they had been performing specialist duties and, in many cases, although doing a valuable job, people skills were not high on their list of managerial abilities. Station personnel (or at least factions of it) would exploit any weakness in their "new" Station Commander or actively seek ways in which to undermine their authority. For some, returning to an operational role at a station proved too stressful, and they simply could not hack it.

The Station Commander concept was meant to bring a high degree of stability and continuity to station management. However sickness and stress led to a number of ADOs, now Station Commanders, to opt out by taking early retirement. This in turn brought about higher than expected vacancy levels. (Hence my own temporary promotion to Deptford.) However, most significantly, it was the Brigade's own principal management and their inability to manage the changeover to Station Commanders (including ensuring adequate resources and funding) that brought about such a protracted period of "teething problems." I was the third Station Commander posted to Deptford within five months. Despite filling all 120 Station Commander posts now many stations, like Deptford, were on their second or third change. Retirements, promotions and transfers out of the Brigade meant that another ADOs promotion round was now necessary to fill these increasing vacancy levels. Naturally, I was delighted. I was also prepared.

My desire to rise to the next exalted rank was both determined and focussed. The normal interview process was to be preceded by "assessment" testing. This was something still relatively new to the Brigade but would in fact accompany all future senior officer appointments. Clearing the first hurdle (there were three tests in all) – my interview was not what you would call a walk in the park. However, my exposure to Brigade Headquarters and an awareness of most of the current policy issues affecting the Brigade, plus my limited work on the Station Commanders project meant I was more than adequately briefed to fend off the in-depth questioning of the promotion board. (The right place at the right time for once.) I was so positive that the Chairman of the board said at the conclusion of my interview, "You really want this job, don't you?" Without a word from me he continued, "You won't be disappointed." But I was!

Despite being found suitable for promotion, and with a considerable number of vacancies to fill, the Brigade took its time putting promotees into post. I remained at Deptford, a temporary ADO. I was also the only ADO on my rota group camping out at Clapham, the others living outside but close to the B Divisional boundary. This meant that I was central and closest to the busier stations within the division and could, and did, have exceptionally busy nights when the cards fell just right. But turning up to the "big one" and making pumps fifteen or twenty whilst taking command until relieved still sadly eluded me. However, the experience, and satisfaction, of commanding a six-pump BA fire could prove just as challenging. Especially so when working with unfamiliar crews and basing my command judgements on a rapid assessment of their operational ability, which could be an unknown quantity.

I had been very fortunate and enjoyed a reputation, within the B Division at least, as both an experienced and sound fireground officer. My operational judgement was readily accepted by crews on the fireground. I knew the four divisional control unit crews and was aware of their capabilities. This made fireground communications and incident command that much easier and more effective. I was soon to discover just how fortunate I was having this kind of rapport and how hard it becomes when you are a new face.

Barking!

Notification of my promotion, when it came, was a bittersweet experience. With most of my "travelling" boxes still unpacked at Deptford I was informed that I had been promoted to Assistant Divisional Officer. I was now the Station Commander of Lima 27 Barking. I had been at Deptford for just over four months and the station was to get its third Station Commander in less than nine months, some continuity. It turned out that I was Barking's third Station Commander. With no replacement nominated, temporary or otherwise, and no one to hand over to I left a welcome note on my desk and the new occupant to benefit from my labours and the continuing smell of new paint. I left Deptford.

Thankfully I was allowed the use of my B Divisional car to transport my gear to Barking. It was somewhere I had never been and had no real desire to go to either. Barking fire station turned out to be a rather smart looking two-storey fire station with its four large appliance room doors giving access to a wide station forecourt that led directly onto the east bound side of the A13. (I had to be told where to find it and if I reached Dagenham, I had passed it!) The station's pleasing design incorporated semi-circular ends on either side of the appliance room that provided light and airy station accommodation and office space. On one side and adjacent to the station was, once a pleasant two-storey house that had accommodated a senior officer and his family. Now it provided a rather up-market camping out base for those senior officers performing their twenty-four-hour duty shifts within the Division. It was certainly far superior to the grotty flat I left behind at Clapham.

Barking fire station was located within the Brigade's L Division and whose whole geographical area was once outside the "old" London Fire Brigade boundary and it showed. All of the L Division fire stations comprised of either the former East or West Ham fire brigade, or those previously in the Essex Fire Brigade. They were a hotchpotch collection of fire station designs that gave testimony to the area's mixed history of County Borough and County Council. This highlighted the respective approaches that had been made to funding its local fire service. I was also to discover that despite the twenty years that had elapsed, since amalgamation with the formation of the GLC, that many of the older L Division hands still hankered for their former regimes. The old lags would try to "convert" new recruits with their message, "It was much better before in Essex or West Ham." For some new entrants, whose childhood and teenage lives were spent growing up in those areas and provided fond memories of those pre GLC days, it was a message that frequently was warmly received.

I had always lived and worked south of the River Thames. I was a South Londoner. Being posted to the other side of the river, albeit in the North East of London, was totally alien to me. My orientation was all to cock. I was now working in this strange and, at times, hostile environment. Even finding my new station proved problematic, despite its reported size and the fact that it was located right on the A13.

First, however, I had to report to the Divisional Headquarters based at East Ham and to be welcomed (after a fashion!) by the Divisional Commander. East Ham fire station was a red brick building and a quirky looking fire station. The former headquarters of the East Ham fire brigade (and its only station), its appliance room looked far more suited to the original horse drawn steamers that would have pulled out of the small arched bays rather than their modern counterparts that now loomed uncomfortably large in the limited space behind the closed wooden and glass doors.

I was interview by the Divisional Commander in his office that once was occupied by the Chief Officer of this one station fire brigade. There was talk of the man before me being destined to hold a similar rank, he was one of the Brigade's rising young stars. Newly promoted to Deputy Assistant Chief Officer (DACO), he was tall and slim with a full head of wavy blond hair and piercing blue eyes. Considered handsome, he spoke with the confidence that matched his good looks and managerial ability as a principal officer. He was just as effective on the fire ground. Awarded a national gallantry medal for a daring hook ladder rescue in London's Bayswater district whilst serving in the A Division, his career, sadly, would come to an unexpected and premature end. He would be discovered at the foot of a staircase at Aldersgate (the former London Salvage Corps HQ now owned by the Brigade). He had suffered serious head injuries and the circumstances of his "alleged" accident was shrouded in mystery. It kept the rumour factory going for months as the speculation about the who's and why's grew. His injuries were so severe from this fall (or attack) that he had to be medically retired, never returning to duty. Now I stood before him for our one and only meeting. Whilst congratulating me on my promotion it was no warm and friendly welcome. He made it clear that I had not been his choice of candidate to come to his Division. On this we were in total agreement. I did not want to be here either, only I did not say so. But here I was and I would make the best of it.

I might as well have been posted to some obscure and distant fire brigade in the British Isles. I was totally out of my comfort zone. I knew no one and thought no one knew me. After my brief exchange with the Divisional Commander I was handed over to his deputy, the DO1 Operations, my line manager. The day was just getting better and better as his lukewarm reception ended with his comment, "You have been sent here with an outstanding reputation. Let's just see how bloody good it is, shall we." My subsequent tour of the Divisional headquarters dissolved into a blur as more new faces were introduced and new names committed to memory only to be almost as quickly forgotten as the next batch were lined up to say hello.

Finally, I was released and told I could make my way to Barking, which I eventually found after getting lost in a, none too complicated, one-way system and finding myself ending up in Stratford! (Which was not even in my new division!) The names on the road signs were just that, names. They held no meaning for me. Anywhere south of the river I could gauge the direction I wanted by reading the road signs even if it did not give my final destination. I could get to Tooting by heading in the direction of Streatham, to Erith by aiming at Bexley. I would get there. Here I did not even know there was a Thurrock or Wennington? I thought this was clearly going to be fun. By the time I worked out the route to emergency calls, then tried to get there, the crews would surely have put the bloody fire out and all gone home.

Barking fire station, as the divisional camping-out base, would be my home when I was on twenty-four-hour call, if I was still not wandering around the L

Division totally lost. The Division covered a large area of Greater London, you could fit three B Divisions into it. It ran from Plaistow in the west (nearest the City) to Wennington on the capital's eastern boundary with Essex. Hainault and Romford were at its most northerly points.

First impressions are important. They can be a fair indicator as to how much, or how little, work has got to be done to get things up (and maintained) to a certain standard. The problem was however that the Brigade had no universally applied benchmark by which to measure the "standard." There were considerable variations and differences between the eleven divisions as to what that standard was. I was seeing at first hand that, despite whatever individuals might have thought about the Clarkson and Butler regimes in the B Division, they had established and maintained, exacting standards within their jurisdiction.

Finally arriving at Barking, I walked in to the station's watch room and rang one bell to summon the officer in charge of the watch. A man in his late-thirties arrived and reported. He was a temporary Station Officer and his fifteen years' service had all been spent in the L Division. His base station was somewhere else in the division that was just a name to me, location unknown? He was one of my four watch officers and I was his third Station Commander since he had been temporary at Barking. He seemed an affable enough chap and I asked him to show me around the station and the appliances. It was not long before he asked me the inevitable question, "How long do you intend to stay?"

"Until I get moved on." I replied. "Well don't bother getting settled in, the last one tried and then he got shifted somewhere else." What a great first day I thought and it is not even lunchtime yet.

The tour of the station was informative and gave me a good first impression of how it was run by this watch officer. I would do the same with each of the other three before getting them all together for a station management meeting to discuss my findings and listen to their comments. By then I would have also inspected the station records and assessed the level of administration. Thanking him and getting him to instruct his drivers of the PL and pump to top up their respective water tanks (which were under three-quarter full) and his crews to check all the hose on the appliances, (I had found two hose coupling washers missing which could cause unwanted and unnecessary water damage when the hose was pressurised.) finally I made my way to my office. There was no note from the last occupant saying, "Welcome", just an in-tray containing the minutiae, that makes a station tick, to work my way through. But not now, later.

At last a familiar face poked his head around my office door and said, "Hello Pikey." It was Brian Reardon and we had worked together whilst I was in Brigade HQ. Brian had been promoted too but had returned to his old stomping ground. He also happened to be a "black" London cabbie so his "knowledge" would not have him fumbling around in his atlas, reading it by torchlight, trying to figure out how to get to Upton Park or Wanstead Flats at 3am.

As we chatted, we walked into the ADO's day room, a makeshift common room and the twenty-four-hour ADO's TV room, come-lounge at night. The surrounding stations' ADOs used Barking as a central meeting point, although it was far from central. Brian introduced me to some of my own rota group and the other nearby Station Commanders. Conversation was polite but inquisitive about the new boy, me, whilst Brian kept everyone on their toes with his cutting wit and black humour. However, it was not long before the undercurrent of discontent felt by these officers bubbled to the surface. But for now, I just listened, unable, and unwilling, to pass comment on their gripes and frustrations about their lot.

I had my own, more immediate, problems to worry about. I had to get to and from work. My unreliable, Eastern Bloc, MZ motorcycle had finally given up the ghost. My black Mini, and my pride and joy, had been sold to Bunny when I left Brixton fire station. Since then I had been totally reliant on trains and buses. I discovered travelling from my home in Orpington to Barking to be a nightmare without private transport. Station Commanders were permitted to take the red Maestro staff car home when on 24 hours but only if they rode from home. I did not have that privilege. I needed some transport and urgently. I needed something reliable and economical to get me through London's traffic, including the Blackwall Tunnel, with the minimum of fuss. Buying another car was not an option. Finding spare money for such an expensive purchase was in short supply especially as our mortgage was still spiralling upwards with interest rates standing at twelve per cent (inflation was at ten per cent) and petrol at the "heady" price of one pound eighty-eight pence a gallon. I needed wheels but not something that used too much petrol. So I invested in a "zippy" Honda motorbike. I had pushed that bloody MZ as far as I had ridden the damn thing, well maybe not, but it seemed like it, especially as the wire throttle cable would snap every time I needed to go somewhere in a hurry. So with a two-hundred-pound loan from my dear Mum, to cover my own shortfall, I had my own transport once again.

My newfound mobility also provided me with an opportunity to learn some of the unfamiliar landscape of East London. I soon discovered my way around Newham Way and Beckton and even made an exploratory foray into the defunct Royal Albert Docks. The Docks would reinvent themselves with the creation of the London City Airport in 1987 and see the regeneration of the whole surrounding area including a regatta centre and its international cruise ship terminal.

With the first couple of weeks under my belt I was feeling more positive about my surroundings. I was getting to know Barking's four watches and the backlog of paperwork had been cleared. I was feeling upbeat about my new station and thought "I can make a go of this." I was starting to get my teeth into some divisional projects too, not least were the unusual transformations taking place at the vast derelict British Gas works site at Beckton, known formally as Beckton Gas Works.

Stanley Kubrick was preparing to shoot his award-winning film "Full Metal Jacket" and one of his principal locations was right on my station's ground, a vast disused gas works in Newham. The gas works was to portray the ruined city of Hué in Vietnam. Working from original photographs taken in 1968, buildings on the site had actually been blown up to achieve the dramatic impact of authenticity he sought. The film's art director used a wrecking ball to knock specific holes in certain buildings over the course of a couple of months to do the same. My first visit to this recreation of a war-torn city was quite surreal. Palm trees on the Beckton marshes! Utilising the skill, which film makers bring to their craft, areas of the gas works had been transformed to construct a replica of a city under siege from American firepower and bombing. It was impressive to say the least. Whilst the gas works was "under attack" other areas of Barking were showing the signs of considerable regeneration and proposed dramatic developments. This was going to be an exciting place to be over the next couple of years. I was looking forward to the prospect of being involved in drawing up emergency plans and contingency arrangements during the construction, and then the commissioning, of at least some of them. Sadly, I never took into account a quote from John Lennon who wrote; *"Life is what happens to you while you're busy making other plans."*

After three weeks of operational inactivity whilst on a twenty-four-hour duty I finally got my first ordering to a fire and I knew how to get there, well at least part of the way. My regular daily excursions away from the station had made me familiar with most of the major routes around the station's ground and which direction to take to head off to the other nine stations in the Division. In the late evening I was ordered to a four pump, persons reported, fire in East Ham. Checking the address (that was in a maze of back streets) I saw it was about five miles from Barking fire station. I pulled out of the fire station with my single blue flashing light indicating that my little red car was in fact an emergency vehicle. Turning left and heading up the A13 I turned north up the North Circular Road where the extent of my memorised route to this blaze was rapidly coming to a standstill. Where next? Stopping and asking the way was clearly not going to inspire public confidence in the fire service's knowledge of their area. Trying to read the atlas in the darkening interior of the car whilst trying to manoeuvre through the traffic did not seem to be a very bright idea either. In desperation I pulled in to a side turning to re-group. I checked the atlas and tried to commit the second half of my journey to memory. Setting off in a determined attempt to reach the address I finally came upon the incident more by accident than design. My arrival was much too late to make any impact on the command of this particular fire, which involved a two-storey terraced house. There were no people involved in the property, just a report that proved to be groundless. Speaking to the Station Officer in charge of the incident it was clear that he had everything covered and had commanded his crews in a professional manner. Which was far more that I could say for myself. I was feeling amateurish and below par. Driving around blindly was unacceptable and I resolved to drive about on day duties until I had a better feel for the area I was now covering.

Any opportunity I had to get a better understanding of my immediate vicinity was very short lived. With only weeks under my belt as Barking's Station Commander I was called to Divisional Headquarters and told in very blunt terms that I had been posted. The DO 1 Operations made no secret of the fact that he thought I had orchestrated my own transfer out of the Division. I was surprised as he was about my unexpected move and told him so in equally forceful terms, saying that I was more than happy to remain in the Division. It was not going to happen. Somebody at Brigade Headquarters had made a decision to send me back south of the river; my transfer was immediate. Once again clearing my locker and personal effects the temporary Station Officer I had first met came over to say goodbye. News of my transfer had preceded my drive back from Divisional Headquarters. Wearing a rueful smile, he put his head around my office door and said, "I told you not to get settled in."

Back South

Once again, I was in a new Division facing a new Divisional Commander and getting an all too familiar welcome. It was October 1985 and now I was to be the Station Commander of Eltham Fire Station, my third station in less than six months. I was beginning to feel travelsick! The Divisional headquarters was in Lewisham, an imposing multi-bay fire station, which occupied the ground and first floors; the E Divisional Headquarters occupied the second floor whilst former senior officers' accommodation (now largely unoccupied) took up the third and fourth floors. What was most unusual, for me at least, was that Eltham still had its Station Commander in post. I would finally get to hand over properly and get to learn something about my station without having to discover it for myself. With a minimum of fuss, I was sent off to Eltham to replace the retiring Station Commander.

Eltham fire station was built in 1904. It was a fine example of the red brick upper floors (it had two) and ground floor white Portland stonework that was so typical of the Edwardian fire station design, much favoured by the then London County Council. The fire station now sat in a long terrace of properties, shops to one side and a public house on the other. There was no rear entrance to the station and the two fire engine bays were separated from the street by just the width of the public pavement. The understated splendour of the fire station gave just a hint of an era now long past, of Eltham at the turn of the twentieth century, with the fire station holding centre stage in what would have resembled a small-town High Street. Eltham then lay on the very edge of the London County Council boundary with the County of Kent just up the road, whilst it stood only nine miles from Charing Cross in the Borough of Woolwich. A year before the station was opened, one of Eltham's most famous sons was born in 1903. He was Bob Hope but not the only notable to originate from the locality. W.G. Grace, the world-famous cricketer and later, Sir Stephen Courtauld would also become synonymous with the area.

Now in the London Borough of Greenwich, Eltham fire station's ground contained a mix of suburban and urban housing whilst the ground, nevertheless, retained an unusually high quotient of green space with large areas of woodland and open spaces. Its ethnic and racial mix was that of somewhere like Harrow although Eltham was deemed to be within an inner London Borough. Its retiring Station Commander was a former E Divisional ADO of some considerable standing. It was clear that he had used both his status and reputation to good effect because he had established a well-appointed office in a former resident's flat. Whilst it was not pretentious it was far superior to the drab surroundings of Deptford and a considerable improvement on Barking's attempts to convert the former residential accommodation. My welcome by the extant Station Commander was both warm and friendly as was his genuine desire to make me familiar with my new surroundings in the last days of his over 30 years' service. He was an able and effective administrator and it was immediately apparent that this relatively quiet station had not taxed his considerable experience and talents one iota.

Although Eltham had two fire engines the second appliance was one of the Brigade's small fleet of foam tenders. It was an aging beast that carried bulk supplies of foam and had the capability of pre-mixing the foam via a complicated system of pipes (which I never understood) to deliver foam directly onto a fire. This appliance did not get very many calls and actually getting it to work was an even greater rarity. This in itself presented training issues for the station's drivers as they were expected to maintain a certain skill level. Arriving at an incident and not being able to get the foam tender to work would be totally unacceptable. It was not the only training issue at the station. Eltham was the E Division's quietest station and in the previous year (1984) had only received five hundred and seventeen calls on its own ground and was in the bottom ten stations for "make ups" having had only two four pump fires in the same year, compared with the top station (Stoke Newington) that had twenty-three make ups on its own ground. Looking at the station fire register it seemed that 1985 was not going to improve on those figures. With the wryest of smiles my guide advised me "Don't do all your paperwork in the morning else you will have nothing to for the whole afternoon."

I had never served at a quiet station and the prospect was not appealing. What was appealing however was that my home was now within striking distance of the Divisional boundary and I no longer had to camp-out in fire brigade accommodation. I would ride from home on my night duties and my children waited eagerly for the phone to ring so that they could watch me drive away with the blue light flashing on top of the car. I was looking forward to covering an area I actually knew and arriving with a reasonable chance of the action still going on. There was a tiered system of senior officers being called out to operational incidents by the mobilising control. Unless it was a straight ten pump fire (or above) or a major incident an ADO was the first to be notified and ordered on if it was a six to eight pump fire. He was also informed of all special risk calls or multiple calls to any incident and could make the decision as to whether to attend or not. I always started to drive towards an incident (without the lights and horns) until I either heard the "stop" message or a priority was sent and then I would be already mobile and en route. Whenever an ADO moved onto an incident then the duty Divisional Officer would be informed and he too would make a decision whether to attend or not.

I was not to be disappointed on my very first night riding from home although my wife found the whole experience surreal. In the end we both slept on the lounge floor downstairs, as she did not want the telephone to wake the children in the middle of the night. When the call did come it did so at a most inopportune moment and despite our attempts to keep the noise to a minimum, I saw two excited faces peering out of the upstairs window. The revolving blue light reflected off our white garage door with my anxious wife looking out the front door as I drove away to a six-pump fire, somewhere in East Greenwich. As far as my wife was concerned, it was one thing for me to attend calls on night duties with my crew at a fire station, it was a completely different story driving away from our house to an emergency. It was something she never got used to.

The local South London paper had wanted to cover the story of Eltham's new Station Commander. It was to be an ironic piece. For as the article was appearing in the following week's editions I was once again packing my boxes. I had not even been at the station for two months when I was told by my Divisional Commander I was temporary promoted to be the latest, in a long line of, Divisional Officer (Training). I would be working out of the Divisional Headquarters at Lewisham. I thought my interview to Assistant Divisional Officer had gone reasonably well but I did not realise just how well. Although only a temporary Divisional Officer (and priding myself for having committed all the names of Eltham's watch personnel to memory) I bade farewell to yet another fire station. As a Station Commander I had a batting average of one new fire station every two months; so much for the concept of continuity.

Big changes

I seemed to be locked into a curious two-month cycle before being hoisted somewhere else new! Moves were afoot and, whilst I was totally unaware of what they were, I was clearly not destined to stay at Lewisham very long either. Big things were happening within the Brigade and even bigger things were happening to the Labour controlled Greater London Council (GLC). It was being abolished. Ken Livingstone's high spending socialist policies (many of which I agreed with and supported) had put the GLC on a collision course with the Conservative Government lead by Prime Minister Margaret Thatcher.

The Government had been pushing for the abolition of the GLC for the past few years. When it finally published the Local Government Act (1985) the Bill faced considerable and concerted opposition and was only narrowly passed into law in Parliament. In the autumn of 1985, the Act received its Royal Assent and the final nail was hammered into the coffin of over a hundred years of London wide local government. The GLC (and the other six affected Metropolitan authorities) would cease to exist from the 1st April 1986. The Thatcher government's actions meant that the Brigade would no longer be answerable to the GLC as Fire Authority. A new quango was to be established, the London Fire and Civil Defence Authority (LFCDA).

The dictionary definition of a quango states that it is, "An organisation that is able to act independently of the government that finances it." This was never going to happen. In the years that followed, regardless of whatever Party was in power, their authority and sway seeped into many aspects of the Brigade's development (or lack of it in some cases) because the Government ultimately had control of the purse strings in the form of the "central government grant (CGG)." CGG was the major component supplemented by the Borough's precepts. There was, and is, always a power struggle between the spenders and the savers. Ultimately H.M. Treasury pulled the strings. Already the then Home Secretary had given strong hints that the new fire authority would be told to impose a freeze on recruitment (There is independence for you!).

London's Chief Fire Officer, Ron Bullers, now had both the looks and build of an older John Wayne. He had his work cut out as he and his principal management team made every effort to ensure that the Brigade continued to operate with its customary efficiency and effectiveness regardless of the massive external forces at work. He made no secret of the fact that the next few months would undoubtedly be a testing time for Brigade management at all levels. Not only were we about to get a new (and untested) Fire Authority, but the Brigade was about to introduce a radical new structure. No more eleven divisions but five Areas instead. Each Area Command would contain about the same number of fire stations and the Brigade area was to be divided into five wedge shaped slices, the points converging on central London. Some divisions would be split and divided whilst others absorbed in their entirety into the new Command area, but we were not there yet. However, the five Area Commanders (designate) had all been selected to aid the transition; Brian Butler was to be the South East Area Commander.

The South East Area Command would absorb six stations from the former B Division, five from the H Division and all twelve stations contained within the E Division. Never a Brigade Headquarters animal, Brian Butler wanted his feet in his new command area as soon as possible and had already set his sights on the E Divisional Commander's office as his Lewisham base. This was much to the dismay of its occupant, the then E Divisional Commander, who had to find a new office for himself and now unceremoniously hoisted his deputy out of his!

Brian Butler arrived early on a February Monday morning. It was particularly early for him as he was not noted as a morning person. I was in my office, packing those damn boxes yet again, when my attention was drawn to a commotion coming along the corridor and to an all too familiar sounding voice saying, "What the f---?" The Area Commander (Designate) was attempting to open his "new" office door and failing. His key would not go in to the Yale door lock. Angrily summoning the duty staff officer, he demanded the spare key kept in the staff office safe. This also failed to open the door and would not even fit in the door lock. The observant staff officer noted that something had been pushed into the lock having first been given a liberal coating of "super glue." A now very irritated Area Commander (Designate!) did not find the situation as amusing as the unthinking Staff Officer. Within seconds of the opening salvo of an almighty bollocking, the poor man was left to reflect on his untimely display of amusement at Brian Butler's expense. I had to host a still seething Commander (Designate) whilst a locksmith was summoned and a replacement lock fitted. There was an uncharacteristic smirk on the face of the E Divisional Commander when he arrived at Lewisham about an hour later. Some say they saw the tell-tale marks of dried super-glue on his index finger!

While Brian Butler made his presence felt at Lewisham, which was a culture shock for many working there, I returned to Brigade Headquarters' second floor. Major building works had greatly restricted the available space for parking at Lambeth. Although a temporary car park had been rented in a back street not far from Lambeth, parking remained a thorny issue. There was also a feeling of organised chaos within the Brigade Headquarters complex. Central Operations had been re-branded and was now called the Programme Office. I soon discovered that not many people seemed to know what the Programme Office was meant to be doing and those that did, did not appear too keen to share the information. Although I was more comfortable arriving here the second time than I had been the first time around, little stands still in Brigade Headquarters and many new faces were gracing the offices that filled the second floor. I appeared to be just the latest.

What talents I had to ease the Chief's woes as to the consequences of the GLC's abolition were never explained to me. Why I was sent to Brigade Headquarters was a total mystery, not only to me but to the principal officer to whom I had been told to report. The Assistant Chief Officer in charge of the Programme Office clearly had a lot on his plate and finding me something to do did not appear to tax his considerable managerial talents to any great extent. There must have been an item on his "must do" list that said, "Check all available furniture." Ticking it off his list he gave a rather vague instruction about conducting a furniture audit of the whole headquarters complex. I was thinking, "It would be rather useful to actually find some of my own." Within a short while I managed to get myself sorted out and even got my name on a door. (The tiny office was that of my kindly mentor on my first exploration into headquarters.) Now there were three of us sharing this narrow piece of real estate and it was like sitting in the cinema because every time someone wanted to pass behind me, I had to stand up or squash myself up against the desk.

The task, I thought to be a bit of a doddle, turned out to be not that simple. Naively I thought (being Brigade Headquarters) that each department would have a similar inventory to that found at fire stations. (In fact, there was even a Brigade Order that said they each had to have one.) For any new officer in charge arriving at a fire station this was one of his very first tasks, to conduct and sign off the station inventory, much to the relief of the other watch officers who had been trying to cover for some missing gear or equipment but which now became the new guy's problem. In theory the same was meant to apply to all other Brigade establishments, with the departmental head being responsible for ensuring the inventory was accurate, up to date and all additions and subtractions were properly recorded. "Inventory, what inventory?" was the reply I got, not only from my own principal administration officer, but the next two departments I tried as well. Thinking back to my days at a fire station I thought, "Talk about one rule for them, another for us!"

Without the aid of inventory sheets, the only available way of ascertaining the amount of furniture held around the headquarters sites was to undertake a head count of what was there. Feeling that this definitely was not the best use of my talents as a senior officer I reluctantly set about my task. But in fact, there was a rather urgent need for this collated information. Without future access to the GLC's supplies department and with the possibility of a moratorium on expenditure (at least until the new authority got its act together) there was no centrally held data of what furniture and office resources were available to assist with the setting up of the five new Areas. Bums were going to be on seats but no one knew if there were enough seats to go round and even if they were, were they in the right place? I soon became "Mr Unpopular" as department after department was visited and stashes of furniture, that had been hidden away, were discovered and which added to the growing list of desks, chairs-office, chairs-easy, filing cabinets and other assorted office hardware. I was beginning to understand why a uniformed officer had been given this "bum rap," my uniform seemed to carry a bit more clout and keys were soon found that otherwise might have been conveniently mislaid for the audit and inspection.

That was my sole contribution to this new world order. With a determination that would have done credit to any sleuth, my collated list was sent to my Assistant Chief only to get immediately lost in the ether of the more weighty issues of the interim arrangements for the new Fire Authority and the implementation plans for the five Area structure. In any event I never heard any more about it as departmental principal heads were increasingly locked away in ever more meetings preparing for the big day.

The creation of a replacement Fire Authority, that would have power over the Brigade, was not the only new development at Brigade Headquarters. Construction work to the Brigade's new Command and Mobilising Centre (CMC), that had turned Lambeth's main yard into a building site for the past couple of years, was nearing completion. The three-storey, white sided, building resembled a child's Lego brick design. It sat in, or rather dominated, the south-west end of the headquarters complex. Standing on the site of the former bandstand and the "infamous" Lambeth bar it also absorbed the Officers' Club. But with all the headquarters senior officers' residential accommodation vacated and converted to office space the Officers' Club belonged to another era and had long since ceased to serve any purpose.

It had taken five years since the original design philosophy was approved and the site cleared and the foundation stone laid for the Command and Mobilising control centre. Fortunately, despite the numerous changes in the Brigade's organisation and some operational procedures, the design brief still held good, which was more than could be said for the operating software. There were substantial delays, as with so many high specification computer programmes located in the public sector. But when up and running, CMC as it was called, would replace the other three mobilising control rooms with a single Brigade wide control and mobilising centre. Not only that but all aspects of the control officer's function would be catered for under this one roof, from recruitment and initial training to their continuation training and senior management selection. There would be a reception area, catering facilities and changing areas and washrooms and toilet facilities. Even the facility to provide for wheelchair access, both for staff and visitors alike, was incorporated into the design brief and delivered.

Much of the design work was ground-breaking. In terms of fire brigade mobilisation there were stringent levels of system security to ensure maximum availability for mobilising. Both the computers and the staff needed the right environment to work efficiently. So although this box-like building looked simplistic from the outside, it gave no clue to the integrated and clever design that incorporated all the extensive needs of both people and technology that this radical departure from the old mobilising system demanded. Naturally, the central hub of the complex was the control room itself. It contained a forward-facing control consul from where control staff would receive 999 calls and with the aid of computer software recommended the correct response to the calls received. Great reliance would eventually be placed on data transmission, whereby fire engines would be fitted with a "button box" that would send a signal to the control's computer to identify where every fire engine was at any one time; whether at the station, mobile, attending an incident or unavailable.

Because all of our eggs would, eventually, be in one basket, greatly enhanced security and fire prevention was paramount both during the design stages and when fully operational. Elaborate entry control systems, not previously employed in the Brigade, would deny all unauthorised access. The building was fully air conditioned and therefore sealed. Every perimeter door was electronically linked to the security system and were the sole means of escape and not fitted with any door handles on the return (out) side. When operational the control and other authorised staff would be able to move around inside the building with coded entry cards that would limit them to defined zones relative to their role and status. Because of the mass of electronic equipment throughout the building, water as an extinguishing medium in the event of a fire was a "no-no." There would also be a strict no smoking rule. The main computer suites would be covered by a total flood inert gas (Halon) system and the fixed diesel tanks for the emergency generators had foam pourers fitted for fire brigade use. The CMC's fire alarm was independent of the rest of the Brigade Headquarters complex and had its own alert and evacuation signal as well as a comprehensive smoke detector system to provide early warning of fire especially in remote areas of the building, or during night time hours, when only the control room accommodation was occupied.

In the event of the necessity to totally evacuate the control a fall-back facility was catered for and would be established at Clapham fire station. It would have all the necessary, albeit basic, facilities to provide for emergency mobilisation of the Brigade. A fall-back micro-computer within CMC would provide updates of the movements of the Brigade's resources so vital information could be used at Clapham to update the wallboards.

A vast amount of planning within the Brigade had to cater for all these imminent changes that were about to unfold. A new Fire Authority, the five new Area Commands, a new control facility, plus three new GLC fire stations, which had been opened the previous year and the Brigade had just commissioned a new fireboat, the London Phoenix.

However, as regards CMC I was just another interested onlooker when I arrived back at Headquarters. Like so many others I wondered if the consultants would ever get the software problems sorted out and when, and if, the Control room would become operational. In fairness the GLC, and before that the LCC, had been the great provider for the Brigade. In all that time there had been a clear understanding between it (the Fire Authority) and the Brigade about the demarcation of responsibilities and the roles the various parties had. The new LFCDA was a totally unknown quantity made up from local Borough Councillors who in many instances had no previous understanding (or indeed interest) in the workings and machinations of London's fire brigade. The Brigade was one of many services provided for by the GLC and now we were to be on our own, without the former support or back up services it provided or having access to the resources that came with working under the umbrella of the GLC. The GLC's fire authority was housed in County Hall. A home had yet to be located to house the new authority and the staff that would make it functional.

There was one other small matter that took up my time whilst at headquarters. It was the imminent promotion round to substantive Divisional Officer III. When I was not scouring basement stores or long forgotten offices for random bits of furniture, I had my head stuck in policy papers honing up on the latest bit of "must know" information for my promotion board. Being at headquarters gave me one other distinct advance over divisionally based officers, access to a wealth of information about various aspects of Brigade funding, fire prevention initiatives and technological advances within the fire service. Those heads of departments or sections that I had not managed to alienate by discovering a horde of recently, undeclared, furniture offered to give me some one to one tuition on the topics of the day and provided me with a better understanding of the Brigade's revenue and capital expenditures. Yet the best piece of advice came from my old mentor (Geoff Townley) who rang me up and told me to read a quality newspaper every day. I chose *The Telegraph*. It served me well as it covered, in depth, the Governments line on the abolition of the GLC. It also gave a thorough analysis of the likely implications for the running and funding of the new fire authority. It enabled me to offer a view; even if the view was one I borrowed from *The Telegraph*.

The promotion interviews were held over two consecutive weekends and the interviews ran throughout the whole day. All candidates were given a timed slot and told to report to Brigade Headquarters and wait their turn on the allotted day. Gerry Clarkson, as Deputy Chief, chaired the three-man board and early whispers were that every candidate was being put through the wringer with a broad sweep of gruelling questions. David Rees, my training school instructor was now the Station Commander of Soho fire station and was to go in just before me. He was incredibly laid back about the whole affair whereas I was feeling somewhat nervous, not so much about the subject matter but facing up to Gerry Clarkson and recalling all too clearly his passing shot to me as he left the B Division. Attempting to look as little "devious" as possible, I went into the fray and gave my best. Both David Rees and I got phone calls that told us we were successful. We were both posted, as substantive Divisional Officers, to the South East Area Command, back with Brian Butler, from April 1st 1986.

Hampton Court

On the very last day of the GLC's existence the Brigade had to deal with, whilst not its biggest blaze of the year, one of the capital's most nationally significant fires and one that had tragic and fatal consequences. So as well as providing an insight into this particular incident, it is interesting to note the chronology of the fire and, with the clarity of hindsight, make some personal observations on what was an all too familiar problem of "drip fed" attendances to make up fires.

What became clear from the subsequent Royal Inquest, the Government's own inquiry, and the painstaking forensic examination, was that this fire had started some considerable time before the first call to the fire brigade was made. It was thought that the blaze may have started in the early hours and that the most probable cause was spread from a naked flame (a candle) on the upper floor of the Palace.

Hampton Court Palace is a royal palace in the London Borough of Richmond upon Thames, located in south-west London. It has not been lived in by the Royal Family since the 1700s. The palace contains many notable and rare works of art and furnishings from the Royal Collection, mainly dating from the two periods of the palace's construction; Tudor (Renaissance) and late Stuart to early Georgian. Throughout the twentieth century Hampton Court established itself as a major London tourist attraction. Contained within its buildings were fifty "grace and favour" residences that were given over to esteemed servants and subjects of the Crown. It was the elderly occupant of one of these grace and favour apartments whose nightly habit of always taking a lit candle into her bedroom had set in train a sequence of events that would be both disastrous for her and the Palace.

The first call to the fire brigade was made at 5.43am. Four fire engines from Twickenham and Kingston, a turntable ladder from Heston and Sutton's damage control tender and hose laying lorry turned out from their respective stations, in response to the call from Hampton Court Palace. Croydon's fire control unit was also ordered as part of the initial augmented attendance to this special risk. Directed by Palace staff, the crews from Twickenham and Kingston made their way to the affected apartments to assess the extent of the blaze. Crews in BA made their first exploratory search to determine the possible extent of the fire, whilst others secured the initial water supplies and hose lines were laid out. Despite having four pumping appliances already in attendance, thirteen minutes after receiving the first call the officer in charge sent a priority message, "Make pumps four." This was followed five minutes later by his first informative which indicated that the whole of the gallery ceiling was alight and that it was not possible to ascertain the full extent of the fire.

Both Twickenham's and Kingston's fire station grounds cover large areas of south-west London. This naturally means the fire engines from surrounding stations, attending the blaze, had considerable distances to travel to reach Hampton Court Palace, taking vital minutes to arrive at the scene. Within those precious minutes the intensity of the fire grew, superheating surrounding combustible materials and thus allowing the heat to rise to very high temperatures, whilst enabling the uncontrolled spread of the fire to broaden its scope to rapidly increase the affected area. Fire can grow with astonishing speed once it gets a hold. This fire had got a hold and it was spreading, having consumed the first apartment, and was now seeking fresh fuel to consume.

Seven minutes after making pumps four, pumps were made six. The list of urgent tasks that the officer in charge was having to prioritise was daunting. Three residents were believed to be involved and unaccounted for; a rapidly worsening fire situation was stretching his crews; reinforcing crews had to be briefed and even then, he had to juggle the demands of search and rescue and actual firefighting. Plus, there were the considerable pressures on him to initiate salvage operations. The London Salvage Corps had long since ceased to exist. Despite the requirements of the 1947 Fire Services Act, (that placed a duty on every fire authority "to ensure efficient arrangements for ensuring reasonable steps are taken to prevent or mitigate damage to property resulting from firefighting") the Brigade had yet to give sufficient emphasis to salvage training. Training that could replicate the standards of the former Corps. (Salvage work remained an afterthought for many and that lack of pre-planning came home to bite you at incidents such as this. This deficiency now came into focus as these national treasures were at risk, not only from fire and smoke but from water damage too.)

Fortunately, pre-planning at the Palace had taken account of the possibility of a serious fire or flood. The Palace staff, including its own salvage squad, had been actively engaged in the rescue work of removing and protecting the affected historic paintings and artefacts. Working in sometimes difficult conditions, and with the aid of available Brigade personnel, the salvage plan was put into action. Almost all these invaluable works of art and irreplaceable treasures were saved for the nation. The same cannot be said for the actual fabric of the building. With all this frantic activity still on-going, ironically, the Palace's automatic fire detection system finally operated at 6.15am.

The arrival of increasing numbers of Brigade senior officers resulted in further evaluations of the situation and a change of command as more and more pumps were requested. Pumps were made eight forty-four minutes after the initial call and then; "Make pumps twelve," twelve minutes after that. By now this disastrous fire had engulfed the whole of the State apartments, which covered an area some forty metres by twenty metres in a building that was described as, "three-storeys high." At make pumps twelve a new officer of higher rank took on the mantle of "incident commander" and attempted to put his plan of action into play. This was easier said than done, given the complexity of the Palace and the lack of access for the firefighting crews. Also, the fire ground description of the wing as "three floors" was simply misleading. Its upper two floors that were erupting into fierce flame, created a false impression as the high vaulted ceiling of both the ground and first floors made the building at least the equivalent of five-storeys.

An additional damage control tender had already been requested to support the salvage work being undertaken under the direction of the Palace's conservators who led their own salvage crews. Now with the intensity of the fire burning its way through the pitched roof, that was itself surrounded by an ornate stone balustrade, one-hundred-foot turntable ladders were increased to three. Many of the crews wearing breathing apparatus struggled, in their heavy equipment, to gain a better foothold to assault the blaze from within, and remained severely hampered, not only by heavy smoke logging, but by the very nature of this historic building. Security was naturally very important, given the treasures the Palace contained. Getting through secured doors and entrances was difficult and sometimes impossible. With every minute's delay the fire grew stronger and gained a firmer hold.

That was not all that was hampering the Brigade's efforts to get to grips with this fire, which was clearly gaining the upper hand. Water supplies within the Palace's ground were insufficient to meet the needs of our major pumps that were now supplying many thousands of litres of water per minute to the various jets that were being directed on to the blaze; some with greater success than others. A water relay was therefore set up and established from outside the Palace perimeter. The Water Board's "turncock" ensured that all available water was diverted to provide the Brigades needs and ensured there was no loss of the pressure to the hydrant fed supplies. The fire within the grace and favour apartments continued its insatiable search for more fuel. Having moved upwards and outwards it was now affecting the very structure as it ate away at the timber rafters and joists that supported the roof and upper floors. The heat of the blaze rose in to the hundreds of degrees centigrade (over 1,200 degrees Fahrenheit.)

The main early morning news story on the BBC and ITN was the dramatic blaze at Hampton Court Palace. The clamour of the media to cover this "breaking news" story was one more pressure to add to the growing list of tactical considerations of the Incident Commander. The primary consideration for any London Fire Brigade officer has always been focused on the preservation of life and property. Despite the many additional duties falling to the Brigade to perform, rescues and firefighting was still the major component and the one area where the public expected us to excel. The command of fireground incidents, including search and rescue, and incident severity, naturally varies with the scale and complexity of the fire being fought. There is, however, one constant in the deployment of the crews that weighs heavily in the mind of the Incident Commander. That is the interface and interaction with the structure, its occupancy, its inherent features, hazards and characteristics in a fire.

Assistant Chief Officer Roy Snarey had taken charge and losing the Palace was not on his agenda, and certainly not "live" on national television. This brash Nottinghamshire man had been in the Brigade all his considerable service but he had lost none of his Nottingham accent. Highly intelligent, this principal officer had set about co-ordinating his team of senior officers as soon as he had taken command. He hit the ground running and was determined to contain the blaze and not allow the fire to spread outside the existing fire zone. By 8.30am he had his BA men and firefighting crews in position. His water relay was laid and the radio message was sent from the major Control Unit, "Steady progress being made." The partial collapse of the central section of the roof eased the smoke logging slightly and after adjusting the position of the firefighting crews he made pumps twenty. He was now in a position to contain and, by boundary cooling, finally press home with his attack and extinguish the blaze.

In doing so he was very conscious of the balance of risks that had to be taken by the firefighters within the blazing building. For them there was the ever-present danger when fire-fighting within a burning structure, regardless of any particular building construction. Both firefighters (regardless of rank) and the Incident Commander have to constantly evaluate the potential risks and benefits before committing themselves to action that may provide no meaningful gain. It was an unwritten law of "London fireman" especially the former smoke-eaters and their "old school" senior officers that the only way to fight a fire was from the inside. But risk has always to be measured and assessed in a controlled and calculated manner. No building, or property is worth the life of a firefighter. But firefighters have lost their lives and this has continued. It is, sadly, the nature of the job.

So interior firefighting, by its very nature, involves inherent risks. The level of risk to be taken is clearly different when life is involved as opposed to property alone. In this case Roy Snarey's view was clear, the remainder of the Palace would be saved. With those firefighters already in attendance and with the aid of the reinforcing crews soon to arrive, he would have the fire surrounded and then press home the attack with a renewed vigour and drive. He would manage this despite the fact that many had been battling the blaze for three hours and were re-entering the fray for a second or third time – having changed their BA cylinders once, some twice, after working to their maximum duration.

Only one person remained unaccounted for. A substantial collapse of the State apartments' upper floors occurred as the fifteen pumps, three turntable ladders and two damage control tenders arrived to relieve the night watch crews. The collapse hampered progress, as the charred timbers and fallen brickwork and masonry blocked access routes and made the continuing search both difficult and dangerous. By 10.45am the crews had penetrated deep into the search area and the removal of the heavy debris was being undertaken by teams working in relays. The charred remains of Lady Daphne Gale were located late in the morning amongst the debris of her former apartment that was now unrecognisable. She was carefully removed and taken by ambulance to the local mortuary.

Both the Queen and Prince Charles, who was nursing an injured arm from a prior accident, visited the scene of the fire and were escorted inside the building by a principal officer whilst the crews continued to work. The Queen was clearly distressed and anxious about the extent of the damage to one of her Royal Palaces. She was joined in this tour of inspection by the then Home Secretary Kenneth Baker (who had Ministerial responsibility for the fire service nationally). In his subsequent news interview, he praised both the efforts of the Brigade and the Palace's staff for their gallant and heroic efforts to save both the Palace and many of the national treasures held within the wing. He was able to confirm that, in fact, only two paintings were completely destroyed. However, the State apartments, the King's Audience chamber and the Cartoon Gallery were not so fortunate. Half the first floor and three-quarters of the second floor and the roof were totally destroyed by fire. Much of the debris was carefully removed by the fire brigade crews. Special attention was paid to salvaging the timber joists and beams, so that subsequent re-construction could be based on, and benefit from the craftsmanship of the earlier skilled workers who had built the Palace two centuries earlier.

In the weeks and months that followed, first up was the Royal Inquest. (Required for, "All bodies found lying within the limits of the Monarch's palaces.") This recorded Lady Gale's death as accidental and as a direct consequence of the lit candle that she was in the habit of taking into her bedroom. The Government Inquiry conducted by Sir John Garlick had been ordered by the Secretary of State for the Department of the Environment, Nicholas Ridley. Sir John's findings were presented to Parliament on the 3rd July by the Secretary of State. Amongst Sir John's conclusions was his contention that it was highly unlikely that an earlier discovery of the fire would have averted the death of Lady Gale. The Palace's fire detection system had inadvertently been rendered inoperative. He criticised the arrangement that allowed the fire alarm system, with design shortcomings, to be installed and then handed over with a less than adequate commissioning process.

Sir John discovered that there had been a "turf-war" as regards the jurisdiction of Hampton Court between the Department of the Environment and the Royal Household. This had contributed to an unsatisfactory state of affairs as to the responsibility and accountability for the Palace. He made recommendations for improving the automatic fire alarm system as well as changes in the procedures for its use and in the training of the staff concerned. In his statement to the House, Mr Ridley made special note of Sir John's praise towards the devotion and courage of the Palace staff and its salvage squad in seeking to protect life and property once the fire had been discovered. Whatever the Brigade's own contribution to the salvaging of the Nation's treasures from the Palace were, the Members of the House never got to hear about it. It was never mentioned.

Shooters Hill

With a commanding view of central London from its top third floor windows, Shooters Hill fire station stood at the junction of Eaglesfield Road and Shrewsbury Lane, just a short distance from the Dover Road. This had once been the Capital's main horse drawn coach route between London and the Port of Dover. It remained an important transport route until the construction of the Rochester Way relief road that extended the A2 down towards Kidbrook and Greenwich Park. With the exception of the Brigade's one-hundred-foot radio mast that stood in a secure compound next to the fire station, the fire station dominated this elevated residential area of Shooters Hill. Another of the peripheral LCC fire stations built in 1918, it retained all of its imposing Edwardian presence and had more recently undergone a major internal refurbishment. This had transformed the former residential accommodation into much needed extra station accommodation and also provided a training suite and offices that took up all of the top floor.

My promotion and return to Lewisham, the headquarters of the newly formed South East Command, saw me as one of many transferred senior officers sent to work under its Area Commander, Assistant Chief Officer Brian Butler. He had, during my short absence at Brigade Headquarters, set up an implementation team to bring about a smooth transition in what, for the Brigade, was the largest reorganizational change since the creation of the Greater London Council in 1965. I retained my former role in a much-enlarged training team and was reunited with Divisional Officer Barney Franklin (Brixton and the Royal Tournament). He had been promoted to Divisional Officer Grade 1 and was put in charge of Command Training and was my line manager. Unlike the other heads of section, Barney opted to work from Shooters Hill rather than Command headquarters at Lewisham. No great fan of the Area Commander, he considered our lofty vantage point far more civilised than the pressurised environment of the Command headquarters.

Over the next two years Barney and I would become a formidable team. He with his sage like wisdom and highly developed intellect and me with an abundance of enthusiasm and drive, which Barney frequently described as trying to hold a tiger by the tail!

Whilst not starting totally from scratch we did have a mammoth task in front of us. Not least was the problem of finding and then integrating our establishment of three Station Officers and eight Sub Officers, plus a dedicated administrative support officer into a cohesive training team. We inherited three training Sub Officers from the former E division plus Peter Jansen (the cabbie from Brixton who had since moved on). He had been the B division's driving instructor and had opted to work in the South East Command. The hunt was now on for suitable candidates to bring us up to full strength. This would be urgently required to deliver a much-expanded Command training regime to support the twenty-three fire stations and improve their own local training.

Sadly, as with the introduction of Station Commanders, what resources there were, were thin on the ground and even those were not fairly distributed. The South East Command consisted of the former E division and parts of the B and H divisions. The South West also had parts of the B and H divisions plus the whole of the former K division. Each division had had its own divisional training team and associated training equipment; videos, TVs, training aids and HGV driver training vehicles. With the notable exception of the equipment allocated to the E division, the remainder of all the training equipment held south of the Thames was located in the South West Area and therefore outside our Command boundary. Barney and I argued that we were entitled to a fair share. Sadly the deputy Area Commander of the SW Area had other ideas and considered possession to be nine-tenths of the law. Despite repeated requests, asking for what any reasonable person would consider ours anyway, he steadfastly refused to transfer the equipment. Talking was getting us nowhere; it was time for action and an "over-the-border" raiding party.

My co-conspirator was Peter Jansen. He knew the exact location of the B Divisional training equipment. Armed with only a dodgy docket, authorising the release of the said equipment, he left Shooters Hill on his furtive mission in his HGV training lorry. He returned some hours later, wearing a very self-satisfied smile. Which was a lot more than the South West's deputy Commander was wearing. Informed of his now almost empty training suite, he went ballistic and was baying for my blood. My own deputy Commander, taking the call from his fuming counterpart merely reminded him that, "Possession is nine-tenths of the law," before hanging up. Ringing me he said, "I suggest you don't go into the SW Area for a while, unless you fancy singing soprano-that is!"

There were four separate training venues in the South East Command; Southwark's breathing apparatus chamber; a comprehensive BA training facility and classroom at Erith fire station; a large (top floor) training suite at Greenwich fire station and our own offices and training rooms at Shooters Hill. Whilst Shooters Hill was well appointed and now reasonably well equipped, the same could not be said for Erith's BA training room. Its BA chamber was adequate but not in the same league as Southwark's, but it had good heat and smoke facilities. It was the adjacent classroom that let the site down. Poorly laid out and appointed, it was not intended for the increased usage that the enlarged Command area would place on its limited facilities.

We had inherited the two, long-standing, E division BA instructors. Both were excellent trainers and held temporary Sub Officer rank although they were substantive firemen. After explaining the accommodation problems to Barney following my site visit, I said, "There is a solution you know. Let the trainers convert it." Armed with a diagram of their proposed alterations and suggested improvements to the layout, there were clear advantages including increased training capacity. Convinced, Barney authorised the "DIY" changes. Getting the necessary materials and funding meant we would be flying by the seat of our pants, but with Barney's nod of approval the "boys" got to work.

Frank was one of the two BA instructors. He was very tall and lanky, highly animated at times but had a heart of gold and loved his work as a BA instructor. It was something he was exceptionally good at. A former ET fireman from Lewisham he brought a wealth of experience to his instructor role. He also happened to have been a competent kitchen fitter before joining the fire brigade. His side-kick and fellow instructor was Doug. A bit of a cockney and with a reputation of a "ladies' man" he was just as proficient with a saw and a hammer as he was with a BA set. The pair of them set to work on the "unofficial" conversion of their classroom and teaching area. Initially their enthusiasm was only matched by the dust and debris that was rapidly filling the training room. After my first exploratory visit to view progress I told Barney, "Give it a few days" before letting him inspect the site lest it brought on a seizure. But the lads "did good." With the assistance of some Command funding (which Barney managed to liberate from under the nose of the Area Commander) and a couple of dubious petty cash vouchers to cover the cost of paint, the training room now had a greatly improved layout. Frank and Doug had enhanced the hanging and storage arrangements for the Command training BA sets, provided a new cylinder storage area and enlarged the BA maintenance and assembly area. The classroom also took on a much lighter and airier feel. These much-improved facilities were inspected by the Command's Building Manager and passed muster and were also signed off by the Fire Brigades Union Health and Safety representative.

Things were moving at a pace in the Brigade and not just in establishing the five new Area Commands. The Chief Officer had a particular bee in his bonnet. He was introducing a new, brigade wide, training course for all qualified firemen and leading firemen. Called "Refresher Training," although much needed, it had little to do with the Chief's belief that it would drive up standards. It had much more to do with enforcing his vision of competency and dealing with a tiny minority of those who were considered to be under-performing, although that was never given as the official reason.

The Firefighter refresher programme was the largest training programme to be devolved to the fledgling Area Commands. Nothing quite like it had been tried before and was totally typical of ***all things Clarkson***, a man not noted to do things by halves. Every leading fireman and qualified fireman was required to attend a two-week refresher course once every two years. The syllabus incorporated an existing two-day BA refresher, a new two-day first aid refresher (both assessable) and incorporated practical ladder handling, pumps and pumping, road traffic accident procedures and a general fire brigade update on discipline and related topics. Selling this compulsory course to fire station personnel had not been easy and had not gone down well. There was a great deal of apprehension (and misinformation) about the refresher training which led to back sliding from some "old hands" nominated to attend the initial courses.

Barney and I shared a great deal of apprehension too. We had yet to find our full complement of trainers to deliver this imminent "refresher" training. With two Station Officer and two Sub Officer vacancies still to be filled, regardless of what the Chief wanted, without them we could not deliver his latest policy directive. Whilst Barney crafted an advert for the Station Officer positions, I set about some head hunting for the two Sub Officers. Two individuals quickly rose to the top of the list. One came willingly whilst the other, initially at least, came screaming and hollering having been talked out of leaving his beloved fire station for South East Training.

Doug Massey was the younger of the two. Bright and enthusiastic, he was a fireman at Greenwich and had recently passed both his Sub Officer's written and practical exams, but had yet to take his Leading Firemen's interview. Peter Gwilliam, on the other hand was an established Sub Officer and serving at Dockhead. He was a tall powerful man with a wonderful sense of humour and fun (although he did not consider his move that funny). He was an exceptionally talented trainer especially when teaching his specialism, road traffic accident procedures and techniques. Both were ideally suited for the job. They were knowledgeable, experienced firefighters and very conscientious. Peter got the short straw, as he was already a substantive Sub Officer, whilst the other seven trainers were all firemen given temporary rank of Sub Officer for as long as they were in the training team. But Peter would cover the two Station Officer positions whenever they were unavailable due to sickness or extended leave.

With Barney's selection of the two Station Officers we finally had a full complement and were ready to deliver the much heralded, but anxiously awaited, refresher courses as well as the other regular training events.

The Brigade's central training department was responsible for all the refresher training policy and the distribution of all course material and trainer guidance. Hastily arranged Training Officers' seminars, at Brigade Headquarters, soon identified a huge disparity between what they (Central Training) expected us to deliver and what the five Area Commands had the resources to deliver. There was universal agreement amongst the five Area Training Officers that someone was living in cloud cuckoo land and it was not them. Struggling with a non-negotiable timetable, we were expected to deliver the programme regardless of the problems and deliver we did, although some Commands were far more successful than others. The South East soon became the lead Command, both in terms of the quality of its training and the throughput of personnel, able to maintain a consistently high standard and pass rate.

There were teething problems, naturally, such as course nominations going mysteriously astray at fire stations. But word was getting around that the course was actually beneficial. There were favourable and constructive comments, even from the "old hands," doing the rounds about the value of this much needed refresher. In fact, the refresher programme was delivering far more than we expected. More and more watch officers were asking to attend the course as their junior personnel were returning to station made more aware of some current procedures than them. Ladder handling was a prime example. The amalgamation of the former divisions into the South East Command had left a legacy of variations in how fire station crews were to handle the forty-five-foot Lacon ladder. Our two Station Officers were the Refresher course directors and were also delivering the approved method of Lacon ladder handling. (The same as the approved method taught to recruits at training school.) So successful were they in their teaching that all Command senior officers were given familiarisation and training by them so that they, in turn, could better monitor the practices operationally and at station level.

The heavy demands placed upon Barney and myself by the refresher programme had scant regard for our rostered leave days. With one or the other of us required to undertake the course introductions, conduct BA practical assessments and lead the end of course debriefs we were occasionally meeting ourselves coming back! But our commitment had its own rewards and that was the incredible comradeship that was engendered within the whole of our training team. The HGV driving instructors also mirrored the efforts of the general trainers, so that the professionalism of the whole training team was reflected both in the feedback by trainees and the positive comments received from Station Commanders. We were in danger of becoming a victim of our own success.

More and more demands were being placed on the training team. Lacon ladder handling was extended to all Command fire stations and other peripatetic training was taking place, delivering training direct to fire stations. Peter Gwilliam developing his own Road Traffic Accident road show. Other local ideas and initiatives were piloted and later adopted by the other Commands.

In addition to the regular large, six pumps or more, and smaller scale four pump exercise programme, the Area Commander required all senior officers to train, in their respective rota groups, at simulated Command and Control exercises. Barney was in his element with these exercises, as he scripted differing scenarios that involved senior officers commanding imaginary major incidents. We had in the Area a defunct hospital complex, which was an ideal venue for our exercises. We employed both major and forward control units for a large-scale simulated exercise. Our team duplicated fireground communications to make the whole procedure as "real" as possible. This "realism" was of great benefit and exposed senior officers to most "lifelike" command and control simulations, which occasionally soon took on an authentic feel as individuals responded to and made decisions about the radio messages and other sources of information coming into the control unit. Occasionally it all became too realistic as the nominated incident commander, totally absorbed in the fireground scenario, ordered the "observing" officer off his control unit because he was impeding his thought processes.

In common with all senior officers within the Brigade, Barney and I were not immune from the other responsibilities that came with our rank. Discipline inquiries and major Health and Safety investigations were part and parcel of those responsibilities. Barney, however, had many and varied talents and among them was his proven ability as a "presenting" officer in discipline cases. A fire service disciplinary tribunal was much like a court martial in the military and the presenting officer is similar to the prosecution in that he was required to present the facts of the case to the presiding officer, no less than a principal officer. Barney was a gifted presenting officer both at tribunals and at appeal (heard before selected Members of the Fire Authority). Barney's intellect, his command of the English language and his razor-sharp wit brought to mind John Mortimer's creation of *"Rumpole of the Bailey"* (played so effectively by Leo McKern in the Thames Television series of the late nineteen seventies and early eighties). It was rare that the accused walked free when Barney presented a case. He also brought his considerable skill in to play when he devised and ran a series of mock discipline tribunal exercises, in which untried senior officers took on the role of presenting officers and the accused friend (normally a remember of the Fire Brigades Union in real discipline cases). Sadly my own efforts as presenting officer against a highly articulate and more able colleague, who took on the role of accused friend, floundered on his introduction of some late evidence that I had not anticipated. The accused walked free that day needless to say.

Barney did have one notable failure and that was getting me to understand the nuances of the apostrophe! I guess in the present day I could have come up with some feeble excuse about being dyslexic but the truth was I never grasped the concept of good grammar at school. It still remains something of a mystery and I still put the damn apostrophe in the wrong place. Getting it right was more down to luck than judgement despite the best efforts of my tutor and our private lunchtime tutorials. Report writing was an essential skill of any senior officer. I had to work harder than many of my peer group to avoid the dreaded red pen of the Area Commander whose vetting of reports matched that of any hardened Fleet Street news editor.

Funerals

Attending brigade funerals and cremation services was, sadly, quite a regular event. It was our Area Commander's unwritten policy to always send a Command senior officer on these occasions although he would frequently attend in person, especially where it was an in-service death or that of a retired colleague. Brigade operational personnel killed in the line of duty continued to occur at all too frequent intervals. News of such tragic events would often be broadcast by the national news media at the same time as the in-house notification to station personnel. The subsequent funeral or cremation service united the brigade in a shared sense of loss. It was a long-established custom that for those killed in the line of duty that their coffin, draped in a Union Flag, was borne to the funeral on a fire engine (normally a turntable ladder) especially adapted for the task.

More commonly, it was only a teleprinter message that told the wider brigade of the sudden or unexpected death of a serving firefighter or a retired member, and gave notification of funeral arrangements. Unexpected and untimely deaths were always difficult losses for the respective families to bear. Some Area Commanders, in a genuine desire to ensure a fitting tribute, provided what they thought to be the appropriate level of a "brigade assisted" funeral. There was no consistency in the guidance given to officers liaising with the bereaved families, regarding what was the appropriate level of the brigade response for the funeral or cremation, simply because there was no in-house guidance available, anywhere. (Serving members would be medically retired in incredibly short order if it was known they had a terminal condition and had been given little time to live. This provided a more favourable financial provision for their spouse and children, if any, under the terms of the Firemen's Pension Scheme.)

One of the most frequent attendees at Brigade funeral services was none other than our own Area Commander. Upon returning from his attendance at the latest funeral, a fireman who had succumbed to a short but terminal illness, I was summoned from Shooters Hill and told to report to his office, pronto! Sitting reflectively behind his desk he told me that he was very concerned at the range and differing levels of the "Brigade" funeral services. Despite his evident compassion for this particular family he said, "Today's service arrangement was over the bloody top! It detracted from the arrangements that should only be afforded a serving member of the brigade. Someone, anyone, who has paid the ultimate sacrifice and been killed at an incident. Go and sort it out." My summons was at an end.

With that as my only brief it seemed I had to devise and introduce a funeral protocol that officers, in any of the Command Areas, could use as an aide-memoir and thereby provide a consistent approach. Dismissed with just a wave of his arm and charged with my unusual brief, I sought the aid of some helpers. I selected two Station Commanders, who I press-ganged into assisting me with my task. I had some personal experience of working with the bereaved when accompanying the Welfare officer and meeting with families to discuss possible funeral arrangements. My two, volunteered, colleagues had been involved in arranging brigade funerals for retired members in recent months. However, with no internal written guidance available to us it seemed logical to seek the aid and expertise of the professionals in trying to put something appropriate together that catered for the range of differing circumstances. I decided who better to advise us of the ceremonial side of things than the military.

I had previously had contact with two of South London's largest undertakers when organising Brigade funerals, so I went back to them to seek their advice. My two assistants headed off to the Woolwich Barracks to speak to the commanding officer of the Royal Artillery. I thought that the military would have standing orders for just about every conceivable situation and funerals would be no exception. They did, but the Army's level of ceremonial was far in excess of our needs and we would never need to provide a firing squad to deliver a ceremonial volley over the graveside!

I did not think there was anything wrong with a little bit of plagiarism (We never took credit for the Army's work). By cherry-picking the Royal Artillery's funeral standing orders, and including the invaluable contributions of the two undertaking firms, our version of a funeral aide-memoir was prepared and submitted to the Area Commander for his approval. Setting out the Command guidelines to funeral planning, in a logical sequence, it offered practical guidance to any officer assigned this unenviable task. Its simple, step-by-step advice set down for the first time a protocol for funerals. It detailed the most appropriate responses for the three types of ritual prior to, and for a burial or cremation. They were; Brigade funeral with full honours; a brigade funeral and; a retired member's funeral. This was not rocket science but this thin little booklet covered everything that was required, before, during and after a funeral or cremation whilst being cognisant of the families' wishes. I reserved the highest standard for any firefighter killed in action or as a direct result of injuries received at an incident.

The booklet, with diagrams and images of an honour guard/pallbearer was printed and circulated throughout the South East Command to every senior officer. However, it soon took on a much wider distribution as senior officers from the four other Area Commands requested copies. It was destined to be the "benchmark" for the whole Brigade after it was later endorsed by the Deputy Chief Officer and subsequently circulated to all uniformed departmental heads. Even other Fire Brigades requested the easy to follow guidance and quickly adopted it as their own. (The original edition remained in use right up to my own retirement and ensured that firefighters killed in the line of duty were laid to rest with dignity and the appropriate level of honours.)

The 1980s was the political decade of Margaret Thatcher, running as it did from her election as Prime Minister in 1979 to her political demise in 1990. It was a decade of many changes and one in which she once famously said, "You turn if you want to; the lady's not for turning." But something was turning and incredibly fast. Having formed over the Atlantic it was now heading towards the British and French coastlines at considerable speed. On the 15 October 1987 the "Great Storm" swept across southern Britain and northern France bringing death and destruction in its wake. Given the enormity and scale of this extraordinary weather event it was amazing that the death toll was only measured in tens and not in the hundreds. However, in the English southern countryside millions of trees were uprooted and destroyed by this hurricane force wind. Sevenoaks was renamed "Oneoaks" by the press in the days following the hurricane as the full enormity of the damage became more widely known. Technically it was not an actual "hurricane" but was declared a "rare event" by the Meteorological Office instead. They stated that the last recorded storm of this magnitude was two hundred and eighty-four years earlier in 1703. (It turned out to be not such a rare event either because three years later, in 1990, the January "Burns Day storm" was of a similar intensity.)

Just over one month later another devastatingly rare event was unfolding. On the evening of 18 November thirty-one people were to die in the worst underground fire during peace time within the nation's capital city. The King's Cross fire, which started in an escalator, made partly of wood, lead to a tragically catastrophic fire. What initially appeared to be a small fire developed rapidly and when an unexpected flashover occurred it filled the extensive ticket hall with flames and dense smoke. The four fire engines sent from Clerkenwell, Soho, Manchester Square and Euston were soon on the scene, Soho's engine the first to arrive at 7.42pm. Totally unaware of what was about to unfold, the crews started to investigate the modest blaze in the busy underground station only to be caught up, within minutes, in the total pandemonium caused by the explosive force of the expanding volume of burning gas and superheated smoke.

Station Officer Colin Townsley was from Soho fire station and was in charge of the first response. (Although thirty fire engines and over one hundred and fifty firefighters would subsequently be deployed to combat this killer blaze.) He was below ground on the station concourse when the flashover occurred. Unhappily he was not wearing BA. He was overcome by smoke and subsequently died from the effects. The Public Inquiry that followed, found from the position of his body in relation to others, that he had been helping a traveller in difficulty. This was at the base of the exit steps to Pancras Road, after a frantic search had been initiated for passengers and fire crews alike, now reported trapped by the conflagration engulfing the underground station. Despite desperate attempts to revive him efforts were to no avail because he was dead by then. He left a widow, Linda, and two teenage daughters. He was later awarded the George Medal, posthumously.

His funeral, ten days later, unified the Brigade in its deep sense of loss, not only for Colin Townsley but also for the other thirty individuals who died that fateful evening. Sixty other victims received injuries ranging from severe burns to smoke inhalation. Senior officers from the Northern Command, Colin

Townsley's local area, were the lead officers and co-ordinated his public memorial service. Brigade Headquarters had requested that the South East Command oversee his private, family, cremation service and were tasked with putting that part of the funeral plan together.

On the 28 November a turntable ladder, laden with wreaths and floral tributes, became the funeral hearse to transport the flag-draped coffin of the late Colin Townsley on his last journey. It carried him from his much-loved fire station at Soho to his last resting place. The most prominent of all the numerous wreaths on that vehicle was from his own Red Watch at Soho fire Station. Just one word, woven into the colourful wreath with white chrysanthemums, spelt out their sense of grief and loss; "Guv." Shaftesbury Avenue, the home of Soho fire station, came to a complete stand-still as the lengthy procession prepared to move off.

His coffin lay across the vehicle. Placed on the Union Flag was a black cushion on which his white Station Officer's helmet was displayed along with his fire service long service and good conduct medal. Standing to stiff attention, three on each side of the turntable ladder and guarding their "governor" were six of Soho's Red Watch, now his pallbearers. Bare headed, but wearing their best fire tunics and white ceremonial Brigade belts and white lanyards, their solemn faces told of the sadness of their unenviable duty. With police motor cycle escort, the long funeral procession, with its two-flower decked red fire engines and two black hearses filled to overflowing with floral tributes, headed northwards as the first of that day's honour guards paid their tribute to a fallen colleague; and to many their friend.

The bright and colourful cortege left the fire station in its wake as it made stately progress through London's traffic to King's Cross station, where it stopped for a few moments silence. Standing there on that chilled November morning were rank upon rank of uniformed firemen and women, not only from London but from Brigades that represented virtually the whole of the United Kingdom. Almost two thousand onlookers had also gathered filling the station forecourt and Underground entrance as the members of the fire service, police and London Ambulance services drew up to attention. The procession came to a halt by the barricades, hidden by flowers, and close to where Colin Townsley had died in suffocating smoke.

Moving on to St Paul's Church in Covent Garden, a smaller crowd watched as the carefully rehearsed pallbearers gracefully slid the coffin from the turntable ladder before lifting it, in one smooth movement, on to their shoulders. Between the three-deep rows of firefighters, forming the honour guard, they bore the coffin in to the church and onto the waiting bier for the memorial service to be conducted by the Bishop of Fulham. This historic church, built in the heart of London's theatreland, was the parish church for the Parish of Covent Garden within which was Soho fire station. It was a fitting setting for the public memorial service. After the moving service, the pallbearers once again hoisted the coffin shoulder high to carry it through the silent congregation and return it to its place on the turntable ladder.

For all of us involved in ensuring that the funeral provided a fitting tribute to a "hero" and his family the ceremonial was testing the aide-memoir to the full. It seemed to be working as intended. Thorough preparation and pre-planning was now delivering the appropriate level of formality. My involvement in this saddest of days for the Townsley family was to oversee the private cremation service that was to take place in a South London crematorium. (The Townsley family lived locally in Lewisham.) After leaving St Paul's Church the funeral procession moved south of the River Thames with police outriders clearing a path through London's traffic, it made its way to Hither Green Crematorium.

I had already measured the height of the crematorium door opening to ensure that when the coffin was carried in by the pallbearers the black cushion and Colin Townsley's helmet cleared the door frame. Cremation services can, and frequently do, run like a conveyor belt. Mourners often leave by one door whilst the next grieving family enters by another, fitting their twenty- or thirty-minute services in to the crematorium's busy schedule. As soon as the date of the service was known, I had met with the Crematorium Superintendent and secured three half hour slots for the Townsley family.

Linda Townsley and her children wished to have a private cremation service to say their final goodbyes to a husband and a much-loved father, with only their close family and personal friends present. Their wishes were paramount in my planning and a watchful South East Area Commander checked, then rechecked, my arrangements. There was considerable press interest in the whole of the day's activities. Despite repeated requests for privacy at the cremation, the simply laid out, gated entrance of the crematorium made excluding the intrusive and pushy press photographers almost impossible. Although the police presence did manage to keep this inconsiderate horde outside the boundary railings, they nevertheless wanted their "pound of flesh." The noisy clicking of cameras was clearly audible as the procession stopped momentarily at the entrance to the crematorium. This noise suddenly stopped when two of the honour guard confronted the press corps and promised to stick their cameras "where the sun don't shine." Their obvious outrage let the assembled media gathering know that they meant it too.

To accord with the family's wishes only a limited honour guard from the South East Command greeted the cortège and the principal mourners as they finally arrived at the crematorium Chapel. Turning silently on to its cleared forecourt the turntable ladder stopped adjacent to the chapel's entrance doors, parallel to its wide porch. The Area Commander took the salute facing the draped coffin. Family and friends now gathered by the entrance to watch the removal of the coffin for the last time. The Soho pallbearers discharged their painful duty with grace and had perfected the coffin's removal with the meticulousness expected of their professional counterparts. Maintaining their quiet dignity, that did them all great credit, they made a seamless entry into the

Chapel and placed the coffin onto the catafalque. As the doors of the Chapel slowly closed, the honour guard removed the floral tribute and wreaths and carried them solemnly to the family viewing area. Those on the turntable ladder had been secured with wire, as had the white helmet to the coffin. Armed with their (issued) wire snips my team of helpers carefully removed the wreaths that had been adorning this vehicle whilst I made my way to the crematorium "furnace" to await the coffin after the committal.

After cutting the white helmet from the coffin, collecting his medal and the Union Flag, I said a personal goodbye to an officer, who although I did not know personally, I felt was a kindred spirit. I saluted the now bare wooden coffin and returned outside. With the service now over, and the numerous flowers and wreaths filling all the available space in the viewing area, family and friends gathered and mingled. Some were reading the many expressions of sorrow on the cards, whilst others offered a sympathetic word or their heartfelt condolences to the immediate family. The fortitude that the pallbearers had demonstrated throughout the day started to waver as, now out of the public gaze, their own emotions surfaced. As Linda Townsley and her two girls prepared to leave, Brian Butler the Area Commander, made one final symbolic gesture to the family. Moving over to her as she sat in the limousine, he presented her with her late husband's Station Officer's helmet and returned his medal. (She would later be collecting another medal; his posthumous George Medal.)

The aide-memoir had served its purpose. It would now gather dust on a shelf or be stuck in a bottom drawer until the next time. Sadly, and tragically, there would be other times. But now, when those situations arose, one thing had now firmly been established across the whole Brigade. Full honours would be reserved for those unfortunate individuals that had paid the ultimate sacrifice and had died in the line of operational duty.

It's a fair cop guv!

The Area Commander was playing chess and the Command senior officers were his personal chess pieces. We were on the move, well some of us at least. Rumours had been rife for a while that, "the old Man" had that certain glint in his eye which could only mean transfers were in the offing! They were, and my time in Training was over. In January 1988 I was ordered to return to Lewisham and join the Operations Team. However, before I departed the training team had a little, and rather pleasant, surprise in store for me as a parting gift. A video taken of that special evening had as its title, "It's a fair cop guv," and she was!

Shooters Hill fire station housed not only the fire station and training offices, but on the same site, in a separate single-storey building, was the Echo Club. This had been the former E Divisional social club and was still being run as a properly constituted licensed social club. Decked still in its festive decorations, the whole team, with their wives and partners, gathered for a belated Christmas buffet. The two guests of honour were Dennis Buckley, a tall slim bald-headed man, who was the Command's Senior Divisional Officer.

Dennis was head of the Command Fire Prevention Branch (re-branded as Fire Safety) but he also had responsibility for Training on the Command's principal management board.

The second was Peter Slevin, the Principal Administration Officer. Whilst he matched the Area Commander in intellect and brainpower, he outshone him in terms of his veracity and integrity. A foot shorter than Dennis and with a full head of dark hair, that had the first wisps of grey, he had a slight but athletic build. Both were in stark contrast to the Area Commander, who had not been invited to the bash by Barney. They both willingly entered into the warm and convivial atmosphere of the evening.

There was a sudden, and unexpected, pause in the conversations and friendly chatter as a uniformed presence entered the clubroom. A young, and highly attractive policewoman, walked in obviously looking for someone. That someone happened to be me. The allure of her sensual perfume and her seductive pout, as she moved closer, told me there was something extraordinary about this lovely, blonde, petite constable. Then to the obvious delight of all the men in the room, and with a disapproving look from one or two of the wives, my "kiss-a gram" got down to business. She planted a first long passionate kiss on my mouth. With the cry of, "You're not meant to be enjoying it," ringing in my ears she invited me to remove her uniform. Never one to refuse a request from a lady, I obliged. Its removal exposed an even more appealing sight. She wore a black lace bodice, revealing an ample cleavage, skimpy black panties and matching suspender belt supported black stockings that covered her slim and elegant legs. Now in her "working" attire she read aloud the short amusing rhyme, which said that she was my leaving present from all of the trainers. By the lustful looks on some of their faces I thought they wished they were leaving too.

Her none too discreet unveiling was recorded by video camera for posterity (or maybe just to show the Area Commander what a good time he had missed!) She then invited me to remove the frilly garter she wore high on her exposed thigh, using only my mouth. Kneeling down before her with my hands behind my back and displaying an adroitness that surprised everyone, especially me, the garter slid down her smooth silk stocking with an assured ease. Thinking I could be in trouble with the wife when I get home, to shouts of, "Do it again." to prove it was not just a fluke, confirmed that I would be. All too soon my exotic pleasure came to an end. After assisting her back into her police uniform and receiving a kiss good-bye she was off to her next engagement.

That was not the end of the evening's surprises however. Two of our trainers had secured examination success in the latter part of 1987 and Barney Franklin had invited Dennis Buckley to hand over their certificates. Doug Massey had passed both his Station Officer's examination and the Graduate of the Institute Fire Engineers' exam. One of the BA instructors had passed both his Leading Firemen's written and practical exams and was to be made a substantive Leading Fireman. Barney explained to the amused gathering that Doug's certificate had come framed, whilst the other had not. So, discarding the framed certificate he had made two new frames for both recipients. Producing a tatty plastic carrier bag, he lifted out the Leading Fireman's certificate, its rough balsa wood and cardboard construction looking every inch the amateurish and flimsy creation Barney had intended. Whilst Dennis delicately took hold of the framed certificate, lest it fall apart, he reminded his audience that, "The Command has a budget of twenty-four million pounds and most of that goes into the Area Commander's office; what's left over goes on Peter Slevin's plants; what little remains I see comes to Training. These framed certificates are a reflection of how we view you lot in Training." Receiving the second, and supposedly more prestigious, framed certificate that was equally crude and shoddy, Dennis noted that the balsa wood had actually been sanded down. Meanwhile Barney held up the plastic carrier bag and reminded everyone that Doug's came with its own executive carrying case!

It was a great way to leave. I felt honoured by the kind tributes that were paid to me that evening. That evening was far more, of course; it was a tribute not only to the two recipients and their individual achievements but to what everyone had achieved since we had first come together, twenty months earlier. It had been a privilege being part of a very special team. Barney and I had laid some very sound foundations on which others could, and would, build. It was with a rather heavy heart that I left Shooters Hill for the very different environment of the Command Headquarters at Lewisham. I, for one, was not too sure if this was such, "A fair cop, Guv."

Lewisham HQ

The Command Headquarters at Lewisham had a different, and much less pleasant, atmosphere from the lofty oasis of sanity that Shooters Hill provided. For one thing Shooters Hill lacked, thankfully, the autocratic and domineering presence of an Area Commander that seemed to pervade all of Lewisham's offices. There everyone was mindful, some fearful, of his ever-watchful gaze. He was, without a doubt, a very effective Area Commander but his management style made Attila the Hun look like a pussy-cat.

I was now one of three Divisional Officers in the Operations Group who monitored and audited the operational performance and readiness of fire station crews. This really meant monitoring, and mentoring, our respective Station Commanders. Auditing the watches helped us judge how well or how badly a Station Commander was doing his job. Each of us had responsibility for a third of the command fire stations. My seven stations were contained within the Borough of Greenwich, five of whom had an experienced former Assistant Divisional Officer as Station Commanders and all of them were older than me. Woolwich and Eltham fire stations had temporary Station Commanders, and had had a succession of them, which made continuity of station management problematic at these stations, if not outright difficult.

The Operations Group was led by Peter Jones; a well-grounded six-footer whose forward thinking and sharp analytical brain set him apart from his peers. This well thought of young man also happened to be a kind and considerate individual. He was someone who possessed the relatively rare skills of being able to balance a high and demanding workload with bringing harmony to his team. His ability to deliver calm, capable and rational decisions and judgements under, occasionally, extremely stressful situations made him a force to be reckoned with. His views, not always in line with those of the Area Commander, would be articulated by this able advocate and nine times out of ten seen to win the day. If you needed a role model this was your man. He would soon rise through the ranks of the London Fire Brigade before departing as the deputy Chief Officer of Cambridgeshire, then becoming the Chief Fire Officer of Gloucestershire before securing the County's Chief Executive Officer position. His management style was different from others, especially so from that of some of his peers. In a way, that made working at Lewisham a challenging and enlightening experience for me, rather than being a chore.

Establishing a working rapport with all seven of the Station Commanders was easier said than done, especially with those resentful of the fact that their own careers had not progressed as they had hoped; but at thirty-eight years of age I was not exactly a spring chicken either. My initial round of station visits provided me with an opportunity of a one-to-one exchange with each of the Commanders and a chance to see, at first hand, their individual management styles and systems. More important were my subsequent follow up visits to their watches to see if what I had been told were their ideas and methods, had filtered down and been effectively applied. Clearly in some cases they had not. The watch visits showed up disparities in individual management styles, but given that there were twenty-eight individual watch officers this was only to be expected. However, of more concern for me was that across the group, as a whole, there was a lack of any co-ordinated planning process. This seemed, to me, to be a significant issue.

It seemed so to Peter too. After some discussion with the other two DOs, he approved my co-ordinated annual planning initiative, in my group of seven stations. Whilst my colleagues may have given their tacit agreement their body language revealed their inner feelings. It was clear that they preferred a station inspection regimen that centred on the prescriptive and relied on compliance with various policies and procedures. This was necessary, of course, but remained only part of the overall solution to monitoring the effectiveness of good station management. It did not necessarily aid individual officer's development. So after some positive marketing on my part and listening to, and addressing, the concerns of my Station Commanders that, "This was not all some five-minute wonder," they bought into the proposal. They found it difficult to disagree with the argument that all too often fire station management would gravitate to "fire-fighting" in a reactionary manner. Better, surely, to plan and schedule agreed work plans and ensure there was an effective follow up procedure in place.

Within a relatively short period of time the seven work plans were submitted and signed off by Peter Jones, who was by now showing real interest in the scheme. He was more than just interested too, as they became integrated into the Command's philosophy of group management. Little did I know then that this was but a precursor to the formal introduction of work-plans across the whole of the Brigade, following yet another top management review. Not that it had anything to do with my apparent foresight, rather we were entering a period of even greater scrutiny for efficiency and effectiveness within a cost-conscious environment that was being driven by our Fire Authority.

But before this happened Peter upped and left. He was destined for greater and higher things and I found myself, unexpectedly, projected into his position as head of the Operations Group. This was much to the dismay of my two, far more able, colleagues who smiled though gritted teeth at my temporary promotion to Divisional Officer Grade 1. I had been getting a real feel for my group of stations, admittedly some better than others, but none more so than the busiest of the seven, Plumstead.

I found impromptu and unannounced visits to a fire station were always a better indicator to how things were running than telephoning first to a make an appointment. I had been caught out more than once as a young Watch Officer when one bell was rung, announcing the arrival of a senior officer and summoning me to the station watchroom. Also, after nearly twenty years at a fire station, you learn to tell the difference between the odd watch "off" day when e.g. fire gear is not stowed away correctly, and a much bigger problem when a watch is not managed properly – or worse the watch is managing the officer in charge. Out of the twenty-eight individual watches within my Group, it was inevitable that there would be "problem" individuals, maybe even the odd watch. Station Officer "Darky" Knight was not so much a problem, rather he was an out of the ordinary type of chap!

I had known of Darky since he was the Station Officer at a busy East London fire station located in the Whitechapel Road. I was a Sub Officer at Southwark and we served on the same watch. We met infrequently on the fireground but Darky had a formidable reputation, both as a good fireground officer but also as a scallywag when it came to life at the fire station. There were a few notable and notorious watches around then; (especially in the C division), stations where firemen were not thrilled to have to stand-by, and Darky ran one of them. He could be often found on night duties either playing the drums or pulling pints in the adjacent pub (still on duty!) only leaving when the shouts came in. With its hard living and hard playing his watch could instil fear into the poor "raw" junior buck who had an out duty to "Charlie 24", although Darky was neither cruel nor vindictive. He was an accomplished character, however, where his people thought it really mattered; on the fireground. Although he probably did not have quite as many make-up fires as legend bestowed on him, he nevertheless, had enough. When he made pumps a straight ten or fifteen you knew you had a real goer on your hands.

His brief foray into temporary higher rank, as an Assistant Divisional Officer, all ended in tears! His laid-back station management style did not transfer easily into that required of running a Division. His sleight of hand in adjusting the riding figures on a particular night shift (the total number of personnel on duty) could not match those actually required to ride the engines and keep them all "on the run" (available). Subjected to a disciplinary inquiry he was found guilty as charged, given a fine and posted out of the Division. Although he never personally paid his considerable fine as it was paid for him. A "whip round" from those at his station and the surrounding stations easily raised the few hundred pounds that Darky had been awarded as a punishment.

Now, in the last couple of years of his lengthy service, he was the watch officer at Plumstead in charge of the Green Watch. My first meeting with Darky did not bode well. Arriving unannounced at the station, I strolled into the station from the yard passing the open appliance room doors that gave direct access onto the street. Plumstead's two fire engines stood in readiness, waiting for the next shout, as I walked into the ground floor station watchroom. Entering the vacant watchroom I went to ring one bell to summon the officer in charge when I saw the station safe, secured to the wall by heavy brackets, was open. Not only open but it still had the safe keys hanging in the lock! Shutting the safe and pocketing the keys I rang one bell.

The swarthy figure of Darky (hence his name!) reported. Whilst not overly tall he had a certain presence and certainly had a streetwise charm. I said nothing about the safe as we toured the station and inspected the appliances. Whilst not the best inspection result ever, it far exceeded my expectations and was to a standard I would have been pleased to show a senior officer if he had turned up, unexpectedly, to "turn me over." The subsequent discussion with the watch was equally pleasing if not actually pleasant. To them I was just yet another senior officer inspecting their station, an outsider, and someone whose motives might lack sincerity. Although respectful, their questions were blunt and to the point. I felt comfortable with this frank and robust exchange and answered all their questions with honesty and conviction. Giving as good as I got, I was even invited to stay for tea.

I had met two of the Green Watch previously whilst they were on their refresher courses. It had been a positive experience for them and Barney and I were, apparently, seen as not so bad; as senior officers go that is! The word had obviously got back to the station. After a couple of hours, I went to leave and Darky, as custom and practice dictates, walked me to my car. "Anything else Station Officer?" I asked. "I was rather hoping you would give me back the safe keys," said a clearly humbled man. With a rebuke and reminder if it happened again, he would need more than a whip round to get him out of the mire I departed. But as it transpired, I would see more of this station sooner than I expected.

A week or two later I was sitting at home during the early evening when the phone rang. I was on twenty-four-hour duty although not the duty DO, but the phone ringing was nothing out of the ordinary. The same could not be said of the message or the messenger; it was Darky. "There has been a bit of a problem at the station, could you come in to sort it out?" he said. "What is the problem?" I asked. "There has been a fight!"

I arrived at the station a little after 7.00pm and the atmosphere was subdued and pensive. Darky was waiting in the yard strangely out of his depth for once. "The White Watch Station Officer and one of my lads have had a bit of a bust up." That was an understatement as it had been an all-out brawl. I knew the White Watch Station Officer, having recently sat on the Station Officer promotional panel that saw him elevated to his current rank. He was sitting in the station watchroom and holding his head, which had as much to do with his feeling of shame as any injury he had received. The other party had been taken upstairs; an experienced Green Watch fireman, he was one of the two refresher candidates and who I thought had come across as a reasonably decent sort of guy. Both knew that with me now present their unthinking actions could have far reaching consequences.

Having listened separately to both sides of the story I came to my decision; one that I hoped I would not live to regret. There had been some history between the two protagonists going back to when Doug, the White Watch Station Officer had once served on the Green Watch. At the change of watch earlier that day, with the White Watch going off duty and the Green Watch coming onto shift at 6.00pm, an argument flared up between the two. This rapidly developed into a fight with Doug landing the first punch. The discipline route and a full inquiry would have been the only possible course of action in some of my colleagues' eyes. This would require me to formally caution the pair, report it to the Area Commander and leaving it to another Divisional Officer to sort it all out. That would have no doubt resulted in a tribunal and an outcome that would see Doug busted by at least one rank, maybe two, and the fireman posted to another station. I wanted a result that saw common sense rule the day and not the outcome of prescriptive formal discipline regulations.

Andy Dark served on the Green Watch and was the Command's Fire Brigades Union representative. He was on duty that night and was fully aware of the difficult situation that now presented itself. Taking the pugilistic pair into the privacy of the Station Officer's office I spelt out the two possible options. They arrived at my preferred solution. It was simple; they would keep any future dispute between themselves outside the confines of the fire station. Asking Darky and Andy Dark to join us the antagonistic pair extended each other a sincere apology before shaking hands to seal their agreement. "This incident stays strictly on the station," I said, "and it ends here."

Much to my relief, and surprise, it actually did. Darky contacted me at the end of the following shift to report that the truce was clearly working. Plumstead's Station Commander, who had got a whisper of some incident at the station had confronted Darky and was told, "Wasn't much and anyway the occifer came and sorted it all out."

My last meeting with Darky probably epitomises this extraordinary character and how his life was more suited to the "old school" London Fire Brigade. Plumstead's pump had been responding to a fire call on Thamesmead when its driver had taken a downhill corner much too fast and clipped a kerb rather hard, very hard in fact. The combination of the fire engine's speed and the momentum of the four thousand-five hundred litres of water in the engine's tank turned the fire engine over onto its left side. It bounced and slid almost a further two hundred feet down the road before finally coming to a grating halt. It was a small miracle that this ten-tonne engine had not hit anything else or that anyone inside or outside the fire engine was neither killed nor seriously injured.

I was ordered onto the incident as the duty Divisional Officer and was the first senior officer to arrive. Other reinforcing crews from Bexley had already removed Plumstead's shaken and clearly shocked crew from the fire engine, which was lying on its side and blocking the road leading towards Thamesmead. I pulled up clear of the engine's skid marks and its array of debris and dislodged equipment; I got rigged in my fire gear whilst absorbing the scene, before walking down towards the crews. The police, who had arrived before me, had already closed the road to traffic in preparation for their accident investigation. Darky saw me moving down the hill and rose from his sitting position on the kerb side and put his fire helmet back on his head. He stood erect, composed himself and then marched, literally, like the Guardsman that he had been, towards me before stopping at attention three feet away ram-rod straight. He gave a swift smart military salute. I thought his arm would drop off with the ferocity of his salute. "Station Officer Knight. All present and correct, except the engine of course Sir!" After checking that he and his crew were alright I asked, "So what the f*** happened Darky?" After listening to a somewhat dubious explanation I sent him back to care for his men.

Having ensured that Plumstead's pump crew were not seriously hurt, just walking wounded, and none required hospitalisation, I set about the task of starting the major accident investigation which the situation demanded. The police were preserving the scene and together we were finding out what happened whilst noting the conditions and actions that influenced this "cock-up" which I was officially looking into as "an adverse event."

Whilst arrangements were made to transport the crew back to Plumstead, and a senior officer ordered into the station to oversee the taking of formal statements, my own investigations ran parallel to the police accident investigation. The Brigade photographer was ordered to record the scene and I sought possible witnesses. No one seemed to have actually seen what caused the engine to turn over but plenty commented on the aftermath. The investigation became complicated with the possibility of a brake failure. The fire engine was impounded and removed, as were the vehicle logbook and its workshop maintenance records. Brake failure proved not to be the cause, but only after a forensic examination of the badly damaged engine at the Brigade's Lambeth, vehicle workshops undertaken jointly by the Brigade's senior vehicle examiner and the police accident investigator. There was much report writing and a considerable hoo-hah from our vehicle driver, who having been suspended from driving duties promptly went sick with stress, still insisting on his brake failure story. The results of the police investigation told another story however, one that was mirrored by my own conclusions, based on the evidence. The driver was going too fast for the road conditions even allowing for the fact he was responding to an emergency call. No formal action was taken by the police against the driver who eventually returned to work but refused to drive fire engines anymore. That turned into a saga itself, in the Industrial Relations arena, before he was finally removed from the approved list of Brigade drivers, reverting to ordinary firemen duties. Darky retired soon after and the Brigade lost another one of its more notable personalities.

Accidents to personnel were all too common but one off-duty mishap had almost fatal consequences for a fireman from Greenwich fire station whilst working at his part-time job. Responding to "Code 1" on a pager meant an ordering to an operational incident, maybe a make-up fire or a major incident, but not this time. Contacting the mobilising control for details I was told to attend Greenwich Hospital's Accident and Emergency department after I had spoken with my Area Commander as a matter of urgency! This was out of the ordinary but the control officer could offer no further information other than what he had just told me.

"Pike Sir", I stated as I was put through to the Commander who was clearly expecting my call. "An off-duty fireman has just been admitted to Greenwich A&E," he said. "He is undergoing major heart surgery as we speak. He is in a critical condition. His wife is on the way to the hospital now. Stay with her and do what you can. Ring me when you get more information." With that he hung up. I sped my way through Lewisham and on to Greenwich District Hospital uncertain as to who, or what, I might find. My officer's uniform looked similar to that of a policeman. Only a closer inspection of the cap badge would tell the uninformed observer that I was actually a fire officer, not a police officer but this did have certain advantages. This was one such occasion.

After a brief exchange with the A & E receptionist, who assumed I was a police officer investigating the accident, I was pointed in the right direction. The ashen-faced figure of an off-duty fireman, also from Greenwich, told me who to aim for. He had accompanied his friend in the ambulance whilst the crewman tried desperately to keep his chum alive. The wife had yet to arrive and his presence would make my task that much easier. He was still clearly in shock and after I explained why I was there he related his story.

The pair had been laying slabs in a private garden where they were working. His friend, using an electric angle grinder, cut the slabs to size before they were laid. For whatever reason, he used the grinder without its protective guard and the cutting disc (the size of a dinner plate) caught in a slab and jammed. In trying to free the blade the grinder kicked back and the spinning cutting disc struck the unfortunate man full in the chest. The spinning disc, moving at over one thousand revolutions per minute, cut through his mate's rib cage like a hot knife through butter. Before the unfortunate man could release his finger from the trigger grip the disc continued its destructive path, carving its way into his chest cavity before striking his heart and cutting it open. In an instinctive reaction he finally threw the grinder away from himself before collapsing, bleeding profusely. All this happened in a matter of seconds. Without the prompt intervention of his friend he would have died within minutes.

Applying direct pressure to the man's open chest wound, unaware of the damage done within, he shouted for help. Waiting for the ambulance seemed an eternity as he tried to stem the flow of blood whilst his friend lapsed in and out of consciousness. Now a team of heart surgeons were trying to save the man's life and his chances of survival were not looking good.

The staff car, that the Area Commander had dispatched to collect the injured man's wife, arrived. The young wife was clearly fearing the worst when she saw me waiting to greet her and to offer what little comfort I could. That I was able to tell her husband was still alive, and that the doctors were trying to save his life, gave her a glimmer of hope and some slight colour returned to her pallid and waxen face, which would have been very pretty in differing circumstances.

Shown into a private waiting area all we could do was wait. Each hour passed painfully slowly. Throughout the small talk and numerous cups of tea and coffee the anxious wife steadfastly clung to the belief that her man would pull through. Finally, a concerned looking surgeon walked through the door to tell her that the repair to her husband's heart had been successful. "You have an incredibly fortunate husband, another eighth of an inch and he would have died where he was. The prompt action by your husband's friend no doubt helped save his life." For the first time, since her arrival at the hospital, tears filled her eyes and crying she fell into the arms of her husband's friend. Consoling her, as tears of relief ran down his own face, he thanked the surgeon who was waiting to say that the husband was not out of the woods yet and that the next twenty-four hours would be critical. Leaving the pair in the hands of the medical team I briefed the Area Commander whilst they went to see the patient who was now in intensive care.

Arrangements were made to collect the wife daily to see her husband for the duration of his stay. He did return to full duties after a lengthy period of convalescence. His wife, who had not experienced any earlier contact with fire brigade officers other than meeting some of her husband's watch, was genuinely moved and grateful for the constant support that the Area Commander had ensured was made available to her. The same could not be said for her husband, however.

Back on their watch at Greenwich there was a marked contrast in the attitude of the two, the injured man and his friend. One acknowledged and remained genuinely grateful for the rapid and constant level of support that had been extended by the Command's senior officers. The other, who now carried an ugly vertical scar in the middle of chest, gave no such indication or acknowledgement. Suspicious of anyone in management he continued behaving in a cavalier fashion. Anyone foolish enough to use a powerful grinder without its protective guard, was someone who required monitoring. And he was.

Senior Staff!

Between the summer of 1988 and the end of 1989, I was chopping and changing roles. Whilst remaining predominantly in the South East Command I had a brief spell back at Brigade Headquarters. I was spending more time in the higher, albeit temporary, rank of a DO1 than my own. Stepping into the shoes of Peter Jones and emulating his standards was out of the question. I could never match his intellectual ability or managerial skills. It was an impossible task and I did not even try to compete. He had a highly developed ability to think, reason and understand at a level well above his pay grade. I was not stupid but if we had both been studying for a degree Peter would have walked away with a First Class Honours whilst I would have struggled to secure my ordinary pass.

Running the Operations Group was an interesting and valuable learning experience, frequently a demanding one too. I was happy being my own man and bringing my own talents to the role. However, the early morning (8.00am) telephone briefing with the Area Commander would occasionally have me scratching my head thinking, "How the hell did he know about that?" It was his custom not to arrive at the office until around 10.30am but he touched base every morning to see what was happening. Trying to anticipate the Area Commander's in-depth telephone questioning, occasionally an interrogation, of the events of the previous night (even those outside my sphere of influence) showed me how closely he monitored the Command's pulse let alone the effectiveness of his private, informal, widespread network of informers! It seemed I was expected to know it all. Sadly some of my own peer group, with their own selfish agendas, did not always choose to share this vital information, especially, if it could be seen to undermine my ability. This fact was not lost on the Area Commander, given his Command headquarters informants. I rapidly rose to the challenge.

The arrival of a transferred DO1 from Brigade Headquarters brought my six-month term of office to an end. Expecting to return to the Operations Group and my seven Greenwich borough fire stations I found myself with a new role; the Commander's senior staff officer. Whilst my organisational abilities were appreciated, including managing the Operations Group, it was considered I could appear a little too ambitious and needed to be reined in. The reining in, it seemed to me, meant I was no more than a "gofer" for the four members of the principal management board. One of my early lessons was getting to grips with the Commander's newly installed traffic lights system that governed access to his office, or inner sanctum as he like to refer to it. Red, amber and green lights had been installed above and outside his office door. Red meant; can't come in. Amber was; "get ready to come in," whilst green meant; "get in here quick."

Woe betide anyone who jumped those lights! When the first of the two latest brain waves of the recently appointed new Chief Officer, Gerry Clarkson, landed in the Commander's in-tray. I was once again let off the leash.

The Chief Officer was now flexing his considerable muscle having been in post for some little while. He was looking to extend his empire and it appeared that he had the London Ambulance Service, or at least part of it, in his sights. He was seeking to introduce Emergency Medical Technicians (EMT's) into the Brigade, more widely referred to as paramedics. Even he considered himself to be an impatient man once stating he wanted, "To see us set and achieve new standards and objectives almost overnight." So why spoil a "good" idea for the sake of some preparatory research! Having already set out his stall in the pages of the in-house magazine the Chief's belated request to conduct a feasibility study landed on my Area Commanders desk and it swiftly found its way to mine.

Anything that enhanced the first aid capability of fire crews got my vote. I had first-hand experience of trying to deliver, and maintain, the basic level of first aid training in the Command. Then the Chief (for reasons that were never fully explained) had pulled the plug on the refresher programme, which despite its rocky start was, without a doubt, one of the most important training initiatives to hit fire stations in over a decade. His brainchild now was to improve the level of emergency medical first aid in the Brigade along the lines of those operated by many European and American fires services. Personally I thought he had been watching too many American television action drama programmes. Some of these had popularised and even promoted the growth of the paramedic service in their major city fire departments.

The type of paramedics the Chief had in his mind originated in the USA. They had started with just six paramedic teams, in three separate pilot studies, in differing locations within two of the fifty States. They were not even termed paramedics then; that evolved later when a US television series, called *"Emergency"*, brought these new highly skilled and innovative band of medical first responders and rescuers to the public's attention in the early 1970s.

An American fire service Battalion Chief, James O. Page, is credited with pioneering the paramedic programme and seeing its expansion into almost all of the State's full-time fire departments. Initially there was a considerable variation in the quality and range of training which these fire brigade based emergency medical technicians received. It was set by what local hospital managers thought was needed and what the City or County could afford. This resulted in tremendous provincial differences. Instruction ranged from little more than enhanced first aid courses, to on the job trauma training, leading eventually, to a nursing (paramedic) university level qualification.

Rationalisation came in the early 1980s with many counties passing laws to protect the title of paramedic (or its local equivalent) from use by anyone except those qualified and experienced to a defined standard. With the spread of this concept to Canada and parts of continental Europe the practitioners of this accident and trauma treatment were, almost universally, following a system of learning accredited by their own countries' medical authorities.

There were no emergency service paramedics operating within London in that winter of 1988. (The first qualified rapid response paramedics would not arrive in London until 1991 when they were introduced riding powerful motor bikes.) The London Ambulance Service (LAS) remained the capital's primary source of emergency medical first aid at any incident. If it were required, the additional support and backup of an emergency medical team could be dispatched from the nearest hospital's Accident and Emergency department. Some emergency ambulance staff were trained, and qualified, to a higher level than the ordinary emergency ambulance crew; the LAS's equivalent of an "emergency medical technician," although there was no formal recognition of this role by the other emergency services.

Whatever was in the Chief's mind he did not share it with me. I had travelled to the States, on holiday, and seen at first hand paramedic units in action. I had also visited some of their crews and seen their ambulances and rescue units at local fire stations. There was no easy like for like comparison between the US fire departments and UK fire brigades in respect of providing emergency medical services. Funding arrangements and organisational responsibilities differ both for UK fire brigades and Ambulance services in respect of emergency medical services from their American counterparts. Certainly in the States that I visited the paramedic units were comprehensively equipped and their crews, although members of the fire department, predominately rode only those units. Some of these were essentially an emergency ambulance, whilst others were rescue vehicles carrying specialist rescue equipment but both were crewed by paramedics (EMTs). Highly trained in their specialist role, the paramedics had nevertheless undergone fire department basic training and in most cases had operational experience riding with an Engine Company, Ladder Company or Rescue Company before training and transferring as a paramedic. They retained their firefighter status although undertaking this specialised paramedic role.

Despite the extremely tight deadline imposed on my enquiries into the issues of introducing EMTs into the Brigade I required pertinent information if my conclusions were to have any credence. This required getting details from the horse's mouth and since I was not gifted in European languages, it meant contacting my opposite numbers in the United States. Phone calls to Los Angeles, New York and Chicago linked me to officers who could impart first hand experiences and avoid anecdotal evidence that would invalidate my findings. It became immediately clear that paramedic services were costly to implement. Continuation training was another significant factor as was the provision of dedicated paramedic vehicles, either ambulances or small rapid response rescue trucks. Although in some locations, money was saved by paramedic trained firefighters riding with Engine Companies and their "pumper" carried advanced life saving equipment such as a defibrillator.

Making contact with the London Ambulance Service was far more problematic than contacting fire departments in the States. The LAS Headquarters was only a few miles away in Waterloo Road, near Waterloo Bridge, but industrial unease was beginning to build within its service. The idea of the Brigade usurping its existing emergency technician role, however limited, had not gone down well with ambulance crews after our Chief Officer went public. (LAS ambulance crews would join the national ambulance strike, over pay and conditions, the following year. It would last six months, ending in March 1990, when an improved pay deal was finally accepted.) Formal contact seemed unwise, but I knew the Station Manager from the local ambulance station near Brixton fire station who was now an LAS Training Officer and was based at their headquarters. He agreed to meet me, unofficially, and proved to be a most helpful source of information. He detailed the range of training that LAS crews underwent and the logistics involved in assessing and providing coverage for their EMTs on a London wide basis.

The Chief was being overly ambitious in his desire to bring in a system of improved emergency first aid based on the American system, or European for that matter. The simple fact was that neither the Fire Authority nor he as Chief Officer had statutory authority to implement such a scheme. Without that authority, the necessary funding for paramedic (EMT) training and the provision of dedicated vehicles could not be considered legitimate. Authority and duties were granted, imposed and contained through the then Fire Services Act (1947). Whilst the Act gave discretionary powers with regard to equipping and attending special services, a quasi-emergency ambulance service manned by firefighters operating from fire stations was, in the unofficial opinion of one of the Brigade's legal team, pushing our luck too far.

The report completed and handed to the Area Commander he questioned me thoroughly and often in an aggressive manner. (Mimicking the questioning that he might well receive from the Chief when he presented "his" findings.) The report was sent to the Chief Officer and no further mention of the introduction of EMTs or paramedics came down from on high.

Just before Christmas that year, on the 12th December 1988, the Clapham rail crash occurred. Thirty-five people died and five hundred were injured, of which nearly one hundred were seriously hurt, making the crash one of the worst in recent times. Declared a major incident, all the emergency services – but especially the brigade and the LAS – worked side by side and in harmony in difficult and daunting conditions to rescue and recover the trapped and injured. Some of the less fortunate passengers had to be operated on, by medical teams, in-situ before they could be released. The Brigade and LAS attending that incident brought their respective skills to bear. The success of such close co-operation (and which was replicated at many other less high publicised incidents) made me think that the Chief's proposals were an unwarranted duplication of service provision, already available to Londoners.

(The London Ambulance Service would go to expand their paramedic core. With all UK paramedics later classified as ambulance practitioners able to achieve and maintain strict standards of clinical care, including the administering of certain drugs, the first LAS (Level one) qualification was introduced in 1996.)

It seemed as the "paramedic" door closed another one opened and this had "Annual Review" written on it. In October that year Brigade Headquarters had hosted an Open Day, which was the Chief's cover story for holding a drill display. Attended by the Home Secretary, the Rt Hon Douglas Hurd, it was a demonstration of fire brigade skills before an invited audience from the Federation of World Volunteer Firefighters and headquarters staff and their families.

I had been actively involved in putting some aspects of that day together which showed the progress of the London Fire Brigade from the Victorian streets of London to a fire scene from the 1970s and up to the present day. The display involved both on and off duty volunteers plus members of the Fire Brigade Society; the band of the Army's Blues & Royals, who set the tone for the proceedings with a selection of well-known tunes.

My exposure to this event was literal and there for all to see. In a dramatic 1970s fire scene, involving a gas blast in a block of flats, a volunteer was required to be the "live" casualty. A hook ladder crew had to rescue this individual then lower him, by line, from the sixth floor of the drill tower. I volunteered to be the casualty. Wearing jeans, a shirt and trainers I gave an Oscar winning performance as I sought urgent help from my rescuers. Placed in the loops of the lowering line and suspended sixty feet above the ground the crew took my weight before lowering me down the outside of the drill tower. As I hung, suspended, from the sixth-floor window the line tightened around my knees and my chest. It had the undesirable effect of pulling my shirt up and my jeans down. For the whole sixty feet down the audience were treated to my exposed posterior! They seemed to find my embarrassing predicament highly amusing. But bare buttocks aside, the whole afternoon was deemed to be a considerable success and the Chief wanted more.

Summoned once again to the Area Commander's comfortably appointed office, with its deep pile carpet and large illuminated tropical fish tank, I was told of the Chief's intention to reinstate the Brigade's Annual Review. It was to be held over a weekend during the summer of 1989. One day was to be set aside for the general public whilst the other would cater for members of the Brigade and their families. Sitting contentedly behind his wide desk the Commander told me that the Chief had designated him the Review's Arena Master. (I had no idea what he meant either?) It was my job to make it all happen. Working from Lewisham and Brigade Headquarters I would link up with the Press and Public

Relations Division who would control the funding for the event. So much for being reined in I thought, whilst secretly relishing the task ahead.

By the spring of 1989 much progress had been made. However, sadly, the Annual Reviews did not come to pass. The combined effort of all those involved in the planning had secured all the necessary volunteers, plus undertakings from outside agencies to give their active support, such as the ambulance service and the police. The stumbling block was securing the attendance of on-duty personnel and appliances to the event. The operational personnel themselves were quite willing to participate; they had done so for the Open Day. It was the Fire Brigades Union who influenced the Fire Authority to put the brakes on and that put the final nail in the coffin of the Chief's plans to bring back the reviews. The Union executive, despite lengthy negotiations, had refused to co-operate and without their active support it would have been difficult, if not impossible, to deliver the review. The Chief was extremely pragmatic about it all and anyway, he had plenty of other irons in the fire. He preferred not to get into a dispute with the Fire Brigades Union over this particular issue. I would, however, deliver a review, two in fact, but not just yet.

Matters Maritime

The honour of dining in the Painted Hall at the Royal Naval College in Greenwich was one of the privileges bestowed on the South East Area Commander by the College. The occasion, this time, was the "dining out" of the Brigade's retiring deputy Chief Officer. The Painted Hall remains, in my humble opinion, one of the finest dining halls in the western world, not that I have eaten in any of the others! Fortunately that is also an opinion shared by those that actually know about such things. The dining room was part of the Court of King William of Orange. The sumptuous wall and ceiling paintings are by James Thornhill and took him some nineteen years to complete.

The Royal Naval College's origins were the Naval equivalent of the Army's Royal Hospital at Chelsea, as a refuge for injured and disabled sailors, originally provided for under the patronage of Queen Mary II around 1690. The Royal Naval College survives today, more or less, as originally planned by Sir Christopher Wren. The painted hall was the venue for the lying-in state of this nation's most revered sailor, Admiral Lord Nelson after his death at Trafalgar in October 1805. His body was later taken up river by Royal barge to be interred in the crypt of St Paul's Cathedral.

Now senior officers from the South East Command and other principal fire officers gathered in this hallowed hall for a feast. It was a fine feast too and in such a magnificent setting. The College kitchens and its chefs were famed for their fine food and culinary expertise. Whilst it may not have met the extraordinary standards of previous banquets (no stuffed swan or suckling pigs) it was certainly a meal befitting the majesty of our setting. Silver dishes came and went as the College waiters scurried to and fro from the adjoining kitchens. For nearly two hours I was immersed in the sense of history that this hall engendered as I joined my fellow officers around the tables on the main dining floor. Naturally, the principal guests, on the top table, surveyed the scene from their elevated position on the stage of the painted hall.

To the clatter of knives and forks, the clinking of elegant table glass and with the rustle of crisp napkins in the background, I could not help but be absorbed in a military tradition that had spanned the centuries within this very room; the formal Mess dinner. Along our tables, candles in elegant candelabra, cast their shadows and filled the hall with a surreal light that brought life to the lavish works of art hanging on the walls and the painted ceiling, which had given the room its name.

There was no formal Command Mess Club then; that would come later, but even so there were certain conventions and rules for evenings such as these. One was the price tag that was put on the evening. It covered the cost of the guest of honour's meal, his drink for the evening and a retirement gift. The cost also covered the Area Commander's meal and his drink. (Although he always denied it!) He also set the dining "rules" and controlled the seating plan. The pecking order was rank related; the higher your rank the nearer you sat to the top table. But where you sat within your peer group was subject to his current whims and fancies. (This was not a unique trait as I was later to discover when dealing with Chief Officers.) But for tonight it was an auspicious occasion that turned into an incredible evening and a treasured memory linking the finest Naval traditions with that of the Brigade's in our all male enclave. (Ladies were not invited for the simple reason that, then, there were no female senior fire officers.)

Zeebrugge – Herald of Free Enterprise

As a young recruit I learned about radio telephony (RT) procedures from our instructor, an ancient and weathered looking riverside Station Officer. He had served during the blitz, and was at the time not much older than ourselves and related a story demonstrating the importance of effective communications. It was based on a fictional cock-up in the First World War's British trenches. Young soldiers were used as "runners" and they had to pass messages to and fro between the front line and the staff officers located, safely, behind the front line. These young men occasionally had to pass the message from one to another before the last man could relay the message to its intended destination. On this particular day, an officer in the front-line trenches gave his runner an urgent dispatch; "Send reinforcements, I am going to advance," and urged him on his way. The message was passed, under heavy enemy fire, from runner to runner until the last man stood panting before the General. "Come on man spit it out," said the general. "Yes sir. The message is; send three and four pence I am going to a dance."

Sitting in the RT classroom that day, which was a specially adapted room, where we recruits sat in front of small individual booths equipped with headphones and a two-way radio (similar to those found on the Brigade's appliances) the instructor wanted to reinforce this amusing anecdote. Writing down a short message on a message pad he showed it to the first recruit before telling him to remember it then whisper the message to the man next to him. The second student then repeated the message to the third man, and so on until the message reached the last person who had to write down the message as told to him. I was somewhere in the middle of the line and felt sure that I passed on the message exactly as I was given. But when the first and last message were compared, the last message bore very little resemblance to the original!

For the avoidance of doubt therefore it was standard operational practice for all fireground messages to be written down, then repeated back to the originating officer before it was sent by RT to the control room. Not doing so could lead to confusion. An imprecise message would either give a wrong impression of an incident, or worse, an inappropriate response to any assistance that had been requested.

An urgent message was received in the Brigade's Operations Room on the evening of 6 March 1987, sent by the Maritime rescue services responding to a disaster in the English Channel. It was a request for the use of the Brigade's thermal imaging cameras. Now the basic principle of only doing exactly what you were asked to do was forgotten for some inexplicable reason.

The cross-channel ferry *Herald of Free Enterprise* had capsized shortly after leaving the port of Zeebrugge. The roll-on, roll-off car and passenger ship, operated by Townsend-Thoresen, was heading for Dover when a fatal error allowed water to pour into the car deck via an open bow door. In ninety seconds the eighty crew and four hundred and fifty-nine passengers found themselves in a ship that was on her side, half submerged in shallow water one kilometre from the Belgian coastline. Many were trapped inside the ship and one hundred and ninety-three passengers and crew would die as they succumbed to hypothermia in the freezing waters of the English Channel. With an international rescue operation in full swing, involving the Royal Navy, RAF Search and Rescue Crews, the British, French and Belgian Coastguard, and Dutch salvage specialists, a call for assistance was made to the Brigade's Operations Room at Lambeth from the Rescue co-ordinators. They requested the Brigade's thermal imaging cameras in the belief that the heat seeking properties of the cameras would assist in the recovery of live casualties, both trapped in the ship and adrift in the cold water. How this simple request got misinterpreted or grew into something else was never made public. But rather than do what was asked of us, to gather the equipment and transport it by the fastest means possible to the RAF station at Manston and then onward to the rescue crews at the scene, the request took on a life of its own.

I was the duty Divisional Officer and was at home when I received an urgent telephone call from the Command staff Station Officer telling me, "A ferry has capsized in the Channel involving hundreds of casualties and the British/French rescue team have requested the Brigade's thermal imaging cameras and our assistance at the scene of the operations." I could not believe what I was being told and asked, "Are you really sure about all this? Who set this up?" I was told that the Operations Room duty officer was liaising with the RAF and that Operations Room were making arrangements for four cameras to be transported to Lewisham. I was to co-ordinate the movement of the equipment to its delivery point. I was also to secure two additional cameras, making six in total, so that they could be forwarded to the scene of the rescue. Dressing and heading into Lewisham at considerable speed, I listened to this breaking news story on my car radio whilst having doubts about just what the Brigade could possibly do, other than provide the requested equipment. I covered the eight miles to Lewisham in record time.

I discovered that in addition to myself, the Area Commander, who had also been informed of the "urgent" request, had ordered in a further Divisional Officer and the duty ADO to Lewisham. (It was a well-known adage in the Brigade that if you had a problem throw a senior officer at it, the bigger the problem – then throw more!) One camera had already been removed from Lewisham's emergency tender and the other taken from the SE Forward Command Unit. We had the requested six thermal imaging cameras, ready and waiting.

Whilst the combined efforts of the rescuers at the scene were battling to save lives and rescue trapped casualties from the stricken ship, in the dark ice-cold water and in the most difficult, daunting and dangerous of circumstances, a separate and quite unnecessary rescue mission was unfolding within the Brigade. It was gathering apace at Lewisham. Despite my doubts about the effectiveness of our TICs in these particular circumstances (and the fact that we carried no underwater diving equipment whatsoever) I was tasked with putting together a list of possible equipment that could be taken, as well as the requested cameras. This was managed with the able, and genuine, assistance of the Staff Station Officer, the officer in charge of Lewisham's emergency tender with additional input from my fellow senior officers. The list was compiled and considered by the Operations Room duty officer and agreed. A decision was taken by the South East Area Commander (who was at home in the company of a bottle of scotch) that the whole emergency tender crew; the Forward Command Unit and its crew; myself, and the other two senior officers should take themselves, and the ad-hoc equipment, plus the all-important requested thermal imaging cameras to RAF Manston, located on the Kentish coastline near Dover. Our gallant band of would be rescuers had been joined by the Brigade's duty Deputy Assistant Chief Officer (DACO) who had been tasked by someone, even higher in rank, to lead this un-requested and unnecessary task force.

It was the longest shout I had ever driven on. For over sixty miles, from Lewisham to RAF Manston, our convoy of five vehicles comprising senior officers' cars led by the Forward Command Range Rover carried men and equipment through south east London's almost deserted streets and on into the Kent countryside. We passed quickly through towns and villages as our two-tone horns and blue flashing lights cleared a path as we sped past what little traffic there was on the road.

The organisation of the RAF was truly impressive. Waved though the guarded entrance gate of RAF Manston we were escorted to an enormous waiting Hercules aircraft with its loading bay doors wide open and its loading ramp run-out, we looked into its spacious interior. With the four thundering propeller engines already running, the crew were eagerly waiting to take off. Also waiting there on the runway, standing by his car, was the South East Area Commander. His driver was sitting impassively behind the steering wheel. We carried the equipment into the noisy aircraft under the watchful gaze of the RAF flight sergeant who was the loadmaster. Then, whilst we parked our vehicles in the adjacent parking area, the DACO went off to speak to the Area Commander. The DACO was clearly a diplomat, he convinced the Area Commander to stay put. It was not his place to lead this group. (A group that had never been requested in the first place.)

Finally, with the Area the Commander looking on, and the throbbing of the powerful engines filling our ears we took off, as we sat pensively in the Hercules' cavernous hold. Quickly passing over the English coastline I knew that somewhere beneath us a real-life drama was being played out. I hoped that lives were being saved by the professionalism, skill and training of those undertaking the rescues. We neither had the necessary equipment nor the right clothing (not to mention the training) to add any value to those gallant and Herculean rescue efforts. In fact we were so far out of our comfort zone that I considered our presence could only be a hindrance rather than a help!

Clearly the rescue co-ordinators must have thought so too, because once we landed on a remote military airstrip, somewhere near the Belgian coastline, that is exactly where we stayed. The cameras were never even collected, let alone used. They sat there, in their boxes, keeping us company as we waited, hour after hour, until finally the following day we were flown back to Manston. I drove back to London with three despondent crew members from Lewisham's emergency tender for company.

Our feeble, yet well-intended efforts, paled in significance when compared to the heroic actions of so many involved and caught up in the Herald of Free Enterprise disaster. Five of the ship's own crew were awarded national gallantry medals. Michael Ian Skippen, the ship's headwaiter, was posthumously awarded the George Medal (Britain's second highest civilian bravery award after the George Cross) for his outstanding courage and heroism at the cost of his own life. A passenger, Andrew Clifford Parker, was also awarded the George Medal for the actions he took with total disregard for his own safety. Eight members of the international rescue team at the scene were also recognised by Her Majesty the Queen for their extreme heroism, two from the Belgian Navy, four from the Royal Navy and two civilian divers from the Tijdelijke salvage tug company.

A sad footnote to this tale was to be found in the lists of those known or believed to be among victims of the disaster. In the days that followed all the victims were either recovered from the water or removed from inside the part submerged ferry. Three members of the brigade, two leading firemen and a fireman, were known to have travelled on the ferry and remained unaccounted for. The fireman was Stephen Smith from the South East Command. Barney Franklin, my immediate boss in South East Training, spoke fluent French and was given the unenviable task of travelling to the disaster's temporary mortuary to identify the body. Not knowing Smith personally, and utilising a brigade photograph taken from records, he had to move from victim to victim until he had a match. He found this duty imposed upon him harrowing and when relating this story to me upon his return tears filled his eyes and he wished, very sincerely, that he would never, ever, have to perform such a similar undertaking again.

Ship and Ports

Of all the courses that the Fire Service College (FSC) ran at its extensive, and unique, training facilities in Gloucestershire, one of the most physically demanding and stimulating was the Ship and Ports Firefighting course. The College provided a range of first-class programmes to ensure that both junior and senior officers were afforded the skills they needed to protect the public. The FSC played a key role in the provision of learning and development for fire service personnel throughout the UK and from abroad. The levels of realism achieved were, and remain, impressive.

Having previously attended a range of development and specialist courses at the College, I was familiar with its vastly improved student facilities, which included individual bedrooms in modern accommodation blocks. Each block had a laundry and limited kitchen amenities that had replaced the former dire lodgings of the old RAF station, which were all the facilities that the then Fire Service Technical College could offer. But a radical and innovative building programme swept all that away and the College reinvented itself into a world class Fire Service College. The only reminder of its former RAF function was the wide runways that now gave access to purpose built commercial and industrial "real fire" training buildings and installations strategically placed along its route. It was, in the mid-eighties, state of the art stuff. Even part of one of the two runways had been converted into an extensive wide section of modern motorway. Here fire crews would respond to multi vehicle accidents and incidents, carefully devised and set up by the course staff that accurately replicated the real thing. In fact many of the scenarios were so realistic that for a number of students these incidents would be amongst some of the most serious incidents they were likely to confront.

That could be said of me too because in that summer of 1987 I returned to the College to experience, at first hand, the rigours of fighting a ship fire. Even if it was constructed from concrete and was located miles from the nearest sea!

The *"Sir Henry"* was another of the College's full-scale purpose-built real fire training facilities. This large concrete ship, complete with engine room, a forward and aft hold, full size bridge and crew accommodation stood four-storeys high. Although square in shape (the pointy bit at the front and the roundy bit at the back looking as though they had been sliced off by a giant knife!) it still covered an area 60-foot-long and 40-foot-wide. On one side of *Sir Henry* stood a full-size replica quayside complete with warehouses whilst on the other side of the ship was an open water area, simulating a dock. Access to the ship, on this side, was afforded only by a small boat and then a climbing up a gangway ladder that led to the ship's upper decks.

Our course was made up of twenty students, either ADOs or DOs, from different Brigades around the country. I was one of three London officers and none of us had ever attended a real ship fire. (I did not think that going to one on a canteen van counted and was too embarrassed to mention it anyway.) Many of my fellow officers had however practical experience of ship fires. One covered the Port of Bristol, others the once great shipyards of Newcastle and the Tyne or Liverpool's docks and Southampton's container port. Their consensus view was stated simply but powerfully during our introductory session with the course director (himself a DO) and his three junior course staff. It was summed up by a small but wiry "Scouse" ADO who acted as spokesman and said, "A serious ship fire places extreme physical and mental strain on crews that are required to work in the most adverse of conditions. Frequently the build-up of heat, combined with high humidity, pushes the BA firefighters' tolerance levels to their limit when they suddenly find themselves in surroundings that are hard to replicate operationally anywhere else."

Even if *Sir Henry* was just a concrete replica ship, we were all too soon to discover just how accurate his description was and two of our number would be pushed beyond their limits of endurance. But on day one of this three-week course the Course Director satisfied himself by outlining the course. With a combination of practical and theoretical input we would, hopefully, at the end of the course be able to demonstrate a sound working knowledge of ship construction and the implications that has on firefighting and rescue operations. We should also be able to recognise; "the key information required to maintain safe working conditions on and around a vessel and, finally, recognise the level of resource requirements to support the successful resolution of a ship-board fire incident." Which basically means how to put out an on-board fire.

Exposed to a wealth of maritime experts, who comprehensively covered their individual topics, some overly so, we became versed in the varied aspects of detecting and containing fires on vessels, utilising a wide range of on-board detection and suppression systems. Ship stability was covered at some length by more than one speaker. Clearly, they were concerned that when a fire brigade attends a serious ship blaze thousands of gallons of water (now measured in litres) can be poured into a burning ship every minute. As if to emphasise the point one speaker reminded us that the aim was, when a ship fire is in harbour or a port, to extinguish the blaze and not actually sink the ship in the process.

This was very much a hands-on course, starting at the College's Olympic sized swimming pool. Lifejacket drill had us wearing full fire gear. I had experienced, at first hand, the folly of trying to take to the water wearing boots and leggings when as a young fireman I had run into the Thames. Add the weight of a sodden fire tunic to the equation and the likelihood of keeping your head above water for any length of time in deep water would challenge even the strongest of swimmers. We would never have made a synchronised swimming team as we first jumped in to the deep end of the pool and then floated around aimlessly supported by our flotation devices. But the point was well made; do not go on to the water unless you or your crews are wearing a lifejacket, especially when wearing a BA set.

The course content included both ship fire simulations and visits to specialist sites. These visits included port areas, merchant and Royal Navy ships; all contained in the courses remit. Real-fire exercises were carried out in-house and this was something that the College had become very good at, sometimes too good. Within the College's considerable workforce was a civilian team called fireground staff. It was their job to set the fires in the real fire training buildings, in our case *Sir Henry*. It was an arsonist's dream! Large robust metal cribs would be filled to the brim with timber or sometimes just stacks of timber pallets and, on cue, ignited within the various training buildings. The internal temperatures could be increased still further by electric or gas fired heaters. Smoke was added by a combination of chemical smoke canisters or smoke generators. Naturally, crew safety was a vital ingredient in all practical drills and powerful extractor fans could rapidly remove the smoke in an emergency. Plus there were course staff designated as safety officers and wearing breathing apparatus within each "fired" building. That said the conditions were very realistic and although the amount of heat was monitored it nevertheless could, and did, reach very high levels and for some (the less experienced or less physically fit) these temperatures took their toll. The combination of physical exertion and the effects of heat exhaustion affected some more than others. Occasionally individuals would, and did, succumb in these energy draining conditions

The *Sir Henry* was the focus of all our operational exercises. We would lead or be led in the five "real fire" ship incidents that were intended to confirm, or otherwise, our understanding of the earlier theory. These exercises had us performing the respective roles of the officer commanding an appliance crew, the officer in charge of the first attendance or the officer in charge of the incident; when we were not any of the above, we formed the fireground crews. Only five of our number would get to be an "incident commander." This was something that was generally par for all practical courses at the College. With normally, twenty students per course the time allocated could not cater for twenty separate exercises.

It was from the post-exercise debriefs that important lessons were learnt which could benefit us all if we were ever an incident commander for real. With a rueful smile there was one other "role play rule" which the Course Director had to explain, "You can make pumps whatever you f****** like, eight, ten or more, but you will only get the four fire engines turning up that you lot ride!"

Even the nominated Incident Commander had to walk, the short distance, from the exercise assembly point to the incident when he was ordered on to take charge.

We fought engine room fires, an accommodation blaze, a fire in a hold and undertook a waterborne assault. On each occasion the "fireground" staff lived up to their reputation of putting realism into these exercises. The internal temperatures rose rapidly within the enclosed confines of Sir Henry as these legalised pyromaniacs honed their craft to perfection. Without the protection of a breathing apparatus set the combination of the heat and the smoke made penetration into the ship's interior impossible. For two of our course's more elderly attendees the real fire conditions, and the strenuous effort required of them, proved too much. One collapsed coming out of the ship and the other was brought to safety by the course "safety crew" monitoring our progress inside the ship. The safety crew had to wear anti-flash hoods and gloves to afford some additional protection from the punishing conditions. During those three weeks it was for many, including me, as real as it gets.

Course staff took on the role of the Master of the vessel, the First Officer or Harbour Master, or whoever else was considered appropriate. From these officials the officer in charge of the first attendance or the Incident Commander had to elicit important information. By asking the right questions fire brigade officers could get a grasp of the situation, including actions already taken. As the exercise scenarios progressed so did our understanding of ship incidents, increasing our skills and knowledge. Concepts that were taught and discussed in the lecture room were applied in practice as we at least improved, if not actually perfecting, our ability to tackle fires in ships and vessels.

This understanding was greatly enhanced by one particular, instructive, guest speaker prior to our three site visits. He was an experienced First Officer serving in one of the more prestigious cruise line companies. In setting out his responsibilities regarding the safety and security of a ship, he explained that he acted for the Captain (who remains at all times in sole in command of the vessel). The first officer's safety duties included both firefighting and damage control. He was the "scene" leader and would report via radio or intercom to the ship's Captain who, normally, would remain on the bridge. From here the Captain would co-ordinate operations. The first officer (or Chief Mate on merchant ships) has special responsibilities to keep the ship, and its people on board, safe. This includes keeping the ship seaworthy during a fire and monitoring its stability. Understanding the ship's stability and trim is key to keeping the ship seaworthy. Explaining that in the UK and North America first officers (and Chief Mates) must be licensed, he explained that it is also usual in the UK for the first officer or chief mate to hold a Master's Ticket so that he or she can take over from the master if necessary.

Using a visual presentation he explained the various types of fire suppression and detection systems commonly found both on cruise and merchant shipping. (Many of the systems were similar, if not identical, to their land-based counterparts to be frequently found in commercial and industrial premises.) Yet despite their sophistication our speaker casually remarked that the best defence remains, "Planning for possibilities." Both Halon gas injection and high mist water systems are among the tools in the Captain's armoury to combat fire (dependent of the nature of the risk it had to cover), but water remained a universally applied medium. Stressing it was important, within the pre-planning process, to estimate the amount of water needed for a given fire scenario and its potential effect on the vessel's stability, you plan to "dewater" preferably concurrent with the firefighting operations. Firefighting on board ship must take account of the potentially destabilising effect of the very water used in an attempt to extinguish the fire. The timely use of drains and scuppers, fixed and portable pumps or ejectors to direct the excess flow either overboard or to the lowest point in the ship was essential. Water placed high in a vessel and contained can cause the vessel to list to one side or the other. For every degree of list the greater the effect the weight of water places on the trim of the vessel. Unless it can be effectively removed it can have a most detrimental effect on the vessels stability and the ability to douse or extinguish a serious blaze.

Naturally, at sea a severe list can have disastrous consequences. Both the ship and the crew can be placed in extreme danger. Even in harbour a fire brigade's overzealous attack with water on a serious blaze can (and has on occasion) cause the capsizing of a vessel, unless there are concerted efforts to maintain the craft's stability and "dewater" by whatever means possible.

Getting into his stride, with his captive audience listening intently, the knowledgeable and enthusiastic first officer filled the full afternoon session with details of a ship's centre of gravity and the importance of understanding its centre of buoyancy. The effects of wind, and water being introduced into the "'tween" deck spaces, were also covered in detail. None of which we could actually apply to the *Sir Henry* whose concrete mass made it unsinkable no matter how hard we tried to do otherwise. This is more than could be said for the stricken *Empress of Canada*, a large freight and passenger ship that had docked in Liverpool many years earlier. An ultimately very serious fire broke out on this vessel and after vast quantities of water were introduced at high level the ship started to list towards the quayside. It kept on listing. The fire was successfully extinguished, but only because the ill-fated ship capsized into Liverpool dock, fully three quarters submerged.

To enforce our theoretical input a range of special visits were programmed to maritime facilities on the South coast. The first was to the Royal Navy's fire-fighting (and salvage) school at Portsmouth and then to the Southampton Container Terminal.

All RN recruits undergo a basic firefighting course before going to sea. There are more extensive courses for ratings who will be leading crews or maintaining on-board training. Whale Island was a reclaimed shore establishment and home to *HMS Phoenix*, the Navy's firefighting and damage control school. Then located on the nearby Tipner and Horsea Island, it would close in 1993, to be replaced by a new ultra-modern complex on *HMS Excellence*. It was at Phoenix that trainee firefighting crews would learn the skills necessary to both attack a blaze on-board ship and undertake containment by utilising "boundary cooling" and also perform search and rescue. RN ship's firefighting crews are nominated at the start of each watch. On discovery of a fire it is this watch that is responsible for fighting a fire whilst other personnel report to their respective assembly points.

Much of the basic training we saw consisted of exercises in hatch/hold entry and were conducted in a steel firehouse constructed to mimic ship's holds. Their crews' breathing apparatus sets were compressed air and their fire tunics were based on a heavy woollen fabric known as "Fernaught." This material looked as if it provided good protection but also looked bloody hot to work in! It is the ship's fighting team, under the command of a ship's officer that establishes an HQ from which operations are controlled. When RN ships are in port it is to here that a local authority fire officer would be directed to appraise the situation. The duty watch officers would also be available to provide information and services, such as control of ventilation systems and the operation of fire and salvage pumps during firefighting. Our RN training school staff were highly motivated and over a tea break, tales of them riding the Green Goddesses as young sailors (in the first Firemen's national strike) were regaled over a plate of biscuits. I could see at first hand that the Royal Navy's firefighters were of a much higher calibre than the poor young Army squaddies who just pointed their hoses and hoped for the best.

We were the overnight guests of the Royal Navy, staying at *HMS Excellence*. This unique establishment is also the oldest RN onshore training facility. Alongside its many proud and important traditions, it also provided forward looking and progressive training programmes. We were greeted by the officer of the day, a Captain, who made our party immediately feel welcome. Pointing to the carved words on a plaque inside the entrance lobby; "***It is upon the navy under the providence of God that the safety, honour and welfare of this realm do chiefly depend,***" he smiled proudly and said, "We remain the senior service gentlemen." Clearly aware of the early history of the fire service and its strong preference to employing seamen as firemen in Victorian times he continued, "We share some common bonds of heritage, gentlemen, so you should feel at home here." Looking at the grandeur of our accommodation I was not too sure about that.

Naval stewards were waiting to show us to our individual rooms for our overnight stay, which naturally were called cabins. A trip, even by RN staff and trainees, to the local pub was termed, "a run ashore." After a quick freshen up we were all expected in the Officers' Mess for an informal gathering, prior to our evening meal. It was clear within moments of entering the Officers' Mess that the senior service places great emphasis on its officers' ability to act as excellent hosts. With a ratio of almost one-to-one, the uniformed Naval officers, comprising of Lieutenant Commander rank and above were superb ambassadors for the "senior" service. There was clearly a "hosting" element that all RN officers must pass in their training curriculum. With a genuine and sincere friendliness our hosts entertained us whilst showing considerable interest in our particular course and in the fire service generally. Over pink gins and a liberal consumption of similarly proofed beverages, stories were exchanged and a real warmth developed in this uniformed, yet informal, gathering.

At length a Captain announced, "Gentlemen, dinner is served," and our naval escorts politely gathered us up and guided us through to the magnificent dining room. It was easy to imagine the grandeur of the formal mess dinners held in this stunning setting. Naval officers' mess kit, smart uniformed stewards and elaborate table settings added to the sense of naval history that seemed to seep from the very walls. With our meal served under the watchful gaze of past naval heroes, of a bygone age, peering down from the numerous portraits, it was impossible not to be moved by the obvious sense of pride that the Royal Navy instils in those that train and work here. At the end of this highly enjoyable meal and entertaining evening our course director rose to pay thanks to our Royal Navy hosts. In his broad "Geordie" accent he expressed both our pleasure and the honour we all felt in sharing such a memorable evening in the company of such an august gathering. He was not merely being polite, it was heartfelt.

Breakfast was in stark contrast to the boisterous and animated conversation of the previous evening that had continued long into the night. It was as though our hosts had suddenly signed up to a silent order! Their faces peered over "ironed" copies of that day's broadsheets, held cunningly upright by polished hard wood sticks that kept their papers straight. It was, apparently, customary in the senior service to have one's breakfast in peace. A polite nod here and there was all we got. So, "when in Rome" we followed suit and consumed a hearty breakfast with only a stifled "pass the tomato ketchup," whispered across a dining table.

Our next port of call, literally, was the Southampton Container Terminal in Hampshire. Southampton is one of the UK's busiest and most important ports, second only to Felixstowe. Handling in excess of thirty-five million tonnes of cargo annually, this natural deep-water harbour with its unique double tide allows the port to accommodate the world's largest vessels, from deep-sea container ships to giant cruise liners.

Whilst being given a brief summary of the history of containerization by our guide, I was looking up at the huge, docked, container vessel prior to us boarding this gargantuan ship. The much-travelled metal containers were stacked like Lego blocks, one on top of the other, towered skyward until almost level with the ships bridge which stood over one hundred feet from the water line.

A vast amount of the world's tonnage of annual cargo is packed into "intermodal" shipping containers. (Identical to those that rose above us.) The origins of intermodal containers can be traced back to the United States in the

1950s. Although the American Defence Department is widely credited with the systems widespread adoption for transporting cargo and goods, it was on the back of designs by Malcolm McLean (a former trucking company owner) who worked to develop, and then introduced, the modern intermodal containers. These shipping containers, made of corrugated metal, could be easily swapped between different modes of transport, for example, such as ships or rail cars and lorries. Each container was slightly over eight feet wide and eight feet high and were measured by reference to their basic minimum length of twenty feet, or their TEU multiples. Now in worldwide usage, handling ports, hubs or distribution centres calculated throughput by assigning a value to each individual container. A twenty-foot container scored one, a forty-foot container scored two. Southampton handled nearly one million TEUs a year and was still expanding in growth.

Each container was given a unique (international) identification code. It was combination of three letters from the Latin alphabet and six numbers. This code provided information as to the container's owner or operator and the container's individual registration number. From this information details of where the container came from and where it was destined can be derived, vital for ensuring that the containers are packed in sequence and unloaded with minimum delay at the respective ports of call. We discovered that container ships do not go to every port, but discharge at major hubs. Southampton was one such hub. Here containers were offloaded from one vessel, stacked and then collected by another vessel, which serves different ports.

Standing on the ship's expansive and high-tech bridge the ship looked even bigger and wider as we looked down on to the container decks. It was hard to believe the computerised system of packing and offloading worked so well, or indeed at all. To our unaccustomed eyes, containers were seemingly lifted off at random whilst others were loaded onto the ship. But it was highly organised and meticulously managed by the ship's First Officer as the dockside container crane gantry was positioned for the next discharge or delivery. Reinforced metal rails guided the individual container in to or out of the ship's holds when placed below decks. Below or above deck each container was individually secured to prevent movement in transit.

It was clear to us that fire occurring within a container and spreading to the storage areas on these vessels had serious, if not potentially disastrous, consequences. Fire on board any ship is a serious emergency. As with all shipping it could be the human element, either by default or poor/insufficient monitoring, that posed the greatest risk. Whilst the engine room and crew's accommodation were covered by fire detection and suppression systems; only those containers below deck were under the umbrella of a fire detection system. Those located above decks, tightly packed and immovable, would not share anywhere near the same degree of protection. Only in port, with local fire brigade support, would there be a possibility of containing a relatively minor outbreak. At sea the crew's ability to minimise spread and prevent a serious outbreak would be significantly hindered by the prevailing conditions, such as collision or storm damaged containers, and the actual seat of the fire. It would take more than just training in the *MV Sir Henry* to prepare us for such dire eventualities. The evidence from previous serious container ship fires did not bode well for a successful outcome in anything other than a minor fire.

We left this interesting and informative visit at Southampton wiser but all hopeful that if a container ship did catch fire it was in one of the other course member's patch and not our own. Although in my case, even on the lower reaches of the Thames, such ships as we had seen here were infrequent visitors. I for one was very pleased.

Our course at the College was non-assessable. However, for some of our number it proved to be a physically demanding experience; for two overly so. It gave us all a new found respect for the hazards of fighting fires in ships and a wider appreciation of the potentially dangerous outcomes of poorly applied firefighting tactics, including that of gauging a ship's stability. The exercises enforced, as with all incident command, the vital importance of speedy and effective liaison, in this case with the ship's master or its captain. As ever, this would be in addition to sizing up the incident and assessing the risks commensurate with firefighting and lifesaving. I had gained a new found knowledge. Sadly (or fortunately!) for London officers like myself there would be little or no opportunity to apply this knowledge in practice. The *Paraguay Star* would remain my one and only real ship fire in over thirty year's operational experience. Even then I only watched!

During the latter part of 1989 until April 1990 I was in a transient state. Short-listed for the DO1's promotion interviews saw me make a hash of the whole affair. My brief and robust first feed-back session with my Area Commander succinctly summed up my abysmal performance when he told me, "You made a right dog's-dinner of that didn't you!" That was an understatement. My discomfort at trying to interpret the promotion board's sophisticated questioning, no doubt highlighted by my waffling answers, did me little credit. The experience came as a big reality check. I had never failed at a promotion interview before, securing each promotion at the first attempt. This interview was in a different league and I clearly did not possess the skills and attributes necessary to secure the next rank.

I felt I had let down my Commander and the two officers that had penned my promotion report and recommended me as, "Highly promotable." Not on that performance. Yet despite this set back I was sent back to Brigade Headquarters as a temporary DO1 to work for the new Assistant Chief Officer (Training). He had just returned from the Fire Service College where he had been its deputy Commandant. His secondment at an end, he had re-joined his former brigade to fill the vacancy as the uniformed head of the Training department. Arriving within days of each other, it was a case of the blind leading the blind as we got to grips with our unfamiliar surroundings and adjoining drab offices in the equally dowdy setting of the non-descript office block, of

Queensborough House. However, we were still on the Albert Embankment and adjacent to the Brigade's headquarters building.

I was thrown in at the deep end, into the ethereal world of headquarters departmental politics. I was head of the training policy unit. I had to be as I was the only bugger in it! A so-called colleague was a senior non-uniformed manager, an academic who clearly had studied under the Sir Humphrey (Yes Minister) school of management. Whilst being seemingly very supportive he believed in Sir Humphrey's philosophy of, "It's necessary to get behind someone before you can stab them in the back." Having expected to head up the policy unit himself, his considerable energies were now directed at thwarting the operational training manual initiative at every opportunity. A project that I had inherited and was now expected to deliver.

The Brigade's Training department went through periods of peaks and troughs. This was one of the troughs. Funding for the department was barely adequate and its resources were stretched, if not to breaking point then very close. The Brigade's training school at Southwark was woefully inadequate, its buildings outdated and the facilities pitiful. There was no promised improvement in the budget allocations to indicate that this would change in the immediate future. Morale amongst both its uniformed and civilian staff was not high. This was something my new boss was not about to improve any as he set about re-establishing himself in the headquarters pecking order with his principal officer colleagues. It was a talent this squat man, who spoke in a distinctive manner and with a slight lisp, was more than capable of doing as he prepared the ground for his eventual promotion to Deputy Chief.

My time at Queensborough House was inconsequential. I found the subdued atmosphere and the constant sniping mind-numbingly wearying. It was only the fact that I was wearing my uniform that reminded me I was still working in the fire brigade. Isolated at the end of a plain and uninteresting corridor on the third floor, my featureless office did little to break the monotonous days. My principal excitement was looking out of dirty windows on to the railways tracks below that formed the main line routes into Waterloo Station. Running parallel to the River Thames from Vauxhall, the lines crossed a vast array of railway arches and the noise of the steady passage of commuter trains, trundling over the tracks many times an hour, seemed my only link with the outside world. I was not cut out to be an office worker.

Jim McMillan was an Assistant Chief Officer. He was one third of my promotion board and had been charged by the Deputy Chief to give feedback to its unsuccessful candidates. He was also a former head of the Training Department, and it was largely due to his strength of personality that Training rose to one of its more memorable peaks, before he was transferred to become the Area Commander South West. Seen as a contender for the position of Deputy Chief, or higher, he was now back at headquarters leading Technical Services and in charge of procurement, research and development and fleet management. He was the lead officer in re-equipping all operational personnel with totally new fire kit following the King's Cross fire. That disastrous fire showed that the old-style fire tunics, leggings and rubberised gloves to be out-dated and in need of replacement.

This able and articulate principal officer had one other special attribute. He was an incredibly nice human being. He engendered respect and loyalty in his staff for all the right reasons and was well regarded by all those that he came in to contact with. I was no exception. Extended a friendly handshake as I entered his modest but comfortable office, he beckoned me to a chair before saying, "I thought you were going to faint during your interview, all the blood drained from your face and you looked ashen." I knew I left the interview room with my tail between my legs but I was unaware of my physical appearance before the three-man board.

Pulling no punches he continued, "You had no confidence in yourself David and it showed. It was your interview technique that let you down. You are capable of better but need to have belief in your own abilities and express your ideas more effectively." He was telling me nothing I had not worked out for myself and I was hopeful that I had a possible solution at hand. As it turned out it delivered far more than I expected.

Watershed

In the final months of the eighties I returned to the Fire Service College for the last time. I was attending my Divisional Command course. This nine-week residential course was broken down into two four-week modules with the middle week spent with an outside organisation undertaking a work-study. This was a personal development course. One that prepared senior officers, open to all UK fire brigades, for middle management. It was also a prerequisite for attendance on the College's Brigade Command Course, which prepared individuals for principal officer rank.

In October 1989 twenty Divisional Officers from different backgrounds and with various talents came together to learn something about themselves. We worked in small syndicates, two larger fixed groups, individually and we all came together for the visiting lecturers. My group's senior civilian tutor was a tall slim Welshman, David Thomas. He was normally a senior tutor on Brigade Command Courses but had agreed to cover a vacancy on our particular course. This elegant and sophisticated man, who was in his early fifties, was called upon to gauge our interpersonal and communication skills and, with the uniformed course director, monitor our individual perceptiveness, enthusiasm and participation throughout the course.

More importantly David acted as our group's mentor as we individually progressed through this learning experience. Whilst the senior uniformed course staff led the case studies and monitored problem solving exercises involving work-related situations, David's considerable skills were utilised in the assessment of our written, spoken and non-verbal skills. He also undertook the psychometric testing and observed the group's dynamics that later provided individuals with a personal indicator of how we each looked at things and the way we went about deciding things. The same tests were carried out on Brigade Command course students. David had recorded all the data over a number of years and had identified the "preference" strengths of those individuals, he had tested, and who had reached Chief or Deputy Chief Officer rank. Needless to say my particular type of **I**ntroversion; **IN**tuition; **T**hinking and **P**erceptive (INTP) did not fit into this particular, high achieving, quadrant!

The highlights of the course were wide-ranging but two particularly stood out. One was a visiting lecturer, a professor in Psychology and the other our visit to the Oxford Union debating society. The Professor had the stature and girth of Danny de Vito and armed with just a piece of chalk this highly accomplished tutor held us riveted to his subject matter. Armed with his encyclopaedic mind, and free of any prepared notes, he delivered his crash course in psychology in a series of extended lectures spread throughout the whole course.

It was his manner to move from one side of the lecture theatre to the other and back again as he gave us the benefit of his considerable wisdom into various behavioural theories and studies with hardly a pause for breath. He was passionate about his subject and was able to transpose even the most complex of ideas into easily understood concepts with the odd jotting on the blackboard to highlight a particular point. In the second half of the course we thought we would conduct an experiment on our Professor to test one of the case studies he had explored but, we hoped, without his knowledge.

He had previously spent a session explaining "operant conditioning." This is a means by which human or animal behaviour could be altered or affected by stimuli or targeted response. This could enforce or change actions or conduct. This can be done in either positive or a negative manner. (Training a dog and reinforcing what is being taught by giving it a reward or praise is positive; beating it instead would be negative.) Having agreed our strategy the Professor arrived in the lecture theatre and within a very short time was in full flow, in his normal animated fashion, on that day's subject. Even when writing on the blackboard he would still move from one side to the other. Every time he moved to the right, we would show interest and smile and whenever he veered to the left we would not smile and feign disinterest. Within forty-five minutes we had him just working from the right-hand side of the room. Finally, asked by one of our number why he was standing only on the right his wide smile was indication enough that he was more than receptive to our practical demonstration as to how pathways in the brain can be activated.

Our Thursday evening visit to an Oxford Union debate was an illuminating and highly entertaining affair. With the two prominent guest speakers adding their weight to the arguments for and against the motion, we were treated to a gladiatorial contest where the only weaponry on display was wit and intelligence. We witnessed a master class in the ability to think and present an argument clearly and logically. The Oxford Union had for many years been an established forum for high class debating. It had hosted many notable guest speakers including a number of American Presidents, and some of this country's most prestigious speakers honed their eloquence there.

Our College debates may not have matched the standards witnessed at Oxford. However, our debates and discussions, both within our syndicate and group, were robust and, at times, forceful yet without ever being hurtful to others. Research into the various topics had to be thoroughly prepared. When presented to your peers you would soon find they were not shy in coming forward to highlight some inadequacy in your argument, or your analysis of the issues at hand.

Somewhere along the line, but certainly in the second half of the course, during a one-to-one session with David he uncovered a vestige of my past that I had shut away. He had discovered a trigger from my secondary schooling that I had wanted to forget but had remained a burden I carried through life. I admit I was not the brightest of school kids. Whilst I struggled to get to grips with English language, its grammar and its punctuation, I was drowning when it came to French. Our French master, who really was French, would ridicule and humiliate me in front of classmates for my poor pronunciation or for mixing up my nouns with my verbs. I dreaded those "double" mid-week French sessions. I felt physically sick on the day of his class in anticipation of the degrading treatment I knew I would receive. I was the class fall guy. He would shout my name, "Peek," (for he could nor pronounce Pike) and then have me stand and make a buffoon of myself as I tried, and failed, to recite that day's phrases which we had been meant to commit to memory. Needless to say I never passed my French GCE, or even the school certificate.

My lack of academic achievement was my Achilles heel, something that I was very conscious of. My Area Commander had an excellent command of English and, despite the support and encouragement that he gave me, because my own style of writing did not mirror his own, he would "red pen" my reports seeking changes and amendments. It was, on many an occasion, soul destroying. As David dug deeper so the recognition of these underlying causes came slowly to the surface. I felt like the Straw Man from the *Wizard of Oz*. I wanted a "literate" brain. I am sure that my English teachers at school must have been as frustrated as I was. The fact is they failed to make me appreciate and understand the formation of words that would have aided my spelling, or to grasp the concepts of past, present and future tense.

I had needed to prove something to myself on this course. I was enthusiastic and committed, as I knew I would only get the chance to do this once. With a dictionary as a constant companion my handwritten work was presented on time and the feedback was surprisingly positive and even complimentary. I was told, probably for the first time, that I wrote in a "crisp" fashion; with a "distinctive but clear style of writing." This evaluation was mirrored by similar feedback from David and the course director on my spoken and non-verbal skills. For me, at least, the course had been a voyage of self-discovery. With both tutor and course director taking a close detailed look at our individual managerial and interpersonal skills, the course was a watershed for me. Only I did not fully appreciate it at the time.

My time serving in the South East came to an abrupt end in April 1990. I was now back at Shooters Hill, only this time as the temporary head of training. Barney had been promoted to Senior Divisional Officer and moved to the Home Office. I had served under Assistant Chief Officer Brian Butler for four years and he thought it was now time for me to move on.

I rarely, if ever, sneaked off early. Quite the reverse in fact, unless it was for some clandestine assignation and then I would book off duty. But on this particular afternoon I was driving back from Biggin Hill fire station around 4.15pm and was so close to my house I thought "bugger it" and went home much to the surprise and delight of my wife. About forty-five minutes later I was paged and told to contact the Area staff office and after ringing them I was put through to the ACO's office.

Telling my two teenage children to make less noise least they give my location away I waited for the Commander to pick up. Announcing myself he said gruffly, "Where are you?"

"The bastard's got the bloody cars bugged now," I thought as I lied, "Returning to Shooters Hill from Biggin Hill Sir."

"Get your arse in here I have something to show you." Putting my uniform back on and leaving a now not so pleased wife putting my dinner in the oven to keep warm I returned to Lewisham.

I found a deserted second floor when I arrived save for the light showing at the ACO's outer office at the far end of the long corridor. He was sitting in his customary position, behind his desk and in contemplative mood and supping on a glass of whiskey. It was obviously not his first. Standing in the open office doorway I was beckoned in and invited to sit on the corner sofa. "I have been having a think about my Command senior officers and their current postings," he said looking into his whiskey glass. There had been whisperings for days about a possible reshuffle of post holders but especially the Station Commanders. He looked up from his rapidly emptying glass and stared at a large white magnetic board that stood in the corner of his office, diagonally opposite his desk. It had been obscured from my line of sight by the open office door. My attention now drawn to it, I saw individual magnetic cards each with a name of a South East senior officer written on them and placed against positions on the Command's organisational management chart.

I was told he had spent the whole afternoon with his principal management team going through his reshuffle, something that was not an infrequent occurrence and designed to keep us all on our toes. I was not immediately taking in all the information on the board when he asked me, "Notice anything?" There was a lot to absorb, but one thing was blatantly obvious. However, before I could speak, he continued, "You ain't on it. You are posted to Central Operations, Brigade Headquarters as of 8.00am Monday." Today was Friday. "You need some exposure. This will do you good." The interview was over and his gaze drifted back into his whiskey glass and the need to get a refill soon.

Shell-shocked I made my way back home. I was disappointed to be leaving the Command and apprehensive about working in Central Operations, which had changed considerably since my last spell there. I was not a headquarters policy animal. I knew where my strengths lay and getting embroiled in the cut and thrust of the frequent headquarters "petty" politics was not high on my agenda. I also questioned my belief in my own intellect, something I thought was essential for delivering the quality demanded of Central Operations. Much to my surprise I enjoyed my new posting, although the drive to and fro from Lambeth soon became a real ball ache. Given some meaningful projects to get my teeth into I was receiving positive feedback from the ACO of Central Operations, Ken Knight. His wife had, sadly, only recently died following a short illness and he was losing himself in his work. This masked a personal grief but he maintained a highly effective, decisive and intelligent management style. He would eventually rise to the very highest position in the British fire service, Her Majesty's Chief Inspector. Yet despite his own personal loss he was very people orientated, an excellent motivator and totally different from Brian Butler. I could get to like it here after all.

Pall-bearers from Soho fire station carrying the body of Station Officer Colin Townsley. GM. who perished at the Kings Cross Underground fire. November 1987.

Copyright. *London Fire Brigade/ Mary Evans Picture Library.*

The iconic frontage of the London Fire Brigade's Lambeth headquarters building on the Albert Embankment, SE1. (The building was subsequently sold off in 2007.)

The Prince of Wales on a visit to the Fire Service College-Morton-in-Marsh and yours truly is presented together with course colleagues. 1987.

Firefighter's, under the command of Area Commander Brian Butler, at a bridge collapse at St John's, Lewisham following the extrication of the two construction workers killed in the collapse.

Copyright. *London Fire Brigade/ Mary Evans Picture Library.*

Chapter 14

Press and PR

My sudden move into Press and Public Relations (Press and PR) came as a complete surprise to me. It was an even greater surprise to my boss within Central Operations. He had been out-manoeuvred by Chris Thompson, a Senior Divisional Officer and the uniformed head of the Brigade's Press and Public Relations Division. He was one rank below that of a Deputy Assistant Chief Officer (DACO), the rank held by my boss. Whilst quietly striving away on some policy directive or other I was summoned into the DACO's office and told, without ceremony, I was posted (again!). The DACO was seething. He was almost incandescent with rage as he shouted at me, "Did you orchestrate this move?" I had absolutely no idea what he was talking about and my shocked face clearly said so as I stood there speechless. "What move?" I finally asked. "Your posting to Press and PR." Stunned, I told him, "Well it's bloody news to me."

The short, heated, discussion that followed, more accurately described as a shouting match, was shared by most of those in the adjoining offices and put news of my imminent departure well and truly in the public domain. My new posting was just a couple of offices further down the second-floor corridor since Press and PR shared the second floor with Central Operations. Packing my stuff once again into cardboard boxes, I changed offices and started my new and totally unexpected role.

Press and PR was a mixture of uniformed, non-operational and civilian staff. Gordon White, a former journalist, was the Division's Head. A brilliant wordsmith, he had an extremely demanding and frequently stressful role of trying to balance "five star" corporate hospitality and event planning demanded by the Chief and Deputy Chief on a "three star" budget. With the support of Helen Atha, another ex-professional journalist, they were responsible for most of the internal and external communication, promoting the Brigade via the media and fending off adverse criticism when the "mire hit the fan" after an operational problem, or because of negative reaction to the Fire Authority policies, such as a fire station closure.

Chris had himself only recently been transferred in to head up Press and PR's uniformed side. This now included myself and one other Divisional Officer plus a collection of operational and non-operational staff. Press and PR had undergone substantial staff cuts in recent years due to budgetary reductions. Even though its former uniformed complement had been significantly reduced it was still expected to maintain the same level of service as that prior to the cutbacks. The Brigade's Treasurer was quoted as saying, "You should not be adversely affected," as he sliced into the Divisional budget. These were extremely challenging times, for although Gordon was a media wizard his management expertise when trying to marry up the "quart" of the Chief Officer's and the Deputy's demands with the "pint pot" of our available resources, occasionally fell short. Juggling the demands of the Brigade's Corporate Board, handling the media and organising and delivering the Brigade's ceremonial duties was taking its toll and Chris had been sent in to "beef" up the Division. Although I had not worked with Chris directly, we both served together in the South East Area Command under Brian Butler. But Chris had incurred the wrath of the Area Commander and been posted. Chris was a Brigade headquarters animal and thrived in its environment. He had recently been promoted to his current rank and sent into Press and PR. He needed a fixer and a proven organiser to help him meet the objectives that he had been set. He set his sights on me and got the backing of the Chief, and despite the protestations of my boss, got me.

My own move into Press and PR coincided with much bigger moves within the Brigade Headquarters complex. The place was in a state of flux and musical chairs, or rather musical offices, was the flavour of the month. The top four floors of the Brigade Headquarters building had once been allocated for residential accommodation of principal and senior officers.

However, following changes to the duty system and a revised accommodation policy, these officers moved out piecemeal. Empty space will always find an occupant and these flats were gradually given over to office space. Now all eight floors of the whole headquarters building had been designated as offices, with the exception of Lambeth fire station that occupied the ground and first floor. The Chief and his Deputy had got newly appointed, and lavish, office suites at either end of the seventh floor that, naturally, befitted their rank and status!

Press and PR came out as one of the winners in this accommodation reshuffle. The division moved up to the vastly superior accommodation of the fourth floor, previously occupied by the Deputy Chief Officer. However, with a nice sense of irony, especially given the many dodgy dealings that the "old" PR team had become embroiled in with (allegedly) dubious budgets, we were to share the fourth floor with the Fire Authorities Internal Auditor and his team of accountants and investigators.

The Blitz

The broadcast of Neville Chamberlain's historic radio announcement that, "This country is now at war with Germany," was followed by the evocative sound of air raid warning sirens filling the Lambeth streets surrounding Brigade headquarters. Against the noise of anti-aircraft guns firing their salvos in the distance and the roar of enemy planes overhead, the display started.

Getting the Brigade's Blitz commemoration, including the display, off the ground was easier said than done. It was something that required "all hands to the pumps" if we had the remotest chance of pulling off this mammoth task. The

Chief Fire Officer, Gerry Clarkson, had wanted a fitting tribute to mark the fiftieth anniversary of the Blitz, not only on mainland Britain, but particularly on London. His aim was to pay tribute to the vital role the fire service had played then and the ultimate sacrifice three hundred firemen made in helping save the nation's capital from mass destruction after the wholesale blanket bombing by the German Luftwaffe during 1940-41.

Getting an invitation, or rather a summons, to the Chief's inner sanctum was a rare event for me. However, I joined Gordon and Chris for his briefing and I soon discovered why I was poached. I was the one tasked with the job of making most of the proposed commemoration happen. The Chief held court sitting behind his palatial desk whilst we three sat pensively, well I did, on easy chairs at the far end of his well-appointed office. Dressed in his crisp white uniform shirt and tugging at his City of London crested cuff links he outlined his "big picture" for the commemoration. Sadly, it was all big picture and almost totally devoid of detail. "We need a Royal," he said as he listed his demands. This was not a negotiation but fortunately he was in a good humour and receptive to our suggestions as he continued down his "wish list."

He had chosen St Paul's Cathedral for the Service of Commemoration and Lambeth headquarters was to host the weekend display. As none of us had got a bollocking nor been shouted at we thought it was a good meeting. All we had to do now was make it all happen.

That evening, over a couple of bottles of wine, Gordon, Chris and I sat in Chris's office (which doubled as the Press and PR conference room and adjoined Gordon's office) and reflected on the Chief's list of must haves. The Chief had decreed that he wanted a Royal personage at St Paul's and an invitation to every City of London Worshipful Livery Company and Guild. (The Chief had recently formed the latest City of London Guild, The Guild of Firefighters, hence the cuff links!) He also wanted every London borough Mayor and the Lord Mayor of the City of London to attend wearing their ceremonial dress and chains of office. Already we felt a "corporate" headache coming on as we looked up Debrett's to take an instant course in protocol and precedence in processing. It was evident that by the end of the second bottle a third was needed as the full enormity of the undertaking began to sink in.

Turning Lambeth's large drill yard and the whole of the rear block's four-storey facade into a show arena and getting it all to represent a scene from war time London was an interesting exercise to say the least. However, being the Chief's pet project helped me enormously with the organisation of the Brigade's most high profile and prestigious event of the year. The mention of his name removed potential barriers to my seemingly strange requests, such as filling over a thousand sand bags and putting brown masking tape crosses on the hundreds of individual panes of glass that made up the front windows of the rear block, the backdrop for the "wartime" arena.

Of course this was not the only thing happening within the Brigade during that memorable year. Four new pieces of kit were being introduced that would change how we looked, most notably at incidents, and would greatly improve firefighter safety and deliver a better level of service to the public. The old-style helmet, based on the original cork helmet, was assigned to the history books as the new "Pacific" helmet that incorporated a protective visor replaced them. Nomex fire tunics had already replaced the old black woollen fire tunics, with their two rows of silver buttons, and now Nomex over-trousers would replace the yellow leggings and give firefighters greater personal protection. For those working in dangerous environments that demanded breathing apparatus an automatic distress signal unit (DSU) was placed on every breathing apparatus set. It would activate itself whenever a BA wearer was immobile for more than twenty seconds. After a pre-alert signal (if it was not reset) the full alarm signal would sound summoning urgent assistance. Lastly, a Halmatro rapid intervention set was placed on every frontline pump ladder that year. This meant that every London fire station had, for the first time, hydraulic self-contained cutting and spreading equipment for immediate use at road traffic accidents.

All these innovations had received Fire Brigade Committee approval and funding to make it happen. This was the same Committee that now approved the funding of a Blitz commemoration and exhibition; invitations to retired Auxiliary Fire Service (AFS), National Fire Service (NFS) and London firemen and women to the Blitz events and to provide them all with refreshments. Unfortunately, this funding did not extend to everything in the Chief's big picture and certainly did not cover what I planned as regards the display.

I thought finding sufficient personnel and period appliances would be a major problem. That was until one afternoon I received a telephone call from a rather strange sounding individual who said he could help. The display could not have taken place, (funding or no funding) without the active participation of this very special band of people; the Fire Service Preservation Group. They were an exceptionally enthusiastic group of fire engine "buffs" that restored and owned vintage and wartime fire engines and support vehicles as a hobby. None were more enthusiastic and "quirky" than my caller, the main contact with the Group and who was also its Secretary and principal activist, Ted Roberts. A truly delightful man who, sadly, had the distinction of looking exactly like the TV character "Fred Scuttle" created by the late Benny Hill. I only ever saw him dressed in his second hand fireman's undress uniform, with his badge-less uniform cap worn at an oblique angle on his head and with his NHS glasses perched on the end of his nose. "Fred" attended plenty of meetings and was always dressed the same. He made lots of promises, all of which he delivered.

This Group, was comprised of both serving firemen (many from London, and others from the surrounding fire brigades) and others who worked outside the fire brigade environment. However, they all shared one thing in common, and either owned or had access to vintage fire engines. Many were actually used during the blitz. A dozen or so of which, Ted assured me, would turn up for the two one day displays in September. I would have wartime fire engines, London taxies pulling trailer pumps and even a dispatch rider's motorbike. There was only one small caveat, none of them would be able to turn up until the actual evening before that weekend's performances, which was more than a little stressful.

Planning for this display was like preparing for a military operation. I had to locate and then ensure that all the essential components were in place. Despite the invaluable assistance of dear old "Fred Scuttle" I still had a considerable shopping list before I could even start to relax. In response to the frequent enquiries from the Chief about progress I gave only one response, "Everything's fine Chief." If only!

I used my contacts and called in favours and was more than ably supported by my team, even though we had hardly had time to get to know one another before embarking on this epic production. We made scale plans and models, which allowed us to study every aspect of the three main elements of the display in detail. My small band of operational volunteers from the C Division worked wonders and willingly agreed to perform all the ladder work and carry out the "live" rescues in the display. This was in addition to promising their services at St Paul's.

It was clear we would need sponsors to cover those costs the Brigade could not cover. I struck gold when an advertising company said they were willing to make and erect all the scenery around the drill tower and to cover the Preservation Group's fuel costs. This was a real boost and for the first time I was able to say, "Everything's fine Chief" and mean it.

I spent much of my annual leave that August writing the script for the three-act display much to the dismay of my wife who thought I might have just as well stayed at work. I returned to duty with a completed script for the Blitz display, which was to be an hour-long show. Act one would be a tribute to the firemen and women of the London Fire Brigade and the Auxiliary Fire Service who, with the other emergency services and voluntary organisations, worked on the front line during the Blitz. The tribute would include a parade of wartime appliances and supporting vehicles. I had promises from the London Ambulance Service, the Metropolitan and City of London Police plus St John Ambulance Service and the Women's Royal Voluntary Service. All said that they would participate and provide authentic period vehicles and uniforms for their attendees. I just had to feed them all.

Act two was a glimpse of the training activities undertaken by members of London's fire force in preparation for the expected aerial attacks on the nation's capital. My own in-house team came up trumps here. They would incorporate a sense of humour and fun into the proceedings, especially within the physical training exercises and the dire attempts of the AFS men to learn squad drill. Keith Blenkin was a star with a marvellous rendition of a cross between Mr Pastry (a television and film comic from the 1950s and 60s) and Flash Harry from St Trinian's. Keith actually looked like Mr Pastry in real life and portrayed the typical London spiv joining the fire brigade in 1938/9.

Act three was to be the main arena event. The scenario was to be a late September afternoon towards the end of 1940; heavy bombing raids had inflicted extensive damage upon the capital since the 7 September, the start of the blitz. London's firemen and women had already faced major conflagrations and many other large fires in and around the City of London, riverside areas and

London's extensive dockland. Crews that had fought these fires throughout the previous nights are depicted snatching a few hours rest.

Leaving the French coastline formations of enemy bombers are heading towards their intended target, London. We expected the sound track of the air raid sirens to shatter the silence of our large crowd of specially invited firefighting veterans who would be gathered to watch both commemorative performances.

I had first met Basil Rietz at Earls Court in 1982 when I had arranged the London Fire Brigade's guest performance at the Royal Tournament. He was "the voice" of the Royal Tournament and he willingly accepted my invitation to provide live commentary for the weekend displays. He had the perfect voice for this occasion and although working from a script he could readily ad-lib when the situation required it. (He sounded rather like Richard Burton or Anthony Hopkins and he could wax lyrical about some small interesting trifle that would have an audience captivated.)

Mike Hebard was a retired London policeman but was fascinated by fire engines. He owned a considerable fleet of historic vehicles and did a lot of film work, supplying and driving his vehicles in period dramas. We had been closely involved in earlier projects and we had just clicked. He was incredibly generous with his time and his machines and, providing the cost of his fuel was met, he would add his considerable support and resources to the display. But with no Preservation Group vehicles available until the night before the event, rehearsals consisted of just Mike and his trustees, plus the C Division volunteer corps practising with Mike's immaculate (circa) 1939 pump and TL in its stunning London Fire Brigade colours and livery.

Everything was now almost in place. The Blitz exhibition, which was admission free, filled Lambeth's expansive seven bay appliance room that had been made available for the occasion. The exhibition had been widely advertised throughout London. It was open to the public every weekday from the 19th to 29th of September. It included an impressive array of especially commissioned original Brigade Blitz black and white photographs; these together with other artwork and memorabilia attempted to recapture some of the hardships and spartan conditions the wartime firefighters had to endure as well as the enormity of the bombing raids, thrust upon them. It was incredibly well attended and received critical acclaim from the curatorial staff of the nearby Imperial War Museum.

The display was sandwiched in the middle weekend of the ten-day exhibition. Veterans, living in all parts of the country, had been invited to the weekend reunion. They were traced largely through the efforts of one of their former members who had maintained a register of contact addresses. Hundreds made the journey that weekend to London and to Lambeth. An emotional reunion for some, but all were rewarded for their efforts by a sunny late summer's day and a reunion that rekindled memories of shared experiences and brought together long-lost colleagues.

By now I had managed to transform (with considerable assistance) the headquarters drill yard and rear block frontage to represent a scene from wartime London. Our sponsors had built and erected full-sized advertising hoardings either side of Lambeth's nine-storey double fronted drill tower. Hand painted artwork on the hoardings replicated adverts of the period, reminding the public to always carry their gas masks as well as, "Careless talk cost lives." Over two thousand sand bags had eventually been filled and used to camouflage the modern security hut by the rear entrance gate and provide authentic looking protective barriers in front of the doors to the rear block and the entrance to the drill tower. Office windows now resembled their wartime counterparts with every pane covered in a brown sticky cross (meant to stop flying glass in a blast).

Our Brigade workshop staff had built a replica gas main for me. It would fracture during the simulated bombing raid and be ignited by remote control by our in-house pyrotechnic team. (The Brigade's scientific advisors who normally attended and advised on chemical incidents.) However, they loved to get involved in my antics and blow something up given the opportunity!

With a frantic last-minute rush of activity that was (and probably still is) typical of fire brigade working the lighting, the sound effects, the PA system and the pyrotechnics all arrived on site and were erected, positioned, tested and secured. Warning notices were hand delivered to all the surrounding properties to reassure the local residents that they were not being invaded or that the Thames was breaching the river's defences when air raid warnings sounded over the coming Saturday and Sunday afternoons. There was a genuine buzz of excitement now both within PR's own staff and many of the other Headquarters departments. The sceptics who were so convinced that, "This ain't going to happen in the time frame set by the Chief," suddenly were no longer so vocal. The first phase of the commemoration had not only arrived, it was on time.

With a, "I might be late tonight," said to my wife I left home that Friday morning. Some fine tuning was the order of the day whilst Gordon fended off last minute queries from the Chief and Chris had me going through his, "What if?" interrogation process, just to make sure everything that should be in place was in place.

"Fred Scuttle" and his formidable band of enthusiasts did not disappoint. They, with their fire engines, started arriving late Friday afternoon and the last of the fifteen fire engine crews finally drew up about seven in the evening. They could either make or break the weekend's display with their fire engines going in or out of the arena at the wrong time, or crews going left instead of turning right, maybe even getting lost driving around the block! I greeted lots of Fred Scuttle look-a-likes, but all were clearly intent on making the weekend work. I was in for a pleasant surprise too as my merry band listened attentively to my briefing and studied their action sheets for the initial parade and final scene. The only dress rehearsal went like clockwork thanks to my team of "stage-hands" working to my radioed instructions and releasing the fire engines in the correct order and on cue. It was a show after all was said and done. After giving them all a slap-up feast in the headquarters canteen, well a hot meal at least, it was off to bed. Too exhausted to drive home that night I joined this merry throng and we all bedded down for the night at Aldersgate on borrowed army camp beds.

For both the Saturday and Sunday performances our special guests started to arrive well before the allotted time of 12am and made their way around the exhibition. At 2pm our war-time band, hired for the occasion, started to play and by 2.15pm our visitors began to take their seats on the tiered headquarter balconies and excited chatter mingled with the big band music of Glen Miller and Ted Heath. Basil was in fine voice and made the formal introductions to the afternoon's performance and gave a moving welcome to all.

My pre-briefing to everyone involved in the parade, including the other emergency services, seemed to do the trick and it passed off perfectly. Act Two went much the same way as laughter filled the air as Keith created havoc within the PT class and his comical attempts at marching. As our brave wartime firemen exited the arena to the sounds of Vera Lynn singing the *"Bluebirds over the White Cliffs of Dover"* a noticeable hush fell over the arena as it emptied in preparation for the final act.

The wailing of the air raid sirens gave their soulless warning of the afternoon's imminent attack. As they faded away a new noise filled the arena, the roar of enemy aircraft engines high overhead. It was so realistic that many of the guests were actually looking skyward as the sound effects reverberated off the surrounding tall buildings that overlooked the arena. Shouts of surprise from the audience greeted the first of a series of loud explosions that had erupted on the flat roof of the rear block. On the top of the drill tower a lone firewatcher raises the alarm as the first signs of a fire take hold within the lower floors of the drill tower. Smoke and flames (created by red flares) spread upwards from floor to floor within the tower and smoke is carried on the breeze over the arena adding to the increasing sense of realism. In the distance the sound of fire engine bells are heard as the first wave of fire engines, in their grey war-time livery, are released from the rear of the Brigade workshops and speed into the arena. A second wave enters from the Thames embankment side and the combined weight of the crews bring numerous jets to bear on the blazing drill tower as the C Division lads pitch ladders and enter the burning building.

As the audience's attention is drawn towards the arrival of the TL and its crew prepare to rescue the trapped firewatcher further loud explosions ripple their way across the roof of the rear block. The whole width of the roof area is bathed in a red burning glow (caused by the pyrotechnic teams over enthusiastic use of their flares). The occasional cough is now filtering out from the audience as smoke continues to swirl around the yard and a motorcycle dispatch rider enters the arena to take a message and speeds off to summon further reinforcements. As he passes the gas main it explodes violently and real flame shoots skyward and the gas main burns freely at the fractured flange. Five further engines arrive including taxis pulling trailer pumps as all available space, including the rear block forecourt, is utilised in a carefully choreographed action. Each crew is performing their own individual "party" piece but the whole attack on the fire scene appears both co-ordinated and effective. Jets are being got to work on the rear forecourt via trailer pumps lifting from a large inflatable emergency dam and are directed on to an area of blank brick wall. (Which was something that would come back to haunt me all too soon!)

After twenty minutes of frantic activity the representation is over. Everybody that need rescuing is rescued. All the fires are safety extinguished. Sadly, this did not reflect the reality of what our wartime guests had to face during the blitz, not just once but night after night during that grim period in the capital's history. But now to the rapturous applause from the balconies above them our gallant heroes that afternoon took their curtain call. After, that is, the short ride around the block to bring everyone back into the arena (without hopefully anyone missing the turning into Lambeth High Street). Here they all reassembled and took their final bow. Afterwards the guests were invited to meet the Preservation Group and to take refreshments within the exhibition area. Both performances were equally successful and the fear of a possible heart attack, caused by the extremely realistic explosions, thankfully failed to materialise. After Sunday's performance a rather rueful principal officer commented as he passed me in the commentary box, "It is a shame we don't control our real make up fires with such polish and panache."

Immediately after Sunday's performance I was, inwardly at least, preening myself like a peacock! Circulating around Lambeth's drill yard I was thanking and congratulating the cast when I was summoned to report to the Chief, who was also circulating and "meeting and greeting." Chris was already standing with the Chief and doing his very best to put a feather in my cap. The Chief, it seemed, was preparing himself to have to anoint me with a, "Well done Mr Pike." I even managed a formal congratulatory handshake and an official photo to record a fleeting moment of praise for posterity. Then it all started to unfold. Rather rapidly as it happens, as the Chief's personal driver furtively sidled up to him and whispered something in his ear. Whatever he said he was clearly not the harbinger of good news! The Chief's face suddenly changed and took on a distinct grimace and that grimace was directed straight at me.

"Problem Chief?" asked a diplomatic Chris. "Yes there is." replied the Chief through gritted teeth as he tried unsuccessfully to maintain an outward appearance of calm as the retired AFS and NFS continued to heap praise on his commemorative enterprise. Telling me to, "Make yourself scarce until I see what's up." Chris went off with the driver in the direction of the rear block and towards the Chief's lock up garage that, until a few moments ago, was the target of the afternoons Luftwaffe's bombing attack. Meanwhile the Chief was left standing in the middle of the yard receiving even more accolades from those eager to relate their tales from the real blitz.

Chris returned after a short while and his own sense of pride in the afternoon's success was hard to find in the concerned look he now wore on his face. "You had better go and hide in the bottom of the drill tower until the Chief is out of the yard," said Chris. "Why?" I ask. "Well," explained Chris, "The bloody three-thousand gallons of water that was in the bloody inflatable dam until the bloody Preservation Group pulled the bloody stopper out is now in the Chief's effing garage."

"What is the problem then?" I foolishly asked, thinking that the driver would not have parked the car in there. Not today! "Here's the rub." continued Chris "The Chief has put his 'dodgy' new kitchen in his garage, intended for the house he is having renovated in Bromley and now most of it is floating!" With an, "Ooh" I scurried off in the direction of the drill tower.

The fact that the Chief was warned about the display detail and the fact that he failed to mention his "unofficial" storage would have no bearing on his apportioning of blame. It would all be down to me for not being sufficiently clairvoyant and foreseeing this problem. I could forget all about my one, and only, invitation to the seventh floor for the Chief's post display piss up and bun fight to congratulate the events principal organisers! So without even a canapé smuggled out to me I gave grateful thanks to the volunteers from the Brigade and the members of the Preservation Group. They had contributed so much and it was they who made the whole display possible.

With the Chief up and me down the last of the invited guests departed the exhibition, many still exchanging stories or reminiscences as they strolled across the yard and heading home their separate ways. Clearly it was not the only story being exchanged that Sunday afternoon for news of the "garage" debacle had spread and found hanging on the Chief's garage door some wag had pinned a notice. "Flood damaged kitchen for sale, must collect."

Although the "garage incident" was never mentioned again by the Chief I was still attempting to keep a low profile whilst simultaneously trying to arrange his biggest public relations event of the year. Then just two days after the display another bombshell landed in my lap. Taking a phone call from a colleague in the Brigade's property group he asked me casually, "How much money you got in your display budget?" It was a strange question to ask so I naturally inquired, "Why?"

"Well we want five thousand quid for a new squash court parquet floor, that's why." A small single airbrick, four inches by nine inches, located centrally in the fifty-foot-high rear brick blank wall, was all that was needed to let the water in. It was below where two jets of water were meant to be directed high onto that wall. Unnoticed by almost everyone, but certainly by me, the airbrick had not gone unnoticed by the dear old preservation group "plonkers" who used it as a target as they aimed their powerful jet at it. In a wall containing thousands upon thousands of bricks it was like searching for a needle in a haystack but they had found it exactly. Upon inspection, the said squash court floor looked like the aftermath of an earthquake tremor. The previous flat surface had erupted, at least a point five on the Richter scale, and unsightly bulges and a large crack ran right across the floor as the swollen and sodden parquet blocks expanded and forced themselves upwards. "The whole floor has got to be replaced plus you got a lot of very unhappy headquarters squash players to contend with," said my grinning Property colleague. Fortunately for me the Chief did not play squash and Gordon, thankfully, refused to pay anyway. The replacement floor costs being put down to some little known about contingency fund that Property Group had squirreled away for a rainy day.

Princess Diana

Gordon's letters, seeking a Royal presence to the commemorative service at St Paul's, had been prepared much earlier and sent up for the Chief's signature. So had those inviting the one hundred and three Worshipful Companies, all London Mayors together with other important civic leaders and the heads of military and emergency service organisations to the service. Personal invitations to the veterans were signed by Gordon and over three thousand individual letters were posted.

This was the largest mailshot ever undertaken by the PR Division and it necessitated its own computer programme so as to accurately list the invitees, record what group they were in and to monitor the responses and any contact information. Steve Burton, who had recently joined the Division to help set up expenditure monitoring, had excellent computer skills and established a framework that ensured every invitation could be logged and tracked. Replies and details, especially from the retirees (who would frequently ring up to chat, at length, about the invitation and wanted to tell their own story) were gathered and recorded. This data collation was ground-breaking stuff and had not previously been possible, something that had caused occasional problems and embarrassment especially when someone's name inexplicably fell off the invitation list to some high-profile function or other. There was one other significant "little" worry that was the capacity of St Paul's. It could only accommodate two thousand six hundred seated guests. With three thousand invites sent out we would have a problem if they all wanted to attend.

Whilst the Blitz exhibition was still open to the public in Lambeth's appliance room, the PR team tried to return the remainder of Brigade Headquarters to some semblance of normality after the weekend displays and to find a home for two thousand sandbags! I was now fully occupied with making the final preparations for phase two, the commemoration service to be held at St Paul's Cathedral in only four weeks' time.

The Chief was euphoric for once, although still not best pleased with me. He had a reply to his request for a *minor* Royal but had not expected one from the private secretary to Her Royal Highness the Princess of Wales and she "was pleased" to accept his invitation. A considerable air of excitement filtered down from the Chief's offices and a sense of anticipation greeted this news within the Division. Chris and I had attended Paddington Fire Station the previous year to co-ordinate the visit of Her Majesty the Queen Mother. The visit had gone exceptionally well and the Brigade was, it seems, still in the good books of the Royal household.

I, on the other hand, was not quite so euphoric. I was still trying to balance my postgraduate Diploma in Management Studies course I had started three weeks earlier, with getting this show on the road. But the attendance of Princess Diana (as she was to be later better known) suddenly made the organisation of this event a lot easier to sell to those whose help we needed. I had already cut my teeth on planning a service at St Paul's the Christmas before when given the task of arranging the Brigade's Christmas Carol service there. This was a regular annual event for the PR Division so it was not a case of having to re-invent the wheel, just tweaking up the previous organisation. The major hurdle with any big Brigade event was the Chief's VIP guests list. Seating arrangements could be fraught with difficulties as he inevitably made last minute changes with someone falling out of favour, or him promising someone a seat in the front rows of whatever was being arranged.

I had met Reverend Stephen Wayne previously, along with a Chief Inspector from the City of London Police, responsible for Royal visits in the City of London, last December. We had all got on famously and now found ourselves working together again on this Royal visit. Stephen, who worked in the Dean and Chapter's office was bright and funny, in fact a real hoot. This young, and newly married man, was as quick witted as he was intelligent and he also happened to be the Dean's curate. He brought a wonderful perspective into the planning process which assumed that if the Dean and Chapter's wives got good seats at the service we could get away with almost anything within reason.

The Chief Inspector, who was about my age, also had a similar temperament and the three of us would go for a couple of pints to sort out that day's particular business. Dealing with Mansion House (the official residence of the Lord Mayor) was not so informal but Colonel John Howard, the City Marshall, was incredibly helpful and a first-rate facilitator when it came to solving tricky problems of protocol. He even managed to keep the Chief in his rightful place.

I had learnt that dealing with a Royal visit, for example to St Paul's, was like playing pass the parcel with whoever the Royal personages might be taking the part of the parcel. The Lord Mayor of London (or his deputy) had to meet and greet the Royal outside St Paul's and escort them to the Dean and Chapter waiting inside the Great West Door. (Protocol you see.) The Lord Mayor or deputy would then take his seat and the Dean and Chapter would escort the Royal(s) to their seats. Protocol ensures our Chief does not get a look-in until after the service when the Dean and Chapter present the Chief to the Royal visitor and other presentations can be made. That took care of thirty-five of the guests, plus the Royal Party, which only left two thousand five-hundred and sixty-five other guests to corral and get seated in the cathedral prior to Her Royal Highness's arrival.

Not noted for doing things by halves the Chief had also decreed that there would be a commemorative march past before the service comprising of the emergency services, voluntary organisations, and as many of the veterans who felt able and willing to take part. Still not flavour of the month I got my instructions via Chris or Gordon, who were briefed on his latest bright idea, and could I, "Look into it." The Chief thought it would be most appropriate if he actually led this march past riding a horse! I thought he would look more like Humpty Dumpty doing that but fortunately Colonel Howard saved the day (and our embarrassment) by insisting that only the City Marshal could lead a march within the City. But if the Chief wanted to ride his horse behind him who was he to say no. When Gordon briefed the Chief next on progress, he conveniently forgot to tell the Chief the last bit saying that only the City Marshal could lead the parade on horseback. This was rather fortunate as I had enough on my plate already without looking for a bloody horse for the Chief to ride.

My plan for managing the happenings outside the cathedral was to divide and conquer. The actual march past would consist of over 500 personnel. It would consist of contingents from the Brigade, the Army, RAF, City of London Police, Metropolitan Police, Ambulance Service, WRVS, St John Ambulance, The Salvation Army and two marching bands. The Brigade's Colour party would lead the main body of the march and a wartime LFB fire appliance (courtesy of dear Mike Hebard) would lead in the veterans. However, bringing the City of London traffic to a grinding halt, whilst we marched through its streets, was never an option. Especially given the strong military presence which posed a real security threat from a potentially lethal IRA bomb attack. There were also serious concerns as to just how far the veterans could be expected to march. Neither of these issues were particularly new to the Chief Inspector or Stephen Wayne. They suggested the march start from the north side of the Cathedral for the uniformed contingent, and staying within the tight security cordon surrounding St Paul's. Not quite what the Chief had in mind with his grandiose plans, but then he was not meeting the cost of providing the considerable security arrangements that the event was now demanding. The Chief Inspector, who clearly understood the demands being placed upon me, said he would fax the Chief if necessary, saying that this was the only option available to us to maintain the required security cordon with the resources allocated to the event. Of course, if the Chief wanted to cough up some cash…but that was never going to happen.

The inclusion of both a "high value" Royal visitor and a military presence pushed security high up our planning agenda. This was still pre 9/11, and before the "ring of steel" encompassed the City with its major security cordon after the murderous IRA Baltic Exchange terrorist bombing attack in April 1992 (that caused three deaths and £800 million worth of damage), but security was still tight. The Chief Inspector insisted on sniffer dog searches both on the night prior to the service and an hour before the service was due to begin. Additionally, armed protective officers would sit in the congregation near the Royal party. Admission to the Cathedral had to be by ticket only and a team of armed City of London police officers would be present to monitor all guest arrivals.

Fortunately the veterans did not pose such a security threat. Aldersgate was only a half a mile away from St Paul's and this was considered a suitable safe place for them to meet, form up and then march to St Paul's with a police escort. Even then the veterans then had to produce their tickets to get into Aldersgate and to enter St Paul's Cathedral.

Colonel Howard was as good as his word when it came to providing us with the promised support and access to his military contacts. The trumpeters of the 13/18th Royal Hussars were secured to provide the royal fanfare for HRH's entrance into the Cathedral. His old regiment, the Grenadier Guards, would provide the band and bandmaster and would play in the Cathedral whilst the invited guests were arriving. I knew little of Colonel Howard's ceremonial role so he invited me one afternoon to Mansion House to explain it. Over tea and cucumber sandwiches (no really, they were!) he gave a brief history on the role of the City Marshall. Created in 1595 by Queen Elizabeth I she had given powers to a Marshall to maintain order within the City of London. Although his powers diminished over the centuries, he was still the Lord Mayor of London's peacemaker and had to lead, challenge and escort those few military regiments still entitled to march through the city. He would lead our parade on horseback, in full ceremonial regalia, and then formally escort the Lord Mayor of London when he arrived at St Paul's.

The next important meeting at St Paul's was with a police Inspector attached to Scotland Yard's Royal and Diplomatic Protection Department (SO14). He was Ken Wharfe and this SAS trained officer was originally chosen to head up security for the Queen's grandchildren, heir apparent Prince William and Prince Harry (who affectionately called him "Uncle Ken"). He had become the Personal Protection Officer to the Princess of Wales three years earlier in 1987. He was extremely affable and with a warm smile immediately put one at ease. He had already got the "ins and outs" of the security arrangements from the City of London police but wanted me to walk and talk him through our arrangements. We wandered through the Cathedral whilst I outlined our arrangements and answered the frequent questions he asked. He said he would be in touch again and passed me his card with his private contact number, before thanking me for a thorough and useful briefing. I did not think, although important, our meeting was all that special but it clearly ticked all the right boxes. Apparently far more boxes than had been anticipated.

The young Royal Princes, Prince Harry (six) and William (eight) were on half term holidays the week of the commemoration and after our meeting it was suggested by the Princess of Wales' private secretary that the boys accompany their mother to the service. Suddenly we had three Royals not one. It would be the young Prince's very first (unofficial) combined public engagement. (The first was credited to Prince William the following year when in 1991 he attended a St David's Day service in Cardiff, Wales.) When the Chief heard of the news it was reported that he looked like the cat that got the cream!

Everything seemed to be falling into place with reassuring ease. St Paul's, the City of London Corporation and the City of London Police were pulling out all the stops to make the commemoration service work. Maybe the fact that the Bishop of London, the Lord Mayor of London and the City of London's Police Commissioner were all attending may have had something to do with it? The knack was trying to keep it all simple and if not exactly simple then certainly uncomplicated. This was all fine in theory but it fell to Chris and Gordon to sell my plans to the Chief. With a little stretching of the truth such as, "Cannot do that Chief, City of London Police security requirements," it seemed to work. My plan approved, it just need implementing. Breaking it down into manageable components, PR staff were now allotted roles to make it all happen. Steve Burton and a female colleague drew the short straws as they had the unenviable task of sorting the London Mayors from the Livery Companies and keeping them marshalled and all in order down in the crypt until they were told to "process."

Other PR staff would welcome the eighty-plus veterans who wanted to march from Aldersgate to St Paul's, via Aldersgate Street then New Change and into Cannon Street, finally stepping into St Paul's Churchyard. I was to co-ordinate the whole march and oversee the uniformed contingents whilst Chris and Gordon did the high-profile stuff. This meant Chris getting the Chief to the right place at the right time and Gordon looking after the VIP guest arrivals within St Paul's. None of this would have been possible without the considerable number of off-duty personnel who had come forward and volunteered to act as stewards, ushers or to take part in the Brigade's uniformed marching contingent. The Army and RAF had a clear advantage when it came to the marching but the Brigade more then held its own when it came to smartness. None more so than the Brigade's own colour party and Assistant Chief Officer Brian Butler who would head the Brigade's marching contingent.

With only two weeks to go, the Dean and Chapter had finally approved my request to repeat the highly popular Blitz exhibition at St Paul's. It was set up in the vast expanse of the cathedral's crypt with the Brigade museum's staff and exhibition team working into the very small hours to erect, and later, staff it. (In fact the exhibition proved to be so successful that the Dean requested it be extended by a further week.) Finally, and with only a limited number of City of London road closures approved for the march past, the City of London Corporation promising to provide the decorated dais, on which Her Majesty's Inspector of Fire Services, Sir Reginald Doyle would stand to take the salute with our Chief standing by his side, the last pieces of the jigsaw fell seamlessly into place. With briefing sheets finalised and circulated, setting out what was happening, when, and who was responsible for it, all I could do now was hope it all worked.

The actual day started at 7.30am in St Paul's Cathedral car park, by Cannon Street, with a "synchronise your watches" moment as I gathered all the key minders for last checks and to ensure that everything was in place and, of course, wishing ourselves good luck. The City of London police dog team had completed their sweep of the Cathedral for explosive devices early (they had arrived at 5am) and the Corporation of London had worked throughout the previous evening erecting street barriers and positioning the dais directly opposite and facing the Cathedrals South door. The carpeted dais was bedecked in colourful flowering plants and green and white ivy trailed down the front. A short flight of carpeted steps gave access to the platform from where the salute would be taken. "If that does not impress the Chief then I do not know what will," said one of the volunteer stewards. I was thinking, "Thank you Colonel, I owe you one."

Not all the stewards or "minders" were at my briefing. A few were already waiting at Aldersgate (the former London Salvage Corps Headquarters, now taken over by the Brigade) to greet the eighty plus veterans who were to march to St Paul's. We had asked the veterans to be at Aldersgate not later than 9am for a 10am "kick off." But when I arrived there just after 8am most had already arrived and were enjoying cups of tea or coffee and avidly digging into the refreshments laid on for them. "Some have been here since 6am," said one of my PR stewards as I grabbed a welcome first cup of coffee of the day. Already there was a wonderful feeling of esprit de corps as faces were recognised and conversations struck up. My attention was drawn however to one elderly dignified gentleman standing on his own by Aldersgate's open appliance room door and looking out into the street. Walking over to him I asked if he was alright. He turned to face me and tears were welling up in his eyes. "I was last standing in this street in December 1940," he said. "In this very street and none of these modern buildings were here then. The office buildings, on either side of the road, were burning out of control from the ground floor to the very top. Most were six floors high and flames were coming out of every opening, where once the doors and windows had been. It was so hot we couldn't even walk up the street. I told myself afterwards that I never wanted to come back here again and have to remember that night. But I am so glad I did." Then he reached out to shake me warmly by the hand and said, "Thank you."

Back at the Cathedral, and filing their way down into the crypt in dribs and drabs, came the Masters and Wardens of the City's Worshipful Company Liveries and Guilds who had to be separated from the arriving London Lord Mayors and Borough Mayors. All had to be sorted into their Order of Precedence. The Liveries starting with the Mercers (General Merchants) followed by the Bowyers (Longbow makers), Fletchers (Arrow makers) and so on to Paviours and Patternmakers. Bring up the rear were The Guild of Firefighters, (the Chief's own creation) of which he was the founding Master. The first 12 Companies were known as the Great Twelve City Livery Companies and woe betide us if we forgot!

With my two-protocol whizz-kids down in the crypt frantically trying to tick off individual names as each group prepared to robe and put on their tricorne ermine trimmed hats, and don their chains of office, things were getting a bit chaotic. First they attempted to politely ask the respective groups to form up in the required order. But when this failed, and in the best traditions of fire brigade crisis management, they went to Plan B. Each one getting a chair to stand on and positioning themselves on either side of the crypt, Steve Burton (in his best Arsenal football supporter's voice) shouted, "Right, now listen up. Livery Companies over here, Lord Mayors and Mayors over there and when your name is called please step forward and line up." Plan B worked out just fine.

The marching contingents gathered on the north side of the Cathedral and in St Paul's Church Yard taking up almost the whole length of St Paul's. They included representatives of the voluntary organisation's that had stood cheek by jowl with the wartime firefighters, The WRVS, the Red Cross, Salvation Army and St John. Whilst London's emergency services could not vie with the marching ability of the military on parade that day their immaculate turnout would have warmed even the sternest of Regimental Sergeant Major's hearts as they formed up, in columns, in their allotted positions.

Colonel Howard was resplendent in the ceremonial dress of the City Marshal. In his red and gold military frock coat, gold epaulets and white plumes flowing from his black and gold hat he cut an imposing figure. Sitting astride his magnificent horse he readied himself to lead the five hundred strong column. Lined up behind him was the marching band of the Metropolitan Police Force (not yet a police Service!). The London Fire Brigade's colour party was in front of the marchers with the Brigade's standard flanked by the honour guard, their ceremonial "No 1" dress uniform of black fire tunic, with chrome buttons, white belt and red sash. Standing ramrod straight, a throwback to his national service days in the Grenadier Guards regiment, was Brian Butler. He was wearing the Queen's Fire Service Medal that he had been awarded in that New Year's Honour list and which hung next to his other medal, the MBE. He stood in front of the eighty uniformed London firefighters selected to represent the Brigade, all in their undress uniform, and today wearing the white gloves that were issued to all the marchers for this special parade. Behind them were the RAF Regiment, the Grenadier Guards and the City of London Police each adding their own flair to this imposing and striking assembly and who were paying tribute to all those being honoured today.

The veterans had by now formed up to attention in columns of four outside Aldersgate. Led by the Pipe Band of the West Yorkshire fire service dressed in their parade uniform of bearskin busbies and traditional highland kilt, complete with dirk and sporran, they followed the wartime turntable ladder that had been stationed at Soho fire station throughout the blitz. The TL looked as new as its red bodywork shone in the bright sunshine, and the sun's rays reflected off the chromed outlets of the fire pump deliveries. Mike Hebard and his crewmember sat in their wartime firemen's uniform with their "tin hats" perched on their heads. The pipe and drum band would play all the way to St Paul's and with the sound of bagpipes warming up, the veterans made ready to depart.

Precisely at 10am three things happened at once. Both bands started to play. My two "parade masters" gave the order, "Atten-shun" and with the order, "By the left quick march," both contingents started their journey to the West Doors of St Paul's. With the sound of the Metropolitan Police band filtering down into the crypt the lines of Mayors and Worshipful Companies made their way up the stairs that lead in to the North and South transepts.

With St Paul's open now for the arrival of guests Chris and Gordon had already been very busy. Chris had gathered up the Chief and Sir Reg and ushered them safely onto the dais. Gordon was meeting and greeting VIPs and directing them either inside the Cathedral or to watch the parade. Lining the steps leading to the Great West Door was the Brigade's honour guard (recruits borrowed from training school for the occasion) waiting for the Royal arrival and that of the Lord Mayor of London Sir Hugh Bidwell and the City of London's civic and honorary heads. Inside the Cathedral the Band of the Grenadier Guards started to play and over forty other uniformed and non-uniformed Brigade stewards supplemented the staff of St Paul's to meet guests and direct them to their seats.

I was by now just an observer but watched with satisfaction, and relief, as the City Marshall came into view and turned into Paternoster Row. He would then turn right into New Change and in to Cannon Street itself. Waiting on the dais were the Chief and Sir Reg and I could not help wondering if the Chief was thinking, "I should be riding that bloody horse" as they saw, and heard, the first contingent drawing ever closer.

A free agent, I was now able to move around the Cathedral's perimeter. I felt like the director of a play, the performance had started and there was not a lot I could do, for now. Stephen Wayne, the Chief Inspector and I had been over the arrangements a hundred times. Our respective superiors had scrutinised our plans and so had Scotland Yard. If we had missed some vital ingredient it was a bit late now to try and add it.

Making the most of my temporary freedom I walked down New Change to Cannon Street to watch the arrival of the veterans. The distinctive sounds of the pipe and drum band echoed off the tall city buildings. The TL had reached the roundabout leading into New Change, about four hundred yards away. I had planned that that the veterans would arrive there just as the last of the uniformed contingent entered Cannon Street. But clearly there was a bigger gap than expected but it was nevertheless a notable achievement that the men and women marching today maintained the pace they did. What stood out, above all else, about this group of seniors was their "joie de vivre." On seeing, to their right, the unmistakable sight of the dome of St Paul's set against the clear blue sky there was a noticeable spring in their step.

Their obvious pride in taking part reminded me of the symbolism that the dome stood for during the height of the blitz. The blitz exhibition within St Paul's crypt told that story and I had taken time out during the week to refresh my memory.

Pre-planning had greatly expanded the fire service nationally with the formation of the auxiliary fire service in 1938. A campaign sought to recruit the hundreds of men and women needed to bolster the numbers necessary to combat the anticipated bombing that had already devastated Warsaw and Rotterdam. Whilst the AFS were paid the princely sum of three pounds per week they received sixty hours of basic training. Fortunately the anticipated onslaught failed to materialise in the first few months of hostilities.

While the Nazis continued their invasion of Norway, Belgium and France the men of the fire brigade continued their wait for the anticipated enemy attack. Frustrated and disappointed firemen in the AFS were given extra training and worked on equipment maintenance, which included lots of cleaning and sandbagging, anything to fight their boredom. By mid-1940 morale was low, their accommodation was basic, washing facilities inadequate and even uniform issue was in utter chaos, some firemen were only issued with a uniform cap and an axe! The phoney war brought public resentment to the fore as many who had signed up for the AFS were labelled draft dodgers. The situation got so bad by the summer of 1940 that thousands had left the AFS to go into other war effort work or to join the armed forces.

On the 7th September 1940 everything changed. Put on immediate stand-by, crews got into their fire gear and started up their converted London taxis and the trailer pumps. Air raid sirens sounded over London followed by the crescendo of a horrendous barrage. Swathes of enemy aircraft were seen over London, bombs rained down on the docks and the East End and the City of London. On and on the bombers came. At Surrey Docks one thousand pumps were in attendance. Warehouses and acres of timber were burning like a furnace. Many other fires were one hundred pumps. Suddenly the firemen and women were heroes. Still the bombers kept on coming and the firefighters took their place on the capital's front line. For fifty-seven nights these intense attacks continued only to suddenly and apparently cease. Then on 29th December a major attack centred on the City of London especially all around St Paul's. Water supplies failed in some places and the Thames was so low it could not be used to augment the water supply. Fourteen firemen were killed that night and fifteen hundred fires raged throughout greater London. The Blitz lasted until May 1941 with intermittent raids over the capital, and then it was over. During the Blitz thirty-two thousand civilians were killed and eighty-seven thousand were seriously injured. Two million houses were destroyed (sixty per cent of these in London) in the Blitz.

Watching the veterans now, heading toward me, I suddenly felt very emotional. I did not know if it was the relief of seeing the project come to fruition (and without a major glitch, so far!) or the sight of these senior citizens' obvious pride in representing so many of their colleagues who had waited fifty years for their achievements and sacrifices to be publicly recognised. But, in truth, it was the flood of personal reminiscence that I had listened to whilst taking phone calls from those so eager to attend today's service and them saying that, "Nothing would stop me getting here," that filled my head. There were so many stories, some of incredible bravery, by ordinary Londoners armed with just hoses which, they knew, would never protect them from the conflagrations they faced. They stood firm not just once but every time the enemy flew over the capital disgorging the thousands of incendiary devices that reaped death and destruction on its population and its buildings.

I was not the only one with a lump in the throat or wiping a tearful eye as the fire service's very own *"Contemptibles"* gave their salute to the Chief Inspector of Fire Services and then proudly continued onwards towards the West face of the Cathedral, there to finish their historic march. Many of those faces striding proudly along were complete strangers but a few were instantly recognisable. Marching side by side were Charlie Watson and Ken Thorne from my own first days at Lambeth fire station. As their marching contingent was halted and the order given, "Dismissed," the Honour Guard was brought to attention as they climbed the steps leading into the Cathedral. Meanwhile the TL was positioned in St Paul's Church Yard, whilst the pipes and drums continued to play as the last of the guests arrived for the service.

The march past finished just after 10.30. Now everything centred on the arrival of our Royal guests, the Princess of Wales and her two sons at precisely 10.55am. "No sooner, no later," is what we were told by her Private Secretary. Other than a bomb threat or the fire alarm sounding nothing was going to stop the order of service, agreed between the Dean and Chapter, the Lord Mayor's office and St James's Palace. It was, for now, their party. At 10.45am the Dean and Chapter, with the Bishop of Stepney, left the Dean's aisle on the south side of the cathedral and proceeded to the West Door of the Cathedral. Besides the

Bishop and the Dean, The Very Reverend Eric Evans, were the Precentor, the Archdeacon, the Reverend Canons plus the Chaplains and Deans Verger, all in a reverential column that slowly made its way to the Cathedral's ceremonial entrance. The Great West Doors are aptly named. These solid and ancient wooden doors stand 30 feet tall and are only used on ceremonial occasions such as today. The entrance of the hierarchy of the Cathedral was just a taster of the ceremonial dress that would be seen today as they slowly walked past the watching congregation in their ornate and decorative vestments. Ceremonial dress was the order of the day and the Dean and Chapter were particularly colourful in their copes (capes) of blood red and elaborately embroidered gold thread. The garments glistened as they caught the sun's rays shining into the Cathedral. Woven into these copes were symbolic hand-crafted tapestries and motifs, unique to St Paul's Dean and Chapter.

Even before the Dean and Chapter had reached the Great West Doors, the Worshipful Livery Companies and Guilds and the London Borough Mayors, who had been released from the crypt after having been put into their order for processing, now proceeded to their places in the Cathedral. For many in the congregation it was the first time they had seen Livery Companies, with their Guild Masters, Wardens and Beadles, all properly attired in their respective company regalia at close quarters. Steeped in tradition and ceremony, we seemed to step back in time two or three centuries as the lines of colourful capes of differing colours, some trimmed with fur others with silks, complemented the hats and caps that were once so fashionable in the sixteenth century. As they snaked their way from one crypt entrance the London Mayors entered from the other on the far side of the Cathedral. Whilst there were fewer Mayors than Livery Companies, they were none the less colourful. In traditional mayoral dress they wore ornate chains of office with the Borough crests hanging on their chests. It was a close-run thing as the two groups converged who wore the best hats? Probably the Mayors had the edge, as they moved up the aisle in their black tricorne hats overflowing with delicate white feather trimmings.

Outside, and unseen by the congregation, the Lord Mayor of London, Sir Hugh Bidwell in his magnificent black and gold trimmed Lord Mayor's ceremonial garments had arrived in the company of the principal Sheriffs and guarded by Colonel Howard, the City Marshal, on one side and the Sword (which he actually carried) on the other. The Sword was another ceremonial office holder and he wore a large round fur hat that looked like a hairy cake sitting on his head! Bringing up the rear was the Lord Mayor's Clerk bedecked in his full wig and gown that indicated his position as an officer of the law. As greetings were exchanged with the Dean and Chapter exactly on time at 10.50am, The Choir, the college of Minor Canons, the Prebendaries and the visiting Clergy proceeded to their places in the quire to the sound, for the first time today, of the Cathedral's magnificent organ. An air of anticipation filled the Cathedral.

A free agent (and with security clearance) I was moving discreetly around the Cathedral and was getting a ringside view of what would be a once in a lifetime experience. Although not a religious person I had fallen in love with the interior of St Paul's since I first I stood with my back to the, closed, Great West Doors and looked up through the nave towards the high altar and tried to absorb the breath-taking beauty before me. Stephen Wayne had extended the very kind courtesy of giving me a private conducted tour of the Cathedral one afternoon and showed me many of the interesting places "off limits" to the normal visiting public. Now this exquisite Cathedral was full to capacity, not an empty seat to be seen. The recital of the Grenadier's Guard band had resonated throughout this vast imposing architectural masterpiece to be then followed by the religious and civic ceremonial accompanied by St Paul's organ. With its seven thousand, one hundred and eighty-nine pipes and five keyboards it is the third largest organ in the United Kingdom. Now standing in the shadows of the West Door, I thought the anticipated hush of the congregation added its own special magic and atmosphere to the occasion. I felt very humbled and honoured just to be a small part of it. But for many of the congregation, the firefighting veterans (in a year that saw Nelson Mandela released from prison, Iraq invading Kuwait with one-hundred thousand soldiers and seven-hundred tanks and saw Margaret Thatcher quit as Prime Minister) this day, above all others, is one they would remember for many years to come.

I knew exactly where I wanted to be next and when I needed to be there. I moved outside to the top of the Cathedral's steps to witness the arrival of the Royal guests. They drove in to St Paul's Church Yard exactly at 10.55am. As Sir Hugh Bidwell stepped forward to greet Her Royal Highness and the two young Princes, she looked simply stunning. She stepped from her limousine wearing a coral pink two-piece suit with collar, cuffs, buttons all in purple together with matching coloured shoes and handbag. Wearing a wide upturned coordinated hat she led her sons up the steps between the honour guard of firefighters accompanied by the Lord Mayor with her personal protection officer, Ken Wharfe, and her RAF aide-de-camp behind them. Confident and smiling happily she looked and was beautiful. I could not help but notice that all eyes centred on her and she brought a smile to the face of everyone watching, as the young Princes walked sure-footed in her wake.

Slipping back into the Cathedral's pillared portico and facing the Great West Doors I followed the Royal party's progress as the Lord Mayor handed over to the Dean and Chapter who welcomed the Royal guests to the Cathedral. In a touching gesture the Dean bent low to say hello to each of the two young Princes whilst a Wandsman led the Lord Mayor and the Sheriffs to their place in the Quire. As the Royal party reached the threshold of the Great Doors a fanfare, played by the trumpeters of the Royal Hussars. The sound fills the Cathedral and on its cue everybody stands. This was immediately followed by the organist playing the introduction to the first hymn, *"Praise to the Lord, the Almighty, the King of creation,"* and the congregation start to sing. Whilst the Dean and Chapter escort The Princess of Wales and her sons to their places, the Colours of the London Fire Brigade, and those of the Guild of Firefighters are presented and placed upon the High Altar.

I secreted myself in the crypt, following the proceedings from the commemorative order of service. The Dean's bidding, prepared by Stephen, was moving and paid a fitting tribute to the contribution of the men and women of the fire service during the Blitz and the three-hundred of the London Fire Brigade and Auxiliary Fire Service who lost their lives protecting London. In a particularly poignant line that Stephen wrote for the Dean he said, "*We give thanks for the bravery and courage of those who worked beyond the call of duty to save life and property; they braved bombs, fire, rubble and shrapnel, putting aside concern for their own safety in the service of their fellow citizens.*"

As the Bishop of Stepney prepared to give his blessing, that was the cue to gather up the Chief Officer and the presentation party and take them to the Great West Door to await the Royal Party. It had been previously agreed with St James's Palace that Her Royal Highness would meet the Chief Officer after the service and half a dozen other individuals could be presented to her Royal Highness. (This group included the only London AFS fireman ever to be awarded the George Cross. He had served during the blitz at Soho fire station.) The Princess would then sign the Brigade's visitors' book and Chris would greet the Royal party outside St Paul's, at the foot of the steps, and show the young Princes over Mike Hebard's TL. To say that I was slightly envious of Chris would be an understatement, but I knew my place in the scheme of things and meeting a beautiful Princess was not one of them!

However, I did get a small walk-on part as looking after the visitors' book fell to me. The Brigade's visitors' book recorded all Royal, and other significant VIPs, visits dating back to the Royal opening of the Brigade Headquarters in 1937 when King George VI and Queen Elizabeth (the Queen Mother) were the first signatures in the current book.

Confirmation that the Princess was happy to sign the visitors' book gave Chris and Gordon a bit of a problem. Neither owned a pen befitting the Royal hand and Chris summed up the problem by saying, "We can hardly give HRH a bloody 'Bic' to sign the book with." So promising not to spend the whole year's PR budget I was dispatched to the West End to purchase a pen suitable for the Royal hand. John Lewis's in Slone Square was my first port of call and upon seeing their considerable array of fountain pens, all without prices, I considered that if I have got to ask the price then I cannot afford it, at least not without the risk of a prison sentence for the misappropriation of public funds. Shooting over to the Army and Navy Stores in Victoria Street I threw myself on the mercy of the store's duty manager and outlined my dilemma. Clearly a Princess Diana fan he parted with a gold plated Sheaffer fountain pen (and box) for a knock down price. (A price, at which I could still have taken my wife and kids away for a weekend break!) Returning to Lambeth, I put the pen in a safe place and was prepared to guard it with my life.

Following the presentations the Chief escorted Her Royal Highness to the Brigade's visitors' book and I passed the Chief the pen, with a cheaper Parker (back-up version) safely in my pocket just in case! The Princess graciously signed the visitors' book and the Chief, now totally besotted with his newfound Royal companion, passed the pen back to me. As no one ever asked for the pen back I did not offer it. I took the pen, and its box, home for safe keeping as a treasured memento of the occasion, and it still is.

Little did I know then that the pen would reconnect with the now Princess Diana. In the early hours of Sunday 31st August 1997 my son rang home, from a nightclub in Brighton, to break the tragic news. Diana had been fatally injured in a car crash in Paris and she had died a short time after. Her death provoked a nationwide outpouring of grief on an unprecedented scale. Now retired, I took the early morning train to Victoria and walked the short distance to Buckingham Palace. There, with hundreds of others, I placed my flowers, already many feet deep, in front of the tall ornate railings of the Palace. However, the largest floral tribute, that filled the whole of the roadway leading to her Royal residence at Kensington Palace, remained in place for weeks after her death.

The public shock and sense of national loss was so great that later that same week books of remembrance were opened in St James's Palace. Once again, I took the London train to join the thousands of others that lined The Mall and queued patiently all day to sign the books. Harrods had sent vans to provide free refreshments and no one lost their place in the queue whilst comfort breaks were frequently taken. Friendships were struck up with the people directly in front and behind as we waited hour after hour and moved, ever so slowly, towards St James's Palace. After nearly seven hours of queuing I finally walked into St James's Palace and sat down in the special booths where the books had been placed. The was no rush, no one said, "Hurry up please," as individuals composed their thoughts and left personal messages and their annotations to someone whose life had been so tragically cut short at the age of thirty-six. From my pocket I removed a pen. Not just any old pen but the pen that Diana had used to sign that visitors' book almost seven years earlier. As I wrote my message of condolence, I recalled the day that she added so much by her mere presence and her genuine ability to connect with people. Having written my private thoughts I lit a candle in her memory and went home with a mixture of emotions that is difficult to describe let alone understand.

But now this young vibrant Royal Princess and Prince William and Prince Harry were walking out into the bright sunshine and there at the bottom of the Cathedral steps was Chris waiting to greet them. He introduced Mike Hebard who invited the young boys up on to the fire engine and Prince Harry did not need asking twice as he climbed aboard and sat smiling behind the big steering wheel with a smiling mother looking on. Prince William needed a little more encouragement as he was helped up and he rang the large fire engine bell much to the delight of the press photographers and press core eager to get that "special" picture of the young Princes' first outing.

The Royal party made their departure before the congregation exited the Cathedral as Her Royal Highness moved onto her next engagement, the State visit of the President of Italy. Suddenly it was all over but not before Stephen, the Chief Inspector and I held a debrief a few days later over a celebratory meal, and a few pints, in The Anchor restaurant in Bankside overlooking St Paul's, across the River Thames. I would be back at St Paul's at Christmas with another Carol Service and another Royal would be signing the visitors' book. (But not with a certain pen!)

What heinous crime had I committed, or what I had done to the Chief Officer in a former life (or this one)? Whatever it was, he could never actually bring himself to say, "Good job Pike." At least not to me. (Unless it was all to do with his soggy kitchen units!) Even to this day, I still find it sad that he never once extended a heartfelt thank you for the work and effort that went into putting those commemorative projects together. But with it all now over I drafted letters of thanks for all those who gave so willingly of their time, and had contributed so much to its ultimate success. The letters were sent to the Chief for his personal signature before being sent to the individual recipients and a copy placed in the personal record file of all those who were within the Brigade. Chris sent one other name up for the Chief's moniker and I duly received a copy of my own bloody letter.

However, I did receive a wonderfully moving and handwritten letter from Colonel Howard expressing his understanding and appreciation of the work that went into the St Paul's commemoration. In his own words he wrote, "*It was an occasion I shall certainly treasure long, and one in which I was very proud to take part.*" That summed up my sentiments exactly. I knew that the words "thank you" to be a powerful motivator when delivered with conviction and felt it poignant that the head of my own organisation failed to see any value in them.

Mayhem-mastermind-manhunt

There were a lot of uniformed operational senior officers within the London Fire Brigade. Some might argue too many when compared to the number of actual incidents that warranted their attendance. Having to attend a major incident simply did not occur as frequently as it once had done, say, in the early seventies. Since then improvements in the conditions of service and the total number of senior officers had grown significantly especially following the cessation of the former senior officers' residential duty system. Now actually taking a commanding role of a major fire or incident was becoming a rare event for some officers. This was not improved by the inconsistency in the Brigade's approach to delivering and assessing the command capabilities of Brigade officers, including its senior officers. Although a serious fire involving the tragic death of two firefighters would soon bring such problems under much closer scrutiny.

Some Command Areas were keener to deliver command and control training than others. I had helped devise and deliver such training in the South East Command, but it was a programme that was not universally taken up across the four other Area Commands and it was totally non-existent at Brigade headquarters.

With the introduction of Station Commanders, and later the five Area Commands, the mobilisation of senior officers to incidents was originally meant to be based on their geographic location. This meant that the nearest appropriately ranked officer was ordered onto an incident to assess the situation and/or to take charge as required. This worked reasonably well outside normal office hours but the five Area Commanders did not like the idea of Headquarters officers, working at Lambeth HQ or Southwark Training Centre (T/C) being ordered onto incidents in their Areas because they were the nearest, being mobilised before their own Area officers. So we officers were not high on the mobilising list regardless of how close to an incident we may have been.

All Headquarters officers, including Southwark T/C, were divided either between the five Areas so as to provide operational cover in the Area where they lived, or were put on the Headquarters senior officer's operational rota. The "press officer" was one of these headquarter operational roles. The nominated post holder covered the whole brigade area, regardless of where he lived or worked, during his twenty-four-hour operational duty periods. Working in Press and PR this became my principal operational duty on twenty-four-hour duty and frequently during my eight am – five pm day shifts when the nominated officer might be out of the brigade area or tied up in a meeting.

On the incident ground dealing with press and media was very ad-hoc. Some officers could see the value of good working relationships with news and broadcast outlets whilst others saw their presence as an unwanted intrusion and a bloody nuisance. A two-page memorandum gave the only guidance on providing information to the press and even that was directed to dealing with local press inquiries received at a fire station. Twenty-four-hour news channels had yet to make the leap that would, in a few years, come to dominate the delivery of instant news stories and cover tragic happenings around the globe with their *"breaking news"* stories. News stories vied for position on scheduled news programmes or broadcasts. A "newsflash" only broke into the regular schedules if it was of national significance, such as a Royal dying or a major aircraft or rail crash.

The Press and PR Division was responsible for the Brigades only press office. Its press officers were civilian staff and their duties were an add-on to their normal managerial or specialist PR function. Three, including Gordon, provided out-of-hours cover and would provide direct press liaison if required for developing major incidents or multi fatality fires. They were in most instances the "fire brigade spokesman" even though one was female.

Before I was "pulled" into Press and PR I had not given much thought to the duties of the incident press officer either. As an Area operational officer I was one of many that focused on my command and control responsibilities and assumed that the senior officer nominated to cover the "press officer" function had a similar understanding as to what their role entailed. I was amazed to discover that there was no guidance to offer Headquarters' officers who were rostered for this duty on their operational rota.

I was also directly responsible for the day-to-day supervision of the brigade's four photographic crews. With two photographers per watch each had their own photographic vans equipped with various cameras and video recording equipment. The brigade had a long history of taking and maintaining a photographic record of major and other significant incidents. This was in addition to providing photographic evidence used for fire investigation, breaches of fire safety requirements and all fatalities. Recording "live" events at incidents rested largely on the shoulders of the individual watch photographers and their particular photogenic eye. All were accomplished "amateur" photographers. (Two were professional if you included their own photographic businesses.) But some had a better eye than others in capturing the spectacular or were just lucky at the moment of a dramatic rescue or had their camera ready the instant a gas cloud erupted violently into a ball of burning flame.

I set down on paper the operational problems I had identified that involved the current media liaison officer's role, or lack of it! We needed to get our act together and this required some training and then putting into operational practice. It would, hopefully, be giving a much better level of support to those covering the brigade's press office. Chris, was an excellent manager and his simple philosophy was, "Do not bring me problems, bring me solutions." So at our next regular Divisional Heads of Section meeting I spelt out the problem, its likely causation and then suggested a way forward. Not least of my proposals was bringing the headquarters uniformed senior officers up to speed as "press officers."

I had previously attended the Civil Defence College at Easingwold in Yorkshire learning about Emergency Planning. (It turned out to be a wonderful week spent at a large country house, within its own private grounds, where I learnt to play croquet after dinner on the immaculately laid lawns!) The principal speaker, in an otherwise boring week of emergency planning seminars, was the Metropolitan Police's Director of Media Relations. He would later go on to be the Communications Director for the Home Office. He delivered a masterful power point presentation on the strategies for successful "operational media relations." It was his contention that the handling of the media at operational incidents had similarities irrespective of the emergency service involved, be it the police, fire brigade or ambulance service.

Under his heading of "*Mayhem-Mastermind-Manhunt*" I explored, with other attendees, the media's insatiable appetite to pursue newsworthy happenings. The brigade's most obvious involvement would come to the fore in the *mayhem* phase. Here the incident is live, the situation fluid and possibly fraught with many difficulties, not least the possibility of injuries and fatalities still on going.

Mastermind is where our professional opinion or judgements can be called into question when compared to the panel of instantly available "experts" as they provide analysis on the unfolding situation or its aftermath. Finally there is the *Manhunt* phase embarked upon by the media frenzy for answers. Why did it happen, and always, who is to blame?

Our guest speaker held nothing back as he guided us through this minefield of potentially damaging media relations, especially if you got it wrong. Highlighting examples from his own experiences as head of the Metropolitan Police's media team he illustrated the benefits of good practice and spelt out the pitfalls of bad media exposure. His most memorable summation was, "If you think preparation is expensive, try chaos!" Now armed with his thought provoking and illuminating presentation notes I had the key elements of our own in-house training package. I made my pitch and Gordon not only saw merit in progressing the training but signed me up for a short television interview course at the City of London University's media studies faculty. I was off to get a better feel of what could be incorporated into our own series of senior officer media seminars.

This short course, and it was short, dealt with aggressive and searching media interviews and identified best practice when working before "live" television cameras. The course participants, in various middle management roles, were from both the private and public sector and all had an active involvement with media liaison. Amongst our group of a dozen or so was an eminent clinical psychiatrist, a somewhat timid lady in her early forties. However, she made the rest of us, including the tutor, feel rather uncomfortable because we, wrongly, assumed that our every move was under her watchful gaze. So I was amazed that when it was her turn to come under the glare of the University's studio camera lights in our interview exercises that she froze. She could not answer a single question or even speak about her own field of expertise. It obviously came as a complete shock to her too and despite the reassurance of our media tutor, a television journalist, she only marginally improved on her second and then third attempt. Much to her obvious discomfort a lesson was learnt, do not put people up for live camera work or live interviews who are uncomfortable being there. It shows and can have disastrous results.

We were taught the importance of avoiding jargon. Organisations love this form of communication and most, it seems, generate their own particular variant. The brigade was no exception, willing and able to generate more than most. It is a language, which is rarely understood or used by other people. To most individuals in the public domain it is often unintelligible and meaningless. Whilst it may be an indispensable means of communication at work it can, and does, easily confuse outsiders. In a series of cleverly contrived studio interviews we were individually put under the spotlight with one clear instruction, no jargon or in-house acronyms. It proved harder than we all thought and for one poor soul, utterly indoctrinated in his company's jargon, impossible.

Armed with this new found media "expertise" Chris and Gordon put me through my paces when I returned to work and evaluated the proposed seminars before I took it out to my fellow officers, tasked with the "press officer" role. The seminars went down extremely well with colleagues, many of whom had received no formal input, on an operational role that they had been performing regularly. There was also a noticeable improvement in the quality of information sent to the press office. But the greatest benefit from all this media training was of a very personal nature and all too soon I would be tested in the real world of breaking news stories. A large warehouse fire in East London that would have, sadly, tragic and far reaching consequences.

The Statue

The Chief's demands, in the twilight of his career, were becoming more and more challenging. His demands were challenging the limited resources of the Division. With little else to be accomplished, his roles as Chief Fire Officer, Master of the Guild of Firefighters and recent election to Chairman of the Firefighters Memorial Trust combined all of his considerable energy and talents on commissioning a special sculpture; a permanent memorial to the nation's firefighters who had died in the course of their duties during the Second World War.

Never a Freemason, I had previously rejected the Chief's invitation to join the Guild of Firefighters, something that I had considered to be in a similar vein. I had little dealings with his latest project, The Memorial Trust. So I was rather surprised when I found myself, once again, heading off to St Paul's to organise the Chiefs most significant, and his last, high profile VIP event. Much had, in fact, already been accomplished by the Chief (wearing his various caps) to raise the necessary funding to meet the significant costs of the monument and securing its siting within the City of London and in the very shadow of St Paul's Cathedral itself.

I was now a familiar face at the offices of the Cathedral's Dean and Chapter. The Very Reverend Thomas Eric Evans was still Dean (and would remain so until his death in 1996). With a welcoming nod this gentle and talented man took even the most complex of high-profile services in his stride. Seemingly unflappable, he said, "What have you got for us this time?" Although from his knowing smile I was pretty sure that he already knew. If anything was happening in the shadow of St Paul's this well-connected man would already have wind of it. But if he did know he had not shared the information with Stephan Wayne, my contact once more at St Paul's. Outlining the brief handed down on high by my Chief, and over morning coffee, Stephen's concerned look was followed by, "You want to do what?" before he continued, "He does not do things by halves does he," as he tried to absorb the full implications of the brief, our last combined project together.

The Memorial Trust had been formed the year before. Among its aims was to negotiate a site, to the south of St Paul's, where a suitable memorial might be placed. This national memorial was being crafted by its sculptor John Mills and it would be something that was rarely seen in life-sized works of art. Still at the artist's studio the statue, aptly named "Blitz," would show three bronze wartime firefighters engaged in firefighting. Mounted on an octagonal bronze base the names of all the men and women who, sadly lost their lives during the conflict, were moulded in to its sides. The completed memorial, when the sculpture was joined to the base, would be over 12 feet high.

"Have you ever done an unveiling before?" Stephen asked. "Not a bloody great statue." I replied, "Have you?"

"No" he said, "but I wish you the best of luck. I am sure you will work something out!" Neither of us really convinced as the logistics and the magnitude of our undertaking started to unfold. "Has he (the Chief) really found a spot near St Paul's?" continued Stephen. "Apparently so," I replied. "Just across Cannon Street, facing the Cathedral's south side, on New Change Court. Influential friends I guess."

"God knows how he gets away with it," smirked my ecclesiastical friend. "I will have to ask him at Evensong!"

Sir Winston Churchill (then still The Right Honourable) once called the Blitz firefighters, "The heroes with grimy faces." Paying a moving tribute to their valiant wartime efforts before a packed House of Commons he was commenting on the extensive and extended bombing raids on London and other British cities devastated by this onslaught. Yet despite the national feeling of gratitude that prevailed for these "heroes" of the country's fire services, no national memorial was ever commissioned to formally recognise the ultimate sacrifice of over one thousand of their number, until now.

The London County Council had erected a small memorial wall and a scroll of honour to the three hundred London firemen and women who had perished, in action, during the blitz and the latter years of that war. The memorial, located in the main entrance lobby of the Brigade Headquarters, was a striking montage of iconic wartime images, including that of St Paul's. At the Brigade's annual Remembrance Sunday Service, tributes of poppy wreaths were laid in honour of our fallen comrades.

Despite whatever personal misgivings I had about the Chief, his Machiavellian ways, his cunning and the wily schemes accredited to him, he deserved full credit for what he was trying to achieve now. This he had largely orchestrated singlehanded. I would do my very best, albeit in a supporting role, to ensure the day was a truly memorable occasion, especially for those that had waited so long for this national recognition to materialise.

Stephen had a genuine interest in the London Fire Brigade. Something that had grown since we first worked together two years earlier. Now curious as to what form the memorial would take I told him our Chief worked in mysterious and, sometimes, unconventional ways. The original idea for the monument's design came from a smaller bronze statuette. It was commissioned in 1984 by Cyril Demarne (the former Chief Officer of West Ham Fire Brigade). He had loaned it to the London Fire Brigade where it was displayed at the headquarters Blitz memorial. It had been Demarne's personal memorial to fallen colleagues who had died during the awful bombing raids in East London. His son-in-law, the sculpture John Mills, had created this small bronze which became the maquette for the Memorial Trust statue.

It was the unveiling of that original statuette that brought about the realisation that there should be a larger, permanent, memorial in a prominent position, possibly in the capital city. The now eight-foot-tall art work tells the story of three firemen, a Sub Officer and two blitz firemen in action as in any great fire anywhere in the country during the blitz. The interdependence of these men and their comradeship, so typical of the service, intensified by the horror of warfare on the home front, was given as the reason by John Mills for their compact grouping. In a link with the times, the names of all the 1,027 men and women who lost their lives was cast in the same font as that used in the 1939-1945 wartime rations books.

Excluded from the personal briefings given to Gordon and Chris by the Chief (I was still persona non grata after his kitchen units were sunk by the Fire Service Preservation Group!) they nevertheless gave me my head when it came to putting the organisation of this big day together. They seemed to have more faith in me than I did to pull this thing off. Where do you start to learn the intricacies of statue unveiling? There were certainly no unveiling instruction manuals in the Brigades comprehensive library and "googling it" was too far into the future!

Whilst I was worrying about how to meet the Chiefs exacting brief the well-oiled machinery of the Division was forging ahead with the event's other necessary arrangements. Gordon had crafted another of his carefully baited letters that he hoped would hook the Chief's required Royal presence. The reply, from Clarence House, when it arrived went first to the Chief's secretariat and there was considerable glee when the Chief read that Queen Elizabeth, the Queen Mother had graciously agreed to both attend the service and unveil the statue. With visions of my first (and last!) unveiling going all horribly wrong and draping the Queen Mother in yards of cloth as it fell, unceremoniously, from the statue, I thought it was time to seek the help of the experts. I made some telephone calls. The solution came in the form of a return call from the Ministry of Defence and an invitation to meet Wing Commander Peter Storey, who was in charge of the Royal Air Force's ceremonial office.

Chris and I headed off to their offices in Whitehall where we were greeted and escorted through the maze of corridors that lead to the RAF's ceremonial offices. Wing Commander Peter Storey was a tall handsome officer who had a welcoming smile and firm strong handshake. "Just how can I help you?" was his opening gambit and it was music to our ears. Armed with a photo of the completed statue, taken at John Mills' studio, Chris passed it to Peter Storey who studied it for a few moments before saying, "I see your problem."

The three firefighters in the eight-foot high statue were portrayed tackling a blaze. Two firemen hold the hose and direct the branch (jet) whilst the Sub Officer, facing in the other direction, points towards the fire with one arm whilst summoning assistance with the other. The combination of arms and the branch were prefect foils that would prevent the free fall of any material placed over the statue for its unveiling.

While an attractive WRAF clerk brought in coffee and biscuits Peter said "Were you the chaps that put together the march and service at St Paul's last September?" Chris said we were and then, very modestly, gave me the credit for putting much of the Brigade's organisation together. I sat their looking rather embarrassed knowing that I was just part of the team responsible for its overall success. "The lads from the RAF regiment, who attended it, said it was almost up to the RAF standard." said the smiling Wing Commander reaching for his phone. "Flight Sergeant, come in here please." We were joined by an immaculately turned out Flight Sergeant, with creases down his trousers you could cut your fingers on. Introductions made, our newcomer was apparently their "Mr Fix-it" and suitably briefed he went out again to consider our problem. "Oh did I mention?" said Chris "The Queen Mother is doing the unveiling." I went back subsequently, unaccompanied, to see the Wing Commander who insisted that I call him Peter. We got on famously, too well according to my Deputy Chief!

With The Queen Mother attending and the Rt Hon Kenneth Baker (the Home Secretary) representing the Prime Minster who had declined the Chief's invitation; Stephen, myself and the Chief Inspector of police came together to prepare our joint plans for this event. Armed with the, almost finalised, plans I accepted Peter Storey's invitation for him to look them over but giving particularly attention to the fine detail involving the actual unveiling. Having assured me that things were progressing well in sorting out just how to unveil the statue, I received his affirmation that our scheme, as outlined, could work. It really had to because we had no plan B! "I see you follow the RAF's K.I.S.S. management philosophy. ("Keep it simple stupid," he said. "Best way and normally delivers the goods.")

Chris and Gordon had bought into the plan too and they now had the unenviable task of getting the Chief on side. I on the other hand had two unrelated summons, one far more pleasant than the other. The first was to report immediately to the Deputy Chief (who was out of the loop on all things unveiling!) on the seventh floor. This odious and arrogant individual would soon be the Brigade's youngest ever Chief Fire Officer at the age of forty-four. His renowned sense of self-importance and general contempt of others won him few fans outside his immediate circle, somewhere I had no desire to be. "I met with a friend of yours yesterday evening at a formal function in the City," he said as I was shown into his half of the seventh-floor executive suites. "A Wing Commander Peter Storey of the RAF who apparently, and misguidedly, considers you to be someone of importance in this Brigade!" He almost spat out the words as he continued, "I put him right of course," before telling me to shut the door behind me whilst his small mouth held its scornful and contemptuous smile as I left the room.

The second summons was far more pleasurable; in fact it was a real treat. I was off to meet Sir Martin Gilliat that evening and you could not have imagined a starker contrast between two people. Sir Martin John Gilliat was one of the Royal Households longest serving members. He was also one of its most efficient and popular members. He had been the Private Secretary, and an Equerry, for over forty years to Queen Elizabeth the Queen Mother and shared much of her public and private life. Born in 1913, at 78 years of age he moved with the agility of someone thirty years his junior as he walked purposefully towards me while I waited in the Dean's Aisle, our agreed meeting place.

He was an utterly charming man. Despite his familiarity with St Paul's and its lay-out he was here on a reconnaissance mission, but one that was not just about looking at the venue which, he said, he knew intimately. It was all about meeting us and seeing what was expected of his Royal charge. He quickly grasped the detail of the event and we walked through the entire route contained in the proposed programme already provisionally agreed with Clarence House.

His subtle questioning tested the thoroughness of our planning. "How many steps did you say led down from the cathedral's South door?" (The Queen Mother's route to the statue after the service.) I had not actually said anything about them but provided the correct answer from memory whilst he, Stephen and I walked down them towards New Change Court. "Correct," he said as we reached the bottom step before crossing Cannon Street to inspect the unveiling site.

The Corporation of London had already completed the monument's footings and were preparing the plinth for the bronze base on which the combined statues would be mounted, which had been negotiated by the Memorial Trustees. We were just left with the responsibility for making the big day go like clockwork. Our elegant and grey-haired inquisitor did not miss a trick as his razor-sharp mind sought to identify any potential flaw in our arrangements, which might pose the slightest problem, or potential embarrassment (which was never going to happen) to The Queen Mother. Curious about the actual unveiling he dug deeper. "What happens now?" he asked. "Her Majesty will simply pull on a ribbon around the statue," I said, sticking to the clear brief given to me by Peter Storey. His Flight Sergeant was still working on a "cunning plan!" The mention of Peter Storey's name, in passing, brought an instant look of recognition and a smile, on Sir Martin's face. "I know the Wing Commander," he said. "I am sure everything will be just fine. I will see you gentlemen on the day." Satisfied he briskly walked away, back to St Paul's and his waiting car, leaving us to ponder just what exactly will happen once the ribbon is pulled?

It certainly was not the charisma of the Deputy Chief that had won the unsolicited support of Peter Storey over to our cause but he was clearly committed to it. Having already promised the RAF trumpeters to provide the Royal fanfare, one of whom would also sound the *"Last Post and Reveille,"* he delivered on his promise to crack the problem of the unveiling, or rather his Flight Sergeant did. My last meeting with him, as the big day was rapidly approaching, ticked off the final item on our "to do" list. The clever Flight Sergeant had devised, and tested, a device that could safely unveil the memorial. "It's more of a hoist actually," said the very cheerful and satisfied Flight Sergeant clearly eager to explain more. I was even more eager to hear about it. "It is a blooming big scaffold pole, well two actually," he said. The look of concern was clearly showing on my face as he continued. "No it won't look like a bloody scaffold pole; it looks more like a very long skinny crane. It works just fine. It really does." Thinking just how to break it to the Chief that the Queen Mother would be working with some old scaffold pole I was certain this would easily top my soggy kitchen unit's debacle.

The unveiling and dedication was under the total direction of the Firefighters Memorial Trust. However, you could easy be forgiven for thinking it was entirely a London Fire Brigade affair as regards the organisation for overseeing and arranging both the service at St Paul's and co-ordinating the arrangements for the unveiling. The Chief may well have been wearing his Memorial Trust's Chairman's cap to promote the occasion but he was skilfully utilising his position as head of the London Fire Brigade to ensure that every available in-house resource was throw at this event. His trusted lieutenant, and a member of the Board of Trustees, was Ken Knight, my former Assistant Chief Officer and still head of Central Operations. Whilst I was out of the Chief's loop, I was certainly not out of Assistant Chief Officer Knight's, the power behind the throne as regards the Memorial dedication. Despite Gordon and Chris briefing the Chief I was still required to update Ken Knight and give him my personal assurances that everything was going to plan. Ken Knight would soon be promoted, first becoming the Chief Officer of Somerset before returning to London as its Chief Officer a decade later. He would become the only London Chief Officer, now called a Commissioner, to be knighted in over sixty years. It was a richly deserved accolade for this multi-talented individual whose elevated position never seemed to adversely affect his deep sense of fair play and his humanity.

The invitees to this service were coming from all over Great Britain. Representatives from virtually every United Kingdom fire brigade combined with the numerous veteran groups, and the Chief's rising list of VIPs were putting the cathedral's seating capacity under considerable strain. Once again, the Dean and Chapter had negotiated prime seating arrangements for the Chapter wives which put an additional strain on the Chief's personal oversight of his seating arrangements, particularly of the front rows.

But, as with all high-profile events the PR Division found itself responsible for, this was not the only ball that was up in the air at the same time of the unveiling and which the combined talents of Chris and Gordon had to manage. They still had to oversee and deal with the considerable day-to-day demands that operational incidents, press inquiries and scheduled visits to Brigade placed on the Division and its limited resources. Early evening would frequently find Chris and I ensconced in his office, sharing a bottle of wine, with Chris doing his normal, "What if?" cross-examination and I listened to the day's news and learnt of its dramas whilst Gordon was darting between the Chief and the Deputy getting ever more tasks allocated to his team. That was the nature of the Press and PR role and we were simply there to support a much bigger picture, the public face of the London Fire Brigade.

The Brigade was no stranger to St Paul's. Over the years it had built up an excellent rapport with the Cathedral's authorities. We also had a wide network of reliable Brigade uniformed and non-uniformed personnel who volunteered as stewards and ushers when requested. They were very used to seeing people into the Cathedral and, after the service was over, politely letting them make their way out in their own good time. This time, however, there was a significant difference. With almost two thousand six hundred people in the Cathedral for the Service we now had to get them out again as quickly as possible. Then get them across Cannon Street and to regroup in New Change Court for the unveiling, all without it looking like a disorganised stampede. It seemed like a logistical nightmare especially as the Cathedral authorities remained insistent that the Great West Doors would only let Her Majesty the Queen Mother in, not the congregation out!

The final briefing to all the important players was delivered on Friday 3rd May, my wedding anniversary. At home I was not the flavour of the month since I was tied up with rehearsals for the service and unveiling that evening at St Paul's. The dais, as promised by the City of London, had been delivered and erected and was now under police guard as part of their comprehensive security precautions for tomorrows big event. On that bright warm May evening the honour guard, who were actually going to unveil the statue, rehearsed their drill. I had elevated myself to the temporary status of Queen Mother! The RAF had been real lifesavers. Their clever, and simple, device was already in its position by the statue. It was as the Flight Sergeant described, two long lengths of scaffold pole joined together and held securely in the vertical position by a heavy concrete base. With a three-foot high wooden box, wrapped around the base of the pole, it looked every inch like a twenty-five-foot high, very thin, flag pole. All except for one thing. A third of the way down from the top was another scaffold pole hinged at its base to the main pole and at an angle of about forty-five degrees. On the top of the angled pole was hanging a white cord that ran through a pulley on the top of the main pole, then continued down the side towards the ground. The whole thing had been painted white. By pulling down on the cord it would raise the angled arm and lift whatever that was secured to it. Just like the arm of a crane moving upwards through an arc to its uppermost point.

Firmly secured to the cord hanging down from the hinged arm were two enormous Union Flags that totally covered the whole of the monument. The two flags had been sewn together along the top and down the long edge nearest the poles leaving the other long edge and bottom open. With the hinged arm angled over the top of the statue the Union flags hid the statue from public view. The enveloping flags were held closed by a long white ribbon that was wound around the bronze base and prevented the flags moving in the gentle evening breeze. As I stepped forward, aka The Queen Mother, to pull on one end of the ribbon I gave the signal for the two firemen performing this delicate task to pull slowly, but firmly, down on the cord. It took three attempts to get the timing just right, but on the third go whilst they slowly pulled steadily down, the hinged arm moved gracefully upwards, lifting the flags and revelling the statue in all its glory. In a surreal moment of realism the rays of the red setting sun caught the three bronze figures giving the impression of them once again bathed in the reflected glow of the blazing conflagration they were depicted fighting.

On the morning of the 4th May and under clear skies and warm sunlight it was, once again, a case of all hands on deck. An air of excitement and anticipation was obvious in our smartly turned out uniformed volunteers and the Division's staff as we all gathered around The Salvation Army's canteen van, parked in St Paul's Churchyard, for a welcome "cuppa" of tea or coffee. Still with three hours to go, much had already taken place the previous evening. Barriers now surrounded the Cathedral to prevent unauthorised entry by the public and despite the relatively low-key military presence, armed City of London police patrols made frequents stops and had already searched the whole site in preparation for the big day.

I thought it highly probable that the Queen Mother's own excitement to the unfolding day would not be matching that of our own. She had attended St Paul's Cathedral so very many times during her 55-year reign and probably even before her husband, George VI, was crowned King after his elder brother, Edward's abdication in 1936. Now, at the age of 91, she would return once again to perform her Royal duty. However, for the very many veterans attending today The Queen Mother could not have been a more fitting regal presence as the guest of honour at today's service to unveil the memorial. Not only did this dignified and refined Royal matriarch hold a position of immense respect and affection in the hearts of the general population. But to those of a certain age, the wartime images of her husband and herself touring London and the devastated cities, immediately following the Blitz bombing raids had done much to bolster the Nation's spirits, and showed that they too shared in the Nation's pain.

With my final checks completed, the safety briefings given and shared exchanges of, "Good luck," we all went about our allotted tasks. By 9.30am Chris was giving the corpulent uniformed figure of the Chief a tour of inspection of New Change Court and the veiled monument. The white satin ribbon, waiting to be pulled, was under the very watchful eyes of the two very tall City of London policemen sent to guard it. Gordon was doing his "front of house" manager bit as he dutifully paced the West Door front steps mindful of the imminent arrival of various VIPs. The VIP arrivals followed a well-rehearsed sequence of events. Each of the key players knew the role they must play and the cues that they would take from others. The Brigade had, by now, earned the admiration of both the Cathedral's Dean and Chapter and the Lord Mayor of London's office and could be relied upon to play our part with the professionalism and (their words) "the panache" which they associated with events organised by the Public Relations Division of the London Fire Brigade.

By 10.30am, and to the sounds of the Hampshire Fire Service band playing in St Paul's Church Yard, first Lord Bramall (the Lord Lieutenant of London) and Lady Bramall arrived followed shortly after by the Home Secretary, Kenneth Baker. All were greeted by a justifiably proud looking Chief Officer whose "wheeler dealing" had brought about this important day. His determination and drive had secured a fitting memorial to the fallen heroes whose names were now inscribed on its base. While principal guests exchanged brief greetings with the Chief, a steady, and constant, stream of guests were making their way into the Cathedral and being directed to their seats.

Exactly on time at 10.55am the Queen Mother arrived at the front steps of St Paul's. Met by the Lord Mayor *locum tenens (*deputy*)* there was not the slightest sign of this nonagenarian being in her dotage as she purposefully climbed the steps to the Great West Doors, flanked by her Lady in Waiting and Sir Martin who carried his trademark tightly rolled black umbrella in one hand and his bowler hat in the other. Dressed in a violet coloured coat and matching hat, with an open lace veil that covered her face, her Majesty had the looks and complexion that would have been the envy of younger women. From my vantage point I watched as Her Majesty was introduced to the Dean and the

Cathedral hierarchy and then as the royal fanfare sounded Her Majesty was shown to her seat by the Dean whilst the Chapter made their way to the Quire.

The first hymn, *"He who would valiant be,"* (by John Bunyan and Percy Dearmer) was my choice and unbeknown to anyone, other than Stephen, who had agreed to put it in the Order of Service as a personal favour to me. A lasting favourite from my childhood days at Edmund Waller Junior School I had wanted to hear it sung in the Cathedral by its wonderful choir and this particular congregation. It also had a much deeper meaning. I was no great fan of the Chief (and he certainly was not a great fan of me!). However, in setting his sights on providing the Blitz memorial project and making it all happen, it was my small personal tribute to him. It was a testament to the man's dogged determination to see the memorial through to its successful fruition. He certainly had been "valiant" and as one of the definitions of a Pilgrims put it; he was "someone that had undertaken a special journey." I could not think of a more fitting way to say, "Well done Chief," even if he would never guess the significance of that wonderful hymn that all those around him were now singing with such feeling.

The Dean, in his bidding, reminded the congregation (if they needed reminding) why we had all come together today. Eloquently with his voice filling every corner of the Cathedral he spoke of the commemoration to those firefighters engaged, during the dark days of the Blitz, in fighting a common foe in towns and cities throughout Britain. In tones that clearly expressed his own emotions he continued, *"To those that perished in the conflict, those firefighters who died in the cause of justice and freedom we will offer and dedicate an emblem and memorial."* It was a theme upon which the Bishop of Coventry built during his sermon.

Detailing the air raid of 14 November 1940, when the city's historic cathedral was destroyed in the firestorm, the Bishop told of Coventry's near destruction. The fire brigade headquarters, which suffered a direct hit, had its command and control disrupted making it difficult to send firefighters to the most dangerous fires first. Water mains were damaged by high explosive and there was not enough water to tackle many of the fires. In that one night more than four thousand homes were destroyed, along with three quarters of the city's factories. There was barely an undamaged building in the city. A hospital, churches and a police station being among the roll call of destruction. The air raid reached such a new level of destruction that Joseph Goebbels later used the term "Coventriert" (Coventrated) when describing similar levels of destruction of other "enemy" cities and towns.

In a moving recollection of the catastrophic damage to his city and the death and suffering it caused, the Bishop spoke movingly of the gratitude of a nation, unified behind that of its King George and Queen Elizabeth, to those who gave their time, their skill and their determination to bring order out of the chaos. In praising the outstanding work of the fire service during the Blitz he paid a special tribute to those that lost their lives in the service of others. Those who some members of the congregation knew and whose memory they continually treasured.

During the last hymn the Union Flag was returned to its Colour party who marched solemnly back down the Nave and, once out of sight, doubled over to the memorial site. After, and with the congregation again seated, the Queen Mother was escorted to the Dean's Aisle (on the south side of the Cathedral) where individuals, nominated by the Firefighters Memorial Trust, lined up ready to be introduced to the Queen Mother by the Chief. They were joined by an array of visiting, high-profile, clergy who witnessed these friendly proceedings followed by presentations to Her Majesty including the creator of the maquette and the statues, a bearded John Mills.

With the Queen Mother comfortably occupied in the Dean's Aisle that was the signal to move the whole of the congregation out of the Cathedral, to get them across Cannon Street and to reassemble them behind the roped barriers in New Change Court. This was a first for the Cathedral's stewards but for our volunteer stewards, used to getting people out of buildings in a hurry, they set about their controlled "evacuation" with a quiet and calm relish. Speedily they cleared the north and south transepts by utilising the respective transept doors whilst those towards the rear of the nave were politely herded out the main entrances on either side of the firmly closed Great West doors. With the south transept now clear the front rows of VIPs could be moved. With slightly more decorum they were directed out via the south door and grouped, still all together, adjacent to the dais.

In a cunning move, proposed by Stephen, to give us some extra time to reassemble the gathering the Dean now escorted the Queen Mother and her party into his office, off the Dean's aisle, for some liquid refreshment. It was rumoured that Her Majesty's favourite tipple, gin coloured pink by adding Dubonnet was on offer. With the presentations over, and the Chief and the others in the line-up, I hurried across Cannon Street ready for the final phase.

With the last of the congregation exiting the Cathedral I walked through the south transept to check that all was in readiness for the Queen Mother. Something unusual suddenly caught my eye, something in the corner of the transept. It was something that should not be there, a lone flag! It was the very flag, or rather standard, that the Retired Members standard bearer should now be displaying among the Honour Guard on New Change Court, but the silly sod had left without it. How could he not remember the bloody thing? Mumbling to myself as I grabbed the flag, "His only job and he's managed to cock that up!" I exited the South Door to the sound of the pitter-patter of Royal footsteps making their way along the Dean's aisle. With the best dignified trot I could muster I returned the flag to its forgetful, and very embarrassed, owner. He appeared to be frozen to the spot, too afraid to retrieve the flag, which, the empty leather cup of his standard holder told him was missing!

Almost everyone was now in position. Peter Storey, who had been standing alongside his Air Marshall, gave me the thumbs up sign and a wink of approval as I, rather unnecessarily, reminded the honour guard tasked with hoisting the unveiling flags to, "Pull slowly and steadily lads," before, nervously, taking up my own privileged position.

Once again it was pass the Royal parcel. The Dean escorted the Queen Mother to the South Door. The Lord Mayor-*locum tenens* escorted her down the steps and into her waiting car. Driven in a majestic U-turn Her Royal Highness was transported the fifty feet from one side of Cannon Street to the other, following Lord Mayor-*locum tenens* in his official car. He alighted and stood on the kerbside next to the Chief, who was now wearing his Chairman of the Board of Trustees head, (something that was totally lost on the majority of the gathering) and jointly they greeted Her Majesty and conducted her to her place on the dais.

The service of remembrance and the dedication of the memorial was to have been an inter-denominational affair including the Jewish faith. It would have been had the Chief Rabbi accepted his invitation to attend but Saturday was the Sabbath and the unveiling was deemed a "prohibited activity" so he could not attend. But the Bishops of Coventry and Fulham, the Archbishop of Southwark and the Moderator of the Free Churches all joined the Dean and Chapter to conduct the final part of the service.

As a lone RAF trumpeter sounded *The Last Post* a reverential hush fell over the assembly, as both the Union Flag and the standard of the Retired Members Association were slowly lowered in a token of deference to fallen fire service comrades. After the moment's silence *Reveille* was sounded and the Queen Mother gracefully moved towards the microphone, in front of the memorial, and addressed the congregation. Although her words were few, her distinctive voice carried the crowds with her as she spoke of her pleasure at being able to attend this dedication and of her admiration for those honoured and remembered by the memorial. Looking at the hundreds and hundreds of faces now looking intently at her it was obvious that she was not the only one finding pleasure in her being here.

How I got the distinction of standing by the draped statue remains a mystery to me. But there I proudly stood, flanked by Chris on one side and the Chief and the Queen Mother on the other. Maybe the Chief wanted to point the finger of blame at me if the memorial statue inexplicably did not unveil as planned! But, thankfully, as the Queen Mother moved closer and gently pulled on the end of the white satin ribbon it fell to the ground. As it fell the two Union Flags covering the memorial rose gracefully upwards revealing the "Blitz" statue and its bronze inscribed base. To the loud and enthusiastic applause of nearly three thousand people witnessing this historic moment there was clear and obvious approval for what they were seeing for the first time.

With the unveiling completed, Chris and I looked at each other with an intense sense of relief but also a feeling of tremendous pride in being involved in this memorable day. Full credit goes to those who worked so hard and so diligently in bringing the concept of the memorial to reality, not least of all the Chief himself. But now a warm carnival feeling came to the morning's proceedings as the Queen Mother went on a short walk-about meeting and greeting some of the congregation and receiving more and more floral bouquets. Some of those gathered there she clearly knew; the Air Marshall, Lady Bramall and Kenneth Baker to name but a few but others, total strangers, were made to feel equally important as she exchanged niceties and spoke warmly about the importance of the day. She was right of course it was, but for so many, myself included, her presence made it all the more unforgettable.

On the bell

It might seem that with all the previous pomp and other general PR work that actually attending fires and maintaining an operational role fell off the fence. That was certainly not the case. With two twenty-four-hour operational duties normally required each a week there was ample opportunity to keep one's hand in whilst monitoring or attending multi-pump fires or significant special service incidents. I was responsible for, as their line manager, the Brigade's eight operational photographers who worked out of the Press and Public Relations Division. I was their uniformed line manager.

The Brigade had a long history of "firemen" who acted solely as its official photographers. I had re-discovered some of the rare original glass negative plates that, whilst not totally lost, had been forgotten about and had been stashed away, collecting dust, in an unused storeroom. I had some of these photographs developed and the quality of the prints was quite exceptional, so much so that a selection were mounted and framed and put on display in and around the Brigade Headquarters building and Southwark's Training Centre.

After the Second World War there was only one photographer attached to each of the two watches. Watches were later increased to three by the time I had joined the Brigade in the mid-sixties, and later still the photographers were increased to two per watch. With the creation of the fourth watch I had responsibility for the eight operational photographers, who each held the rank of temporary Sub Officer, in recognition of performing these specialist duties. Most were substantive firemen, one was a Leading Fireman but they all had one obvious thing in common; a photographic eye and the skills and ability to develop their own work. There always had to be at least one photographer on duty to provide Brigade-wide cover. Each duty photographer had their own operational photographic van with one was nominated to take the operational role whilst the other would perform other photographic duties. However, if the first was already attending a call and a photographer was required operationally then, in most circumstances, he would drop what he was doing to attend the incident. Their operational role always took priority.

Fatal fires, arson or suspicious fires, infringements of fire safety and dramatic images of fires in progress or crews in action all fell to their remit as the Brigade's official visual recorders. Unless directed otherwise it was also their photogenic skills and professional eye, which captured some remarkable images either in still life (and frequently death!) or recorded the action onto video. Some major incidents required both photographers to attend and combine the use of still camera and video recording, sometimes supplementing the national and local broadcasting outlets' own images and footage.

Gillender Street

The drive through London's traffic on that July afternoon was fast and intense. I was responding to a serious fire in East London at Hays Business Services, located in Bow. This was no commonplace response either, as information had been received from the fireground that two firefighters were missing. Something had obviously gone terribly awry, and even as I was leaving Lambeth HQ and heading through the City of London, herculean efforts were being undertaken by emergency breathing apparatus crews to try and locate and rescue their colleagues. The missing firefighters had entered this burning warehouse in breathing apparatus but were now dangerously overdue.

What had seemed like a quiet day in the Division, especially in the Press Office, was suddenly turned on its head by the information coming in from the Brigade's control room. I was the duty Press and Liaison officer and was ordered on to the incident. Given the severity of the news filtering through, I took the unusual step of taking with me one of the non-uniformed press officers to help her gain experience. Leslie was able and intelligent, rather brash, and a single lady in her late twenties. Grabbing the press officer's mobile phone, which was the size of a house brick then, and her identification surcoat we prepared to leave for the scene, but not before informing Gordon and Chris of my intention of taking Leslie with me. With still no news of the two missing firefighters I expected that Gordon would either accompany me to the incident or drive himself. This was clearly not going to happen. Gordon was not on par, his demons had resurfaced and he had shut himself away mentally, a prisoner to the depression and private feelings of hopelessness these moods occasionally brought on. He had sought relief from the intense pressures placed upon him in his role as head of the Division by finding solace in drink. It had made matters worse not better, and whilst he would eventually rise to the challenge and seek help for his problems, it was not going to happen today and not now. So leaving Chris behind to deal with Gordon, we left Lambeth as the Chief Fire Officer was being briefed of the unfolding events at Bow.

To set the scene; the fire in Gillender Street was in a medium height brick and concrete high security data and records storage warehouse. What was immediately noticeable was the almost total lack of any normal window openings, what glazing there was was covered in metal grills and security fixings. The lack of such openings did not bode well for anyone trapped inside and desperately seeking some, or any, source of fresh air. Even whilst I walked to the control unit to book-in, the desperate and strenuous efforts of the breathing apparatus crews inside the building were continuing, trying to locate and, hopefully, lead to safety their two missing colleagues whilst others were valiantly trying to contain the serious blaze in the core of the building. For both these groups the conditions within the enclosed warehouse were daunting. The desire to locate their overdue comrades pushed the endurance of the emergency BA crews beyond their normal limits, yet still they refused to give up their search. This was a difficult fire to tackle in normal circumstances, the heat being contained within the structure because of the compartmentalised nature of the fire floor and lack of ventilation points. In the near total darkness the choking smoke and noxious fumes made entry without breathing apparatus an impossibility. For the crews inside it was like working in an oven. Ventilation had been a particular problem in tackling this blaze and was now making the very urgent task of search and rescue all the more challenging.

Having booked myself and Leslie in with the control unit crew it was clear she was moved by the sombre mood that was becoming evident as the seconds turned into minutes and the likelihood of a happy outcome was looking more and more remote. The emerging crews who were now recharging their BA sets on blue plastic salvage sheets spread out on the ground knew exactly what the conditions within the warehouse were like. These men were clearly suffering the effects of extreme heat and some were having to be administered oxygen. This told the graphic story of the physically demanding environment they had just left and, for many, would soon be re-entering.

I was instructed to report to the incident commander, Assistant Chief Officer Albert "Joe" Kennedy. Leslie remained by the control unit still trying to absorb the enormity of the events that were unfolding before her. Joe, as he was affectionately referred to, was a formidable fireground commander. He was the North East Area Commander. This was his patch and these were his people. Joe's features had the look of a pugilist (which he had been in his younger years) and he retained the physique of one. He was still more than capable of taking care of himself in or outside the ring. However, this intelligent and gifted fire officer cared passionately about those in his charge. The concern and pain he was feeling, waiting impatiently by the BA entry control point for the emergency crews to bring out the missing firefighters, was written across his face. Having nothing to add to the process I stood aside, a mere spectator, as the tragic sequence of events started to unfold.

The muffled, yet urgent, calls and the rapid movement of the hastily exiting breathing apparatus emergency crew, as they raced down the concrete staircase from the upper fire floor, brought a momentary sense of hope as the first missing firefighter was returned to the fresh air. Willing hands swiftly moved forward to render assistance to their fallen colleague but the face of Joe Kennedy told its own story of the futility of their humanitarian, yet vain, efforts. Whilst his crews administered cardiac massage and resuscitation to the man lying on the ground before him, he knew already it was too little, too late. It was a scene that was repeated all too soon as the second missing firefighter was carried down and passed out through the warehouse entry point. He too was clearly beyond medical help. That, however, did not stop the desperate attempts of those waiting by the entrance to try to revive him. Despite the dozen plus firefighters that had died at incidents in my twenty-four years of operational service this was the first time it was being played out before my eyes. The feelings of sadness, anger, frustration and wretchedness combined within me to start the inevitable questions in my head. How could this be possibly be happening? This was not meant to happen, not with the safety procedures that should, and seemed to be, in place.

Joe Kennedy was a highly accomplished, respected and experienced fire officer. He started his career, 29 years before, in Essex fire brigade before joining London in the enlarged London fire brigade in 1965. He had been commended twice for his bravery and officership at two difficult special service incidents. He left London to serve in Essex as a Divisional Commander before returning to London in principal officer rank. He had been the officer in charge of the major Oxford Circus underground fire in 1984. This was a precursor for him commanding the Brigade's actions at the King's Cross fire where both a member of the Brigade perished and thirty-one members of the public died. Although officially off-duty he attended and assumed control at King's Cross and received his third commendation, the Brigade's highest gallantry award, for his outstanding command role at that incident. Now despite the enormity of the tragic events unfolding before his eyes he realised, the consummate professional that he was, this was not the time to grieve or lose his focus. He still had a serious and difficult fire situation to contend with and to extinguish.

Joe Kennedy knew me and the role I was performing at this incident. Seeing the Chief had arrived and was standing by the Brigade's control unit, waiting to be briefed, he told me to follow him as he went to report to Gerry Clarkson, the Chief Officer. Standing in Joe's wake it was an emotional Joe Kennedy that told the Chief, "We have lost two of our men Chief." Regaining his composure he then provided an accurate summary of the fire situation, his plan for dealing with it and his belief that he didn't need any additional resources to achieve it. (He had already made this a twenty-pump fire.) Telling Joe to return to commanding the incident the Chief said he would put in train the major (fatal) accident investigation and deal with the media. I was already mentally preparing a draft press statement. News of this fatal fire had been leaked to the national press and a local radio station had broadcast, unconfirmed, reports that firefighters had died.

The police had made a very effective job of placing a total cordon around the whole of the affected site. They had corralled the growing media scrum near the main gate of the Hays Business Services warehouse in Gillender Street. The Press were clearly eager to discover exactly what had happened and with their who, how, what and why questions (that are their stock in trade) they were chomping at the bit. A mix of some twenty to thirty press reporters and television crews were waiting behind the police lines as I approached to give an "off the record" briefing before the Chief spoke to them officially. Removing my helmet the solemnity of my expression conveyed confirmation of the rumour that firefighters had died. Having introduced myself I said the Chief would be willing to give a statement and answer questions on one stipulation. This stipulation was that none of the press would request to know the names of the fatally injured firefighters. Explaining that the next of kin had yet to be informed, it was our intention that they would hear about their sons' or husbands' demise from us and not via the media. That said I confirmed that two firefighters had died whilst tackling the fire in the building behind me. Returning to advise the Chief, he then met with the press and gave a comprehensive briefing and paid a heartfelt tribute to the two firefighters whose bodies were now waiting to be removed to the local mortuary where a post-mortem would have to be conducted to determine the exact cause of death.

Meanwhile Leslie, who had been keeping the Brigade's press office fully updated of the unfolding and tragic events by mobile telephone, had decided to put it to much greater, and more beneficial use. Circulating amongst the crews waiting to re-enter the building or changing the compressed air cylinders on their BA sets, she allowed them to make calls home, reassuring family and loved ones that they were okay.

After nearly four hours of determined fire-fighting, in difficult and harsh conditions, crews had contained the blaze to a large storage area on the second floor. The day duty Green Watch tour was over and relief crews brought fresh faces to complete the task that had been started. I returned Leslie to Brigade headquarters and thanked her for her initiative in the wise, but unaccustomed, use of the press officer's mobile phone. She remained locked in her own thoughts and said very little as we drove through the evening rush hour traffic of East London en route to Lambeth and then on to our respective homes.

I did not arrive home until late evening and no sooner had I walked through the front door than my pager went off once more. A code 1, an operational ordering. I was heading back to Gillender Street, this time to assist the South East Area principal officer charged with conducting the Health and Safety fatal accident investigation. The conditions within the warehouse, whilst still very uncomfortable, had improved to the point where crews could enter without breathing apparatus. Emergency lighting provided illumination to and on the fire floor, but other than the damping down of the fire compartment all other movement by crews within the second floor of the warehouse was greatly restricted. All equipment used had been left in situ, untouched, including the personal uniform and the breathing apparatus sets that the late Terry Hunt and David Stokoe had been using and wearing. I was to direct the operations of my photographic team recording evidence both inside and outside the warehouse. Having first recorded all the evidence on stills photographs I then worked with the video photographer. We re-traced the exact path that had been taken by Silvertown's crew as they made their entry into the warehouse interior, who whilst wearing breathing apparatus sets, had deployed a BA main guideline to mark their route in their search for the fire.

As the name implies a guideline does just that. It enables a breathing apparatus crew, entering a large or complex building, to search whilst being able to retrace its steps to their entry point and thus to safety. Working in BA is never straightforward. Working with a BA guideline is not clear-cut and can be complicated, especially when other guidelines are brought into use. Regular training was meant to enable BA crews to work effectively and confidently with these guidelines. The reality was the infrequency of use and lack of realistic training facilities and scenarios, meant station personnel were, in many instances, known to be wanting. (This was discovered and highlighted during the Firefighter refresher programme, which was introduced and subsequently cancelled by the Brigade.) Neither did watch training records accurately reflect which station personnel actually did what at a drill or training session, only that they had attended, or witnessed, a particular training activity or event being undertaken. So individuals might have seen a guideline in use but not actually used it. No individual training records existed at this time.

A few minutes after ten that night, I entered the ground floor entrance facing Gillender Street with the video operator. The external double doors gave access to the internal concrete staircase that led to the upper floors. This was the starting point for Silvertown's crew who were ordered to lay out their guideline in their search for the fire on the upper floor. Two of its members, one of whom was only a probationer and who would not usually enter such a demanding and serious fire, would not be returning alive. The beginning of their guideline was indicated by a yellow round disc with the letter "A" engraved on to it. From any one entry point only two guide lines may be laid out, an "A" and a "B" guideline, and these may run for many hundreds of feet as one three-hundred-foot guideline runs out and a second or third is added and the guideline extended. As we climbed up the staircase I held on to their guideline with my left hand. As my hand moved along the guideline it passed over the regularly spaced tags, made of smaller diameter white cord, that were fixed to the guideline. These two pairs of tags were six inches apart and the first pair were knotted at the end of each of the two legs and this made it shorter than the other pair of tags. The second pair weren't knotted, just two six-inch legs hanging together. When firefighters are working their way along a guideline it is the knotted tags that indicate which way you have to travel to find your way back to the entry point. Long legs "going in" and knotted legs "going out." The guideline can only be made up one way in its carrying bag so that it will always come out the correct way and the knotted tags will always lead crews to the exit.

As we moved ever higher the residual heat was radiating from the brick and concrete walls. As we reached the second-floor mezzanine, the fire floor, the heat was such that the lens of the video camera had to be constantly wiped to clear the effects of the heat. Snaking their way up the staircase were two charged lines of hose that the initial crews had laid out in their failed attempts to locate and tackle the fire within the labyrinth of storage areas and passageways that filled this floor. Silvertown's guideline had been laid clear of the floor, tied off at regular intervals to suitable anchorage points as the crew had made their way higher and higher and on to the warehouse's upper floor. Having travelled the full length of their first guideline they would then have connected a second guideline that could take them another three hundred feet before having to connect a third. As we reached the top landing the entrance to the fire floor lay before us, exposing the maze-like area that Silvertown's crew had entered some seven hours earlier. They, unlike us, did not have the luxury or benefit of seeing the wire mesh cages and breeze block walls that turned the floor space into a veritable rabbit warren of storage areas and enclosed spaces. They had to move forward blindly, shuffling their feet as they went and groping for fixings for their guideline. Next to the doorway, just inside it, was the discarded fire tunic of one of the two dead firefighters. His BA set lay elsewhere, now depleted of its life-giving contents.

My role was to record the evidence and give commentary to the laying out of Silvertown's guideline and what I saw. But it was impossible not to be drawn into the events of that day and to relive the actions of Silvertown's crew as they had moved steadily forward, seeking the fire that was generating the most punishing conditions. How and why Terry Hunt and David Stokoe got separated from their comrades was a matter of pure conjecture at this point. Even the clarity of hindsight was not going to undo the damage done and bring back either of them. It was simply not possible to remain unmoved by the undoubted fear, the sense of foreboding, and desperate feeling of isolation that they must have felt and which ultimately engulfed them both. Within this claustrophobic atmosphere of extreme heat and near total darkness they surely must have realised the extreme nature of their plight. The pained cries, sometimes screams, for rescue on their breathing apparatus communications sets would not only haunt those desperately trying to respond, but others that just had to listen to the last words the pair would ever speak. Now those pleas to save them still seemed to linger and reverberate around in my head as we recorded the evidence that showed they died not only separated from their crew but from each other. Though their audible distress signal units continued sending out the penetrating summons for help, and their low cylinder pressure warning whistle continued their shrill warning the pressure gauge needles on their respective breathing apparatus sets would have moved ever closer to empty. Finally, when they tried to take a breath and no air flowed into their respective facemasks, the desperation of the two would have been unimaginable. In utter desperation one removed his depleted breathing apparatus set completely, the other his facemask. They would have known the dire consequences but desperation drives out logic.

The remainder of Silvertown's crew simply had no choice but to return to the entry point lest they also ran out of air and suffered the fate of their missing mates. They exited with the plaintive cries of their colleagues ringing in their ears. However, by returning outside they were at least not adding to the problems of the rescue crews or hindering the extensive search for the lost pair whose air supply would be dangerously low. To have remained meant they would have most probably succumbed; unconsciousness and death would have been inevitable.

Something here had so obviously gone horribly wrong. We, in the Brigade, were used to dealing with the crises of others but it is difficult to rationalise the situation when it happens to us. It would take the subsequent combined internal investigation of the Brigades, the Health and Safety Executive (HSE) and the Fire Brigades Union to analyse and explain the full sequence of events that lead to this devastating happening. The findings of that inquiry would identify failings that went far beyond the actions of that tragic day and would find shortcomings in a range of operational training practices and policies. So concerned were the Health and Safety Executive at their own conclusions that they served the London Fire Brigade with two statutory Improvement Notices, a first in the Brigade's long history. Changes to operational practices and training would follow but by the very nature of the firefighter's profession lives would still be claimed in the years ahead.

This building's outward appearance gave little indication of the fiercely hot and smoke-logged conditions that lay within and which were likened to tackling Hampton Court maze with closed eyes. Without physical contact with the life-giving guideline, finding a way out would have been a matter of pure luck. For Terry Hunt, aged 34 and David Stokoe, aged 25, their luck ran out.

The funerals of both men were distinctly differing affairs. David, who had only completed twenty month's operational service, was given a private family service, at the request of his parents. The Chief Officer, friends from Silvertown and colleagues from his training school squad, were present to pay their respects. Terry Hunt, a father of two, was buried with full Brigade honours. A firefighter for twelve years he had served at Kingsland Road before transferring to Silvertown fire station in 1989. Gillender Street would prove to be Gerry Clarkson's last major operational incident as Chief Fire Officer. He retired soon afterwards to be replaced by his deputy Brian Robinson, and at the age of forty-four, the youngest Chief Officer of London in modern times. It would fall to the new Chief Officer to draw up strategies to deal with the aftermath of this particular incident and to implement and action the Improvement Notices of the HSE.

The Baltic Exchange – St Mary Axe

Less than 24 hours after the surprise result of the 1992 general election, which saw John Major's Conservative Party returned for a record fourth term, the Provisional IRA detonated a murderous fertilizer bomb on the evening of the 10th April. Their target was the Baltic Exchange, located in St Mary Axe in the City of London. It left three dead and injured 90 innocent members of the public.

Sitting at home, on 24-hour duty, there was no indication of the devastating carnage that this terrorist attack had inflicted upon the Baltic Exchange and the surrounding area. The *Nine o'clock News*, that evening, had given extensive coverage to the general election success of the Conservatives, the highest turn out in recent times (77%). I had just witnessed one of the most dramatic elections in the UK since the end of the Second World War. The result had taken most of the "pollsters" by surprise as they had shown the Labour Party, under the leadership of Neil Kinnock, narrowly ahead of the Tories. With the recession in the UK deepening and continuing public unhappiness about the British involvement in the first Iraq War, I was one of those who had expected a Labour victory. The newsflash of a bomb explosion in central London coincided with my pager showing a Code 1, an operational ordering. Suddenly all thoughts of yesterday's election disappeared from my mind as I found myself responding to this bomb explosion in the heart of the City.

By the time I had covered the 17 miles from home to St Mary Axe, in a little under 25 minutes, the deputy Chief had already taken charge of the incident. (He had been attending a social gathering in the City at the time of the detonation.) My arrival coincided with Assistant Chief Officer Brian Butler booking in at the Brigade's control unit. Following a brief exchange with the Deputy, he was nominated as a Sector Commander, covering one half of the extensive bomb-damaged area, including the Baltic Exchange building. Seeing me waiting by the control unit I was ordered to follow him, my Press and PR role being handed on to someone unknown to me.

Had I been around in the Blitz I am sure that what I witnessed would have been a familiar sight to those heroic wartime firefighters. I had never seen devastation on such a vast and widespread scale. Masonry, debris and the contents of the bomb-damaged offices littered and obstructed the road. Fire was still burning in the crater that had been the site of the Provisional IRA's van explosive device, which had caused such carnage. Two things were noticeable above all else, one was the vast amounts of fallen glass and the other was the endless reams of paper that covered the surrounding streets. Whole multi-storey office blocks were totally devoid of their glazing. Layers of razor-sharp glass cluttered the paved squares forming what looked like an ice-covered lake and the glare of distant, undamaged, lighting was reflected off the surface of the glass. The glass was treacherous to walk upon and a slip could prove lethal to anyone foolish enough to try without protective clothing and sturdy boots.

With the possibility of the injured being trapped within the affected building's fire brigade ladders were pitched to upper floors and crews were now in the process of making systematic searches under Brian Butler's direction. It was not known then just how many casualties or deaths would be attributed to this murderous attack. Crews were allocated to individual buildings and they checked them floor-by-floor, searching for those possibly caught in the blast or injured by flying glass or debris. I was allocated the Baltic Exchange with crews from nearby stations. The Baltic Exchange seemed to us to have caught the full force of the explosive blast. The structural damage was substantial. It was known that the security guard who worked there remained unaccounted for and was possibly inside the building. However, despite the determined efforts of the crews, penetration deep into the building was restricted due to the hazardous conditions posed by the building's dangerous structure. It would need the approval of the City of London building surveyor before a more thorough search of the Exchange could be made and that would lead to the eventual discovery of Thomas Casey's body, who died at the age of 49. He was not the only fatality. The two others who fell victim to yet another gross example of the IRA's mainland killing campaign were Mr Paul Butt, aged 29 and Miss Danielle Carter, who was only 15.

The Baltic Exchange was all but destroyed by the one-ton fertiliser bomb that was detonated at 9.20pm. The now, world famous, "Gherkin" designed by Lord Foster would ultimately stand on the site. The total cost of the damage was estimated as £800 million, of which £350 million was considered to be losses to the world's international shipping contracts markets. This loss was said to exceed more than the total damage costs of all the previous Northern Ireland's terrorist related bombings.

Moving On

Promotion rounds were in the offing. Chris Thompson was up for his Deputy Assistant Chief Officer's promotion board and the much-awaited Divisional Officers (Grade One) promotion round was set in motion after my previous one was aborted. Whilst Chris was quietly confident of getting short-listed for his promotion interview, the Divisional Officers' round was something of a convoluted and drawn out affair. My round would come in three distinct stages; fail the first two and you never saw an interview. Naturally there was an application form where all candidates had to respond to the detailed job description. Your written submission had to demonstrate your experience and/or knowledge to meet the job specification. Returned applications could run to numerous pages of script and many did, as individuals tried, some more successfully than others, to address and meet the demanding selection criteria.

The second round in the selection process were the, now familiar, assessment centres. Ours concentrated on the candidates' ability to interpret data and pass a verbal evaluation test, which was a demonstration of your ability to understand and evaluate the logic of different kinds of arguments. The grades were A to E. A and B were above average; C was average whilst D and E were marked below average. Having previously taken these tests in the aborted round I was invited to either keep my existing results or retake the assessment centre tests. I stuck with what I had, thinking that I was very unlikely to improve on the good scores I had already achieved. (Secretly I was sure I had been sent someone else's results as I could not recall doing that well!)

Dependent on how individuals were rated in stages one and two they were either invited for interview or received a, "Sorry to inform you" letter. However, returning to the actual applications, all ranks were now mandated to go through this process to secure promotion to higher rank, even principal rank. Completion of these forms was not without a degree of skulduggery either, if you were in the know. A certain senior officer seeking principal rank had duly completed his application and, as you do, made a copy. His completed application was a work of art: if ever there was a model answer for an application for higher promotion, this was it. Having successfully secured his promotion someone had either found, or borrowed, the copy and copied the copy. It was doing the rounds on the headquarters black-market. Whilst no one copied this application verbatim, it was nevertheless an excellent guide to ticking all the right boxes in the various selection criteria, which with a little tweaking and adjustment here and there many did. It was all very good stuff. Obviously individual experiences and knowledge had to support your application, but if it was supported by the key buzz-words and current management jargon you could make it sound as if you knew what you were actually talking about. This was all about getting to the interview room and then selling yourself on your individual merits. (Or not, as the case may be.) After the previously cancelled interviews, this was a highly competitive round and anything that could give you the slightest edge was not to be sniffed at.

With my application form now duly completed, all fourteen pages of it, I would have to forward it to Chris, as my line manager, to assess my application and grade the twelve selection criteria as; not being met; met or exceeding the requirements of a particular criterion. Those who had a copy of the "model answer" certainly did not advertise the fact. (Even how it was circulated remains a bit of a mystery in itself.) My fellow Divisional Officer, with whom I shared an office, had also applied for this promotion round. He had yet to start his application form and the closing date for all applications to be submitted was fast approaching. As he had to work that weekend duty he asked if he might look through my completed application and I thought it churlish not to let him do so, as I had access to the "mother lode" when it came to completing application forms. Leaving that Friday evening, pleased with my completed tome I asked for my application form to be left in my office drawer so I could forward it first thing on Monday morning. My so-called colleague had that Monday off, having worked the weekend duty, and had slid his completed application under Chris's office door before leaving the headquarters building on Sunday evening, before going home.

Monday morning and my application followed a similar route and both found their way to Chris's in-tray awaiting his attention and comment. It was not until the following day that I was unceremoniously summoned into Chris's office and the expression on his face instantly told me that something was seriously awry. Chris and I had shared an exceptionally good working relationship, there had never been a major disagreement between us even though he was a hard taskmaster. In fact, he had posted out of the department each of my three previous opposite numbers because they either couldn't deliver what he wanted or just were not up to scratch. My current opposite number was number four. Standing in the obviously disquieting atmosphere of his office, without even an invitation to sit which was so out of character, I was feeling like someone whose hand had just been caught in the till holding a handful of fivers! "Why is your application almost identical to the person you share your office with?" he asked, clearly irritated by even having to ask the question. I knew exactly effing why but was not about to say. In answer to his question if I had copied the other's application, I left him absolutely in no doubt that I hadn't.

Slamming shut my office door I returned to confront my now not so close colleague. I promised him immediate and extreme physical violence if he did not go and sort this matter out, right now! After I let go of his uniform lapels, he left our office in the direction of Chris's. It was some considerable time before he returned looking both flushed and extremely embarrassed. In what I believed was a sincere apology he said he had simply run out of time over the weekend and had plagiarised my application. I thought had he at least managed to put in some independent thought and some original ideas, whilst giving due consideration to key concepts, with a fair sprinkling of the all-important current buzz-words he might have got away with it. Withdrawing from the promotion round he also soon withdrew from Press and PR completely. Chris was eagerly looking for number five, his replacement.

Although I was recommended, and considered above average by Chris, I was not looked upon so favourably by the Assistant Chief Officer of the Brigade's Fire Safety Department, under whose umbrella Press and PR now fell. Despite having virtually had no contact with the man, and he having little knowledge of me he marked me down to only "promotable." The fact that his own Divisional Officers, who were seeking promotion in the same round and working directly to him, did not received the same downgrading only made me more determined than ever to prove Chris right and him wrong.

I felt my success at the subsequent interview board was undoubtedly aided by my recent achievement in securing my Diploma in Management Studies. I had successfully completed a two-year postgraduate course thanks to the Brigade who had, kindly, sponsored me. Part day-release and part residential course, it was a demanding learning curve for me. A salutary lesson in effective time-management when balancing my fire brigade work with the demanding schedule of the frequent assignments and other course work. It also happened to be somewhat of an emotional roller-coaster ride during the second year. A flirtatious liaison with a much younger, and highly attractive lady who worked for Kent County Council as an auditor, made our extended residential weekends on the south coast titillating to say the least. Her infatuation with me, an older man, paled into insignificance compared to my besotted feelings at being fancied by someone nearly fifteen years my junior. In an ironic twist this bright, blonde and beautiful twenty-something had an older female colleague on the same course, who was utterly determined that her younger companion was not going to have a fling with this forty year plus "fireman." That was until "Miss Prim and Proper" had it off during a residential weekend in Margate with another course member and started her own affair. My stunning, younger, course mate may have well behaved alluringly but her true focus was firmly set on achieving the highest possible marks, something she succeeded in doing. Whilst I had managed a credible pass, I unexpectedly won the praise of my fellow students by being voted the individual who had made the most significant contribution to the course. I certainly had tried hard with her.

With the results of the promotion rounds promulgated a delighted Chris Thompson was now a Deputy Assistant Chief Officer. He was heading back down to the second floor as the head of Command and Mobilising and in charge of the London Fire Brigade's mobilising control room at Lambeth. I was deemed promotable but without a suitable slot to fill, I and three other successful candidates, had to wait for vacancies to occur. Press and PR seemed in an unaccustomed state of flux. Chris's first replacement was the out-going Chief's "Mr Fix It." A tall rotund, man he had the personality and ego to match. If Gordon found him hard to get on with, he was too polite and well-mannered a professional to say so publicly but the replacement was soon moved on. I became the temporary head of the uniformed side of Press and PR whilst my civilian opposite number, an outspoken Yorkshire lass, scurried up the corridor and planted herself in Chris's old office clearly wishing to make a statement!

In my last couple of months the new Chief Officer, Brian Robinson had two prestigious events which the Division was blessed to make happen and I had to oversee. The first was the Brigade's annual Sports day. This was to take place at the Crystal Palace National sports stadium. Having such a well-known and "professional" venue it attracted far more entrants than in previous years and we were able to put on a full sporting programme, including a five-kilometre cross-country in the adjoining Crystal Palace park. Whilst the race started and finished in the stadium, the runners followed an extensive circuit around the park, marked out with directional signs that indicated the runners' route. At two or more intersections stewards were placed to ensure the signs were not moved and to keep the runners on the correct path. Unfortunately, I failed to check that all these stewards had an ounce of common sense when it came to navigational skills. One of our own, a non-uniformed woman of plump proportions, was charged with directing traffic, or rather runners, at the far side of the park near the boating lake. Not only had this lady placed herself in front of the directional sign, but she also took it into her head to send the runners in the wrong direction, towards Penge High Street and Beckenham! Having entered the race myself but happily trotting along the rear of the pack, not least because I could not keep up with the front runners, I found myself almost in the lead when I reached the "silly bitch" still happily sending runners completely the wrong way. Competitors now clearly aware of the error and competing against cars and lorries that, they were assured, would not be on their route had turned around and were explaining in very graphic terms what they thought of the steward and her navigation skills. My running companion that afternoon was none other than the Chief's wife (to be) who was saved from the impromptu detour and the less than salubrious experience of window-shopping down Penge High Street.

The new Chief's first major ceremony was to be an Honours and Awards presentation. I had stayed in contact with a fellow student from my Diploma course, the Chief Executive of the Commonwealth Institute. So when the Chief requested a high profile, and appropriate, venue for his first Award ceremony he seemed taken with the possibility of holding the ceremony there. Gordon and I had sounded out the venue and we were offered the Institute, with all the trimmings, at a very competitive price which was within budget and which seemed to please the Fire Authority, not least because of the ethnically diverse setting for such a high-profile event. It was in fact a highly successful evening and delighted both the Chief and the Chairman of the Fire Authority who seemed to enjoy it immensely and vying to take the credit for coming up with the novel idea of using such an interesting and impressive venue. Of far more importance, to me, were the actual recipients themselves and who had been invited to the gathering along with their close family, or nominated friends.

The Commonwealth Institute is an exhibition centre based on a large circular design on various levels. In the centre of the main building, and at its hub, was a round, raised, mezzanine floor space something like a pedestrian roundabout that was connected to the upper and lower floor levels by stairways. This floor space acted as the main stage, or arena and families and friends, seated at large round tables looked down from the upper level onto the presentation area. A principal uniformed officer sat at each of the round tables and hosted that group. Individuals being awarded citations, medals and bravery awards were discreetly gathered up and taken by the stewards to the lower tier, from where they would make their entry on stage, when their name was called to receive their individual award before making their way up the stairs to re-join their family or friends. As a famous personality of the nineteen-eighties and the nineties (Kenny Everett) would say, "It was all done in the best possible taste." (In a return to my own award ceremony, conducted at the then Greater London Council's County Hall, I had the recipient's own Area Commander, or Assistant Chief Officer, read out their Royal Warrant or bravery citation.) It may sound like we replicated an Oscar or BAFTA ceremony but the feedback from the recipients told us we had found a winning formula. Sadly, it was all very short-lived as the favourable pricing we received from the Institute was not repeated, but the Chief had established a new benchmark for his award ceremonies and, to his credit, he managed to maintain them through the strenuous efforts of Gordon and the PR team.

Finally, a new Senior Divisional Officer arrived, and with him came a noticeable change in the atmosphere within the Division. He was pedantic and this did not bode well with the creative and flexible approach that most of us, "delivering the goods", felt was necessary to get the job done to the standards now widely expected of us. His catch phrase, "I mean this sincerely" soon lost all sense of sincerity as his genuineness increasingly came into doubt. There was an uneasy tension between us that lasted until my departure, on promotion, in October 1992.

The Museum

Among the so-called many assets of the Press and Public Relation Division of the London Fire Brigade was the niche Brigade museum. Located at Southwark Training Centre and housed within Winchester House, it would be most remiss of me not to make comment on it, nor to mention of its place within the culture of the Brigade and the people that worked there. This is my last Press and PR recollection before I move on to pastures new. However, my personal involvement with the museum, that ran throughout my time in the Division, brought a special sense of achievement and holds a singular, and particular, place in my many career memories.

The museum, despite the fact that it had been around in one form or another since post-First World War, was frequently seen as the poor relation. It was a "nice to have," not a "need to have" in the eyes of some brigade policy makers. In spite of the fact that it was the official custodian of the Brigade's heritage and the safety deposit box for most of its unique and irreplaceable artefacts, funding for its continuing upkeep was regularly kept on a knife-edge. Its location within Winchester House, certainly since the nineteen-sixties, was a major factor in its continuing existence, although that existence often found it surviving hand-to-mouth. This was certainly the case when frequent budgetary cuts were looked at and it was targeted as an easy candidate to reduce running costs within the Brigade. However, some creative accountancy, and not a certain amount of skulduggery, always seemed to save the museum and its unique collection of equipment, uniforms and appliances from the axe. Plus there was a noticeable soft spot from most, if not all, of the Brigade's recent Chief Officers to see the heritage collection maintained and at their personal disposal to impress the not infrequent VIP visitors to Winchester House. Some were far more committed to the museum than others, so the museum continued along on its seesaw existence never really making it out of the backwater.

The late eighties and early nineties saw an improvement in the museum's fortunes with the creation of two full-time staff replacing the retiring museum guide and minder. The enthusiasm of these new staff members was rewarded by an allocation of limited funds to improve the displays and undertake some much needed, but limited, conservation of artefacts and memorabilia.

I have always been fascinated with Victorian properties. With its ornate architecture, elegant proportions and intricate detailing they were clearly built to last and be admired. They have stood the test of time too. The London Fire Brigade has many such fine examples, fire stations that were testament to the skills of the Victorian architect and builder. That is with one notable exception, Winchester House, home of the London Fire Brigade's first Chief Officer Captain (later Sir) Eyre Massey Shaw. In the late 1980s the place was actually in danger of falling down, if not completely, then suffering a very embarrassing collapse. The maintenance of this building, that was around one hundred and fifty years old then, required a considerable amount of work and upkeep and both had been sadly lacking. Winchester House had not featured high on over a decade of annual budgets when fire engine replacements and operational equipment took much higher precedence. However, with the building Grade II listed by English Heritage, and the main staircase taking on an uncharacteristic and dangerous list to starboard, the Fire Authority finally gave its approval to use public funds to undertake major structural repairs and to preserve the fabric of the Brigade's most historic and important heritage site.

My own tenuous link with Winchester House was that the Brigade museum occupied the first floor and part of the second floor and the museum came within my Public Relations role. The large semi-basement, running the length of the house, was also used by Press and PR for furniture storage and we had use of the small, very basic, basement kitchen. Scullery with a cooker was a more apt description that still, nevertheless, managed to turn out the most sumptuous meals thanks to the culinary skills of our "uniformed cooks" despite the appalling facilities.

Winchester House's main ground floor, consisting of three large and one small reception room, plus the imposing entrance hall and staircase was known as the Massey Shaw suite. The rooms, with their Victorian furniture and period decor had been an unpublished perk of the Chief Fire officer for the last twenty years or more. It was a sort of "grace and favour" facility that went with the post. The Greater London Council had funded a revamp of the Massey Shaw suite in the late 1960s and since then it had been a favourite haunt and bolthole of Chiefs past and present. Its relaxed and informal setting was ideal for wining and dining "friends" or for winning over policy changes with either local or national political decision makers. The Victorian dining room hosted many such functions and its guests could not fail to be impressed as they dined, under candle light, in what many considered was the spiritual home of the Brigade.

Special medal presentations were organised there and the Lord Lieutenant of London would bestow upon the recipients either citations or medals at these award ceremonies, conducted within the Massey Shaw suite. However, now embarrassed by its rapidly deteriorating (and unsafe!) state these ceremonies had to be moved to another venue. The whole interior looked tired and had lost its lustre. Many items of the period furniture looked just as sad and were in need of long-awaited restoration and repair. The years of budgetary neglect had taken its toll and it showed. Both the interior décor as well as the fabric of the building was in desperate need of some tender loving care.

The museum had its "curator" and he had an assistant. (Curator was however just an honorary title and neither had any formal museum qualifications.) They oversaw the day-to-day running of the museum, conducted public and private visits and generally looked after the artefacts. I looked after them. Although not formally trained in conservation and preservation work, they were, nevertheless, totally committed to their roles. Both had gained a wealth of knowledge about the museum's extensive collection. I was then (and remain) a great fan of the Brigade's unique museum. Being so openly supportive of the museum and promoting it to anyone willing to listen, I was taken to the museum staff's bosom. As long, that is, as I remained loyal to them and argued for their annual maintenance budgets to remain intact! This support for the museum extended to both Chris Thompson and Gordon White and it is to Gordon's great credit, and his close association with various London Chief Officer's, that he coerced and persuaded them to keep the museum funded, even if the allocation of funds only just kept the museum's head above water at times.

Presented with detailed reports by principal officers on the state of Winchester House, the Fire Authority Members had very little option but to agree to fund its restoration. This was a win-win for the many fans of the museum, especially given the stance taken by English Heritage who said demolishing Winchester House and clearing the site was simply not a viable alternative strategy. Given the extensive nature of the structural building works and the resultant restoration works, both English Heritage and Southwark Council (the local Planning Authority) stipulated that the house's ground floor interior and frontage be returned to its former "glory."

With my natural bias towards both Winchester House and the museum I was delighted when my museum role was expanded, and I found myself the "liaison" officer with the in-house property services group who were project managers for the imminent structural building works and subsequent refurbishment. Falling under the spell of Winchester House, many years earlier, had not been hard for me. I had thought, since my time at Southwark fire station, that if the Brigade had a soul or a heart this iconic building was where it lodged. Although rather neglected and forlorn in recent years I could still sense the Brigade's historic past and it was easy to imagine the ghost of Captain Shaw moving from room to room. It was, after all, his family home for very many years. This former army officer in the North Cork Rifles, a tall elegant man, transformed the then Metropolitan Fire Brigade into the land's finest professional fire service. He was a real tour-de-force and he not only left his mark on the Brigade but on London's social scene too. Among his many upper-class friends were the Prince of Wales and his entourage who would accompany Captain Shaw to major fires. The Prince of Wales even had his own Royal fire gear, complete with a silver-plated fireman's helmet.

The weekly drills and displays at the Metropolitan Headquarters in Southwark Bridge Road were great social occasions. But in 1883 Captain Shaw was seriously injured at a fire, which left him with a permanent limp. Whilst recovering at home, the Prince of Wales and other members of the Royal family drove to visit him at Winchester House. The entourage arrived in three open carriages whilst cheering crowds of onlookers lined Southwark streets to greet the Royal party. Captain Shaw remained at the head of the Metropolitan Fire Brigade until 1891, when he fell out with the LCC's Board of Works who wanted more control over the Chief's powers. (Was it ever thus!) Shaw's career was remarkable. His Brigade grew with him in both efficiency and reputation. He saw the number of land stations increase by about fifty per cent during his term of office. Although Shaw was a strict disciplinarian he was nevertheless highly regarded by his men. Over six-foot-tall and with a goatee beard and long moustache, he exhibited a striking presence. Nicknamed the "long-un" or the "skipper" by his men he produced three ground-breaking textbooks on fire protection. He sought out the very latest ideas and inventions concerning fire extinguishing and lifesaving apparatus and his training manual were widely believed to be the most definitive source of guidance and instruction of their day and was the first published "fire service drill book." He also revolutionised mobilising.

When I was visiting or "fronting" events at Winchester House, it was not hard to imagine the "great" man stepping through the double doors of Winchester House into the large, once elegant, hallway before turning left and striding through his formal drawing room on the elevated ground floor to his adjoining office. However, now with the contractors actively pulling more down that putting up the place resembled a bomb site. Because of extensive renovations to the frontage, including all the windows facing Southwark Bridge Road, the museum exhibits and artefacts had to be removed to safety and were placed into storerooms, lent by the Training School. It was a stressful time for the two Museum staff as they tried, unsuccessfully, to cope with the ever-increasing levels, and layers, of brick dust and debris that at times were in danger of engulfing their domain.

Slowly, but surely, a transformation was underway; if not a total transformation, then a splendid restoration. The museum staff had artfully ingratiated themselves with the external contractor's project manager. They offered him numerous cups of tea and extended him the sanctuary of their somewhat dusty office, rather than have him use his chilly and spartan site hut to have his lunch in. Little did he realise then that this kindness would not come cheap. Anything and everything they could cajole out of him, like extra non-specified work in the museum, was pushed for and largely achieved. I had a similar success story with our in-house team of project managers. I managed this after wining and dining the visiting English Heritage advisor, who was monitoring the ongoing work, and getting him on board for a little scheme I had up my sleeve.

Winchester House was originally built as a family home. Its upper two floors, (it only had two) now housed most of the museum and its exhibit rooms were originally the bedrooms of the family and their servants. These rooms ran off the corridors located at the back of the house. It was in these series of rooms that exhibits were displayed and visitors had to walk in and out of separate rooms to look at the various displays. This was a greater problem on the first floor, as the rooms there were somewhat smaller and only two had a connecting door linking the two rooms together. I needed some walls knocked down to allow visitors to wander through the whole exhibit and not just in and out of each room. It is important to point out here that the two principal in-house project managers were also fans of the museum and what it stood for. They were genuinely enthusiastic about enhancing the visitor experience and, with the blessing of English Heritage, they put in amendments to Southwark Council to carry out these additional alterations and better still coughed up the extra funding from the project's contingency budget. The work, once completed, would allow a one-way system to be established that would take a greater number of visitors through the history of the brigade and avoid the congestion that had previously marred the experience, if more than a dozen people visited the museum at any one time. (Tours, which were by appointment only were always escorted.)

I had been a keen gatherer of Victorian collectables and objets d'art for some time and had managed to "salvage" the odd Victorian cast iron fireplace or earthenware corner sink from burning derelict buildings whilst serving at fire stations. With the collusion of my two willing museum helpers, and some gentle arm-twisting of the site project manager, we all came together over two consecutive weekends to recreate a new exhibit for the museum, a Victorian firemen's gear room. With the two new openings knocked into the dividing walls and proper doorways now in place, it was time to call in all those cups of tea and lunchtime use of the museum office. Our very willing contractors helped install the ornate, but typical, fireplace that would have been found in such a setting and the wall-mounted corner sink, complete with its large brass tap. We painted the walls in characteristic drab cream and brown colours and hung the firemen's uniforms from pegs, with their tall black leather boots and real brass helmets. Together with a wooden table and brass oil lamps (with flame effect bulbs) it all looked very authentic when finished and was much favoured by all who visited the museum. In a nice touch of realism one of the museum staff brought in a very live looking furry toy mouse and had its head sticking out of a "mouse-hole" he had drilled into in the skirting board. This gave far more than just one visitor a shock, when they spotted the head and whiskers of this little brown rodent looking back up at them.

With the majority of the major structural works completed and the painstaking replacement and restoration of the ceiling mouldings, plaster cornices and carved mouldings on the wooden doors well in hand, it was now time to consider the remaining décor. Much to my amazement, and the in-house team's relief, it was left to me to select the hand printed wallpapers that would now adorn the ground floor walls. Apparently, they were happy, ecstatic actually, in the knowledge that if the Chief did not like the choice of wallpaper, they could simply point the finger of blame at me. It was a challenge I relished.

Armed with an instant course in block print wallpapers of the period by a friendly face at the Wallpaper History Society, I was advised to head off to Cole and Son (Wallpaper) Ltd, located in Mortimer Street in the heart of London's West End. Here I was received most warmly even though, quite rightly, I was treated as a complete novice when it came to their specialist (and very expensive!) product. With some eighteen hundred block print designs in their collection, not including their screen print range, there were a great number of quality wall coverings at their disposal. From the curious and slightly aloof, look I received from the well dressed and extremely well-spoken Cole's sales representative and wallpaper consultant I was clearly not in their stately home or ultra-expensive mansion league. This was clearly not a DIY store! However, much to my relief this elegant chap soon warmed to my request for his assistance when I showed him the external and internal photographs of Winchester House that I had brought along with me. His curiosity aroused, as to why a uniformed fire officer was seeking to purchase his product, he diplomatically guided me away from the highly priced block prints to those he clearly thought we were more likely to be able to afford. Seeing one design I liked the look of I innocently asked the price? Still not in the upper price bracket, one roll still cost more than all the rolls required to completely redecorate my three-bedroom home. I was not allowed to spend more than sixty pounds a roll and the lofted rooms of Winchester House required quite a few rolls.

In the end I compromised, selecting two block print designs for the drawing and dining rooms and two screen prints for the "ladies" waiting room and the large replica Massey Shaw office. Cole's invoices were to be sent to the Brigade's Property Group for payment and would record the favourable "fire brigade" discount I had managed to negotiate as their contribution to restoring our heritage site.

Hanging this delicate paper, when it arrived, was an art form in itself. It tested the skills of decorators brought in to undertake the work. The walls were pasted, not the paper. No paste could be allowed to come into contact with the printed side of the paper and only specialist, and equally expensive, paste would suffice! This was no job for your off the shelf Polycell or Solvite pastes. Sadly, the first hanging in the dining room did not go to plan and one wall had to be completely stripped and re-papered, at the cost of a few hundred extra pounds.

With the paper going up and the latter stages of the restoration well in hand I was left with only one more problem to resolve. What to do about the furniture? The furniture collection of the Massey Shaw suite, spread over the four rooms, were something of a mismatch of Victorian and, later, Edwardian furniture. However, they included five or six valuable pieces. Such as the imposing grandfather clock, the large hardwood dining table and twelve place setting chairs, inlaid occasional tables and a period sofa (come chaise longue). Sadly the collection was not enough to set Sotheby's alight; especially given their much-needed restoration.

There was an expectation that all the furniture should now match the splendour of the, almost, fully renovated and redecorated suite. My choice of wallpapers had found favour in high quarters and whispers had been passed down from on high to, "Do something about the furniture," but without a name being attached to these instructions! Some monies had been earmarked from the museum and PR budget to undertake a limited amount of furniture restoration and re-polishing, but it was woefully inadequate. In fact it would fall short by a few thousand pounds of the projected costs.

These were extremely cost-conscious times in the Brigade. The Fire Authority's Scrutiny Committee would soon be going over the project budget and its expenditure with a fine tooth-comb. This was no time for any dodgy manoeuvring of funds to cover this much-needed work, which had not been included in the original estimates. But keen to see the overall scheme finished, with the contents looking as resplendent as the renovated décor I had an idea. Whilst *probably* not actually illegal, it would push the boundaries on Authority procurement policies to the limit (and beyond!). They would have me hung, drawn and quartered if they got wind of what I was planning, and ultimately executed.

Among the collection of period furniture, both within the suite and within our storerooms, were quite a few pieces (bookcases and tables and alike) which, whilst genuine Victorian items, did not actually harmonise with the suite's layout, even before the renovation. These items of furniture were discards, handed down by the former London County Council at County Hall. Heavy and well made, they were nevertheless principally items of old office furniture. Made of mahogany, walnut and oak they had been sent to Winchester House in the years before the Greater London Council, as newer and modern office furniture was brought into service at County Hall. Left in various storerooms and in use in the museum, whilst most were not up to the standard for display and use in Winchester House, they had both a clear Victorian pedigree and considerable monetary value.

Tasked with the job of locating a professional antique furniture restorer and French polisher, I sought the advice of the curator of a local Southwark museum and contacted their suggested nominee. We met at Winchester House and he promised to undertake a detailed survey of the pieces to be restored. Although a one-man-band he nevertheless presented some extremely impressive testimonials of his work, which included both Stately Homes and national museums. He soon presented a thorough and professional appraisal of the work required. He stated he could undertake some of the work on-site but other pieces would have to be removed to his workshop for more detailed restoration. What became immediately clear was that there were insufficient funds in our budget to complete the work he had identified. During our inspection of the furniture it became clear that this soft spoken and bohemian craftsman was not only interested in the actual work he had been asked to look at, he was also fascinated by both the setting and the house's history.

He considered my suggestion that he undertake a complete inventory and list all the work required before saying he would need a further visit, for which there would be no charge. I had already discovered that our own inventory of all the antique furniture, both on display and stored, was rather sparse. Only the major and most valuable items were listed. Even some of those had not been individually photographed, as required, for record and insurance purposes.

The return visit and his in-depth survey took a whole day. I joined him for a working lunch at Winchester House. This we enjoyed, without the knowledge or permission of the Chief, in the now very pleasant surroundings of the Massey Shaw's renovated drawing room. Munching on our "sarnies" and served tea and coffee by an equally conspiratorial museum curator, I broached the subject of how we might possibly pay for the necessary restoration for which we clearly had insufficient funds! Intrigued he listened patiently to my proposal (which I had already mentioned to Gordon but in the loosest of terms). I explained to the restorer the possibility of a barter to cover the shortfall in funding. His sense of intrigue turned into active interest as he finally agreed to send me two completed, but separate, lists. One would be the official list and the other would be definitely very unofficial. List A was the official version of his findings and his estimate of costs. List B was a complete run down of every item of furniture, most of which was stored away, and would give a brief description, its state of repair and estimated market value.

Getting all this restoration undertaken was simply not going to happen, not without some creative accountancy or sleight of hand. Firstly, there was not enough money in the Public Relations "pot" to pay for all the work. Secondly, asking for additional funding from the Fire Authority was not only very complicated, what with its competitive tendering policies, but once the full cost of the work was known it was almost certainly doomed to failure. Our nominated restorer and contractor was only deemed acceptable to the Authority because of the low cost of his "official" estimates and the limited and specialist nature of his work. The total amount of period furniture we had under our remit could perhaps be likened to an iceberg. Only one third of it was on public view, the other two thirds were largely unknown, stashed away in various storerooms or laying hidden in the disused former Brigade control in the basement of Lambeth headquarters. In a deal that would easily have done credit to the television portrayal of the likable character called *"Lovejoy"*, (played wonderfully well by Ian McShane) a bargain was struck. (Lovejoy was an antiques dealer whose scruples were not always, shall we say, the highest. He was considered to be a "divvie" by his fellow dealers which was taken to mean he was one of those with an uncanny knack of recognising a good deal when he saw it.) So in exchange for two or three items from the B list, plus his official payment, all the required work would be undertaken within the Public Relations budget. Our restorer would also undertake a two-year follow up programme to carry out minor works and re-polishing at no additional cost. His agreed restoration work would take a month to complete.

In the meantime the Victorian drawing room, the replica of Massey Shaw's office and the dining room were still in need of a few well-placed pieces of furniture, to put "the icing on the cake." Armed with the B list, and some dubious moves that were well below the radar of those that mattered, I trotted off (very early) to the Friday morning Bermondsey Antique Street Market and toured the adjacent antique warehouses in the lee of Tower Bridge, to do a little horse-trading. These warehouses once housed vast quantities of imported tea, coffee and spices. Their bare timber floors absorbed the aroma, over very many years, of what was stored on the various floors. It was still possible to discern what was stored where, as a distinct bouquet lingered in places where the lack of ventilation allowed the build-up of these once powerful odours.

Finding nothing of interest in the street market I explained my particular quest to the owner of a well-stocked four-storey antiques warehouse in the shadow of Tower Bridge. After carefully studying the list he said he was prepared to barter. He eventually exchanged an American love seat (circa 1890), a lady's mahogany dressing table and full length Victorian cheval mirror for the balance of tables, a bookcase and all the chairs remaining on my list. In an unexpected, and delightful, act of generosity he also donated some imitation, but authentic looking, mantelpiece china and other appropriate objets d'art as his personal contribution to the Massey Shaw suite. Under the cover of a weekend duty, and an almost deserted Winchester House, we undertook the furtive delivery and collection of our exchanged furniture. The new pieces blended in perfectly, we enjoyed a wonderful sense of achievement and pride in the finishing touches being put to the Massey Shaw suite. My co-conspirators and I were sure that Sir Massey would have thoroughly approved.

When the Chief Officer finally came to view the fully restored Winchester House and its revamped museum layout, including the original Victorian appliance room which now once again housed the two gleaming steamers and the horse-drawn manual fire engine, (less the horses!) he beamed with obvious delight. He then escorted selected Members of the Fire Authority around the site saying how wisely and carefully the Authority's funds had been spent. Hosting a small reception that was held in the drawing room of the Massey Shaw suite, he carefully pointed out the newly acquired items saying how fortuitous it had been to find them in one of the old storerooms. Displaying a wide smile, that went from almost ear to ear, he said how nicely they had cleaned up with a little bit of spit and polish. The glint in his eyes, as his gaze caught mine, said that very little got past this man and with a knowing smile he continued to hold court in his favourite "grace and favour" bolthole.

Despite the favourable reception the formal re-opening of the museum and Winchester House received in various quarters, there were forces at work, which if not actually against the operation of the museum, would make its continued existence extremely difficult. In fact, the Fire Authority had charged the Press and Public Relations Division, *"To come forward with proposals in respect of the Brigade Museum to achieve its operation on a commercial basis and as a self-financing venture."*

This requirement, whilst problematic for the museum and its staff, was a godsend for myself and a tightknit group of us on my Diploma in Management Studies course (Public Administration). Each of the six project groups in the postgraduate undertaking had to produce an individual "opus" based on a relevant and current case study within the public sector. The completed case study, together with its proposed business and strategic management plan, had then to be formally presented to the host organisation. Each of the studies demanded a critical analysis of a topical management issue and consideration of the relevant operational systems. In our case, that was the Brigade's museum and the drive to make it less reliant on in-house funding. Whilst Gordon was fully supportive and gave his approval to the study, and believed in our ability to deliver a viable plan, others viewed us with considerable scepticism particularly members of the Brigade's principal management board (Chief Officers' Corporate Board). However, as things turned out the study, when presented, surprised many with its insight into the thorny issues involved. The report provided the most comprehensive and enlightening study of the museum operation and its potential for future commercialisation that had ever been undertaken.

In defining (the status of) the current problems and critical issues facing any possible commercialisation of the museum, the report highlighted the background and political climate that was driving this course of action. The major consideration was the consistent pressure being placed on local Authorities by central Government to reduce expenditure. To this end the Brigade's Corporate management board had recommended a reduction in the museum budget. The museum, however, did not operate in a vacuum, although internally many thought it did. Local Authorities, nationally, had been evaluating the need for museums to become more market oriented. Local and national museums were increasingly being driven to raise additional revenue, particularly through donations, sponsorship and trading opportunities.

Our detailed researches, which involved national museums, demonstrated that the Brigade museum already made a significant contribution in kind to the Brigade. Empirical evidence had highlighted that, for example, museums such as the British or Science Museums added to the reputation and understanding of the Nation through the knowledge it acquires and disseminates. So in calculating the break-even point, or self-financing position, of the Brigade museum (which is taken to mean the museums zero net-costs to the Fire Authority) then the museum's contribution to the Brigade should be awarded a financial value, and that value must be taken fully into account. This existing contribution was considered to be in terms of the status it brings to the organisation, enhancing its prestige by the dissemination of information both internally and externally. These elements were argued, both by our study group and national museum bodies, to form an integral part of any financial calculation. The museums contribution was (and remains) in kind. But this contribution has a quantifiable financial value that could be further enhanced, and we argued, significantly.

The report was presented to a joint audience of Brigade principal management and the DMS external assessors. It was delivered in Winchester House itself. Whilst being principally an academic piece of work, for our Diploma finals, it was nevertheless acknowledged as a thoroughly well researched study that offered viable and deliverable options to meet the Brigade's self-financing and commercialisation requirements. The report's forty-five-minute visual presentation, its conclusion and ten recommendations were highly commended by the Course's principal assessor and was said to be one of the most comprehensive and professional presentations delivered by any DMS students in recent times. That said, the report would all too soon just collect dust within the Brigade! If anything, its conclusions were too comprehensive and its recommendations turned over stones that some clearly wished left untouched.

The recently promoted Chief Officer, whilst radically different from the outgoing Chief in many ways, was no less smitten and attached to his perks when it came to Winchester House. The possibility of the Massey Shaw suite being hired out for corporate hospitality and/or business lunches and evening dinners was a definite "no-no" in his book, despite the fact it would have attracted substantial income. (In fact it was firmly believed that Winchester House and the Massey Shaw suite would have met the needs of a niche market and with a quality product could have made the museum self-financing on its own.) However, Brian Robinson, the Chief, clearly had his own private agenda when it came to the future of the Museum and Winchester House.

His intention was that the status quo be maintained whilst paying lip service to commercialisation, this keeping the Authority's politicians happy. There would eventually be a shop located in the museum and some tweaking of its budgets but in essence Winchester House would remain untainted by wholesale commercialisation. The active drive to make the museum self-financing was placed firmly on the back burner. My own small part in the restoration of Winchester House and the re-design of the Brigade's museum would prove a lasting legacy of my time within Press and Public Relations. It was one of which I remain immensely proud.

Three envelopes!

This was the twilight of my time in Press and PR. The days were rapidly counting down and I was eager now to move on. An uneasy truce existed between me and my replacement; who was a rank higher than me. His obsession with wanting to know the ins and outs of everything, the minute detail of the planning of the various PR events was undermining the devolvement of authority that had been steadily handed down to the staff during the previous two years. The PR staff had responded magnificently to this transfer of responsibility and had risen to the challenges that they had been set. They knew where to go for advice or guidance and were given support when required. This was now being eroded and it was not assisted by the obsequious nature of the individual who would soon be the only Divisional Officer in the Division.

With my departure date now common knowledge, this chap came to seek my advice about holding the fort on his own, as I was soon to be off. By its very nature, anything we did or tried to do within Press and Public Relations, left us only as good as the last task we had performed. Forget the Chief's lunchtime meeting sandwiches and you were in the doghouse for weeks, regardless of the outstanding or high-quality work that we might have delivered immediately before. It was how we were measured and judged, somewhat unfairly, but true nevertheless.

So in response to his question I told him the tale of three envelopes. "When I go," I said, "I will leave you three envelopes numbered one to three. When you are about to get your first serious bollocking for some PR cock-up or other (and you will) open the first envelope. It will tell you to blame me, say it was all Pikey's fault; he left me an insufficient brief. When you are about to get your next major bollocking open envelope number two. It will tell to offer a humble apology, say sorry and offer a grovelling promise that it will never, ever, happen again. When the third significant finger wagging session follows another PR disaster open the third, and final, envelope. It will simply tell you to prepare three envelopes!"

The 50th Anniversary Blitz drill display at the LFB's headquarters at Lambeth and a reconstruction of an enemy bombing raid during late 1940. September 1990.

Copyright. *London Fire Brigade/ Mary Evans Picture Library.*

Firefighters suffering from the effects of extreme heat at the Gillender Street warehouse fire in Bow, which cost the lives of two of their colleagues; Firefighter Terrance Hunt and Probationer Firefighter David Stokoe. 10th July 1991.

***HRH Princess Diana, with Princes William and Harry enjoying Mike
Herbard's wartime turntable ladder following the Blitz 50th commemorative
anniversary service in St Paul's Cathedral. September 1990.***
Copyright. *London Fire Brigade/ Mary Evans Picture Library.*

***Eighty former London firemen and firewomen, all Blitz veterans, march from
Aldersgate to St Paul's Cathedral prior to the Blitz 50th commemorative
anniversary service. September 1990.***
Copyright. *London Fire Brigade/ Mary Evans Picture Library.*

***HRH. Queen Elizabeth, The Queen Mother, unveils the Blitz Memorial
statue in Old Change, opposite St Paul's Cathedral. May 1991.***

Copyright. *London Fire Brigade/ Mary Evans Picture Library.*

The remains of the IRA truck bomb burning outside the Baltic Exchange that killed three innocent civilians. 10ᵗʰ April 1992.

Copyright. *London Fire Brigade/ Mary Evans Picture Library.*

Some of the extensive devastation caused by the IRA terrorist bombing of the Baltic Exchange in St Mary Axe in the City of London on the 10th April 1992.

Copyright. *London Fire Brigade/ Mary Evans Picture Library.*

The Victorian, Portland stone, Metropolitan Fire Brigade relief restored to its former glory and mounted in the Brigade's Training Centre entrance lobby at Southwark. 1994.

Remembering those that paid the ultimate sacrifice for doing their duty.

Chapter 15

The Last Rung

In the autumn of 1992 the winds of change were blowing. Only, then, I had no idea just how hard and how much they would affect me. For now, however, only a gentle breeze was coursing its way through the ranks of the London Fire Brigade. But the storm was brewing.

In the late 1980s and early 1990s there had been fourteen rungs on the London Fire Brigade's promotional ladder. The first rung was, and remains, that of recruit firefighter. The last was that of the exalted rank of Chief Fire Officer. That title would change and two senior rank positions would disappear altogether in a radical management shake-up. But these were things to come. For now I had managed to climb up nine of those rungs. I had become a Division Officer-grade one (DO1). This was the highest of the three national Divisional Officer grades. It also happened to be the point where I levelled out. Something I thought that was no mean achievement for a "know nuffing" boy from Samuel Pepys secondary modern school. Maybe one more rung could have been doable? But I lacked the academic flair and the intellectual capacity to climb beyond the tenth rung and secure principal officer rank. Besides, far too many of my peer group did have those qualities and were eager, if not hungry, to push their careers ever higher. Some managed to do so at any cost. I knew the extent of my own capabilities and was comfortable, and happy, with that fact. I remained content to pass on whatever management talents I had "acquired" to those who were either prepared to listen or the "wannabees" who just watched and cherry picked my skills and knowledge in their personal quest to reach principal rank. Many of my, then, subordinates would rise to achieve their goal. They included both the future Chief Fire Officer of London, a title that would be re-branded "Commissioner," and the Chief Officer of the West Midlands Fire Brigade.

It's October 1992 and it seemed to me I had come full circle. Overjoyed by my recent promotion, it was not lost on me that I had also returned to the very place that I had started. I was back amongst the recruits at Southwark Training School, now designated a Training Centre. The word "school" had been removed from the Brigade's increasingly politically correct lexicon and, together with its positive discrimination policies, it was providing people, places and jobs with ever more upbeat and flowery new titles and labels.

Many could be forgiven for thinking that Southwark Training "school" had changed little, in looks, since 1965. (Sadly the majestic Metropolitan Fire Brigade frontage in Southwark Bridge Road had been demolished in the late 1960s.) One or two cosmetic modifications had been made; the cobbled drill yard (once London's largest enclosed cobbled area) was now largely replaced by asphalt. A start had, however, been made on the much-needed major refurbishment of the site and the first, limited phase had included the Museum and Winchester House, in which I had played a part, was completed. That first phase had also included improved and revamped accommodation for the recently formed "Operation Training Team (O.T.T.)." This team had been created after the Health and Safety Executive issued two improvement notices on the London Fire Brigade in the wake of the deaths of two firefighters in an East London warehouse fire in Gillender Street. O.T.T. now occupied the converted former residential accommodation above Southwark fire station. It had been transformed into spacious teaching areas in addition to well-appointed office space.

My arrival coincided with the commencement of the next phase in this major (£2.6 million) redevelopment of the Brigade's Training Centre. I was now in charge of the Brigade's recruit firefighter training. I learnt that my brief also included responsibility for the Centre's considerable administrative staff and the day-to-day management of the site. I reported directly to Robert (Bob) Marks, a Deputy Assistant Chief Officer who carried the title "Commander-Training." It was Bob Marks who had overall responsibility for the Training Centre, its people and its various functions. My new job was, nevertheless, challenging as I all too soon discovered. It seemed that news of my previous, successful, role in the upgrading and refurbishment of the Museum and Winchester House had preceded me. As had my ability in managing to squeeze a quart out of a pint pot, at least as far as the project's budget allocation was concerned.

Bob Marks was a giant of a man, both in stature and personality. He had a face more suited to that of a battered, bare-knuckle, street fighter than a fire brigade principal officer. Even without these boxer-like features he had acquired a formidable reputation as a hard man. His looks just helped his image. It was rumoured that when the Chief Officer had once commented on what skills Bob carried in his managerial tool bag he said, "It contains only one thing, a bloody big hammer." I quickly learnt that this was far from the truth as Bob proved himself to be a skilful and able principal manager, and someone who happened to be both thoughtful and considerate. I would also discover that he was a demanding taskmaster who, nevertheless, was a pleasure to work for.

I had previously built up a good rapport with Bob during my time working within Press and Public Relations. This was, no doubt, helped by the fact he now sat in a nicely refurbished office and behind a desk that had, allegedly, once been used by Captain Eyre Massey Shaw himself. This, I had ensured was placed in the Commander-Trainings' office, as part of the Winchester House refurbishment.

October also saw another new starter at Southwark Training Centre. He too had been a junior fireman and an old "mucker" from my Southwark fire station days. Ray had recently returned from his secondment at the Fire Service College in Morton and had also been successful in the recent DO1s promotion. He was to head up the Operational Training Team. This team included the specialist firefighter courses and advanced firefighter training. Sadly, we would all too soon lock horns after I was ordered to conduct an inquiry into his enthusiastic over-spend of his budget. The outcome was a "slap on the wrist" for Ray and provided for a strained relationship between us throughout my time at the Training Centre. Fortunately that cannot be said for Bob and myself. We got on like a "house on fire." He proved himself to be both a wise advisor and an effective mentor. Not only to me but to others that took the time to get to know him better.

The Fire Service was, and remains, a hierarchy. It had too many layers of management and still does. Although I managed firefighter recruit training, I was answerable to the Commander (Training). He in turn reported to the Assistant Chief Officer (Training). Although that Assistant Chief was a full member of the Brigade's Corporate Management Board, he too was answerable to the (1) Chief Personnel Officer (a civilian post), (2) the Deputy Chief and (3) ultimately the Chief Officer. I was way down the pecking order, yet within my own sphere of influence I oversaw the recruit trainers, the senior trainers and the recruits themselves, plus most of the civilian support staff in the Training Centre. This, in theory at least, meant having control of a significant proportion of the Training Centre budget. However, most of the money was taken up in staff costs, especially the recruits themselves, which came under control of the Chief Personnel Officer. So in reality I had very little financial control at all.

My own office accommodation and that of my fellow recruit section officers proved, if proof were needed, just how dire the fabric of training facilities had slipped over the years. The appalling state of the accommodation extended also to the recruit trainers and the recruits themselves. It was a direct consequence of years of neglect and under-funding that had seen the Brigade Training Centre as the poor relation when it came to a fair share of the Fire Authority's capital budget. It was a testament to the trainers' outstanding commitment to their role that they had tolerated these deplorable conditions for so long. The poor recruits simply got no choice!

Significant funding had been finally agreed, and was now in place, to allow for a massive capital expenditure for site refurbishment. The issuing of the Health and Safety Executive's two Improvement Notices had impacted heavily upon the Brigade's operational policies and procedures with regard to many aspects of operational training. Southwark's profile suddenly became far more significant and, ironically, was the principal beneficiary of that tragic fire. However, the refurbishment would necessitate considerable upheaval and that centred predominantly on the recruit section and its civilian support team. I had made a conscious decision that if there was to be discomfort, due to the building works, then I and my senior trainers should share equally in any disruption. So we moved lock, stock, and barrel into the former, dilapidated, recruits' locker room (less lockers!) and shared an "open-plan" office. Portakabins were brought on site to accommodate a reduced recruit intake; this cut the normal twelve squads to nine. Similar temporary accommodation arrangements were made to house the recruit trainers. This decision, to rough it, turned out to be a real winner. Not only did it let the whole team know we were all in this transitional phase together, but it also allowed me to see my team at work, close up and personal, and for them to see me.

Both the trainers and senior trainers were to be closely involved in the planning and design of the much-needed improvement to the site's training facilities. Again this was a conscious decision on my part. It would see their input help deliver the Brigade's first ever dedicated fire-sciences' laboratory. I had argued, successfully, that this important part of the recruits' syllabus could be more effectively and economically delivered by external science teachers. It was put out to tender and did secure a better service provision than the recruits received previously. But this was not the only element of the recruits' training syllabus that was under scrutiny.

Recruit training and beyond

Early 1993 and recruit training in the London Fire Brigade was on the cusp of major change. I had seen to that. Given the job (with an extant remit) of conducting a key review; not only of the in-house recruit training but of the training, and development, of firefighters throughout their probationary service, and on to their four yearly "qualified" status, I had presented my report, with its key conclusions and recommendations.

My radical review had covered recruit basic training practices; the Brigade's probationary procedures; and the out of date qualified "fireman's" examinations. I had discovered, or rather confirmed, there was significant room for improvement. I took a detailed look at our recruit course syllabus and its timetable. I had also drawn comparisons with other major British fire brigades' practices. My investigation had looked beyond our own parochial boundaries and I viewed the recruit training practices of both the Metropolitan Police and the Ministry of Defence Fire Service to see what lessons might be learnt. The review, in highlighting the inadequacies of the then LFB's operational probationary procedures, suggested ways in which it could be considerably improved.

The third element of the review gave prominence to the failings of the out of date examinations necessary to acquire the re-named "qualified firefighter" status. The problems were widely understood, but had not been acted upon. The suggested way forward argued what needed to be done to rectify this. This process would provide an objective assessment to determine the skills and appropriate knowledge level of those wishing to be awarded "qualified" status (and receive the financial rewards that this status provided). However, progressing this final part was easier said than done. This was largely due to the barriers imposed by the Fire Brigades Union. (This was the very organisation that had used the "qualified fireman's" (sic) status so effectively to pursue the membership's wage claim, in the first national firemen's strike that lasted from November 1977 to January 1978.)

What had struck me, so powerfully, when I returned to Southwark was the apparent familiarity of the recruits' basic training programme. In many ways it mirrored the basic training I had undertaken when I first joined the Brigade 27 years earlier. Some equipment had changed, new procedures had been introduced (to take into account the changes to operational policy and imposed legislation such as Equal Opportunities and Health and Safety at Work) but in many ways the course had only been tweaked at the edges. It had not undergone any significant modernisation, whilst life at a fire station clearly had.

There was a Home Office national syllabus for the training of whole-time recruit firefighters. Published in 1974, it had remained unchanged for nearly twenty years. In setting out the technical and practical elements of a recruit's formative training it had allotted a total of 450 hours of basic training, the equivalent of an eight-week, full-time, course. Individual fire brigades could, and did, differ in both their approach and attitude towards recruit "operational" training. London, for example, had gone from a 12-week course in the 1960s and 70s to a 16-week recruit course in the 1980s. London had also provided recruit training courses for smaller rural fire brigades. These Brigades either lacked the resources or facilities to undertake their own recruit training programme, or their annual firefighter recruitment needs were so small so as to make training recruits locally uneconomic.

In more recent times the breathing apparatus course for London's recruits had been incorporated into their basic training and was bolted on to the end of the recruit course. This followed the recruit's final practical and theoretical examinations. Those recruits passing their BA course (now deemed probationers) were posted to their individual fire stations. Serious misgivings about the placement of this BA training, in the last part of the course, had been expressed – in private – by many of the recruit trainers. These concerns had been clearly not vocal enough or someone higher up had not been prepared to listen to them. Either way it remained an ongoing, worrying, issue when I arrived at Southwark.

My detailed study into the areas of the review lasted eight weeks. I was assisted in my task by a small team of operational senior officers, two from Southwark TC and one seconded from North West Area. Our visits to other Brigades and organisations, the numerous interviews and analysis of Brigade policy and other data resulted in our conclusions and recommendations being presented to Bob Marks, the Commander-Training, by late spring. Agreeing with our findings, he referred the full report to higher authority, the Brigade's Principal Training Managers, including the Chief Personnel Officer, seeking their endorsement. We had clearly pinpointed a number of major concerns connected to the development of a firefighter (But nothing that the Chief Inspector of Fire Services had not already brought to the Brigade's attention a year earlier). Among our findings were: the, then, structure of the LFB's recruit course had failed to provide "best practice" when compared to other Brigades and emergency service organisations. In particular there was a failure to provide the recruits with an introductory BA course that exposed them not only to the use of BA, but used that BA in a range of basic drills. BA at this stage should be used in conjunction with combined ladder and hose drills. These skills could be further developed once they were posted to fire stations.

There existed a breakdown in communication between the Training Centre and individual fire stations. Most, if not all, watch officers were unaware of the details of the recruits training syllabus and the elements of basic training covered by their, now, probationary fire-fighters. There existed an impression of what skills and knowledge a recruit may have acquired, but this varied station by station, watch by watch. Obviously recruits not reaching the required pass standard would not be posted to a fire station. However, there existed a wide variation of understanding just exactly what those standards were.

As for the subsequent progress of a "probationary" firefighter I had found that there was no consistency in how the five Area Commands monitored or reported on a firefighter during their probationary service. The Areas also lacked common standards of assessment to deem if a probationer was suitable as a whole-time firefighter prior to confirming their appointment. After an appointment was confirmed the same problems existed with the progress of a firefighter on to their "qualified" status. Neither the candidate nor the assessing officer had their performance monitored against any defined standard. (As in the way, for example, that someone might demonstrate their ability of the required skill and knowledge level necessary to pass a driving test. Here national standards set a common standard regardless of where the test was taken and which examiner might conduct a test.) A probationary firefighter's period of probation followed no formal training programme. The minimum probationary period, of 12 months, had remained the same since it was introduced in 1945. It now failed to reflect the enormous changes to the duty systems since that time. (There were only two watches in 1945 whilst in 1993 there were four. A probationer in 1993 had twenty-five per cent less time in which to acquire operational skills and knowledge and to be measured against the extant criteria- which itself was outdated having last been published 1966.)

Lastly, came the considerable inadequacies associated with "The Qualified Fireman's Job." The concept of this role was originally based purely on the financial remuneration for a senior fireman whose earnings were intended to be comparable with those of a skilled craftsman in industry. A series of inquiries into the workings and conditions of the fire service (*Prices and Incomes No 32 – Fire Service Pay – 1967; Fire Service and its Personnel 1969*) were superseded by the Holroyd Report of May 1970. Among Holroyd's findings was the recommendation for the introduction into the fire service of a new grade of "qualified fireman." This new grade would not be involved in any supervisory duties. Although the original timescale for senior firemen was based on three years' service, Holroyd's findings established the need for individuals to be qualified in the full range of duties and skills required in firefighting operations. The Holroyd Committee recognised the need and value in providing encouragement of "extremely competent" firemen who do not seek promotion or who were unlikely to gain it."

The 1970s was a period of considerable industrial unrest throughout the United Kingdom. The British fire service was not immune from that unrest or the demands of its members, via the Fire Brigades Union, for better working conditions and pay. Following hot on the heels of the Holroyd Report came the Cunningham Inquiry whose terms of reference was to evaluate the fireman's job. Cunningham came out in favour of the position taken by Holroyd in the recognition of the acquisition of skills by firemen, but more importantly, the testing of those skills. Cunningham put forward proposals to the National Joint Council (NJC). This was the employers and employees negotiating body for determining the pay and conditions of all ranks up to and including Sub Officers. (A separate NJC committee dealt with the pay and conditions of Station Officers and above – Chief Fire Officers and Firemasters (in Scotland) had separate arrangements entirely.)

Cunningham's proposals, which had been agreed at the NJC, provided for a top point in the firemen's pay scale. This could be awarded subject to a minimum of four years' service combined with the satisfactory completion of the required tests. London introduced the "qualified fireman's" rate of pay in 1972. To be eligible a fireman had to be qualified in BA; to have had either passed the Leading Fireman's practical examination or undertaken the tests prescribed; to have held an HGV licence or agreed to undertake HGV training or an equivalent skills course; and to have undertaken basic fire prevention training and thereafter be prepared to perform fire prevention duties.

All too soon the HGV requirement, or the equivalent skill, element became a contentious issue with the London Region of the FBU. It challenged its inclusion in the required signed undertaking of prospective qualified firemen. The brigade backed down and it was not enforced. In the years that followed a major part of the brigade's original published syllabus was negated by the withdrawal from service of first, hook ladders, then the 50-foot wheeled escapes, and the discontinuation of "live" carry downs at station level.

Despite the considerable concerns raised at local level as to the falling status of the qualified fireman's (now termed firefighters) examination no alternative proposals were forthcoming from the Training Department. Variations in the standard and quality of first aid and BA refresher courses also impacted on the range of skills and knowledge available to personnel undertaking the "qualified" examinations. The London Region of the FBU had successfully pursued an agenda that resulted in the examinations being still further diluted, by limiting the choice of subjects being selected by the candidate, contrary to the NJC working party proposals. Despite the recognition of the inappropriateness of the existing qualified firefighters' examination by the Assistant Chief Officer Training in 1987 no changes were implemented by the then Chief Officer despite the concerns of the ACO(T).

Finally, during his annual inspection of the Brigade in 1992 Her Majesty's Inspector of Fire Services made adverse comment on the "flawed" system of London's qualified firefighters' examination in his annual inspection report. The lack of any formal system of development was the focus of his concerns. That report also made comment on the Brigade's probationary procedures and lack of feedback on the effectiveness of recruit training.

My review had not just been about the Brigade putting its own house in order, albeit belatedly. It had been driven to do so by the Chief Inspector's public concerns. With the impact of the two, unprecedented, Health and Safety Inspectorate improvement notices still fresh in the mind of the Chief Officer, they had cast long shadows in every aspect of operational training. The development of a firefighter, from recruit to "qualified" status was no exception.

I had long aired my views about the steady loss of value of the four-year qualified firefighters' examination and its detrimental effects. My concerns, like those of so many other like-minded officers had, sadly, fallen on stony ground. By February 1993 firm proposals were in place to introduce a development programme, starting with recruits through to the qualified firefighter. My report had found favour at the highest levels of the Brigade. Not that it actually told principal management anything they did not already know!

However, what it did provide was the means to implement a development programme as a whole package and they had bought into it or, at least, so I thought. With my recruit trainers getting a voice to correct the problems associated with recruits undertaking BA training far too late in their basic training, the trainers wholeheartedly supported the recruit course changes. My proposals also brought forward radically amended reporting procedures of recruits heading into the five Areas. These new "end of course" reports identified exactly what individuals had done in their basic training and the grading they achieved throughout their assessments. Area Training senior officers combined, for the first time, with Southwark's senior officers and conducted the recruits' final assessments. This became far more transparent than just Recruit section senior officers conducting the final recruit exams and tests. Area Officers were fully engaged and now aware where the probationer firefighters were expected to start from on the next phase of their development programme.

With approval given for the next two recruit squad intakes to pilot the revised course, it was deemed to be a success: not only by the central Training Department chiefs but by all the Area Training Officers, who had been invited to observe both the midpoint and final assessments. Full implementation of phase one of the firefighter development course (recruit training) came into being in August 1993.

However, the initial euphoria would soon slowly be eroded. Although the changes to the recruit course remained, and were signed off by the Fire Brigades Union, significant other factors were already in play. Separate brigade studies had been directed towards the identification of operational "competencies." The results of those studies would, eventually, redefine the measurement of operational standards and the performance indicators required to assess the standard required of not only firefighters, but each individual operational rank within the fire service.

With procrastination and "huffing and puffing" by the in-house Competencies Team, unhappy that our proposed firefighters' development programme had been given the "green light," even as an interim measure, they lobbied hard for its halt. Their own detailed "role mapping" exercise of a firefighter, whilst completed, remained unpublished. The team created barriers to the brigade-wide introduction of our suggested development programme. We had pushed hard for the equivalent of the Betamax system of video recording whilst they had gone with VHS, and we all know the outcome of that particular battle. It was alleged that we had measured and determined inputs and not the outcomes required of "competency." Likewise London Fire Brigade would eventually move from "ranks" to "roles." However, that would not be until the start of the next millennium and happily, well after my retirement. The competency national role-mapping exercise, which would be based upon London's ground-breaking work, had some way to run in 1993; and even then it still had to get NJC agreement before its implementation. It would be finally approved in 2002.

The Fire Brigades Union also threw their "hat into the ring" and entered the debate. Ironically, it was the FBU who made concerted objections to any change in the status quo, as regards inclusion of the qualified firefighter's phase in to our proposed development programme. The fact that the original NJC document "The Qualified Fireman's Job" was the cornerstone of the Fire Brigades Union's case in seeking its wage claim during the 1977 national firemen's strike seemed to have conveniently skipped their memories. I had been an active supporter of that strike. I firmly believed in the case put forward in the agreed NJC document. I saw the value of having firemen (now firefighters) earn their qualified status and be deemed skilled workers with an enhanced rate of pay. The FBU's stance seemed hypocritical to me. They appeared prepared to see that "skilled" status completely eroded, due to the dire assessment process, as long as their members received their "qualified" rate of pay. Such was life and the FBU. These factors combined to prevent the adoption of our suggested firefighter development programme; officially that is. However, in lieu of any viable alternative, our probationer programme would be used as the "unofficial" benchmark in all five Area commands. Whilst at Southwark the revised recruit course was secure, for now at least. It continued to deliver enhanced basic recruit training that received wide acclaim. It was to remain that way until I left the Brigade due to my medical retirement.

Shouts

You might be forgiven for thinking that attending fires and other "shouts" had all but been put on the back burner. Well not exactly, although it did seem that the price of promotion had meant a marked decline in the number of times you were called out operationally. It was certainly the case that you were "out of the loop" when compared to the Area Duty Station Commanders and the Duty Divisional Officers who were normally notified of all interesting calls or first ordered onto shouts. Although I was on the South East command operational rota I could, in theory, be ordered to anywhere in the greater London. There were the odd midnight summonses to a major blaze somewhere in the South East Command whilst posted at Southwark T/C. However, it could be where I was at the time of receiving details of an emergency call that gave me the opportunity of witnessing a drama as it unfolded.

So on a Saturday morning, whilst working my double 24-hour weekend duty, I was alone in my shared office at Southwark. I was catching up on my paperwork. The whole place was deserted. I had only the loud ticking of the office wall clock for company and I was on my umpteenth cup of coffee of the morning. Somewhere in the South East Command a four-pump fire was in progress. I had been notified that the duty DO had gone on in support of the Station Commander. In the distance I could hear the station yard bells summoning Southwark fire station's crew to their second call of the morning. Shortly afterwards I got a "Code 2" message on my pager. This required me to contact the mobilising control immediately. I thought it would be information regarding the four-pump fire but was disappointed it was not a "Code 1." This would have meant an operational ordering and ample reason to leave the mundane paperwork behind.

Having given my call sign to the control officer I was told that Southwark's crews had been ordered to a "man threatening to jump" from the twelfth floor of Guy's Hospital tower block, on Southwark's ground. The appliances had been ordered to make a "silent approach" at the request of the police already in attendance. Silent approach meant no two-tone horns should be sounded in the immediate vicinity of the call. A South East Station Commander had been ordered onto the incident and was coming from Bexley, some 12 miles away. I immediately booked mobile to Guy's Hospital.

The scene, upon my arrival, was one of controlled inaction. Southwark's two fire engine crews and the TL crew from Barbican were standing by in the private road giving access to the tower block. A police Inspector was talking to Southwark's officer in charge and the pair were looking up the tower block, a short distance away. We all saw the same thing; a man sitting, well crouching actually, on a ledge over 100 feet from the ground. There was another man, standing close to the man crouching, but not close enough to be able to reach out and touch him. It seemed there was an exchange going on between the two men, whilst out of sight of the two men I was told other uniformed police officers were standing by at a nearby window. A tense quiet aptly describes the setting whilst the Inspector explained that the man threatening to jump was known to be mentally disturbed and that the second man, standing, was a hospital psychiatrist. A dialogue had been established and the crouching man was being encouraged to return inside the building. For a busy inner-city hospital an unusually eerie calm surrounded the tower block site. That was until, in the distance, the noise of a two-tone horn sounding could be heard drawing ever closer.

It could, of course, be another emergency vehicle passing the hospital or perhaps an ambulance bringing someone into Guy's busy A&E department. However, the look on my and the other fire brigade crews' faces said we all recognised the distinctive sound of the two-tone horns. It was the type that were fitted to all Station Commanders' Maestro cars. By the pained look on the Police Inspector's face so did he. The scene above us was one of controlled negotiation, whilst 12 floors below it was anything but serene. Our embarrassed gaze was now focused on the arrival of the Station Commander who was stepping from his car that he had pulled in behind the parked fire engines. Its two-tone horns now silent for the first time.

Our initial embarrassment now turned to dismay as this fire officer exited his car and surveyed the scene many floors above him. He was in a world of his own, seemingly oblivious to what was around him on the ground. His thoughts were focused, as were his eyes, and he clearly knew what to do next. In a voice that reverberated right around the hospital complex, and without any warning, he bellowed, "Don't jump!" at the still crouching man. Fortunately he was the only one that did not jump because we all did including the Inspector who was now minded to arrest him on the spot. Thankfully, and with our eyes averted towards this late and extremely loud arrival, the man on the ledge was being assisted away from the edge of his precarious position and into the safety of the hospital. That was not the only outburst to resonate from this incident. Placating the still fuming Inspector by promising to deal with the Officer who had a foghorn for a mouth I undertook to bollock him. My exchange with this officer took place immediately afterwards back in my office at Southwark. I, for one, was pleased the place was deserted. As for the officer concerned, he was left fully aware what "silent approach" meant, only his reminder was not delivered in such a fashion.

Rainham Marshes

Going to a fire on relief was, generally, boring. Being sent in the middle of the night, on relief, was even more so. Getting sent to an incident on relief was something that was not just restricted to fire station crews. Senior officers were just as likely to get involved in lengthy "relief" firefighting operations.

Whilst the hectic pace of an incident, in the initial stages, may well have calmed down, the requirement to continue operations and, hopefully, bring the incident to a safe conclusion nevertheless placed the responsibility for the actions of the attending crews (and their safety) squarely on the shoulders of the officer deemed the "Incident Commander." The "baton" of command could be passed down as well as up. I was to relieve a Deputy Assistant Chief Officer who had been left in Command of a 20-pump fire, in the unimpressive surroundings of Rainham Marshes in East London, after the Assistant Chief who had commanded the blaze at its height had departed for the comfort of his bed.

My steady drive was uneventful as I crossed South London, passing through the Blackwall Tunnel, and I turned right on to the A13. (You were not allowed to attend a relief ordering "on the bell.") I was headed back into the L Division, somewhere I had not returned to since my brief stay whilst Barking's Station Commander. As I passed my former fire station a solitary fire engine, from another station, stood guard in one of its bays. It was there to cover the fire station's ground. Barking's fire engines had been amongst the first appliances to attend the fire that I was now nearing. I passed by Dagenham and, over to my right, I saw a distant orange glow shining through the mass of smoke rising high into the night sky. How, I wondered, could such a large fire occur in such a desolate and barren looking place as this? The Marshes covered a considerable area of land that ran between the River Thames and the A13. It extended some three or four miles in length. I drove passed the odd, medium sized, industrial unit as I turned right into the Marshes and continued heading in the direction of the orange glow. Flickering blue lights, in the distance, confirmed I was still heading in the right direction.

One, then another fire engine, linked by hose lines, greeted me as I reached the main control unit parked in Coldharbour Lane. I had received little information about the incident prior to my departure from home. However, the 90mm diameter hose I had been driving past for the last half a mile and the relay pumps told me that getting water on to the fire in sufficient quantities in its early stages had clearly been a problem. I was not the only one arriving either, as the first of the ten relief pumps were driving down the road behind me.

There was a quiet orderly calm on the Control Unit as I booked in attendance. I reported to the Deputy Assistant Chief, the Incident Commander. I knew of him rather than knew him so it was all rather formal, which was fine by me. The initial tasks to be allocated to the relief crews attending had already been worked out. The first two pumps to arrive had been designated to relieve the pumps providing the water relay. A pump had been set into a high-volume water main about half a mile away and one intermediate pump positioned to boost the water pressure to feed the fire ground pumps. The fireboat had been ordered to the incident but a combination of tides, a vast exposed muddy foreshore and the distance to the fire made pumping water from the fireboat impracticable – so it had been sent back to its base.

As we walked towards the fire the Incident Commander briefed me as to the situation. "Without a good water supply the fire just got away," he mused. "It was not until the hose-layer arrived that we were able to get a sufficient supply of water to attack the fire." The smell of burning and smouldering rubber and plastics filled my nostrils. Those materials had combined to make this a particularly intense fire even if it did not a pose a risk to anything around it – not least because there was nothing around it, except the Marshes! The nearest building must have been at least 500 metres away.

Fire engines filled the asphalt access road. Some crews were ready to depart whilst others had to wait to be relieved. A cluster of hose lines littered the wide, gated, entrance to the site. The open gates – like the extensive site's perimeter fence – were constructed of corrugated metal sheeting nailed to an eight-foot-high timber framework. Whilst a thick plume of smoke still rose into the night sky it now had the unmistakable mixture of steam combined with the acrid fumes. As it drifted upwards an informed observer could tell that the fire was no longer in the driving seat. Flames were, however, still visible and some rising above the height of the boundary fence. They too had lost the ferocity of a blaze burning out of control. Passing through the entrance and strolling into the site I saw, for the first time, the full extent of the fire that had required 20 pumps; first to surround it and then press home the attack on the blaze.

What I had been looking at was a bloody big scrapyard. It would in years to come possibly be re-branded a recycling centre. Whilst it predominantly contained waste plastics and rubber there were other equally combustible products that had added fuel to the fire. The site covered an area equal to about four football pitches. Mounds of smouldering and burning rubber tyres, together with used plastic goods were separated by narrow access paths, used by the site's forklifts and small grab crane. These paths had resembled fast flowing streams that ran to one side of the site and there found the exit at the perimeter fence. Black contaminated water seeped into the surrounding marshes. None of the site's plant had survived the intensity of the fire and was totally destroyed. In one corner the skeletal remains, of what once had been the site office, provided the only marker to where it had once stood.

I had been shown the fireground plan used for the containment of this fire. It recorded where jets had been positioned and which crews were working where. The plan would be adjusted as relief crews were put to work. However, it was quite clear that my four-hour stint as the Incident Commander was not going to see this particular fire extinguished.

Returning to the control unit I was met by my other "relief" senior officers – five Station Commanders. None of whom appeared too enamoured of the task ahead; a trait which seemed to be matched by the rest of the relief pump crews as they reported in and allocated their specific tasks.

Six jets were still at work in the yard. Deep-seated pockets of fire were continuing to burn at many hundreds of degrees Centigrade. The way the waste was stacked and the properties of the rubber and the plastic prevented even powerful jets of water penetrating right into the mound and extinguishing these pockets of fire. The heat generated from below and radiated from the fire had, in many places, melted and welded the plastic together so as to form a "skin" over considerable swathes of the waste material. Clambering over this waste could be very hazardous. It was possible for the "skin" to give way without warning and an unsuspecting firefighter could easy fall through into a "hot spot" and be engulfed in fire. So now having formally taken over command I set about completing the changeover with the relief crews.

Changing over inevitably means a temporary break in the water supplies as relief pumps are set in and hose lines are disconnected and changed from one fire engine to another. Unnecessarily long delays need to be avoided as fire will take any opportunity with a break in the attack to regain a firm foothold. There has been many a tale of a lacklustre change over allowing a fire to flare up again, very occasionally with embarrassing consequences, especially for the Incident Commander. I was not going to have that happen here. I divided my senior officers to cover the two halves, or sectors, of the fireground. One additional Station Commander would act as a Safety Officer for each sector. The fifth Station Commander would remain in charge of the control unit. With all ten relief fire engines in attendance the clock was now running; they would have at least three hours to get to grips with the deep-seated pockets of fire throughout the site before the next wave of relief pumps arrived.

Messages, sent via the control unit, were required at regular intervals. My first said all reliefs had been implemented. That was followed by others saying what progress had been made. Later I would determine what other relief pumps would be necessary. The control unit staff had been working for over six hours without a break. The crew said they were OK, but I would include a relief control unit with the next change over. One of the most demanding aspects of this duty is making sure that all the crews were gainfully employed. Damping down a fire was a necessity but in the wee-wee hours if a crew could skive off and sit on their fire engine, rather than pour water on the remains of a fire or turn over the debris, they would. Not all, but there were a few "scallywags" who would always try it on if they could. But a watchful eye kept the momentum going and a first "steady progress" message was followed by a second. In fact sufficient progress had been made to reduce the next relief down to six pumps plus the necessary senior officers, and to get the control unit crew relieved.

With the dawn the handing over process was repeated. I passed the command baton onto another senior officer and thanked the five Station Commanders and the control unit crew for their efforts. In all honesty the task had not taxed any of us, but it was a job that had to been done and it was our turn to do it. A final visit would be made by the local station the following day, and this incident would be closed down. For now I made my way back to Southwark Training Centre, a hot shower and a change of uniform, reasonably confident that I would not pick up another relief ordering two nights running. However, an ordering to an incident – well that was a different matter entirely.

The building site

The builders were back and in force. They were to spend the next 36 months striving to deliver what had been essential for a very long time; a modernised training facility that was fit for purpose. They were about to start the second phase, of a four-phase programme. This particular phase would see over 50% of the site shrouded in ground to roof scaffolding and the builders erecting six-foot timber hoardings. We were denied access to our main drill yard, the canteen and the three storey North and West Block teaching areas. Both the recruit and other operational training would be restricted to outside the "building site", which actually didn't leave a lot of available space to undertake practical training. In fact space had become something of a premium.

However, it would be to the credit of all those involved that no major conflicts, between us and the contractors and more importantly trainers fighting over the limited training space, arose. Without the Training staff's understanding and co-operation, throughout the extended occupation of the Training Centre by a whole raft of different skilled workers and general labourers engaged in transforming the site, no end of problems could have arisen. But they didn't. That is not to say there was not the odd niggle that needed to be sorted. Such as the recruit squad who let their jet suddenly get out of control and soak some contractors, who only a few minutes earlier had been taking the "mickey" out of the lads playing at "firemen" on the drill tower adjacent to the scaffolding where the contractors were working.

Working around this building site, which took up the hub of the Training Centre, made adjustments very necessary. The total number of recruits undergoing training at Southwark, at any one time, could vary considerably. It had been dependent on the projected wastage and retirement rate of the operational workforce. As many as sixteen squads, one hundred and ninety-two recruits, had been undergoing recruit training, in various stages of their basic training, in recent times. With the building works given a start date the total number of recruit squads in training were to be reduced to nine. This was considered to be a manageable number given we were sharing a building site. Valuable training space also had to be used to accommodate "porta-cabins", shipped into the site, that provided temporary locker and changing facilities for the reduced number of recruits, their trainers and other site staff. A temporary canteen and kitchen also had to be added to the mix, again in Portakabins. With so many temporary cabins, some stacked one on the other; the site was rapidly taking on the look of a container depot.

However, the Training Centre modernisation scheme and associated building works was a vast project and the general consensus of opinion, certainly from the Recruit section, was no pain, no gain. The work would cause far more disruption than the combined Winchester House and museum restoration. Juggling the remaining drill yard space and providing access to the drill towers taxed the considerable talents of those responsible for drawing up the revamped recruits' weekly timetable. Occasionally tensions spilled over, especially when two squads tried to use the same drill space at the same time and neither trainer was prepared to give way and seek alternative space, not that there was any!

That was not the only difficulty that had to be overcome regarding the modernisation programme. Southwark Training Centre's establishment allowed for a civilian senior administration officer post. The incumbent had been promoted and moved on before my arrival. His position had remained vacant for months. Whilst Bob had delegated me the day-to-day task of site liaison, with both the in-house Property Services team and the site contractors, neither he nor I were sufficiently IT literate to set up and monitor the computer project management systems that this task demanded. However, I knew a man who could.

Steve was a non-uniform junior manager. Despite his youth he was sharp, as bright as a button and an absolute wizard when it came to all things IT. Unfortunately, he was working in Press and Public Relations and they were not keen to lose him. During a telephone conversation that would have done credit to the film *"The Godfather,"* I made him an offer he could not refuse. He willingly accepted and came over to join my Recruit Training team. With a temporary promotion as part of the deal he became my joint deputy, alongside Ron Dobson, who was my DO 3. Together we would make a formidable team. My enthusiasm, organisational skills and drive combined with their brain power. (Both Ron and Steve would later secure principal officer rank with Ron becoming London's Fire Commissioner. A title that was to replace that of Chief Fire Officer.)

With the contractors finally on site, work started on the long-awaited redevelopment of Southwark Training Centre that would see the blueprint become a reality. The plans to turn the inadequate and antiquated amenities into modern and multipurpose training facilities had taken a tortuous route. Numerous delays and fears over adequate funding had caused a decade of amended proposals. Procrastination about alternative Training Centre proposals had caused both frustration and schemes shelved. Proposals had included building a custom-made training complex in Averly, Essex; then developing the former RAF site at Biggin Hill was investigated. Both were deemed prohibitive with estimates in excess of twenty million pounds. Finally the wholesale redevelopment of the existing Southwark site became the only viable and affordable option. This not least because of central Government's determination to see local authorities restrict their overall spending. London's Fire Authority finally approved a £2.6 million phased implementation over four years. (The refurbishment programme, when finally completed, actually came to £4.7 million.) Whether my posting to the Training Centre was just a happenstance that coincided with its redevelopment I never knew, but for me it provided both an interesting and a rewarding experience.

The MFB stone reliefs

You might recall, at the beginning of my story, I mentioned the grand Victorian building that Captain Eyre Massey Shaw had had constructed when he transferred the headquarters of the Metropolitan Fire Brigade from the City of London to its new site in Southwark Bridge Road. The Greater London Council had the building demolished in the late 1960s and, in my opinion; an impressive London landmark had been lost. (Sadly, it proved to be one of many, demolished in a time when concrete monoliths increasingly took the place of once graceful architecture that had fallen on hard times.) There was little to register where that building had once stood except a narrow band of grass and a couple of trees behind the cast iron boundary railings of the Training Centre and Winchester House. One of the striking features of that once elegant building had been the grand entrance arch with its hand carved reliefs mounted on either side. They featured images of the Metropolitan Fire Brigade. Both beautifully sculpted, they displayed brass helmets surrounded by a circular fireman's belt; a fireman's axe; a long nozzle and period copper riveted hose. A work of art, they weighed hundreds of pounds each, and were interlaced with flickering flames that had been crafted into the solid blocks of Portland stone.

The reliefs, plus the MFB insignia that formed a five-foot high triangular shaped badge cut from smaller interconnecting blocks of Portland stone, had been salvaged when the rest of the building had been carted away by the demolition men. Who had had the foresight to put the reliefs to one side remains a mystery. Maybe there was once a proposal to have them all put on display? Whatever the intention was it had never come to pass. The stonework had lain, in the open, behind the former recruitment hut, for over twenty years.

I had previously seen the reliefs, and the various bits of the badge, laying uncared for when I had been heavily involved with the museum restoration project. I had tried, unsuccessfully, to get them restored and put on display. Just where, I was none too sure. However, I had already pushed my luck as far as it would go by managing to squeeze extra money out of that project's budget. I had been told by John Turner, the in-house project manager, "No can do Pikey."

John Turner was a tall, good-looking, some might say suave, non-uniformed senior manager in the Fire Authorities Property Group. Highly skilled in his own discipline he and a colleague were the Brigade's project officers during the first three phases of the Southwark redevelopment programme. John also had another endearing quality: he was totally supportive of the London Fire Brigade and had a particular interest in its cultural heritage. He had combined his professional skills and fondness for the history of the Brigade to excellent effect in the restoration of Winchester House. He also found some slack in the budget for that project to indulge my requests for extra works within the museum and the refurbishment of the ground floor Massey Shaw suite.

Having told me, "No can do Pikey," to resurrect the carved reliefs, he had added, "I will see what I can do in the next phase. Little did the poor man realise that I would be at Southwark when the next phase unfolded. I was back on his case, big time, to remind him of his undertaking. As Baldrick so often said in Rowan Atkinson's *"Blackadder"*, "I have a cunning plan!" An integral part of phase two was the creation of a new reception lobby and visitors' entrance for the Training Centre. Its simple, yet stylish, design was intended to project both a professional and pleasing impression to visitors and trainees attending the Brigade's premier training centre. I had requested the stone work be incorporated into the entrance lobby scheme, suggesting the carved reliefs be set into an inside wall of the new lobby and the MFB badge be erected on the grassed area by the entrance door to the reception. I had immediate success with the reliefs but I would have to wait to see how the budget went as to having the badge erected.

All the original stonework had fallen into a very sorry state of repair, especially the carved reliefs. A specialist stonemason had to be contracted to undertake the careful restoration necessary and to mount the two reliefs, one above the over, set into the high ceilinged, entrance lobby wall. Mounted flush, and carefully restored and polished, they made a surprisingly effective contrast between the new and the old. It was with considerable pride that I had seen the reliefs returned to their former glory and once more put back on public display. Fortunately, sufficient monies were later found to erect the MFB badge, together with a plaque, to mark the site of the former Brigade Headquarters building.

It was Christmas Eve 1993. The training centre would close over the Christmas break, but after that morning's recruits' parade, everyone was first invited into the "old" MFB appliance room, cleared for the occasion, for a glass of mulled wine, a hot mince pie and a sausage roll. There had been an air of anticipation as Bob Marks announced that the recruits and their trainers would be able to use much of the revamped accommodation when they returned in the New Year. The building contractors, who were already on their Christmas break, had largely finished phase two – and within budget. Not that many present were too worried about the budget. They were just keen to get into the new accommodation. Sadly, my team and I were still to be left in the former locker room since the creation of the recruit section new open plan offices was in the next phase.

By lunchtime most had left to get home early. In a private moment of celebration Bob Marks, John Turner (who had been invited especially) and myself opened a bottle or two in Bob's office and drank a toast to the success of the recent renovations and to the old Chief himself – Eyre Massey Shaw. He had been an active moderniser in his time and we were certain he would have approved of what we had accomplished in his former fire brigade headquarters.

However, this was not what we were there to discuss. Phase two had been all but completed. I had spent the previous couple of weeks physically going over the building and modernisation works with a fine toothcomb to identify any "snagging" which the contractor would have to correct before it was formally handed over. I had found a few minor issues but the task had been completed to an exceptionally high standard. News had also come down from on high that (whilst the other phases had yet to be completed) the most crucial aspects of the redevelopment work were done and the Chief had wanted a formal opening of the Training Centre in the New Year. Gordon White had already phoned to give me the heads up and said he had been drafting a letter of invitation destined for a member of the Royal Household.

Royal re-opening

Early in the New Year, and back in the Commander's office, Bob Marks confirmed that a reply had been received to the Chief's invitation. Her Royal Highness the Duchess of Kent had been "pleased to accept" and a date had been set in March to formally re-open the Training Centre. "The Chief wants you to organise the display," said a smiling Bob. Normally such tasks would fall to Press and Public Relations to co-ordinate, but it seemed that I had little choice in the matter. Not overly fussed by having to put together the Royal road show at the training centre, I did however, have serious concerns about what impact the visit might have on recruit training, Royal or not. Explaining my concerns I added I wanted to discuss the options with my recruit team. "Fine," he replied, "Just as long as the Chief gets something to impress HRH with." Meeting over.

Recruit training was an expensive business. I have no doubt it still is. (Now in the 21st century training the LFB's recruits is also privatised.) My job then, or rather that of my trainers was to get recruits through their intensive basic training and to pass them out successfully. It was not to fail them.

I had 49 uniformed operational personnel (including trainers and my management team) under my wing. Plus there were the non-operational and administrative staff; craft and manual personnel who I had direct control of regarding their general supervision, standards of performance and the maintenance of discipline. However, the real "life and death" decisions were only made in conjunction with those above me. That included whether a recruit, who had failed their training course, should have their services terminated or not. So the prospect of a recruit, or recruits, underperforming because we had to put on a "Royal" show did not sit lightly with me. Nor, for that matter, did I imagine would it sit lightly with any of the squads of recruits who were eager to do well at either their intermediate or, more importantly, their final assessments.

Suddenly I felt like I was back in Press and Public Relations. Out came my "little black book" and I made telephone calls to get the ball rolling. One of the first people I contacted was Basil Weitz MBE, who had done such a wonderful job of providing the commentary at the Blitz 50th anniversary commemorative weekend at Lambeth. "Yes I am free," he informed me, "and I would love to be involved."

However, my team of senior trainers and Ron shared the same concerns as me. Put simply, the building works had already impacted heavily on the recruits' training programme and they did not need any more, unnecessary, disruptions. Together we arrived at a solution. HRH would see exactly what the recruits did during their basic training and at the point each squad was at in their course. A little bit of embellishment was necessary but no serious breaks in their training occurred and with full access to the main drill yard restored all practical training had been making up any lost ground. Bob had bought into the plan.

Whilst Bob and Gordon White had been taking care of the Chiefs worries about meeting and greeting the Royal visitor, the staff on site all came together to either give up some of their time, for a few after hours rehearsals, or to assist with the proposed Royal activities. Supporting Brigade reviews, or public displays had not been top of the Chief's agenda unless, of course, there had been some political gain to be made. But mixing with a Royal, well that was right up his street.

However, it seemed to me, in some small measure, to be an appropriate return to the past. Southwark had been, in the days of Eyre Massey Shaw, and until 1937, the LFB Headquarters. It had been the natural venue for the regular public displays, in fact they occurred most Saturdays throughout the summer months. Once very popular, they had entertained quite a social gathering. The rich and famous had gathered for a free show and to witness the firemen demonstrate their ladder and rescue skills with great aplomb. A frequent visitor in Shaw's time was Prince Edward, The Prince of Wales. He was even pictured sauntering around Southwark's drill yard, casually dressed, and fully immersed in the drills that Massey Shaw had arranged for him. The Duchess of Kent's visit would be the first formal Royal visit to Southwark training centre in over half a century.

The recruits' drill programme, although the centrepiece, was only one part of Her Royal Highness's tour. She would visit some of the new teaching classrooms, the science laboratory and see trainee facilities, plus a proposed ride on a fire engine. The Brigade had taken delivery of a new hybrid aerial appliance, a combination of a turntable ladder and a hydraulic platform (ALP). Enquiries made of HRH's private secretary as to whether the Duchess would be willing to ride in the "cage" had been favourably received. The Duchess, it appeared, had no fear of heights

The visit turned out to be a great success. The recruits put on a remarkably good show, given they had no previous experience of such events. The young men and women taking part did themselves proud and in doing so reflected very well on the Brigade's recruit training standards. The Chief beamed but not as much as Bob Marks who had been given the honour of escorting Her Highness around his domain. With music from Mike Oldfield's *"Tubular Bells"* accompanying the recruits' physical fitness demonstration and Jean Michel Jarre's *"Oxygene"* playing in time to a turntable ladder demonstration, Bob's worries, after seeing the earlier rehearsals vaporised. Basil provided a master-class in commentating whilst the senior recruit squad performed their pass-out drill to the highest standard. Something they hoped they would repeat in a week's time when it would be for real. Our Royal visitor was delighted by her visit to the Training Centre.

Even those who had been somewhat cynical about a Royal re-opening felt it seemed a most fitting and gratifying reward after all the immense amount of work and effort by all concerned (that had been dedicated to the project both by the training centre personnel and the Property Services Group). Other development work was to follow including the construction of the firehouse, which was some way off. I would not be around to see the project to fruition, I was unaware of that fact as the Chief gathered up his immediate circle of acolytes and disappeared into Winchester House's Massey Shaw suite for a self-congratulatory drink.

South West Operations

We all possess some degree of ambition. Some are far more driven by it than others. I had managed to achieve, in the latter part of my career, what I had wanted. Even if in 1994 I did not realise just how "latter" it had become.

As a young fireman, almost thirty years before, my driving ambition had been to be a good fireman. With the guidance and direction of some helpful mentors, a few incredible characters, and some experienced practitioners of their craft, slowly but surely, my skills and knowledge increased and my goals had shifted towards seeking higher rank. I had had the luck and good fortune to see that ambition realised. It would not have possible without the assistance of some excellent teachers who had pushed me to develop good habits and try to avoid the bad.

In those early formative years my watch Station Officer was, to me, like a God. He appeared to be the ruler of his own domain. That became my early goal, to be the boss of my own watch. Although, by the very nature of a hierarchical organisation, this was never wholly achievable. But it appeared so at the time. When that day arrived, as my earlier recollections of Brixton highlighted, it was a wonderfully fulfilling period covering five years of a career, spanning nearly thirty-two years. Now in senior rank I felt I had reached a plateau of personal achievement; well almost. I had one burning ambition remaining, but with work still in hand at the Training Centre I had put that aside and concentrated my energies on what had to be done there. That was until one day I received a summons to report to the Commander's office. No explanation was given, which in itself was most unusual. I knocked and entered Bob Marks office and found he was not alone. Seated there was the South West Area Commander. I knew this Assistant Chief Officer only by reputation and I had had only minimal personal contact with him. As I walked in, he rose to shake my hand, which immediately made me very wary. A tall man, considered to be good-looking, he was in his early forties. Privately educated, well-spoken, as a Divisional Officer he had been the Chief Officer's staff officer. He worked briefly with Brian Butler in the South East Area as his deputy, but it was not a pairing that worked well. Returning to Brigade Headquarters he was subsequently promoted to Assistant Chief Officer and held the Training portfolio before becoming the latest South West Area Commander. Very "politically" astute and ambitious, he did not have the fireground reputation of some of his fellow Area Commanders. He was, however, a very close friend of Bob Marks, a fellow freemason, and even more importantly he out-ranked Bob!

Introductions having been made Bob left the room. "Bob tells me you have done an excellent job here David. I attended the Royal opening and that was a fine piece of organisation on your part."

"Thank you, Sir," I replied. Whilst rapidly trying to work out what I had done to incur the wrath of the South West Area? You were not normally summoned to make small talk with a principal officer. This conversation had to be going somewhere but I had no idea where. After delivering a couple more ego boosting compliments about my work, he changed the subject and talked about his current Divisional Officer-Operations and in less than flattering terms. This individual had secured promotion to another Fire Brigade. He was none too complimentary about this officer's talents and gave the distinct impression that he was glad to see the back of him. I knew the person in question. I had taken over his job at the Training Centre when he had gone to the South West. Whilst sharing the ACO's views of the individual I knew better than to express them, at least not to him. I remained silent and waited.

"How do you feel about taking his place?" he asked. "What again!" I thought. At the same time a voice in my head was saying Yes, Yes, Yes. I tried to remain poker faced. "Does Bob know what you are here for?" I inquired. "He knows that if you agree it has been cleared at a higher level. That will do." I felt I was on the "horns of a dilemma." I welcomed the chance of doing this job but not at the expense of letting Bob, and my own team, down. I was not indispensable; nobody ever was in the Brigade. But my personal values of loyalty and commitment to see a job through was, and still remains, a strong principle of mine. "Can I discuss this offer with Bob?" I requested. "Yes, but I want your answer by 5pm today." The interview was over. He got up and left. As he did so Bob returned to his office. It was obvious that Bob was annoyed about one of his officers being headhunted, but was gracious towards me in discussing the matter.

Bob and I had built up an excellent rapport whilst I had been his Head of Recruit Training. We had moved forward the standards of recruit training together and developed a much-improved end of course reporting system. It had been universally accepted by the five Area Commands as a better system, of benefit both to individual probationers and their officers in charge responsible for delivering their continuation training. As for my role in the redevelopment of Southwark, I had become one of his most trusted officers with a proven ability to deliver the goods.

"So what do you think?" I asked. "That is more a question for you to answer than me," he replied as we settled down into the occasional armchairs where we had so often shared a glass of wine at the end of a long, occasionally stressful, day. "This is something that I have wanted to do, become the DO1 Ops in an Area," I said. "I have done about all I can do here. The refurbishment of the site is 70 per cent completed; the Royal re-opening went well according to the Palace and, more importantly, the Chief! Ron is more than capable of taking my place and will see the remainder of the project through." Well aware of my organisational and managerial strengths, I was conscious of my intellectual limitations but certain I could hold down such a post. Never believing I was destined for principal rank it had never been my ambition either. There had been far too much stiff competition, nearly all of whom were far more worthy and talented.

Bob confirmed what I already knew. He told me that although he felt I possessed the qualities to hold Senior Divisional Officer rank it was never going to happen, not whilst the present Chief was in post. "He doesn't like you," uttered Bob. Which was fine with me as the feeling was entirely mutual. Saying that he would like me to stay, he continued. "The Training Centre will manage without you. It will manage without me too, soon." He had been informed that he was not destined for further promotion. (He would seek his own exit strategy and would be medically retired in the very near future.) His view was that the position offered was an excellent opportunity; I had the talents required to deliver what the Area Commander required of the post holder. His advice was that I shouldn't hesitate in accepting. I didn't and rang the SW Commander confirming my acceptance of his offer. "Fine," he said, "You start next Monday, four days' time."

I never did get to enjoy the new, open plan, office suite I had helped design. Those who did said it was an exceptional working environment. Light, a pleasing setting whilst functional it enhanced the management and supervision of the recruit training team. What I got however was a new working environment – Croydon, the Area headquarters for the South West Area.

The three-storey building had once been the Headquarters of the Croydon Fire Brigade. Now it housed not only the single-storey multi bay fire station, but a greatly expanded South West staffing complement. Originally the accommodation was generous and spacious for the Chief Officer of Croydon and his small contingent of senior officers. With the creation of Greater London it became the Southern Command Headquarters and still managed to liberally service the needs of the management team that worked there. When the three Command Headquarters were disbanded it was then a Divisional Headquarters, responsible for the 11 stations in the Division, and housed the Divisional Commander's senior officer corps and support staff. Now it served the south-west area of London and catered for the 1,200 plus operational staff which it was responsible for. Space was at a premium and Portakabins littered the periphery of the site housing various administrative support units where civilian and non-operational staff had to work. However, my office was on the Area Commander's floor, where other heads of departments were also accommodated.

I had transferred my gear to Croydon at the weekend, eager to start on the Monday morning. The previous occupant had already departed for his new Brigade so I didn't have the luxury of any formal handing over, not even a good luck note! I worked through the weekend putting some semblance of order to my office, which it clearly had lacked and made it more user friendly. Ensuring that my coffee percolator was up and running, I left Sunday evening satisfied that the space would, hopefully, send out the appropriate message about the new occupier?

My first day had been spent meeting heads of the other departments, being introduced to the workings of the Area Headquarters and its various component parts. It soon became a blur of names, faces, and information overload. But I did get to meet my own management team during that first afternoon for an informal gathering. The three group Divisional Officers shared a common office on the ground floor of the Headquarters complex. I chose to meet them in their office. It was a useful way for me to see, at first hand, them in their own working environment which turned out to be in an untidy state and the charts and monitoring systems, at first sight, appeared poorly kept. Each of the three officers had a monitoring and mentoring role for a group of stations, although each of those stations was headed by a Station Commander. It was he who was responsible for their individual stations and the four watches in the first instance.

Whilst Head of Operations, on a day-to-day basis, in practice it meant I was still accountable to my Area Commander and his principal management board. Having developed my formative Area management skills in the South East Command, under the control of its legendary Area Commander Brian Butler. I found this to be an extreme change in Area management style. They were juxtaposed. I had moved from a totally autocratic approach to an almost democratic style, well on the uniformed side at least. Whilst Butler had closely controlled his section heads, this Commander was more hands off than hands on. This I felt, in part, explained my predecessor's apparent lack of effective operational monitoring and other measures to check how his twenty-three Station Commanders were maintaining operational readiness and effectiveness at station level.

What measures there were, I soon discovered, were applied without much conviction or enthusiasm, something that the SE Commander would never have tolerated. I found it hard to believe, despite my four years away from front line Area management, that such a disparity could exist between the two Commands south of the Thames.

Two of the principal managers now in the SW had been moved from the SE because Brian Butler had found them wanting. Their managerial skills were not suited to the type of ship he ran. So despite my extended time at Brigade Headquarters I was still labelled, initially, by these particular officers as a Butler man, part of the South East mafia. It was down to me to prove otherwise, not that I felt I had anything to prove. I was a round peg in a round hole.

Comfortable with my brief and without being complacent, I welcomed the probable challenges ahead. I had a crystal-clear vision of my role and the expectation of the required "service delivery" by operational personnel. It was all "service delivery" then, plus "key monitoring indicators" and other such jargon. Communicating what I expected and why, became my first priority. Twenty-three stations with 92 watches made personal individual visits time consuming and winning the hearts and minds of the front line needed a strategy.

There still was no clearly defined method of assessing the important operational areas that had to be uniformly applied across the five Area Commands. As strange as it may seem, each Area Commander had either adapted existing systems of monitoring or developed their own methods. Some were better than others. Of course the true measure of how well crews performed could only be assessed on the incident ground, when their training and knowledge was applied in practice and the outcomes could be measured.

My own operational philosophy had been both consistent and relatively straightforward throughout my career. When those bells rang, "we" went out on the engine(s) in response to a call for assistance regardless of what it was. The public had a rightful expectation that when the fire crews arrived, we would do our professional best to resolve the situation – whatever it was. That is what we were trained and paid for. So after firefighters became "qualified" (normally after four years' service) or promoted they should have acquired the necessary skills and knowledge to apply them in a wide range of circumstances and conditions. Most did, but a few either couldn't be bothered or chose not to. It was these individuals that could tarnish the reputation of the Brigade and possibly even put lives at risk. Something, I felt, was totally unacceptable. What do they say about, "One bad apple?"

My arrival at Croydon had not gone down well with at least two of my new team. One clearly had his arse in his hands because he had not been given the job I was now doing, especially as he had previously done it on a temporary basis. His opening gambit had been, "Welcome, I've put in for a transfer out of the Area, OK?" The next one up, a double degree holder but seriously lacking in social skills had also expected the job. In fact he considered himself to be the only possible candidate and wasted no time in telling me so. This is going well I thought! The third guy, a Station Commander "acting-up" as a temporary Divisional Officer remained non-committal. So I assumed he, at least, was staying and not wanting to bail out just yet.

By the end of that first week I was summoned to see the Deputy Commander so he could gauge my first impressions. He was a forty-something year old Cornishman with a paunch. Stating that I had some work to do pretty well summed up my first thoughts. Mine were a fresh pair of eyes and the standards required were not new; subjective at times certainly, but in some of the operational areas matters had clearly gone off the boil. It was time to turn up the gas again. In the weeks and months that followed much of that work was well under way, some had even started to pay dividends. But it was not all doom and gloom; there was much to commend the South West for. They were much less orientated by line management than the South East and preferred the functional management approach, certainly on the operational side. Station Commanders were actively encouraged to resolve their problems directly with the functional heads or members of their team. There were five functional areas; Operations, Personnel, Training, Technical Services and Fire Safety. (As an aside there had always seemed to have been the same headings throughout my career, only the post holders changed.)

By that summer I had met with every one of my 23 Station Commanders individually, visited every station at least once and had sat down with over a third of the station watches for a "fireside" chat. I had been comparing what I was told by the Station Commanders with what I found when visiting their stations. I was also able to compare what I had discovered with the views expressed by my three Divisional Officers and the results of their programme of station visits and inspections. Given the numbers involved many of the South West stations were managed to a more than acceptable level. Sadly there was still no Brigade wide definition of just exactly what "acceptable" was. Most of the stations were up to par, however a few individual watches had been a cause for concern.

My "Ops" team had also changed. It sounded rather like a result from a football league table; lost two, drew one, won two. One of the team had gone before my feet were firmly under the table. He had disappeared to Brigade Headquarters with his tail between his legs because he felt I was sitting in his chair. One of the other DO's thought it acceptable to bunk off, most days, to get home early. This silly man always found an excuse to be near his home, on the far side of the Area, late in the afternoons. Warnings to desist fell on deaf ears and he soon found himself back at a fire station. Somehow I had managed to win over the only substantive member of the original team. He said it was actually refreshing to work for someone who did not have any hidden agenda. This I took to be a compliment. But given that his social skills were still rather questionable I could not be too sure. Lastly, I had acquired two exceptionally talented, young(ish), officers who complemented each other. Terry was a well-grounded and experienced South West Station Commander who had run his various stations very well indeed. He had set good standards and was able to communicate them to others without alienating people in the process. The other I had headhunted from Southwark. Vij was an exceptionally bright, good-looking Asian. He had a sound operational background as a junior officer and had been promoted to a day related Assistant Divisional Officer position at the Training School. Vij was one of the very few from an ethnic background to have been promoted to higher rank in the early 1990s. I had seen him work and was impressed with what he had achieved. His ethnicity was neither here nor there as far as I was concerned. He was clearly destined for greater things in the Fire Service but needed some Area, operational, experience. I had offered it to him and considered it would be a worthwhile investment for both of us. The Ops Team had gelled well and station inspection programmes were working. The results were showing improvements where previously there had been concerns.

Croydon, as the Area headquarters also housed the Command Staff office. Each watch was headed up by a Station Officer and contained a Sub Officer, three Leading Firefighters who between them crewed the Forward control Unit and the larger Area Control Unit. The Station Officer normally took charge of the main control unit whilst the Sub Officer went out on the Forward Control Unit. These control vehicles attended make up fires and special service incidents or those requiring a greater degree of incident command and control. They responded mostly in their own area but could also be ordered anywhere in the Brigade if the local control unit(s) were unavailable for any reason.

Each Headquarters' watch also had a small complement of firefighters. They drove the BA and general-purpose lorries. The four watches were overseen by a day related Assistant Divisional Officer. The duty Staff office watch collated the daily fire station "rider" figures, ensuring that normal levels of crewing were maintained, as far as possible, across the Area. They also monitored those figures to make sure they should not fall below minimum standards of fire cover. When that happened, and it did, the "stewards' inquiry" and an investigation was necessary into how and why it had occurred.

It fell to my team to monitor these figures and to watch for trends, especially any spikes in sickness and absence levels. It had also been necessary to ensure that there was a sufficient balance of skill qualifications at fire stations to keep all the fire engines "on the run", including the various specialist appliances at all times on each watch. Appliances taken off the run, due to insufficient skills had not been a major issue during my first couple of months at Croydon. However, the early summer period brought higher levels of annual leave allocation and with it came a worried looking staff ADO knocking on my door to report that we had to order in HGV or aerial drivers from other Areas to keep our fire engines on the run. That had sent worrying "smoke signals" to principal officers at Brigade Headquarters that not everything in the South West was managed as well as it should be.

Details of the recorded number of trained "skilled" personnel in the Area told a different story from that which had been coming through my door. A story that clearly indicated we didn't have enough qualified personnel on some of the watches to cover our summertime daily needs. The answer to this problem proved to be a simple one. Those with the skills were not necessarily where the skill requirement was most needed. Far too many were on the wrong watch or at the wrong station or both. On paper we had an excess of HGV motor drivers. How it had been allowed to come to pass was not the question then; that could come later. How to resolve the problem had been a pressing issue.

As the first stage in rebalancing the problem I had got every Station Commander to list the skilled personnel that were required at each station and compare them with what were actually available. I had already calculated the minimum area skill requirement per watch, it was not rocket science. The fact that I then expected Station Commanders to manage the skills profile of their stations, and to encourage personnel to take skill courses or move personnel between watches, to overcome any imbalance in skills necessary came as a total shock to some. This had been my first major issue I had to contend with and I was being watched with interest from above as well as below.

The South West had had a noticeable difference in its management style to those I previously experienced. It was one where I could get on with resolving a problem providing I kept the Commander's deputy in the loop. I did not have to report, cap-in-hand, to explain every twist and turn as I had been required to do elsewhere. So with the riders' figures still giving cause for concern, some shifts much more than others and still requiring stand-bys from other Areas, it was acknowledged that this was a not a problem that would be solved by waving a magic wand – even if I had one.

Other than the Personnel Section, which had a civilian in charge, the other operational sections each had a uniformed Divisional Officer as its head. Meeting with the heads of Training and Technical Services (who had the job of dealing with the Fire Brigades Union joint secretary) I had outlined my plan.

Training Section had previously responded to requests for training section courses from individual stations by adding the names to a list. The training had then been allocated on a first come basis. They had not provided the training on a priority needs basis. Neither had there been a close rapport between Training Section and Operations Team in the recent past. Whilst Training Section had a role and overview in development training, and the needs of those seeking career advancement, they did not have the same appreciation when it came to the requirement of skill training required by the Area as a whole. Informing the DO1, in charge of the Training Section, that my team would first reprioritise all existing skills course applications, and would in future, then allocate skills training courses on a priority basis. (Something that lead to the maintenance of the required skills level, and also meet the anticipated shortfalls due to retirements and/or the promotion of station personnel.)

The Joint Secretaries (Brigade and the FBU) had had an excellent understanding in the South West. Whilst the FBU Secretary could argue his corner for his members' concerns, in the appropriate arena, he did not go out of his way to seek confrontation or make unnecessary trouble. John Spragett was the DO in charge of Technical Services. He had been the long term temporary DO1, covering a vacancy, and was very good at his job. He had already raised the problem of the skills shortfall with the Union as some of its members had been declined short notice leave because there had been insufficient skilled personnel available to allow them leave. Explaining that the skills problem could not be resolved overnight, John had explained my strategy for resolving the issue. One that had required the voluntary transfer of personnel across watches, at station level, to rebalance skill shortfalls. Additionally station to station, voluntary transfers, were arranged between the respective Station Commanders, temporary transfers were arranged to cover shortfalls whilst other watch personnel were given priority for appropriate training courses. Had the skill shortfalls not been resolved by way of the amicable voluntary movement of personnel, either on a temporary or permanent basis, then compulsory transfers would have been put in place. With the deputy Commander buying into the way forward, whilst the rider figures continued to cause the odd hiccup the solution proved to be remarkably successful. Much of that was due to the Station Commanders given the authority to run their stations and the co-operation of the South West operational personnel who, in large measure played ball. With only a couple of individuals reacting strongly to their unavoidable enforced transfer, by the following summer the area was again self-sufficient and maintained a steady level of skills cover.

Sadly, my association with the Command Staff office had one other very close connection. One that I would have gladly not have been required to undertake. Rod Higgins had been a Leading Firefighter on the Blue Watch. An experienced "leading hand" he was well versed in all things Staff and had been both conscious and efficient in his duties. He had one other outstanding quality, he cared passionately for others and their welfare. He had, for many years, been closely associated with major fundraising for the Fire Services National Benevolent Fund. Then what had seemed like a normal day turned in on itself when news of Rod's sudden and tragic death spread like wildfire, first around the Area Headquarters, and then the area and beyond. He had been an exceptionally keen motorcyclist. Taking a fancy to buying a new motorbike he had gone to road test a powerful bike that had caught his eye. He never returned from that ride; he died when he came off the bike at speed. A later inquest would record an "accidental death." Summoned to see the Commander I was tasked with arranging Rod's "service" funeral. It was a sad and very moving affair that took place near his family home. Friends and family joined his widow and teenage son in their grief at the loss of a loving husband and wonderful father. We had seen, all too often, just how fickle fate could be when the innocent were swept up by the "Grim Reaper", at a fire or some other fatal incident. You think you get used to death but every so often you would be painfully reminded of the fragility of life. Just how precious it is and how unfair the unexpected can be. Someone who had given so much became a memory at such a relatively young age.

Last big blaze

The first of fifteen calls had summoned the crews of Kingston and the surrounding fire stations to a fire at Kingston University, Penryhn Road, South West London in October 1994. It had formally been the Kingston Polytechnic but had been elevated to University status, like so many other London Poly's, in the late 1980s. Roofing contractors had been undertaking major works on one of the University's central facilities and had started to resurface a flat roof of a three-storey building. It was quite an extensive facility at that, some 60 metres by 60 metres. Kingston's crews had seen the huge pall of thick black smoke rising into the morning autumn sky en route, and some distance away, so already knew whatever was happening it was no false alarm.

Area command staff had a different summons to an emergency call from the normal fire stations call bells. It had the sound of the "warbler," a characteristic sound that would vibrate around the Area headquarters telling the staff office control unit crews they had a shout. Such was the warning to the duty South West Area staff officers informing them a "make-up" was in progress that required their presence. Even without the distinctive resonating of the warbler, individual pagers had been activated and the "bleeping" demanded an urgent response. My pager was but one that had shown a Code 1, an ordering to a "shout."

Earlier that day, on the roof of the University building, the contractors had fired up the industrial sized bitumen boiler. It had been left and the gas fed flames had started to heat the metal cauldron containing its full load of blocks of black bitumen. The blocks soon melted whilst the temperature had risen and the bitumen increased in volume. Shortly before 10am, still unsupervised the boiling pitch had flashed over and burning bitumen poured down the sides of the pot onto the roof. Heat and flames had spread to the contractor's materials nearby which in turn had ignited the timber battened semi-pitched tiled roof.

As Kingston's fire crew responded, and the fire grew in intensity, the building's fire alarm had sounded its warning and a full-scale evacuation of the premises was in progress. What would have been uncertain at that point was whether all the contractors had escaped from the roof and if the occupants of the three-storey laboratory and offices had made it out to safety?

Vij Randenjia had been in my office as the warbler sounded and our pagers bleeped simultaneously. We were on the same operational rota group and were performing our 24-hour duty. Vij was the Area duty Divisional Officer. Contacting the Lambeth mobilising control, we were both ordered on to the fire at Kingston where the officer of the first attendance had radioed his priority message, "Make pumps eight – persons reported."

To the general public it must have appeared quite a convoy of fire engines and fire cars as we covered the eleven miles from Croydon to Kingston University. Croydon's fire rescue tender had taken the lead and in good time, amply aided by the cacophony of two-tone horns clearing a path we made our way through the mid-morning traffic of first Mitcham, then New Malden and finally onto Kingston.

By our arrival it had been confirmed that no one was involved in the fire, which had now taken a considerable hold on the roof. Crews had deployed jets and firefighters, wearing compressed air breathing, had made their way up to roof level. An eight-pump fire gets more than just eight fire engines. Specialist fire engines, like the fire rescue tenders and the control units had increased the total to 14. Added to which there were six, or more, senior fire officers' cars, all sufficient to cause considerable disruption on the University campus. I had arrived just behind Vij. After we had rigged in our fire gear, I told him it was his fire, until I said otherwise or he had made pumps plenty. He had taken charge of smaller incidents before but this was his first large fire. It was a good learning opportunity, so why spoil it for him I thought.

A quick look around confirmed that the duty Station Commander, from Sutton, appeared to have got a grip on things. The initial crews appeared fully committed to the tasks in hand. A control pump had been established, that the main control unit would soon supersede. However, that always took a few minutes to set up and it provided the opportunity for us to have a better look at the fire situation and see what was happening; always a useful thing to do.

We found the incident commander near the contractor's scaffolding that had afforded the fire crews, in their breathing apparatus, easier access to the roof. Details of what had already been done was explained to Vij, and what still needed to be done. I listened in. The likelihood of the fire spreading beyond the building was unlikely. But it would be a foolish fireground commander who took such things for granted. With the formal hand over complete Vij had assumed command and told the Station Commander to carry on overseeing the firefighting operations on the roof. The main control unit had set up and established its fireground radio communications network for the senior officers, all of whom had now arrived.

Telling Vij I would act as the Control Unit DO, I watched as he briefed the senior officers what he required of them. Having detailed the safety officers and other roles he maintained close contact with the Station Commander he had taken over from and who was his eyes and ears on the ground. The attack on the fire was being driven home but the fire still had to be surrounded. The deputy Commander, who had booked mobile to the incident after our departure from Croydon, had arrived and booked in attendance. He did not have to take command, not yet, and told me, "I'll think I will just look and monitor what is going on Mr Pike."

Despite the two fire rescue tenders being in attendance, and the 10-breathing apparatus sets its crews brought into play, the BA crews were running short of air and would need to withdraw and change their air cylinders. Although the fire was coming under control the Station Commander had requested reserve BA crews as a precautionary measure to cover the unforeseen. Vij had looked uncertain for the first time that morning. If the fire had suddenly got out of control, he would have had no hesitation in making pumps more. But he was doing well and more importantly, learning. I was confident the fire was going nowhere but out. If Vij had made pumps ten, to get his two extra BA pumps, he would have had to relinquish command. Something that, sadly, happened all too often and where the baton of command would be passed from one incident commander to another without an effective plan of attack having been given sufficient time to be implemented. I had been there and had it happen to me. Suggesting to Vij rather than make-up he could request two "immediate" relief pumps carrying BA, I got a very old-fashioned look from the deputy Commander but, much to his credit, he did not interfere. The message sent, the pumps had arrived post haste and with the fire now surrounded it was possible for Vij to dispatch his stop message at 12.19 pm.

Meanwhile I had a wander around the fireground and chatted to some of the crews. They had done a good job, which is probably a lot more that can be said for the roofing contractors. The rest of that day relief fire crews would be engaged in hacking away at the damaged roof timbers and roof covering and damping down. The crews had saved 80 percent of the roof and prevented significant fire spread to the floor below. The Station Commander was congratulated on a job well done and Vij: well he could not help but look quite pleased with himself. His first command of a major fire. That however was not the end the tale. The command debrief would follow, something that had not been welcomed with universal glee.

PRCs. (Performance Review of Command.)

Long before I had reached the final rung on my promotion ladder it was my practice to hold informal watch debriefs after a decent working job. Although, sadly, this was not the case during my formative years at Lambeth, where such practices appeared to be frowned upon. However, someone, somewhere, must have introduced me to the idea and when I was a Sub Officer at Southwark it became the norm.

Occasionally, and it was occasionally, formal debriefs had been conducted at either Divisional headquarters or at a designated fire station. Here crews were meant to discuss the incident or fire of note and hopefully learn from their actions. Sadly, all too often these sessions became rather defensive. Attending officers in charge (and crews) would defend their actions and decision making regardless of the possibility of other courses of action being available. Frequently by the end of the debrief, and sometimes before, the discussion left many feeling that they must have attended a totally different incident to the one that was being discussed. The most enduring image I had of these structured Divisional debriefs was how not to conduct one.

Later, as a watch related Assistant Divisional Officer, I had made it my custom to gather, or visit, the initial crews attending any notable incident that I had attended. We would talk about the crews' actions in an informal yet frank and honest manner. Some watch officers were cynical about my motives and the value of such practices, especially where the officer was more senior in service than myself. (I was only 28 when first a temporary ADO.) The look on these individuals' faces told its own story of what they were prepared to bring to the table. The unspoken comment spoke volumes such as, "Who are you to say what my actions should or could have been?"

The vast majority of those I came into contact with, especially junior officers and those like myself, new to the rank of Station Officer, found the informal debriefs of value. Despite the increasing growth of bureaucracy within the Brigade, a report for everything, I had not been in the habit of making formal reports of these debriefs. However, when necessary I would undertake one-to-one follow up discussions when warranted. I was not, of course, the only individual undertaking informal or station based debriefs. For those of my generation, and who had attended the Fire Service College or in-house operational courses, the debrief was a way of life. Unfortunately, for many, once the course was over the value of the debrief, back at the station, was quickly forgotten or frowned upon by the unconverted who saw little point in them.

Some thought a debrief too time consuming. It conflicted with other managerial duties of a senior officer. In all the time I was at Brixton there was only one senior officer – ADO Roger Vaughan – who conducted the type of debrief where individuals were encouraged to speak openly about their actions and thought processes. I am not saying that there were not others of a similar ilk, but I did not come across them. Sadly, other senior officers who conducted debriefs that I had attended made it clear they had a different agenda to Roger. They were there to kick butt or settle old scores with individuals or particular crews; not a positive learning experience.

By the late 1980s and with the creation of the five Area Commands, things had started to improve and some definite policy direction was given to operational debriefing. None more so than in the South East Command, under the command of Assistant Chief Officer Brian Butler. However, there was still a wide discretion as to how and when these were delivered in the individual Areas. Fortunately Brian Butler gave more credence to the value of operational debriefing than some of his contemporaries. Changes to operational practices, because of the feedback from debriefs, were rare. Whilst debrief reports might contain salient points from which lessons could be learned, the lines of communication between the Areas and the Central departments, particularly Central Training, were poor. The systems were also lacking to analyse and evaluate the raft of information provided and then act upon it. That, unfortunately, remained the domain of Health and Safety accident investigations, which had achieved considerable structure and were considered both thorough and searching. If principal rank debriefs had been held for deputy assistant chief officers and assistant chief officers, conducted by the Deputy Chief or the Chief, about their actions at major incidents no one was saying, not publicly at least.

The London Fire Brigade had been pulled up by the bootstraps, after the issuing of two improvement notices, following the tragic deaths of the two firefighters in Bow. The Health and Safety Inspectorates action had driven the Brigade to formalised arrangements for debriefing of officers on their command role following incidents. Called PRCs they were facilitated by a principal/senior officer that was one rank above the officer in charge of the actual incident. An operational senior officer from the Operational Performance and Training Inspectorate (OPTI), who had attended the incident in an observing capacity, would attend the PRC. OPTI had been created after that fatal fire in Bow and the issuing of the improvement notices. Its officers were required to audit the operational performance of the Brigade. One of the many ways they had of doing so was attending incidents, but most notably six pump incidents and above, and monitoring the command roles of the various officers attending. There had been a fair degree of mistrust and scepticism in the early days, when OPTI arrived and wandered around with their identification surcoats over their fire kit. But gradually, they came to be a non-threatening presence and were seen as more of a help rather than a hindrance.

PRCs had to be arranged as soon as possible after the incident. Each officer that had performed a "command" role as the incident commander was required to attend. The PRCs were not minuted and were designed to be non-confrontational and not a means by which disciplinary proceedings could be brought to bear on the actions of officers in a particular command chain. A typical six pump fire debrief would include the officer in charge of the first appliance on scene, the officer in charge of the first attendance, the officer in charge of the incident and the senior monitoring officer attending, if not the actual incident commander. Only those individuals, plus the officer conducting the PRC and the OPTI officer would be summoned to the PRC. The aim was to identify what had been seen, the response to it and why?

Some Areas had put more into the PRC process than others. The South West had been very committed, so much so PRCs were arranged after all four pump fires. I, or a member of my Operations Team, conducting the process. With six pump fires and above an OPTI officer would be present. I had both conducted and been involved widely in PRCs and considered them a very worthwhile experience. The knack, for the facilitator, was to remove any barriers that prevented command decisions being discussed in an open and honest way. Sometimes this was easier said than done, especially if a particular course of action was seen, in hindsight, to have been wanting. Frequently, as the discussions developed, some actions were discovered to have been less effective than first thought. It was the general habit that make-up fires in London, certainly up to ten pumps, went up in multiples of two; i.e. four, six, eight and ten. An officer could, of course, immediately "make pumps" a straight ten or fifteen pumps if the situation demanded it. However, it was virtually unheard of to have a five or seven pump fire! So if an officer arrived at a fire and deemed it sufficiently serious, he would "make up." In more cases than not it would start as a four-pump fire, adding "persons reported" if people were believed involved or rescues were required. Although there is evidence to show the first officer on scene requesting reinforcements in double figures, say making, "pumps 10" or "12" for example. But let's just consider a PRC following a four-pump fire for a moment.

The question might be posed to the officer who had "made pumps" at the incident, "What did you see and what was your plan of action?" If it happened to be a small two-storey semi-detached house with just one room well alight, then the resources that came with four pumps might be more than adequate to deal with the tasks in hand. If, however, it were a middle terrace four-storey house, with one or more rooms alight, and people were trapped in the property and the officer concerned had still only requested four pumps, the supplementary question would most likely be, "What was your plan of attack and what were your priorities?"

In considering the plan, a quick assessment is made as to what reinforcements are required. This takes into account calculating the risks, allocating firefighters to the various tasks required e.g. firefighting, including any search and rescues. It might be discovered that the estimated number of personnel attending might then be insufficient to cover all the tasks that needed to be performed. If pumps had been made four and only 20 firefighters attended (four times five firefighters per engine) safety could have been compromised and unnecessary risks taken. Where additional pumps were then urgently requested it was generally recognised, certainly within the PRC, that probably the initial assessment had been understated. As the effectiveness of the PRC process grew, officers were encouraged to avoid such under-estimations. However, that said, five pump fires never became the norm. Whilst four pump fires remained the predominant make up category those fires, or special services, that may have started at four pumps and suddenly grew to six, now more often started at six. The message was getting across and with the improved command and control training that had been cascaded down to fire stations, better decision-making was making its presence felt.

Which brings me back to the PRC for the ten-pump fire at Kingston University. As each officer, in turn, went through their action plan of what they did and why, whilst not textbook perfect the action plan was sound, well thought out and implemented with due consideration given to the resources necessary to follow it through. That was until it came to my turn. Whilst my advice to Vij had been given with the best of intentions, it could not be defended when set against the criteria that should have applied. It was the practice of a past generation of fire officers. With a mild admonishment delivered from the deputy Commander for the advice I had given, the incident itself was considered a success. After the PRC Vij repeated his thanks for the learning opportunity whilst the deputy Commander, over a private chat and a cup of coffee, admitted, "I probably would have done the same as you David. Too few opportunities to gain command experience these days."

"New look."

Just prior to leaving Southwark training Centre I had been interviewed by Fiona Murphy, a journalist from a national daily broadsheet newspaper. Following up the aftermath of the Health and Safety Inspectorate's improvement notices that were served on the Brigade she tried to assess the concerns raised about the fitness of firefighters and the hierarchical nature of the Brigade. Whilst I had argued that, "standards had to be improved," I had been drawn into a wider debate put forward by the then Chief Officer, Brian Robinson, and his agenda for significant change within the Brigade. The Chief had argued the Brigade was too top heavy and there were too few major fires to find out how "good we were." (Maybe the fact that most fires started out as relatively small and that fire station crews skilfully kept them that way conveniently slipped his mind?)

However, *The Times* article went on to provide him with a platform to reiterate his intention to reduce the uniformed management down to just six ranks. Arguing that single room fires, the bread and butter of the fire brigade, "don't prepare you for running a 20-pump fire ground" he was also quoted as saying, "You cannot learn on the job any more." To say his comments raised concerns amongst the majority of operational senior officers would be an understatement. Many, myself included, held the view that the man had lost touch with what was really happening at local level, the result of him being a Headquarters animal for far too long.

Without giving due recognition to the organisational failings of the past, something that had seen in-house senior officer command and control training and simulations consistently given a low priority, and no suitable fire ground assessment procedure having been put in place to determine someone's suitability for higher rank, he spoke of his determination to instigate his management changes. He seemed, to many of us, driven by the wider move to "commercial" market forces in his desire to change the Brigade. Something that had already caused similar restructuring changes of other public organisations like the National Health Service. We had already adopted business related budgetary procedures, with business units, that mirrored commerce and had differing parts of the Brigade deemed "customers" and "service providers." None of which had inspired much confidence, or understanding, to those outside Brigade Headquarters as to which direction we seemed to be heading? Revisions to the ranking structure was not the only issue the Chief had in train. The five Area Commands were to be reduced back to three. Ironically the very structure when I joined thirty years earlier. (The Brigade had subsequently moved to 11 Divisions, then the current five Areas) It was to come full circle!

July 1995 saw the Chief's proposals become a reality. My rank ceased to exist in London, together with that of the deputy Assistant Chief and the lower Divisional Officer grade. They were promoted, subject to assessment, to the higher grade two. I had been moved down – although retaining my original DO1 pay scale. The Officers' Committee of the Fire Brigades Union had washed its hands of my DO 1 colleagues and myself. We had become casualties of the reorganisational changes.

It was not lost on most informed members of the Brigade that the severe financial restrictions of the time imposed harsh constraints and pressures on the fire service generally. 1995 would see some of the most stringent fiscal measures in recent years due to central government policies. Neither was it lost on us that historically there had been a steady growth in the size, and breadth, of the senior officer corps in London. I had been part of that expansion. Devolving responsibility downwards had always appeared to be the least palatable option in earlier reorganisations, not least in the creation of the Station Commanders. The growth in so many officers had restricted, not improved, individual access to command experience. However, we were where we were and change was the order of the day.

The transition was a rather surreal experience for me. The thought of returning to be a group Divisional Officer, with a small group of stations to oversee, did little to excite me. I had loved my role and the challenges it had brought. Rarely was it the same old "blah blah", there was always something going on with 23 fire stations lurking in my in-tray to excite the grey cells.

My final year in the Brigade saw me out of the operational loop completely. The decision of the Authorities Medical Examiner was pending. I did not know if I was to be permanently medically retired or not. The focus of his attention was a longstanding injury to my back. Others were far more sceptical about my medical referral. They considered it had far more to do with the Brigade's principal management decision to re-organise and remove the existing Command structure and eradicate the Divisional Officer (Grade 1) position – my rank!

Even before my medical referral I had already been placed on "light duties." I had developed severe carpal-tunnel syndrome in both wrists. I had to wear medical wrist supports before two minor operations would eventually correct this painful condition. However, I had managed to conceal my back condition for some time. I had collapsed and lapsed into unconsciousness at home in 1991. My subsequent referral to a hospital consultant, and the extended physiotherapy treatment, brought confirmation of the nature of the problem. It was delivered by my GP, who told me I had a permanent degenerative injury to my lower back. Whilst it was not necessary for me to be as physically active as a firefighter would be at a fire station, I nevertheless maintained a regular personal training regimen. I had kept myself very fit. Maintaining that fitness programme I had managed my back condition without any further relapse. (Or discovery by actively avoiding all contact with the Medical Examiner!) But with my rank now disestablished I put my future fate in the hands of the Medical Examiner.

The Chief's managerial "new look" was a done deal. However, he also had other policy areas that were up for review. The Chief had required an urgent appraisal of the current river service provision. In fact he had already earmarked the type of craft he wanted as a replacement fireboat. He was seeking a report that would support its proposed purchase. The new Southern Command had Lambeth's fireboat on its patch, its Commander had to come up with the required report. He had, in turn, delegated the task to myself and another "defrocked" DO1, Alan Smith. Alan's sudden need to wear his glasses at work coincided with the decision to dispense with our rank. This meant that he too was referred to the Medical Examiner. Something he already knew would result in his medical discharge from the service.

Working first from a spare office at Croydon, and then later Lewisham we were deemed surplus to requirements and had no fixed abode. However, we delivered on our brief handed down from on high. Told to bring forward policy options, directed to the Brigade's waterborne provision or support, the Commander said we were to consider ourselves "consultants" and he expected a comprehensive report. I recalled, with a wry smile, the very words the Chief Officer had once uttered when berating the role of consultants. "They are someone who borrows your wristwatch to tell you the time!"

I had known Alan throughout my career. We had started at Lambeth together in the 1960s but on separate watches. We had had regular contact in the intervening years. He was both contentious and meticulous. A Scotsman and a former soldier he still had a military bearing with his cropped fair hair and a tall lean figure. Although a private individual he was, like myself, extremely pragmatic and felt that our report was to be our "swan-song." Agreeing at the outset to ignore the Chief's known preferences we conducted a proper and thorough review. When discussing our strategy we decided we were not interested in whatever time the Chief's wristwatch was saying, we looked for a far more accurate timepiece.

We had unfettered access to all river service policy and related archive material. We soon discovered we had opened a can of worms. The prospect of delivering an objective assessment of London's river fire services, and its future direction, gave us an uninhibited determination to express our findings free of any "political" restraint. We took to our task with relish. Our comprehensive report investigated all the factors involved in providing and maintaining London's fire and rescue service, but with particular reference to its riparian risks. Our findings were verified by the either the Authority's Treasurer or Head of Legal Services. We had studied the, then, current published research information, which had highlighted strategic policy issues relating to and future use of the River Thames.

It came to light that there was no "statutory" responsibility upon London's Fire Authority to provide fireboats for normal fire-fighting purposes. Nor had it any statutory responsibilities in the provision of non-fire river related incidents, i.e. search and rescue. Neither did it have any legal powers to purchase equipment not related to its statutory functions. However, first the London County Council (LCC), then the Greater London Council (GLC) and now the London Fire and Civil Defence Authority (then London's Fire Authority) had all chosen that path and provided and maintained a fireboat as an integral part of its operational strategy.

The River Thames (within the greater London area) had undergone massive change by 1995. (Something that has continued to the present day.) In the 30 years prior to our report, modernised shipping and storage methods had revolutionised the Thames-side panorama. No longer did cargo discharge on to wharves or lighters (barges) for onward carriage. That fact had led to the domestication of old wharves and warehouses and an eventual explosion of dockland developments of both offices and housing.

Other craft had been considered to replace the Brigade's then aging fireboats. A hovercraft was one likely contender. The prevailing financial climate had been the principal factor in not progressing the hovercraft option. Subsequently, and after a highly successful trial introduction, the Sea-truck (a shortened landing craft) was deemed a suitable fireboat. Again the lack of finance was cited for its non-introduction.

In 1979 the GLC again reviewed its fireboat provision in direct response to continuing Government fiscal pressure, and in recognition of the significant changes to the nature of the capital's river and its associated riparian risks. The down-river fire station was closed. Only one fireboat was retained at Lambeth despite very serious concerns being expressed as to the site's strategic suitability. Just prior to the GLC's abolition in 1986 the Council's Fire Brigade Committee approved the then Chief Fire Officer's report for the purchase of a new fireboat, the *London Phoenix*. Missing from that report were salient factors that could have influenced the Committees approval. The London Fire and Civil Defence Authority (a quango) had been created on the 1st April 1986. They did not challenge the approval of the new fireboat.

In 1991, as part of an "expansionist" Fire Cover review, proposals were put to the Fire Authority to enhance the Brigades waterborne provision. The then Chief (Gerry Clarkson) wished to upgrade the facilities on the *London Phoenix* and introduce a second fireboat with additional waterborne rescue capability. These proposals, brought forward without any supporting evidence of detailed riparian risk assessments or proven risk re-categorisation, appeared more like a bolted on "wish list" to the main Fire Cover review. Maybe they were, because no subsequent reports were ever submitted to the Fire Authority on the acquisition of a second craft? It was not long before we discovered why no supporting evidence was sent to the Fire Authority Members. There was none.

From all the available data for river and riparian special risks, much to our surprise and amazement, we had discovered no agreed brigade policy guidance, or criteria, for the attendance of a fireboat. In fact considerable variations existed in the pre-determined attendance to where a fireboat was even mobilised. It was found that many premises to which a fireboat would be ordered on receipt of a 999/fire alarm call were a considerable distance from the actual river frontage. Also there were thoroughfares adjacent to the Thames to which the fireboat was ordered that had absolutely no riverside risk whatsoever!

Our 62 conclusions did not make pleasing reading for the Chief. They identified a number of, hitherto unreported, important safety considerations. We had not provided him with the necessary evidence to purchase an immediate replacement fireboat of his liking. Rather we had set in train a means by which the operational performance standards for future fireboats would have to be first established, then implemented and lastly measured. Not a bad "swan song" all things considered.

Last day

The last occasion I wore my uniform was incredibly special for me. It was also the last day I served in the London Fire Brigade. I had already left Croydon, my nominal base, two weeks before and had been using up the remainder of my annual leave prior to my medical retirement on the 31 May. I, together with my family, had been invited back to Southwark Training Centre as the guest of honour and asked to inspect the morning parade of the recruits. Having no idea what had been planned I gladly accepted.

The day had meant an early start from our Orpington home as the parade, as always, was held promptly at 8.30 am – retirement or no retirement. Accompanied by my wife, grown-up son and daughter we were collected by Doug Massey, the principal organiser, and driven the fifteen miles through the morning rush hour traffic to Southwark. Months of enforced "light-duty" had added a few extra pounds around my waist-line but I had managed to squeeze into my best undress uniform without putting the seams under too much strain.

En route Doug explained that the parade was a low-key affair, coffee before the inspection and then home again. For me this was just fine as I had always wanted to depart with minimal fuss, but it seemed fitting that I should finish at the very place I had started four decades earlier. Doug also mentioned, in passing, that Southwark was hosting some important management training event that day and parking might be a bit tight when we arrived. He said he would drop us off at the reception lobby to the Training Centre, park, and come back for us.

What followed was a series of surprises; each one brought a bigger lump to my throat as the emotions kicked in. Walking into the entrance lobby I was pointing out the MFB reliefs, and the plaque HRH had unveiled, to my family when I heard a familiar voice behind me. It was Bob Marks, who had already retired, but returned to say farewell and he was leading a group of my former staff. With my wife being given a stunning bouquet of spring flowers we were made most welcome and much hand shaking and hugs followed. A Senior Divisional Officer was now the Commander of the training centre, we had worked in Press and Public Relations together, and he said that my family, Bob and I should follow him into the yard where the recruits were waiting. That was not all that was waiting.

Walking out from the entrance lobby I had turned the corner and faced the main drill yard. There lined up, in three long ranks, were over 100 recruits in their best No 1's standing smartly to attention. What I had not noticed, either side of the dais that we were being guided to were the long line of uniformed officers. Seeing them I instantly recognised many familiar faces, close friends, others were trusted colleagues, some were Senior Divisional Officer's, most were Divisional Officer's and Station Commander's whilst others were Station Officer rank. We all had one thing in common, we had worked together and enjoyed the experience, me more than most probably. Hands were shaken and kind words exchanged as I was finally asked to take my place on the dais where my family were already seated and waiting. Looking to the side of the drill yard I saw the many faces in the tiered rows of seats, people whom I had worked closely alongside in recent times and who had come to say their goodbyes. Among them John Turner, Gordon White and Rick Adams, together with colleagues from the South East and the South West Area. With more kind, and amusing, words from Bob Marks during his short speech to the assembled gathering he paid a flattering tribute to both my time at the Training Centre and in the wider Brigade. Calling a Recruit Trainer forward, who had been a career long personal friend, I was presented with a surprise retirement gift. The gift was a small wooden box, beautifully crafted out of a piece of former timber drill tower sill. It still had the ruts caused by years of hook ladder usage showing in the lid to the box. The box was a wonderful piece of carpentry and on opening the box I saw the gold ring, cuff links and tie clip all bearing the London Fire Brigade crest. I found my emotions hard to contain. My brief speech of thanks was heartfelt as were my comments to the recruits standing on parade, the future firefighters of the Brigade.

Just when I thought things could not get any better, they did. With the parade over and the recruits dismissed I was asked to walk round to the front of Winchester House as there was someone waiting to see me. There was, Mick Hebard had brought two of his vintage fire engines. One was the wartime turntable ladder I had once ridden when it was on the run at Lambeth, the other was a Dennis Pump Escape complete with its hook ladders and first floor ladder. Standing in front of these fire engines were members of my "old" Brixton White Watch, resplendent in black cork helmets, period fire tunics and their boots and leggings. Next to them was a recruit squad, in their latest fire kit standing by a modern Pump Ladder. It was all too much to take in and with a tear or two in my eyes I shook hands and said more emotional thank you's. That was not the last I saw of the two old fire engines. With my wife and grown up children driven home in the Pump Escape, Mike and I rode side by side in the "open" turntable ladders through south London's streets to our Orpington home. It had been a truly memorable occasion, noteworthy for so many reasons but not least because it was devoid of any principal officer.

The Brigade was changing. Some would argue that it was constantly evolving. But for those of a certain generation, like myself, who had witnessed and experienced a steady yet progressive pace of change, what lay ahead would turn out to be radically different. It would be for the next generation of London's firefighters, the very firefighters I had inspected on that last day, to experience. The Brigade's management structures would soon be more akin to a supermarket chain than to an emergency service as the generic title of station and group manager replaced the former names of fire service rank holders. I had always thought banks were managed. Fire Brigade's had officers who ordered, instructed, commanded and led.

Future global events, such as the 9/11 attacks on New York's Twin Towers, would bring about the repeal of the 1947 Fire Services Act and a new legislative framework that would make the Fire Service more responsive to the needs and demands of the 21st century. Every fireman, or woman, of whatever rank thinks their time in the Brigade was the best. I know mine was. However, I was now a creature of the last part of the 20th century. It is for someone else to continue the story.

Appendix I

Summary of the London Fire Brigade's (LFB) gallantry entries on fire station Honours and Awards boards 1965 to 1996

Author's Not: This, sadly, is not a complete listing as not all records were available for research. However, over 90 per cent have been identified and recorded below. This summary is based on the LFB as it was formed in 1965 following the creation of the Greater London Council's – London Fire Brigade. It had an eleven-division structure; A to L Division. (There was no "I" Division!)

*Although the brigade reorganized in 1986, and the 11 divisions were absorbed into the five Area Commands, for ease of reference the stations are listed as in the Greater London Council-London Fire Brigade Divisional Structure. The individual location entries are shown by year, giving name of the recipient and the gallantry honour awarded. Any station not highlighted, in **bold**, does not mean that gallantry honours were never awarded to personnel from that particular station but rather at the compilation of this record information relating to such an award was not available.*

The London Fire Brigade's highest gallantry award was a Chief Officer's **Commendation,** next came a **Chief Officer's Letter of Congratulations**. In either case an individual had demonstrated exceptional courage and bravery working in a hostile and dangerous environment. For any individual bravery award to be placed on the station Honour's board, or that of a fire crew, it had to be issued by a Brigade principal officer of at least Assistant Chief Officer rank or issued by an accredited outside organisation such as the Royal Humane Society. (Royal Humane Society awards are shown "RHS.")

Brigade Headquarters – Lambeth and Southwark Training School.
1969. Sub O James Holland (Southwark T/S) CFO's Letter of Congratulations.
1969. Sub O James (Jim) McMillan. CFO's Commendation and **Queen's Commendation.**
1974. T/DO John Simmons. CFO's Commendation.
1974. ACO Trevor Watkins. DFC. KPFSM. CFO's Letter of Congratulations.
1974. ADO Gerald Clarkson. CFO's Letter of Congratulations.
1982. L.Fm Ernie Cornwall. Chief Staff Officer's Letter of Appreciation.
1982. Non-Op Fm Paul Davies. CFO's Letter of Congratulations.
1985. DO Joe Bishop. Certificate of Merit from the President of Mexico. **MBE.**

1985. ADO Paul Quick. Certificate of Merit from the President of Mexico. **MBE.**

1985. T/Stn O John Elliott. Certificate of Merit from the President of Mexico.

1986. DO Joe Bishop. Diploma of Honour. President of El Salvador.

1986. Stn O Ian Pegram. (Southwark T/C) Diploma of Honour. El Salvador.

1986. Sub O Des Hayes. (Southwark T/C) Diploma of Honour. El Salvador.

1986. Mr Neil Gale (PAO) CFO's Letter of Congratulations.

1990. Non-Op Stn O Sean Jupp. CFO's Letter of Congratulations.

A Divisional HQ – Paddington. 1965-1986.
North Area HQ 1986-

1968. DO Arthur Nicholls. CFO's Commendations and **Queen's Commendation.**

1968. ADO Edward Harrington. CFO's Commendation and **BEM.**

1969. ADO Fredrick Hurcombe. Certificate of Merit-Binney Awards.

1974. ADO Tom Rowley. CFO's Commendation.

1974. ADO Roy Baldwin. CFO's Letter of Congratulations.

1988. Stn O Alan Pryke. CFO's Letter of Congratulations.

1988. DO Clifford Shore. CFO's Commendation and **MBE.**

A21 Manchester Square until 1968; then A21 Paddington

1968. Fm M F Jackson. CFO's Letter of Congratulations.

1969. Stn O Alexander Pilbro. CFO's Commendation.

1969. L.Fm Gerald Fuller. CFO's Commendation and **Queen's Commendation.**

1969. Fm Peter Mars. CFO's Commendation and **Queen's Commendation.**

1969. L.Fm Robert Fielder. CFO's Commendation and **BEM.**

1969. Fm Michael Ruffle. CFO's Commendation and **BEM.**

1970. Fm David Wilson. CFO's Commendation.

1970. Fm Peter Mynors. CFO's Commendation.

1970. Fm Christopher Reynolds. CFO's Commendation.

1970. Fm Kenneth Palan. CFO's Commendation.

1971. L Fm Ray Cleverdon. CFO's Commendation and **BEM.**

1971. Fm George Simpson. CFO's Commendation.

1971. Fm Ken Salmon. CFO's Commendation.

1971. T/L Fm Howard Winter. CFO's Commendation.

1971. Fm William Willis. CFO's Commendation and **BEM.**

1972. Fm Francis Nice. CFO's Letter of Congratulations.

1972. Fm David Pare. CFO's Commendation and the **Queen's Commendation.**

1973. L Fm Ken Salmon. CFO's Letter of Congratulations.

1974. Fm Hamish Pettit. CFO's Commendation (Posthumously).

1974. **Fm Hamish Pettit. Queen's Commendation. (Posthumously).**

1974. Stn O Neil Wallington. CFO's Commendation and **Queen's Commendation.**

1974. Fm Raymond Chelton. CFO's Commendation and **Queen's Commendation.**

1974. Fm David Webber. CFO's Letter of Congratulations.
1976. Stn O Graham White. CFO's Commendation.
1976. L Fm Nicholas Martin. CFO's Commendation.
1976. Fm Peter Bundey. CFO's Commendation.
1976. Fm Paul Upton. CFO's Commendation.
1976. Fm Richard Crowther. CFO's Letter of Congratulations.
1976. Fm Byron Mathews. CFO's Letter of Congratulations.
1976. Fm Douglas Halligan. CFO's Letter of Congratulations.
1979. Stn O Graham White. RHS Testimonial on Vellum.
1979. Fm Jeffery Hale. RHS Resuscitation Certificate.
1979. Fm Derek Spicer. RHS Resuscitation Certificate.
1988. L Fm Des Hayes. Presidential Commendation (Armenian Disaster). **BEM**

A22 Manchester Square.
1969. Fm Brian Robin. CFO's Letter of Congratulations.
1969. Fm John Hughes. CFO's Commendation.
1969. Fm Paul Stevens. CFO's Commendation.
1969. Stn O Fred Alcock. CFO's Letter of Congratulations.
1972. Fm Bernard Barklamb. CFO's Letter of Congratulations.
1972. Fm Jack Buzelin. CFO's Letter of Congratulations.
1973. T/L Fm Roy Beer. CFO's Commendation.
1974. Fm Daniel O'Dwyer. CFO's Letter of Congratulations.
1975. A/L Fm Maurice Montgomery. CFO's Commendation.
1975. Fm John Kline. CFO's Letter of Congratulations.
1981. Sub O Peter Holmes. CFO's Commendation and **Queen's Commendation.**
1988. Stn O Peter Osborne. CFO's Letter of Congratulations.

A23 Euston.
1969. L.Fm Richard Ellicott. CFO's Commendation.
1985. Fm John Gray. CFO's Letter of Congratulations.
1985. Fm Terrance Harrison. CFO's Letter of Congratulations.
1988. Ff Anthony Hanlon. CFO's Commendation and the **BEM.**
1988. Ff Michael Hurwood. CFO's Letter of Congratulations.
1990. Sub O Terence Gall. CFO's Letter of Congratulations.
1990. Ff Anthony Sterling. CFO's Letter of Congratulations.

A24 Soho.
1971. L.Fm Patsy O'Brien. CFO's Commendation.
1974. Stn O Keith Hicks. CFO's Letter of Congratulations.
1974. T/L Fm Eric Hall. CFO's Commendation and **Queen's Commendation.**
1974. Stn O Keith Hicks. CFO's Letter of Congratulations.
1974. T/Sub O Ian Macey. CFO's Letter of Congratulations.
1974. Fm Donald Clay. CFO's Letter of Congratulations.
1974. Fm Edward Temple. CFO's Letter of Congratulations.
1974. Fm Peter McCarlie. CFO's Letter of Congratulations.

1979. Fm Trevor Browse. CFO Letter of Congratulations.
1983. Sub O John Slone. CFO's Commendation and **Queen's Commendation.**
1983. Fm Mark Blackman. CFO's Commendation, RHS Certificate of Merit.
1983. Fm Walter Slade. CFO's Letter of Congratulations.
1983. Fm Martin Fitall. CFO's Letter of Congratulations.
1988. Sub O Steve Short. CFO's Commendation.
1988. Stn O Colin Townsley. CFO's. CFO's Posthumous Commendation.
1988. Stn O Colin Townsley. Posthumously awarded the GEORGE MEDAL.
1988. Ff Peter Hale. CFO's Commendation and the **Queen's Commendation.**
1988. Sub O Vernon Trefry. CFO's Commendation and **Queen's Commendation.**
1988. Ff Robert Molton. CFO's Commendation and **Queen's Commendation.**
1988. Ff Stewart Button. CFO's Congratulations and the **Queen's Commendation.**
1988. Ff John Edger. CFO's Congratulations and the **Queen's Commendation.**
1988. Ff Steve Bell. CFO's Congratulations.
1988. Ff David Priesman. CFO's Letter of Congratulations.
1988. Ff David Smith. CFO's Letter of Congratulations.

A25 Westminster.
1969. Sub O Roger White. CFO's Commendation.
1972. Sub Officer David Jefferies. CFO's Commendation.
1974. Sub O Ron Morris. CFO's Commendation and **Queen's Gallantry Medal.**
1974. LFm Peter Lidbetter. CFO's Commendation and **Queen's Gallantry Medal.**
1982. Fm Stephen Coleman. CFO's Commendation and **Queen's Commendation.**

A26 Knightsbridge.
1970. Fm Anthony Suen. CFO's Letter of Congratulations.
1972. A/Sub O Norman Pratt. CFO's Letter of Congratulations.
1974. T/Stn O Roy Dunsford. CFO's Letter of Congratulations.

A27 Chelsea.
1982. Fm Ian Nivison. CFO's Letter of Congratulations.
1986. Fm Anthony Davies. Letter of Commendation from the High Sheriff of London.

A28 Kensington.
1968. Fm J Clements. CFO's Commendation.
1968. Fm J A Murphy. CFO's Commendation.
1971. T/Sub O Colin Livett. CFO's Commendation.
1971. Fm Leslie Austin. CFO's Commendation.
1971. Fm Richard Thomas. CFO's Commendation and **BEM.**

1971. T/Sub O Colin Livett. CFO's Commendation and **BEM.**
1976. A/L Fm William Smith. CFO's Letter of Congratulations.
1981. Stn O Steven Close. CFO's Commendation.
1981. Fm Malcolm Burns. CFO's Commendation.
1981. Fm Stephen King. CFO's Commendation.
1981. Fm Robert Lovegrove. CFO's Commendation.
1981. Fm Kevin McDowell. CFO's Commendation.
1981. Fm Noel Phillimore. CFO's Commendation.
1981. Fm Thomas Richards. CFO's Commendation.
1981. Sub O Thomas Tilling. CFO's Letter of Congratulations.
1981. L.Fm Gordon Heeley. CFO's Letter of Congratulations.
1981. Fm Roy Davies. CFO's Letter of Congratulations.
1981. Fm Eric Flood. CFO's Letter of Congratulations.
1981. Fm Peter Johnson. CFO's Letter of Congratulations.
1981. Fm Frank Turner. CFO's Letter of Congratulations.
1984. Fm Noel Philmore. CFO's Commendation.
1986. Stn O Richard Clisby. CFO's Commendation.
1986. L.Fm Thomas Corbin. CFO's Letter of Congratulations.

A29 North Kensington.
1967. Fm Donald Massey CFO's Letter of Congratulations.
1968. Fm Robert Burn. CFO's Commendation.
1968. Fm Graham Holloway. CFO's Letter of Congratulations.
1969. Sub O Desmond Plattern. CFO's Letter of Congratulations.
1969. Stn O Graham White. RHS Resuscitation Certificate.
1969. Fm Maurice Bolwell. RHS Resuscitation Certificate.
1971. T/Stn O David Ellis. CFO's Commendation.
1971. Fm Bernard Cannon. CFO's Commendation.
1980. Fm Renick Joseph. CFO's Commendation.

B Division HQ.-Clapham. 1965-1986.
1968. Sub O John Harding. CFO's Letter of Congratulations and RHS Resuscitation Certificate.
1969. DO Norman Rose. CFO's Commendation and **Queen's Commendation.**
1981. DACO Brian Butler. **MBE** (Brixton Riots.)
1985. ADO Colin Down. CFO's Letter of Congratulations.
1986. DO Roy Larking. CFO's Letter of Congratulations.

B21 Clapham.
1966. Fm Bernard Lewis. CFO's Letter of Congratulations
1966. Fm Brian Swabey. CFO's Letter of Congratulations.
1967. Fm Terrance Davenport. CFO's Commendation and **BEM.**
1969. Fm Paul Quick. CFO's Letter of Congratulations.
1970. Fm Michael French. CFO's Commendation.
1970. Fm Bernard Lewis. CFO's Commendation.
1979. Fm John Sturgeon. CFO's Letter of Congratulations.

1986. Sub O John Worden. CFO's Letter of Congratulations.
1988. L.Ff Gordon Button. CFO's Letter of Congratulations.

B22 Lambeth.
1968. Fm David Pike. CFO's Commendation and **Queen's Commendation.**
1968. Stn O Donald Brown. CFO's Letter of Congratulations.
1968. L. Fm Ken Bland. Commander's (ACO) Letter of Congratulations.
1968. Fm Les Davidson. Commander's (ACO) Letter of Congratulations.
1969. L. Fm David Crook. CFO's Commendation.
1972. Fm Les Davidson. RHS Resuscitation Certificate.
1974. T/Stn O Ian Peebles. RHS Resuscitation Certificate.
1974. Fm John Marsh. RHS Resuscitation Certificate.
1975. Fm John Crowley. Commended by the Recorder of London-Criminal Court
1981. Fm Stephen Honour. CFO's Letter of Congratulations.
1987. Fm Greg Herne. CFO's Letter of Congratulations.

B22 Lambeth-River.
1975. Fm Malcolm Roe. RHS Testimonial on Vellum.
1891. Fm Andrew Sideway. CFO's Commendation.

B23 Southwark.
1977. Sub O David Pike. Commander's Letter of Appreciation.

B24 Dockhead.
1969. Stn O Charlie Dixey. CFO's Letter of Congratulations.
1973. L.Fm Robert Young. CFO's Commendation and **Queen's Commendation.**
1977. L.Fm Robin Burgin. CFO's Letter of Congratulations.
1977. Fm Anthony Hal. CFO's Letter of Congratulations.
1978. T/L Fm Percy Keeping. CFO's Letter of Congratulations.
1983 Fm Martin Ellis. RHS Resuscitation Certificate.

B25 Pageants Wharf (Closed in 1969)

B26 Old Kent Road.
1971. L.Fm George Brown. CFO's Letter of Congratulations.

B27 Deptford.
1978. Fm Alan King. CFO's Letter of Congratulations.

B28 Peckham.
1973. Sub O George Bartlett. CFO's Letter of Congratulations.

B29 New Cross.
1983. Fm James Carroll. RHS Resuscitation Certificate.

1983. Fm Barry Morcombe. RHS Resuscitation Certificate.
1987. Fm Edwin Risby. RHS Certificate of Commendation.

B30 Brixton.
1971. Fm James Miller. CFO's Letter of Congratulations.
1971. Fm Raymond Young. CFO's Letter of Congratulations.
1979. Stn O Barry Edwards and White Watch. RSPCA Certificate of Merit.
1981. Stn O David Pike. Letter of Appreciation, Commander Metropolitan Police.
1981. Stn O David Pike. Letter of Appreciation. Honours and Awards Committee.
1981. Fm John Halford. Letter of Appreciation. Honours and Awards Committee.
1990 Ff David Dower. CFO's Letter of Congratulations.
1990. Ff Mark Negus, CFO's Letter of Congratulations.

B31 West Norwood.
1979. Stn O David Pike and White Watch. RSPCA Certificate of Merit.
1981. Fm Michael Harding. CFO's Commendation and **Queen's Commendation.**
1981. Stn O Alan Lowles. CFO's Letter of Congratulations.
1990. Ff Adrian Codd. CFO's Letter of Congratulations.
1990. Ff Christopher Drummond. CFO's Letter of Congratulations.

C Division HQ. Shoreditch. 1965-1986
1985. ADO Graham Holloway. CFO's Commendation.

C21 Shoreditch.
1968. Fm Robert Arrowsmith. CFO's Letter of Congratulations.
1975. Fm Robert Furlong. CFO's Commendation and the **BEM.**

C22 Kingsland.
1972. Fm Hugh Robinson. CFO's Letter of Congratulations.
1976. T/Sub O Fredrick O'Hare. CFO's Letter of Congrats.
1979. Stn O Keith Fisher. Binney Memorial Award for Bravery.

C23 Stoke Newington.
1970. Fm Chris Roper. CFO's Letter of Congratulations.
1970. Sub O Raymond Smith. CFO's Letter of Congratulations.
1971. Fm Henry Blackford. CFO's Letter of Congratulations.
1973. Fm Melvin Howes. CFO's Commendation.
1974. Stn O Albert 'Joe' Kennedy. CFO's Commendation.

C24 Whitechapel.
1968. Fm Francis Harvey. CFO's Commendation.
1973. Fm Ernest Allen. CFO's Commendation and **Queen's Commendation.**

1973. Fm Michael Cooper. CFO's Commendation and **Queen's Commendation.**
1977. Stn O Michael Whitty. CFO's Commendation.
1977. A/L Fm Julian Ketteridge. CFO's Commendation.
1978. T/Sub O John Bryant. CFO's Commendation.
1978. Stn O Michael Whitty. CFO's Letter of Congratulations.
1979. Fm Anthony Sandman. CFO's Letter of Congratulations.
1990. Probationer Ff Thomas Whelan. CFO's Letter of Congratulations.

C25 Cannon Street until 1975 then Dowgate.
1976. A/Stn O Malcolm Grout. CFO's Commendation.

C26 Barbican.
1967. L.Fm I H Hallums. CFO's Letter of Congratulations.
1967. Fm. L Wright. CFO's Letter of Congratulations.
1975. Stn O Christopher Wood. CFO's Commendation and **BEM.**
1976. Stn O Christopher Wood. CFO's Commendation.
1984. Blue Watch. Commendation from the Metropolitan Police.

C27 Clerkenwell.
1972. Stn O Derek Edwards. CFO's Letter of Congratulations.
1977. Stn O Keith Fisher. RHS Testimonial on Vellum.
1977. Fm Anthony Morrison. RHS Resuscitation Certificate.
1988. Sub O William Bell. CFO's Letter of Congratulations.
1988. Ff Joseph Bolland. CFO's Letter of Congratulations.
1988. T/L Ff David Flanagan. CFO's Letter of Congratulations.

C28 Islington.
1970. Stn O Thomas Stanton. CFO's Letter of Congratulations.
1974. Fm Douglas Rowe. CFO's Commendation.
1974. Fm Leonard McToldridge. CFO's Letter of Congratulations.

C29 Kentish Town.
1955. L.Fm Ronald Platts. CFO's Letter of Congratulations.
1964. L.Fm Tony Lynham. CFO's Letter of Congratulations.
1968. Fm Kenneth Taylor. CFO's Letter of Congratulations.
1969. Fm John Novak. CFO's Commendation and **BEM.**
1971. Sub O Douglas Horsman. CFO's Letter of Congratulations.
1971. Fm Andrew Levens. CFO's Commendation and the **Queen's Commendation.**
1976. Fm Alan Havens. CFO's Letter of Congratulations.
1978. A/L.Fm Christopher Shaw. CFO's Letter of Congratulations.
1978. Fm Kevin Repper. CFO's Letter of Congratulations.
1978. Fm Christopher Johnson. CFO's Letter of Congratulations.
1986. Sub O Pheasant. RHS Certificate on Vellum.

C30 Holloway.
1973. Fm Roger Chelton. CFO's Letter of Congratulations.
1973. Fm Peter Jones. CFO's Letter of Congratulations.
1978. T/Stn O Graham Knight. CFO's Commendation.

D Division HQ. Ealing. 1965-1986.
1968. ADO Leslie Smith. CFO's Letter of Congratulations.
1968. Fm Bill Ranson. CFO's Letter of Congratulations.

D21 Ealing.
1973. Fm Derek Simpson. CFO's Letter of Congratulations.

D22 Acton
1974. Fm David Harris. CFO's Letter of Congratulations.

D23 Hammersmith.
1967. Stn O James Farley. CFO's Commendation.
1968. Sub O H H Scott. CFO's Letter of Congratulations.
1969. Stn O James Farley. CFO's Commendation.
1969. Sub O Keith Brandon. CFO's Letter of Congratulations.
1968. Fm Herbert Dean. CFO's Letter of Congratulations.
1968. Fm Neil Heywood. CFO's Letter of Congratulations.
1968. Fm Tom Slade. CFO's Letter of Congratulations.
1968. Fm John Wyatt. CFO's Letter of Congratulations.
1970. Fm Brian Dusgate. CFO's Letter of Congratulations.

D24 Fulham.

D25 Chiswick.
1971. L.Fm Colin Russell. CFO's Commendation.

D26 Twickenham.
1967. Fm F Gilbey. RHS Resuscitation Certificate.

D27 Heston.
1973. Fm Peter Farris. CFO's Letter of Congratulations.
1973. Fm Kevin Wright. CFO's Letter of Congratulations.
1975. Fm Terrance Kitto. Commendation and Certificate from the High Sheriff.
1975. Raymond Towells. Commendation and Certificate from the High Sheriff.

D28 Feltham.
1970. Stn O Roy Larking. CFO's Commendation and **Queen's Commendation**.
1970. Fm Jeff Bennett. CFO's Commendation and **Queen's Commendation.**
1970. Fm John Pope. CFO's Commendation.
1970. Fm Colin Watts. CFO's Commendation.

D29 Southall.
1967. Stn O. G R MacDonald. RHS Resuscitation Certificate.
1968. Sub O Brockley. CFO's Commendation.
1989. Stn O Ernest Pearce. RHS Resuscitation Certificate.

D30 Hayes.
D31 Hillingdon.

E Division HQ. Lewisham. 1965-1986.
South East Area Command HQ. 1986-
1984. Con Off David Dawes. CFO's Letter of Congratulations.
1988. DACO Brian Ash. CFO's Commendation.

E21 Lewisham.
1973. Fm Terence Trimmer. CFO's Letter of Congratulations.
1974. A/Sub O John McCabe. CFO's Commendation.
1974. Fm Bryn Cuffe. CFO's Commendation.
1974. Fm Sidney Lane. CFO's Commendation.
1985. Sub O Peter Simpson. CFO's Letter of Congratulations.

E22 Greenwich.

E23 East Greenwich.
1969. Sub O Michael Botten. CFO's Letter of Congratulations.

E24 Woolwich.
1985. Fm Kevin Laybourne. CFO's Commendation.
1985. Fm Les Lockwood. CFO's Commendation.

E25 Plumstead.
1981. Fm Raymond Pryce. CFO's Letter of Congratulations.
1982. Fm Martin Beeston. RHS Resuscitation Certificate.

E26 Shooters Hill. (Closed)

E27 Erith.
1967. Sub O Thomas Lucus. CFO's Commendation.
1981. Fm Paul Hill. CFO's Commendation.
1986. Fm Paul Hill. Area Commander's Commendation
1986. Fm Andrew Parries. Area Commander's Commendation.

E28 Bexley.
1972. Fm Martin Eppey. RSPCA Certificate of Merit.
1972. Fm Leonard Dartnel. RSPCA Certificate of Merit.
1985. Blue Watch. RSPCA Bronze Medal.

E29 Lee Green.
1977. A/L Fm Kevin Beattie. CFO's Letter of Congratulations

E30 Eltham.
E31 Forest Hill.

E32 Downham.
1972. Sub O Richard Elicott. CFO's Commendation.

F Division HQ. Stratford. 1965-1986.
North East HQ.1986-
1985. ADO Trevor Stratford. CFO's Commendation. **Queen's Gallantry Medal.**
1988. ACO Albert (Joe) Kennedy. CFO's Commendation.
1988. Stn O Roger DeMonte. CFO's Letter of Congratulations.

F21 Stratford.
1972. Fm Sidney Balls. CFO's Commendation.
1978. Fm Michael Stothard. RHS Resuscitation Certificate.
1982. Fm Ian Izzard. RHS Resuscitation Certificate.

F22 Brunswick Road until 1970 then Poplar.
1969. Stn O Harold Snelling. CFO's Commendation and **BEM.**
1974. Fm Barry Shipman. CFO's Letter of Congratulations.
1981. Fm Brian Jeffery. RHS Resuscitation Certificate.

F23 Millwall.
F24 Burdett Road (Closed in 1970).
F25 Shadwell.

F26 Bethnal Green.
1982. Fm Martin Powell. CFO's Letter of Congratulations.

F27 Bow.
1967. Fm C Stuart. CFO's Letter of Congratulations.
1977. Fm Stephen McLaughin. CFO's Commendation.

F28 Homerton.
1988. Sub O Edward Simmons. CFO's Letter of Congratulations.
1989. ADO Liam Hackett. CFO's Commendation and **Order of St John Life Saving Medal.**

F29 Leyton.
1968. Sub O James Docherty. CFO's Commendation and the **BEM.**
1968. Fm Arthur Atkins. CFO's Letter of Congratulations.
1983. Fm Robert Howes. RHS Certificate of Merit.

1983. Fm Roy Harold. RHS Certificate of Merit.

F30 Leytonstone.
1974. T/L Fm Thomas Dodson. RHS Resuscitation Certificate.
1989. L.Ff Stephen Dudeney. CFO's Letter of Congratulations.
1989. Ff Jeffery Hickling. CFO's Letter of Congratulations.

G Division HQ. Wembley 1965-1986.
North West HQ 1986-
1980. Sub O Roger Stewart. RHS Resuscitation Certificate.
1980. Fm Michael Hunt. RHS Resuscitation Certificate.
1982. DO Colin Brum. RHS Resuscitation Certificate.

G21 Harrow.
1969. Fm Michael Hadland. Certificate of Merit-Binney Awards.

G22 Stanmore.

G23 Mill Hill.
1986. Blue Watch. RSPCA Certificate of Merit.

G24 Hendon.
1966. Sub. O Leonard Tredwell. CFO's Letter of Congratulations.
1966. L. Fm Leslie Long. CFO's Letter of Congratulations.
1966. Fm Norman Long. CFO's Letter of Congratulations.
1966. Fm Colin Oliver. CFO's Letter of Congratulations.
1966. Fm Christopher Richardson. CFO's Letter of Congratulations.
1966. Fm Colin Wyatt. CFO's Letter of Congratulations.
1966. Fm John Wyatt. CFO's Letter of Congratulations.
1969. Fm Alan Cox. CFO's Letter of Congratulations.
1972. Fm Paul Hale. CFO's Letter of Congratulations.

G25 West Hampstead.
1969. Fm Alan Fosbrok. CFO's Letter of Congratulations.
1974. Sub O Roger Stewart. CFO's Commendation and **Queen's Gallantry Medal.**
1974. Fm David Blair. CFO's Commendation and **Queen's Gallantry Medal.**

G26 Belsize.
1970. Fm Donald MacLean. CFO's Commendation.
1970. Sub O Colin Brum. CFO's Letter of Congratulations.
1974. A/L Fm Alan Trotman. CFO's Letter of Congratulations.

G27 Kilburn.

G28 Willesden.
1969. Fm Michael J Wallman. CFO's Commendation and **BEM.**
1969. Fm Brain Hudson. CFO's Commendation.
1974. Stn O Richard Luckcroft. RHS Resuscitation Certificate.
1981. Fm Peter Bailes. CFO's Commendation.
1981. Stn O Lionel Galleozie. CFO's Letter of Congratulations.
1981. Fm Michael Walker. CFO's Letter of Congratulations.

G29 Park Royal.
1985. Stn O Gardner. CFO's Letter of Congratulations.
1985. L.Fm Steve Davies. CFO's Letter of Congratulations.
1985. Fm Alan Garside. CFO's Letter of Congratulations.
1986. Fm John Hunter. CFO's Letter of Congratulations.

G30 Wembley.
1969. Fm John Hobart. RHS Resuscitation Certificate.
1981. Fm Robert Webb. CFO's Commendation.

G31 Northolt.
G32 Ruislip.

H Division HQ. Croydon. 1965-1986.
South West Area HQ. 1986-
1988. DO Gordon Crompton. CFO's Letter of Congratulations.

H21 Bromley.
1971. Stn O Eric Rutter. CFO's Commendation.
1971. Fm John Elliott. CFO's Commendation.
1971. Fm Barry Redbourn. CFO's Commendation.
1971. Fm Ian Southby. CFO's Commendation.

H23 Sidcup.
1971. Sub O Raymond Davis. CFO's Commendation.

H24 Orpington.
1971. Fm Roland Dean. CFO's Commendation.
1971. Fm Roland Oliver. CFO's Commendation.

H25 Biggin Hill.
1967. Sub O Joseph Southby. RHS Testimonial on Parchment.
1967. Fm Edward Sines. RHS Testimonial on Parchment.
1967. Fm Arthur Killick. RHS Testimonial on Parchment.
1986. L.Fm Dave Fletcher. RSPCA Certificate of Merit.

H26 Addington.
H27 West Wickham. (Closed in 1969)

H28 Woodside.
1969. Fm Robert Kneller. CFO's Commendation and **Queen's Commendation**.
1969. Fm Patrick Millea. CFO's Commendation.
1990. Ff Stephen Cowlard. CFO's Letter of Congratulations.

H29 Purley.
H30 Sanderstead (Closed).

H31 Croydon.
1969. Stn O Ken Birch. CFO's Commendation and **Queen's Commendation.**
1969. L.Fm Victor Kennedy. CFO's Commendation.
1973. Stn O Sidney Imber. CFO's Commendation.
1973. L.Fm John Bissex. CFO's Commendation.
1973. Fm John Brooks. CFO's Commendation.
1973. Fm John Dabkowski. CFO's Commendation.
1973. Fm James Gallagher. CFO's Commendation.
1973. Fm Gerald Winyard. CFO's Commendation.

H32 Thornton Heath until 1971 then Norbury.
1989. Ff Justin Williams. RHS Resuscitation Certificate.
1989. Ff Anthony Ridge. RHS Resuscitation Certificate.

H33 Beckenham.

J Division HQ.-Edmonton. 1965-1986
1972. ADO John Spring. RHS Testimonial on Parchment.
1981. DO Philip Lloyd. RHS Testimonial on Vellum.

J21 Edmonton.
1968. Fm Peter Bull. RHS Testimonial on Vellum.
1969. Fm Colin Shinn. CFO's Letter of Congratulations.
1972. Stn O Vic Bagnelle. RHS Testimonial on Parchment.
1977. A/L Fm Paul Manning. CFO's Commendation
1977. Fm James Welch. CFO's Letter of Congratulations.
1982. Stn O Colin Perry. CFO's Commendation and **Queen's Commendation.**
1982. Fm Norman Jiggins. CFO's Letter of Congratulations.
1982. Fm Robert Henry. CFO's Letter of Congratulations.
1984. Fm Barry Panton. Binney Certificate of Merit.
1985. Fm Anthony Streach. CFO's Letter of Congratulations.
1988. Sub O Peter Banks. CFO's Letter of Congratulations.

J22 Chingford.
1967. L.Fm M Ashby. CFO's Letter of Congratulations.
1977. Fm Christopher Langrish. CFO's Letter of Congratulations.

J23 Woodford.
1968. Sub O J W Hobbs. CFO's Commendation.

J24 Walthamstow.
1968. L.Fm F Leadbeater. CFO's Commendation.
1972. Red Watch. RSPCA Certificate of Merit.

J25 Tottenham.
1967. Fm M W Cheney. CFO's Letter of Congratulations.
1968. Fm Edward Huckle. CFO's Letter of Congratulations.
1968. L.Fm R J Barnes. CFO's Commendation.
1969. Fm Edmund Green. CFO's Commendation.
1970. Red Watch. RSPCA Certificate of Merit.
1984. Stn O Stephen O'Sullivan. RSPCA Certificate of Merit.
1984. Red Watch. RSPCA Certificate of Merit.
1984. Stn O Stephen O'Sullivan. RHS Resuscitation Certificate.
1984. Fm Stephen Molson. RHS Resuscitation Certificate.

J26 Hornsey.
1982. Stn O Brian Strut. CFO's Letter of Congratulations

J27 Finchley.
1973. Stn O James Alcock. CFO's Letter of Congratulations.
1973. Fm Robert Brown. CFO's Letter on Congratulations.

J28 Southgate.
1973. Fm Thomas Tooley. CFO's Commendation.
1977. L.Fm Roy Pearce. CFO's Commendation.
1977. Fm Ronald Skingle. CFO's Commendation.

J29 Barnet.
1966 L.Fm R H Brocket. RHS Resuscitation Certificate.
1970. Fm Keith Wheatley. CFO's Letter of Congratulations.

J30 Enfield.
J31 Coombes Croft (Closed in 1966).
J32 Ponders End (Closed in 1966).

K Division HQ.-Wimbledon.1965-1986.
1969. DO William Norman. (FPO) CFO's Commendation

K21 Wimbledon.

K22 Wandsworth.
1969. Stn O Charles Jarman. CFO's Commendation.
1969. Fm Peter Mogg. CFO's Commendation.
1972. Fm Brian Greenleaf. RSPCA Testimonial on Parchment.
1976. A/L Fm Anthony Dowdeswel. CFO's Commendation.
1976. Fm Ronald Cotton. CFO's Letter of Congratulations.

K23 Battersea.
1967. Fm Alan Brandon. RHS Protection of Life Certificate.
1968. Fm R Winter. CFO's Letter of Congratulations.
1968. Stn O. T J Swift. CFO's Letter of Congratulations.
1973. Fm Charlie Beauchamp. CFO's Commendation.
1973. Stn O Norman Marshman. CFO's Letter of Congratulations.
1976. Fm Brian Middleton. CFO's Commendation.
1976. L.Fm Keith Angle. CFO's Letter of Congratulations.
1988. Stn O Glenn Mills. CFO's Letter of Congratulations.
1988. T/Sub O Stephen Williams. CFO's Letter of Congratulations.
1988. Ff Edward Durrant. CFO's Letter of Congratulations.
1988. Ff Thomas McGoven. CFO's Letter of Congratulations.

K24 Tooting.
1973. Stn O Roy MacGregor. CFO's Commendation.
1973. Fm Victor Davey. CFO's Commendation.
1973. Fm Keith Baxter. CFO's Commendation.
1987. Stn O John Bonney. CFO's Letter of Congrats.
1988. Stn O Charlie Beauchamp. CFO's Commendation.
1988. Sub O Stephen Nellies. CFO's Commendation.

K25 Streatham. (Closed in 1971)

K26 Mitcham.
1971. L.Fm Ron Parke. CFO's Commendation and **BEM.**

K27 Wallington.
1982. Fm John Chapman. CFO's Commendation.
1982. Fm David Williams. CFO's Commendation.
1985. Fm William Buckley. CFO's Letter of Congratulations.

K28 Sutton.

K29 Surbiton.
1974. A/L Fm Richard Davies. CFO's Commendation.
1974. Fm George Davies. CFO's Commendation.

K30 New Malden.

K31 Kingston.
1966. A/L.Fm Peter Humphreys. CFO's Letter of Congratulations.
1966. Fm Welford. CFO's Letter of Congratulations.
1968. L.Fm A R Winslet. CFO's Letter of Congratulations.

K32 Richmond.
1973. Fm Raymond Goodall. CFO's Commendation and **Queen's Commendation.**
1974. Fm Alan Darby. CFO's Commendation.
1975. Fm Richard Fountain. RSPCA Bronze Medal

L Division HQ. East Ham. 1965-1986.

L21 East Ham.
1967. L.Fm R W Walker. CFO's Letter of Congratulations.
1969. L.Fm Kenneth Fuller. CFO's Commendation.
1969. Fm Ian Richards. CFO's Commendation and **BEM.**
1972. Fm Michael Wilson. CFO's Letter of Congratulations.

L22 Ilford.
1967. Fm Brian McAndrew. RHS Resuscitation Certificate.
1990. L.Ff Gary Paul. CFO's Letter of Congratulations and RHS Resuscitation Certificate.

L23 Hainault.

L24 Romford.
1982. L.Fm David Hall. CFO's Letter of Congratulations.

L25 Dagenham.
1980. Red Watch. RSPCA Certificate of Merit.
1982. Sub O John Stone. CFO's Commendation.
1982. L.Fm Fredrick Hughes. CFO's Commendation.
1987. Fm David Dare. CFO's Commendation.

L26 Hornchurch.
1970. Sub O Graham. CFO's Letter of Congratulations.

L27 Barking.
1983. Red Watch. RSPCA Certificate of Merit.
1983. Fm Gary Paul. RSPCA Silver Medal.

L28 Wennington.

L29 Silvertown.
1972. Stn O William Roy. CFO's Commendation.

L30 Plaistow
1968. A/Stn O H A Bottomley. CFO's Letter of Congratulations.
1969. Fm Michael Lambell. CFO's Letter of Congratulations.
1972. L.Fm Fredrick Bird. CFO's Commendation.
1975. Sub O Derek Smith. RHS Resuscitation Certificate.
1980. Red Watch. RSPCA Certificate of Merit.

Appendix II

Roll of Honour

In my lifetime 33 London firemen/firefighters have given their life at operational incidents. They paid the ultimate sacrifice for performing their duty and doing their job. They shall not be forgotten.

1949
Station Officer Charles Fisher   Covent Garden Flower Market. WC2

1951
Fireman Edward Harwood   Broad Street. EC2
Fireman Leslie Skitt   Broad Street. EC2
Fireman Thomas Joy   Broad Street. EC2

1954
Station Officer Frederick Hawking   Langley Street WC2
Fireman Arthur Batt-Rawden   Langley Street WC2
Fireman Charles Gadd   Langley Street WC2
Sub Officer John Skinner   King Street Hammersmith

1956
Leading Fireman Frederick Willoughby   Kensington High Street W8

1958
Station Officer Jack Forte-Wells   Smithfield Meat Market. EC1
Fireman Richard Stocking Smithfield Meat Market. EC1

1962
Fireman James Bardens   Wyndham Road SE5
Station Officer Thomas Carter   Wyndham Road SE5

1964
Fireman Daniel O'Donovan   Hilldrop Lane N7

1968
Fireman Colin Comber   Kings Road Chelsea
Fireman Brian O'Connell-Hutching   Kings Road Chelsea

1969
Sub Officer Michael Gamble   Dudgeons Wharf E14
Fireman John Appleby   Dudgeons Wharf E14
Fireman Alfred Smee   Dudgeons Wharf E14
Fireman Trevor Carvosso   Dudgeons Wharf E14
Fireman Terence Breen   Dudgeons Wharf E14
      Leading Fireman Michael Lee   Goswell Road EC1

_1974_
Fireman Hamish Pettit   Worsley Hotel Maida Vale W9
_1978_
Fireman Stephen Neill   St Pancras Way NW1
_1980_
Leading Fireman Stephen Maynard   MV Rudi M, Regent Canal Dock

_1981_
Fireman Anthony Marshall   Woolworths Wimbledon
Firemen Barry Trussel   St Georges Hospital Tooting
_1987_
Station Officer Colin Townsley. GM   Kings Cross Underground Station NW1
_1991_
Firefighter Terrance Hunt   Gillender Street E3
Firefighter David Stokoe   Gillender Street E3
_1993_
Firefighter Michael Hill   Villiers Road Willesden

_2004_
Firefighter Bill Faust   Bethnal Green Road E2
Firefighter Adam James Meere   Bethnal Green Road E2

Appendix III

Glossary

A.

ACO: Assistant Chief Officer, the third most senior rank in the London Fire Brigade.

ACU: Area Control Unit, mobile control vehicle located at Area Headquarters. Attends special predetermined attendances and all six-pump fires and above. This vehicle provided the focal point for command and control at major incidents.

ADO: Assistant Divisional Officer, the rank above Station Officer and subsequently re-designated Station Commander.

Aerial: fire engine capable of reaching the upper floors (maximum of eight floors) of buildings, i.e. Turntable-ladders, Hydraulic Platforms Aerial Ladder Platforms.

AFA: Automatic fire alarm, term used to describe a variety of automatic heat and smoke detectors that, when actuated, set off a fire alarm.

AFS: the Auxiliary Fire Service, established in 1937, to supplement the existing fire service prior to the outbreak of the Second World War. Disestablished in 1969.

Acting Leading Fireman. Lowest form of the temporary promoted officer.

B.

BA: collective name for breathing apparatus sets which enable a firefighter to enter an irrespirable atmosphere and work. Historically oxygen cylinders were used with BA but now compressed air is predominately used throughout the British fire service.

Baccy Van. The Breathing Apparatus Control Van, maintained at each Divisional Headquarters and ridden by the Staff Sub Officer and Leading Fireman. Attended all four pump fires and above and carried the Stage II BA control boards for fires involving the extensive, or extended, use of BA.

Bardic: small spark-proof torch worn by all firefighters.

Branch: the outlet connected to the end of the hose-line, which enables either a jet of water or water spray to be directed onto a fire or incident.

Brown bread: slang for somebody who has died. (Dead).

C.

CEAG Lamp. A spark-proof, battery, lamp worn with the Proto BA set. Certified electrically against gas (CEAG).

CFO: Chief Fire Officer, Operational head of the Brigade, later re-designated "Commissioner."

CMC: Command and Mobilising Centre, which replaced the former three fire controls, and where all 999 emergency fire brigade calls were processed.

Conflagration: a fire of such intensity that jets of water have virtually no effect on it.

D.

DC: Divisional Commander. Senior/Principal Officer in charge of a Divisional area.

DO: Divisional Officer, senior ranking fire officer.

Dry Riser Main: a pipe built into high rise buildings with outlets on each floor to enable firefighters to attach charged lines of hose at ground floor level, then carry hose to any floor in the building and attach the hose and be supplied with water at high pressure. Some very tall buildings have "wet risers" where the pipe is already charged with pressurised water.

Donning and starting up: Putting on a breathing apparatus set, turning it on and breathing from the set.

DSU: Distress Signal Unit, worn on a breathing apparatus set and used to summon assistance by other firefighters in case of an individual/crew becoming trapped or collapsing unconscious.

F.

FCU: Forward Control Unit, a small control unit crewed by two staff officers and sent to four pump fires and above or other specific incidents where additional command and control officers are required.

Fire: the rapid oxidation of gaseous, liquid or solid fuel in atmospheric air.

Flash-over: a sudden intensifying of a fire when an inrush of oxygen occurs, perhaps because a window or door is opened often with deadly effect. Also known as a back-draught.

G.

Goer: a fire that is burning fiercely or "going" well when fire crews arrive.

Guv or Guvnor: a term of address used by firemen/firefighters for a watch Station Officer.

H.

Hook ladder: a thirteen-foot wooden ladder fitted with a hinged tensile steel hook and used to scale buildings by hooking the ladder over the window sill of the floor above.

Hook belt: a special belt worn by firemen that enables them to hook onto a hook ladder.

HP: Hydraulic Platform, a fire appliance with elevating beams and a cage or platform at the head from which firefighters could carry out rescues and bring the rescued to the ground. It also allowed firefighting from an elevated position.

Hydrant: a water supply point from a water main found in nearly every street and located under the surface of the pavement and marked by a yellow descriptive H plate showing the size of the main and distance from the marker.

Hydraulics: the science of the flow of liquids, and particularly the firemen's science of moving water from one point to another.

J.

Jet: allows pressurised water from a hose line to be directed onto a fire or other incident.

Job: LFB lingo for a working fire.

Jumper: a person who is threatening to jump, or who has already jumped, off a building or under a train.

Junior Buck: name given to a probationary fireman or the most junior member of a watch.

K.

Knock-off: Turning off the water supply from a fire engine pump or hydrant.

Knots and lines: a drill where fireman/firefighters practice tying different knots and use the different lines they carry on fire engines.

L.

Leggings: separate plastic coverings for firemen's legs worn from the thigh high boots to the waist and held up by a belt and "dog-clips."

Line: rope cut to specific length and used either for rescue or general-purpose tasks.

London Salvage Corps: organisation funded by Insurance Companies to attend fires or other incidents in order to reduce or prevent resultant damage. No longer in existence.

M.

M2FH: the radio call sign of the fire brigade control that was based at Lambeth HQ and mobilised the central London fire stations and co-ordinated mobilisation for all major fires in the greater London area.

Make-up: an incident where the number of fire engines are increased (made-up) over the initial attendance to deal with a fire or special service incident e.g. a six-pump fire.

Multiple calls: an incident where the mobilising control receives more than four/five separate calls to the occurrence in a short space of time which indicates an incident is genuine.

N.

N.F.S: National Fire Service, formed in 1941 to provide a unified fire service during the Second War World in the UK and disbanded in 1947.

Nominal roll board: a roll board of the individuals riding a fire engine and carried on it. It is handed into the control unit at any make-up fire to facilitate the taking of a roll-call in the event of an evacuation of fire service personnel.

O.

On the bell: driving fast to a fire or emergency call in a fire engine with the officer ringing the engine's bell, in later years using two-tone horns and with blue flashing lights switched on.

Ordering: a mobilising message for a fire crew or senior officer given by the fire brigade control via teleprinter, radio or telephone. Origin from the phrase "You are ordered to," or "Order your pump to."

P.

Persons reported: an urgent radio message sent to control to indicate that persons are reported to be trapped or are clearly involved in a fire. An ambulance is ordered to a fire as soon this message is received.

Pump Escape: a dual-purpose pumping fire engine that carried a 50-foot wheeled escape rescue ladder.

Pump Ladder: the replacement dual-purpose pumping fire engine that was brought into service when the wheeled escape ladders were withdrawn in the early 1980s.

Proto: a breathing apparatus set that uses oxygen and which air is supplied to firemen via a re-breather bag and with a nominal duration of one hour.

Pyromaniac: a person who repeatedly fails to resist the temptation to light fires.

R.

Riders: members of the on-duty watch riding the fire engines at a fire station.

Running call: an emergency call made direct to a fire station by a member of the public or by flagging down a fire engine in the street.

S. Seat of the fire:
the fire's point of origin, the fireman's efforts are made to attack the seat of a fire whenever possible.

Shout: an emergency workers' term for an operational call, especially firefighters.

Smoke eater: a term used by firemen for a colleague who frowned on the use of breathing apparatus and who could, seemingly, endure endless smokey conditions whilst fighting a fire in a building.

Smoke issuing: fire brigade term for smoke seen emanating from a building.

Special service call: a non-fire emergency call.

Station Commander: an Assistant Divisional Officer who commands the four watches at a fire station.

Station Officer: rank of the officer in charge of a two or multi appliance fire station watch.

Stiff: LFB lingo for a dead body.

Sub Officer: deputy to a Station Officer or in charge of a single appliance station.

T.

Tally: 1. A name tally that is attached to a breathing apparatus set and has to be handed to the BA control officer whenever a fireman enters an incident requiring BA. The time of entry is recorded on the tally and an exit time calculated from the wearer's cylinder contents. 2. There is also a hose delivery tally. One is attached to each pump outlet and indicates the station name of the appliance and the delivery outlet number. This tally is attached to a jet at large incidents and lets crews know which pump is supplying them with water and allows the pump operator to identify and react to their instructions.

TL: Turntable ladder, a hundred feet in height when fully extended.

The Job. A term used to describe working in the London Fire Brigade or another fire brigade.

Turncock: Works for a Water Undertaking and is responsible for providing water at an adequate pressure to the fire pumps at the scene of a fire.

Turning over and cutting away: Performed in the aftermath of a fire to ensure all signs of a fire are completely extinguished.

Turn out: Mobilising of fire engines (appliances) from a fire station to an emergency call.

W.

Watchroom: the communications centre of a fire station and where the log book is kept and maintained; emergency calls are received via the teleprinter and in times gone by, where firemen would keep watch twenty-four hours a day.

Working rig: Once blue overalls but replaced by lightweight trousers and tee shirts/shirts and sweatshirts.

Working job: A fireman's/firefighter's term for a serious fire or special service call.

Myself and Bob Marks (former Commander-Training) reunited on my last day in the Brigade at Southwark TC. May 1996.

Brian 'Bill' Butler. MBE. OStJ. QFSM. Founding President of the Brigade's Retired Senior Officer's Mess Club presides at my dining-out from the London Fire Brigade. October 1996.

Presentation by Jim McMillan QFSM. President of the Retired Senior Officer Mess Club to yours truly upon my departure for pastures new following my five-year tenure as the 'founding' Secretary for the Mess Club. 2001.

*Colleagues and friends say farewell at my dining-out at the Royal Blackheath
Golf Club in October 1996.*